The Overthrow of Colonial Slavery
1776–1848

The rich texture of the anti-slavery movements is described with verve and passion ... Mr Blackburn's authoritative study is a brilliant evocation of the diverse nature of New World slavery in the Revolutionary Age.
Newsletter of the British Association for American Studies

This is an immensely readable and valuable book.
Richard Rathbone, *Marxism Today*

... an absorbing piece of sustained argument ...
Robert Stewart, *The Spectator*

... making skilful use of the last half century's accumulation of research into the history of slavery, Blackburn has put every serious student of the subject in his debt ... an admirable work.
Peter Fryer, *City Limits*

Blackburn has a fascinating story to tell ... an important book.
John Mortimer, *Sunday Times*

... the agreeable thing about Mr Blackburn is that he really likes to find out what actually happened ...
Eric Christiansen, *The Independent*

The Overthrow of Colonial Slavery is a valuable book for socialists who wish to trace the tortuous paths through which modern capitalism emerged.
Alex Callinicos, *Socialist Review*

I liked the broad sweep of this book and its hard-headed treatment of the European colonial governments.
Colin Thubron, BBC2 *Cover to Cover*

The author never lets the detail of his European and anti-colonial narratives fog his basic commitment to the capacity of the slave populations to act in furtherance of their own liberation.
Paul Gilroy, *New Society*

The Overthrow of
Colonial Slavery
1776–1848

———◆———

ROBIN BLACKBURN

V

VERSO

London · New York

First published by Verso 1988
Reprinted 1990, 1996
© 1988 Robin Blackburn
All rights reserved

Verso
UK: 6 Meard Street, London W1V 3HR
USA: 180 Varick Street, New York, NY 10014-4606

Verso is the imprint of New Left Books

British Library Cataloguing in Publication Data

Blackburn, Robin, 1940–
    The overthrow of Colonial Slavery 1776–
    1848.
    1. Slavery. Abolitionist movements,
    ca. 1770–1861
    I. Title
    322.4'409034

ISBN 0–86091–188–8
ISBN 0–86091–921–8 Pbk

US Library of Congress Cataloging in Publication Data

Blackburn, Robin.
    The overthrow of colonial slavery, 1776–1848 / Robin Blackburn.
        p.   cm.
    Bibliography: p.
    Includes index.
    ISBN 0–86091–188–8.   ISBN 0–86091–901–3 (pbk.)
    1. Slavery–America–Anti-slavery movements–History.   2. Slavery
–America–Emancipation–History.   I. Title.
HT1050.B54 1988
326'.0973–dc19

Printed in Great Britain by Bookcraft (Bath) Ltd.
Typeset by Columns of Caversham, Reading, Berkshire

List of Maps

For Gemma and Christopher

Contents

Acknowledgements

I would like to thank Perry Anderson and Mike Davis for most helpful advice on a draft of this book. The following kindly commented upon portions of the manuscript or of earlier drafts of the project of which it forms a part: Neil Belton, Hugh Brogan, Paul Buhle, Malcolm Deas, Caroline Fick, Elizabeth Fox Genovese, Fred Halliday, Winston James, Gareth Stedman Jones, Octavio Rodriguez, George Rudé, Larry Siedentop, Ben Schoendorf, Mary Turner and Ellen Meiksins Wood. I am grateful to all the foregoing for their help while, of course, absolving them from responsibility for any errors the text may contain. I would also like to thank Alejandro Galvez, Lynne Amidon, Gregor Benton, Elisabeth Burgos and the staff of Canning House Library for their help in locating research materials.

Without the extraordinary support and patience of my colleagues at New Left Review and Verso the book could never have been completed.

I would also like to thank Susan and Reg Hicklin, and Barbara and Ian Webber, for their generous hospitality while I was writing and researching.

Finally I must thank Margrit Fauland for her encouragement and for tolerating the anti-social behaviour which composition seems to entail.

Robin Blackburn, January 1988

For Gemma and Christopher

Contents

List of Maps

Acknowledgements

I would like to thank Perry Anderson and Mike Davis for most helpful advice on a draft of this book. The following kindly commented upon portions of the manuscript or of earlier drafts of the project of which it forms a part: Neil Belton, Hugh Brogan, Paul Buhle, Malcolm Deas, Caroline Fick, Elizabeth Fox Genovese, Fred Halliday, Winston James, Gareth Stedman Jones, Octavio Rodriguez, George Rudé, Larry Siedentop, Ben Schoendorf, Mary Turner and Ellen Meiksins Wood. I am grateful to all the foregoing for their help while, of course, absolving them from responsibility for any errors the text may contain. I would also like to thank Alejandro Galvez, Lynne Amidon, Gregor Benton, Elisabeth Burgos and the staff of Canning House Library for their help in locating research materials.

Without the extraordinary support and patience of my colleagues at New Left Review and Verso the book could never have been completed.

I would also like to thank Susan and Reg Hicklin, and Barbara and Ian Webber, for their generous hospitality while I was writing and researching.

Finally I must thank Margrit Fauland for her encouragement and for tolerating the anti-social behaviour which composition seems to entail.

Robin Blackburn, January 1988

Introduction:
Colonial Slavery in the
New World c. 1770

Behold the peace that's owned by him who feels
He does no wrong, or outrage when he deals
    In human flesh; or yet supplies the gold
To stir the strife, whose victims you behold . . .
Perhaps the Cuban merchant too, may think
In guilt's great chain he's but the farthest link.
Forsooth, he sees not all the ills take place,
    Nor goes in person to the human chase;
He does not hunt the negro down himself;
    Of course he only furnishes the pelf.
He does not watch the blazing huts beset,
Nor slips the horde at rapine's yell, nor yet
Selects the captives from the wretched band
Nor spears the aged with his right hand . . .
He does not brand the captives for the mart,
Nor stow the cargo – 'tis the captain's part . . .
    His agents simply snare the victims first,
They make the war and he defrays the cost . . .
    To human suffering, sympathy and shame,
His heart is closed, and wealth is all his aim.

The Slave-Trade Merchant (1840), R.R. Madden

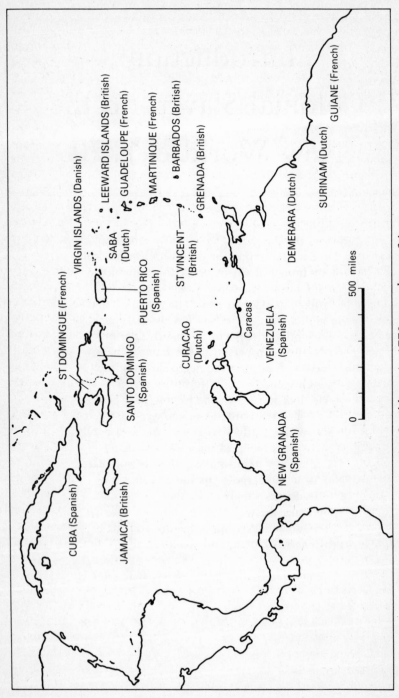

The Caribbean in 1770: see also p. 34

CUBA (Spanish)

JAMAICA (British)

ST DOMINGUE (French)

SANTO DOMINGO (Spanish)

VIRGIN ISLANDS (Danish)

PUERTO RICO (Spanish)

SABA (Dutch)

LEEWARD ISLANDS (British)

GUADELOUPE (French)

MARTINIQUE (French)

BARBADOS (British)

ST VINCENT (British)

GRENADA (British)

CURACAO (Dutch)

Caracas

VENEZUELA (Spanish)

NEW GRANADA (Spanish)

DEMERARA (Dutch)

SURINAM (Dutch)

GUIANE (French)

0   500 miles

Introduction

Around the year 1770 there were nearly two and a half million slaves toiling in the fields, mills, mines, workshops and households of the New World colonies. Slave labour supplied the most coveted and important items in Atlantic and European commerce: the sugar, coffee, cotton and cacao of the Caribbean; the tobacco, rice and indigo of North America; the gold and sugar of Portuguese and Spanish South America. These commodities comprised about a third of the value of European commerce, a figure inflated by regulations that obliged colonial products to be brought to the metropolis prior to their re-export to other destinations. Atlantic navigation and European settlement of the New World made the Americas Europe's most convenient and practical source of tropical and sub-tropical produce. The rate of growth of Atlantic trade in the eighteenth century had outstripped all other branches of European commerce and created fabulous fortunes. Yet this imposing nexus of empire and slavery was about to enter a terminal crisis.

The period 1776–1848 witnessed successive challenges to the regimes of colonial slavery, leading to the destruction either of the colonial relationship, or of the slave system, or of both, in one after another of all the major New World colonies. The contestation of empire and the contestation of slavery were, in principle, dissimilar and distinct projects. Yet in this period they became intertwined, as colonists resisted imperial rule and as the slaves themselves sought to exploit any weakening in the apparatus of social control. All the colonial powers permitted slavery and all the slave systems were integrated within one or other of the transatlantic empires. Large-scale plantation slavery had developed in the seventeenth century Caribbean as a result of private enterprise and freelance initiative; after a few decades of virtual autonomy the planters had acquired the interested protection of England or France, powers which had the naval strength to keep marauding pirates, privateers and colonial rivals at bay. The new slave systems developed within a colonial shell and generated large commercial profits and customs revenues for the imperial metropolis. But for the plantations to prosper, the imperial authorities had to resist the temptation of over-regulating and over-taxing the plantation commerce.

The structures of empire were more immediately vulnerable than those of slave subjugation and exploitation. Slaveholder power was concentrated in the Americas; imperial power was strung out across oceanic sea-lanes and depended on the more or less willing allegiance of the possessing classes in the colonies. As European settler populations reproduced themselves across generations they developed institutions and resources which reduced reliance on the metropolis. By the latter

3

half of the eighteenth century colonial elites throughout the Americas were acquiring greater self-confidence, whether they were involved in slaveholding or not. The buoyancy of Atlantic trade was such that the commercial monopolies were bursting at the seams in 1770. In the aftermath of the Seven Years War (1756–63) all of the imperial powers recognised the pressure for greater colonial autonomy and sponsored projects of reform. The colonial challenge to metropolitan officials and merchants represented an aspiration to self-government: it was at once a claim to greater economic freedom and an assertion of an embryonic new American identity and civilisation. American demands for liberty and self-determination strengthened attacks on oligarchy and arbitrary rule in the Old World. Yet rejection of the *political* regimes of the Old World did not necessarily imply fundamental changes in *social* institutions. One of the aims of this book is to find out why the crisis in the mode of political domination sometimes detonated a crisis of the social regime, especially the institution of slavery.

This introduction aims to give a sketch of the colonial slave systems of the mid-eighteenth century, establishing their characteristic strengths and weaknesses, on the eve of that 'Age of Revolution' in which they were to play a highly significant role.

The systems of mercantilist control sought to direct colonial trade, and engaged tens of thousands of officials to this end. Britain permitted a species of imperial free trade and did not at all respect the colonial monopolies of its rivals. French merchants were allowed to re-export plantation produce free of duty and received a bounty for the slaves they sold to the planters in the Antilles. The royal bureaucracies of Spain and Portugal asserted direct control of the silver and gold produced in their American possessions. Colonial monopolies in principle enabled metropolitan merchants to skim off a surplus and impede inter-American trade. But the very vigour of Atlantic commerce tended to overspill the prescribed boundaries. Smuggling is likely to have accounted for at least a tenth of all trade despite the customs and excise officials and the regular naval patrols. Notwithstanding Portugal's weakness, and the trading concessions extended to Britain, the merchants of Lisbon and Oporto held their own in the Brazil trade, even if this meant selling British textiles for Brazilian gold. By the 1760s the main *raison d'être* of the Dutch islands was as centres for unregulated commerce.

The different patterns of colonial development produced the division by territory of the New World slave population in 1770 set out in Table 1 below.

Table 1 Estimated Slave Populations of the American Colonies 1770

	Slaves	*Total Population*
British America	878,000	2,600,000
(British North America)	(450,000)	(2,100,000)
(British Caribbean)	(428,000)	(500,000)
Portuguese America (Brazil)	700,000	2,000,000
French America (Caribbean)	379,000	430,000
Spanish America	290,000	12,144,000
(Spanish Caribbean)	(50,000)	(144,000)
(Spanish Mainland)	(240,000)	(12,000,000)
Dutch Caribbean	75,000	90,000
Danish Caribbean	18,000	25,000

The size of the colonial slaveholdings did not reflect either the geographical size of the different empires or priority in colonisation. Spain, the first and still the largest colonial power in the New World, ranked only fourth as a slaveholding power. Britain and France, which had no slave colonies in 1640, now possessed the most flourishing slave plantations in the New World. The total slave population of Brazil may have been larger than that of the French colonies, but the estimate is uncertain and slavery was somewhat less concentrated in the export sector. Brazil was a colony of Portugal, but Portugal was almost a semi-colony of Britain so that much of Brazil's slave-produced gold came to London. Britain and France had the commercial vigour to create the most productive slave colonies even if the Iberian powers still held sway over immense mainland empires. And, in contrast to the Netherlands, Britain and France had been able to mobilise the requisite strength to defend their colonial conquests in the New World. Though capitalist social relations were more highly developed in Britain than in France, the vigorous development of French commerce and manufacture in the eighteenth century nevertheless ran Britain a close second. French exports of refined sugar or of cotton manufactures exceeded those of Britain in the 1760s; cheap colonial raw materials, supplied under special privileges and exemptions, helped to make possible an enclave of accumulation that employed wage labour.

The use of African slaves had enabled Britain to vault to the premier position as an American colonial power, developing its American possessions until their exports overtook those of Spanish America. By the 1770s the slave colonies of the French Antilles were bidding to overtake the British West Indies. The annual value of colonial exports in the early 1770s amounted to £5.6 million for the British colonies, £5.2 million for the French colonies, £1.8 million for Brazil and £4.9 million for the whole of Spanish America. British merchants and manufacturers held a larger lead in supplying colonial markets; their exports to the Americas as a whole were at least twice as great as those of the French. Transatlantic commerce required approximately half a million tons of shipping and employed more than a hundred thousand seamen and dock-workers. Britain's profits on the Atlantic trade derived chiefly from the effective capitalist organisation of marine transport, manufacturing supply and commercial finance; French commercial profits, which in gross amounted to a half of the colonial export trade, were more dependent on mercantilist monopoly.

In the mid-eighteenth century Britain and France were, according to widespread contemporary testimony, the most powerful, the most splendid and the most dynamic states in the world. In their different ways Versailles and Westminster were the exemplary governments of the age. Following Portugal, Spain and the Netherlands they had established a worldwide network of colonies and trading bases. These were the first truly global, trans-oceanic empires in human history. The New World was thought to be the crucial testing ground by such leading statesmen as Pitt the Elder and Choiseul. Even the Abbé Raynal, who endorsed the new philosophical critique of slavery, believed that sugar plantations had replaced gold mines as the sinews of empire. In his *Histoire des Deux Indes* (1770) Raynal urged the Spanish authorities to promote the plantation economy of Cuba so that it could rival the achievements of the Virginian planters, who supplied all Europe with tobacco, or those of the planters of St Domingue, who supplied half of Europe with sugar.

The Atlantic and Caribbean loomed large in eighteenth century wars. Britain and France protected their empires with navies that comprised sixty to eighty 'ships of the line' each, with a swarm of smaller vessels; Spain's naval forces were only a little smaller and included the effective *guardacostas* of the Caribbean. The Netherlands, defeated in Brazil in the seventeenth century, was only a minor American power. British and French conquests in the Caribbean were only sustained because of the deployment of massive naval power and the availability of a steady stream of emigrants. After the Treaty of Ryswick in 1697 there had been few territorial changes in the Caribbean but the threat was there. However, by 1770 an important turning point had been reached. Britain's victories in the Seven Years War had enabled her to eject the French from North America. From this time forward internal upheavals overlaid and displaced imperial rivalry as the key to change in the hemisphere. Slaveholders were to play a leading part in these upheavals, whether in the thirteen English colonies of North America in the 1770s, or in the French Antilles in 1788–93, or in Venezuela, New Granada, Peru, and Rio de la Plata in the 1810s and 1820s. The slaveholders of Brazil, and of the British and Spanish Caribbean, played their cards in a different way, avoiding upheaval so far as possible but making their presence felt all the same. American slaveholders in this period were distinctly less conservative than the wealthy and powerful elsewhere; whether mine-owners in Mexico or landowners in Europe. Some observations on the character of the slavery found in the Americas of this epoch will help explain this.

The species of slavery that prevailed in the Americas in the eighteenth century should not be seen as a relic of the Ancient or medieval world. The colonial systems were of very recent construction and were highly commercial in character. They spanned an ocean and were locked in rivalry. The slaves were drawn exclusively from Africa and the great majority of them were subjected to harsh labour regimes. By contrast previous forms of slavery had been less far-flung, less commercial and more heterogeneous. The slaves of the New World were economic property and the main motive for slaveholding was economic exploitation; to this end at least nine tenths of American slaves were put to commodity production.[1]

In other societies slavery has had a chameleon-like ability to adapt to the surrounding social formation; like a social false limb it has extended the powers of slaveholders in forms appropriate to the given society – perhaps enlarging a lineage or supplying a trusted core of administrators. In the eighteenth century Americas the use of slaves in agriculture and mining helped to extend the scope of mercantile and manufacturing capital and supplied industrialising regions with needed inputs and outlets. Elizabeth Fox Genovese and Eugene Genovese have identified the impulse to mercantile accumulation as the propulsive force behind the rise of the new slave systems. The New World partnership of merchants and planters led to the creation of an integrated manufacturing and agricultural enterprise. The slave plantations themselves incorporated those advances in agricultural technique compatible with co-ordinated gang labour. The entrepreneurs directing them were usually willing to adopt innovations in processing methods and they had the resources to purchase the products of capitalist industry and commercial farming. The New World planter, purchasing inputs in partial exchange for the commodities supplied, could increase output in response to market pressures far more rapidly than the feudal lords of

Eastern Europe and on the basis of greater complementarity with manufacturing capital. The plantation itself embodied a feat of productive organisation and invigilation. The slave gangs in the fields and the slave teams in the mills were mobilised for labour that was coerced, intensive and continuous. Manuel Moreno Fraginals has explored the ways in which the sugar mills anticipated some of the methods of an emergent capitalist industrialism, with its precise calibration of labour inputs and subordination to mechanical rhythms. The tightly coordinated labour process of the late eighteenth century sugar 'plantation' half resembled the industrial 'plant' of the future.[2]

Yet these Marxist authors rightly distinguish between New World slavery and a regime of generalised commodity production. The slaveholding enterprises still had roots in so-called 'natural economy' – that is, subsistence cultivation and internal, 'uncommodified' labour. Slaves grew much of their own food, built their own huts and thus, unlike the wage labourer, did not chiefly depend on goods purchased on the market. The slave plantation could usually survive, if necessary, from its own subsistence cultivation and manufacture. The fact that planters had this 'reserve' of natural economy, as Jacob Gorender has called it, reinforced their capacity to survive times of war, revolution or commercial depression.[3] Like the peasant or farmer, and unlike the manufacturer or merchant, the planter could withdraw from the market for long periods and keep his enterprise in being. But he was not bound, in phases of expansion, to the resources of the estate; with beckoning markets his prospects were limited only by his capacity to buy in slaves, supplies and equipment as needed. European peasant cultivators or feudal serf-lords, by contrast, were hemmed in by 'natural economy' and constrained by the given size of the family or estate labour available to them. The capital tied up in his plantation meant that the planter was not prone to relapse into autarchy. Building and maintaining a plantation entailed ongoing economic costs which acted as a spur to renewed commodity production as soon as it was possible; and the economic value of slaves was such that the planter who could not make a profit out of them himself was induced to sell them to someone who would. Once again neither the peasant nor the serf-lord was subject to comparable economic pressure. Since the slaves covered their subsistence needs in only two days labour each week, including nearly all their sparse 'free time', the rate of surplus extraction and gross profit was very high. The slaveholding planter was thus an entrepreneur with both the ability and the motive to be responsive to market pressures. The expansion of supply depended only on the cost of clearing land, of acquiring slaves and equipment, and of paying salaried supervisors.

8

Europe's craving for exotic commodities was such that these costs could be amply met.[4]

The characterisation offered here refers to the predominant form of American slavery in the eighteenth century. In Spanish America and Portuguese Brazil there were also residues of an earlier, more diffuse pattern. It is necessary to distinguish between the *ancillary* slavery of early Spanish or Portuguese colonialism and the *systemic* slavery, linked to plantations and commodity production, which was dominant by the eighteenth century. The 'ancillary slavery' of the Spanish did not involve colonies with slave majorities or the exclusion of slaves from all responsible posts or the denial of human attributes to the enslaved. The introduction of slaves helped to consolidate an imperial superstructure of exploitation that was not mainly based on slave labour. Spanish wealth and power derived from the conquest and exploitation of the indigenous peoples of the continent; outright enslavement of the Amerindians was tried but proved either impossible or so destructive as to be counter-productive. The Indian communities of the sixteenth century Caribbean islands and littoral had been disrupted and demoralised by invasion and overwork; their peoples were destroyed by appalling epidemics, or were absorbed as the conquerors took Indian women. Some fled to inhospitable and marginal swamps, or held out on rocky islands and in jungle backlands. But on the mainland the Spanish conquerors were able to substitute themselves for the previous ruling strata of the Inca and Aztec empires, exploiting Indian communities that were subjugated but not enslaved.

Captive Africans had been introduced to Spanish America to make up for de-population of the worst-hit areas and to strengthen the presence of the colonising power; to sustain centres of administration and lines of communication and to serve the personal needs of the conquerors. The eighteenth century use of slaves in Spanish America retained some of this long-established pattern. African slaves worked as domestics, porters, foremen, dockers, seamstresses, barbers, gardeners, artisans; slaves did toil in gold mines in New Granada, and on sugar estates in Cuba or cacao groves in Venezuela, but these were still fairly modest enclaves in the Spanish imperial economy of 1770. Its silver was mined by wage workers, mostly of Indian extraction but with some blacks or mestizos, or by tribute labour from the Indian villages. Imperial administration in Spanish America directly promoted and co-ordinated economic activity; royal administrators supervised the supply of food and labour to the mines, allotted mining concessions, purchased tobacco and took charge of the flow of silver back to Europe. There were leaks, of course, but this *extensive* system of imperial exploitation contrasted with the *intensive* regime of micro-exploitation on the slave plantations elsewhere in the Americas. It also helped to inhibit the creole elite who were well aware that the imperial state was a direct and crucial factor in their extraction of surplus labour from the underlying producers. By contrast planters directed a self-contained process of surplus extraction, with the colonial state stepping in to levy taxes, establish awkward regulations and furnish external protection. The Spanish American silver mines in the 1770s were yielding fabulous bonanzas – hence the impressive value of Spanish colonial exports – but this left the Spanish American mining proprietors much less interested in colonial autonomy than was the case with the planters.

The Brazilian slavery of the 1770s, with sugar estates in the North East, gold fields in the South, and widespread use of slaves in workshops, households, farms and ranches in every province, reflected the variety of the colony's history. The Portuguese in Brazil had first set up sugar mills in the late sixteenth century and, with Dutch help, developed crucial features of the commercial slave estate. In Brazil as in the Caribbean the indigenous Indian communities were decimated by disease and driven back by conquest. Portuguese merchants had been the first to develop the Atlantic slave trade, supplying slaves cheaply from their own trading posts on the African coast. Newcomers from Africa found escape far more difficult and dangerous than did the Amerindians. Moreover the captive Africans came from societies where agriculture, mining and social relations of enslavement were all more highly developed than was the case for the Amerindians of Brazil, the Caribbean or the North American littoral. Brazil attracted a stream of Portuguese settlers but the landholders (*fazendeiros*) found it easier to overwork captive Africans than to deny all rights to immigrant servants from Europe. The labour force of the early seventeenth century Brazilian sugar mill remained mixed, combining scores of servile Africans and Indians with a dozen or more Portuguese immigrants; and processing was not integrated with agricultural labour as most cane was supplied by independent farmers (*lavradores de cana*). The term plantation was not used of the Brazilian sugar estate.

The early Brazilian colonists demonstrated the profitability of sugar cultivation, using a mixed labour force with a growing predominance of African slaves. Further advance to a full-blown systemic slavery was blocked by erratic demand in Europe, by Dutch invasions and occupation (1624–54) and by a cumbersome and expensive annual fleet system. The discovery of gold in Brazil in the late seventeenth century gave the Portuguese monarchy a powerful incentive to retain the mechanisms of 'extensive' imperial exploitation. The fleets facilitated imperial control and taxation as well as offering protection. But while gold exports were safely convoyed to Europe the sugar trade was choked. Brazilian slaves continued to produce sugar but in this almost closed economy many were also employed in supplying local markets with foodstuffs and manufactures. The Iberian powers obliged merchants to sail with the annual fleet down to the 1760s; the spontaneous growth of commercial agriculture was inhibited, so that greater scope was given to the Dutch, English and French.[5]

The breakthrough to large-scale plantation production was made by British and French planters, backed by independent Dutch merchants, in the Caribbean around 1640–50. Systemic slavery had to be colonial in character because the slave plantations needed naval and military guarantees to protect them from rivals and the threat of slave revolt. While ancillary slavery helped to reproduce empire, empire helped to reproduce systemic slavery. The plantation was run as an integrated enterprise with privileged access to European markets; soon all menial labour was performed by slaves. Instability and war retarded the plantation development of Jamaica and Saint Domingue until the Peace of Utrecht in 1713 established more favourable conditions both for plantation development and for the organisation of a large-scale slave traffic.

The British and French colonies became, like Brazil but unlike Spanish America, colonies of settlement, as the original inhabitants were killed, marginalised or forced out. Export agriculture itself helped to finance colonisation, as merchants extended free passage to European servants willing to work on the plantations for three or five years. More than half of the white emigrants to colonial North America arrived as indentured servants; the French and British Caribbean also absorbed tens of thousands of these tied labourers, who could be purchased more cheaply than slaves. Altogether some 350,000 servants were shipped to the British colonies up to the 1770s. The white servants or *engagés* could be harshly exploited but they did not offer the planters the chances of building up a stable work force. White servants or *engagés* eventually had to be set free; the Africans were condemned to a lifetime of bondage. In the first decades of the eighteenth century the tobacco planters of Virginia and Maryland also came increasingly to rely on slave labour rather than on indentured servants from England. White servants had defined legal rights and some expectation of finding support within the colonising community, both from the authorities and from the common people. Captive Africans had few rights and virtually no ability to enforce them. They might evoke pity but not solidarity from non-slaveholding whites. White colonists enjoyed a measure of freedom unknown in the Old World while blacks were subjected to a more systematic and ferocious system of enslavement than had ever been seen before.

New World colonial slavery developed in the wake of capitalist advance in seventeenth century Europe. By the 1760s some 60,000 slaves were being brought to the Americas each year, roughly ten times the annual intake of the 1650s and fifty times the number introduced by Spain and Portugal each year in the 1560s or 1570s. Prior to 1580 it is likely that European immigrants outnumbered slave entries to the New World; between 1580 and 1650 the number of African captives arriving in each year was roughly the same as the number of European immigrants. With the rise of 'systemic' slavery slave 'imports' rose proportionately as well as absolutely. The first New World colony where African slaves comprised the majority of the population was the British island of Barbados in about 1645, to be shortly followed by the other British and French controlled islands of the Lesser Antilles, then by Jamaica in the 1660s and St Domingue in the 1690s. African captives only began to be shipped to North America in large numbers in the first decades of the eighteenth century. The discovery of gold in Brazil at the end of the seventeenth century more than doubled the annual import of slaves into that territory. The development of the British and French Caribbean meant that the numbers of African slaves landed in the New World certainly exceeded the number of European immigrants in the period 1650–1700. But it was not until the eighteenth century that a huge disparity opened up with some six million African captives arriving in the New World, five or six times the number of Europeans. At least a million slaves died in this century alone in the course of the notorious 'middle passage' from Africa to the New World, and untold numbers died before reaching the African coast.

This surge in the slave trade reflected a vast increase in the output of the slave plantations. Brazil's entire sugar output in 1620 had been only 15,000 tons annually, a figure probably not exceeded until the 1750s; the tiny island of Barbados alone produced 15,000 tons in the 1670s. By 1760 the British and French slave colonies produced 150,000 tons of sugar annually, rising to 290,000 tons in the years 1787–90. The construction of slave plantations in Virginia and Maryland raised tobacco output from 20 million lbs in 1700 to 220 million lbs in 1775. In 1700 there were some 100,000 slaves in the British colonies and 30,000 in the French colonies; at this time there are unlikely to have been as many as 100,000 slaves in all of Spanish America, or more than 150,000 in Brazil. Thus, despite appalling mortality rates, the slave population of the Americas multiplied six times over from about 400,000 in 1700 to 2,400,000 in 1770, with the British and French colonial slave populations expanding most rapidly.[6]

Why were the Americas the site for this phenomenal expansion and why did it entail slavery? Capitalist development in Europe generated new wants that could not be met from European resources. The New World had the climate and soil needed to grow the exotic produce craved by Europeans and maritime transport was cheap. But the Americas were not peopled by cultivators dedicated to commodity production. Indeed the sub-tropical coastal regions most suited to produce these crops were severely de-populated following the disastrous impact of European conquest. The cultivation of plantation products involved the kind of labour which repelled voluntary migrants; the more so since the abundance of land in the New World offered an alternative that was widely preferred to labour on the plantations – even if, as was often the case, this meant fighting the indigenous inhabitants for possession. Portuguese, Dutch, British and French merchants found that it paid handsomely to sponsor the development of plantations. But they only succeeded in staffing them by securing a supply of slaves from the coast of Africa. Competition in the Atlantic marketplace submerged any scruples they had about trading in enslaved Africans, or putting them to forced labour on the plantations, or making money out of the produce of slaves. Prior to about 1760 there were astonishingly few protests at the mass enslavement of Africans despite the fact that, as will be seen in the next chapter, slavery had long disappeared from North-western Europe. New World slavery solved the colonial labour problem at a time when no other solution was in sight. It thus proved to be highly congruent with commercial and manufacturing accumulation in the centres of capitalist advance in Western Europe; first and foremost those in Britain, the Netherlands and the French Atlantic sea-board and its hinterland.

What maintained demand for the slave produce? The plantation products were popular pleasures, with demand for sugar and tobacco often acting as the lure drawing widening circles of the population into a commodity economy; the taxes on these products also supplied a useful revenue for the major states. The new pattern of social relations led to incomes being earnt in money rather than kind; sweetened beverages and tobacco were both a consolation and spur, while light, washable, bright textiles made life more pleasant and healthy. Europe's thirst for plantation produce, which it seemed impossible to slake, allowed the supply of sugar, coffee, tobacco or cotton to double in a decade without a collapse in price. Traders and planters were encouraged to pursue the almost limitless prospects of expansion which attended the construction of slave plantations. The new culture of commercialised consumption was oblivious of the human cost that its satisfactions entailed.[7]

What were the internal tensions generated by colonial slavery? In 1770 the British and French authorities were most at risk from rebellious colonists. The British and French settlers, and their descendants, did not believe that being colonists should deprive them of rights; this sentiment was, of course, strongest in the older British colonies of North America but it was also to be found in the French Antilles.

The specific strength of British and French colonial slavery was the decentralised, planter-controlled apparatus for containing the slaves. The strength of Iberian colonisation was concentrated in centres of administration in the colonies themselves.

Colonial slavery bred its own characteristic social antagonisms. Even the wisest of ministers found it difficult to allot privileges and penalties in an effective and coherent way given the spontaneity of the Atlantic economy and its unpredictable responses to changing tastes and changing methods of production. The tobacco planters of Virginia, the sugar planters of the French Antilles and the gold mine concessionaires of Brazil had the disadvantage that their products had achieved a high degree of visibility. Prone in any case to resent merchants and excise officials they were subjected to mercantilist restrictions which made them feel, as Washington once put it, 'as miserably oppressed as our own blacks'. The planters of the British West Indies accepted their position more easily since they knew that the colonial system delivered to them a protected metropolitan market, saving them from the necessity of competing on equal terms with the more efficient French plantations. Likewise the sugar planters of Spanish America or even of Brazil were not yet sufficiently dynamic to feel a keen sense of frustration; though this was not the case with the cacao planters of Venezuela who challenged and evaded the monopoly claims of the Caracas Company in every way they knew until they secured its liquidation in the 1780s.

Aside from a few privileged big-wigs the slaveholders of the New World had a lively dislike of colonial officials since they wished to run their own affairs and since colonial officialdom had the job of administering mercantilist regulation. But at least colonial garrisons gave them some protection. Slaveholders were prone to a more intimate antagonism towards metropolitan merchants and their local agents, especially when, as was so often the case, they were indebted to them. Bringing a slave plantation to the point where a crop could be sold was a protracted, expensive and risky undertaking. The planters often had recourse to credit in buying slaves, equipment or provisions. They often fell into the clutches of the merchants after a war, a hurricane, or a slave revolt had wiped out their crop or an epidemic had carried away half or more of the overworked slave crew. Typically the merchant charged high interest on loans to planters and could get away with doing so because of the risks involved. But all this meant that the slaveholding planter was giving the merchant-creditor a prior claim on super-profits that had not yet even been produced. The very cash laid out in acquiring a slave represented discounted future surplus to be appropriated by putting the slave to work. There was here a nexus of antagonism between planter and merchant that often intensified hostility to colonial systems which awarded national mercantile monopolies. Usually local merchants aroused less suspicion or hatred since they might be partners in evading mercantilist restrictions and metropolitan creditors. But the relationship between planters and merchants was never an easy one. This included antagonism to slave traders wherever planters felt that they could get along without extra slave purchases. It could even prompt impatience with slavery itself, a sort of desperate longing by the slaveholding planter to jump out of his own skin and into that of some more sovereign landholder and agriculturalist.

The relationship between planters and other layers of the free population of the colonies, while also ambivalent, admitted of more cordiality. The planters bought provisions from small-holders and some supplies from local manufacturers. They engaged the services of overseers, book-keepers, lawyers, doctors and the like. In the plantation zone itself the larger planter would be acknowledged as leader of the local community, holding such posts as magistrate or Colonel in the militia. Despite tensions associated with patronage the planters could usually attract support from other free colonists in confrontations with the metropolis. This planter-dominated axis was strongest in the North American plantation zone but was also found wherever plantation development had taken place. The metropolitan powers had been obliged to allow the colonies to develop their own military capacity both as an insurance against servile revolt and as an auxiliary to metropolitan forces during the wars of imperial rivalry.

Throughout the Americas planters, slaveholders, and the local merchants linked to them, were restive and unruly colonial subjects. This was true in South America and the Caribbean as well as North America. But naturally the prevailing balance of social forces and the vigour of the slave-based economy encouraged variations in the precise goals and methods adopted. The possession of slaves conferred status, and running a plantation gave a habit of command. The planters of the mainland tended to be bolder in defying imperial authorities; those of the Caribbean, perched on large slave majorities, were fiercer in word than deed and often preferred to lobby for influence in the imperial centres. But whatever their location planters inclined to think of themselves as autonomous agents with an enlightened and rational outlook on life. The species of quasi-capitalist economic rationality embodied in the slave plantation encouraged this outlook and often tilted it in an anti-mercantilist direction. Striving to get a competitive return out of his estate the planter resented commercial restrictions which prevented him from buying the cheapest supplies and selling to any willing customer. British West Indian planters felt these resentments less intensely because empire free trade allowed them to buy cheap North American supplies, cheap English metal implements and textiles, and to find outlets for as much sugar as they could produce. Virginian and Maryland planters looked at it differently because by selling tobacco direct to Europe they could cut out the middleman's commission. The planters of the French Antilles and of the plantation enclaves of Spanish America knew that metropolitan merchants paid them less because of their monopoly privileges and would have liked to have direct access to British manufactures and North American supplies. The owners of gold mine concessions in Brazil felt such resentments less keenly, partly because their concessions depended on royal licences and partly because the mining economy was in decline by the 1770s as deposits were exhausted.

Britain's colonial empire in the Americas allowed a large measure of colonial self-government. It had been held together by its own commercial coherence, by the strength of the Royal Navy and by fear of the Indians and of France. With the exception of Virginian tobacco Britain absorbed by far the greater part of the plantation produce of its colonies. For reasons of dynastic and national aggrandisement France maintained a large naval and colonial establishment; sections of the aristocracy and bourgeoisie both found a nesting ground in the colonial system. But the French colonial *conseils* were as jealous of their rights as the metropolitan *parlements* and probably more representative of the local possessing classes. Britain and France extracted a commercial surplus from their colonies but did not levy large direct revenues from them. The royal governments of Spain and Portugal had a much weaker European base and had come to rely on American revenues generated by the mining economy and some plantation trade. In fact the flow of colonial revenues to Madrid and Lisbon both required and financed a colonial establishment whose spinal column was supplied by an aristocratic military caste. African slaves and free people of colour were still used as an auxiliary force to underpin imperial fortifications, arsenals, naval yards and communications. In 1770 both Spanish and Portuguese America almost entirely lacked the autonomous vigour of the English and French territories; the local-born ('creole') elite had at best a secondary role in government and was, outside plantation

16

enclaves, generally sunk in provincial torpor.

The most independent and vigorous slaveholders in the Americas were to be found in English North America and in the French Caribbean; towards the close of the eighteenth century some planters in Portuguese Brazil and the Spanish Caribbean began to emulate them. The arc of planter resistance to imperial control – moving from the former to the latter – furnishes one of the themes of this book. It began with the British colonies of North America partly because the planters there were more strongly positioned but also because the imperial power had long tolerated internal colonial autonomy. The strongest Atlantic states, Britain and France, had been willing to concede more to colonial self-government than did Spain or Portugal, weaker as European powers but with formidable imperial bureaucracies. In the year 1770 colonial slavery was strongest where imperial authority was weakest, in the English colonies. Similarly slavery was weakest in Spanish America where metropolitan authority was exercised in the most dirigiste fashion. France and Portugal occupied intermediate positions. Since slavery was inversely proportional to the exercise of metropolitan authority it is not surprising that the first exercise in independence was to make a rather large contribution to boosting the slave systems.

The British empire, though less exacting and constrictive, was also less useful to the North American planters than was the case with the other imperial systems. The departure of the French, and with them of the need for British military protection, also revealed that the empire had long lacked the intrinsic productive rationale which was still retained, to a greater or lesser extent, by the other large empires. French absolutism conferred privileges on the merchants of Bordeaux and Nantes but also helped the Antillean planters. The slave trade was subsidised, planters with a title of nobility were exempt from taxation and the colonial garrisons helped to maintain roads, ports and those systems of irrigation which made St Domingue so productive. The planters of North East Brazil could also compile a similar list of imperial favours in the 1760s, as Pombal sought to foster the plantation economy. By contrast the infrastructure of empire impinged on Virginian planters more simply as a constraint and not a support. This is not to say that narrowly economic motives dictated the pattern and sequence of colonial rebellion; but so long as they were effective the structures mentioned here had an impact on mentality as well as on economic calculation. As for the Spanish American mining proprietors, they were more thoroughly beholden to the imperial authorities than any planter since they depended on them, as noted above, for supplies, labour, licences and transport.[8]

In the Old World the 'intensive' commercial and manufacturing development of the Low Countries had led to a momentous clash with the then most powerful 'extensive' empire, that of the Spanish Hapsburgs; a similar impulse to national liberation appeared in those regions of the New World where there was an intensive development of commerce, farming and planting.

Slaveholding in the Americas was heavily concentrated in the tropical and sub-tropical zone of the Caribbean and of the immediate hinterland of the Atlantic coasts of North and South America. While there were still huge expanses not yet effectively colonised or controlled by an imperial power there were also sectors of the colonial economies in which slavery played a secondary or negligible role. The 25,000 or so black slaves in New England in 1775 were not crucial to farming or ship-building; the coerced cooperation of the slave gang had no commanding productivity edge in mixed farming and manufacture as it did in the cultivation and processing of the plantation staples. However the merchants, farmers and sea-captains of New England found that the slaveholding planters were good customers and resented attempts to limit their trade with the West Indies; as yet there was little they could supply to Europe. The ranchers of South America often engaged some slaves – they sold dried meat to the planters and wished to sell hides and skins more freely to European merchants. The slaveholding gold miners of New Granada and cacao planters of Venezuela smuggled vigorously but still resented metropolitan controls.

The maintenance of colonial slavery had produced different patterns of racial privilege, with different potentials for conflict. In all the colonies whites enjoyed special status and advantages. By 1770 all American slaves were black though not all blacks were slaves. Lower class whites and native Americans owed their freedom from outright enslavement to the resources of communal resistance. Slaveholders appealed to the racial solidarity of whites, and sometimes they even urged Indians to help them maintain black enslavement; but only in the English colonies was there so small a free black population that nearly every black was a slave. In Spanish and Portuguese America sufficient numbers of slaves, or their offspring, had obtained manumission to create a sizeable free black and mulatto population. The free blacks and mulattos were sometimes regarded by the authorities as a counterweight both to the slaves and to the creole elite; they occupied an intermediate status in the caste system and were permitted a separate, if still subordinate, identity. In Brazil the Portuguese had formed black regiments with black officers in their struggle to eject the Dutch; the Spanish also formed black militias in the eighteenth century. The ranks of the Brazilian *Henriques* or the Spanish American *pardo* or *negro* batallions were often recruited from slaves purchased by the state and offered their freedom in return for a lengthy term of service. Since purchasing slaves for the armed forces was expensive they were sometimes seized from enemies of the Crown. In the French and Dutch Caribbean free people of colour were almost as numerous as the white colonists and received some official recognition as a subordinate buttress to the colonial slave system. The complex racial hierarchy of the Spanish, Portuguese and French colonies contrasted with the bipolar, black or white system in the English colonies with their comparatively large white colonial population. In the plantation colonies of North America a majority white population only barely tolerated the presence of free blacks; in the British West Indies, with their massive slave majorities, the whites found it expedient to be somewhat more accommodating to free blacks and mulattos. In all the colonies free blacks and mulattos could themselves own slaves, but in the English colonies this was quite rare. New World slavery coded 'black' skin as a slave characteristic; free people of colour might be led to deny their blackness – or to deny slavery. Slaveholders of partly African descent shared with 'white' slaveholders a concern for their rights that impelled them towards this difficult choice.

The slaves of the Americas in 1770 were more intensively exploited than any group of this size in history. Yet the immediate threat to empire came not from the exploited but from a colonial alliance including many of the exploiters. While imperial garrisons and squadrons were sometimes available to subjugate slave revolts and contain maroons the planters preferred to stamp out resistance by means of their own patrols and militia. Metropolitan forces had the primary function of protecting colonies from external attack. It is for this reason that the British victory in North America in 1763 was too sweeping for its own good; it emancipated the colonists from their fear of the French and Spanish.

Those who built the slave-based enterprises in each colony were united by language, cultural identity and economic interest; and they had the resources to hire employees and to secure allies amongst the non-slaveholding free population. The slaves, by contrast, had been torn from different parts of a huge continent; they spoke different languages and had different traditions. The sequence of capture, sale and shipment was itself traumatic. Those captive Africans who came from the more developed regions were more vulnerable, both more familiar with slavery and less familiar with life in the forest than the Bushmen who seem to have comprised a disproportionate number of the maroons. Every effort was made to prevent slaves developing a common outlook or interest, by sowing division within the plantations and preventing communication between them. The slave populations were always a source of apprehension to their masters; but this fear did not paralyse the slaveholders who believed themselves to be better schooled in the necessities of slave control than metropolitan functionaries.

Colonies with large slave majorities could not have survived for over a century or more if they had not reproduced the subjection of the forced labourers effectively. The extraordinary destructiveness and profitability of the plantations continually re-created a labour force that had had little opportunity to discover itself. The slave crews condemned to labour in the plantations of the tropical and sub-tropical zone had such high mortality and low fertility that it required a slave trade of enormous proportions to maintain or increase population levels. Had it not been for this influx the slave populations of the Caribbean colonies would have declined by two, three or four per cent each year in the mid-eighteenth century. Caribbean planters bought more male than female slaves because of their unwillingness to take on the expense of natural reproduction. Between 1700 and 1774 half a million slaves were introduced to Jamaica yet the slave population rose by only 150,000 between these two dates. The fact that the newly arrived slave in the Caribbean had a life expectancy of only seven or ten years, and that the plantation crews were continually replenished by purchases, made more difficult the construction and transmission of a new collective identity. On the other hand the dire prospects of plantation existence did encourage individual escapes and occasional mass breakouts.

Slave conditions and plantation security varied markedly from colony to colony. The 450,000 slaves of English North America were subjected to close and detailed invigilation by their owners, who typically possessed only a few dozen slaves, if that. The whip, the prayer book and the planters' control of foodstocks helped to keep them hard at work from sun-up to sun-down, with evenings often devoted to processing or manufacture. However a milder climate, plentiful land for raising fresh foodstuffs, and the less intense requirements of tobacco cultivation, meant that North American slave populations avoided the very high mortality rates characteristic of the sugar plantations; blacks in North America multiplied almost as fast as the whites. North American planters faced higher slave prices but much lower interest rates, giving them an incentive to encourage the natural reproduction of the slave labour force. Family ties made North American slaves less willing to run away or revolt than those in the Caribbean.

The low survival rate of Africans in much of the New World partly reflected the fact that they were concentrated in the tropical lowlands where disease took a heavy toll on all immigrants. But overwork, and the consequent neglect of subsistence, certainly helped to kill the slaves. At least two thirds of the Africans arriving in the New World were sent to sugar plantations. In the Caribbean and Brazil the sugar plantations regularly imposed a sixteen or even eighteen hour working day on the slaves; there was nightwork in the mill, and, rain or shine, field work in the day during the long planting and harvesting cycle. The slaves were given bare rations and expected to feed themselves by working for a day, or a day and a half, each week on plots given to them for the purpose. The Caribbean plantations typically contained hundreds of slaves each; the brutalised overseers and drivers to whom they were entrusted did not even have the owners' dubious motive for treating his chattels with some care, namely that they would lose value if he did not. In Spanish and Portuguese America the lot of the plantation slave was generally no better and that of the slaves in the gold workings actually worse – in the latter case there was not even a harvest cycle to limit over-work and exposure to water or weather inflicted heavy mortality. The relative cheapness with which new captives could be bought from the slave merchants and the great value of slave produce – whether sugar or gold – gave a terrible commercial logic to the practice of using up the lives of the slaves in a few years of intense labour. And so long as slave crews were wracked by disease and overwork they found it difficult to resist their oppression collectively.

Throughout the plantation zone the slaves were subjected to, and threatened by, repeated floggings, quite apart from other forms of punishment; slave women were abused by the white men; and the plantation community, if such it can be called, often abandoned to under-nourishment and disease, despond and lassitude, when not galvanised by brute force to attend to the implacable rhythms of plantation labour. The material conditions of slave existence were undoubtedly worse in the Caribbean and Brazil than in North America, where crops and climate were less exacting. On the other hand the large size of plantations in the Caribbean diminished the cultural impact of the slaveholders; this factor favoured African survivals and, eventually, the discovery of new sources of communal identity. Throughout the Caribbean creole languages and dialects, heavily influenced by African vocabularies and structures, became the chief medium of communication. The large rice plantations of South Carolina tended to this latter pattern, with the inhabitants of that region developing a language of their own, Gullah, just as islanders did in many parts of the Caribbean.

The diversified and traditional pattern of slaveholding in Spanish America, and to a lesser extent in Brazil, encouraged the more privileged slaves to develop their own subordinate incorporation within colonial society and to look forward to the day when either they or their children would be freed. Special religious brotherhoods furnished a cultural medium and a form of social insurance for the comparatively large free black and mulatto population.[9] In the Spanish and Portuguese colonies there were quite a large number of semi-autonomous slaves, plying a trade or working land under their own direction. Allowed to keep a proportion of their earnings they could buy their freedom, or that of a relative, over twenty years or so – in so doing they also gave their owner the resources to buy a new young slave and thus to perpetuate his or her role as slaveholder.

American slaveholders found it convenient to foster and rely on a layer of more permanent, skilled or responsible slaves who had mastered the complex requirements of plantation agriculture. These were awarded petty privileges and in return were expected to help invigilate or drive their fellows in the slave gangs. Members of the slave elite had extra rations, could choose a mate, and enjoyed at least a margin of manoeuvre in negotiating the pace and content of plantation labour. Often the Caribbean planters would hand over to their chosen 'head people' all the clothing, foodstuffs and rum destined for the slave crew as a whole. In this way the slave elite had a vested interest in the authority structure of the plantation. It is important to recognise the internal strength of the plantation regime. In principle each plantation was a world to itself and only the most privileged slaves were normally permitted intercourse with other plantations. Even the field slaves had some reason to fear life in the wild and to feel tied to the estate, where they would have their own plots and personal attachments. Slave resistance to the plantation regime was endemic, taking a reformist as well as revolutionary form. Slaves would negotiate, via the drivers and overseers, for larger gardens or an extra evening to work for themselves. The absoluteness of the juridical category of slavery may prevent us from seeing all features of the actual slave condition that were important to the slaves themselves. While the plantation regime was a shock to the newcomer those habituated to it came to discriminate between good and bad conditions, good and bad drivers or overseers. They would still long to be free but other objectives could appear more immediate and practical – a larger garden or making life difficult for a hated overseer. By working slowly and 'stupidly', or seeming indifferent to threats and punishment, the slaves could sometimes bargain for better conditions. The plantation owners and local authorities had superior fire-power, and would use the utmost brutality to maintain servile subordination, but planters and managers sometimes discovered that negotiation was the best way to get the harvest in; the bleak alternatives available to the blacks severely limited the bargains they could strike.

In the French and British sugar islands, where slaves comprised 80–90 per cent of the population, the planters were evidently far more beholden to the guarantee afforded by the colonial state than was the case on the mainland. In the last resort they could always call upon the help of metropolitan garrisons and 'ships of the line' even though they preferred to count only on their own forces. In practice the small size of the Caribbean colonies and the proximity of militia forces greatly reduced the opportunities for slave revolt or escape. Considerations of security and commercial advantage could, however, dispose Caribbean planters against their own national metropolis. During the Seven Years War Britain was able to occupy parts of the French and Spanish Caribbean with the active collaboration of local planters.

The entire colonial process whereby certain West European states carved out empires in the Americas, and developed mines or plantations in them, can be described in terms of a prodigious growth in social powers, some of these co-ordinated by states, many others propelled by private centres of wealth and power. The African captives were introduced into a social formation where the slaveholder disposed not only of the fire-power of his henchmen, but also of the support of his neighbours and clients. Without foodstocks bought in by the planter or his administrator starvation might ensue. Planters and colonial officials controlled local information systems and made recalcitrant blacks the victims of exemplary violence. Even the Amerindian populations were often hostile to black rebels or runaways.

In normal times the slave was trapped within an insidious and many-sided structure of oppression in which slaveholders disposed of economic and ideological resources, as well as political and military guarantees; by contrast the enslaved were divided by background and situation, cut off from their origins but isolated in their new habitat, and enmeshed within vast and complex systems of territorial control, economic exchange and social mobilisation.

Rivalry between the various empires helped to set the scene for attempts by colonists to assert a larger sphere of autonomy and gave some opportunities for slave resistance: only one decade between 1660 and 1770 was not marked by war between one or other of the Atlantic states.

Colonial mercantilism had protected the infancy of the slave systems and national slave trades but output rose most vigorously as chartered monopolies were disbanded and mercantilist restrictions lifted. Some planters felt sufficiently confident of their position to claim self-government and commercial freedom for the colonies; others preferred to sponsor reform within the metropolis. A few were reactionaries with a stand-pat position and a privileged niche in the prevailing order. Slaveholders did not have a uniform outlook or situation but they tended to the side of progress and at least some of them rose to be amongst the outstanding revolutionary leaders of the age. With the industrial revolution still very much in its infancy in 1770 there was nothing to compare in the Atlantic world with the boom in plantation output and trade over the preceding century and a half. In socio-economic terms the slaveholders of the New World had created a new species of slavery and had been obliged to invent, almost from scratch, the legal and ideological underpinnings of a slave system. This historical experience endowed them with a certain confidence in their own capacities. However there was to be no Declaration of the Rights of Slaveholders. The revolutionary slaveholders chose to stress other identities, and other common interests, usually uniting all free-born citizens. At the limit some planter revolutionaries disavowed not only the slave trade but also slavery as inconsistent with civic liberty and national integrity; they discarded that aspect of their double or triple identity which they found most difficult to justify and preferred to see themselves as citizens and as men of enterprise and learning. That slavery was the ugly side of New World progress was not difficult to understand even for a slaveholder. Slavery was thought degrading long before the moralists and economists explained their own objections.

In his classic study of the *Age of Revolution* E.J. Hobsbawm surveyed the *economic* impact of Britain's industrial revolution and the *political* impact of the French Revolution. There is much in subsequent European and American development, and in the modern world, which can be traced to the momentous implications of this 'dual revolution'. However the history of New World slavery demands attention to another set of forces and impulses: those generated by the *political* impact and example of the Hanoverian state, the Atlantic's premier power, and the *economic* impact of the revolutionary events in North

America, the Caribbean and South America. Even those who fought against Hanoverian Britain found much to admire in it; its political institutions, as we will see, were to be widely imitated in the Atlantic world of this epoch, and came to be associated with plantation slavery uneasily co-existing with half-baked abolitionism. Likewise the Revolutions of 1776, 1789 and after had prodigious consequences for the economic fortunes of slavery in the Americas. They broke down mercantilist barriers to the expansion of the plantations and gave an impulse to the spread of slavery on the mainland; at the same time they gave occasion for a succession of momentous eruptions against slavery in the Caribbean. The literature on the 'Age of Revolution' tends to concentrate on Europe, albeit that R.R. Palmer and J. Godechot stressed the revolutionary democratic impulse of the revolt of the thirteen North American colonies. But developments in the slave plantation zone after 1776 – the rise of new states based on slavery, or the spread of revolution and emancipation from Haiti to Spanish America – have not been given attention commensurate with their significance. The present study, devoted as it is to a vital chapter in the history of New World slavery, will explore this somewhat neglected American dimension.[10]

Of course there is no consensual understanding of the 'Age of Revolution' in Europe, even among Marxists. Hobsbawm's work was notable for addressing the international complexity of a continent-wide and epochal process of 'bourgeois revolution' in which politics and economics advanced in counterpoint rather than unison. The class struggles of this epoch were by no means confined to the struggle of a rising capitalist class against an obsolete feudalism. Small producers, wage labourers, artisans, petty functionaries, non-capitalist 'bourgeois' all played a part. Sometimes they formed alliances with capitalist interests or helped to remove obstacles to capitalist advance. But a characteristic feature of the 'Age of Revolution' is that popular forces also intervened to safeguard their own interests as best they knew how. This epoch of 'bourgeois' progress did eventually produce national state structures more conducive to capital accumulation than the *anciens régimes*; but it also gave birth to democratic movements and institutions that acted as a check on the power of capital. The course of events in the Americas was to have a similar complexity, marked by popular class struggle as well as bourgeois revolution. This secular and contested process raised American slaveholders to a pinnacle of wealth and power at one moment only to dash them to pieces at the next.

That slaveholders from the Chesapeake to Rio de Janeiro could be protagonists of 'bourgeois revolution' and capitalist development is, of course, thoroughly paradoxical since they were not themselves bourgeois or capitalist, even if their mercantile associates can be so described. And there is the further problem that while the rise of capitalism in Europe in the seventeenth and eighteenth centuries manifestly promoted the development of the slave systems in the New World there does, nevertheless, seem to be some link between capitalism and the rise of anti-slavery. In several outstanding studies the abolition of slavery or the slave trade has been identified with the purposes or outlook of a new capitalist and imperialist civilisation. It has been argued that the critique of slavery cleared the path for regimes of industrial wage labour or the imposition of a bourgeois hegemony on every layer of society. Similarly, in a non-Marxist idiom, the advance of rationalisation or of industrial society or of market relations is held to have driven back the primitive social form of enslavement. If slavery developed in the wake of capitalism, as I have insisted above, how was it that capitalist advance also prompted anti-slavery impulses? In the course of this book an attempt will be made to resolve the paradox of how capitalism at once needed regimes of unfree labour and yet unleashed forces which helped to challenge American slavery.

In *Capitalism and Slavery* (1944) Eric Williams developed the argument that slavery belonged to the old world of colonial mercantilism and was rendered redundant by the rise of wage labour in the metropolis and the spread of European colonial rule in Asia and Africa. While *Capitalism and Slavery* contains much powerful argument and marvellous illustration it propounds an explanation of abolition according to which industrial capitalists did away with the slave trade and colonial slavery for essentially economic reasons. Reference is made to broader social tensions and to slave revolts but the main weight of explanation is borne by capitalist economic interest. British abolition is approached as if it were a largely self-sufficient national process and the fate of slavery in independent America is not investigated, either as a test of his thesis or as an influence on British emancipation. Williams did not blink the fact that the development of capitalism and slavery had been intimately related. But he minimised the explanatory problems by holding that slavery had produced capitalism rather than the other way about. In contrast to the Marxist understanding of the origins of capitalism, Williams did not take the measure of agrarian, manufacturing and mercantile capital accumulation in the pre-industrial epoch. For him the New World slave systems, far from being a consequence of capitalist development, were a disposable ladder up which it had climbed. In the end his 'dialectical' schema of capitalism using and discarding slavery is mechanical and unsatisfactory.

In *The Problem of Slavery in the Age of Revolution 1776–1823* (1975) David Brion Davis advances a more comparative and complex interrogation of the abolitionists, illuminating the ways in which they helped construct a new bourgeois hegemony, even while moving against a more primitive mode of exploitation in the plantation zone. This impressive work focuses chiefly on the ideology of abolitionism, presenting only in summary form some of the early struggles over emancipation. While metropolitan controversies are much illuminated the pattern of resistance and accommodation amongst the slaves themselves is not integrated into the analysis. The experience and aspirations of the slaves of this epoch are far more difficult to identify and document than the thoughts of leading abolitionists, but this does not dispense us from making the attempt.

Eugene Genovese's outstanding essay *From Rebellion to Revolution* (1979) explores the development of the slaves' own anti-slavery, arguing that its scope and trajectory were transformed during the epoch of bourgeois democratic revolution. In these sustained works of interpretation, informed by wide-ranging research, Davis and Genovese both qualify and nuance the thesis linking anti-slavery to the rise of bourgeois society. Davis shows that abolitionists often aimed beyond a purely capitalist revision of social relations, while Genovese brings out the ways in which slave resistance was made to prevail against bourgeois egoism and reminds us that bourgeois democratic revolution in Europe itself often involved popular forces imposing democratic progress on reluctant, timid or treacherous bourgeois. Davis and Genovese draw attention to the tensions and contradictions that this entailed and place the rise of abolition movements, and the enactment and outcome of emancipation, in a context of class struggles both within the plantation zone and in the metropolis. Drawing on these approaches the present work seeks to construct a Marxist narrative of the actual liberation struggles in the different areas of the Americas and to establish to what extent anti-slavery, either in intention or result, transcended the bourgeois democratic or capitalist dynamic. The narrative reconstruction offered also seeks to acknowledge the contribution made by slaveholders to a wider bourgeois revolutionary process, to the dismantling of colonial slavery and to the birth of new slave systems. This has involved bringing together colonial and metropolitan politics in a country-by-country account of the fate of slavery in each colony in the revolutionary epoch.

In the 1980s there are signs that the study of abolitionism is becoming a specialised branch of study disconnected from the history of slavery. Abolitionism is seen as an important expression of middle class reform rather than as a response to struggles in the plantation zone itself. That abolitionism led to emancipation tends to be assumed without investigation. Thus abolition is understood as a vindication of capitalist advance, of the spread of a market model of society and bourgeois confidence in progress. In such work the focus tends to be upon the evolution of social thought and feeling amongst the metropolitan middle classes. Little attention is paid to metropolitan class struggle or to contests concerning the purpose and character of the state; and even less attention is paid to events in the plantation zone itself, to slave resistance and to the role of former slaves in determining the outcome of the emancipation process. While a theoretical critique of these approaches is needed a narrative which traces the advances of slavery and anti-slavery in the Americas can make its own contribution to suggesting their inadequacy, as this book seeks to do.[11]

If historians of abolitionism are prone to ignore events in the plantation zone there is also a flourishing school of 'slavery studies' which abstracts from the context supplied by metropolitan politics and economy. Slave life and black resistance are studied in isolation, without reference to their impact on metropolitan decisions. Academic specialisation and division of labour has its own justification but the reasons for the destruction of colonial slavery cannot be grasped if metropolitan abolition and the struggles of the plantation zone are allotted to different departments of knowledge.

The still unsurpassed model for understanding the struggle against slavery is *The Black Jacobins: Toussaint L'Ouverture and the San Domingo Revolution* by C.L.R. James (1938). In this work James establishes the impact of revolution in the Caribbean on events in the metropolis and explores the extraordinary fusion of different traditions and impulses achieved in St Domingue in the 1790s. James' story illuminates the essential workings of capitalism, racialism, colonialism and slavery – and the complex class struggle to which they gave rise in St Domingue; it conveys a marvellous sense of the eruption of the masses in history. With a sensibility attuned to the cosmopolitan forces of the age he follows the transatlantic revolutionary impulse as it criss-crosses the ocean from Saint Domingue to Paris and back to the Caribbean again. This is both far more satisfying as explanation, and far more compelling as narrative, than those accounts of struggles concerning colonial slavery which never look outside the plantations or, even worse, never leave the drawing rooms or debating chambers of the metropolis. In some quarters it is supposed that narrative history has little to offer and is incapable of identifying deep-seated structures of economy, mentality or political life.[12] The present work was under-taken out of the conviction that if they are real and effective such structures will also be visible at the level of events. And in the further belief that socio-economic forces and the discourses of ideology are so inherently antagonistic and contradictory that they open up a space of political choice and action which must also be registered if the dynamic of historical development is to be grasped. The attempt to construct a narrative therefore puts conflicting interpretations to the test. It can help to establish the respective weight and significance of the different forces and factors at work. In the accounts offered below I have tried to place struggles over colonial slavery in context and to show that anti-slavery was often imposed on metropolitan decision-makers by external pressures. Marxist research, in the works of such writers as James, Genovese, Gorender and Fraginals, has already made a notable contribution to our understanding of the making and unmaking of slavery in the Americas. But the bearing of this body of work on the mainstream of capitalist development and class struggle has been insufficiently appreciated, and this furnishes an additional reason for the present study. The conclusions offered remain partial and tentative in a field where research and debate advance at a rapid rate.

The first chapter surveys the sources of anti-slavery in the mid-eighteenth century Atlantic world – in popular sentiment, in slave resistance and in philosophy. But it required the crisis of empire for anti-slavery to become a question of practical politics; subsequent chapters trace the eruption of anti-slavery themes in the imperial and revolutionary crises which punctuated the history of the Atlantic powers down to the middle of the nineteenth century. The systems of colonial slavery unravelled very nearly in inverse order to that of their formation, with the crisis of the British and French systems preceding, and helping to precipitate, that of the Iberian powers. It has been suggested that American slavery had an expansionary impetus often frustrated by colonial mercantilism and it is therefore not surprising that the crisis of the colonial systems was provoked by growth rather than contraction. It was altogether appropriate that Hanoverian Britain, aggrandised by slave-related commerce, should have been the first state to be humbled by its own colonists, in 1776–83, and then, in the 1790s, the first to be defeated by insurgent slaves. The planters of English North America were not the richest in the New World but they were embedded in the most dynamic colonial social formation and they were the best placed to challenge metropolitan power. Chapters 2 to 4 explore anti-slavery in Britain and North America, setting both the American Revolution and the rise of abolition in the context of the political order and culture from which they emerged. In subsequent chapters the overthrow of French colonial slavery is similarly considered in its context, that of the crisis of the *ancien régime* and the eruption of revolutionary forces in France and the Caribbean.

Accounts of abolition and New World slavery often pass rather rapidly over the impact upon them of the revolutions in the French Caribbean and the emergence of Haiti, a black state. It is almost as if James' *Black Jacobins* dispenses them from considering the momentous concomitants and consequences of the only successful slave revolt in history. In fact James' work should be an inspiration to trace through the impact of the 'first emancipation' on the subsequent struggles over colonial slavery in other parts of the Americas. The detailed account given in chapters 5 to 9 of the disintegration of slaveholder power in St Domingue, of the birth of Haiti, and of the latter's impact on slaves and slaveholders, on the strategists of empire and on the free-floating milieu of adventurers and revolutionaries, seeks to remedy this deficiency, with help from the welcome recent spate of monographs on this subject by Caribbean historians. I hope to show that it is scarcely possible to exaggerate the impact of the Haitian revolution on the fate of colonial slavery.

This conclusion and others emerge from chapters which trace the progess of slavery and anti-slavery in the United States, Spanish and Portuguese America, the British West Indies and the French Antilles. They underline the paradox that while this period of 'bourgeois democratic' revolution and capitalist advance strengthened and extended slavery in sóme parts of the New World (the South of the United States, Cuba and Brazil), it also set the scene for anti-slavery currents which secured significant slave emancipations in almost every decade from the 1780s to the 1840s and beyond. There can be no doubt that this paradoxical correlation poses a major challenge to historical explanation.

It has recently been claimed that a commitment to historical progress can no longer be sustained. Certainly the history of New World slavery allows of no simple or linear conception of historical advance. But when all due account has been taken of cross-currents and contradictions, the movements for American independence, for republican liberties and for slave emancipation do represent epic achievements in human history and in the making of the modern world. Despite the mixed results of anti-slavery in this period the sacrifices of slave rebels, of radical abolitionists and of revolutionary democrats were not in vain. They show how it was possible to challenge, and sometimes defeat, the oppression which grew as the horrible obverse of the growth of human social capacities and powers in the Atlantic world of the early modern period. More generally they are of interest in illuminating the ways in which, however incompletely or imperfectly, emancipatory interests can prevail against ancient law and custom and the spirit of ruthless accumulation.

Introduction

Notes

1. For the many varieties of slavery see Orlando Patterson, *Slavery and Social Death*, Cambridge, Mass., 1982; I attempt a definition of this variable institution in a contribution to Leonie Archer, ed., *Slavery*, London 1988.

2. Elizabeth Fox Genovese and Eugene Genovese, *Fruits of Merchant Capital; Slavery and Bourgeois Property in the Rise and Expansion of Capitalism*, Oxford and New York 1983; Manuel Moreno Fraginals, *El Ingenio*, 3 vols, Havana 1978; see also Richard S. Dunn, *Sugar and Slaves*, Chapel Hill 1972; Michael Craton and James Walvin, *A Jamaica Plantation*, Toronto 1970; Gabriel Debien, *Les Esclaves aux Antilles Françaises: XVII–XVIII Siècle*, Basse Terre, Guadeloupe 1974.

3. Jacob Gorender, *O Escravismo Colonial*, São Paulo 1978 (p. 242 for the argument referred to above).

4. These and other features of the formation of colonial slavery in the New World up to 1776 will be explored systematically in a companion study to the present work entitled *The West and the Rise of Slavery*.

5. J.H. Parry, *The Spanish Sea-borne Empire*, London 1966; James Lockhart and Stuart Schwartz, *Early Latin America*, Cambridge 1983, pp. 98–101, 181–252; James Lang, *Portuguese Brazil: the King's Plantation*, New York 1979, pp. 115–52, 205–18. For the wider context see Eric Wolf, *Europe and the People Without History*, London 1984.

6. The data in this and previous paragraphs have been drawn from Ralph Davis, *The Rise of the Atlantic Economies*, London 1973, pp. 257, 264–5; Fraginals, *El Ingenio*, I, p. 41; Paul E. Lovejoy,'The Volume of the Atlantic Slave Trade: a Synthesis', *Journal of African History*, vol. 23, 1983, pp. 473–501; David Eltis, 'Free and Coerced Transatlantic Migrations', *American Historical Review*, vol. 88, no. 2, April 1983, pp. 251–80.

7. For the consumer dynamic behind plantation development see Sidney Mintz, *Sweetness and Power*, London 1985.

8. For an illuminating exploration of the ways in which empires have imposed productive co-ordination see Michael Mann, *The Sources of Social Power*, Cambridge 1986, pp. 145–55, 250–98.

9. A.J.R. Russell Wood, *The Black Man in Slavery and Freedom in Colonial Brazil*, London 1982, pp. 128–60; but see also Ronaldo Vainfas, *Ideologia e Escravidão*, Petrópolis 1986, pp. 93–115.

10. Though Hobsbawm himself certainly does register, briefly but emphatically this American dimension, see *The Age of Revolution*, London 1964, pp. 69, 110.

11. For an example of this approach see Thomas Haskell, 'Capitalism and the Origins of the Humanitarian Sensibility, Part 1', *American Historical Review*, vol. 90, no. 2, April 1985, 'Part 2', *American Historical Review*, vol. 90, no. 3, June 1985; see also the 'Forum' on these articles in the *American Historical Review*, vol. 92, no, 4, 1987, pp. 797–878, with critiques by David Brion Davis and John Ashworth and a reply by Thomas Haskell.

12. François Furet, *Interpreting the French Revolution*, Cambridge 1985, pp. 184–204.

I

The Origins
of Anti-Slavery

Branco diz o preto furta
Preto furta come razão
Sinho branco tambem furta
Quando faz a escravidão

(The white says the black steals
The black steals with reason
The white master also stole
When he made slavery)

Brazilian song of slavery days

...the king and his other lords ... found there [Mile End] threescore thousand men of divers villages and of sundry countries in England. So the king entered in among them and said to them sweetly, 'Ah, ye good people, I am your king. What lack ye? What will ye say?' Then such as understood him said: 'We will that ye make us free for ever ourselves, our heirs and our lands, and that we be called no more bond, nor so reputed'. 'Sirs', said the king, 'I am well agreed thereto. Withdraw ye home into your own houses and into such villages as ye came from ... and I shall cause writings to be made and seal them with my seal ... containing everything that ye demand'. . . . These words appeared well to the common people, such as were simple, good, plain men.

Froissard's Chronicle (1381)

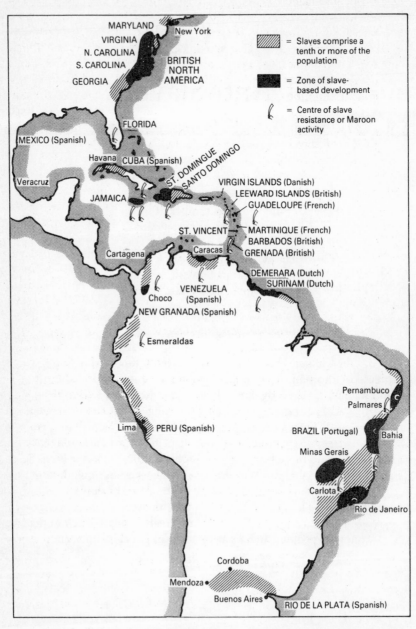

Legend:

- ▨ = Slaves comprise a tenth or more of the population
- ■ = Zone of slave-based development
- ʃ = Centre of slave resistance or Maroon activity

MARYLAND
VIRGINIA
N. CAROLINA
S. CAROLINA
GEORGIA
New York
BRITISH NORTH AMERICA
FLORIDA
MEXICO (Spanish)
Havana CUBA (Spanish)
Veracruz
JAMAICA
ST. DOMINGUE
SANTO DOMINGO
VIRGIN ISLANDS (Danish)
LEEWARD ISLANDS (British)
GUADELOUPE (French)
ST. VINCENT
MARTINIQUE (French)
BARBADOS (British)
GRENADA (British)
Cartagena
Caracas
DEMERARA (Dutch)
SURINAM (Dutch)
Choco
VENEZUELA (Spanish)
NEW GRANADA (Spanish)
Esmeraldas
Pernambuco
Palmares
Lima PERU (Spanish)
BRAZIL (Portugal)
Bahia
Minas Gerais
Carlota
Rio de Janeiro
Cordoba
Mendoza
Buenos Aires
RIO DE LA PLATA (Spanish)

Zones of slave-based development and of slave resistance around 1770

Prior to the mid-eighteenth century authoritative opinion in Europe and the New World, whether religious or secular, had always accepted enslavement. In the very first book of the Old Testament Noah was held to have condemned a portion of humanity, 'the sons of Ham', to perpetual bondage because Ham had seen his father naked. The Judaic justification of enslavement had been adopted by Muslims and Christians; the notion of a hereditary taint was thought to justify racial slavery. The Emperor Justinian promulgated a slave code in the sixth century which admitted property in persons, hereditary bondage and the powers of slaveholders though prohibiting gratuitous abuse and allowing for the possibility of manumission; regulations inspired by this code were extended to the New World by the Iberian powers while the revival of Roman law in the late medieval epoch also strengthened respect for property. The philosophers of Antiquity had offered no fundamental criticism of slavery; the same can be said of the early Christian fathers, the theologians of the medieval Church, the leaders of the Reformation and Counter-Reformation. The Christian view that the servant or slave owed faithful service to the master is found from St Paul to Luther and beyond. Slaveholding was not only recognised by the Catholic Church but tolerated in Rome through into the eighteenth century. Neither Luther nor Calvin questioned chattel slavery; Luther, deliberately taking the extreme case, argued that it would be wrong for a Christian slave to steal himself away from an infidel Turkish owner.[1]

The international treaties of the European states acknowledged and regulated the trade in Africans; the Treaty of Utrecht in 1713 had done so quite explicitly in the case of the *asiento*, the slave trade to Spanish America. England, France, Portugal, the Netherlands and Denmark all had chartered trading companies engaged in the slave traffic; and if most states also permitted free enterprise in the Africa trade this was because it had proved more effective at boosting the supply of slaves to the colonies. Grotius, advocate of the *mare liberum* as well as of the natural rights doctrine, accepted slavery as a legitimate institution. While tradition sanctified slavery so did the new doctrines of 'possessive individualism', since the slave was indeed property, a chattel whom the slaveowner had normally acquired through some perfectly legal transaction. The lot of the slave was widely acknowledged to be unenviable, and even pitiable; yet it was still held to be the best or only way of introducing heathens and savages to civilisation.

Since the publication in 1808 of Thomas Clarkson's *History of the Abolition of the British Slave Trade* it has been common to identify the origins of Anti-Slavery with the works of the learned men who first published critiques of slavery or the slave trade. Yet to approach the subject in this way involves a serious distortion. It is both true and remarkable that philosophical attacks on New World slavery – that is to say on the institution itself rather than on cruel excesses of particular masters or traders – were extremely rare prior to the middle of the eighteenth century; Bodin made a pointed critique in 1576 after which there was a prolonged silence until the appearance of Montesquieu's *Esprit des Lois* in 1748, with its critical passage on the enslavement of blacks. But the rise of anti-slavery tapped a popular revulsion to bondage and untramelled private power which long preceded the critiques of colonial slavery. And, of course, the slaves themselves, if the opportunity presented itself, did not wait for the approval of philosophers before striking out for their freedom. This chapter will survey the emergence and meaning of anti-slavery in its various forms. It will seek to put 'philosophical' anti-slavery in its context and to indicate the ways in which the philosophers and political economists sought to respond to an anti-slavery impulse that they did not invent.

Paradoxically, the rise of colonial slavery had not changed the popular consensus, on both sides of the Atlantic, that the condition of the slave was odious and that slaveholding menaced the liberties and condition of the free-born. Popular anti-slavery was more than aversion to becoming a slave: it embraced the notion that slaveholding and slave trading should not be allowed within a given territory. As an element in the popular culture of early modern Europe it must be considered here since it furnished a springboard for later abolitionist appeals. While the techniques of abolitionist agitation were innovatory the anti-slavery feeling it tapped was both traditional and spontaneous. The roots of primitive abolitionism undoubtedly reach back into the Middle Ages. Slavery was a marginal but not insignificant force in feudal Europe, the lords regarding slaves, when they could secure them, either as an adjunct or as an alternative to serfdom. The supply of new slaves dwindled when the frontiers of Christendom stabilised, as enslavement had been promoted by clashes between radically distinct cultures. In Eastern and Southern Europe, especially the Iberian Peninsula, the pattern of warfare remained conducive to enslavement, and there was some scope for employing slaves in agriculture. In Northern and Western Europe the consolidation of serfdom was associated with a diminution of outright slavery: mixed general farming, with extensive use of the heavy plough, gave no productive advantage to cultivation by slave gangs and encouraged the lords to concentrate on controlling land rather than labour. Individual slaves, when available, were acquired to work the lord's own desmesne lands or to operate the mill; but such slaves or their offspring eventually acquired the status of freedmen. In the fourteenth and fifteenth centuries the devastating impact of the Black Death, the spread of peasant revolt and a growth of trade in necessities as well as luxuries encouraged serf-lords in many parts of North West Europe to commute labour services into rent. The strengthening of economic property relations supplied the context for a class struggle against all forms of bondage.[2]

Popular resistance to bondage reflected not simply an anxiety to avoid becoming a slave but also a fear of the outsize power which slaveholders could wield in dealings with free persons. This 'egotistical' anti-slavery might detest both slave and slave-owner, as a threat to the independence of the free. Those of slave origin might be used as bailiffs or henchmen. Where serfdom was in decline slavery became both more valuable to the lords and more vulnerable. It disappeared from neither East nor West Europe, though in the latter it did change its name. 'Servus', the old term for slave, rose in the scale of social esteem, being transmuted into 'servant'. The term 'slave' spread in Western Europe, reflecting the 'slavic' origin of many European slaves by the fourteenth and fifteenth centuries. The privatisation of wealth and power in late feudal and early modern society furnished new space to chattel slavery but also stimulated opposition from the common people. While some slavery survived in Western Europe, especially Italy and the Iberian peninsula, it was far more common in the East, though there too it gradually diminished as serfdom was consolidated. The relatively greater physical and economic insecurity of life on the Eastern marchlands helped to create conditions conducive to slavery and encouraged self-sale by those in a particularly vulnerable situation. In the East land was plentiful in relation to labour giving a premium to control of the latter; in the West the relative scarcity of land allowed the lords to prevail where they could control access to it without the need for strict personal bondage.[3]

In the class struggles in Western and Northern Europe the towns became a point of support in resistance to, or evasion of, the harsher forms of bondage. The medieval communes liked to proclaim that the 'free air' of the city or town was incompatible with bondage. Toulouse in 1226 and Pamiers in 1228 adopted charters which made them refuges where slaves automatically became free; the Kings of France chose to encourage this principle. The *affranchisement toulousain* aimed to undermine the power of local serflords and to boost the population and resources of the town. Sovereigns who exercised the power of emancipation gained the freedmen as perfect subjects, free of awkward obligations. In some towns and cities the protection of civic freedom led to the exclusion rather than manumission of slaves. The cantons of Switzerland also exercised bans on the entry of those of a servile condition. The townsmen of North Italy did not stop the rich buying slave domestics but Venice did exclude slaves from the municipal fleet and from fine cloth-weaving. The guilds and *arti* of late medieval Europe asserted a principle of occupational autonomy and dignity that was inimical to slavery. Municipalities and monarchs could both be persuaded that slaveholding was an institution that undermined the integrity of the social order, removing a special category from the restraint of law. So far as sovereign authorities were concerned the powers of the slaveholder were potentially a derogation of their own power. In most of Western Europe both municipal laws and royal decrees came to make a presumption of liberty and to offer their citizens or subjects relief from personal bondage. But they also tolerated a private sphere of power and wealth where chattel slavery remained. Venice possessed plantation colonies in the Mediterranean and permitted slave-owning both in its possessions and at home. Despite the survival of domestic slavery Renaissance Italy produced an ideal of civic virtue incompatible with widespread bondage. Machiavelli had little to say about slavery but he did argue that a healthy Republic needed a sizeable free citizenry, and would be corrupted by lordly pretention or an idle gentry. And he pointed out that even in a kingdom not founded on extensive civic liberty it still behoved the monarch to guarantee the personal security of his subjects, as did the King of France. On the other hand small pockets of slavery and indentured service for foreigners were acceptable to Machiavelli and to Italy's civic patriotism. The slave trading activities of Venice, Genoa and Ragusa prompted controversy but thrived nevertheless. In contrast the muncipalities of France and Northern Europe sometimes succeeded in completely suppressing extremities of personal bondage within their limits. The struggles of Hussites, Lutherans and Anabaptists in Germany and Central Europe ventilated a doctrine of Christian freedom and equality with pronounced secular overtones; hostility to slavery was probably more intense in the countryside than in the towns since it was likely to be less circumscribed in its effects there and since slaveholding was in any case linked to luxury and civilisation. There was no late medieval or early modern 'abolition' but there was a molecular restriction of slavery backed up by a widespread popular belief that the rich and the powerful should not be allowed to dispose at will of the bodies of the common people. The daily workings of a social formation in which economic power and unfree labour were assuming new forms continually renewed and replenished detestation of bondage.[4]

Medieval laws did not aim at the system or coherence of modern legislation, nor were they comprehensively enforced, so slavery often survived in the interstices of the social formation. But by the time that the Netherlands, England and France were setting up slave colonies in the New World the institution had virtually disappeared in the metropolis. Even in Spain and Portugal, where slavery persisted, it was of declining significance, though African slaves were introduced to the Canary Islands and the Madeiras. The monarchs of Aragon and Castille had adopted an elaborate but mild slave code, as part of the celebrated *Siete Partidas* of Alfonso X, 'the Wise'. This code conceded many rights to slaves, including that of purchasing manumission and, in cases of abuse, that of demanding sale to another master; it echoed Justinian but should also be seen as an Iberian response to the municipal and royal emancipations of other parts of Western Europe, though it sought to regulate rather than eliminate bondage. During the first half-century of Spanish colonisation of the New World this custodial tradition was given a new twist when the catastrophic decline of the Indian populations and royal distrust of the *conquistadores* led to promulgation of a ban on the enslavement of Indians in the 1540s. This selective royal abolitionism actually paved the way for more extensive imports of African slaves, who were deemed more capable of enduring the rigours of bondage. While Bartolomé de las Casas had denounced the enslavement of Indians two other sixteenth century Spanish American clerics, Tomás de Mercado and Alonso de Sandoval, attacked the excesses of the slave trade. But even such critics did not attack the very principle and institution of enslavement; their protests helped to strengthen the case for regulation. The Church as well as the state believed that the slaveholder needed tutelage; slaveholders in New Spain could be denounced to the Inquisition for ill-treating their slaves and there were a few cases of this sort. The slave codes of the Catholic powers gave a certain protection to some household or urban slaves but large slave-worked enterprises in the countryside were to develop beyond the scope of secular or religious invigilation and here regulations beneficial to the slaves were a dead letter.[5]

In England and France slavery had withered away without ever becoming illegal, as Thomas Smith was to point out in *De Republica Anglorum* (1565). After outlining the distinction between chattel slaves and serfs bound to the estate he declares: 'Neither of the one sort nor of the other do we have any number of in England. And of the first I never knewe any in the realme in my time; of the second so fewe there be, that it is almost not worth the speaking. But our law doth acknowledge them in both these sortes.' Smith's explanation for this development pointed both to religion and to alternative methods of securing a labour force: 'I think in France and England the chaunge of religion to a more gentle humane and equall sort . . . caused this old kinde of servitude and slaverie to be brought into that moderation . . . and litle by litle extinguished it finding more civil and gentle means and more equall to have doone that which in time of gentility (heathenesse) [i.e. pagan antiquity] servitude or bondage did.'[6]

It is difficult to believe that the powerful were naturally more gentle and humane in England and France than in other parts of Christendom; in the English case the ferocious Statute of Labourers of 1349–51 certainly suggests otherwise. Therefore it is the possession of other 'means' to the same end (presumably, labour control) that must bear the main weight in explaining the eclipse of serfdom and slavery. Popular revolt, not mentioned by Smith, also helped to determine the choice of means, even, as with the English Peasant's revolt of 1381, when it was defeated or deflected. Some combination of market power and state power could deliver landless labourers into the hands of landlords or their tenants with no need for the aggravation of direct bondage. Serfdom and poll taxes united the exploited; markets could divide them. Popular pressure did not directly produce abolition but it did encourage ruling authorities to present themselves as guarantors of elementary personal freedom.

Standing as a rampart between the feudal order and the threat of peasant revolt, or urban disaffection, the centralised repressive apparatus of the absolutist regimes made serfdom redundant. The construction of absolutism did not require intensified personal bondage nor did it extinguish particularist privileges. The proponents of monarchical power were often distrustful of the spontaneous privatisation of social relations, as forms of mercantile and agrarian capital accumulation established themselves in the social formations of Western Europe. They elaborated a model of kingship which left little space for metropolitan slaveholding. They insisted that the sovereign's custodial power should stretch evenly over all subjects.

Jean Bodin, one of the earliest exponents of the new theory of sovereignty, also produced what is probably the first critical discussion of slavery in *Les Six Livres de la République* (1576). He pointed out that whereas all philosophers justified slavery, practising lawyers were different: 'Lawyers, who measure the law not by the discourses or decrees of philosophers, but according to the common sense and capacity of the people, hold servitude to be directly contrary to nature.' Bodin's observations on this topic were directly inspired by the French municipal tradition of *affranchisement*. He pointed to the wisdom of French Kings in banning the harsher varieties of servitude and urged that, in view of the cruelties and dangers to which slavery must give rise, it would be 'most pernicious and dangerous' ever to allow slaves to enter the country. At a time when France had failed to establish New

World colonies Bodin attacked the slavery practised by Spain and Portugal in the New World, but does not mention the use of slaves in the French galleys.[7]

The status of slave had previously formalised and accommodated the presence of aliens or of persons lacking any birthright and entirely absorbed in the household of their owner. The refusal to admit this status signalled the birth of a new civic consciousness in which all were to be subjects or citizens. The absolutist regimes and early bourgeois states both conceded a civic identity that did not fit with slavery. The English Parliament was persuaded to accept slavery as a punishment for vagrants in 1547 but abandoned the legislation after a popular outcry. A famous English judgement of 1567 prevented a traveller from bringing back a bondsman from Russia on the grounds that 'the air of England was too free for a slave to breathe'. The French cult of civic liberty was no less vigorous. In 1571 the Parlement of Guyenne described France as the 'mother of liberty', and declared that slavery could not be tolerated there. When a Dutch captain brought a boat-load of African slaves to Middleberg in 1596 the municipality obliged him to free them. The Grand Council of Mechlin declared in the early seventeenth century that all slaves brought to Flanders by the Spanish would be free upon arrival.[8]

Those who first proposed American colonisation, such as Walter Raleigh or the Dutchman Usselinx, urged that it should be based on free immigration. The Dutch revolt, the calling of the French Estates General in 1618 and the English Civil War all gave occasion for assertions of metropolitan freedoms. An indictment of the English Star Chamber in 1640 cited the judicial anti-slavery decision of 1567, and constitutes the only surviving written record of it. An English Member of Parliament, attacking the sale of captive royalists as indentured servants in 1659, declared indignantly: 'We are the freest people in the world.' In a similar vein the Bishop of Grenoble described France in 1641 as 'the freest monarchy in the world' while Massillon declared that monarchs must remember: 'You do not rule over slaves, you rule a free and fiery nation, as jealous of its liberty as of its loyalty.' The celebrations of English and French liberties had an element of myth-making about them but at least such myths conceded to popular anti-slavery.[9]

New World slavery developed a novel ferocity, scale and focus. As noted in the introduction it was overwhelmingly economic in character and soon battened exclusively on those of African descent. Plantation slavery in the Americas, though barely contested other than by slaves themselves, ground out the lives of millions of captives with an implacable commercial frenzy. The New World did not simply reproduce the prior features of slavery in Europe, the Mediterranean or Africa. It brought about what might be termed a *degradation of slavery*, violating on a massive scale even traditional notions of what slavery meant. In most previous slaveholding social formations slavery had been both a marginal and a various institution: slaves had not been wholly concentrated in the meanest and most burdensome occupations. But as the slave systems established themselves in the New World it became impossible to conceive of an 'honourable' slavery; there were no slave administrators or soldiers and very few acknowledged slave concubines. Under the impetus of the Atlantic boom enslavement intensified and accumulated. Slavery had a new permanence. In many social formations enslavement had been a means whereby alien individuals were incorporated into the host society, with the prospect that either they or their children would eventually rise out of slavery. The great majority of Afro–American slaves were destined to die in slavery, as were their children; the prospects were especially poor for field slaves and for slaves in the British colonies.

Despite their intense and radical moralism the protagonists of the Dutch revolt and the English Commonwealth accepted and promoted black slavery in the Americas. In the period 1630–1750 the British Empire witnessed an increasingly clamorous, and even obsessive, 'egotistical' revulsion against 'slavery' side by side with an almost uncontested exploitation of African bondage. Thus John Locke, who owned stock in the Royal Africa Company, justified slavery as a means whereby Africans were rescued from a worse fate. But when writing of his own country's institutions in *Two Treatises of Government* he roundly declared: 'Slavery is so vile and miserable an Estate of Man, and so directly opposite to the Generous Temper and Spirit of Our Nation; that 'tis hardly to be conceived, that an *Englishman*, much less a *Gentleman*, should plead for 't.'[10] Locke was here attacking the patriarchal political philosophy of Filmer, disciple of Bodin and apologist for monarchical authority; he had no intention of challenging the appropriateness of slavery for commoner Africans.

The very process whereby the new slave colonies were created reflected both the popular revulsion against slavery and the ease with which it could be kept within ethno-centric limits. English or Irish indentured labourers or French *engagés* could not be abused in the manner of a slave because of the solidarity they could elicit from free colonists. Because captive Africans were alien, heathen and black the free colonists were less inclined to identify with them. Secular and civic identities tended to be more exclusive and localistic than the religious ideologies which they displaced. But they were also more intolerant of the claims of the slaveholder, who might easily overbear other citizens.

The majority of English or French settlers to tropical and sub-tropical America arrived as unfree labourers. But their contracts as servants or *engagés* offered them some protection; masters were often taken to court by their servants or by friends of their servants, something which could scarcely happen in the case of slaves. The English or French servant had rights as a subject which could not be claimed by the captive African. Servants or *engagés* were also better placed to run away; their chances of escaping detection in areas of colonial settlement was certainly greater than those of blacks. The Europeans of this epoch did not have the racial conceits of a later colonial epoch but they preferred to see blacks put to the deadly work of the plantations rather than perform it themselves.[11]

By the later seventeenth century some travellers to the new Caribbean colonies recorded their shock at the inhuman treatment of the blacks, as did George Fox, the Quaker, or Aphra Behn, the writer. But their comments did not amount to consequent opposition to the very idea of slavery. Fox urged slaveholders to treat their slaves with care and consideration, if they cared for their immortal souls; he suggested that thirty years of labour should lead to manumission. Aphra Behn's novel *Oroonoko* (1688) specifically indicted the enslavement of an African Prince who, she made clear, stood apart from his race; he instigates a revolt whose failure, it is broadly hinted, stemmed from the subservient nature of those he was trying to arouse. Both Fox and Behn were outraged by the inhumanity of the plantations without yet seeing beyond slavery, a mixture that was echoed in some private letters or journals, in isolated acts of kindness and in the precarious tolerance sometimes extended to small numbers of black freedmen and women. As a core of responsible slaves, creole slaves and Christian convert slaves developed the racial definition of slavery became more pronounced; but this maturing of the slave societies went hand in hand with a consolidation of the material interests of slaveholders.[12]

In the introduction it was observed that the racial slavery of the New World imposed an especially sharp dilemma on free people of colour. The first challenges to slavery and the slave trade from this quarter came from the Portuguese Empire; they were both more sustained and more effective than the early, isolated queries of the Spanish clerics. In the years 1684–6 the Holy Office received a number of petitions attacking the brutality of the slave trade and protesting at the 'perpetual enslavement' visited upon descendants of Africans taken to the New World, even those who were Christian and 'white'. The Brazilian mulatto Lourenco da Silva de Mendouca composed and presented a number of these protests; he was the lay Procurator of one of the religious brotherhoods permitted to free and enslaved blacks and mulattos in Brazil and Lisbon. These protests received backing from the Capuchin Order, active in seeking converts in the Congo, which pointed out that few African victims of the slave trade could be said to be justly enslaved. In March of 1686 the Holy Office endorsed condemnation of the way the slave trade was being conducted in an apparently sweeping resolution. Not only was no sanction, such as excommunication, proposed for slave-traders but the resolution itself became a dead letter, not to be mentioned again for well over a century. The shelving of the resolution is explained in the minute of a Vatican Secretary of State who pointed out that the slave trade was a source of revenue and a vital imperial interest for their Most Catholic Majesties the Kings of Spain and Portugal.[13]

The Vatican's momentary support for the protests of Lourenco da Mendouca may have helped to inspire the promulgation of the French *Code Noir* of 1688. Regulation was absolutism's preferred solution to the excesses of the burgeoning new slave systems. Under the terms of Louis XIV's code free people of colour were to share the rights of other colonists. Both this clause and others favourable to blacks were often to be flouted, sometimes with the active connivance of royal administrators, as the momentum of plantation development accelerated.

If the horrors of the slave trade were multiplying in the late seventeenth and early eighteenth century, so were the profits of those engaged in it. This certainly helps to explain why the few scattered early protests were stifled and ignored. But it must also be borne in mind that the protests were limited by the very terms in which they were couched. Rather than rejecting enslavement root and branch, they focused instead either on pastoral concerns – the treatment of slaves, especially if actual or potential converts to Christianity – or on the moral perils of being a slaveholder. Even the most vehement critics of slavery at this time inclined to compromise their views and to impale themselves on the following dilemma: either they accepted the established order, in which case they advocated a pastoral amelioration of slave conditions rather than the overthrow of slavery; or they rejected King and Church in the name of a private sphere, in which case the morality of slaveholding became a matter of individual conscience. Radical anti-slavery required the existence of a secular public space and a preparedness to argue that even a thoroughly pious and humane slaveholder would be perpetrating injustice.

In Pennsylvania Quakers did have secular responsibilities prompting four Dutch-speaking Friends of Germantown to address a searing reproach to a Pennsylvania Meeting in 1688. The Germantown petition comes closest of all the early protests to making out a radical case against slavery, though even here the question was probably still seen as one of private conscience for a small group of co-religionists:

> There is a saying that we should doe to all men like as we will be done
> ourselves; making no difference of what generation, descent or colour they
> are. And those who steal or rob men, and those who buy or purchase them,
> are they not all alike? here is liberty of conscience, wch is right and
> reasonable; here ought to be likewise liberty of ye body, except of ye evil-
> doers which is another case. But to bring men hither and to rob or sell them
> against their will, we stand against. In Europe there are many oppressed for
> conscience sake; and here there are those oppressed wh are of a black colour
> ... This makes an ill report in all those countries of Europe, where they here
> off, that ye Quakers doe here handel men as they handel there ye cattle ... If
> once these slaves (wch they say are so wicked and stubbern men) should
> joint themselves – fight for their freedom.– and handel their masters and
> mistresses as they did handel them before; will these masters and mistresses
> take the sword at hand and warr against these poor slaves ... have these
> negers not as much right to fight for their freedom, as you have to keep them
> slaves?[14]

Such questions were not allowed to disturb the Holy Experiment in
colonial settlement. The Germantown petition was tabled by the
Philadelphia Quarterly Meeting; it was not public in character and
reached only a handful even of Quakers. At this time slaveholding and
slave-trading had powerful representatives in the councils of the Society
of Friends just as they did in the Vatican.

Captain Johnson's *History of the Pyrates*, published in London in
1724 and sometimes attributed to Defoe, represents another early
manifestation of anti-slavery spirit, this time entirely secular in
character. This work recounted the real or apocryphal story of a French
buccaneer, one Captain Misson, who came to the conclusion that
religion was no more than 'a curb on the minds of the weaker which the
wiser sort yielded to in appearance only'. Misson maintained that:
'Every man was born free and had as much right to what would
support him as the air he respired.' He held that monarchy only existed
to justify inequality and that government was only legitimate if it
prevented the wealthy and powerful from oppressing the weak. The
slave trade could never be justified in the eyes of 'divine justice' and
Christians who practised the slave traffic proved that 'their religion was
no more than a grimace'. According to Johnson's account Misson led a
buccaneer crew of 'new-fangled pirates' amongst whom 'regularity,
tranquillity and humanity' prevailed. Many of the French members of
his mixed crew were Huguenots from La Rochelle. When they captured
slaves they freed them and invited them to join as equals. Misson and
his crew established the colony of 'Libertalia' on Madagascar; slavery

was to be outlawed and money kept in a common treasury but land held in private possession. The government of 'Libertalia' took a 'democratical form where the people were themselves the makers and judges of their own laws'.[15]

Johnson's book broadcast an attack on slavery even if its author had embroidered for effect the stories it contained. The early history of the colony of Georgia affords documentary evidence that popular anti-slavery feeling could take forms inimical to black as well as white bondage. Predating the philosophical critiques by several years it is probably the first civil and public petition against slavery. When Georgia was established in 1735 it was proposed to ensure that it remain an asylum for orphans and debtors by banning the introduction of slaves. A move to abrogate this ban prompted protest in 1739; it was entered by eighteen Scots immigrants, a number signalling their support with a mark rather than signature. The petition, mixing the egotistic and altruistic, advances economic and practical as well as ethical objections to the introduction of slaves;

> I. The nearness of the Spaniards, who have proclaimed Freedom to all slaves who run away from their masters, makes it impossible for us to keep them without more labour in guarding them, than what we would be at to do their work. II. We are Laborious, and know that a White Man may be by the Year more usefully employed than a Negro. III. We are not rich, and becoming Debtors for Slaves, in case of their running away or dying, would inevitably ruin the poor master, and he become a greater slave to the Negro Merchant, than the slave he bought could be to him. IV. It would oblige us to keep a Guard-duty at least as severe as when we expected a daily invasion . . . V. Its shocking to human Nature, that any Race of Mankind, and their Posterity, should be sentenced to perpetual slavery; nor in justice can we think otherwise of it, than they are thrown amongst us to be our Scourge one Day or another for our Sins; and as Freedom to them must be as dear as to us, what a Scene of horror must it bring about![16]

While the first or second objection are compatible with racial animosity towards blacks the last clause strikes a more generous and universal note. This petition did not prevent the gradual introduction of slaves to Georgia and the formal legalisation of slavery there in 1750. But it probably gives a good idea of 'common sense' objections to slavehold-ing, a common sense later often to inform the action of free citizens who opposed slavery.

These isolated and sporadic protests showed that the popular anti-slavery reflex, though often blinkered and egotistical, had not been entirely perverted by racial privilege. The growth of black enslavement into a vast and permanent system stimulated fears of slaveholder power and of slave revolt. The epoch of the Enlightenment and of the first attempts to codify the principles of political association and socio-economic organisation allowed the question of the legitimacy of civil institutions to be posed in a new way. If the philosophers did not invent anti-slavery they did educate and generalise it. They also elaborated it to the point where it could inform public policy. Civic boasts about 'free air' had often been hot air. At last some philosophers and moralists were prepared to examine the merits of the anti-slavery ideal or myth. In so doing they also shaped and modified it to new concerns.

In the *Esprit des Lois* Montesquieu devoted the best part of one chapter to ridiculing conventional justifications for the enslavement of Africans in the New World. His remarks were to be widely quoted by early abolitionists, though in fact they fell short of a thoroughgoing anti-slavery. In a parody of arguments for black slavery on the plantations he unmasked the crude interests and racist assumptions which these usually conveyed: 'The Europeans, having extinguished the Americans, were obliged to make slaves of the Africans for clearing such vast tracts of land. Sugar would be too dear if the plants which produce it were cultivated by any other than slaves.' Because of their substantial accuracy such remarks could be taken cynically as well as ironically. Others were somewhat less ambivalent:

> It is hardly to be believed that God, who is a wise Being, should place a soul, especially a good soul, in such a black ugly body ... The Negroes prefer a glass necklass to that gold which white nations value so highly. Can there be a greater proof of their wanting common sense? It is impossible to suppose these creatures to be men, because, allowing them to be men, a suspicion would follow that we ourselves are not Christian.[17]

This oblique disavowal was re-inforced by the contention that slaveholding was incompatible with the spirit of true liberty and provided fertile soil for the growth of despotism. The slaveholder was encouraged to be arbitrary, pleasure-loving and cruel while the slave could do nothing from a motive of virtue. However, Montesquieu also conceded that enslavement might sometimes be a necessary evil:

> There are countries where the excess of heat enervates the body, and renders man so slothful and dispirited, that nothing but the fear of chastisement can oblige them to perform any laborious duty: slavery is there more reconcilable to reason; and the master being as lazy with respect to his sovereign, as is his slave to him, this adds a political, to a civil slavery.[18]

In these few, swift clauses the former *President* of the Bordeaux *Parlement* contrived to join together deprecation of the slaveholder with justification of metropolitan authority, aspersions on the morality of the planters with readiness to concede that enslavement might be a sad necessity in tropical climates. Montesquieu favoured generous recognition of the rights of the *parlements* and other intermediary institutions between sovereign and subject, but his references to colonial disobedience argue little sympathy with colonial autonomism. The French colonists were known for their hatred of the *exclusif* which bound them to Bordeaux and a few other ports; they distrusted metropolitan officials, and conducted themselves in such a rude and riotous manner when aroused that they discredited the impulse to constitutional reform, as in Martinique's *Gaoulé* of 1718. It is difficult to believe that the *Esprit des Lois* did much to create anti-slavery opinion but, once that opinion had formed, it supplied a prestigous reference point. Montesquieu's real contribution lay in the scorn he expressed for white racism, a salient feature of slaveholder ideology, and it is this which explains why he was taken to be a prophet of the anti-slavery cause.

The Scottish philosopher Francis Hutcheson, in his *System of Moral Philosophy* (1755) advanced arguments which were also to be cited by opponents of slavery. His arguments were not as radical as those of the Darien immigrants but they were embedded in a philosophical system that sought to temper 'possessive individualism' with more ample humanitarian and ethical considerations. And as a professor at the University of Glasgow he enjoyed a certain eminence. He held that slavery and the slave trade were a violation of 'all sense of natural justice', of Christian morality or a proper sense of 'liberty'. He wrote: 'Scarce any man can be happy who sees that all his enjoyments are precarious, and depending on the will of others of whose kind intentions he can have no assurance. All men have strong desires of liberty and property, have notions of right, and strong natural impulses to marriage, families and offspring, and earnest desires of their safety.' Hutcheson condemned slavery both because it failed to respect this natural human propensity to reproduce and because it violated the principle that 'each man is the natural proprietor of his own liberty'. He refused to accept that servile acquiescence could justify slavery since:

> The labours of any person of tolerable strength and sagacity are of much more value than his bare maintenance. We see that the generality of healthy people can afford a good share of the profits of their labour for the support of a young family, and even for pleasure and gayety. If a servant obliged himself by a contract to perpetual labours for no other compensation than his bare maintenance the contract is plainly unequal and unjust; . . . he has a

perfect right to further compensation, either in some peculium, or little stock
for him or his family, or in a humane maintenance for this family. Such a
servant whether for life or a term of years, is to retain all the rights of
mankind, valid against his master, as well as all others, excepting *only* that
to his labours, which he has transferred to his master; and in lieu of this he
has a right to the maintenance as above mentioned, or to the wage agreed
on.[19]

In this and other passages Hutcheson started out from radical hostility
to slavery but veered towards qualified endorsement of humane forms
of permanent service. Many American slaveholders encouraged slaves
to have families, to cultivate a garden plot or even to have a 'frolic'
when the harvest was in. The slave did, in theory, retain some human
rights; for example, it was not usually lawful for their owners to kill
them unless gravely provoked. Slaveholders did claim to control much
more than simply the labour of the slave; yet in the end it was control
of the slaves' labour which was the crucial concern. Hutcheson's
observations on the slave trade also suggest that the principles of his
reasoning did not quite allow him to reach the conclusions at which he
aimed. He wrote: 'No damage done or crime committed can change a
rational creature into a piece of goods void of all right, and incapable of
acquiring any, or of receiving any injury from the proprietor.' This
seems clear enough, but Hutcheson goes on to take seriously the
argument that the slave-trader and slaveholder qualify for some
compensation for the costs of taking captive Africans to the New
World:

> Thus suppose that a merchant buys a hundred such slaves; so that his whole
> charges on the voyage, and prime cost of the captives, adding also a
> reasonable merchant's profit upon the stock employed, amount to a
> thousand pounds. These captives are his debtors jointly for this sum; and as
> soon as the value of their labours beyond maintenance amounts to this sum,
> and the legal interest from the time it was advanced, they have a right to be
> free.[20]

Hutcheson is here, for the sake of argument, supposing that slave-
traders were rescuing Africans from an original captivity. He optimisti-
cally estimated that slaves could work off their debt in ten or twelve
years, though presumably slaveholders would, if they wished, have
produced different calculations. Hutcheson did produce something of
an immanent critique of slaveholding but, in themselves, his ideas could
suggest a reform rather than outright abolition of slavery and the slave
trade. Part of his difficulty lay in a wish to attack slavery but not to
infringe legally acquired property rights or to question long-term

indenture, or even service for life, such as still survived in the coal mines of eighteenth century Scotland. At a more fundamental level Hutcheson was concerned to assert that the activities of men of commerce and wealth should be answerable to general principles elaborated by moral philosophers, members of an academic or clerical establishment.

The first European thinker to attack slavery unequivocally since Bodin was probably the Scottish jurist George Wallace in his book, *A System of the Principles of the Law of Scotland*, published in 1760. Though this work was itself to remain fairly obscure its sections on slavery were widely reprinted. Wallace's discussion of slavery concluded:

> For these reasons every one of those unfortunate men, who are pretended to be slaves, has a right to be declared free, for he never lost his liberty; he could not lose it; his prince had no power to dispose of him. Of course the sale was *ipso jure* void. This right he carries about with him and is entitled everywhere to get it declared. As soon, therefore, as he comes into a country, in which the judges are not forgetful of their own humanity, it is their duty to remember that he is a man and to declare him to be free.

For Wallace it was quite simple: 'men and their liberty are not *in commercio*.' Wallace's anti-slavery radicalism came more easily to him in consequence of his unusual lack of respect for private property: 'Property, that bane of human felicity, is too deeply rooted in society, and is thought too essential to the subsistence of it, easily to be abolished. But it must necessarily be banished out of the world before an Utopia can be established.' Wallace further insisted that slavery should be abolished even if it meant economic loss; it would be intolerable for mankind to be abused 'that our pockets may be filled with money, and our mouths with delicates'. However, he added: 'Set the Nigers free, and in a few generations, this vast and fertile continent would be crowded with inhabitants.'[21] Free men would, he believed, be more industrious. Like other members of the Scottish school Wallace wrote at length on the need for a more liberal family statute.

Wallace's anti-slavery argument was extensively drawn upon by Louis de Jaucourt, who used it verbatim in his contribution to the *Encyclopédie* on the slave trade, published in 1765 in the sixteenth volume. Rousseau's attack on slavery echoed Wallace's radicalism and added to it arguments against the validity of self-sale into bondage. Wallace's observations on slavery were reproduced by the North American Quaker Anthony Benezet in 1762, who compiled the first collection of writings directed exclusively at slavery and the slave trade; this pamphlet, *A Short Account of that Part of Africa inhabited by Negroes*, was itself much reprinted on both sides of the Atlantic.

Benezet drew on travellers' reports as well as the arguments of philosophers to demonstrate the cruelty and immorality of slave trading.[22]

The case against colonial slavery was to be greatly strengthened by the fact that it could find some support in the new political economy, most particularly in the central dogma concerning the productive superiority of free labour. In the moral system of classical political economy the interests of the independent producer were the ultimate touchstone and the activities of traders were suspect. Both the Scottish political economists and the French Physiocrats argued that slave labour was costly and inefficient; in Adam Smith's view the expense of slave labour could only be borne by the planters because of their monopolistic privileges. Slave labour was held to be expensive because of the slaves' high mortality and low fertility, because their owners capital was tied up unproductively in human chattels and because the slave had no motive for working hard or effectively. It is interesting that such arguments began to gain ground throughout the Atlantic world in the mid-eighteenth century. They appear almost simultaneously in writings published in the 1750s and 1760s in such places as Philadelphia (Benjamin Franklin), Paris (Marquis de Mirabeau), Glasgow (David Hume) and Havana (Felix de Arrate).[23] The analysis of slave labour implied some general knowledge of the workings of the slave systems, even if they concluded too hastily that slave labour tended to be unprofitable or inefficient – few of those who wrote on slave labour had observed a slave gang at work and were thus unfamiliar with the compensations of coerced co-operation, however expensively obtained.

The critique of both slave labour and colonial mercantilism was to find classic expression in Adam Smith's *Wealth of Nations* published in 1776. The arguments of Smith and the Physiocrats had a special resonance amongst the professional middle classes – lawyers, doctors, academics, administrators – as well as amongst independent producers resentful of mercantile tutelage. In these cases occupational *amour propre* encouraged a belief in the virtues of free labour and a distrust of slaveholders. Smith's political economy reflected the vigour of a social formation where capitalism was still compatible with widespread economic independence, for mechanics and artisans as well as commercial farmers and manufacturers. Some American planters also welcomed Smithian and Physiocrat economics. The critique of mercantilism was far more thorough and effective than the critique of plantation slavery. Many planters conceded that indefinite reliance on the slave trade would prove ruinously expensive and believed that their slave labour force could be self-reproducing; and a cessation of slave imports would even boost the value of their slaveholdings.

The outlook of early anti-slavery received its most rounded presentation in another work of the Scottish Enlightenment, John Millar's *The Origin of the Distinction of Ranks*, first published in 1771 and reprinted three times within a decade. Millar radiated confidence in the emergent bourgeois order while seeking to identify and remedy its weaknesses and inconsistencies. It was the contention of this work that: 'The introduction of personal liberty has ... an infallible tendency to render the inhabitants of a country more industrious.' This conclusion was reached via a longer and more systematic discussion of the demerits of slavery than was to be found in Smith or Hutcheson: 'when the arts begin to flourish, when the wonderful effects of industry and skill in cheapening commodites, and in bringing them to perfection, become more conspicuous, it must be evident that little profit can be drawn from the labour of the slave'. In Millar's view the slave could not be expected to acquire 'dexterity' and 'habits of application'. Moreover the slave-based enterprise was inevitably over-capitalised:

> when we compute the expense attending the labour of the slave, not only the charge of his maintenance, but also the money laid out in his first acquisition, together with all the hazard to which his life is exposed, must necessarily be taken into account. When these circumstances are duly considered, it will be found that the work of the slave, who receives nothing but a bare subsistence, is really dearer than that of a free man, to whom constant wages are given in proportion to his industry.

Wages will ensure hard work and will sustain an adequate system of reproduction of the labourer: 'No conclusion seems more certain than this, that men will commonly exert more activity when they work for their own benefit than when they are compelled to labour for another.' Moreover:

> To promote the populousness of a country, the mechanics and labouring people should be maintained in such a manner as will yield the highest profit from the work they are capable of performing; and it is probable that they will more commonly procure the enjoyments of life according to this due medium, when they provide for their own maintenance, than when it depends on the arbitrary will of a master, who, from narrow and partial views, may imagine that he has an interest in diminishing the expense of living as much as possible.[24]

In this critique of slavery a central point is its supposed unprofitability. Though Millar erred in making this assumption his itemisation of the costs borne by the slave-owner showed a better grasp of plantation economics than some planters themselves possessed; his error lay not in his computations of the expense of slave labour but in his failure to consider the superprofits which coercive co-operation on the plantation could produce. To a considerable extent the purpose of Millar's discussion is to construct slavery as foil to his own view of the direction social progress should take. Millar's lengthy chapter devoted to this topic is complemented by an even longer discussion of the family, which he sees as incompatible with slavery and indispensable to the workings of a free labour system. He observes a tendency to the liberalisation of the family regime: 'In all European nations which have made the greatest improvements in commerce and manufactures great liberty is enjoyed by the members of every family; and the children are no further subjected to the father than seems necessary to their own advantage.' But Millar certainly believed that authority within the family had a natural rather than wholly contractual basis and he is disposed to justify this. While rejecting traditional patriarchy Millar also observed: 'The tendency of a commercial age is rather towards the opposite extreme, and may occasion some apprehension that the members of a family will be raised to greater independence than is consistent with good order or a proper domestic subordination.'[25]

Millar's measured condemnation of slavery on the grounds that it was inimical to personal industry, profitable economy and family life corresponds closely to the average abolitionism of the Atlantic world in the latter half of the eighteenth century; the fiercer moral indictment and rejection contained in the work of Wallace, his less well-known fellow countryman, had an impact, by contrast, on a narrower band of anti-slavery radicals. The latter only acquired wide influence at times of crisis, though even then the measures they proposed aimed at purifying rather than overthrowing the established order. Radical abolitionism aimed at slavery as well as the slave trade and was prepared to challenge property and the state in the name of universal human rights. Moderate abolitionists thought that gradual and non-expropriatory measures could strengthen the moral standing of the state and of the predominant social order; however even moderate measures demanded a willingness to qualify property rights and the workings of the market.

One of the most remarkable, radical and widely disseminated attacks on slavery to be published in the pre-revolutionary epoch is to be found in Raynal's *Histoire des Deux Indes* first published in 1770 and going through fifty five editions in five languages over the subsequent thirty years. The book, which drew on drafts from several hands, contained a comprehensive survey of the American colonies; it expressed sympathy for the demands of American colonists and hostility to the projects of British imperialism. The passages on slavery in this work were drafted by an early utopian socialist of colonial extraction, Jean de Péchmèja, and were discrepant with the moderate reformism found in other sections. They point with outrage to the involvement in slavery of the Church and of the monarchs of Europe. Those who dare to justify slavery are said to deserve the contempt of philosophers and a dagger from the slaves. It is pointed out that it would be just to carry fire, sword and emancipation into the lands of any European sovereign who upheld slavery and the slave trade. Slave revolts and the communities of runaway slaves are pointed to as a portent of the future.

> These enterprises are so many indicators of the impending storm, and the negroes only want a chief, sufficiently courageous to lead them to vengeance and slaughter. Where is this great man to be found, whom nature perhaps, owes to the honour of the human species? Where is this new Spartacus, who will not find a Crassus?[26]

As in the case of Millar the passages from Raynal use reference to New World slavery to express a view of metropolitan institutions – in this case to call in question the authority of Church and King. For Europeans anti-slavery always had a link to the destiny of their own society and only a few rare souls pursued it purely for its own sake. For obvious reasons this was not the case with the anti-slavery of the slaves themselves. And as we have seen European anti-slavery, whether popular or philosophical, was keenly aware that slaves had and would contest their bondage.

The prevalence of slave resistance, despite formidable and usually overwhelming odds, was a fact of great significance. For the escaped slave or maroon the struggle for existence would be ardous indeed, even without the hazards of militia patrols and well-armed, well-mounted slave catchers with tracker dogs. The planter, overseer and all free employees would be armed with cutlasses, pistols and other firearms; they and their neighbours were united by fear of the slaves. In principle being a slave meant being exposed to tight physical controls and the risk of daily physical abuse; resistance was met by punishments of extraordinary savagery designed to terrorise the slaves. Outbreaks were also discouraged by the divisive privileges, petty palliatives, rewards for good behaviour, and disguised bargaining alluded to in the introduction; the elite of slave headmen, and a few headwomen, drove the slave gangs but did set some limits on planter power. The diverse origins of the slaves assisted planter control but a Governor of Virginia warned in

1710: 'we are not to Depend on Either their Stupidity, or that Babel of languages among 'em; freedom wears a Cap which Can without a Tongue, Call Togather all those who Long to Shake of the fetters of Slavery.'[27]

The liberty the slave aspired to would be that of freedom from unremitting toil, from daily abuse and from being at the continual command of another. The tyrannical world of the plantation could make even the dire prospect of life in the wild seem inviting. Its intimate control of the slave was so far-reaching that it was likely to provoke a new conception of freedom, influenced by, but not limited to, African memories. The American present as well as the African past necessarily influenced slave resistance and the maroon communities. Sometimes rebels struck up an alliance with American Indians, as happened on St Vincent with its 'black Caribs', who gave British occupation forces much trouble in the early 1770s. In other cases maroons came to terms with the colonisers. And just as life on the plantation was marked by forms of communal resistance so revolts could lead to practical compromises with the colonial or slaveholding regime.

Slave conspiracies and revolts punctuated the history of the slave colonies. They were more damaging where there were large estates, slave majorities, terrain suitable for maroon resistance and a slack or distracted colonising population. Thus Jamaica was notable for the frequency of revolts and the stubbornness of maroon resistance from the time of its capture by the British in the 1650s down to the 1760s. In the 1730s and 1740s the colonial authorities negotiated agreements with some of the main maroon bands, linking them to the colonial administration in return for undisturbed usufruct of tracts of land. One of the last big risings was 'Tacky's Revolt' in 1760–1. On this occasion about a dozen plantations in the vicinity of St Mary's Parish on the North coast were raised and as many as four hundred slaves involved, many of them of the Coromantin nation; the rising was only suppressed after many months of fierce fighting and the mobilisation of militia units, regular troops and two groups of maroon auxiliaries, with the latter bearing the brunt of the fighting. About 400 slave suspects and rebels were executed and 500 deported to other British colonies.

A rebel captured in Tacky's Revolt vouchsafed the following remarkable plan to his guard, a Jewish militiaman, according to an account written in 1774 by the Jamaican planter Edward Long:

> You Jews, said he, and our nation (meaning the Coromantins), ought to consider ourselves as one people. You differ from the rest of the Whites and they hate you. Surely then it is best for us to join in one common interest, drive them out of the country, and hold possession of it to ourselves. We

will have (continued he) a fair division of estates, and we will make sugar and rum, and bring them to market. As for the sailors, you see they do not oppose us, they care not who is in possession of the country, Black or White, it makes no difference to them; so that after we are masters of it, you need not fear that they will come cap in hand to us (as they now do to the Whites) to trade with us. They'll bring us things from t'other side the sea and be glad to take our goods in payment.[28]

Long, animated by his own hopes, fear and prejudices, may have embellished the story. Nevertheless the dream of American independence was not to be confined to planters and reflected something of the vigour and confidence of those who had built the plantations – a category that most emphatically included the slaves.

Another, possibly more authentic, and certainly more typical, statement of the rebel outlook was to be found in the words used in Surinam in 1757 to colonial representatives who wished to negotiate with a rebel band:

We desire you to tell your governor and your court, that in case they want to raise no new gangs of rebels, they ought to take care that the planters keep a more watchful eye over their own property, and not trust them so frequently in the hands of drunken managers and overseers, who wrongfully and severely chastising the negroes, debauching their wives and children, neglecting the sick ... are the ruin of the colony, and wilfully drive to the woods such numbers of stout active people, who by their sweat earn your subsistence, without whose hands your colony must drop to nothing, and to whom at last, in this disgraceful manner, you are glad to come and sue for friendship.[29]

This group eventually reached an agreement under which they received arms, ammunition and supplies; in return they promised not to raid the plantations and to return all escaping slaves.

The small-scale acts of resistance within the plantations could, under favourable circumstances, coalesce into a general attack on the slaveholder regime while still not formally challenging the juridical institution of slavery. Thus there was a slave revolt on an estate near Ilheus in Brazil in 1789 which led to a prolonged struggle between the owner and the slave crew. The slaves of the plantation withdrew to the woods taking with them some valuable equipment. They offered to return to the plantation on condition that (a) they could veto the appointment of overseers (b) Fridays and Saturdays were to be free as well as Sunday (c) they were given canoes and nets for their fishing (d) they had freedom to perform their own songs and dances (e) the staffing of the mill was increased (f) rations of food and clothing were increased. In this extreme case the slave demands went far to dismantling slavery without the institution itself being named.[30]

The songs and dances that the Brazilian slaves wished to perform were a vital element in the Afro–American culture which sprang up with varying inflexions and combinations in each separate colony and district. Like other components of Afro–American culture – religion, language, myth – the music and songs of the blacks were shot through with a painful ambiguity: they helped to affirm an identity distinct from that offered by slaveholder society but they also helped to make intolerable conditions more supportable. The political forms of slave resistance sometimes echoed African models – Akan kingship or Jaga military organisation – but with the risk of alienating other slaves or being inappropriate to American conditions. The widespread cult of 'voodoo', found in many parts of French tropical America by the later eighteenth century, echoed Dahomeyan myths but had a rich syncretistic diversity that was elaborated according to the inclination of each separate grouping and its *houngan* or priest. The precise ideological content of the various Afro–American cultural forms may have been of less significance from the point of view of anti-slavery than the very fact that they provided a medium of communication removed from the invigilation of the masters and their overseers.[31]

Though wars and internal commotions gave an opportunity to some slaves to make a break for freedom, they also tended to boost the vigilance and fire-power of the slaveholders and their patrols. The slave populations remained fragmented and subjected to the disciplines and hierarchy of each separate plantation. Slave rebellions only threatened to engulf a whole colony on two occasions before the 1790s: the Danish island of Ste Croix in 1733 and Dutch Berbice in 1763. In both cases third-rate colonial powers had failed to mobilise sufficient force to guarantee slave subordination and had to call on help from outside.

From the mid-1760s slave rebellions became far rarer in Jamaica as the colony embarked on rapid growth. Likewise there were few slave revolts in St Domingue, the most dynamic sugar colony of all, prior to the historic uprising of 1791. Colonies that were growing and prosperous attracted settlers and could afford the upkeep of patrols, militia units and garrisons. Slave *maronnage* was more of a problem at the periphery of the slave systems or in colonies that were stagnating. There were particularly large numbers of fugitive slaves and maroon communities inland from the South American littoral, in New Granada, Venezuela, the Guianas, Surinam, Brazil and the River Plate. And following the expulsion of the Jesuits in the 1760s the estates they had formerly owned in Spanish America were the scene of a chain of revolts. The North American interior, with its strong Indian nations, was less hospitable to the runaways, though in Florida the Seminoles struck up an alliance with Spanish blacks. In normal times slave conspiracies and rebellions did not pose a mortal threat to the slave systems. This very fact encouraged a sense of security amongst the American slaveholders and a belief that the colonial relationship could be challenged with little risk. But understandably those who depended on a slave elite, as did many Caribbean planters, inclined to greater caution.

The foregoing survey of the crucial sources of anti-slavery has also indicated their limits. The European anti-slavery prejudice tended to be egotistical and ethnocentric; and even at its most generous it came from those who were largely excluded from political power. The philosophical critique of slavery was predominantly, though not exclusively, moderate and reformist in its implications or even purely speculative and rhetorical; and it too was the work of writers rather than those with direct power or responsibility. The planters lived in fear of slave revolt, but the slaves had to contend with the fragmentation of their own communities and confronted a ferocious and integrated apparatus of coercion and control. Finally all three species of anti-slavery existed at a considerable remove from one another and as late as 1770 still did not represent any concerted threat to the slave systems. The rise of anti-slavery reflected pressures at every level of the social formation, and significant advances were only to be made in the context of crises gripping the whole society, drawing large numbers into political life, bringing together the most diverse forces and influences and putting in question the organising principles of power.

The construction of the colonial systems and the development of new patterns of production and consumption had assembled new labouring populations; wherever these labourers came from they brought with them conceptions that could challenge the power and arrogance of the slaveholders and slave-traders. The new environments into which they were plunged eventually allowed them to discover new sources of solidarity and points of resistance. The whirlpool of Atlantic economy mixed up races, languages, religions and nationalities as it recruited the seamen, dockers, clerks, lawyers, notaries, craftsmen and labourers that it required. Even the slave relationship was bent and broken in the port cities; as the Brazilian slaveholders said, the urban slave was already half free. Poor or outcast whites often spoke the same pidgin or creole as the slaves. The systems of colonial slavery did not simply set planters against officials and merchants, or slaves against masters. They also set up the most strange and unexpected associations between those brought into some sort of communication with one another by Atlantic commerce and its tributaries: maroons, smugglers, the 'brethren of the coast', deserters, naval ratings fleeing the lash, seamen jumping ship, religious or political dissidents, soldiers of fortune and renegade priests, Quakers and Freemasons, devotees of the Enlightenment and disciples of African cults. The colonial milieu was turbulent and disrespectful – and its rough and ready egalitarianism and libertinism continually threatened to spill back into the metropolis, together with other smuggled goods.

Both slave resistance and the different species of abolitionism reflected the inherent tensions generated by a dynamic slave sector of a transitional, and therefore incomplete, socio-economic system and political order. The enslavement that was created by the Atlantic boom did not only shatter prior notions of bondage, whether African or European, it also posed a revolutionary challenge to the distribution of power. It created a class of planters and colonial merchants that was unlikely to remain for ever content with metropolitan tutelage. The real or supposed intentions of slave-owners and slave-traders easily aroused suspicion and alarm amongst non-slave-owners, whether inside or outside ruling circles.

The Atlantic boom and the rise of both slavery and industrialism fostered different types of fears, some of which helped to make slavery controversial. It was, perhaps, too early to take the measure of capitalism without slavery, that is of a capitalist mode based primarily on free wage labour. But it was not too early to be concerned at the implications of a sort of hybrid capitalism *with slavery*; that is of a regime of accumulation in which wealth-holders could deploy servile labour at will wherever they found it convenient. Britain and France, possessed of the most flourishing slave colonies, were the states where the spirit of commercial and financial gain seemed to be most highly developed by the latter half of the eighteenth century. It was widely believed, and not without reason, that there was a connection. The surge of Atlantic trade was based on the toil of a motley, mobile and cosmopolitan proletariat of seafarers, port and construction yard workers with a culture of resistance continually stimulated by tussles with employers, colonial officials, customs officers and the press gangs. In 1768 the word 'strike' was added to the English language when the seamen and dockers of London struck the sails of the ships in the port and joined the demonstrations calling for 'Wilkes and No King'.[32]

In 1775 the English agrarian socialist Thomas Spence gave a lecture on the evils of a property system in which the wealthy and powerful monopolised access to the means of life, above all land. 'If we look back to the origins of the present nations we shall see that the land and all its appurtenances was claimed by a few and divided amongst themselves ... so that all things, men as well as other creatures were obliged to owe their existence to some other's property.' He concluded that this private 'conquest or encroachment on the common Property of Mankind' meant that the earth came to be 'cultivated either by slaves, compelled, like beasts, to labour, or by indigent objects whom they [the landowners] first exclude from a share in the soil, that want may compel them to sell their labour for daily bread.'[33] Spence's indictment thus sought to unite a critique of slavery with a critique of the proletarian condition; vindicating the 'common Property of Mankind' it was to inspire a radical anti-slavery in subsequent decades, as will be seen in chapter 8.

The 'New World' had long excited the imagination of common people in Europe. They hoped to find there an independent livelihood and freedom from abusive authorities of all sorts. For many America came to take the place of the mythical lands of Atlantis and Cockaigne.[34] At its most generous this popular utopianism could make common cause with slave rebels. But even in its egotistical or ethnocentric forms it still objected to the lands of the New World being held in thrall to slaveholders and slave-traders. Both revolutionaries and reactionaries were prepared to appeal to this popular sentiment, especially when their backs were to the wall and they needed to rally all the support they could get.

The novelty of the slave plantation, the commercial megapolis, the proto-industrial village, the capitalist factory posed fundamental questions about the relations between production and reproduction, and about the compatibility of new productive forces with a stable configuration of family and state. In the struggles and debates of the age of revolution anti-slavery furnished revolutionaries with a conservative cause and conservatives with a revolutionary cause. It enabled them both to articulate their vision of social harmony and justice.

The discussion of Hutcheson and Millar has already made it clear that the late eighteenth century did give birth to a distinctively bourgeois abolitionism. Bourgeois abolitionism stressed the need to pacify and normalise social relations, to encourage family life, to develop habits of industry and thrift. It was often endorsed by professionals and middle class people who played the role of organic intellectuals of a new social order, to be strengthened by institutions which they hoped would tame and civilise capitalism and its unruly class struggles: representative assemblies, schools, and libraries as well as prisons, police and hospitals. Such outstanding social reformers as Benjamin Rush, Jeremy Bentham, Condorcet, Buxton, Schoelcher and Ramon de la Sagra were also to be proponents of anti-slavery. While such men did promote bourgeois ideals they also felt that the institutions of a 'commercial age' were inadequate or even dangerous. Though an enlightened and far-sighted capitalist might support such bourgeois ideals there was no complete or immediate identity between bourgeois politics and capitalist interest in this age of reform and revolution. At the limit radical bourgeois became 'bourgeois socialists' who believed that capitalist private property itself would have to be done away with. The majority of big capitalists shunned not only 'bourgeois socialism' but even 'bourgeois abolitionism' unless it presented itself as an imperative compromise or concession, so that a decorous anti-slavery from above might allow non-slaveholding proprietors to pre-empt a rude egalitarianism and emancipationism from below.

The issues at stake in the various struggles over colonial slavery had a powerful symbolic meaning for wide layers of the populations of the Atlantic empires and could involve even those remote from the slave estates or commercial centres. Attacks on both the *ancien régimes* and on the ruthlessness of private power and wealth both appealed to the anti-slavery reflex in European popular culture. Widespread though it was anti-slavery sentiment did not necessarily amount to more than mild benevolence or mere political rhetoric. Since abolitionism could so easily be adopted for ideological effect it often crumbled at the first contact with an opposing material or 'patriotic' interest. Once the ideology of abolitionism has been interpreted there still remains the larger question of how, and by whom, the slave systems were destroyed – and with what results. Even a thoroughly satisfactory account of abolitionism as a system of ideas would not add up to an account of the actual forces at work in the overthrow of colonial slavery.

There were, of course, powerful vested interests opposed to abolition in any form since the slave systems made such an immense contribution to the wealth of the Atlantic states. But such opposition was weakened by the conflicts internal to the colonial slave systems – between merchants and planters, creditors and debtors, one colony or branch of trade and another – and some slaveholders found themselves so placed that they could accept or welcome particular abolitionist measures, such as suppression of the slave trade. Some moderate varieties of abolitionism were compatible with a reformed or strengthened slave system, though they might be resisted nonetheless by slaveholders fearful of legitimating anti-slavery.

The 1750s and the 1760s witnessed open stirrings of colonial revolt as well as the beginnings of the sea-change in educated opinion towards slavery. The Seven Years War had more disruptive effects on the systems of colonial slavery than any of the wars that preceded it. It involved all the major Atlantic powers, stirred up a variety of patriotic sentiment and ended in a peace that was pregnant with future conflict. The war moved Quakers in Philadelphia to begin to dissassociate themselves from slavery while the peace set the scene for rebellion within the British and French Empires. Secular political quarrels and a debate on the proper nature of public space gave new openings to the challengers of New World slavery. The rebellion in the British North American colonies will be considered in the next chapter. As a premonition of things to come the French colonists of St Domingue met projects of imperial reform with clamorous resistance in the 1760s and demanded greater autonomy. One of the reform measures which most outraged the colonists had been a project to enrol free blacks and mulattos in special militia units; poor whites had agitated against this, aware that it represented a threat to their position within both the racial caste system and the slave system. The French authorities were able to contain colonial insubordination in the 1760s without compromising plantation security; but French officials urged that civil conflicts of this sort in a slave colony were highly dangerous, disrupting the apparatus of slave subjection more insidiously than an international conflict.[35]

The first decree banning a branch of the Atlantic slave trade was issued in Portugal in 1761 on the advice of the future Marquis of Pombal. Portugal was at this moment anticipating attack by Spain as the two countries joined opposite sides in the Seven Years War. The decree of 1761 banned further slave imports to metropolitan Portugal. Its aim was to encourage slaves to be taken to Brazil rather than the metropolis and to reduce a source of internal instability. Pombal himself disliked the English arrogance that he had encountered as an ambassador in London and sought to dismantle some of the racial caste discriminations which structured Portuguese imperialism. The measure of 1761 was an echo of the Iberian tradition of regulated slavery, but it was also a contribution to modernising Portugal and rendering it more independent of Britain. Pombal was a late baroque prototype of the patriot dictator, an Iberian enlightened despot. He may have been influenced by the appearance of *O Etiope Resgatado* by Ribiera da Rocha in 1758, a work which insisted that the actual slave systems grossly violated the Christian concept of just bondage. This work argued that the slaveholder was the custodian as well as proprietor of the slave's freedom and that the slave should be able to buy it back after twenty or twenty-five years of faithful service. The decree of 1761 was followed after an interval in which anti-slavery had appeared elsewhere in the Atlantic world by a decree of January 1773 which extended freedom to those slaves in Portugal whose parents, grandparents and great grandparents had been Portuguese slaves. Pombal was concerned at the time to stop power slipping away from him. This exceedingly modest instalment of emancipation was not the product of any movement, nor accompanied by large claims. Yet it probably illustrates the way in which anti-slavery was thought to have a mobilising and legitimating potential for regimes which needed to secure popular support.[36]

All subsequent struggles over slavery and abolition must be placed within the wider political context which played a critical role in shaping their outcome. In the chapters that follow it will therefore be necessary to examine the imperial states, which had promoted New World slavery and which fought over its spoils, and the nature of the revolutionary challenges they faced in the 'age of abolition'. As the imperial states broke up and reformed new opportunities were presented to the black rebels or revolutionaries of several different kinds.

The onset of revolutions by no means immediately or automatically spelled the end of slavery. Those American slaveholders who backed revolution did so to challenge the colonial connection and counted on the considerable inherent strength of the slave systems. Anti-slavery only prevailed where there was a protracted accumulation of problems for the slave order and a concatenation of diverse forces opposed to it. The institution of slavery was buttressed by respect for property, disregard of blacks and prevailing definitions of national interest – anti-slavery only made headway as each of these was contested.

Notes

1. William McKee Evans, 'From the Land of Canaan to the Land of Guinea: The Strange Odyssey of the Sons of Ham', *The American Historical Review*, vol. 85, no. 1, February 1980, pp. 15–44; David Brion Davis, *The Problem of Slavery in Western Culture*, Ithaca, N.Y., 1966, pp. 62–121; Herbert Marcuse, *From Luther to Popper*, London 1984, pp. 56–78.

2. The above remarks can only be the most tentative sketch. For a compendious but anecdotal account of the extent of slavery in medieval Europe see Charles Verlinden, *L'esclavage dans l'Europe médiévale*, vol. I, Brussels 1955; vol. II, Ghent 1977; for the wider context, tracing the decline of slavery in late antiquity and early medieval Europe, see Marc Bloch, *Slavery and Serfdom in the Middle Ages*, Berkeley 1975 and Pierre Dockès, *Medieval Slavery and Liberation*, London 1982.

3. For England, with some comparative references, see Rodney Hilton, *Bondmen Made Free*, London 1973, especially pp. 56–9, 232–6; see also Georges Duby, *The Early Growth of the European Economy*, London 1974, especially pp. 172–84; and Perry Anderson, *Passages from Antiquity to Feudalism*, London 1974, pp. 197–211. For Russia see David Hellie, *Enserfment and Military Change in Muscovy*, Chicago 1979; the phenomenon of self–sale is copiously indexed in David Hellie, *Slavery in Russia: 1492–1725*, Chicago 1982. Debates on the transition from feudalism evidently have a bearing on the forces at work in the slow, uneven decline of slavery in the latter Middle Ages. For the privatisation of economic and political power in both feudalism and early capitalism see Michael Mann, *The Sources of Social Power*, pp. 416–50 and Ellen

Meiksins Wood, 'The Separation of the Economic and the Political in Capitalism' in *New Left Review*, 127 (1981), pp. 66–95.

4. The late medieval pattern of slavery and civic anti-slavery is surveyed in William D. Phillips, Jr., *Slavery from Roman Times to the Early Transatlantic Trade*, Manchester 1985, pp. 88–113. For the municipal abolitionism of Pamiers and Toulouse see Verlinden, *L'esclavage dans l'Europe médiévale*, I, pp. 814–9 and R. Limouzin–Lamothe, *La Commune de Toulouse*, Toulouse 1932, p. 230. The struggle for civic freedom may be traced in such classic works as M.E. Levasseur, *Histoire des Classes Ouvrières en France*, Paris 1859 and Mrs J.R. Green, *Town Life in the Fifteenth Century*, 2 vols., London 1894, vol. I, pp. 174 et seq, vol. II, pp. 92–5. For the strength of the guilds even in an oligarchic context see Richard Mackenney, *Traders and Tradesmen: the World of the Guilds in Venice and Europe c. 1250–c. 1650*, London 1987, pp. 229–32. For Machiavelli see *The Discourses*, book I, ch. 16–18, 37, 47, 55, 58; book II, ch. 59; and Quentin Skinner, *Machiavelli* London 1981, pp. 48–77. For egalitarianism and hostility to bondage in North Western Europe see Norman Cohn, *The Pursuit of the Millenium*, London 1957; on the 'politicisation' of popular culture, see Peter Burke, *Popular Culture in Early Modern Europe*, London 1978, pp. 259–69.

5. John Francis Maxwell, *Slavery and the Catholic Church*, London 1975, pp. 67–8, 88–9; Davis, *The Problem of Slavery in Western Culture*, pp. 165–196; Colin Palmer, *Slaves of the White God*, London 1976, pp. 82–119.

6. Sir Thomas Smith, *De Republica Anglorum*, edited by Mary Dewar, Cambridge 1982, pp. 135–6.

7. Jean Bodin, *Les Six Livres de la République*, 4th ed., Paris 1579, livre I, ch. V, pp. 45–66 (*The Six Bookes of the Commonweale*, done into English by Richard Knolles, London 1606, pp. 33, 44). For the context see, Quentin Skinner, *The Foundations of Modern Political Thought*, Vol. 2, *The Age of the Reformation*, Cambridge 1978, pp. 293–300; Perry Anderson, *Lineages of the Absolutist State*, London 1974, pp. 50–1.

8. For the unpopularity of slavery in England in Tudor times see C.S.L. Davies, 'Slavery and Protector Somerset; The Vagrancy Act of 1547', *Economic History Review*, 2nd series, vol. XIX, no. 3, 1966 pp. 533–49; for Guyenne see Verlinden, *L'esclavage dans l'Europe médiévale*, I, p. 851; for Mechlin see Seymour Drescher, *Capitalism and Anti-Slavery: British Mobilisation in Comparative Perspective*, London 1987, pp. 14, 172.

9. John Rushworth, *Historical Collections*, II, London 1680, p. 468; such rulings did not stop a few blacks of indeterminate juridical status being attached as servants or slave domestics to the households of some wealthy magnates in Tudor and Stuart England. For Massillon and the Bishop of Grenoble see Blandine Barret–Kriegel, *L'état et les esclaves*, Paris 1979, pp. 51, 75–6.

10. John Locke, *Two Treatises of Government*, edited by P. Laslett, Cambridge 1960, p. 159; see also pp. 302–3.

11. Richard Dunn, 'Servants and Slaves: the Recruitment and Employment of Labor', in J.P. Greene and J.R. Pole, eds., *Colonial British America*, Baltimore 1984, pp. 157–94; Gabriel Debien, *Les engagées pour les Antilles*, Paris 1947.

12. The doubts of Quakers and of Dutch clergy are noted in Davis, *The Problem of Slavery in Western Culture*, pp. 291–332; see also David Brion Davis, *The Problem of Slavery in the Age of Revolution*, pp. 213–4, n. 1.; Aphra Behn's novel is in many ways very engaging but her royalist convictions do limit her sympathy with the mass of blacks, see *Oroonoko*, London 1986, pp. 32–3, 86–7; see also Peter Hulme, *Colonial Encounters: Europe and the Native Caribbean*, London 1986, pp. 240–2.

13. Richard Gray, 'The Papacy and the Atlantic Slave Trade', *Past and Present*, 115, May 1987, pp. 52–68.

14. For the full text see the valuable compilation by Roger Bruns, ed., *Am I not a Man and a Brother: the Antislavery Crusade of Revolutionary America, 1688–1788*, New York 1977, pp. 3–5.

15. Charles Johnson, *A General History of the Pyrates*, London 1724, pp. 384–434. For the significance of this text and the phenomenon of which it was a part see

Christopher Hill, *Collected Essays*, vol. III, *People and Ideas in 17th Century England*, Brighton 1986, pp. 161–87.

16. Bruns, *Am I not a Man and a Brother*, pp. 64–6.

17. Charles de Secondat, Baron de Montesquieu, *De L'Esprit des Loix*, Geneva 1748, pp. 383–5; Montesquieu, *The Spirit of the Laws*, Aberdeen 1756, book XV, chapter 1. This was the first of many English editions.

18. Montesquieu, *The Spirit of the Laws*, pp. 262–3. For the limitations of Montesquieu's anti-slavery see Davis, *The Problem of Slavery in Western Culture*, pp. 394–5.

19. Francis Hutcheson, *System of Moral Philosophy*, London and Glasgow 1755, book III, ch. 3, section i, pp. 199–200.

20. Hutcheson, *System of Moral Philosophy*, book II, ch. 14, section iii; see the discussion in Roger Anstey, *The Atlantic Slave Trade and British Abolition*, London 1975, pp. 101–2.

21. George Wallace, *A System of the Principles of the Law of Scotland*, Edinburgh 1760, pp. 94–5. Wallace also denied that individuals owned themselves: 'Nobody is the proprietor of the members of his own body; for the property of them belongs not to any private person, it is vested in the public. Therefore no man has a right to mutilate himself. A Fortiori he has no right to dispose of his life.' (p. 99)

22. See, David Brion Davis, 'New Sidelights on Early Antislavery Radicalism', *William and Mary Quarterly*, 3rd series, XXVIII, October 1971, pp. 585–94.

23. Felix de Arrate, *Llave del nuevo mundo*, Havana 1761 (reprinted with an introduction by Julio le Riverend, Mexico D.F., 1949); Davis, *The Problem of Slavery in Western Culture*, pp. 426–8; Fox-Genovese and Genovese, *The Fruits of Merchant Capital*, pp. 272–98.

24. John Millar, *The Origin of the Distinction of Ranks*, London 1781, 3rd edition, pp. 306, 311, 347–8.

25. Millar, *The Origin of the Distinction of Ranks*, pp. 168–9, 170.

26. Abbé Raynal *A Philosophical and Political History of the Settlements and Trade of the Europeans in the East and West Indies*, 2nd edition, London 1776, 5 vols, III, pp. 466–7. This passage derives from the second French edition of 1774.

27. Quoted in Winthrop Jordan, *White over Black*, Chapel Hill 1968, p. 111.

28. Edward Long, *History of Jamaica*, II, London 1774, p. 460. For Tacky's Revolt see Maurice Craton, *Testing the Chains*, Ithaca 1982, pp. 125–39. For a sociology of Jamaican slave revolts see Orlando Patterson, 'Slavery and Slave Revolts', in Richard Price, ed., *Maroon Societies: Rebel Slave Communities in the Americas*, Garden City, N.Y. 1973, pp. 246–92.

29. Quoted, J.G. Stedman, *Narrative of a Five Years Expedition against the Revolted Negroes of Surinam*, London 1796, 2 vols, I, pp. 68–9.

30. Robert Edgar Conrad, ed., *Children of God's Fire*, Princeton 1983, pp. 397–401.

31. On the development of voodoo and the 'fiercely conservative' nature of African culture in the Americas see Roger Bastide, *African Civilisations in the New World*, New York 1971, pp. 133–51. But for a more differentiated account see also José Luciano Franco, *La Presencia Negra en el Nuevo Mundo*, Havana 1966. For the persistence of African forms of slave resistance see Oruno D. Lara, 'Resistance to Slavery: From Africa to Black America', in V. Tuden, ed., *Comparative Perspectives on Slavery in New World Plantation Societies*, New York 1977, pp. 464–80. But see also Stuart Schwartz, 'The *Mocambo*: Slave Resistance in Colonial Bahia', in Price, ed., *Maroon Societies*, pp. 202–26, and the critical survey of received ideas on this question in David Geggus, 'Slave Resistance Studies and the Saint Domingue Revolt', mimeographed paper published by Florida International University, Winter 1983.

32. For revolutionary traditions amongst sea-farers and their links with blacks, both free and slave, see the evocative essay by Peter Linebaugh, 'All the Atlantic Mountains Shook', *Labour/Le Travail*, no. 10 (1982); and also the exchange between Robert Swilling and Linebaugh in *Labour/Le Travail*, no. 14 (1984).

33. Thomas Spence, *Lecture on Land Reform to the Newcastle Philosophical Society*

(1775), in M. Beer, ed., *Pioneers of Land Reform*, London 1920, pp 7–8; see also Noel W. Thompson, *The People's Science*, Cambridge 1984, pp. 42–5.

34. Carlo Ginzburg, *The Cheese and the Worms: the Cosmos of a Sixteenth Century Miller*, London 1980, pp. 112–26.

35. Charles Frostin, *Les Révoltes Blanches à Saint Domingue*, Paris 1975.

36. A.C. de C.M. Saunders, *A Social History of Black Slaves and Freedmen in Portugal*, Cambridge 1982, p. 178.

II

Hanoverian Britain: Slavery and Empire

When Britain first at Heav'ns command
Arose from out the azure main
Arose, arose from out the azure main
This was the charter, the charter of the land,
And guardian angels sang this strain
Rule Britannia, Britannia rule the waves
Britons never never never shall be slaves.

Rule Britannia (1740), Arne/Thompson

Why do the nations so furiously rage together? Why do the peoples imagine a vain thing? The kings of the earth rise up, and the rulers take counsel against the Lord and His anointed.

Let us break their bonds asunder, and cast away their yokes from us.

He that dwelleth in heaven shall laugh them to scorn, the Lord shall have them in derision.

Thus saith the Lord, the Lord God of Hosts: 'Yet once, a little while, and I will shake the heav'ns and the earth, the sea and the dry land, and I will shake all nations, and the desire of all nations shall come.'

Hallelujah, for the Lord God omnipotent reigneth, Hallelujah!

The Messiah (1741), Handel/Jennens

Slavery first became a focus of public controversy in the 1760s and 1770s as Britain's imperial order was plunged in crisis. The first moves against slavery and the slave trade were to reflect the distinctive political economy and culture of the British Empire in the latter half of the eighteenth century. This chapter aims to illuminate this context, to explore the nature of the state which had established a premier position in Atlantic commerce and to identify the sources and limits of anti-slavery in Britain and North America down to the outbreak of the American Revolution.

Hanoverian Britain was evidently some species of early capitalist or bourgeois state. It had issued from the revolutions of the seventeenth century, culminating in the post-1688 settlement, which asserted the political power of a capitalist landowning and mercantile oligarchy. The Hanoverian state helped to guarantee, reproduce and extend the social relations necessary to agrarian, commercial and manufacturing accumulation – independent property and free wage labour. Britain was the largest free trade zone in Europe; with its dependencies, the largest in the world. The state, staffed by several thousand paid employees, claimed direct sovereignty over both metropolis and colonies. A unified government administered the whole national territory through the Treasury, the Departments of State and the Board of Trade. It had at its disposal a formidable navy and a small but effective standing army.

The Hanoverian political order approximated more closely to Max Weber's classic definition of the modern state – a body exercising a 'monopoly of legitimate violence over a given territory' – than did other European states of the epoch, with their 'parcellised sovereignty' and provincial or municipal autonomy.[1] The Crown in Parliament claimed sovereign sway over the entire kingdom and empire. Thus the Union with Scotland (1707) produced a larger United Kingdom, with a single set of sovereign institutions, not a 'dual monarchy'. Yet the sovereignty of the state was still approximate and ill-defined: the early Hanoverian order was dispersed, localised and self-reproducing. In Britain most public employees worked for Customs and Excise, the Post Office or the Ordnance, leaving the great Departments of State with tiny staffs of a few dozen each. The landed gentry and municipal corporations aspired to be self-governing and did not welcome interference from a centralised authority. The political claims of absolutism had been vigorously and indignantly rejected in favour of limited government. Not only was Parliament dominated by the propertied oligarchy, but the latter ran local affairs directly as Lords Lieutenant, County

Commissioners, Justices of the Peace or through membership of a variety of corporations. Parliament determined the national budget but many of the most lucrative public offices were held as private property. Parliament established a framework of legislation, but the laws were interpreted and applied by Justices of the Peace, drawn from the local gentry, who enjoyed lengthy terms of office. Even in Parliament Bills introduced by private Members predominated over government measures, save in the case of the annual budget. In the Commons 'borough' seats, many of which could be bought, outnumbered 'county' seats; while this distribution was no doubt appropriate for an early bourgeois regime, the existence of the 'rotten boroughs' betrayed the immaturity of bourgeois development. The City of London was jealous of its corporate privileges, as were other municipalities. The Bank of England and the chartered companies were private bodies, though established by public statute. The preservation of law and order was the reponsibility of each county or borough, with its militia or special constables. Oligarchic power was thus not a seamless robe but a patchwork.[2]

The structure of empire was of a piece; the governors and officials appointed from London usually needed to negotiate local sources of finance and to establish a cordial relationship with at least a section of the local possessing classes. In North America and the West Indies colonial assemblies, colonial militia and colonial Justices of the Peace were integral to the structure of government. These British colonies could be seen as miniature editions of the metropolitan regime which claimed sovereignty over them. Most of the colonial assemblies had an upper and a lower house; drawn from them was a Council presided over by the Royal Governor or Proprietor. The British outposts in Africa and India were in the charge of chartered corporations – the Royal Africa Company and the East India Company – established by the Crown in Parliament but answerable to their shareholders and disposing of their own armed forces. But before exploring the colonial dimension it will be appropriate to further specify the political and social formula of the regime in the metropolis.

Opponents of the late Hanoverian order were to coin the term 'Old Corruption' to highlight the way in which oligarchic factions gained possession of the state and distributed the spoils amongst their supporters, thus upsetting the 'balance' of the constitution. Though this term evokes a specific, and at times crucial, aspect of the articulation of power in eighteenth century Britain, it does not sufficiently capture the social logic or future dynamic of the Hanoverian order, nor its ability to enlist consent. Precisely because political influence could be bought, there was a definite correspondence between the workings of government and the interests of large-scale property, whether new or old. And while there was fierce competition between rival oligarchic groupings there was also widespread respect for the rules of the game, enshrined in the procedures of Parliament and other ruling institutions; appointments made by one government would often be respected by its successor. If they could muster the required parliamentary strength and time governments could pass what laws they wished, but in their own actions ministers were bound by the law and by the decisions of courts they did not directly control. While the lay magistracy was the gentry wearing a different wig, and the senior legal officers were political appointees, between these two was a professional and semi-independent judiciary with the power to decide cases in the light of precedent as well as legislation. The need for a legal-rational justification and codification of the laws and constitution was elaborated, with its beginnings in the polemics of Locke and Hoadly and its culmination in the systematic compilations and commentaries of the Scottish school, William Blackstone and Jeremy Bentham.[3]

Britain's constitution was a source of intense national pride, even to oppositionists, prior to 1776 – and for the great majority after that date as well. Government was obliged to respect all independent private property and the rights of the 'free-born Englishman'. Indeed most of those who attacked 'Old Corruption' did so in the name of Britain's supposedly ancient 'mixed' monarchy, whose peculiar genius was traced to Magna Carta and Anglo-Saxon principles lost in the mists of time, as T.B. Macaulay was to claim in his *History of England*. In fact Hanoverian monarchy differed fundamentally from its Stuart and Tudor predecessors – it was in the space opened up by that difference that property rights and personal rights could be asserted in a new way. When Locke declared that the principal aim of government was the 'defence of property', he meant this in a larger sense: land, buildings, cattle, offices of profit, privileges and exemptions, the liberties of the subject and the latter's rights over other persons, including wives, indentured servants and slaves, all counted as 'property'. Property was now the real sovereign and the monarch's role was to respect and uphold it, as laid down in the Bill of Rights. The apologists for the Revolution of 1688 and the Act of Settlement – such as Hoadly, the 'constitutionalist' Bishop of Bangor – had a truer appreciation of the innovation represented by the new order than their mythopoeic opponents.[4] Seeking to downplay the revolutionary origins of the state Tory oppositionists and some later reform-minded Whigs constructed a story of constitutional continuity whose categories failed to acknowledge the true novelty of the British capitalist state. That novelty must be a concern of the present study since the fortunes of colonial slavery and of the Hanoverian regime were so closely intertwined.

Though the structure of social power in Hanoverian Britain was essentially oligarchic, the state was formally monarchical. Previous early bourgeois states, also oligarchic in social content, had opted for the republican form, whether municipal or federal. In Britain monarchy had been restored to give stability, continuity and decorum to the workings of the state. The sovereign stood at the head of the permanent executive and armed forces, but also at the intersection of class forces. The oligarchy was no means oblivious to the need to secure a measure of general consent. Popular tradition had long looked to the monarch as a check to the power of wealthy magnates; the Restoration of 1660 was engineered by the oligarchy but gained a degree of popular support and acclaim, in part because it was seen as a deliverance from the untrammelled rule of Commonwealth power-brokers. Monarchy was a form of government which it was easier for the common people to understand and accept than unadorned oligarchy. The monarch could be represented both as the custodian of the liberties of his 'free-born' subjects and a barrier against renewed bouts of Puritan revolutionary enthusiasm. But the restoration of monarchy brought in its train the danger of royal recidivism. The Divine Right of the monarch was as stridently asserted in the years before 1688 as in the heyday of Tudor absolutism. The ejection of James II by the Glorious Revolution made it clear that Britain's ruling class would not permit any reassertion of a substantive and independent royal government; the King's deal with the Quakers had helped to complete oligarchic alienation. The post-Revolution capitalist state allowed the ruling class not only to defend property and contain levelling tendencies but also to make war more effectively, to run an empire, to raise taxes and to guarantee the National Debt – each of which put extra strain on the maintenance of the social order. Monarchy helped to clothe oligarchic rule and to furnish a point of concentration to the various propertied interests. The person of the monarch came to symbolise the more uniform authority and developing capacity of Britain's state administration.

The menace of a renewed royal bid for independent power continued to be feared after 1688 for a structural reason – the Hanoverian propertied classes needed a centralising instance yet were unable fully to control it. Parliament did not sit for the greater part of the year; its members had their estates or business interests to attend to. The King had the power to select ministers and to dissolve Parliament. Parliament itself was only a sample of the major propertied interests and a number of its members would be beholden to royal patronage. At root the problem was that the ruling class itself was organised around landed and commercial wealth, with an inadequate impulse to the generalisation and centralisation of policy. The individual members of the ruling oligarchy, scattered across the country, were naturally preoccupied with their private affairs. Moreover such means of communication and deliberation as newspapers and political association developed unevenly and sometimes against the grain of oligarchic rule.

Both the strength and the weakness of the ruling oligarchy was revealed in its jealous concern for the privileges of the national Church; the monarch was head of the Church and membership of it was essential to all office-holding. Beneath the factional labels post-Restoration Britain was formally a 'one church' state. Under the terms of the Test and Corporation Acts, only Anglican communicants were permitted to hold public office, though well-established dissenters who were willing occasionally to 'conform', by taking the communion, might also be admitted. The Church of England was the ruling class at prayer with loyal tenants, freeholders and labourers; it was conceived of as a barrier against both Puritan and royal excess. The Restoration had been immediately followed by the Quaker Act of 1661 which tightly circumscribed the activities of religious dissidents. The Putney debates and Puritan exaltation bequeathed ideals which mocked the cynical and pragmatic arrangements of the post-revolutionary order. On the other hand Catholicism was thought even more dangerous since it was the creed of royal absolutism and wedded to the interests of a foreign power. The Revolution Settlement led to the Toleration Act of 1689 which licensed the main Protestant sects while still denying individual Nonconformists many civic rights. The Test and Corporation Acts remained in force but Nonconformist congregrations – Baptists, Presbyterians, Independents, Quakers – might obtain a licence to worship in return for specific oaths and undertakings, varying according to their degree of theological concordance with Anglicanism. Over the next three decades, in the factional battles that preceded the Hanoverian consolidation, the Tories upheld every Anglican privilege while the Whigs offered concessions to Dissent in return for useful political support; Nonconformists, numbering about 400,000 in all, could sometimes vote, or make financial contributions, even if barred from holding office in the state or in the chartered corporations. With the arrival of the Hanoverians secular politics pushed religious controversy from the centre stage. But confessional discriminations still overlaid, to an extent even structured, the political and social system. That the oligarchy felt the need for this reinforcement of their dominant position in society was a sign of weakness; that they could sustain it while tolerating Dissent was a sign of strength.[5]

The Hanoverian regime was thus devised to avoid either royal backsliding or Puritan enthusiasm, naked oligarchy or weak republicanism, Leveller democracy or the rule of courtiers. The memorable convulsions of the seventeenth century had prompted those who had ultimately benefited from them to ensure that they would not be repeated. The personal powers of the monarch were narrowly circumscribed by constitutional practice and law. Indeed constitutionally the powers of sovereignty could only be exercised in and through Parliament, with its hereditary and representative chambers. The Crown in Parliament had formidable powers to make war, regulate trade and raise taxes; but without parliamentary sanction it was powerless. The Revolution of 1688 established these principles so firmly that, almost for the first time, British government had the financial resources to do what it wished; a crucial instrument of the new regime was the National Debt, a deep well of public credit which simultaneously allowed it to fight its enemies and to attach to it the loyalty of a wide layer of friendly rentiers.

The Hanoverian regime was, then, a new species of monarchy, whose rule formally derived from the support and consent of a parliamentary oligarchy rather than from Divine Right or royal blood lines. It might provisionally be termed an *illegitimate monarchy* – that is a monarchy whose very lack of an inherent or self-sufficient title to rule paradoxically assisted its acceptance by society. When George I, Elector of Hanover, succeeded to the British throne, he did so on the authority of Parliament's Bill of Rights (1689) and Act of Settlement (1701) and not by virtue of hereditary right. He was, at the time, only fifty-second in line of succession.[6] For a ruling class that intended itself to rule, George's lack of monarchical legitimacy was an extra guarantee against attempts to assert royal power. George's lack of English further reduced the scope for royal intervention. From this date the Cabinet met regularly without the sovereign being present; a Prime Minister, the First Lord of the Treasury, now presided over the Cabinet's deliberations. Yet while the day-to-day affairs of the government were attended to by Cabinet and Prime Minister the sovereign furnished an element of continuity and a focus for loyalty.

The monarch's lack of inherent legitimacy paradoxically allowed the monarchy to become a more popular institution. The weakness of the sovereign was seen as the obverse of the rights and powers of his subjects. While the oligarchy could exercise political power in the King's name, the rest of his subjects could also find a consolation for their exclusion from political power – their liberties as subjects of the Crown. This was as true of the backwoods Tory squire, prone to an instinctive monarchism and distrust of the government, as of independent men completely outside the power system. Those who vaunted the social rights enjoyed by the 'free-born Englishman' held that they had no parallel in continental Europe, and the boast had some substance. The abolition of the last vestiges of English villeinage in the seventeenth century meant meant that all men, and not a few women, were free to move to where the wages and conditions were best – if necessary to emigrate to the New World. The relations between employers and employed were still legally defined as those of 'masters and servants', but the masters' powers were circumscribed by custom and contract, by the servants' mobility and by the existence of a substantial body of 'masterless' men and women. The extension of market relations created new freedoms and new risks; the rigours of the market were tempered by a locally administered welfare system and by a popular propensity to riot if conditions got too bad. The legal rights of the subject also offered a measure of protection from the power of office-holders, though such rights were more easily invoked by the propertied than the propertyless, by townspeople than country folk, by men than women. Those who celebrated the rights of the 'free-born Englishman' would be the frequenters of coffee houses and taverns rather than those subsisting on the poor rates. But this was a secular identity acceptable to many with a heterodox religious background or little religous conviction at all.

The successes of British arms and the profits of empire ensured that the cult of Britain's mixed monarchy was a truly national institution. This was the epoch which gave birth to official and unofficial national anthems: 'God Save the King!', 'Hearts of Oak' and 'Rule Britannia' (1741), with its triumphant and suggestive couplet 'Rule Britannia, Britannia rule the waves/Britons never, never, never shall be slaves.' In another register the thrilling chords of Handel's magnificent oratorios encouraged a species of secular religiosity combining self-confidence and responsibility.

The new sense of a secular national destiny received militant expression in the ideology of 'patriotism', vaunting the glories of Britain, its constitution and liberties. Britain's maritime and imperial vocation was a favourite patriot theme; it received striking expression in the parliamentary oratory of Pitt the Elder in the 1730s and 1740s, leading to war with Spain and France, and indicting the comfortable corruption of Walpole's 'Robinocracy'. Imperial aggrandisement could be seen as a popular cause because it promised to facilitate emigration, encourage colonial development, promote the export of manufactures and boost the supply of plantation produce. France's ambassador to London in the late 1730s was struck by the fact that humble artisans and labourers as well as Peers of the realm took up the patriot cry for a war against Spain to secure and enlarge Britain's American empire. And he was alarmed by the patriots' skill in confecting issues, misrepresenting complex questions and playing upon popular prejudice. The 'War of Jenkin's Ear' was the first fruit of this new-fangled patriot agitation.[7]

Patriotism, rooted as it was in the claims and identity of the 'free-born Englishman', was an ideology which appealed to the radical and expansive wing of the oligarchy and helped to furnish it with a following. It claimed to represent popular interests and aspirations. But oppositional Tories and members of the 'country party' had made their own contribution to the invention of patriotism and of the social ideology of the 'free-born Englishman'. The Tory leader Bolingbroke had elaborated a theory of patriot opposition which gained currency in the 1730s and 1740s. For a sometime legitimist Bolingbroke's patriotism was a curious echo of Machiavelli's Renaissance republicanism: it attacked the corruption of Hanoverian governments as a menace to English liberty and civic virtue. Bolingbroke and the Tories articulated the country gentlemen's distrust of Westminster and of costly entanglements in European wars. But the Tories had themselves played a part in consolidating the imperial and maritime orientation of British policy and the British state: they had sponsored the 'blue water' strategy during the War of Spanish Succession, seen as a cheaper and more profitable alternative to military engagement in Europe, and themselves had responsibility for the Treaty of Utrecht. The great majority of Tories not only accepted the Hanoverians but wished to underline their commitment to the constitution and to a responsible and ordered liberty. Thus the peculiar virtues of Britain's balanced constitution were to be summed up in the following words by an oppositional paper of Tory inclinations, *The Freeholders Journal*, in 1769:

> The constitution of our English government (the best in the world) is no arbitrary tyranny, like the Turkish Grand Seigneur's, or the French King's, whose wills (or rather lusts) dispose of the lives and fortunes of their unhappy subjects: nor an oligarchy where the great one(s) (like fish in the ocean) prey upon, and live by devouring the lesser at their pleasure: Nor yet a democracy or popular state, much less an anarchy, where all confusedly are hail fellows well met. But a most excellent mixt or qualified monarchy, where the King is vested with large prerogatives sufficient to support Majesty; and restrained only from power of doing himself and his people harm ... the nobility adorned with priviledges to be a screen to Majesty and a refreshing shade to their inferiors, and the commonalty too, so guarded in their persons and properties by the fence of the law, as renders them free-men, not slaves.[8]

Thus even the more conservative strand of the ruling ideology was prone, as with the concluding phrase here, to flatter the common people with the compliment of freedom. While the patriot Whigs and radicals paraded the claims of the middling sort the more conservative Whigs and Tories liked to stress that *social* freedom was perfectly compatible with *political* subordination. Those powerful interests affronted by the turbulent and challenging proponents of colonial rights or 'Wilkes and Liberty' were to argue that the free-born Englishmen should be content with being a subject not a citizen.

The possession of New World colonies and the superprofits of slavery gave the Hanoverian regime both a transatlantic safety valve for popular energies and extra resources with which to wage its battles at home and abroad. Every year thousands of Britons went to make their fortune in the New World. Britain's tax system, claiming a third of national income, found its major support in the Customs and Excise. It was characteristic of Hanoverian 'illegitimate monarchy' that taxes falling on the sphere of circulation would be preferred to those directly levied on wealth holders or on the process of production. There was a land tax, but ministers generally strove to keep its incidence as low as possible. The revenue obtained from Customs and Excise, levies falling on commodity circulation, always greatly exceeded those from any other source.[9] The customs duties on tobacco, sugar and the other colonial imports provided a particularly welcome source of revenue since they were less likely to arouse popular resentment in the metropolis than excise levied on the consumption of domestic products. Foreign tobacco or sugar was virtually excluded from the British market but the colonial product still had to pay a sizeable duty. Re-exports paid duty at a lower rate but could still yield impressive revenues. Domestic exports were free of duty and given protected access to the colonial markets. So long as metropolitan interests were not menaced British traders and British colonies were encouraged to penetrate the imperial systems of Britain's rivals. The Methuen Treaty with Portugal (1703) and the *Asiento* clauses of the Treaty of Utrecht were both designed to encourage a clandestine as well as legal trade. Thus much of the slave-mined gold of Brazil and New Granada ended up in the Bank of England or helping to finance the activities of the East India and African companies. While the North American colonies were expected to buy only English manufactures, they were permitted to trade in rice and provisions to the foreign West Indies.

Prior to the imperial crisis the regime of 'illegitimate monarchy' seemed to have a special affinity with empire, with colonial profits and projects greatly assisting metropolitan stabilisation. The phenomenal growth of Britain's colonial and Atlantic trade in the period 1620–88 had not only created new sources of revenue but also reflected and consolidated the rise of a new mercantile and manufacturing establishment directly underpinning the new political regime. The limited monarchy formula had a definite attraction for colonial planters and merchants. They wanted a state that could defend their vital interests while interfering as little as possible in their private affairs. The planter was in any case first cousin to the metropolitan landowner. Both West Indian and North American planters played a part in devising the settlement of 1688–9, both through their representations in London and through the parallel action of colonial assemblies challenging the pretensions of royal governors. Colonial merchants, for their part, knew that trade was one of the foremost preoccupations of the King's ministers and they had many channels for making known their views on government policy.

The richest colonial merchants and proprietors were able, if they wished, to purchase influence or representation at Westminster. This was especially true of the absentee West India proprietors, though the North American colonies also engaged agents to advance their interests in London. In the 1730s a Committee of West Indian Planters replaced the previous informal lobby in making representations to government and Parliament. West Indian merchants for a time had their own separate committee. In mid-century about twenty MPs had links to West Indian planting, about thirty to colonial trade. Cornwall and Devon, with their 'rotten boroughs' and historic ties to West Indian planting, sent no less than seventy MPs to Westminster while such new manufacturing centres as Manchester, Leeds and Halifax sent none.[10]

During the century between 1660 and 1760 all colonial proprietors needed the protection and commercial facilities which the metropolis could provide. While the richer colonists expected royal officials to be pliant they were, on occasion, themselves willing to invoke royal authority to overawe rebels and demagogues of the sort who had caused such memorable havoc in Virginia during Bacon's Rebellion in 1676.[11]

Nevertheless, within the system of 'illegitimate monarchy' the colonies developed a more ample and popular measure of self-government than was to be found in the constituent parts of the metropolitan Union. Scotland or Wales did not have their own assemblies but were directly represented at Westminster. The American colonies were unrepresented at Westminster but had their own well-established representative assemblies. Formally these bodies were convoked by a royal Governor, or the proprietory holder of a royal patent, and owed allegiance to the Crown in Parliament. In practice their traditions of self-reliance, their distance from London and their more representative character gave them considerable autonomy.

The colonial franchises were based on wealth-holding no less than in the mother country but a much higher proportion of adult white males met the property qualification; a third or a half instead of only one in every eight or ten. The colonists were strongly attached to personal independence and civic equality. Planters displayed this assertive impulse no less than farmers, and the West Indian colonists were almost as exigent in their demands as those of North America. The popular aspect of 'illegitimate monarchy' – government limited by the representation and consent of property-holders, concern for the rights of the 'free-born Englishman' – acquired an extra intensity when transported to the New World. The presence of black slaves itself contributed to a sense of equality amongst whites. The levelling up of all whites was, if anything, more generalised in the West Indies or Virginia than in, say, Pennsylvania or New England, where the slave population was small. A Jamaican planter was to remark upon 'the display of conscious equality through all ranks and conditions. The poorest White person seems to regard himself nearly on a level with the richest, and, emboldened by this idea, approaches his employer with open hand.'[12]

The very successes of the colonial system generated sources of tension: between planters and merchants, between creditors and debtors, between those looking to invest in new lands and those concerned to defend the value of existing estates, between one branch of trade and another, between those interested in colonial markets and those involved in the entrepôt trade, between tax-payers and rentiers or contractors. So long as these were shifting and unstable quarrels of interest they could be brokered by factional conflict. They testified to the vitality of empire. The patriot agitations of the period 1739–63 received strong backing from the colonies, notwithstanding quarrels over the precise distribution of expenses and spoils. Down to the very eve of the Declaration of Independence the American colonists united in proclaiming fidelity to the principles of the Revolution settlement and Constitution.

The slave trade and colonial slavery remained virtually unquestioned, until the challenge to empire dramatically extended the social and political agenda. It was, after all, the privileges of the free-born *English* that were being celebrated. One of the earliest examples of the mobilisation of a broad public opinion behind competing parliamentary factions had been a pamphlet war in the first decade of the eighteenth century concerning which ports could enjoy the custom of the slave-trading Royal Africa Company.[13]

Nevertheless Britain's rulers could not entirely avoid the apparent discrepancy between metropolitan liberty and colonial slavery. In the backwash from the Atlantic trade Britain itself acquired a growing population of black slaves, rising to ten thousand or more by the middle decades of the eighteenth century. A number of colonial proprietors brought slave domestics with them to Britain; possession of a black boy became something of a status symbol for the wealthy, even if they had no colonial interest. In 1729 the West Indian planters approached the Attorney General, Sir Philip Yorke, to inquire whether their rights as slave-owners enjoyed legal recognition in the metropolis; they were assured that all legally acquired property enjoyed the protection of the law, including slaves, and that 'baptism does not bestow freedom'. Two decades later Yorke, now Lord Chancellor Hardwicke, reiterated his view that 'there are no laws which have destroyed servitude absolutely'.[14] Though weighty, these opinions did not have the force of legal precedent; there were also judicial decisions which denied particular slaveholder claims in England, leaving the whole question indistinct. The concern of the planters' representatives, long preceding philosophical anti-slavery, came from the knowledge that slave-owning had been and could be challenged by runaways, and those prepared to help them or simply to employ them without asking questions. It seems likely that they did not press for further clarification in the courts because they felt unsure of the outcome. Slaveholders in England wanted the service of their slaves, and in particular to be able to order them back to the colonies at will. They understood that it would be needless provocation to insist upon enacting into English law a full-blown slave code, such as was to be found in the colonies.

Following the rise of a revolutionary challenge to Britain's ruling order its representatives were to retreat into studied empiricism, if not outright mysticism, when it came to examining the principles of the established order. But there was a vital moment in the middle decades of the eighteenth century when the generalising spirit of the Enlightenment was employed to explore the presuppositions of Britain's socio-economic and politico-legal systems. The works of Wallace, Smith and Millar referred to in the previous chapter would be examples of this. But not even Smith's work, with all its analytic brilliance, so directly concerned the practical problems of legislation and government as William Blackstone's *Commentaries on the Laws of England*, first published in 1765. Blackstone's ambitious attempt to codify England's legal and constitutional doctrine was directly encouraged by Lord Mansfield, the Chief Justice. This work was thoroughly permeated by respect for Britain's ruling order and was immediately recognised by British courts as a work of authority. Nevertheless its attempt to enunciate general principles of liberty and order was to encourage not only Jeremy Bentham's crypto-republican gloss, and leading proponents of the North American revolt, but also some early opponents of slavery. In a characteristic passage on English liberty Blackstone wrote:

> The idea and the practice of this civil and political liberty flourish in the highest degree in these Kingdoms, where it falls little short of perfection, and can only be lost or destroyed through the demerits of its owner; the legislature, and of course the laws of England, being peculiarly adapted to the preservation of this inestimable blessing even in the meanest subject. Very different from the modern constitutions of other states, on the continent of Europe, and from the genius of imperial law; which in general are calculated to vest arbitrary authority and despotic power of controlling the actions of the subject, in the prince, or a few grandees. And this spirit of liberty is so implanted in our constitution, and rooted even in our very soil, that a slave or a negro, the moment he lands in England falls under the protection of the laws and becomes *eo instanto* a freeman.

Blackstone's concern here had been to heighten the sense of English liberty, though there were judicial *obiter dicta* that bore out his view. When it was pointed out to him that Yorke had come to a different conclusion and that there were indeeed black slaves in Britain, he changed the concluding flourish in the 1767 edition to the following perilously uncertain formulation: 'A slave or a negro, the moment he lands in England, falls under the protection of the laws, and so far becomes a freeman; though the master's right to his service may probably still continue.'[15]

Elsewhere in the *Commentaries* Blackstone adduced arguments from the logic of contract also tending to undermine the validity of slavery:

> Every sale implies an equivalent to the seller, in lieu of what he transfers to the buyer. But what equivalent can be given for life and liberty? His property likewise, with the very price which he seems to receive, devolves *ipso facto* to his master, the instant he becomes a slave: In this case therefore the buyer gives nothing, and the seller receives nothing. Of what validity, then, can a sale be, which destroys the very principles upon which all sales are founded?[16]

Neat though it might sound at first, this argument was by no means invulnerable since eighteenth century England recognised many forms of property founded neither in purchase, reciprocity nor original title. Moreover English law encompassed a variety of conundrums such as that 'the King could do no wrong' but that his government could; self-ownership might be neutralised by perpetual alienation just as royal power was by ministerial responsibility. Blackstone's argument from contract was stated in terms that flowed from a supposed universal logic, yet Blackstone himself recognised that slaveholding was entirely lawful in the British colonies. However systematic or philosophical his approach Blackstone could not resolve the contradictions of a social order which gloried in inconsistency; only the clash of contending social forces and philosophies could do that. Nevertheless, with the publication of Blackstone's *Commentaries* law as a functional and legitimating ideology had come of age; the monarchy might lack legitimacy but the social order on which it rested craved it. The need for this work may be judged from the fact that it went through nineteen editions in the first seven years after publication.

While those responsible for governing Britain were concerned to recognise and protect colonial slavery their actions did betray an awareness that it could be an inconvenient or vulnerable institution in the colonies as well. The colonial charter given to Georgia in 1733 contained a clause barring slaves from the colony, in the hope that this would provide more opportunities for the poorer class of emigrant and would make Georgia an asylum for English orphans and debtors. The banning of slaves may well have been encouraged by security considerations. Georgia, on the southern flank of the British possessions, was exposed to Spanish attack; it was known that the Spanish authorities would sponsor servile rebellion in case they attacked Georgia.

Similarly, when the British authorities concluded treaties with the Jamaican maroons in 1739, they pledged them to help in defending the island from foreign invasion. Britain itself hoped to play the part of liberator in Central America: the commanders of an expedition destined for Central America in the early 1740s drew up proclamations promising the Indians freedom from the Spanish yoke. Abandonment of the expedition meant that this tactic remained unused.[17]

Britain's war for empire in North America concluded triumphantly at the Peace of Paris in 1763 with the ejection of the French. This victory directly prepared the ground for the momentous conflict which ensued between the metropolis and the mainland colonies. During the wars large concessions had been made to the colonial assemblies. Efforts had been made to bring together the formerly localistic and fragmented colonies in a common military effort. The defeat and disappearance of French power in mainland North America removed a powerful incentive to colonial subordination. The heady rhetoric of 'patriotism' had stimulated both colonial confidence and imperial assertiveness.

The defiance of the North American colonies in the 1760s appeared, to begin with, to be a quarrel within the terms of 'illegitimate monarchy' and of the 'patriotic' exhilaration of the time. The Americans defied first particular parliamentary measures, then the competence or authority of Parliament, and only lastly the House of Hanover; as late as July 1775 the rebels were still declaring their ultimate loyalty to the King. In contrast to the Jacobite rebellions of 1715 and 1745, the British opposition of the 1760s adopted a loyalist rhetoric and drew its main strength from the new social forces associated with the Atlantic boom. Like that of the Wilkesite opposition the language of North American resistance was couched in terms of the rights of 'free-born Englishmen' and exploited the ambiguities of 'illegitimate monarchy'. Patriotic politics not only expressed commercial interests but was promoted with a new commercial flair on both sides of the Atlantic, with mass-produced buttons and pottery, as well as newspapers and pamphlets, broadcasting the themes of civic liberty.[18]

The patriotism of the metropolis and the patriotism of the colonies had largely converged during the war years. But the mobilisation of public opinion on each side of the Atlantic fostered both metropolitan arrogance and colonial insubordination. The relatively weak legitimacy of royal government, and the strength of national conceit, permitted each 'free-born' subject to assume airs of superiority. Benjamin Franklin remarked: 'Every man in England seems to consider himself as a piece of a sovereign over America; seems to jostle himself into the throne with the King, and talks of *our subjects in the colonies*.'[19] But if the metropolitan English were prone to arrogance the colonial English developed their own potent claims and conceits. They wished to jostle themselves into the place of Parliament and entertain a direct relation with the King.

The advent of peace prompted London governments to enhance the integrity of empire. With the departure of the French, Britain's responsibilities and expenses increased as a string of forts and a permanent garrison had to be maintained. The proclamation of a western boundary was designed to curb colonial land-grabbing and the colonial propensity to stir up Indian trouble. The Currency Act (1764) was designed to prevent colonists paying off debts to British merchants in depreciated local currencies. The Sugar Act (1764) aimed to boost revenues and prevent the North Americans from engaging in a clandestine trade with the French islands to the detriment of the British West Indies. British ministers started with relatively modest objectives – that of raising revenue and tightening up administration – but soon discovered that they had gravely underestimated colonial pretensions.[20]

When challenged by the colonists British ministers claimed that all responsible British subjects were 'virtually represented' in Parliament, since its members comprised a sample of the possessing classes. Proprietors resident in the colonies, however, could not accept that they were 'virtually represented' within the London Parliament. With an ocean separating them from the ruling authority American colonists knew they had different needs and interests. They believed that they made a decisive contribution to imperial prosperity. Colonial troops had participated in most of the decisive engagements of the Seven Years War. Britain's navy and merchant marine depended on North American supplies and the output of its naval construction yards. Colonial trade supplied the metropolis with its largest and most dynamic outlets and vital inputs. The North American colonists were able to inflict a series of humiliating reverses on the British ministries of the 1760s. The colonial boycott of British manufactures stimulated an outcry in Britain and forced successive administrations to retreat, all the while proclaiming Parliament's ultimate sovereignty.

The West Indian assemblies were also disposed to defy central authority but were quite unable to sustain early gestures of defiance. Over a half of the West Indian proprietors actually lived in Britain. Slaves comprised the vast majority of the colonial population. Together with the presence of nearby hostile powers this was identified as a great source of insecurity. British troops were needed to guarantee the colonial order, suppressing uprisings like 'Tacky's Revolt' in Jamaica, and to defend the islands from the continuing danger of foreign invasion. The West Indian proprietors were also deterred from schemes of independence by the knowledge that they benefited from privileged access to the imperial market and were well represented in imperial institutions. The West Indian planters and the West Indian merchants had a common interest in protection of the British market for colonial sugar; they had played a part in urging adoption of the Sugar Act, curbing as it did trade with the French sugar islands. In all the circumstances it is surprising that the Jamaican assembly was prepared to extend even verbal support to North American defiance of the metropolitan authority. That it did so testified to the will to autonomy of local representative institutions, even when these were in a highly vulnerable position and had little reason to seek independence.

In North America, with its far larger and more settled population of white colonists, the local oligarchy of gentry and richer townsmen had obtained the support of the mass of freeholders in their periodic tussles with royal Governors or proprietors. In Virginia, which was to play such a crucial role in the challenge to Britain, members of around 400–500 gentry families dominated the magistrate's bench, the county courts and the House of Burgesses; but in elections to the latter body there was often stiff competition for the votes of 25,000–30,000 freeholders since any white man who owned fifty acres with a house could vote.[21] Most of Virginia's slaveholders were much less wealthy than those of the Caribbean; by the revolutionary epoch only sixty-five owned over a hundred slaves compared with at least 500 plantations of this size in the British West Indies. But the tobacco planter who owned between thirty and sixty slaves and 1,000 acres of land was a rich man and disposed of great influence and patronage in his county – the more so if he was a Justice of the Peace and a member of the County Court. However, the planter Edmund Randolph noted that all white Virginians regarded themselves as equally free and independent: 'the system of slavery, however so baneful to nature' nourished a 'quick and acute' sense of liberty and resentment at 'any abridgment of personal independence'.[22]

The Hanoverian regime manifestly permitted far greater autonomy to American colonists than did the Kings of France or Spain. Projected measures of imperial reform in the 1760s did not aim to cancel or even seriously abridge the powers of the colonial assemblies. But they did assert dormant rights and the ultimate sovereignty and authority of the metropolis. During the long years of 'benevolent neglect' the British Government had regulated colonial trade and appointed colonial office holders but had often failed to enforce its regulations or give full and effective support to its officials if they proved unable to work with the local establishment. The British governments of the 1760s and early 1770s were still willing to give ground but not to concede Parliament's sovereignty over the colonies. The colonial rebels and patriots began by proclaiming their loyalty, but the very institutions of 'illegitimate monarchy' encouraged them to treat metropolitan sovereignty as a formality with little substance, somewhat akin to the monarch's own authority *vis-à-vis* Parliament. Some spokesmen for the colonial assemblies claimed they should bypass the authority of Parliament altogether, in matters other than trade and war, and enjoy a direct relationship with the monarch. A flood of pamphlets appeared defending the rights of colonial subjects and colonial assemblies in terms which drew liberally on Locke, Hoadly and the oppositional English writers who have become known as 'commonwealthmen'.[23]

Imperial reform meant not only taxation but also the creation of a salaried colonial administration and judiciary capable of acting independently of the local possessing classes. The colonial spokesmen perceived a danger that initially quite modest imposts would be simply the thin end of the wedge, soon permitting, as in the metropolis, wholesale fiscal exploitation in the interests of office holders, *rentiers* and public contractors who would not be controlled by colonial interests. Trade regulations which had long been a dead letter would at last be enforced. Within the thirteen colonies themselves budding local dynasties already competed for metropolitan favours. It thus fell to a radical new generation of political leaders to articulate colonial opposition to what was seen as an imperial project to rob Americans of effective self-government, to make levies on their property without their consent, to create costly new public offices and generally to foist upon them a 'tyranny' and 'slavery' inimical to the rights of free-born Englishmen.[24]

The thirteen North American colonies were in the full flood of development by the time of the Treaty of Paris; the imperial crisis both reflected and aggravated a check to this growth as metropolitan controls and colonial boycotts interrupted the flow of trade. The North American complex of farming, planting, shipbuilding, petty manufacturing and trading gave a self-reliant strength to the social formation, which depended on the metropolis for no essential product or service. No less than a third of Britain's ocean-going merchant marine was North American in construction and ownership. The slaveholding planters of Virginia, Maryland, Georgia and the Carolinas produced rice and wheat as well as tobacco and indigo. In contrast to many Caribbean planters Virginian planters had no shortage of land for subsistence cultivation; their slave complements, typically numbering no more than a few dozen, were replenished by natural reproduction, not the import of Africans. The North American slave system was far more secure and stable than its counterparts elsewhere in the Americas because of the strength and coherence of the white slaveholding social formation. On the eve of the Revolution there were about 450,000 slaves in English North America out of a total population of over 2,500,000; the major slave colonies, Virginia and Maryland, had no need for further importations. The fact that blacks were outnumbered by whites in every colony except South Carolina gave its own reassurance. On the other hand, the presence of slaves available to perform the most menial labour encouraged racial solidarity and pride amongst the free whites. It encouraged the slave proprietors to extend without anxiety more ample rights and freedoms to other white men. Free blacks constituted less than 1 per cent of the population and suffered many legal disabilities. The pressure exerted by the Indians of the interior furnished another source of solidarity, while British attempts to halt westwards expansion aroused frustration.

The slaveholding planters of North America were natural leaders of their communities. They had experience of fighting their own battles as well as of governing themselves. In the wars with the Indians they had often seized the initiative, while in the French wars the colonial militia had contributed to British military strength. A visitor to old Virginia remarked: 'Wherever you travel . . . your Ears are constantly astonished at the Number of Colonels, Majors and Captains that you hear mentioned: in short the whole Country seems at first to you a Retreat of Heroes.'[25] The poorer whites filled the ranks of the patrols and militia; they accepted this obligation partly because they too feared Indian marauders, or runaway slaves, and partly because they hoped that the planter colonel would hire their sons at harvest time, or buy extra provisions from them, or overlook some petty legal infraction. Class differentiation among the white population in North America, even in the plantation zone, was less polarised and antagonistic than in Hanoverian Britain; slaves, comprising about 30 per cent of the population in the southern colonies, performed the harshest labour. Security considerations prompted the larger proprietors to extend concessions to other whites. Thus Britain's ferocious game laws contrasted with the 'freedom of the range' which permitted the generality of white colonists to graze livestock or shoot game in the continent's unfenced grasslands and woodlands. The fellow feeling between planters and farmers was also encouraged by the fact that the relationship between them was not that of landlord to tenant; indeed the planter was a sort of large edition of the farmer, with both enjoying patriarchal authority over their households.

Like the Caribbean planter the Virginian resented dependence on merchants who extended him credit at high rates of interest. On the eve of the Revolution the planters of the southern colonies owed British merchants about £3 million. But unlike the sugar trade of the British Caribbean the North American staple trade was not favoured by the workings of the imperial system. Virginian tobacco planters resented having to sell at lower prices to British merchants rather than trade directly with the customers in France, and elsewhere in continental Europe, who purchased over four-fifths of their crop. Likewise the farmers, merchants, manufacturers and refiners of the northern and middle states resented the imperial legislation which tried to prevent them from trading freely with St Domingue, Brazil and the Spanish colonies, where they would have been able to find a ready market for their own provisions or manufactures, and buy molasses or raw sugar. Such keenly felt material complaints lent an extra edge to North American anger at the menacing conduct of the London government and stiffened North American determination to build on the practice of colonial autonomy.[26]

The conflict in North America led to a fundamental radicalisation of the critique of the Hanoverian regime. The publication of Thomas Paine's *Common Sense* in January 1776 was both an eloquent call for American independence and the first fully republican indictment of the 'royal ruffians' and their hangers-on. It is reputed to have sold 120,000 copies in North America in its first year. The break with the metropolis could not be sustained by remaining within the assumptions of 'English liberties', but required the birth of a new political discourse of republican legitimacy and of the rights of man. In Britain the actions of George III and his ministers were challenged in the most sarcastic terms, as in the writings of Junius, but few even hinted that monarchy itself should be overthrown. While the ideology of the Hanoverian order made for a particularist vindication of liberty the new republicanism raised questions of universal significance.

The refusal of the British government to give up the substance of sovereignty in North America meant that there was no alternative but to invent a new political order. The custodians of Britain's 'illegitimate monarchy', for their part, felt that empire, royal prerogative, the government's right to tax, to regulate trade and to appoint officers, were all vital attributes of sovereignty and empire that could not be compromised. Both sides in the conflict had a large stake in the continuing prosperity of the slave systems of the New World. But soon both colonial and metropolitan leaders found it necessary to vindicate political arrangements by appeal to principles. And as it developed the mortal struggle led each side to discover new sources of legitimacy, to maximise its own striking power and to sow confusion in the enemy camp. The North American colonists found themselves impelled by the conflict and their new goals to raise a carefully delimited challenge to the slave trade and to slaveholder rights in New England. This corresponded not simply to the logic of political conflict but also to deep social fears.

To men such as Thomas Jefferson or Benjamin Franklin the ideal citizen was an independent property-holder; the independency of such a person could be menaced by indebtedness or mercantile monopoly as much as by arbitrary and unrepresentative government.[27] British rule compounded these various evils in a tyranny which would 'enslave' the colonists if they did not throw it off. By 1776 any exercise of sovereignty was intolerable – to such an extent that it became a major problem for the rebel Confederation itself. Patriot discourse had always focused on the rights of the individual as well as a right to representative government. And it had always displayed a hysteric quality, as if it needed to deploy every device of exaggeration to keep its constituency on the alert. Whether in Britain or in North America the patriot alliance was motley indeed, bringing together artisans, professionals, labourers, farmers, manufacturers and many others. A lively sense of menace fused this broad coalition of the middling sort of people.

The American colonists were apparently partisans of free trade, yet for them the independent producer, whether artisan, farmer, manufacturer or planter, had a political and social value that could not and should not be contradicted by the verdict of the market. Their 'moral economy' only favoured free trade so long as it was compatible with the continued prosperity of the independent producer. Just below the surface there was an anti-mercantile as well as anti-mercantilist reflex in the North American revolt. In 1767, and again in 1774 and after, the colonists chose to hit at Britain by means of a trade boycott. In the eighteenth century merchants were still suspect figures on both sides of the Atlantic. Acting as middlemen they produced nothing. Much of their skill was thought to involve manipulation of the market by 'engrossing' and 'forestalling'. Using credit they acquired goods cheaply, charged extortionate interest and converted producers into their hirelings; in times of dearth, sometimes artificially engendered, they made a killing. Though there were important individual exceptions, merchants in North America displayed no unequivocal enthusiasm for conflict with Britain. As relatively wealthy persons they had more to lose than most; many of them were primarily engaged in a transatlantic trade which the colonial system favoured; only those who wished to expand the carrying trade to the Caribbean directly suffered from the trade restrictions. The generality of North American planters, farmers, manufacturers, artisans and labourers were prone to see merchants as commercial agents of the metropolis with little interest in an independent North American prosperity. The idea that productive activities were superior to mere buying and selling was reinforced by the effectiveness of the first trade boycotts; British as well as North American merchants responded to the boycotts of the 1760s by imploring the London government to withdraw the offending legislation. When the government did back down this seemed an impressive demonstration of the power of the American producer. Some parallel may be seen between the methods and outlook of the protesting North American colonists – with their boycotts, riots and Boston 'Tea Party' – and the typical protests and 'moral economy' of the British populace in times of shortage and high prices. In the course of the American Revolution itself citizens' committees were often established to set fair prices and thereby prevent mercantile profiteering.[28]

Anti-slavery was not a central concern of either the British or the North American patriots. Indeed many of them were so deeply implicated in the workings of the slave system that to have been so would have been rather incongruous. But their discourse of freedom and their commitment to popular politics did incline to anti-slavery gestures. The proposal to suppress a branch of trade was more familiar and easier to accept than that of suppressing a category of property. Even the former slave-traders would not be expropriated but only required to find a different branch of commerce. The suspension of slave imports could even find support among planters, whose slaveholding thereby became more valuable; in North America planters knew that the slave population was self-reproducing while in the West Indies the reproduction rate was rising and many hoped to emulate this North American pattern. Planters were often hostile to the mercantile interest, seen as the agent of indebtedness. Even those North American patriots most implicated in slavery favoured suppression of the slave trade, because they recognised that the continued importation of Africans was a source of weakness and dependence. The more radical patriots, and those without a stake in slavery, were prone to extend the argument, albeit cautiously, from the slave trade to slaveholding itself; and in the northern colonies there was also popular pressure to curb slaveholder rights.

West Indian proprietors did not venture as far in opposition either to the metropolis or the slave trade as did the North Americans, but even they considered partial measures against the slave trade. 'Tacky's Revolt' in 1760 moved a grouping in the Jamaica Assembly to petition for a restraint on slave imports. The Peace of Paris in 1763 led to plans for plantation development in the newly acquired territories. For established planters who lacked the resources for expansion this prospect of stiffer competition was not at all welcome. The Jamaican Assembly asked in 1766 for a tariff on slave imports in the hope of impeding such developments.[29]

The action proposed by the North American colonial assemblies had a more far-reaching significance. In the early stages of the conflict with the London government the Virginian planters, who no longer needed slave imports, called for a ban on the slave trade to reinforce other measures of colonial boycott. The logic of this was strengthened by the fact that British traders were mainly responsible for bringing slaves to American ports. In Virginia, as in Jamaica, the royal Governors refused official sanction to the measures proposed. The colonial leaders, though failing in their objective, were not displeased to dramatise British sponsorship of the slave trade. In the southern colonies the slaveholders stressed their paternalist responsibilties and portrayed the plantation as a large family within whose protective embrace childlike Negroes received shelter and sustenance. The young Thomas Jefferson went further in 1767 and in his capacity as a lawyer took on the case of a free person of colour who had been wrongly held in bondage; such 'freedom suits' were rare in the southern colonies but became quite common in those to the north.[30]

In New England and the middle Atlantic states slaves comprised a declining minority of the population in the period 1750–75. The free artisans and labourers of Boston, New York and Philadelphia often refused to work with slaves, or white indentured servants, on the grounds that it degraded their occupations. The holding of slaves became increasingly problematic in New England since owners enjoyed scant legal protection. In the 'freedom suits' slaves or their friends brought masters before the courts accused of wrongful enslavement, on the grounds that there was some technical error in the bill of sale or that they had promised manumission in return for good service. Such freedom suits were heard by juries who often manifested a prejudice against slaveholding and found against the master. These decisions reflected antagonism to slaves as well as slaveholders. Few slaves had the contacts or means to bring a 'freedom suit', but the effect of these cases was to undermine the legal basis of slaveholding and discourage slave imports to the New England colonies.[31]

The escalation of conflict with the metropolis helped to broaden the social range of those involved in political controversy. In the ports the activities of the British press-gangs were a major provocation, hauling their victims off to the life of the naval rating, incarcerated in insanitary hulks and subjected to merciless floggings. The Royal Navy press-gangs set vigorously to work in the North American ports because of the large numbers of experienced sailors to be found there. Amongst the seamen there were quite a few free blacks and mulattos. The activities of the press-gangs led both to riots and to lawsuits. Lawyers like John Adams and James Otis burnished their patriot credentials by taking up cases which demonstrated the arbitrary and tyrannical conduct of the British and developing the theory of their incompatibility with the 'natural rights' of man. While the British regarded such men as the worst demagogues, a view shared by many wealthy Bostonians, Adams and Otis warned against tumults and bully-boy tactics. They criticised the rich conservatives but did not condone the sacking of their houses. Their doctrine of natural rights sought to elevate and dignify the rude protests of the 'meaner sort'. It had definite anti-slavery implications.

Thus Otis declared in a famous broadside of 1764: 'The colonists are by the law of nature free born, as indeed all men are, white or black.'[32] Attacks on slavery and the slave trade became a point of contact between patriot leaders and the patriot mob, even if racism might sometimes mingle with abolitionism; in some cases the Sons of Liberty and the patriot committees specifically excluded free blacks from membership and in other cases the question may simply not have arisen. In the previously quoted pamphlet James Otis, notwithstanding his declaration that all men were free born, black or white, was also at pains to insist that North American colonies were settled 'not as the common people of *England* imagine, with a compound mixture of *English, Indian and Negro,* but with freeborn *British white* subjects.'[33] Free blacks themselves sometimes opted to throw in their lot with the colonial Patriots, despite the latter's standard assumption of a white American identity. Prior to 1775 British officials made no move to help North American blacks: on the first occasion when British troops fired on a patriot mob – the 'Boston Massacre' of 1770 – one of the victims was Crispus Attucks, a free man of colour. White and coloured artisans and labourers of diverse extraction were brought together in the port towns in cosmopolitan circumstances which encouraged fraternisation in the face of both the authorities and the employers. The experience of shipboard life also encouraged solidarities and friendships across ethnic and religious lines. Opposition to slavery and the slave trade helped to focus more general hostility to merchants, few of whom were ardent Patriots.

The slave-traders offered special inducements to those who sailed with them, but the slaving voyages were not popular because of the brutally disagreeable, degrading and dangerous aspects of life on board for the ordinary sailor as well as the human cargo. One way or another the call for a ban on slave imports enjoyed widespread backing in the north.

The appeal of anti-slavery rhetoric to the patriot mentality makes the greater sense if it is borne in mind that in the larger colonial ports, and in parts of the interior, the patriot cause attracted support from mechanics and labourers for whom some form of bondage or servitude had been a direct personal experience. Apprenticeship and indenture were far milder than the slavery inflicted on blacks but could be onerous none the less, with indebtedness leading to an extention of servitude. The more idealistic patriot manufacturers, such as Franklin, heartily endorsed denunciation of enslavement as well as of endebtedness in the conviction that the terms of service they offered their employees were altogether different. Benjamin Rush and Thomas Paine, who helped to lead the patriot challenge to the ruling oligarchy in Pennsylvania, were both early critics of slavery; Paine's first American writings of 1775 included an attack on slavery and on the slave trade.[34]

In 1771 the Massachusetts assembly passed a Bill banning the slave trade entirely. In 1772 the Virginia Burgesses enacted a prohibitive tariff on the importation of slaves which it denounced as a 'trade of great inhumanity'. These legislative initiatives were both predictably refused the Royal Assent. When the Continental Congress met in 1774 it adopted a resolution banning the slave trade, together with other measures of commercial boycott. The Patriots undoubtedly saw the ban on slave imports as combining moral as well as economic pressure on the metropolis and as a way of rallying the 'common people' to a cause led by gentlemen. The southern planter-magistrates proved themselves eloquent exponents of the natural rights doctrine. A widely published first draft of Virginia's Declaration of Rights proclaimed that 'all men are born equally free'; a statement amended in the version adopted on the grounds that it might give rise to civil convulsion.[35]

The British social and imperial crisis of the 1760s and 1770s was a compound of many elements: colonial self-confidence and metropolitan blundering, commercial booms and fluctuations, the rising incidence of taxation and new demands made by government, the growth of communications and urbanisation, producers against merchants, servants against masters, the increasing penetration of market relations and the introduction of proto-industrial methods, and demands for the representation of new interests and the protection of popular living standards. Many of the conflicts of the time were conceived of in terms of the opposition between freedom and tyranny, liberty and slavery. Standing armies, taxation without representation, mercantile monopolies, abuses of executive power, endebtedness were all thought to embody the threat of *enslavement*. The opposition between freedom and slavery was absolutely central to political discourse, as it had been for more than a century. While radicals fought for representative government conservatives pointed to the wide scope of social freedom. The regime of 'illegitimate monarchy' had justified itself domestically as a political order that allotted to each rank and condition its due measure of liberty. The free-born Englishman did not necessarily share in political power but he did live in a 'free country'. The imperial crisis put this justificatory system to the test at a time when economic commotion and insecurity tested to its limit the primitive and localistic welfare arrangments of the Hanoverian state.

Those hostile to, or suspicious of, patriot politics were to develop an anti-slavery critique of their own. Both in Britain and in North America there were those who saw the Patriots as crude and vulgar demagogues, using an overblown vocabulary to pursue base interests and disrupt the peace. Samuel Johnson was famously distrustful of patriotism – the 'last refuge of a scoundrel' as he put it – and he was also consistently sympathetic to slaves and free blacks. His pamphlet of 1775 denying that North American colonists should expect representation ended with the pointed query: 'How is it that we hear the loudest yelps for liberty among the drivers of negroes?'[36]

As in the case of patriot anti-slavery the proto-abolitionism of those who looked askance at patriot politics was no mere political gambit but often a matter of deep conviction. The rise of patriotic politics, beginning in Britain in the late 1730s, led to wars, increased taxation, and a variety of political and economic disruptions. The more conservative wing of the Hanoverian oligarchy itself had opposed the belligerent venture of patriot politicians like Pitt the Elder. The campaigns of the 'Great Commoner' had been backed by, amongst others, the West Indian magnate William Beckford. Those who opposed patriot plans of colonial aggrandisement fastened on colonial slavery as a particularly disreputable accompaniment of the imperial mission. While patriot politics had a popular dimension there was also a basis for popular opposition to military and colonial adventures; in the short run they led to more press-gangs, higher taxes and a swollen National Debt. The protection afforded to British West Indian sugar planters was attacked in a well-informed pamphlet by Joseph Massie in 1759 as a subsidy extended to British slave-owners at the expense of the British consuming public.[37] A pseudonymous London pamphlet of 1760 by 'J. Philmore' attacked slavery in the most uncompromising and radical terms concluding:

> And so all the black men in our plantations, who are by unjust force deprived of their liberty, and held in slavery, as they have none upon earth to appeal to, may lawfully repel that force with force, and to recover their liberty, destroy their oppressors; and not only so but it is the duty of others, white as well as blacks, to assist those miserable creatures, if they can, in their attempts to deliver them out of slavery, and to rescue them out of the hands of cruel tyrants.[38]

Such sentiments would seem to express antagonism to all factions of the oligarchy. Tories, Whigs and Patriots each had a discourse of popular liberty and no doubt a real measure of popular support. But there was also a strand of opinion which was aghast at the menacing trend of politics and economics.

People in the Atlantic world at this time faced ancient tribulations – epidemics, early death, physical danger – as well as the trials of capitalist modernity: boom and bust, intrusive commercialisation, migrations on a new scale. The family and religion had to respond to more insistent demands for personal identity and definition as the familiar social landscape shifted. A new prosperity did not cancel out uncertainty but encouraged the common people of England and North America to assert a new civic and personal identity. This was a time of revivalist movements, 'Great Awakenings', evangelism and Methodism, on both sides of the Atlantic. In different ways patriotism and anti-slavery may both be seen as secular correlates to this search for new meanings and a more stable and satisfying order, alike in the public and private spheres. The challenge to empire was accompanied and preceded by a generalised malaise, what might be called the 'legitimation crisis'[39] of illegitimate monarchy, evoked by Oliver Goldsmith's 'The Traveller; or, A Prospect of Society', published in 1763–4:

> Calm is my soul, nor apt to rise in arms,
> Except when fast-approaching danger warms:
> But when contending chiefs blockade the throne,
> Contracting regal power to stretch their own,
> When I behold a factious band agree
> To call it freedom when themselves are free;
> Each wanton judge new penal statutes draw,
> Laws grind the poor, and rich men rule the law;
> The wealth of climes, where savage nations roam,
> Pillag'd from slaves to purchase slaves at home;
> Fear, pity, justice, indignation start,
> Tear off reserve, and bare my swelling heart . . .

Even within the ruling class there were to be some whose sensibility was affronted by the slave trade and its toleration by a braggart patriotism. Horace Walpole may have been the first member of the oligarchy to record – in private correspondence – his distaste. During the parliamentary session of 1750 he wrote:

> We have been sitting this fortnight on the Africa Company, *we*, the British Senate, that temple of liberty, bulwark of Protestant Christianity, have this fortnight been pondering methods to make more effectual that horrid traffic of selling negroes. It has appeared to us that six-and-forty thousand of these wretches are to be sold every year to our plantations alone! – it chills one's blood. I would not want to say I voted for it for the continent of America.[40]

Walpole's private abstention reflected a wider distaste for prevailing social and political trends but led to no further action; the first parliamentary challenge to British participation in the slave trade was not to be made until 1779 when, following reverses in the American war, some Yorkshire MPs favourable to parliamentary reform also unsuccessfully proposed a ban on the slave trade.

British and North American Patriots had, at best, a deeply ambivalent and inconsistent record on slavery and the slave trade. Yet their sporadic recourse to natural rights doctrine and anti-slavery rhetoric did encourage others to address the slavery question in a new way.

The religious bodies which took up the anti-slavery cause were those most challenged by the rise of patriotism and those most responsive to the diffuse social crisis. They were attentive to secular events and saw good works, rather than faith alone, as the route to salvation. The two Christian denominations which proved most open to anti-slavery were the Quakers and the Methodists. For both a commitment to anti-slavery, and a concern with social amelioration, allowed them to retain the confidence of members who might be tempted by radical democratic politics. Both regarded worldly riches as a dangerous source of corruption; at the same time, by a familiar paradox, their habits of thrift, industry and self-denial made them successful accumulators or disciplined employees. The Quakers' alienation from the state, and links to the heritage of seventeenth century radicalism, disposed them to be active in the anti-slavery cause. Wesley and the Methodists, by contrast, initially inclined to Tory politics and were respectful of property, though regarding riches with the greatest suspicion. Their identification with the British monarchy put a distance between them and the new Republic declared by, amongst others, American slaveholders; while they could not support expropriatory measures their evangelism led them to be concerned with saving the souls of both slaves and slaveholders.

The patent link between colonial slavery and violence did much to provoke the Quaker reaction. The pacifist Quakers were to play an outstanding part in pioneering anti-slavery agitation. Between 1755 and 1761 the Yearly Meetings of Quakers in Philadelphia and London moved from disquiet at the activities of slave-traders to outright disavowal. In each generation there had been individual Quakers who attacked 'man-keeping' as one of the worst manifestations of corruption and sin; but such prophets had quickly been isolated from their co-religionists, many of whom were bankers or merchants with a stake in the Atlantic system. The first Quakers to make real headway in persuading the Friends to disassociate themselves from slave-trading and slaveholding were John Woolman, a tailor, husbandman and scribe, and Anthony Benezet, a school-teacher, both of Philadelphia. They were men of modest means who urged that slaveholding and slave trafficking were incompatible with a Christian way of life and an offence against that 'sweetness of freedom' which should be recognised in every fellow creature. Not only were there Quaker slaveholders in Pennsylvania, but the Government of the colony was largely in their hands. In the years 1754–7 the pacifist scruples of these influential Quakers were severely tested by a bloody border war against the Indians and patriotic mobilisations preparatory to the Seven Years War. All Quakers were asked to live in conformity with the 'Discipline' of their local Society.

After a discussion of the duties of Quaker witness all members were ordered to withdraw first from the Council and then from the Assembly. Woolman urged that the time had come for a more far-reaching rectification and secured the inclusion of advice against slave-trading in the letter sent out following the Yearly Meeting in 1755. By 1758 the Philadelphia Society decided that slaveholders would not be permitted to hold positions of authority within the Church. Woolman and Benezet pursued a sort of saintly class struggle within the ranks of the Friends, shaming their richer brethren into abandonment of man-keeping. The Quakers most inclined to defend slaveholding were farmers of middling wealth for whom possession of a few slaves was a valuable economic resource; urban artisans were less likely to own a slave, while urban merchants had most of their wealth in other forms. Woolman was an itinerant minister as well as tailor: if he found himself billeted in a house where there were slaves he would always insist on paying for his board and lodging, suggesting that the money be given to the slaves. During the troubled decade of the 1750s Woolman succeeded in gaining the support of the Pembertons, one of the richest Quaker families in America.[41]

Quaker rejection of slavery reinforced, and helped to justify, their rejection of war. In 1761 the London Quakers, who can have numbered few slaveholders within their ranks, lent their influential support to the lead of the Philadelphia Quakers. However, it was not until 1770 that the Quakers in New England adopted a rule against slave-trading. In this first instance Quakers sought to prohibit the buying and selling of slaves, and then slaveholding, within their own ranks. But Woolman and Benezet also looked for allies outside Quaker ranks. Woolman wrote pamphlets addressed to all Christians as early as 1754 and 1756. In the subsequent decade Benezet developed the anti-slavery case on the broadest humanitarian grounds: his writings on the subject drew on Montesquieu, Hutcheson and Wallace as well as travellers' accounts of conditions in Africa. With manumission adopted as Quaker policy Benezet helped to establish a school in Philadelphia for the former slaves and their children. On the other hand, few blacks were admitted to Quaker membership.[42]

The eruption of militant colonial opposition to the British govern-ment put the American Quakers in a very awkward position, since their pacifism prevented them from giving support to colonial revolt; many belonged in any case to a commercial elite which did not favour a break with the metropolis. The rejection of slavery helped to embody the special destiny and spiritual purity of Quakers at a time when they shunned the patriotic cause. The slave trade was a particularly vulnerable target of criticism since it evidently rested on violent and arbitrary acts. Even if the slave-traders acquired their human cargoes through purchase, it took little imagination to see that a huge traffic in captives required wars, raids, kidnapping and tyranny in Africa and harsh measures of intimidation and constraint during the middle passage. Anthony Benezet furnished details of what was involved in his influential *Historical Account of Guinea* published in 1773. In this he reprinted passages from the radical anti-slavery pamphlet of 'J. Philmore', despite the latter's call for slave insurrections to be supported. The onset of the Independence War gave another boost to anti-slavery within Quaker ranks until slaveholding was rejected in principle by all societies; those members who refused to divest would be visited, reproached, and eventually even excluded.[43] In the post-revolutionary epoch Quakers were to become outstanding proselytisers of the movements against the slave trade and, later, slavery. Yet slavery was to be ended in Pennsylvania, where Quakers had ruled so long, by secular radicals at a time when the Friends had withdrawn from political life; the respective roles of Benezet and Paine in this will be considered in the next chapter.

Prior to 1776 the Patriots were only anti-slavery in a rhetorical or instrumental sense. The Quakers renounced slaveholding for themselves but did not yet undertake public campaigns against slavery. Granville Sharp, who became the first anti-slavery campaigner in England in the years 1765–72, occupied a middle ground between political radicalism and religous evangelism. Sharp came from a distinguished ecclesiastical and musical family. His father was an archdeacon and his grandfather Archbishop of York. Lacking conventional ambitions Sharp became a clerk in the Ordnance Office, devoting much of his time to a succession of good causes. He supported constitutional reform in England, believing that government should be brought closer to the authentic principles of 'Anglo-Saxon liberty'. He eventually resigned his post in the Ordnance office because of opposition to the American war. Thereafter his family supported him and, despite the radical flavour of his convictions, his eccentricity and piety set him apart even from the bourgeois radicals. In later years he drew up a plan for a co-operative commonwealth in Sierra Leone, based on outlawing slavery and other forms of accumulated private wealth; all citizens would be guaranteed a decent livelihood though the able-bodied could only claim goods in proportion to their labour. Sharp's radical social and political convictions were inspired by a belief in the 'Mosaic Law' understood as a sort of primitive communism.[44]

Granville Sharp had first been moved to contest the actions of English slaveholders in 1765 when he was concerned in the case of

Jonathan Strong, a runaway slave who was beaten up and kidnapped by the man who claimed to be his owner. Sharp helped Strong to escape from the clutches of his owner, but he was shocked to discover that English courts were prepared to equivocate on the vital question of personal liberty. In this case Sharp failed to obtain rulings which bore upon the legality of slaveholder powers as such in Britain; Strong's owner only fitfully pursued his claim leaving the issue of the legality of slaveholding undetermined. Sharp was outraged to learn from the prosecution that slave-owner rights had been specifically endorsed by Lord Chancellor Hardwicke. Convinced that slavery could not be tolerated by Britain's constitution he combed the statute books and law books for supporting evidence. He found at least some comfort in Blackstone's apparently sweeping declarations concerning slavery.

As we have seen, central to the justificatory system of Britain's Revolution Settlement of 1688 was the view that power was restrained by parliamentary law and civic liberty. Sharp's first pamphlet, *A Representation of the Injustice and Dangerous Tendency of Tolerating Slavery; or of Admitting the Least Claim of Private Property in the Persons of Men, in England* (1769), argued that slavery was incompatible with English liberty and necessarily led to great inhumanity. As well as developing this legal and humanitarian argument Sharp took up a number of other cases of those resisting enslavement by their supposed owners. While pamphlets could be ignored the legal cases taken up by Sharp demanded a practical response from the authorities and attracted the notice of an aroused public opinion. Not until he was approached by James Somerset in 1771–2 did he find a legal case which would test fundamental principles. Somerset was the slave of a Boston customs official who wished to force him to return to the colonies. Sharp's own single-mindedness and unworldly dedication helped him to create a sympathetic climate for vindication of Somerset's right in London, where there was already much concern with the fate of English liberties.

Lord Mansfield, the Chief Justice who had taken unpopular decisions in the Wilkes controversy, was again put in a most awkward situation when called upon to adjudicate the Somerset case. Quite apart from the fact that he owned property himself in Virginia, he was loath to deliver a judgement in the Somerset case and several times sought to postpone it in the hope that it could be resolved without depriving all slave-owners in Britain of their full rights as masters; there were several thousand slaves in the metropolis at this time. Neither Somerset nor his master were prepared to compromise and both received considerable support in pursuing the case to a final judgement. While the slave-owner's costs were met by West Indian planters Somerset's cause was taken up by a coalition of supporters which included radical artisans, fellow blacks and concerned members of the liberal professions. Somerset received dubious offers from individuals willing to buy his freedom but in his concern to vindicate the general principle he insisted on exposing himself to the risks of a judicial hearing. Seven lawyers donated their services to the defence and a large crowd attended the hearings. Mansfield eventually ruled that English law could not countenance the deportation of a servant by a master: 'So high an act of dominion must derive its authority, if any such it has, from the law of the Kingdom *where* executed ... The state of slavery is of such a nature, that it is incapable of being now introduced by justice upon mere reasoning ... it must take its rise from *positive law*.'[45]

Conducted as it was in a glare of publicity the Somerset case revealed how difficult it was to defend the full rights of the slaveholder, given the cult of liberty and the aroused state of public opinion in England at this time. Britain's rulers might be ready to confront rebellion and subversion at home and abroad, but they knew that to do so while openly defending slavery would be most unwise. Moreover the 'high dominion' claimed by the slaveholder was disturbing to the power of the state as well as to the harmony of the metropolis.

Mansfield's judgement essentially concerned a particular slaveholder right – that of being able to deport his slave back to the colonies. It did not remove the presumption that slaves brought to England were bound to serve their masters. Despite its loose ends Mansfield's decision was undoubtedly a heavy blow to slaveholding in England because it denied to slaveholders the positive support they needed. It did not only free a particular individual but gravely weakened the position of all slaveholders in England: the Scottish courts went somewhat further in 1778 ruling that no slaveholder rights could be upheld in that country. These blows to slavery in a metropolitan zone where it was in any case completely marginal were only a very modest beginning, but a beginning none the less, and one achieved directly as a result of slave resistance – the courage of James Somerset – and anti-slavery argument – that of Granville Sharp.

The secular controversy concerning slavery, and the example of the Quakers, put pressure on other religious denominations to declare their position. One of the first to do so was the Methodist leader John Wesley in his 1774 *Thoughts on Slavery*. From the very beginning the evangelical movement had had a strong American connection but George Whitfield and the young Wesley had somehow managed to avoid taking a stand on the question: indeed Whitfield, the single most influential preacher, had himself become a slaveholder. Wesley's pronouncement followed the consolidation of the anti-slavery critique in jurisprudence, moral philosophy and in the witness of the Quakers. Its immediate occasion was supplied by the Somerset case of 1772 and the escalating conflict with the North American colonies. Wesley was not a pioneer of anti-slavery thought but his adhesion both reflected and focused a species of popular abolitionism.

While many Quakers were well established in business John Wesley used open air preaching to reach the neglected and displaced populations created by the new pattern of economy and demography. Wesley's message was politically conformist and theologically eclectic, drawing on Anglicanism, Quaker doctrine, pre-millenarian revivalism and the redemptive message of the Moravian Brethren. Wesley, though highly impressed by the Christian communism of the Moravian communities, thought the 'dung and dross of riches or honour' could be sloughed off by sufficiently intense personal commitment to salvation and good works. He offered a heightened but not unfamiliar religious message to the new populations of the manufacturing and mining districts, a more flexible and open organisation, and a visceral hostility to democratic agitation. Methodism recommended a dour subordination to its followers, but it also encouraged collective self-respect and self-help; loans to those in distress, primitive medicine for the sick and advice on a host of practical problems.[46]

Wesley's attack on slaveholding distinguished the Methodists from their main rivals in the evangelical movement, those who adhered to the Calvinist doctrine of the elect, such as the followers of the slaveholding Whitfield. Methodism had significant transatlantic connections, though the first North American Methodist Conference did not take place until 1784; some of its 15,000 American adherents lacked proper patriotic credentials, whether as recent arrivals from Britain, former Anglicans or outright loyalists. The Methodist message had chimed in well with the doctrines of the 'Great Awakening' in the American colonies. Methodism's moral critique of slaveholding could attract support even in Virginia because of its stern repudiation of licentiousness and brutality. There were many, especially women, who had good cause to rue the encouragement given to the 'boisterous passions' by slaveholding (the phrase was Jefferson's). The wives and daughters of slaveholders, together with many of the common people, knew that their society was marked by violence, drunkenness and lewd behaviour. Evangelical religion promised to establish more restrained patterns of conduct even when slavery was not at issue. And often it was the womenfolk who made sure that the men kept to the straight and narrow path of righteousness, shunning rudeness, brawling, fecklessness and viciousness, including fiddling, dancing, drinking, bad language and fornication. Blacks as well as whites were attracted to the evangelical preachers.[47]

Wesley's *Thoughts* evoke the message of evangelical religion for those uprooted by migration, shoved aside by economic advance or buffeted by political conflict. The slave suffered an extremity of abuse, the slaveholder exhibited a fatal and false pride. Wesley insists that only right conduct and penitence offer salvation. His pamphlet directly addresses the slaveholder:

> May I speak plainly to you? I must. Love constrains me; Love to *you*, as well as to those you are concerned with. Is there a God? You know there is. Is He a just God? Then there must be a state of retribution; state wherein the just God will reward every man according to his works. Then what reward will he render to you? O, think betimes! Before you drop into eternity! Think now, *He shall have judgement without mercy that shewed no mercy*. Are you a *man*? Then you should have an human heart. But have you indeed? What is your heart made of? Is there no such principle as compassion there? Do you never feel another's pain?

While appealing to slaveholders to mend their ways Wesley also consoles the suffering slave with the prospect of their redemption by a merciful God:

> Thou who hast mingled of one blood, all the nations upon earth: Have compassion upon these outcasts of men, who are trodden down as dung upon the earth! Arise and help these that have no helper, whose blood is spilt upon the ground like water! Are not these also the work of thine hands, the purchase of thy Son's blood? Stir them up to cry unto thee in the land of their captivity; and let their complaint come up before thee; let it enter into thine ears! Make even those that lead them away captive to pity them, and turn their captivity as the rivers of the South. O burst thou all their chains in sunder; more especially the chains of their sins: Thou, O Saviour of all, make them free, that they may be free indeed![48]

In addition to such dramatic addresses, awakening the soul of the believer, Wesley also introduces more mundane political and economic arguments, especially those which tend to show that slavery was contrary to equitable exchange and contract, and to England's constitution and common law. As a good Tory Wesley is happy to quote Blackstone. At a time of distressing challenges to the established order Wesley was content to identify a cause to which his followers could wholeheartedly commit themselves with little danger of aiding the revolutionary threat to the British monarchy. It would, of course, be wrong to construe Wesley's denunciation of slavery as no more than a device to undermine sympathy for radical politics or the colonial cause; yet his *Thoughts on Slavery* indicted the wickedness and vanity of slaveholders just at the time when planter politicians were calling into question British monarchy.

As the North American colonists moved into open rebellion Lord Dunmore, royal Governor of Virginia, decided to issue an open invitation to slaves owned by rebels to desert their masters and join the forces loyal to the Crown. This plan had been mooted as early as April 1775. Loyal slave-owners would not be threatened; and as it happened much loyalist support was to be found away from the tidewater region where slaveholding was concentrated. In November 1775 Dunmore, whose headquarters was now aboard a ship in the Chesapeake, issued a proclamation offering freedom to all slaves of rebels who deserted. About eight hundred slaves took advantage of this offer and those who could bear arms were formed into a white-officered regiment.[49]

Dunmore's proclamation scandalised the colonial patriots and drove many moderates to embrace the cause of independence for the first time. There were alarmed reports of the numbers of blacks ready to answer Dunmore's call; only patriot vigilance prevented an even larger response.[50] The governor's action underlined that slavery could be a source of weakness and threatened the moral credentials of the rebels. When Thomas Jefferson came to draft the Declaration of Independence he included in it a denunciation of George III and the British government for having

> waged cruel war against human nature itself, violating the most sacred rights of life and liberty in the persons of a distant people who never offended him and carrying them into slavery in another hemisphere . . . he has prostituted his negative for suppressing every legislative attempt to prohibit or to restrain this execrable commerce: and that this assemblage of horrors might want no fact of distinguished die, he is now exciting these very people to rise in arms among us, and to purchase that liberty of which *he* has deprived them by murdering the people upon whom *he* also intruded them, thus paying off former crimes committed against the *liberties* of one people, with crimes which he urges them to commit against the *lives* of another.[51]

The Continental Congress did not accept this clause of the Declaration, verging, as it did, on an outright rejection of slavery. But with southern support it accepted a ban on slave imports, as a war measure, in April 1776. Patriotic rejection of the slave trade helped to cement an alliance between the slaveholding gentry and those who owned few or no slaves, since small men were prone to see the slave trade as furnishing the large planters with a facility that enabled them unfairly to overbear their neighbours.

Just as Congress shrank from endorsing Jefferson's slavery paragraph, so the British authorities shrank from generalising Dunmore's appeal for slave revolt. Neither side could afford to challenge slavery, but as the Revolution unfolded new opportunities were created for making a breach in the slave regime.

Notes

1. For 'parcellized sovereignty' see Perry Anderson, *Lineages of the Absolutist State*, London 1974; for Weber on the state see Max Weber, *The Theory of Social and Economic Organization* , New York 1966, p. 154.

2. For the Revolutionary foundations see Christopher Hill, *The Century of Revolution: 1603–1714*, London 1980, pp. 220–69; for the centrality of independent property to eighteenth century politics see Roy Porter, *English Society in the Eighteenth Century*, London 1982, pp. 113–58 ; for the residue of particularism see W.A. Speck, *Stability and Strife: England 1714–1760*, London 1980, pp. 11–30.

3. Edward Thompson, following Douglas Hay, argues that law became the central legitimating ideology of Britain's eighteenth century ruling class, and that it elicited a degree of popular consent, in *Whigs and Hunters*, London 1975, pp. 258–69. The term 'Old Corruption' was first used by William Cobbett, but it echoed Tory critiques of the Whig establishment in early Hanoverian times. For a brilliant discussion of the eighteenth century British political order using this term see Edward Thompson, 'Peculiarities of the English', originally published in *The Socialist Register 1965*, pp. 311–62, see especially pp. 319–26, reprinted in *The Poverty of Theory*, London 1978. For a critique of Thompson's analysis see Perry Anderson, *Arguments within English Marxism*, London 1979, pp. 88–97 and *English Questions*, London 1992. John Brewer notes that venality in public office was much less marked in Britain than in France *The Sinews of Power*, Cambridge (Mass.) 1988, pp. 19–21, 72–3.

4. Thomas Babington Macaulay, *History of England*, vol. I, London 1913, p. 23–5; Speck, *Stability and Strife*, pp. 169–84.

5. Those Dissenters who did not subscribe to the doctrine of the Trinity were subject to the most discrimination. The structure of Anglican power and privilege is described by Speck, *Stability and Strife*, pp. 91–119. For the limits of toleration see Michael R. Watts, *The Dissenters: From the Reformation to the French Revolution*, Oxford 1978, pp. 259–67.

6. According to one calculation, see Speck, *Stability and Strife*, p. 169. For a discussion of the wider meaning of monarchy in modern British history see Tom Nairn, 'The House of Windsor', *New Left Review*, 129 (1981).

7. Angus Calder, *Revolutionary Empire*, London 1981, pp. 550–55; Richard Pares, *War and Trade in the Caribbean*, London 1963, p. 68.

8. Quoted in John Brewer, *Party Ideology and Popular Politics at the Accession of George III*, Cambridge 1976, pp. 243–4.

9. Customs and excise accounted for no less than 70 per cent of all revenues in the years 1750–80; in France indirect taxes contributed about a fifth of revenues. See Peter Mathias and Patrick O'Brien, 'Taxation in Britain and France, 1715–1810', *Journal of European Economic History*, vol. 5, no. 3, Winter 1976, pp. 601–50, especially p. 617.

10. Lewis Namier and John Brooke, *History of Parliament: The House of Commons, 1754–1790*, London 1964, pp. 234 *et seq.*

11. Edmund S. Morgan, *American Slavery, American Freedom*, New York 1975, pp. 263–93. This work is fundamental for understanding the politics of colonial Virginia.

12. Bryan Edwards, quoted in Calder, *Revolutionary Empire*, pp. 479–80.

13. K.G. Davies, *The Royal Africa Company*, London 1957, pp. 122–35.

14. A. Leon Higginbotham, *In the Matter of Color*, New York 1978, pp. 313–70, 327; Peter Fryer, *Staying Power: The History of Black People in Britain*, London 1984, pp. 114–15.

15. William Blackstone, *Commentaries on the Laws of England*, Oxford 1765–9, I, p. 123; in the second edition of 1766 the revised formula appears on p. 127.

16. William Blackstone, 'Of Master and Servant', *Commentaries on the Laws of England*, I, London 1773, 9th edn, pp. 423–4. Blackstone elsewhere refers to the 'sacred and inviolable rights of private property' (p. 140). The various contradictory formulas to be found within this work were examined in Jeremy Bentham, *A Comment on the Commentaries*, London 1775; for criticism of Blackstone's ingenious paradox that the King can do no wrong, that he can do no civil act except through his ministers and that the latter are accountable for their actions, see pp. 179–83.

17. Higginbotham, *In the Matter of Color*, pp. 53–61; Pares, *War and Trade in the West Indies 1739–1763*, pp. 70–2.

18. Brewer, *Party Ideology and Popular Politics*, p. 208; Bernard Bailyn, *The Ideological Origins of the American Revolution*, Cambridge 1967, pp. 167–9.

19. Quoted in Hugh Brogan, *Longman History of the United States of America*, London 1985, p. 80.

20. Robert W. Tucker and David C. Hendrickson, *The Fall of the First British Empire*, Baltimore 1982, pp. 187–211.

21. About half of all adult white males qualified for the vote, and of these only about half owned a slave. Charles S. Sydnor, *Gentlemen Freeholders: Political Practices in Washington's Virginia*, Chapel Hill 1952, p. 31.

22. Jack Greene, '*Virtus et Libertas*': Political Culture, Social Change, and the Origins of the American Revolution in Virginia', in Jeffrey J. Crow and Larry E. Tise, eds, *The Southern Experience in the American Revolution*, Chapel Hill 1978, pp. 55–108, especially pp. 64–5.

23. Bailyn, *The Ideological Origins of the American Revolution*, pp. 8, 35–9, 43.

24. The salience of these terms is noted by Bailyn, *The Ideological Origins of the American Revolution*, p. 245.

25. Quoted in Rhys Isaac, *The Transformation of Virginia*, Chapel Hill 1982, p. 109.

26. Tucker and Hendrickson, *The Fall of the First British Empire*, pp. 106–45.

27. Edmund S. Morgan, *The Challenge of the American Revolution*, New York 1976, pp. 139–73; T.H. Breen, *Tobacco Culture*, Princeton 1985, pp. 124–59.

28. Eric Foner, *Tom Paine and Revolutionary America*, New York 1976, pp. 71–106, 145–82.

29. Calder, *Revolutionary Empire*, p. 631.

30. John C. Miller, *The Wolf by the Ears: Thomas Jefferson and Slavery*, New York 1977, pp. 7–8; for the southern paternalist ethos see Jan Lewis, *The Pursuit of Happiness: Family and Values in Jefferson's Virginia*, Cambridge 1983, pp. 221–2. On the tendency of slave trade bans to unify the slaveholders see Duncan MacLeod, *Slavery, Race and the American Revolution*, Cambridge 1974, p. 11.

31. Edgar J. McManus, *Black Bondage in the North*, Syracuse, NY 1973, p. 166. See also Gary Nash, *The Urban Crucible: Social Change, Political Consciousness, and the Origins of the American Revolution*, Cambridge, Mass. 1979, pp. 109–10, 320–1, 343–5. And Higginbotham, *In the Matter of Color*, pp. 84–5. On a later occasion, that of the Boston massacre of March 1770, Adams undertook the legal defence of the English soldiers, partly to demonstrate fair play but also because he disapproved of the conduct of the patriot mob, 'a motley rabble of saucy boys, Negroes and mulattoes, Irish teagues and outlandish Jack Tars'. Hiller Zobell, *The Boston Massacre*, New York 1970, p. 292.

32. James Otis, *The Rights of the British Colonies Asserted and Proved*, Boston 1764, p. 24.

33. Otis, *The Rights and Duties of the British Colonies*, p. 29.

34. Roger Bruns, *Am I Not a Man and a Brother*, pp. 224–45, 376–9, 385–6. Paine is reliably reported to have written an anti-slavery article in 1775 though some conventional

attributions, as in this compilation, strike an uncharactistically pious note.

35. W.E.B. DuBois, *The Suppression of the African Slave Trade to the United States of America*, New York 1904, pp. 15, 25–6, 37–8, 41–2. The natural rights discourse outlook of the southern patriot leaders may have reflected their reading of Hutcheson or Blackstone, but it will also have been formed by an apprenticeship as magistrates in a colony where the often inappropriate practices and precedents of English Common Law needed to be corrected by more generalised principles of justice and greater respect for the common people, if white. Virginia promulgated the first American Bill of Rights in 1775 though its protective clauses were extended only to 'men . . . when they enter into a state of society' thus excluding women, Indians and slaves. Isaacs, *The Transformation of Virginia*, pp. 134, 309.

36. Samuel Johnson, *Taxation no Tyranny*. This text may be found in many places but is given in its political context in Marshall B. Davidson, *The World in 1776*, New York 1975, p. 311.

37. Joseph Massie, *A Computation of the Money that hath been exhorbitantly Raised upon the People of Great Britain by the Sugar-Planters*, London 1760. For a discussion of this see Peter Mathias, *The Transformation of England*, London 1979, pp. 71–89.

38. David Brion Davis, 'New Sidelights on Early Antislavery Radicalism', *William and Mary Quarterly*, 3rd series, XXVIII, October 1971, pp. 585–94, especially pp. 593–4.

39. Jurgen Habermas, *Legitimation Crisis*, London 1976, pp. 1–8, 11–12, 69–75. Habermas has developed this concept in relation to modern capitalist societies and clearly it has a different sense in social formations where capitalism was still emerging in the course of a vigorous and many-sided class struggle. Nevertheless his observations concerning discrepancies between 'life world' and 'system', and between the achievement of social and system integration clearly have a bearing on the impact of capitalist modernity on the first nation to experience it. The relatively weak legitimation of the sovereign power in Hanoverian Britain put an extra obligation on each constituent social activity and enterprise to furnish its own intrinsic justification. In Hanoverian Britain there was no longer an englobing whole which bore responsibility for the whole pattern of social relations. And on the other hand, new social relations were developing which did not correspond to traditional ideologies. The interrogations of the Scottish school, of Blackstone and Bentham responded to this as a problem for philosophy and jurisprudence, but did not thereby meet the affective and existential problem.

40. Calder, *Revolutionary Empire*, pp. 453–4. Walpole was to launch a public attack on imprisonment for debtors in the course of which he reflected on the absurd spectacle of the English making 'such a fanfaronade about liberty' yet condemning a person to prison for the sum of forty shillings. Horace Walpole, *Reflections on the Different Ideas of the French and English in regard to Cruelty*, by a Man, London 1759, p. 10.

41. Thomas E. Drake, *Quakers and Slavery in America*, New Haven 1950, pp. 51–61. See also Jean Soderland, *Quakers and Slavery: a Divided Spirit*, Princeton 1985. For the development of Christian anti-slavery see Roger Anstey, *The Atlantic Slave Trade and British Abolition*, London 1975, pp. 200–38.

42. The impact of patriotism on the Quakers is explored by Davis, *The Problem of Slavery in the Age of Revolution*, pp. 213–254.

43. Drake, *Quakers and Slavery in America*, pp. 71–6, 84.

44. E. Lascelles, *Granville Sharp: The Freedom of the Slaves*, London 1928, especially pp. 22–50. Sharp's plans for a settlement in which labour tokens replace money , private property is strictly limited and lands are worked for the common good will be found in *A Short Sketch of Temporary Regulations (until better shall be proposed) for the Intended Settlement of the Grain Coast of Africa, Near Sierra Leone*, London 1786. For a discussion of Sharp's mixture of radicalism and traditionalism see Davis, *The Problem of Slavery in the Age of Revolution*, pp. 375–6, 388–98.

45. For an account of the Somerset case see F.O. Shylon, *Black Slaves in Britain*, London 1974, pp. 82–124.

46. John Wesley, *Thoughts Upon Slavery*, London and Philadelphia 1774, pp. 51–2, 57. For the background to Wesley's writings on the slave trade, and his detestation of

idleness and luxury, see Stanley Ayling, *John Wesley*, London 1979, pp. 206–7, 262–3, 281–8; Wesley's doctrinal conflict with Calvinist predestinarianism had flared up after 1768, see pp. 269–77.

47. The spread of evangelicalism and Methodism in the American colonies posed a challenge to gentry hegemony until planter patriotism found a popular voice with men like Patrick Henry: see Isaacs, *The Transformation of Virginia*, pp. 243–69.

48. Wesley, *Thoughts Upon Slavery*, p. 36.

49. Benjamin Quarles, *The Negro in the American Revolution*, Chapel Hill 1961, pp. 19–32, 111–33.

50. Merrill Jensen, *The Founding of a Nation*, London 1968, p. 645. See also Peter Wood, 'Black Freedom Struggles on the Eve of White Independence', in Gary Nash, ed., *Retracing the Past*, New York 1986, pp. 132–41.

51. Davis, *The Problem of Slavery in the Age of Revolution*, p. 273.

III

Slavery and the American Revolution

As negroes in Virginia,
In Maryland or Guinea,
Like them I must continue
To be both bought and sold.
While negro-ships are filling
I ne'er can save one shilling,
And must, which is more killing,
A pauper die when old.

At every week's conclusion
New wants bring fresh confusion,
It is but mere delusion
To hope for better days;
While knaves with power invested,
Until by death arrested,
Oppress us unmolested
By their infernal ways.

An hanging day is wanted;
Was it by justice granted,
Poor men distressed and daunted
Would then have cause to sing:
To see in active motion
Rich knaves in full proportion,
For their unjust extortion
And vile offences, swing.

From *The File Hewer's Lamentation* (1784), Joseph Mather

When the Declaration of Independence insisted that 'all men are created equal' and endowed with an inalienable right to 'life, liberty, and the pursuit of happiness' it took a historic leap beyond the particularistic notion of the 'rights of Englishmen'; there were radical implications in the choice of the words 'pursuit of happiness' rather than 'property'. The Declaration was at least open to a generous and universalistic interpretation. Its secular cadences inaugurated a democratic moment in the cycle of bourgeois revolution. But in context it had a predominantly, even exclusively, political significance and intended no challenge to any of the institutions of civil society. The Declaration was asserting principles that regulate government not proposing a programme of social emancipation. After speaking of men's inalienable rights it immediately proceeded to the conclusion:

> That to secure these rights, Governments are instituted among Men, deriving their just powers from the consent of the governed, That whenever any Government becomes destructive of these ends, it is the Right of the People to alter or abolish it, and to institute new Government, laying its foundations on such principles and organizing its powers in such form, as to them shall seem most likely to effect their Safety and Happiness.

A few of the most enlightened revolutionaries were prepared to argue that liberty was the birthright of all humanity and that permanent enslavement was incompatible with the principles of liberty that ought to provide the proper foundations of the Republic. But for the great majority of Patriots 'all men' meant 'all of us'; it did not include Indians, Negroes, women or children. When the Declaration asserted that the North Americans were 'one people' this referred only to the white population. The fine words of the Declaration echoed the Virginia Bill of Rights which no one saw as implying a challenge to slavery. Negroes were not fully 'men' in the sense intended; to most white colonists they were not only without civic competence (like women or children), or untrustworthy and dangerous (like Indians), but also essentially alien and primitive, or even a sexual threat to good colonial stock. It would be anachronistic to attribute modern racism to the founding fathers yet they did find German or Dutch settlers entirely acceptable; and since many blacks were American-born and Christian they could not justify their enslavement or exclusion by reference to African heathenism. Those who did not approve of slavery might still refuse full and equal citizenship to black men. Even Paine had argued, in *Common Sense*, that providence had decreed America as a country for Europeans.

The exclusions implicit in revolutionary ideology stemmed from its starting-point as a revolt of civil society against a tyrannous state. The rebellion was one of already constituted collectivities, of colonial assemblies forming themselves into new states and a Congress. They brought with them an identity inherited from the colonial epoch. In the two key states of Virginia and Massachusetts the continuity was integral. The only state to adopt an anti-slavery clause in its constitution was Vermont in 1777; Vermont was a break-away, not one of the original thirteen colonies, and it was not admitted to Congress until 1791. The first state to adopt legislation against slavery, Pennsylvania, was one where social turmoil was great and the structure of political representation most extensively transformed.

Founding new states proved an arduous and protracted business. The strains of war and of economic dislocation sometimes threw up conditions in which the implicit ethnic assumptions of the American identity could be challenged by the latent universalism of the opening words of the Declaration. After all, black and white children on the plantation, or in the port towns, might easily play together. In the cosmopolitan and multi-ethnic milieux of the ports free blacks faced discrimination but also found some who accepted them as fellow citizens. And the progress of individual anti-slavery measures did not usually entail support for black citizenship or immediate emancipation. Jefferson saw blacks as dangerous partly because he agreed that they had been wronged. To those constructing a new nation the presence of a mass of captive blacks was not welcome. The suspension of slave imports stopped the arrival of further Africans as well as hurting British trade; its abolitionist significance was a propaganda bonus. White radicals and philanthropists, challenged and aroused by the universal appeals of the independence struggle, hoped to see slavery ended, though not always in terms of conferring full citizenship on the existing slave population; Jefferson, like many who deprecated slavery, hoped that emancipated slaves could be settled somewhere outside the United States. Some secular philanthropists joined the Quakers in urging individual slave-owners to prepare their slaves for freedom. The balance of shifting and contradictory feelings towards slavery and blacks changed several times in the early years until the main lines of a settlement emerged around the time of the Constitutional Convention in 1787.

To the surprise of some slave emancipation was generally avoided by both sides in the war. Lord Dunmore's appeal to the slaves of rebel masters at first provoked Washington's anxiety: 'If that man, Dunmore, is not crushed before the Spring he will become the most dangerous man in America. His strength will increase like a snowball running down hill. Success will depend on which side can arm the Negroes

Detail from Trumbull's 'The Battle of Bunker's Hill': the black soldier is thought to be Salem Poor

faster.'[1] This alarm proved unfounded both because Dunmore withdrew aboard a British ship and because British commanders were concerned not to alarm loyalist slaveholders. Though both sides did arm some blacks, they did so with great caution and assigned the modest numbers of black recruits chiefly to support roles. Both Patriot and loyalist commanders counted on white recruits and white support to play the decisive role in the war and they knew that these would be deterred by any wholesale policy of arming blacks. The sight of a black man with a gun was a disturbing one to North American whites, whether North or South, Patriot or Tory. As the struggle dragged on, and both sides experienced a shortage of manpower, such prejudices were sometimes neutralised by force of necessity but never abandoned. In the Northern colonies the Patriot forces probably enlisted more blacks, whether slaves or freedmen, than the British while in the Southern plantation zone the use of black soldiers was confined to British forces and loyalist militia.

Each of the protagonists looked far and wide for allies as the mortal struggle unfolded. Confronting Britain's formidable power the rebels believed that they were justified in seeking allies wherever they could find them; the vital assistance of France made the Patriots allies of a hereditary foe and Catholic tyrant. The British had no scruple in appealing to the Indians and inciting them against the Patriots even though Indian 'savagery' had traditionally been cited in justification of Britain's colonising mission. By comparison with these bold strokes there was to be resolute refusal on both sides to rouse the hundreds of thousands of black slaves to any active role in the conflict.

In the North a number of free blacks took part in early clashes, but Congress at first forbade the enlistment of blacks in the Continental army. The New England state of Rhode Island, acutely short of men for its militia, was permitted in 1777 to form two black regiments. As the war dragged on the commanders of the Continental Army and of the state militias found that maintaining troop strengths was a major problem; the states resorted to levies to raise their Continental quota and to fill the ranks of the militias. In a number of Northern states slaves were accepted as substitutes; in Connecticut slave draftees were automatically manumitted. The Congressional ban on black recruitment was untenable, but great care was taken not to alarm Southern slave-owners. Eventually about 4,000 blacks served with the Continental army, some in an auxiliary capacity. Both sides in the conflict declared that enemy property was forfeit; as a consequence slaves were seized, and put to work as sappers or officer's servants. Despite their recourse to military manumission the British did not imitate the Portuguese in Brazil in the 1640s, or even the Spanish in the 1760s, who had formed black-officered military units. The Patriots of the Northern states were, in this respect, slightly bolder since there were a few black junior officers, such as Salem Poor of Massachusetts.[2]

In the Southern zone the economic significance of the plantations, fear of slave insurrection, and respect for the established racial code inhibited both sides. But the British had less to lose and were desperate to break the costly war of attrition which plagued them after their defeat at Saratoga in October of 1777. Virginia with its slave plantations was seen as the rebel's most vulnerable flank. The British advance in the South in 1779–80 provided conditions in which several thousand slaves escaped to British lines. The British commander at Charleston sought to take advantage of this without provoking generalised slave unrest; he declared that slaves who had left loyal masters would be returned, while those owned by rebel masters would become public property and would be put to work until hostilities ceased, when they might expect freedom. The British Army and the loyalist militias in South Carolina and Georgia recruited blacks in an *ad hoc* and subservient capacity.

The Tory leader Banastre Tarleton came from a major planting family and had no intention of contesting slavery. But as a desperate irregular war proceeded loyalist bands were willing to enroll suitable blacks with no questions asked. Runaway slaves realised that they had a better chance of securing freedom if they went to the British; though a few also offered to serve the French. For their part the British partisans were less attentive to established racial boundaries. A wealthy slaveholding widow in Charleston wrote that when her house was visited by 'abusive' loyalists, accompanied by armed Negroes, she 'trembled so with terror, that I could not support myself', and later 'gave way to a violent burst of grief'.[3]

In the Southern theatre the Patriots recruited no black soldiers though some marched down from New York to besiege Yorktown in 1781 while a few were attached to the Patriot forces in a menial capacity. In the difficult period before Yorktown John Laurens, one of the ablest young American commanders, proposed that 3,000 slaves should be freed and formed into a black battalion which he would command; Laurens was the son of a slave-owner and former slave-trader from South Carolina who now repented his involvement with the Africa trade. Astonishingly enough Laurens obtained a majority in Congress for this scheme, but it was vetoed by South Carolina. The victory at Yorktown in October 1781 removed the military pressure, while John Laurens himself was killed in a skirmish. It is doubtless significant that South Carolina, the one state with a slave majority, should have produced the South's most radical anti-slavery Patriot and that its assembly should have blocked his boldest proposal.[4]

The partisan war in the South, sustained by white militias, played a large part in thwarting Britain's southern strategy and encompassing its eventual defeat. In all the rebel states soldiers were promised land by political authorities short of cash. Virginia, the Carolinas and Georgia offered their soldiers a slave to go with the land. Mixed feelings about wealthy slaveholders co-existed with a widespread aspiration among poorer whites to own a slave; the slave bounty scheme harnessed the colonising impulse to the birth of the Republic.[5]

When the British left Charleston they were accompanied by about five thousand blacks, many of them former slaves of rebel masters; several thousand more blacks accompanied British departures at Savannah and New York. British promises at the peace talks that fugitive slaves would not be evacuated with the British troops were not received in time or were simply ignored. In South Carolina and Georgia there were a few areas where the plantation regime broke down at least momentarily. An irregular loyalist 'Black Dragoon' was reported to be active in South Carolina in 1782–3; later some black irregulars withdrew behind Savannah or marched southwards to Florida; Georgia's border lands witnessed a continuing guerrilla war against the Americans in 1785–6 waged by black 'Soldiers of the King'.[6]

But the majority of slaves proved wary of the British and most slave communities seem to have decided that the very doubtful promises and prospects of the Tories did not justify abandoning their plantations. The overall impact of the seven years war, whether on the plantation regime or on slave numbers, was surprisingly small. The fighting in the South caused great material devastation, and Jefferson was to claim that 30,000 slaves escaped bondage as a result of the conflict in Virginia. But the slave system survived in reasonable working order. The natural growth of the slave population replenished losses. The militarisation of white society during the conflict, with trigger-happy bands roaming the countryside, was a potent deterrent to slave revolt or slave escape. The trade in plantation produce was badly hit by the war, but planters simply withdrew into the shell of 'natural economy', stockpiling tobacco but increasing output of other crops. Easing of the pressure for commodity production made for less overwork on the plantations and greater concentration on subsistence cultivation; women were often left in charge, which would have reduced the incidence of drunken brutality, always a danger in the plantation zone.[7]

The Patriot struggle against the British was accompanied by a constitutional and legislative process which offered some openings to anti-slavery in the Northern states. When the revolutionaries came to devising state constitutions and the framework of a continental

Confederacy, the issue of slavery could scarcely be avoided, even if slaves were seen simply as property, while the rights of free blacks and the scope for manumission also had to be considered. In states with few slaves some bold spirits did suggest that slavery should be ended by legislative means. Emboldened by the constant talk of liberty, groups of black slaves petitioned state assemblies for their freedom, while freedmen demanded the civic rights enjoyed by white men. Up-country farmers and urban artisans often distrusted the slaveholder; and patriotic and enlightened planters would favour individual emancipation and reduced reliance on Africans. The wording of the petitions from blacks typically drew attention to the logic of the revolutionary natural rights doctrine: 'We are endowed with the same faculties with our masters and the more we consider the matter, the more we are convinced of our right to be free.'[8]

The radical 'Constitutionalists' of Vermont and Pennsylvania were the first to move against slavery. Vermont's Constitution of July 1777, after echoing the opening words of the Declaration of Independence, added that 'therefore' no man older than twenty-one years or woman older than eighteen years could be held as a 'servant, slave or apprentice', unless by their own agreement.[9] This clause was drafted by a Philadelphia radical and no doubt corresponded to the radical patriotism of the Green Mountains; it also acted as a barrier against their reincorporation by the government of slaveholding New York. There were very few slaves in Vermont and the numbers freed, if any, are unknown; however, the courts did subsequently rule that slavery was indeed outlawed by the state constitution. The banning of indentured service points to the existence of 'anti-master' feeling, reinforcing anti-slavery.[9]

In 1780 the Constitutionalist majority of the Pennsylvania Assembly, of which Paine was Secretary, adopted an emancipation law by thirty-one to twenty-four votes; the Philadelphia delegation supported the law unanimously, but some Constitutionalist representatives of German farmers voted against. The radical Constitutionalists were by this time fighting a rearguard struggle against the Republican opposition, having failed to sustain the experiment with price-fixing committees. The emancipation measure will have helped to boost morale, and sow discord in the Republican camp. The Republicans enjoyed the support of the wealthier citizens and numbered among their leaders both Benjamin Rush, a veteran anti-slavery advocate, and Robert Morris, whose extensive mercantile interests included involvement in the slave trade. At this time there were some 6,000 slaves in the state and the law was very cautious; nevertheless this was the first law of its type to be adopted anywhere and it was a product of public debate. According to its terms children born of slave mothers would be free once they reached the age of twenty-eight; until then they they would have to toil for their mother's owner to recompense him for the cost of their upbringing. The law required masters to register their slaves by a certain date; some masters refused to do so and thereby forfeited their title to their slaves. The supposedly ultra-democratic Constitutionalists, in a state where slaves comprised a mere 2.5 per cent of the population and where anti-slavery had been long nourished by Benezet and the Quakers, thus postponed the beginnings of emancipation for twenty-eight years and generously compensated the masters; only the intransigence of many slave-owners gave more immediate effect to this modest measure. In one respect the law was genuinely radical; it conferred full civic rights on all blacks freed under its provisions. Opposition to the law focused both on the slaveholders' property rights and on the danger of enfranchising blacks and permitting them to join the militia. These objections were vigorously answered by an anonymous pamphleteer (possibly Paine) signing himself 'A Liberal', an early use of this term as applied to politics. Although the Constitutionalists were soon removed from power, attempts to reverse the law were easily defeated. Though not a member of the Assembly Anthony Benezet had lobbied energetically in defence of emancipation. When he died in 1784 his funeral was attended by a large crowd of mourners, both black and white.[10]

In most Northern states proposals were made to ban slavery when constitutions were adopted, but in no case save that of Vermont were such proposals adopted. At the Rhode Island convention a vague promise was made to look at the matter when 'some favourable Occasion may offer'. In 1784 Rhode Island and Connecticut, two states which had been earliest to recruit blacks, adopted emancipation laws similar to that of Pennsylvania, only on this occasion the slaveholders did not aid the abolitionists by flouting the registration procedures. The solution adopted was again that of respecting the slave-owner's right to his living chattels, 'freeing' those not yet born, but only after they had themselves worked off their notional debt to their oppressors. The age at which those born to slaves were to be freed was somewhat lower than in Pennsylvania: twenty-one for men, eighteen for women in Rhode Island; twenty-five for both men and women in Connecticut. These measures were adopted at times when prevailing property concepts faced a fundamental challenge from advocates of debt cancellation, paper money and anti-mercantile radicalism. Wartime dislocation had fanned the animus against merchants and induced many farmers and artisans to consider extreme measures for relieving the problems of debtors; in Rhode Island, shortly before the adoption of the emancipation law, the legislative had been asked to consider a scheme for taking into common ownership all wharves, warehouses and ships as a means of striking down mercantile profiteering. While these extreme demands were rejected, the government of Rhode Island remained in the hands of radicals who allowed debtors to discharge their obligations with depreciated paper money. Creditors were given short shrift, because their claims threatened to overwhelm farmers and small producers who had been hit by the post-war economic crisis; the Rhode Island emancipation law also allowed personal rights to weaken, though not cancel, property rights. Rhode Island's option was the more impressive in that the state did still contain a few thousand slaves. The relatively small number of slaves remaining in Connecticut made it a less fraught issue. The emancipation measure was introduced to a fundamental statute without fanfare at a time when former loyalists were being admitted to politics; though the state's politics were not as agitated as those of Rhode Island, the discontents which led to Shays's Rebellion in neighbouring regions of Massachusetts in 1786 were also present.[11]

In some parts of New England judicial decisions furnished a different path towards emancipation, one building on the earlier freedom suits but avoiding legislative controversy. The case of Quock Walker in Massachusetts had some similarity with that of Somerset in England. The first ruling on the case in 1781 avoided pronouncing on the general issue and it was only because of the persistence of both parties that the eventual judgement of 1783 was made on wider grounds. The Chief Justice had to make a decision in default of any clear legislative guidance. In 1777 an attempt had been made by some members of the Massachusetts Assembly to free children of slaves born after a certain date, but this had failed on the grounds that it might offend 'our brethren in other colonies'. In the Walker case the Massachusetts Chief Justice found against the master, who had assaulted his alleged slave, because he could find no law which permitted the high-handed behaviour typical of the slave-owner. John Adams commented: 'If the gentlemen had been permitted by law to hold slaves the common people would have put the Negroes to death, and their masters too, perhaps.' The veteran Patriot's judgement as to the social location of the anti-slavery sentiment may have been more acute than his implicit depreciation of popular motives. In the aftermath of the Walker judgement masters continued to claim authority over black servants and there is even a record of some slave sales. But henceforth slave-owning had no public sanction in Massachusetts. In New Hampshire, another state with very few slaves, a similar decision undercut lawful slaveholding in 1783, though once again some slaveholders may have found ways of evading the precedent. The ending of slavery by judicial decision differed from gradual emancipation in that no full slaves were left in the area affected; but it was less deliberate and clear-cut, leaving ambiguities which masters were able to exploit. The Northern laws against slave-trading usually included a ban on selling slaves out of the state, but such bans could be quite easily flouted.[12]

In two crucial Northern states, which together accounted for three-quarters of all slaves outside the South, slavery survived both constitutional and legislative challenges in the revolutionary and immediate post-revolutionary period: New York, with 20,000 slaves, and New Jersey, with 10,000. In these states the assemblies failed to agree even a moderate emancipation law in the 1780s. There was dispute over the rights of freedmen and over the form of compensation to slaveholders; also concern at the possibility that the abandoned children of slaves might become a charge on the tax-payer. Slaveholders in New York were sufficiently influential to secure passage of a slave code in 1788; at around 5,000 the number of slaveholders in the state was roughly equal to the number of artisans in New York City. Political life in New York had been retarded by British occupation during the war and by the influence of well-entrenched and conservative landowners and merchants. Emancipation was openly resisted by the representatives of Dutch farmers; though they only owned a few slaves apiece, this would constitute a valuable part of their estate. The failure of abolition probably also reflected the tactics of false friends, like Aaron Burr, and of feeble friends, like Alexander Hamilton. Burr secured a very radical amendment to the anti-slavery bill but may have known that this would doom the measure.[13]

Alexander Hamilton and John Jay patronised the New York Manumission Society, founded in 1785; the Society charged a high membership subscription and did not even bar slaveholders from joining. Hamilton, one of the authors of the Federal Constitution, was convinced that the Republic needed more authoritative national institutions; a vague abolitionism fitted in well enough with this programme in New York. In the years 1787–9 Hamilton's main efforts were directed at securing acceptance for the Constitution against conservative landowners who did not wish to see their state lose its customs revenues, since this might lead to a tax on land. Abolitionism dignified the 'Federalist' cause but was not allowed to jeopardise ratification; because of its support for protective tariffs and national development Hamiltonian Federalism was at this point a cause with which artisans could identify.[14]

Manumission societies were formed in several states in the aftermath of the war. The Methodists and the Baptists, with their growing

Southern membership, took up an official stand against slaveholding, though the task of persuading individual slaveholders to conform was left to local congregations. In the early 1780s emancipation had been championed mainly by urban radicals; subsequently it was as often taken up by the great and the good. In the North manumission societies came to be patronised by respectable members of society who saw slavery as an unnecessary, primitive and vexatious institution. In opposing it men like John Jay, the first Chief Justice, also advertised their own openness to peaceful and responsible reform.

Free blacks in the North championed emancipation because of family attachments and because they knew the continuance of slavery prejudiced their position; however, even where there was no formal colour bar they often lacked the qualifications for voting or office-holding, which in most states were still limited to those owning some property or paying certain taxes. Several thousand blacks had participated in the Revolutionary War; some of these acquired the vote but no black person reached an elective post. In Philadelphia and some other towns black people formed their own Churches, partly in response to the slighting treatment they received from white co-religionists: the African Methodist and Baptist connections formed as a result developed a strong following and gave expression to a distinctive Afro–American evangelicalism.[15]

Manumission societies were formed in the South as well as the North. Patriot leaders deprecated the moral effects of slaveholding and lauded the sturdy independence of the farmer. In 1782 the Virginia Assembly legalised private manumission and the Manumission Society urged slaveholders to take advantage of this. In fact during the 1780s more slaves were to be manumitted as a result of individual initiative in the South than were to be freed by the emancipation laws in the North. Most Southern supporters of manumission favoured very gradual measures and advocated eventual 'colonisation' of blacks, that is their removal outside the United States. But there was also support in the South for more consequent emancipationist measures; this was chiefly forthcoming from teachers and tradesmen who owned no slaves and from a small number of religious enthusiasts. These Southern emancipationists bravely took up individual cases of mistreatment, kidnapping and re-enslavement of blacks; for a time, but with great difficulty, they promoted black education.[16]

Until 1787 supporters of anti-slavery could assure themselves that abolition was in tune with the spirit of the times and would be bound to triumph. Perhaps for this reason the abolitionist societies devoted much of their energies to local cases and did not set up a nation-wide body to co-ordinate any wider campaign. The setbacks in New York and New

Jersey were seen as temporary and the famous leaders of the Revolution were known to be patrons of anti-slavery, almost to a man.

Acceptance of the need for a national government welled up in the mid-1780s following the eruption of severe conflicts within and between the states. War losses and the closing of British West Indian markets created economic difficulties for many, while radical experiments in Pennsylvania and Rhode Island were deemed dangerous failures by the more comfortable citizenry. The outbreak of Shays's Rebellion alarmed the leaders of the revolution; under the terms of the Confederacy there was no national armed force or authoritative centre to contain or suppress riot and insurrection. The lack of national institutions risked inter-state strife and denied needed support to economic or territorial expansion. The aim of those who framed the Constitution was to furnish a political framework that would guarantee prevailing social relations without shackling or constraining them. The constitutional structure arrived at after much hard debate created a national government with the competence to raise armed forces, to levy customs revenue, and to organise new territories – but otherwise so mixed and divided against itself that it could never challenge or change the society which had produced it. In contrast to the unicameral notions of the Painite radicals, the elective component of the government was divided into two legislative chambers with different franchises, and an indirectly elected head of the executive. Standing apart as arbiter of the whole was an appointed body, the Supreme Court. Also standing apart with their own separate powers and elective systems were the individual constituent states of the Union. These elaborate checks and balances would, it was hoped, not only represent but reconcile established interests while frustrating factionalism and the dangerous implications for property-holders of majority rule. The forms of government should so far as possible discourage by their very design political passions and 'the zeal for different opinions' – including that very generalising impulse which it had been the grandeur of the Revolution to have promoted. The relations of debtor to creditor, propertyless to propertied, slave to master, were to be the unquestioned building blocks of the state. The impeccably republican and elective principles of the constitution elaborately reinvented – in, as it were, algebraic form – the devices of Britain's 'illegitimate monarchy'. In both cases the nominal sovereign was to be denied the power to interfere with the crucial institutions of civil society. Just as Britain's mixed government took the power of the monarch, placed it in the hands of his Ministers, subjected them to the rule of law, erected judges as arbiters of that law, invited Ministers to be answerable to public opinion, made legislation dependent on a hereditary as well as elective chamber, until no branch of government could erect itself into a 'tyranny' – so the Constitution of the United States started out from popular sovereignty, then multiplied, distributed and divided the sovereign power against itself, subordinated it to the rule of law, made judges arbiters of that law, and so on and so forth until there could be little risk that the nominal sovereign would ever rule as well as reign. The similarities between the British and American forms of government were so striking that some authoritative observers, such as John Adams, thought them to be the same. Of course, the structure of American government was tidier and more logical – since it had dispensed with the central absurdity and mystery of monarchy itself, save in its elective presidential form – but this itself was a problem. While colonial slavery could be tolerated in the patchwork of the British Empire, the holding of slaves presented difficult problems for those seeking to devise equitable systems of representation and taxation without giving any openings to future attempts to tamper with prevailing property forms.[17]

In the constitutional debates the question of slavery arose in an indirect but insistent fashion precisely in regard to these crucial attributes of representation and taxation. The key slogan in the struggle against the British had been 'no taxation without representation'. One of the most delicate issues which confronted those devising a constitution was the apportionment of representation and taxation as between the different states and regions. The representivity of the political arrangements invented by the rebels were their prime claim to legitimacy in their struggle against Britain's 'Royal Brute'. The Articles of the Confederacy established a crude equality between the states so far as representation was concerned, but naturally the poorer and smaller states refused to accept that they should be taxed as heavily as the larger and richer states. Slaves contributed largely to both the population and the wealth of one part of the new country. While most Northerners were content to see slaves included as indices of Southern wealth, they were loath to see them counted in any system for relating representation to the size of population. These differences surfaced as early as 1775 when a Northern delegate in Congress proposed that all expenses should be shared proportionally to the size of the total population of each colony. Samuel Chase of Maryland immediately riposted that Negroes were property and should no more be included in a population count than horses or livestock. The Confederacy eventually chose the value of land as the basis for taxation, but the problems of valuing land uniformly made this unworkable. In 1783

Congress eventually sought to return to population as the basis for apportioning taxation. As a compromise between the interests of North and South it was eventually agreed that each slave would count as only three-fifths of a free person.[18]

This 'Federal ratio' was eventually to resolve the problem of apportioning political representation amongst the states in the House of Representatives. Prior to the Constitutional Convention of 1787 it proved impossible to reach any other agreement on a basis for representation than the manifestly inequitable system of allotting the same representation to every state regardless of its size. In the debates on population and representation the Southerners argued that slaves should be fully counted; though, of course, only qualified free white males would vote for the representatives so allotted. Southerners were particularly concerned to establish this principle since they constituted 41 per cent of the free population of the Union and could foresee that this proportion might shrink. Northern delegates found it difficult to agree that Southern slave wealth should be awarded extra representation, while their own wealth counted for nothing. Only the taxation precedent, and their awareness that a solution must be found or no Union would survive, eventually persuaded them to accept that the three-fifths rule should also govern Congressional representation.

The acceptance that slaves as wealth should entitle Southern voters to extra representation built an acknowledgement of slavery into the heart of the Constitution. When Lafayette later chided Madison with the Convention's failure to consider even gradual emancipation, he was told: 'any allusion in the Convention to the subject you have so much at heart would have been a spark to a mass of gun powder.'[19]

In the interests of the Union even Franklin made no attack on Southern property, contenting himself instead with the wry observation that Northern property was different, since 'sheep will never make any insurrection'.[20] The text of the Constitution resorted to shamefaced circumlocution rather than use the dreaded words 'slave' and 'slavery':

> Representatives and direct Taxes shall be apportioned among the several states which may be included within this Union, according to their respective Numbers, which shall be determined by adding to the whole Number of free Persons, including those bound to Service for a Term of Years, and excluding Indians not taxed, three fifths of all other persons.

This was not the only clause in which specific provision was made for slaveholder interests.

The Constitution stipulated that persons 'held to service or labour' who absconded should be delivered up to the party to whom such service or labour was due, whatever the local laws of the state or territory in which they were apprehended. Once again Southern slaveholders saw this provision for runaways as a vital interest. Aware of their special interests and vulnerability the Southern delegates sought to limit the power of the Federal authority to interfere in the domestic affairs of the constituent states. However moderate the emancipation measures of the North might be, they intended to make quite sure that similar laws could not be imposed upon them by a Congressional majority. Many Southerners hoped that the Federal government would be denied any authority to regulate the slave trade, but since trade regulation was one of the few powers it possessed this was asking for a lot. The Union would scarcely have been competent as a sovereign state if its government could not make commercial arrangements, preferably by simple Congressional majorities. Most states, including Virginia, had maintained a ban on slave imports; in a planting economy that had yet to return to boom conditions many slaveholders found they were not at all inconvenienced by this. Following acceptance of the Federal ratio governing representation the Northern representatives perceived an interest in stopping any further influx of slaves into the South. However, slave dealers in South Carolina and some Northern ports wished to protect their business and found some support from others who did not wish to entrust any powers relating to slavery to the Federal government. The Convention eventually reached a compromise according to which Congress would be prohibited from banning the slave trade, or placing a prohibitive tariff upon it, for a period of twenty years. Delegates were united in the conviction that slaveholding had been unshakeably established by the Constitution, though this was a point which it cost the Southern delegates much trouble to explain when they got back home. Great talents had gone into devising a state form that would consecrate prevailing social relations and frustrate the political expression of class antagonisms; but not even the genius of a Madison could entirely succeed in such an enterprise.

The preamble to the Constitution declared that its intention was to secure 'the blessings of liberty to ourselves and our Posterity' and declined to echo the assertion of a universal human right of equality and freedom made in the Declaration. In July of 1787, the month in which agreement was reached on including slaveholdings in the representational arrangements for Congress, agreement was secured to an Ordinance which favoured the generality of the free citizenry. The Ordinance ended slave entries to the Federal territories of the North-west, thus giving greater scope to the smallholder aspirations of the free population. The North-west territories were not thought suitable to plantation development, so the concession did not appear a large one; it did not apply to the South-west. On the other hand, the North-west Ordinance, and the land legislation associated with it, did offer real benefits to intending settlers; and since most of the North-west had formerly been claimed by Virginia the passage of this Ordinance did embody a symbolic concession. While no more slaves were to be sent to the North-west the white settlers also did their best to exclude free blacks.[21]

Neither the travail of the American Revolution nor the conservative consolidation of the early Republic had effected a weakening of the North American slave system – indeed to the careful observer these events demonstrated the slaveholders' tenacity and resilience. Endorsement of the arrangements in the Constitution represented a strategic defeat for North America's diffuse abolitionism. In the aftermath of the Constitutional Convention most of the states passed legislation outlawing participation in the slave trade or imposing a prohibitory tariff on slave imports. It was generally assumed that Congress would ban slave imports as soon as it was permitted to do so; but 1808 was a long way off and much could happen in the meantime.

Radical opponents of slavery were aware that a decisive battle had been lost; Southerners had established as constitutional dogma that Congress had no power to meddle in the domestic affairs of the constituent states. Nevertheless the dispositions of the young Republic looked different from across the Atlantic. The Revolution and its immediate aftermath provided Europe with a definite anti-slavery message or challenge. Emancipation and manumission laws had been passed; their limitations were not studied, or not seen as limitations. It was known that there were some free black preachers, writers and men of learning, but not that free blacks were often denied the same rights as white citizens. Resounding slogans had been launched on the world; the fine print of the Constitution made less of an impression. The slave trade had been suspended for many years and then banned by most states; it could be banned completely in 1808. In their dealings with the outside world the representatives of the New Republic conveyed the impression that slavery was an institution of diminishing consequence for North America. Jefferson's famous *Notes on Virginia* deplored slavery and its corrupting effects even if it also suggested that Negroes were racially inferior; it was composed in response to a request from the French ambassador Barbé de Marbois. Many of the Republic's most illustrious representatives – Jefferson himself, Franklin, Jay, Hamilton – gave their patronage to the manumission societies. Washington was one of the few to keep his counsel on the matter and even he wrote privately of achieving emancipation by 'slow, sure and imperceptible degrees'.[22]

The evolution of Thomas Jefferson's views on slavery in the decade after the end of the Revolutionary War already show the limits of 'planter abolitionism' in North America. In the heroic period of the American Revolution Jefferson evinced a cautious but definite sympathy with the anti-slavery impulse. The freedom suit he had taken on in 1770 and the passage deleted by Congress from the Declaration both testify to the latter. The *Notes on Virginia*, published in 1785 and written two years earlier, summoned up the rhetoric of revolutionary virtue, attacking luxury imports from Europe as well as the slave trade. In an eloquent passage Jefferson warned his countrymen that they could expect sanguinary retribution if they did not find some way of attenuating slavery. Around this time he also proposed that slaves be excluded from the North-western territory; the territory was to be kept for white settlers and land sales were to be used to finance a public education system. Jefferson's writings were always animated by a keen desire to retain and fortify the allegiance of the mass of smallholding farmers. These smallholders were not anti-slavery in any pure sense but there were prone to resent both the presence of blacks and the arrogance of gentleman planters. Jefferson was himself, of course, one of the latter but like Patrick Henry he saw preservation and cultivation of the farmer-planter axis as vital to the health, even the survival, of the Republic. White Southern farmers were prone to disapprove of large slaveholdings but they disapproved even more of schemes for freeing the slaves unless they were to be immediately transported to some distant destination. Jefferson, in tune with such sentiment, always remained a convinced and effective foe of the slave trade. During the war and its immediate aftermath Jefferson's willingness to avow anti-slavery sentiments was at its height and in this he was probably sensitive to the opinion of non-slaveholders in the slaveholding states. Following his return from France in 1789, Jefferson offered no further public criticism of slavery. He politely declined all invitations to speak out on the subject, on the grounds that the time was not yet ripe.

The eruption of a slave revolt in St Domingue in August 1791 certainly encouraged Jefferson's reserve. The arrival of a stream of refugees from the French colonies, many with stories to tell of bloody slave revolt, hardened the white citizenry's support for black slavery, and for restrictions on the activities of free blacks, throughout the United States. Early rumours that the slaves of St Domingue had been encouraged by royalist *agents provocateurs* were given colour when their leaders enrolled in the forces of the Spanish King.

As Secretary of State in 1789–93 Jefferson instructed the American representative in London to demand that Britain should offset the value of the slaves taken from North America in 1783–4 against the debts owed by Americans to British merchants. Jefferson had himself lost thirty slaves when the British occupied one of his estates. However, he would not criticise slaves for running away nor did he ever demean himself by proposing their return. In taking up the question of the British 'abduction' of American slaves Jefferson was, as a politician, adopting a cause he knew to be dear to the heart of many white Virginians; as a statesman he must have known that the British government would never entertain his demand. Neverthless Jefferson's willingness to take up this issue in the early 1790s contrasts with his earlier silence on the matter.[23]

The debates of the Constitutional Convention and the awesome spectacle of slave revolt in St Domingue in 1791 marginalised North American abolitionism while bringing into the open a vociferous pro-slavery sentiment in the Southern states. With the birth of the United States a new and vigorous slaveholding power had appeared, offering commercial facilities and a political ideal to slaveholders elsewhere in the hemisphere. The Republic's merchant marine soon matched British tonnage in the Atlantic; partnerships with Spaniards or Cubans in the mid-1780s led to the rise of a new branch of the Atlantic slave trade.[24]

In North America itself the prospects for abolition were not good and the slave population was growing; in 1776 there had been less than 500,000 slaves in North America; by 1790 there were 698,000 slaves, despite the disruption of the war and the passage of measures of emancipation and manumission. But however cleverly the cracks were concealed, the new order was a hybrid, effectively blocking slavery from developing in major zones of the country – New England, Pennsylvania and the North-western territories. In this sense the abolitionist reputation or aura of the Republic in Europe was not wholly unwarranted.

Notes

1. Quoted in Philip S. Foner, *Labor and the American Revolution*, Westport 1976, p. 178. Just as there was controversy over slave recruitment to the patriot forces so also was there over the enlistment of indentured servants. By 1783 indentured service had disappeared, though there were to be attempts to resuscitate it, as Foner notes.
2. Benjamin Quarles, *The Negro in the American Revolution*, Chapel Hill 1961, pp. 19–32, 111–33.
3. Mary Beth Norton, ' "What an Alarming Crisis This Is": Southern Women and the American Revolution', in Jeffrey J. Crow and Larry E. Tise, *The Southern Experience in the American Revolution*, Chapel Hill 1978, pp. 203–34, 216.
4. Quarles, *The Negro in the American Revolution*, pp. 60–67.
5. William J. Cooper, Jr, *Liberty and Slavery: Southern Politics to 1860*, New York 1983, p. 35.
6. Mullin, 'British Caribbean and North American Slaves in an Era of Revolution', in Crow and Tise, *The Southern Experience*, pp. 240–41.

7. For slave escapes in the course of the war see Allan Kulikoff,'Uprooted Peoples', in Ira Berlin and Ronald Hoffman, eds, *Slavery and Freedom in the Age of the American Revolution*, Charlottesville 1983, pp. 143–74, p. 144. For the resilience of the slave system during the war see Mullin, 'British Caribbean and North American Slaves in an Era of War and Revolution', in Crow and Tise, *The Southern Experience*, pp. 235–67. Proportionately more slaves escaped bondage in South Carolina than in any other state, partly because of heavy fighting but perhaps also because of its special pattern of slaveholding, influenced by the urban culture of Charleston and by large rice plantations on which slaves enjoyed considerable work autonomy. (See Mullin, pp. 236, 240–41.) However, even in South Carolina there were few outbreaks of collective slave rebellion, most of them at the close of the war. See also Peter Wood, ' "Taking Care of Business" in Revolutionary South Carolina', in Crow and Tise, *The Southern Experience*, pp. 268–93.

8. McManus, *Black Bondage in the North*, p. 169.

9. Bruns, *Am I Not a Man and a Brother*, pp. 429–32.

10. Arthur Zilversmit, *The First Emancipation: The Abolition of Slavery in the North*, Chicago 1967, pp. 124–32. The unsettled condition of Pennsylvania on the eve of abolition is clear from Eric Foner, *Tom Paine and Revolutionary America*, p. 133, 184.

11. Zilversmit, *The First Emancipation*, pp. 139–67; Jackson Turner Main, *The Sovereign States 1775–1783*, New York 1973, pp. 333–40. Connecticut and Rhode Island were more deeply affected by the post-war crisis of the 1780s, and acquired more radical state governments, than New York or New Jersey. For radical politics in Rhode Island see Merril Jensen, *The American Revolution within America*, New York 1974, pp. 82–3. Slaves had comprised nearly a tenth of the population of colonial Rhode Island, though, as also in Connecticut, many had been freed in the course of the war either because they were the property of Tories or because they had fought in the militia.

12. Donald Robinson, *Slavery in the Structure of American Politics*, New York 1970, pp. 24–8; McManus, *Black Bondage in the North*, p. 166.

13. Zilversmit, *The First Emancipation*, p. 166.

14. John Jay was one of the slave-owners in the Society; his attitude to his personal slaves is illustrated by the following remark, made in 1798: 'I purchase slaves, and manumit them at proper ages, and when their faithful services shall have afforded a reasonable retribution.' Quoted in Zilversmit, *The First Emancipation*, p. 167n. On artisanal support for Hamilton in the late 1780s see Sean Wilentz, *Chants Democratic: New York City and the Rise of the American Working Class, 1788–1850*, New York 1984, pp. 67, 87.

15. Ira Berlin, *Slaves Without Masters: The Free Negro in the Antebellum South*, Oxford 1974, pp. 79–107; Donald Mathews, *Slavery and Methodism: A Chapter in American Morality, 1780–1845*, Princeton 1965, pp. 293–9.

16. Berlin, *Slaves without Masters*, p. 89.

17. Where government really mattered to them, in their own state, Virginian planters did not tolerate a separation of powers (see Sydnor, *Gentlemen Freeholders*, pp. 86, 92–5). Of course in both the United States and Britain the nominal sovereign, though hobbled by oligarchic restraints, did exercise some real power. James Madison's celebrated Tenth Federalist Paper furnished an extraordinarily lucid account of the purposes of the Constitution; however, its account of the rival interests and views that must not be allowed to tear society apart manages to omit any direct reference to slaveholders, slaves or abolitionists. See Jacob E. Cooke, ed., *The Federalist*, Cleveland and New York 1965, pp. 56–65. That fears for slavery did loom large is argued by Staughton Lynd, *Class Struggle, Slavery and the United States Constitution*, New York 1967, pp. 159, 161–2, 201. Other conservative features of the Constitutional Convention are noted by Jensen, *The American Revolution in America*, pp. 167–220.

18. Robinson, *Slavery in the Structure of American Politics*, pp. 131–58. Though the principle of the 'Federal ratio' was agreed in 1783 the tax measure of which it was a part failed to gain the necessary majority for implementation.

19. Madison, recollecting these events in 1830, is quoted by Lynd, *Class Struggle, Slavery and the United States Constitution*, p. 161. The point made by Madison explains

why, as recent historians have noted, slavery questions were not openly and vigorously debated at the Convention.

20. Franklin's remark is quoted in Robinson, *Slavery in the Structure of American Politics*, p. 148. Robinson has a good account of the Constitutional Convention's deliberations relating to slavery, pp. 168–206. Opponents of the Constitution in the South argued that the very existence of a Federal government with powers to promote national defence and welfare might be turned at some future date against slaveholding (see, for example, Patrick Henry's warning quoted by Robert McColley, *Slavery in Jeffersonian Virginia*, Ithaca 1978, p. 169). In 1790 Franklin challenged the consensus that Congress had no powers relating to slavery by presenting it with an abolitionist petition; this provoked a bitter debate, until the issue was dropped when the Southerners made it clear that they would withdraw from the Union rather than admit Congressional jurisdiction over their 'species of property'. Likewise the amendments embodying a Bill of Rights steered clear of slavery, concentrating instead on the rights of free persons and of the constituent states.

21. Eugene H. Berwanger, *The Frontier Against Slavery*, Urbana 1967, pp. 7–36; Robinson, *Slavery in the Structure of American Politics*, pp. 378–91. For the slavery compromises of the Convention see Lynd, *Class Struggle, Slavery and the United States Constitution*, pp. 153–216.

22. Quoted in Davis, *The Problem of Slavery in the Age of Revolution*, p. 170. Unlike some other slaveholders who paraded their anti-slavery sentiment at this time (such as Jefferson), Washington was at least to free his own slaves in his will and furnish them with the wherewithal to make a living as free people.

23. Miller, *The Wolf by the Ears: Thomas Jefferson and Slavery*, New York 1977, p. 118.

24. Manuel Moreno Fraginals, *El Ingenio*, I, pp. 65–7.

IV

British Abolitionism and the Backlash of the 1790s

On those vast shady hills between America and Albion's shore,
Now barr'd out by the Atlantic sea, call'd Atlantean hills,
Because from their bright summits you may pass to the Golden world . . .
Here on their magic seats the thirteen Angels sat perturb'd,
For clouds from the Atlantic hover o'er the solemn roof.

Fiery the Angels rose, and as they rose deep thunder roll'd
Around their shores, indignant burning with the fires of Orc;
And Boston's Angel cried aloud as they flew thro' the dark night.
He cried: 'Why trembles honesty, and like a murderer
Why seeks he refuge from the frowns of his immortal station?
Must the generous tremble and leave his joy to the idle, to the pestilence,
That mock him? who commanded this? what God? what Angel?
To keep the gen'rous from experience till the ungenerous
Are unrestrain'd performers of the energies of nature;
Till pity is become a trade, and generosity a science
That men get rich by; and the sandy desert is giv'n to the strong?
What God is he writes laws of peace and clothes him in a tempest?
What pitying Angel lusts for tears and fans himself with sighs?
What crawling villain preaches abstinence and wraps himself
In fat of lambs? no more I follow, no more obedience pay!'

America (1793), William Blake

Organised anti-slavery in North America had been the cause of a few dedicated individuals, of a layer of free people of colour and of a number of sedate and exclusive abolitionist associations. To become a member of the New York Society required not only a hefty subscription but the endorsement of respectable proposers and seconders. In Britain in the 1780s a different species of abolitionism was to be born. But before examining this phenomenon it will be appropriate to sketch in the delicate, 'post-operative' state of the British body politic at the time.

The war and defeat in North America was a heavy blow to the morale and credibility of Britain's rulers. Contemporaries were at first exercised at the prospect of losing American markets and at the heavy expense of military operations. Yet the momentum of British capital was such as to take these in its stride; domestic markets absorbed ever larger quantities of the new textiles and manufactures, while there was no dearth of subscribers to the national funds. Once peace was made British manufacturers and merchants found that they could reconquer North American markets with surprising ease. The North American war proved the merest hiccup in the forward surge of industry and commerce. But political and military defeat at the hands of a patriot rabble was an intimate and lasting wound. The triumph of the American Revolution took a heavy toll on Britons' inflated self-regard and gave some encouragement to radical, democratic alternatives to oligarchy and corruption. The parliamentary opposition first placed responsibility for the débâcle on the King and his leading minister, Lord North, but then stitched up a disastrously unpopular deal with North allowing them a share of power, the Fox–North coalition. The collapse of this coalition betokened widespread disenchantment with oligarchic politics. The ruling classes saw that fundamental reforms were necessary if the contagion of revolutionary democracy was not to spread.

During the war itself influential proprietors from Yorkshire, England's largest county, formed an association to press for reforms which would make Parliament more representative and the administration more economical. The Yorkshire manufacturers and merchants had found their trade hit by colonial resistance. The American suspension of the slave trade had highlighted Britain's dominant role in the traffic; the 1779 bill for the suppression of the slave trade had been introduced by a Yorkshire Member. While the moderate and responsible Yorkshire Association appealed to the Hanoverian oligarchy to reform itself, the Society for Promoting Constitutional Information, of which the abolitionist Granville Sharp was a member, began to canvass a wider public with more radical proposals. Yet these opposition forces felt obliged to advance their ideas with greater caution than had been displayed by the oppositionists of the 1760s. The empire faced disintegration and even reformers felt that they should tread carefully. While ministers sought to curtail the permitted areas of discussion, the temper of the populace was both unsteady and uncertain; in 1780 the centre of London had been ravaged by a week of rioting as anti-papist mobs protested at modest proposals to alleviate the disabilities of Irish Catholics. The disaster in North America reflected most directly on the structure of imperial administration and on the system of official patronage that had given the initiative to the King and sustained Lord North in office. The underlying buoyancy of the economy itself encouraged the demand for fairer representation and for an administration more attuned to the needs of commerce and manufacture; at the same time the unexpected concomitants and cross-currents of the first capitalist 'modernisation' left many, even some of its beneficiaries, feeling bemused, anxious and vulnerable.[1]

The government formed in December 1783 by William Pitt the Younger, a man of only twenty-three, reflected the oligarchy's awareness of the need for a new broom. Pitt inherited the lustre of his father's name and, in a short spell as Chancellor, had demonstrated some expertise in financial administration. Pitt presented himself as a champion of economic and political reform. In the election of 1784 Pitt received the backing of the Yorkshire Association. His friend William Wilberforce, Member for the West Riding of Yorkshire, won a famous victory over the candidate of the Whig connection in the county. Yorkshire's large electorate of freeholders and manufacturers gave popular prestige to its representative. Endorsement from the reformers enabled Pitt to stitch together a precarious parliamentary majority, which included Members elected by popular franchises, City interests looking for more effective and economical government, place-holders keen to keep their jobs, dissident Whigs and Tories anxious to settle accounts with Whig corruption.

Pitt's government embarked on a major overhaul and rationalisation of Britain's cumbersome tariff structure and system of financial administration. He had absorbed the teachings of Adam Smith: the Anglo–French Trade Treaty of 1787 was a breakthrough for free trade principles and fostered a welcome export boom. The device of a 'Sinking Fund' restored public credit and gave the impression that the National Debt was to be repaid. Though Pitt's parliamentary managers skilfully deployed the resources of official patronage, some notorious sinecures were suppressed and the Prime Minister himself refused the lucrative emoluments which his predecessors had accepted. After consultations with Wilberforce Pitt supported impeachment proceedings against Warren Hastings, Governor of Bengal and one of the East India

Company's richest and most effective officials. In the new scheme of empire India had an extraordinarily important role and there was anxiety that this should not be compromised by the greed or arrogance of individuals.

The successes of the Pitt administration were marred by a complete failure to push through a single measure of parliamentary reform. Pitt's distinctly moderate proposals failed to attain the necessary majorities. Even those measures which appeared to respect most vested interests within Parliament raised awkward issues concerning how far, and on what principles, representation should be extended. The very wealthy could buy political influence. However, those of middling wealth were only modestly represented and Dissenters formally excluded, though some slipped through the net by taking the Anglican communion occasionally. The North American events had stimulated the expectations of artisans and small producers who were largely excluded from political life and many of whom were attracted to the Nonconformist Churches. The vigour of industrial and commercial growth boosted the importance of such people but also exposed them to the roller coaster ride of the trade cycle.

The blockage on reform disappointed Pitt's reformist supporters just at the time when their expectations were rising. The approach of the centenary of 1688 inspired the formation of 'revolution societies'. The holding of the Constitutional Convention in the United States, and the onset of the last crisis of the *ancien régime* in France, stimulated popular interest in political and representative principles. Britons could no longer be so sure that they possessed the freest and most representative government in the world. But if foreign events whetted the popular appetite for political reform they alarmed many members of the ruling oligarchy, who believed that the onset of heavy weather was the worst time to tamper with the rigging of 'illegitimate monarchy'.

Pitt's failure to alleviate the civic disabilities of Nonconformists caused special bitterness; controversy over confessional privileges and proscriptions carried a freight of political overtones in a country where Puritans had carried through a vital phase of the bourgeois revolution but had seen its fruits taken from them. In the 1784 election many of Pitt's supporters had declared themselves in favour of religious reform, but the Prime Minister knew that his administration would immediately fall if he sought to interfere with the privileges of the Church of England; the King and court, the House of Lords, with its bench of Bishops, and the mass of county and borough Members of Parliament saw the demands of the Nonconformists as undermining an essential bulwark of the ruling order. Thus Nonconformists were obliged to pay tithes to the established Church; while Nonconformist ministers were exempted from such payments, any more general concession would have offered a fiscal inducement to Nonconformity and raised the question of how otherwise the established Church was to be financed. The Nonconformist Churches were distrusted because they were centres of independent opinion. The disqualifications imposed on Nonconformity were designed to insulate and discourage it; Dissenters were prevented from acting as legal trustees, guardians and executors as well as barred from office-holding. In the course of the century the Whigs had suspended particular penalties and prohibitions imposed on Dissent while never granting positive civic equality. Thus Nonconformists had been permitted to organise their own schools and 'academies'; the latter had far more enlightened curricula than Oxford or Cambridge, and included the study of the new trends in political economy and moral philosophy. Blackstone pointed out that technically Nonconformity was 'criminal' even if Parliament had generously agreed to suspend any consequent penalties in view of the 'serious and sober' nature of Dissenting convictions. Lord Mansfield had ruled in 1767 that Nonconformity was no crime, but he left in place most of the practical disabilities imposed on its adherents. From the 1760s the Nonconformist demand for civic equality was couched less in particularistic and theological terms and more in terms of general human rights. The more radical spokesmen of the Nonconformist cause, men like Joseph Priestley and Richard Price, insisted that there should be toleration for 'all modes of thinking' and that a free constitution should not 'deprive itself of the services of any man of ability and integrity on account of his religious opinions any more than on account of the colour of his hair'.[2] The assertion of religious liberties in the United States heightened Nonconformist resentment at the limited but real forms of discrimination to which they were subject. Most Nonconformists realised that social equality and religious liberty had to be pursued with caution and skill to avoid arousing the furies of popular prejudice. The appeal to general 'human rights' was deemed by many to be more promising than harping on the special interests of Nonconformity.

Anti-slavery became a popular movement with a national organisation just at the time when radicals and Nonconformists were becoming disappointed with the Pitt administration. Pitt's motion for parliamentary reform was defeated in 1785 and a motion repealing provisions of the Test Act, opposed by Pitt in the parliamentary debate of March 1787, was defeated. Pitt defended the Test Act on the grounds of expediency rather than principle and supporters of repeal looked forward to further attempts to persuade Parliament of the justice of their case.

A Society for Effecting the Abolition of the Slave Trade was set up in

April 1787 by the Quakers, Granville Sharp and others with leanings towards social reform and evangelical Christianity. Sharp urged that the Society should declare itself for slave emancipation, but the other members of the founding committee believed that suppression of the slave traffic was an adequate first step. The Quakers had already presented a petition to Parliament against the slave traffic in 1783; the Society for Promoting Constitutional Information found it appropriate to support this petition. Granville Sharp, the Society's first Chairman, had recently publicised the scandal of the slave ship *Zong*; in order to collect insurance the master of this ship had thrown overboard sick slaves rather than risk uncompensated deaths. Thus the Society was launched at a time when there was already some public debate on the slave trade.[3] The London Quaker Meeting for Sufferings had set up an Abolition Committee of its own in 1783; it was this committee which drew together the founders of the Abolition Society four years later, supplying nine out of its twelve members.

The Quaker abolitionists, though themselves debarred from politics, were sufficiently wealthy and well-connected to begin the task of making converts to abolition within ruling circles. The exclusion of Quakers from political life, and the character-forming effect of Quaker disciplines, no doubt made its own contribution to their extraordinary business success. By the late eighteenth century such leading Quaker families as the Darbys, Barclays, Lloyds, Gurneys and Pembertons formed a sort of bourgeois elite. They combined prosperity as bankers, merchants or manufacturers with concern for civic regeneration and the spread of social institutions appropriate to the new economic order. They worked for prison reform, poor law reform, and the promotion of libraries, hospitals, Bible societies and Sunday schools. The campaign against the slave trade had a special place in Quaker concerns. Many Quakers had enriched themselves through involvement in the triangular trades. In rejecting the slave trade they assuaged their sense of guilt and combated the dulling of the moral faculties which they feared would result from devotion to business activity. While much Quaker social work was undertaken by women, the Meeting for Sufferings – to which women did not belong – showed that Quaker men could emulate the charity and good works of their womenfolk. As abolitionists and social reformers Quakers stood for the creation of a new social framework which would adapt commerce and accumulation to the needs of the human order. They identified easily with the cosmopolitan tendencies at work in the Atlantic world and put their international contacts at the service of abolitionism. The Quakers did not want to became office holders – to do so would have violated their pacifism and ban on oath-taking – but they did wish to offer moral leadership and to use their wealth and influence in godly ways; if this showed the absurdity of discrimination against them so much the better.

The Abolition Society won two new recruits to the cause who helped to transform its political work and influence: Thomas Clarkson, a recent Cambridge graduate, and William Wilberforce, the West Riding MP and confidante of the Prime Minister. Granville Sharp, Clarkson and Wilberforce were all members of the Church of England; but they all also believed that their Church had lamentably failed to match the piety and good works of many Dissenters. That the Anglican Society for the Propagation of the Gospel itself owned slaves was particularly mortifying to them. While Clarkson and Sharp supported repeal of the Test Act Wilberforce spoke against it in Parliament.

In its first year or so of existence the society directed most of its attention to lobbying members of the government and preparing arguments that could inform policy. Thereafter in the years 1788–92 abolitionism suddenly moved to the centre of British political life and set the pattern for a novel type of reform movement. This was due partly to changes in the methods of the society and partly to the parallel initiative of anti-slavery forces in Manchester and other northern towns.

Thomas Clarkson was engaged as a full-time organiser and propagandist for the society. Clarkson brought to the abolitionist cause a dedicated professionalism in research, organisation and agitation. The slave trade, though widely deplored, was still believed to be an important source of national wealth and strength. The slave-trading interests claimed that it was a 'nursery of seamen'. The small circle of abolitionists were the first to question this belief; one of them, John Newton, had formerly been a slave-trading captain, while another, Sir Christopher Middleton, was Comptroller of the Navy. Clarkson engaged in detailed investigation of the operations of the slave-traders in visits to Bristol and Liverpool prior to launching a public campaign. Scrutiny of the manifests of the slave-trading vessels enabled him to show that both British seamen and captive Africans suffered appallingly high mortality rates. He showed that more British seamen lost their life on the slave ships than in all other branches of British commerce put together, and that the slave trade was less valuable and less profitable than had generally been supposed. In the first fifteen months of its existence the society spent more than £1,000 producing 15,000 copies of Clarkson's pamphlet on the slave trade and 1,500 copies of Anthony Benezet's *Historical Account of Guinea*.[4] But the society's impact was to be transformed by the appearance of a committee in Manchester which attracted widespread support and which caused to be published a summary statement in a string of provincial papers.

On a visit to Manchester Clarkson had received a warm welcome from the local leaders of the Society for Constitutional Information, which stood for universal manhood suffrage. Together with other forces an abolitionist committee had been formed and by November 1787 over 10,000 signatures gathered for a petition to be submitted to Parliament. The breadth of support may be gauged from the fact that the petition had been signed by over half of the adult males living in the city. Manchester stood at the centre of a burgeoning commercial and industrial network; its population had doubled in fifteen years, yet it had no parliamentary representative or municipal corporation. The town had sponsored a number of commercial petitions in the mid-1780s, but with the anti-slavery petition it made a bid to bring together other forces excluded from the formal system of political representation. The public petition had been drawn up despite advice from the London Society that this might be unwise and that resources should be concentrated on individual lobbying of Parliament. Manchester's petition and advertisements calling for its example to be followed were placed in the *General Evening Post*, *Lloyd's Evening Post*, and other leading national and provincial newspapers. Without losing its air of respectability abolition became a popular cause. Local committees were formed in such towns as Birmingham, York, Worcester, Sheffield, Leeds, Norwich, Falmouth, Nottingham and Exeter; large meetings were held and petitions displayed in public places. Edinburgh formed a committee but Scottish participation was limited in 1788. A small abolitionist circle developed even in Liverpool, though general hostility in the slaving port obliged its members to be discreet.[5]

The anti-slavery emblem – a kneeling African in chains bearing the motto 'Am I Not a Man and a Brother?' – became a familiar sight on cups, plates, broaches and pendants; Josiah Wedgewood, who marketed these items with his customary flair, designed the anti-slavery device. Supporters of both political and religious reform were prominent in the ranks of the society. Christopher Wyville and other leading members of the Yorkshire Association endorsed the cause. Nonconformists of every denomination were well represented in the provincial societies; the members of the local committees included many men who had been educated at the Dissenting Academies or the Scottish universities. Manufacturers, tradesmen, doctors, clergymen, lawyers, clerks and artisans constituted the membership of these local committees. Often there was a link between the Abolition Society and local philosophical and literary societies.

Clarkson travelled throughout the country to spread the word and to co-ordinate a campaign of petitions to Parliament. So far as ruling-class opinion was concerned abolition was less threatening than other campaigns for reform. Some of its tactics, such as that of the petition,

The Anti-Slavery device

derived from time-honoured rights of the subject, available for the redress of grievances or the defence of the interests of a commercial lobby. The loyal petition did not question ruling institutions and was, indeed, to become thoroughly parliamentary in its orientation. But it required extensive extra-parliamentary organisation and departed from the usual pattern in that the petitions were presented in the name of the general inhabitants of the community, not from some specific interest, trade, guild or corporation as was more normally the case. Abolitionist campaigning also spoke directly to popular sentiment in a way that echoed both an evangelical meeting and patriot politics.

Clarkson was only one of a number of itinerant speakers. Former slaves and former slave-traders would testify at abolitionist gatherings. Olaudah Equiano (Gustavus Vassa) and Ottobah Cugoano, former slaves who had both suffered the middle passage, could relate its horrors with the authority of experience. While the African voice had been raised in North America it was now accorded an honoured place on public platforms. Cugoano published a pamphlet against the slave trade in 1787, while Equiano's *Life*, published in 1789, was to become an abolitionist classic.[6] At abolition meetings John Newton, the former captain turned preacher, also insisted on the brutalising and corrupting effect of the slave traffic on the white men who took part in it. Abolitionist agitation made a direct appeal to the conscience and to a sense of common humanity beyond caste distinctions. The African was portrayed, in what seem patronising terms, as a man on his knees; but many abolitionists also felt themselves outcasts and supplicants, labouring under civic or religious disabilities; they identified with Equiano's impressive indictment of the commerce in humanity and the degradation of enslavement. The combination of a moral and a political appeal in the abolitionist campaign enabled it to bridge the gap that was opening between reform constituencies and reform politicians. Altogether one hundred and two petitions supporting abolition were presented to Parliament during its 1788 session.

Political leaders responded swiftly to public interest in the slave trade question. In what was possibly an attempt to head off the agitation Sir William Dolben introduced a parliamentary bill to regulate the slave trade, establishing maximum loading ratios for the slaving ships; this became law in the 1788 session. Dolben had been one of the leading opponents of repealing the Test Act in the previous session. The Prime Minister himself expressed the hope that an end to the trade could be devised; the French government was approached to explore the possibility of a joint Anglo–French ban. No doubt Pitt was as affected as many others by reports of conditions on the slave-trading vessels. But the issue was certainly a far easier one for him to take up than political or religious reform. The slave-traders, as distinct from the planters, had few parliamentary representatives. West Indian planters did not favour abolition, since they saw anti-slavery sentiment animating the campaign. On the other hand, the British slave trade of the mid-1780s was supplying large numbers of slaves to the French islands and undercutting the competitive position of the British planters. A joint Anglo–French ban would certainly have hit the French planters much harder than the British. Such considerations did not require Pitt to endorse abolition but, so long as he was sufficiently cautious, they did mean that he could do so while still appearing a responsible statesman. Parliamentary willingness to regulate or restrain the slave trade in turn helped to lend credibility to abolition as a live political question and thereby to stimulate extra-parliamentary representations. Radicals and Nonconformists had no difficulty in expressing a heart-felt detestation of slave trading; they knew that West Indian interests were close to the heart of 'Old Corruption' and they were delighted to discover that anti-slavery agitation could be undertaken with a vigour that would have been impossible in a less disinterested and high-minded cause.

Pitt's failure to make any headway with political reform put Wilberforce in a particularly difficult situation. In the early months of 1787 he withdrew from Parliament and underwent a conversion to evangelical Christianity, though not resigning his seat. Wilberforce was not involved in the activities of the Abolition Society during its first year. During this time he decided to devote himself to the 'reformation of public manners' by means of a new association which would act as the 'guardian of the religion and morals of the people'. The energies which had been frustrated by the parliamentary strength of Old Corruption were to be redirected into an overhaul of the nation's moral life. The King was prevailed upon by Wilberforce to issue a Royal Proclamation against Vice and Immorality on June 1st 1787. This Proclamation furnished the Charter for a Proclamation Society which god-fearing and law-abiding subjects were invited to join. One of Wilberforce's biographers writes of this society:

> Its activities, in which Wilberforce took a vigorous part for many years, were mostly directed against blasphemous and indecent publications, but it busied itself also with attempts to enforce a stricter observance of Sunday among the poor, to suppress such indecorous rustic festivities as 'wakes', and so forth. In 1802 its place was taken by the better known Society for the Suppression of Vice – better known if only as the butt of Sydney Smith's mordant humour. 'A corporation of informers', he called it, 'supported by large contributions' and bent on suppressing not the vices of the rich but the pleasures of the poor, on reducing their life 'to its regular standard of decorous gloom', while 'the gambling houses of St James remain untouched'. These were well aimed shafts and they hit the Proclamation Society as surely as its successor. It was fortunate, surely, that Wilberforce's fine enthusiasm was soon to find a wider and worthier field.[7]

Pitt, disconcerted by Wilberforce's evangelical conversion, urged him not to abandon politics and suggested that he might take up the cause of abolition. Wilberforce had already been approached by Clarkson to take an interest in the slave trade question. Wilberforce began by going over Clarkson's researches and obtaining further information from official quarters. He became convinced that he should lend the Abolition Society his support, though not, to begin with, as a formal member. While Clarkson toured the country speaking to local abolition societies Wilberforce threw himself into the work of preparing a parliamentary bill and to making out an economic as well as moral argument against the slave traffic. Wilberforce's bill was eventually brought before the House in 1789, arousing great public attention. Despite powerful advocacy by Wilberforce, and support from the three most renowned parliamentary orators – Fox, Burke and Pitt – and despite an impressive barrage of testimony from former participants, the opponents of abolition successfully obtained postponement of a vote until Parliament had had the opportunity to hear more evidence. This effective delaying tactic had the disadvantage that the evidence diligently presented to the House by the Abolition Society and others received considerable publicity.

Partly because of an intervening election consideration of the bill to abolish the slave trade was not resumed until the early months of 1791. Following a two-day debate it failed in the House of Commons by 163 votes to 88. Though Pitt spoke once again in favour of abolition he refused to make it a government measure; many of his colleagues and supporters, notably Henry Dundas, voted against the bill. Dundas was, in effect, patronage Secretary to the Pitt administration and controlled all but one of the Scottish MPs. An important part of Dundas's job was to negotiate support for the government's programme with influential parliamentary and imperial lobbies. Dundas supervised Indian affairs and championed the reorientation of British imperial interests towards Asia; but he did not see this as a good reason to ditch wealthy West Indian proprietors who could contribute to the sustenance of the administration. Another key member of Pitt's Cabinet was Lord Hawkesbury, later the Earl of Liverpool, who was the administration's chief expert on overseas commerce and himself a West Indian proprietor. In the Parliament of 1790 there were two or three dozen Members with West Indian interests. They were advised by the Society of West Indian Planters and Merchants to oppose the bill on the grounds of general principle and because a unilateral British gesture would simply give a free run to the French competition. The West Indian group in Parliament was effective in rallying opposition to abolition not so much because of its size as because of its ability to persuade other MPs that it would be wrong for them to sacrifice national advantage, and cast a doubt on West Indian estates. One MP declared: 'The leaders, it is true, are for Abolition. But the minor orators, the pygmies, will, I trust, succeed this day in carrying the case against them. The property of the West Indians is at stake; and though men may be generous with their own property, they should not be so with the property of others.'[8]

At court and in the House of Lords the pro-slave-trade lobby also found powerful champions. The King and the Duke of Clarence – the future William IV – both defended the slave trade and made members of both Houses of Parliament familiar with their views. The King saw the slave trade as essential to national and imperial strength; the Duke of Clarence had served as a naval commander in the Caribbean and testified to the humanity of the planters there. At a time when there was popular clamour for reform in every field it appeared that abolition of the slave trade might be seen as a sign of the established order's weakness rather than strength. In view of the forces ranged against abolition Pitt knew that his administration might well fall if he sought to make it a government measure. On the other hand, by expressing his personal opposition to the slave traffic he was able to salvage something of the esteem in which he had been held by reform opinion.[9]

The parliamentary procrastination of 1789 and the defeat of 1791 in no way dampened the campaign for abolition outside Parliament. Indeed, following the parliamentary defeat energies which had been tied up in the laborious business of preparing evidence were released for agitation in the country at large. Wilberforce announced that he would present another bill in 1792. The course of the French Revolution was not yet such as to divide the British reform movement; indeed all reform currents drew strength from the widespread belief that a new era of progress had dawned. For a time abolition became the reform measure that commanded most support. In the early 1780s the association movement for constitutional reform had presented 50 petititions to Parliament. The 102 abolitionist petitions of 1788 were greatly exceeded by the 519 of 1792: 312 from England and 187 from Scotland, each bearing several hundreds or thousands of signatures. Manchester, with a population of 75,000, sent a petition to Parliament signed by over 20,000 people in 1791. Throughout Britain as a whole the number of signatories to abolitionist petitions rose from 60,000–100,000 in 1788 to 380,000–400,000 in 1792. Abolitionists were widening the boundaries of the political nation, though still observing certain inhibitions: only adult males were invited to sign. Pro-slavery advocates poured scorn on the absurdity of supposing that the views on a commercial question of a group of 'enlightened Cornish miners' had the same weight as that of a similar number of burghers of the City of London. The parliamentary debates on abolition in 1789 and 1791 had appeared to open up a breach in the stony façade of the ruling oligarchy; radicals and reformers of all descriptions sought to press the advantage and widen the space for popular agitation. Even the most nervous Justice of the Peace could scarcely claim that meetings held in support of a cause endorsed by the Prime Minister was seditious or treasonable. The publicity that inevitably attended parliamentary proceedings had a tendency to centralise and focus the disparate concerns and constituencies favourable to radical or reform politics. Wilberforce urged the Abolition Committee to adhere strictly to constitutional channels. He was worried when Clarkson expressed enthusiasm for the French Revolution and was even concerned when some local abolition societies advocated a consumer boycott of West Indian sugar and other slave produce, on the grounds that this might, if successful, take matters out of Parliament's hands. Wilberforce's biographer comments that the movement's achievement was to have shown 'how much could be done to mobilize public opinion outside the walls of parliament but within the liberties of the constitution'.[10]

The Methodists, whose membership doubled within a decade to reach over 77,000 in the mid-1790s, identified strongly with abolition while abstaining from involvement in other reform questions. Yorkshire was a stronghold of Methodism, containing about a quarter of all its British members. The Methodist ranks included large numbers of artisans, miners, small masters and, so far as the female membership was concerned, domestics. In the last years before Wesley's death in 1791 he and Wilberforce became firm friends; Wesley supported Wilberforce's moral crusade and requested him to use his influence with Pitt to make sure that Methodist preachers were not impeded by local Justices.[11]

In the years 1791–2 the international conjuncture became steadily more favourable to abolition. One of the most difficult objections with which abolitionists had to contend was that unilateral British action would simply strengthen the hand of Britain's colonial rivals, especially France. The progress of the Revolution made France appear more preoccupied with internal affairs and more willing to consider anti-slavery measures. For nearly two years domestic preoccupations and planter interests prevented the French National Assembly from debating issues connected with colonial slavery. But in May 1791 supporters of the French equivalent of the Abolition Society – the *Amis des Noirs* – eventually succeeded in pressing through a measure favourable to mulatto rights; by May of 1792 Brissot de Warville, a leading supporter of the *Amis*, was leader of the French government. These developments seemed to promise that any British action would be reciprocated by the French authorities. The outbreak of the slave insurrection in St Domingue in August 1791 could only strengthen the view that Britain had little to fear from French colonial competition and that it was in the best interests of both colonial powers not to further enlarge the numbers of raw and hostile captives held on the small islands of the Caribbean.[12]

By 1792 the main seafaring states of North America had already banned their citizens from participating in the slave trade. In March 1792 the royal Danish government announced that the slave trade to the Danish islands would be ended within ten years. The Dutch trade had already dwindled to small proportions while Portugal represented no threat to the larger powers, least of all to Britain.

The cautious decree in Denmark itself reflected the rise of abolitionism elsewhere and its endorsement by some planter interests. The absolutist government in Copenhagen was anxious to avoid revolutionary turmoil and any maritime clash with other powers. The

First Minister, Ernst Schimmelman, was himself the owner of large slave estates in the Danish islands and a prominent shareholder in the Danish slave-trading company. Schimmelman believed that the Danish slave trade was neither profitable, nor necessary, nor morally justifiable; he would cite the first two considerations when addressing official bodies, the latter when communicating with his evangelically inclined sister. Schimmelman set up a commission to investigate Danish colonial slavery and the Danish slave trade. This commission confirmed that the trade made losses and detected a possibility that the slave population of the Danish islands could reproduce itself without new slave imports. It was pointed out that the slave crews of the Schimmelman estates were close to reproducing themselves naturally due to good treatment. The Danish Commission also pointed to the high mortality among seamen who sailed in the slaving ships. In view of such findings the commission recommended that the Danish slave trade be ended within ten years, the interval to be used to secure properly balanced slave crews. In accepting the commission's report the Danish government hoped to retain control of events and place Danish colonial slavery on a more secure basis; as it turned out slavery in the Danish islands long survived the decree against the slave trade. However cautious, the action of the Danish government, announced shortly before the opening of the British Parliament, was encouraging to the abolitionist cause.[13]

The Commons votes on abolition in April 1792 reflected the pressure exerted on MPs by the impressive growth of opinion on the subject. The two-day debate on the bill was marked by powerful speeches from Wilberforce and Pitt – the latter, consonant with his support for free trade, looked forward to the day when relations between states would be governed by law and morality, and Africa redeemed by means of peaceful commerce. The debate appeared to be going badly for defenders of the trade. Towards its end Dundas proposed that the word 'gradually' be inserted in the abolition bill; this amendment was carried by 193 votes to 125, against opposition from Wilberforce and Pitt. The amended bill, providing for gradual abolition, was then passed by 230 votes to 85. In a subsequent session the Commons voted by 151 votes to 132 that the trade should end by 1796; this was to be the only slave trade vote where Dundas found himself in a minority. When the bill for gradual abolition reached the Lords it met fierce opposition; but instead of simply voting it down the Lords insisted that all the evidence given to the Commons should be repeated in their own chamber. The whole question was thus postponed for at least a year.[14]

After its near-triumph in 1792 the abolitionist movement went into decline. Britain's declaration of war on France in 1793 and the onset of the Jacobin phase of the Revolution divided abolitionist ranks, further radicalising many democrats but provoking a counter-revolutionary mobilisation which drew on support from every level of society. Wilberforce himself showed distaste for the revolution long before the rise of Robespierre and was, indeed, to become a ferocious anti-Jacobin; he was, however, not enthusiastic for war with France. Wilberforce conceded that ruling-class opinion had reason to see a connection between abolition and radical republicanism: 'It is certainly true,' he wrote,'and perfectly natural, that these Jacobins are all friendly to Abolition; and it is no less true and natural that this operates to the injury of our cause.'[15]

The London Corresponding Society was founded by Hardy, Paine and others in January 1792. The precedent set by local abolitionist committees was thus swiftly taken up, sometimes by the very same people. Equiano, a friend of Hardy's, used contacts he had made on abolitionist speaking tours to spread the work of the Corresponding Society in the North of England. Thomas Hardy declared that the Rights of Man 'are not confined to this small island but are extended to the whole human race, black or white, high or low, rich or poor'.[16] The British Jacobins often invoked anti-slavery themes as part of their attack on the British government and monarchy. A large radical meeting in Sheffield in April 1794 passed unanimously a motion calling for emancipation of the slaves in the West Indies. However, the radical democrats and 'rational Dissenters' tended to argue that the introduction of a new political system would be necessary before abolition could be effected and that slavery, not simply the slave trade, could then be overthrown. The Quakers and the Methodists, in contrast, were far more concerned with abolition than any other issue; most became positively hostile to reform, though in 1797 some radical Methodists seceded from the main connection.

The abolitionist movement could not rise above the harsh polarisations produced by the Revolution in France. Events across the Channel in the latter half of 1792 prompted increasing alarm in ruling-class circles and steadily opened a breach within the ranks of radicals, reformers and democrats: these months witnessed the formation of a counter-revolutionary coalition led by the Duke of Brunswick, the sacking of the Tuileries, the fall of Verdun, the September massacres, the abolition of the monarchy, the trial of Louis XVI. It became clear that France was not moving towards a limited monarchy on the British model. The famous polemical exchanges between Burke and Paine made it seem that a choice had to be made between a democratic republic and an oligarchic monarchy, the 'rights of Englishmen' and 'the rights of man'. While radical Nonconformists became semi-Jacobin republicans, moderate reformists, including the main body of Dissenters, rallied to the status quo. Already in April 1792 Burke had assailed those who proposed reform of the Test Act as opening the gateway to 'conspirators' who would 'seize the Tower of London and the magazines it contains, murder the governor and mayor of London, seize upon the King's person, drive out the House of Lords, occupy your gallery, and thence, as from an high tribunal dictate to you'. With these hysterical words Burke had achieved the virtual representation of the moral panic which now gripped the Hanoverian order. Burke's commitment to abolition also suffered and by 1792 he was declaring, 'the cause of humanity would be far more benefited by the continuance of the trade and servitude, regulated and reformed, than by the total destruction of both or either'.[17]

Those identified as Jacobins or Republicans became the target for 'Church and King' mobs; Priestley's house in Birmingham was burnt down and his laboratory smashed – before long he emigrated to America. The key demands of the reformers – repeal of the Test Act, Parliamentary reform, abolition of the slave trade – offered little to the mass of the populace; the programme of the democratic radicals – a republic, manhood suffrage, public education, progressive taxation, more generous poor relief, the end of all types of slavery – was taken more seriously by those who would lose from it than by those who might gain. In the parliamentary arena only the Foxites continued to defend the reform programme. The French Republic's decision to open the Scheldt and to execute Louis XVI led Pitt to support war against it in February 1793. Pitt took this step reluctantly since it threatened his already highly successful commercial policy, but the aroused and belligerent consensus of ruling-class opinion gave him no choice. In fighting France Hanoverian Britain could, it was believed, simultaneously exorcise the spectre of Jacobinism and make major commercial and imperial gains at French expense. A degree of popular and patriotic support could be guaranteed for the return bout against Britain's traditional antagonist. The domestic correlative of this policy was stern repression of every type of malcontent at home. This hit not only at open Republicans, or instigators of strike action, but also at Dissenting ministers who continued to uphold the reform programme: a Unitarian minister was sentenced to seven years' deportation, a Baptist minister to four years' imprisonment and a Scottish advocate to fourteen years' transportation before the end of 1793. However, with the outbreak of war, the main bodies of Dissenting ministers made haste to declare: 'That we hold and ever have held in the highest respect and veneration that excellent form of government by King, Lords and Commons which hath obtained from time immemorial in this country

... That we are firmly attached to his present Majesty ... That we abhor all seditious practices tending to subvert this our excellent Constitution ...' and so on and so forth.[18] The Coercion Acts of 1795 gave the government wide powers to stamp out unauthorised political meetings or publications. Wilberforce played a crucial role in reassuring the freemen of Yorkshire that such drastic measures were necessary. He also interceded with Pitt to ensure that the right of petition was safeguarded. As the threat of French invasion loomed there was a patriotic rallying to 'illegitimate monarchy'; following his illness in 1788 the King was no longer seen as a menace to popular liberties or constitutional government but rather as a decent and honourable man battling with private misfortune.[19] Pitt had not produced political reform but he had an evident distaste for personal corruption.

Looking back with hindsight many years later Wilberforce wrote:'I am myself persuaded that the war with France, which lasted so many years and occasioned such an expense of blood and treasure, would never have taken place but for Mr Dundas's influence with Mr Pitt and his persuasion that we should be able with ease and promptitude, at a small expense of money and men, to take the French West Indian Islands.'[20] It is difficult to believe that West Indian acquisitions had the primacy Wilberforce here accords them since such large issues were at stake in Europe itself. But there can be no doubt that the West Indian theatre was a major preoccupation for the British Cabinet. Dundas and Hawkesbury persuaded their colleagues that priority must be given to the dispatch of large forces to the Caribbean. For nearly two years representatives of the French planters had pleaded with the London government to save them from the triple affliction of republicanism, slave revolt and the *exclusif*. Giving succour to the French planters would, it was hoped, encourage constitutional monarchists, suppress slave insurrection, and open up new fields for investment and trading. In the course of 1793 and 1794 the British proceeded to occupy Martinique, Guadeloupe, St Lucia and most of the west coast of St Domingue. The British were greeted as saviours by most French planters, though they met stiff resistance from the beleaguered republican forces who increasingly made common cause with the insurgent slaves. The Jacobin Convention proclaimed the end of slavery in all French colonies.

Wilberforce supported the war, albeit with misgivings, and remained on intimate terms with Pitt and his Cabinet. It might seem that his abolitionist convictions were hopelessly discrepant with British war aims. Yet in Wilberforce's view there was probably no contradiction between his desire to end the slave trade and his willingness to go along with the government's attempt to roll back servile revolt and republicanism in the West Indies. He had never supported slave resistance or rebellion, or any plans for the expropriation of slave-owners. He loathed regicides and revolutionaries. He seems to have persuaded himself that the British Crown and Parliament would be more easily brought to accept abolition if French power and rivalry in the West Indies were broken; there was, in fact, substance in this view. After the protracted hearing of evidence the Lords had killed the parliamentary abolition bill of 1792. Even though Wilberforce did not think it appropriate to put an abolition bill before the 1794 parliamentary session he devised what he saw as a useful partial measure. He proposed a bill which would end the supply of slaves by British traders to foreign colonies, including those recently occupied. This measure received some support from West Indian proprietors, who had no wish to see the French islands grow at their expense; nevertheless, after failing to gain Cabinet backing, this bill was also defeated in the Lords. Wilberforce's reputation as an abolitionist probably hindered acceptance of what could otherwise have been seen as a simple protectionist measure. In the aftermath of this new defeat, and with the emergence of opposition to the war in Yorkshire and elsewhere, Wilberforce began to call for the opening of peace negotiations with France; however, neither at this time nor later did he call for British withdrawal from the occupied French territories – territories where British arms were the only effective prop of the slave system.[21]

In 1795 Wilberforce again presented a general abolition bill but it was defeated by 78 votes to 61. In the following year a similar bill lost by only 74 votes to 70. These apparently close scores give a misleading impression since Dundas and the pro-slave trade lobby would have mobilised more forces if they had suffered defeat on a first reading. The Abolition Society itself lost much of its vigour, holding few meetings in 1794 and only two in the following three years. From 1797 to 1804 the National Committee of the Abolition Society did not meet at all. Clarkson was overtaken by illness and demoralisation in 1794; he retired from abolitionist campaigning, now difficult or even impossible to sustain outside Parliament, and devoted himself to historical researches. In Parliament Wilberforce was still able to lend the abolitionist cause a semblance of life but debates on the question were ill-attended; since an unlikely Commons victory would have been followed by certain defeat in the Lords hopes could barely be kept alive by the ritual of introducing bills. Burke, a leading advocate of abolition in earlier days, declared himself content with a regulated slave trade in 1792. Between 1799 and 1804 Wilberforce himself became sufficiently discouraged to abandon the practice of the annual abolition bill, though he did introduce some partial proposals and one general bill in 1802.[22]

The fate of the first wave of British abolitionism had been determined essentially by the interplay between the domestic political crisis and the international situation. Abolition had gained a foothold in Parliament and a following in the country because of the narrowness of its target and the breadth of the constituencies which could identify with it. Stopping short of expropriation it had momentarily united plebeian radicalism with bourgeois reformism. But once the popular element was distracted or repressed, and abolitionism reduced to the dimension of a parliamentary caucus, it ceased to make headway. Abolitionism in retreat remained as a symbolic link with the idea of a more coherent bourgeois order and an advance for morality and reform in the heart of the constitution; for this reason it could continue to limp along as a parliamentary cause even after the onset of the anti-Jacobin reaction and at a time when hope for all other reform measures was completely extinguished.

Wilberforce continued to act as the unofficial conscience of Parliament and the Pitt administration, even though at times he censured their actions; since Wilberforce was manifestly in and of the political establishment he helped to conserve its moral title to rule at a time when this was fundamentally contested. In 1795 he spoke of the advisability of peace with France but promoted war against the Jacobins at home. When the government seemed seriously threatened, as during the crisis of 1798, responsible middle-class opinion rallied strongly to it; Wilberforce helped to express and cement this profound loyalty to the established order. His reactions and reflexes were closely attuned to those of the new bourgeois public. To the satisfaction of the Yorkshire manufacturers he sponsored an act in 1799 outlawing combinations of workers. When the Bank of England was on the point of defaulting on its payments Pitt turned to Wilberforce to investigate its operations and restore public confidence. It is scarcely surprising that Wilberforce, from a gentlemanly mercantile background, should have become such a virulent anti-Jacobin in the 1790s, that he was alarmed by huge meetings of Republicans in Islington, the stoning of the King, mutiny in the fleet, revolt in Ireland, or that he felt that Britain's rulers needed, at whatever cost, to reassert moral leadership over a turbulent and threatened social order. In deference to Wilberforce's judgement Pitt was to continue his ineffectual support for abolition to his dying day. The warmth of Wilberforce's relationship with his friend was, however, appreciably diminished by the knowledge that Pitt deferred to Dundas and the imperial lobby, refusing ever to risk his administration by making abolition a government measure. Wilberforce never publicly reproached Pitt; on his death he paid tribute in Parliament to a man who had saved England from 'the revolutionary spirit that has convulsed France and alarmed the whole civilised world'.[23]

David Brion Davis has written of the early British abolitionist movement that, in their broad concern for reforms, they were diffusing 'the needs and values of the emerging capitalist order' and experimenting with 'new methods that would have the effect of ensuring the hegemony of an emerging ruling class'.[24] Davis's judgement is a partial one even if a final verdict must await a consideration of subsequent developments. Abolitionism was both less and more than the instrument of a rising bourgeoisie. The radical anti-slavery of Wallace or Sharp, or of Equiano or Hardy, was first and foremost an attack on a branch of commerce and colonisation that was still highly congruent with capitalist accumulation. The abolitionism of Manchester and the northern towns had a partly bourgeois character and looked to a broad popular alliance to reform or even replace the oligarchy. But it proved unable to sustain the challenge or to promote its own hegemony. Parliamentary abolitionism was different again; it helped an old ruling class to absorb and deflect the challenge of democracy, and to establish *its* hegemony over emergent bourgeois forces.

In their different ways Pitt and Wilberforce were the leading representatives of a British bourgeois politics that was deferential to the old ruling class while reserving its militant qualities for the work of suppressing democratic and republican opinion. Wilberforce was to write of Pitt: 'If only he had tried to "govern by principle", he would have succeeded. And then the whole British body politic would have been cleansed and strengthened. Even so great a cataclysm as the French revolution would have left it unshaken.' As his biographer Reginald Coupland rightly observes, Wilberforce was not here speculating on the possibilities of an historic alliance between 'the real democratic movement in England' and 'the new ideas in France', but rather 'would have us believe that, working within the structure, more or less unchanged, of the old eighteenth century political system, Pitt, single-handed, could have moralised British politics'.[25] Moral hegemony was a sort of anti-politics in this view. Wilberforce's indulgence of Pitt sprang not simply from friendship but from a shared commitment to Britain's ruling institutions.

For their part Republicans also supported anti-slavery, sometimes more consequentially than did the parliamentary champions of abolition. While some were essentially bourgeois radicals, attracted by abolitionism's celebration of the virtues of the wages system, others were small producers, or clerks or artisans, possessed of an almost utopian belief in the power of free labour – by which was usually meant the labour of a *masterless* man, a producer owning or controlling his own means of production. It was for this reason that the abolitionist impulse could outrun the limits of purely bourgeois reform. In the popular anti-slavery campaign, no less than in Granville Sharp's pamphlets, it is often possible to detect hostility to commercial capitalism as well as to the slave trade, though the latter is certainly seen as the former's most monstrous product. The abolitionist idealisation of family life also appealed to these free workers and to their wives and daughters. Women attended some meetings, though they could not sign petitions or join abolitionist committees; Lady Middleton and Hannah More were influential advocates of the cause, the latter writing several pamphlets. The willingness of some women to work for the cause aroused mixed feelings in Wilberforce: 'All private exertions for such an object become their character, but for ladies to meet, to go from house to house stirring up petitions – these appear to me proceedings unsuited to the female character as delineated in scripture.'[26]

The basic options of both mainstream and radical abolitionism contributed to the decline of the movement. So far as Wilberforce and the Methodists were concerned, if anti-slavery threatened the integrity of Britain's established order then it would have to be postponed until it did not. Symptomatically, Wilberforce decided to oppose the withdrawal of British troops from St Domingue in 1797, since this would be ceding ground to French republicanism. John Wesley had exhibited a similar priority when he advised one of his followers to make sure to vote for the government candidate at Bristol in the election of 1789, despite the fact that this man was a leading parliamentary apologist for the slave trade while his opponent was an abolitionist. For its part radical anti-slavery became submerged within a general commitment to the democratic programme and to peace with France; in the face of these concerns, and of widespread harassment, it survived as little more than rhetoric.

As might be expected the abolitionist challenge and its defeat led to important mutations within pro-slavery ideology. The elaboration of an anti-slavery critique was followed, at a short interval, by the development of a new justificatory ideology for slaveholding. During the epoch of the making of the European colonial systems slavery had been justified in traditional ways. Paternalist relations were fairly well entrenched in social life; slavery in the Americas, it was claimed, saved Africans from captivity and heathenism; blacks were 'sons of Ham', condemned to bondage by a biblical curse; and so forth. Defoe's highly influential novels *Robinson Crusoe* and *Colonel Jack* lent themselves to justifications of enslavement. But Defoe was not a consistent ideologue of slavery: if he was 'Captain Johnson' (see p. 45) he publicised the anti-slavery pirates of 'Libertalia' while even his fictions implied that a voluntary service was better than violent enslavement. *Robinson Crusoe* was a 'colonial romance', a parable of 'primitive accumulation' but also the tale of an individual's survival strategy and search for allies. *Robinson Crusoe*, source of more than one genre, bears comparison with the narrative 'lives' of those who had experienced enslavement.

In eighteenth century novels and plays racial stereotypes were still naive and unsystematic.[27] The eruption of anti-slavery led to a certain polarisation. The human universalism implicit in the anti-slavery critique was challenged by a more generalised, even 'scientific', racial doctrine which supposedly justified slavery. In one of the first signs of a new 'learned' racism David Hume added a lengthy footnote on the probable natural inferiority of Negroes to his essay on 'National Character' published in 1755; Montesquieu's observations in *The Spirit of the Laws* may well have prompted this.[28] The first sustained attempt to supply a justification of slavery on the grounds that blacks were sub-human was made by Edward Long; it was initially composed as a response to Granville Sharp. Long subsequently incorporated this racial doctrine in his *History of Jamaica* (1774), a work which enjoyed a certain authority because it gathered together useful data on the slave colony. Long's argument has been summarised as follows by the most recent editor of this work:

> That the trade in slaves and in goods produced by slaves was immensely profitable, not only to the West Indies, but to Britain itself and that it greatly enriched Englishmen in all walks of life; that West Indian slavery was, on the whole, a mild and benevolent institution and that slaves were better off than the lowest classes in Britain; that negro slavery was inevitable and necessary in certain regions of the world; that the slave trade benefited and helped civilize Africa; that virtually all slaves were originally convicted criminals; that in every mental and moral way negroes were absolutely inferior to white men, and that the most constructive thing that could happen to them was to be compelled to work productively.[29]

Long conceded that Africans should not be brought to England, whether free or enslaved; indeed he played on sexual fear of blacks and encouraged horror of racial intermixture. Though Long's racialist notions were thoroughly fanciful, and sometimes utterly bizarre, they did chime in with some of the 'scientific' thinking of the Enlightenment; Long made no appeal to biblical justifications of slavery. The classifications of Linnaeus, first published in the 1760s, and notion of a 'Great Chain of Being', involved the postulation of a hierarchy within *homo sapiens* as well as between the species. Some, like Lord Kames, the highly influential patron of the Scottish Enlightenment, argued that the different races of mankind were separate creations and constituted different species; Long's claim that those of mixed blood were infertile was to be cited in support of this view.[30]

The new racism drew on age-old prejudices, but was far more purposive and polemical than the ethnic conceits that abound in the literature of earlier times. It was not simply idle prejudice but served to justify enslavement, exploitation and discrimination. It was held that blacks must be kept in bondage since they were childlike, lazy and dangerous. Racist doctrines were calculated to justify functioning slave systems; their implications for the slave trade were less clear cut since it could easily be concluded from them that a country would be unwise to import blacks. Despite its abolitionist reputation Jefferson's *Notes on Virginia* contained reflections on the probable low intelligence and distinctive smell of Africans which were often taken up by pro-slavery and racist writers; their tentative formulation made them seem all the more reasonable.

However, if racism was more generalised and systematic than traditional ethnic particularism so were the humanist and philosophical assumptions of abolitionism. The idea of an essential human unity had, of course, been prefigured in the universalistic world religions. In the 1770s and 1780s Christian apologists, like the Scottish divine and anti-slavery advocate James Beattie, defended monogeneticism – a single creation – against the proponents of separate racial origins. However, the world religions usually accorded superior human value to the community of believers, the chosen or elect, while denying those outside such categories the protections extended, at least in theory, to those within them. Prior to the mid-eighteenth century no religion had ever denounced slavery in general terms. In different ways abolitionism, democratic politics and Enlightenment philosophy all contained within them a potential to develop a secular doctrine of universal human rights. But this impetus could be checked or confused, as it was in both the United States and Britain during the last decade of the eighteenth century. The radicalisation of the French Revolution and the eruption of the great slave rebellion in St Domingue aroused the most intense alarm amongst the possessing classes on both sides of the Atlantic. While it might still seem prudent to end the slave trade, an intellectual climate was created in which abolitionists no longer had the initiative and in which the new racism could make headway. Linnaeus's derogatory racial stereotypes were rendered in an English edition in 1795. In this same year the Manchester Literary and Philosophical Society, previously hospitable to anti-slavery, was treated to a disquisition on the inferiority of Negroes by Charles White, a local physician, in which it was asserted that 'in whatever respect the African differs from the European, the particularity brings him nearer to the ape'. This lecture, published in 1799, was to become a standard reference point for British racism.[31]

This new racism was an affair of the educated and official elite rather than of the common people. British plebeians still treated Africans with curiosity and jocular condescension rather than hatred or contempt; blacks would be judged as much by their clothes, speech and beliefs as by their skin colour. Some, like Equiano, married white women at a time when even Philadelphia Quakers looked askance at racial inter-marriage. Following the eruption of anti-slavery the popular dramatised version of *Oroonoko* was adapted to give a more sympathetic view of the mass of enslaved blacks.[32] The mid-1790s witnessed a chauvinist rictus as British national sentiment was mobilised against the French, but at the popular level white racism had little relevance to this. However, within ruling circles the new racism did justify both tolerance of colonial slaveholders, whether British or French, as well as the beckoning destiny of empire. Without Long's phobic intensity this racism could easily assume a paternalist or dominative form, justifying the rule of whites over lesser breeds, and foreshadowing the extention of colonialism in Africa and Asia. The notion of a biological hierarchy was in some ways more congruent with the elaboration of doctrines of class and empire than with slaveholder democracy on the North American pattern. The British lower orders were also seen as needing restraint and discipline: Hume believed there was a natural gulf between labourers and persons of quality as well as between whites and blacks. The Jacobin threat was identified in terms which had traditionally been used to justify enslavement: in his 'Letters on a Regicide Peace' of 1796 Burke reported with horror that the French revolutionaries were addicts of 'cannibalism': 'I mean their devouring as a nutrient of their ferocity, some part of the bodies of those they have murdered; their drinking the blood of their victims.'[33] Notions of racial hierarchy also allowed the imperial mind to identify local allies of colonial rule – superior racial castes, warrior peoples and the like. There was a strand in abolitionism, especially the variant most influential within ruling circles, which saw imperial power as the necessary corrective to chaotic and destructive commercial rapine.

The war in North America had ended with a signal British naval victory in the Caribbean: the West Indian slave colonies had stayed loyal throughout while British maritime strength stood athwart the trade routes to Africa and Asia. While the North American Anthony Benezet argued that the natural virtue of African states and societies had been traduced by the European slave traders, the more respectable varieties of British abolitionism inclined to argue that Africa needed European tutelage. In the mid-1780s Pitt's government had supported a philanthropic scheme to settle black refugees from North America in Sierra Leone; Granville Sharp and some of the leaders of the black community supported this scheme for a 'free colony' in West Africa. Pitt had urged the case for abolition by summoning up the potential wealth of a pacified Africa. As the tide of mass support for abolitionism ebbed the idealistic elements in colonial abolitionism were transmuted into imperial *realpolitik* and notions of Britain's divine right to rule other lands and peoples. The 'enlightened' planter MP Bryan Edwards helped to thwart the progress of abolition in Parliament; but he deprecated the violence of the slave trade and believed that both it and slavery were in need of regulation to prevent abuses. His argument for the invigilation and control of blacks was permeated by the notion of an essential racial hierarchy and antagonism.[34]

In the last years of the eighteenth century it seemed that anti-slavery had reached its limit in England. In the renewed conflict with France the British ruling class had seen an opportunity to smother revolutionary politics, to acquire the remnants of French empire and to rally popular patriotism in support of the government. Yet the advances of British anti-slavery in public opinion and in Parliament had made a large impression in Europe and North America. For a moment it seemed that Britain really was about to abandon the slave traffic, with a large Commons majority promising its extinction by 1796. There were echoes of the rise of British abolitionism in the 1790s in North America: in 1792–4 an attempt to persuade the Connecticut assembly to move from the 'free womb' to complete emancipation only just failed; in 1794 the various American abolition societies came together for the first time in Philadelphia to discuss co-ordinated activity; in New York and New Jersey new attempts were made to devise an acceptable emancipation law. In British North America the parliament of Upper Canada adopted a gradual emancipation law in 1793.[35]

In Britain there had been an unprecedented campaign against the slave trade yet by the 1790s the British slave traffic had grown to extraordinary dimensions. Between the first parliamentary motion for an end to the slave traffic and 1800 about one million captives were taken from Africa by British traders.[36] The chief success that abolitionists could claim was to have brought a measure of emancipation to areas where slavery had been of very small importance: England, Scotland, Canada, New England and Pennsylvania. The main centres of slaveholder power in the New World remained not only unscathed but largely unchallenged.

The anti-slavery impasse of the 1790s would be broken not by petitions to Parliament or Congress but by revolutionary struggles in the slave zone itself. In the Caribbean anti-slavery had acquired champions of a new sort, for whom the destruction of slaveholding was a life and death matter, and who were consequently committed to it body and soul.

Notes

1. For the immediate political impact of the American War see John Derry, *English Politics and the American Revolution*, London 1976, pp. 174–96. Granville Sharp belonged to the more radical wing of political reformers in the 1780s arguing for annual Parliaments and claiming rather improbably that 'the principle of representing property instead of persons' was 'entirely contrary to the principles of the English Constitution' (Lascelles, *Granville Sharp*, p. 105). The significant overlap between abolitionism and political radicalism was, of course, a direct product of the 'legitimacy crisis' of 'illegitimate monarchy'. Drescher has drawn attention to the social tensions that supplied the background to the rise of abolitionism as a movement but he is wrong to counter-pose this polemically to factors of political morale. In his discussion of the background to the abolitionist take-off in 1788 he implies that British opinion, like the British economy, had by this time entirely recovered from the American war. But defeat in North America was to be a lasting trauma for Britain's rulers and made a deep impact on every layer of public opinion; so far from evaporating in a few years it was to rankle and inspire for decades to come, and to bequeath a complex of sentiments that has yet to disappear entirely two centuries later! Seymour Drescher, *Capitalism and Antislavery: British mobilization in Comparative Perspective*, London 1986, see in particular pp. 140–2. The social dimension is also stressed in Betty Fladeland, *Abolitionists and Working Class Problems in the Age of Industrialization*, London 1984, pp. 1–16, for early British anti-slavery.

2. Joseph Priestley, *A Letter of Advice to those Dissenters who Conducted the Appeal to Parliament*, London 1773, quoted in Richard Burgess Barlow, *Citizenship and Conscience: a Study in the Theory and Practice of Religious Toleration in England during the 18th Century*, Philadelphia 1962, p. 197. For Blackstone's dictum and Mansfield's judgement see Barlow pp. 160–6.

3. D.H. Porter, *The Abolition of the Slave Trade in England*, Hamden 1970, pp. 36–7.

4. Roger Anstey, *The Atlantic Slave Trade and British Abolition*, pp. 233–54.

5. E.M. Hunt, 'The North of England Agitation for the Abolition of the Slave Trade, 1780–1800', Manchester University M.A. thesis, 1959, especially chapters 1–3. For the breadth of social support for abolition see pp. 244–5. Hunt notes that the fustian manufacturers supported abolition while 'the opponents to abolition in Manchester tended to be the dyers and calico printers as well as the dealers in African goods' (p. 77). Drescher brings out the innovatory role of Manchester in *Capitalism and Antislavery*, pp. 67–88.

6. Ottobah Cugoano, *Thoughts and Sentiments on the Evil and Wicked Traffic of the Slavery and Commerce of the Human Species*, London 1787, and *The Interesting Narrative of the Life of Olaudah Equiano, or Gustavus Vassa, the African: Written by Himself*, London 1789, 2 vols. For brief biographies of these outstanding anti-slavery advocates see Fryer, *Staying Power*, pp. 98–112.

7. Reginald Coupland, *Wilberforce. A Narrative*, Oxford 1923, p. 55.

8. Coupland, *Wilberforce*, pp. 144–5.

9. For analysis of the parliamentary supporters and opponents of abolition see Anstey, *The Atlantic Slave Trade and British Abolition*, pp. 281–5 and G.M. Ditchfield, 'Repeal, Abolition and Reform: a Study in the Interaction of Reforming Movements in the Parliament of 1790–6', in C. Bolt and S. Drescher, eds, *Anti-Slavery, Religion and Reform*, pp. 101–18.

10. Coupland, *Wilberforce*, p. 160. The extent of Scottish support for abolition reflected not only the Scottish contribution to the anti-slavery critique but, more generally, the strength of Nonconformity there, and resentment at the workings of the patronage system. For other aspects of abolitionist activity see Anstey, *The Atlantic Slave Trade and British Abolition*, pp. 289, 304–6, 315.

11. Ayling, *John Wesley*, pp. 263–4, 311n.

12. That the revolt in St Domingue briefly favoured abolition is clear from David Geggus, 'British Opinion and the Emergence of Haiti', in James Walvin, ed., *Slavery in British Society 1776–1846*, London 1982, pp. 123–49.

13. Joseph Evans Loftin, *The Abolition of the Danish Slave Trade*, Louisiana State University PhD thesis, 1977, see especially pp. 73–4; and Svend E. Green–Pedersen, 'The Economic Considerations behind the Danish Abolition of the Negro Slave Trade', in Gemery and Hogendorn, eds, *The Uncommon Market*, pp. 319–418.

14. Anstey, *The Atlantic Slave Trade and British Abolition*, pp. 286–320; Ditchfield, 'Repeal, Abolition or Reform', in Bolt and Drescher, *Anti-Slavery, Religion and Reform*, pp. 112–13.

15. Quoted in Anstey, *The Atlantic Slave Trade and British Abolition*, p. 276. Wilberforce's opposition to the slave trade earned him an undeserved reputation as a supporter of revolution. The French National Assembly elected him as an honorary member and down to the most recent times he is numbered by French historians as a foreign sympathiser with the revolution (for example, M. Vovelle, *La chute de la monarchie*, Paris 1974, p. 159). At the suggestion of Burke, Wilberforce joined a committee to aid French *émigré* priests (Coupland, *Wilberforce*, p. 158).

16. Quoted in James Walvin, 'British Popular Sentiment for Abolition', in Bolt and Drescher, *Anti-Slavery, Religion and Reform*, pp. 152–3.

17. For Burke on the slave trade see Davis, *The Problem of Slavery in Western Culture*, p. 398. For Burke on the outrageous proposal to repeal the Test Act see Barlow, *Citizenship and Conscience*, p. 287. From the regime's standpoint the Church of England's privileges and position were a matter of the greatest moment. After all the most radical phase of the Commonwealth, the Barebones Parliament, had been brought to an end by a proposal to abolish the tithes payable to the Church (Watts, *The Dissenters*, pp. 146–51). The American revolutionaries' success in disestablishing the Church was an ominous precedent.

18. Barlow, *Citizenship and Conscience*, p. 289. For divergent reactions to the French Revolution within the ranks of the Nonconformists see Watts, *The Dissenters*, pp. 478–87; Watts points out that abolition was one of the few questions which united 'rational Dissent' and Methodism.

19. Linda Colley, 'The Apotheosis of George III: Loyalty, Royalty and the British Nation', *Past and Present*, 102, 1984, pp. 94–129, especially pp. 114–16.

20. Coupland, *Wilberforce*, p. 188. David Geggus, who has made a thorough study of the British archives, concludes that British strategy in the West Indies was 'undoubtedly aimed at annexation and providing an indemnity for the costs of the war'. *Slavery, War and Revolution: The British Occupation of Saint Domingue*, Oxford 1982, p. 85. However, Geggus disputes the idea that the West Indian theatre had primacy for the British government.

21. Wilberforce, anxious as ever not to rock the boat, was cautious and intermittent in his opposition to the war and strove to maintain good relations with Pitt (Coupland, *Wilberforce*, pp. 184, 198–9, 209). He signally failed to combine his opposition to the war and his opposition to the slave trade by supporting the withdrawal of British occupation troops from St Domingue – this was left to the Foxite Opposition who tabled such a bill in 1797 but only to meet opposition from the supposed champion of abolition (Geggus, *Slavery, War and Revolution*, p. 213).

. Coupland, *Wilberforce*, pp. 213–28, 270–74; Anstey, *The Atlantic Slave Trade 3ritish Abolition*, pp. 329–42.

23. Coupland, *Wilberforce*, p. 324.

24. David Brion Davis, *The Problem of Slavery in the Age of Revolution*, pp. 350, 355.

25. Coupland, *Wilberforce*, pp. 325–7.

26. Quoted in Leonore Davidoff and Catherine Hall, *Family Fortunes: Men and Women of the English Middle Class 1780–1850*, London 1987, p. 429.

27. Compare C. Duncan Rice, 'Literary Sources and the Evolution of British Attitudes to Slavery', in Bolt and Drescher, *Anti-Slavery Religion and Reform*, pp. 319–34, especially pp. 323–5. See also Hulme, *Colonial Encounters*, pp. 175–224. Some critics have suggested that imperialist and racist notions were implicit in Defoe's fictions because of their travelogue form. One might as easily argue the opposite and cite the travelogue form of Equiano's memoir. In fact the narratives of both Defoe and Equiano may well have shared the common inspiration of Dissenting personal witness and testifying.

28. David Hume, 'Of National Character', *Essays*, London 1875, I, p. 252.

29. George Metcalf, Introduction to Edward Long, *History of Jamaica*, London 1970, I, p. xi.

30. Keith Thomas, *Man and the Natural World: Changing Attitudes in England 1500–1800*, Harmondsworth 1984, pp. 135–6; Jordan, *White Over Black*, pp. 482–511; Fryer, *Staying Power*, pp. 165–9; Nancy Stepan, *The Idea of Race in British Science*, London 1982.

31. Charles White, *An Account of the Regular Gradation in Man*, London 1799.

32. Generalising about popular racial attitudes in eighteenth century Britain is not easy; but see Jack Gratus, *The Great White Lie: Slavery, Emancipation and Changing Racial Attitudes*, who notes the still comparatively 'innocent' stereotyping of blacks at this time, see p. 188; see also Drescher, *Capitalism and Antislavery*, pp. 33–4, 228; for Quaker qualms at racial inter-marriage at this time see Duncan MacLeod, *Slavery, Race and the American Revolution*, Cambridge 1974, p. 160.

33. Quoted in Hulme, *Colonial Encounters*, p. 327. On class elements in racism see Benedict Anderson, *Imagined Communities*, London 1983, p. 136. David Hume observed: 'The skin, pores, muscles, and nerves of a day labourer are different from those of a man of quality; so are his sentiments, actions and manners. The different stations of life influence the whole fabric, external and internal; and these different stations arise necessarily, because uniformly, from the necessary and uniform principles of human nature.' David Hume, *A Treatise on Human Nature*, Oxford 1983, p. 402.

34. Bryan Edwards, *The History, Civil and Commercial, of the British Colonies in the West Indies*, 4 vols, London 1801.

35. For Canada see John Hope Franklin, *From Slavery to Freedom*, New York 1964, (2nd revised edn), pp. 357–61.

36. Though one French traveller, Brissot de Warville, did note the depreciation of blacks by white 'public opinion' (quoted in J.T. Main, *The Social Structure of Revolutionary America*, Princeton 1965, p. 1981). For a discussion of the pattern of discrimination see Jordan, *White Over Black*, pp. 406–26, and Leon Littwack, *North of Slavery: The Negro in the Free States, 1790–1860*, Chicago 1961.

V

The French Revolution
and the Antilles:
1789–93

Our very good friend the Marquis de la Fayette has entrusted to
my care the key of the Bastille . . . as a present to your Excellency
. . . I feel myself happy in being the person thro' whom the
Marquis has conveyed this early trophy of the spoils of despotism,
and the first ripe fruits of American principles transplanted in
Europe, to the great master and patron . . . That the principles of
America opened the Bastille is not to be doubted, and therefore
the key comes to the right place.

(Tom Paine to George Washington, May 1st 1790)

Soon, to announce morn
the sun will arise on her golden path,
soon shall superstition disappear,
soon the wise man will conquer.

The Magic Flute (1791), Mozart/Schickaneder

The morning comes, the night decays, the watchmen leave their stations;
The grave is burst, the spices shed, the linen wrapped up;
The bones of death, the cov'ring clay, the sinews shrunk and dry'd
Reviving shake, inspiring move, breathing, awakening,
Spring like redeemed captives when their bonds and bars are burst.
Let the slave grinding at the mill run out into the field,
Let him look up into the heavens and laugh in the bright air;

America (1793), William Blake

The colony of St Domingue

The colonial system of France's *ancien régime* was one of its most splendid achievements. Government, colonists and merchants had built the most diversified, technically advanced and well-fortified slave plantations in the New World. They had pioneered New World coffee cultivation, improved the variety of cane used for sugar-making, and extended St Domingue's capacity through elaborate irrigation works. A slave trade bounty and remission of duty on colonial re-exports had promoted an extraordinary development of the French slave plantations, helping to make them Europe's chief suppliers of plantation produce. Between 1770 and 1790 the slave population of the French Antilles rose from 379,000 to 650,000, while their exports reached 217.5 million *livres* (£9 million) in the year 1789, compared with British West Indian exports of about £5 million, produced by 480,000 slaves; in land area the French islands were twice as large as the British. The workings of the *exclusif* meant that as much as a half of the value of colonial produce accrued as mercantile profits to metropolitan interests; while British planters received premium prices for their sugar the French were subjected to monopolistic commercial exploitation. The brilliant prosperity of Bordeaux and Nantes derived from colonial commerce. With some 465,000 slaves St Domingue was the largest and most productive slave colony in the Caribbean in 1789; it had served as a privateer base throughout the century without ever itself suffering invasion. The colony's 30,000 whites and 28,000 or more free people of colour were organised and armed to defend slavery. Guadeloupe and Martinique were amongst the most productive and stable of the colonies of the Lesser Antilles. On Guadeloupe, together with its small island dependencies, there were 90,000 slaves, nearly 14,000 whites and 3,000 coloured *affranchis*; on Martinique there were 83,000 slaves, 10,600 whites and 5,000 *affranchis*. Nearly all free males between sixteen and sixty were armed. The colonial militias acted as auxiliaries to the regular garrisons – roughly 3,000 troops in St Domingue and the same number in the Windwards – and naval squadrons. French Guyana remained something of a backwater with only 10,000 slaves; even fewer were to be found on Ste Lucie and Trinidad, colonies turned over to France by the treaty of 1783. Louisiana, despite its French links, had been ceded to Spain; nevertheless the vigour of the island colonies nourished the dream that they could be stepping stones to a new empire on the mainland.[1]

In purely military and diplomatic terms French participation in the American War of Independence had achieved all that was hoped of it, isolating and defeating the traditional enemy. Since France was the main customer for North American tobacco there was commercial underpinning to the diplomatic and military alignment. Whatever the impasse of the French monarchy in the Old World, in the New World its alliance with the American Revolution had been an astonishingly bold stroke of policy and one apparently crowned with great success. The partisans of an enlightened reform of the political and financial structures of the monarchy were encouraged by American and colonial successes. Nor did they withhold respect, even admiration, from Britain's rulers who had acknowledged defeat with decorum, regained commercial access to North American markets and financed with ease the heavy costs of the war. By contrast French achievements overseas proved to be almost as disruptive in their effects and implications as the stubborn structures of privilege and caste power in France itself. Colonial and American entanglements made their own spectacular contribution to the crash of the *ancien régime* and the travail of the revolutionary order. Few contemporary observers missed the obsession with the New World which was characteristic of French statesmen, philosophers and economists in the eighteenth century, nor the impact of colonial controversies on alignments in the metropolis. The decision to back the revolt of the thirteen English North American colonies disastrously compounded the problems of the old order, with the huge costs of waging war across the Atlantic directly precipitating the final agony of royal finances and the example of representative government stimulating expectations in the French colonies as well as metropolis.[2]

The rapid growth of France's slave colonies in the years before 1789 made its own contribution to the instability of the *ancien régime*. Colonial wealth was a nesting ground of fractious and antagonistic interests prior to the revolution; afterwards it proved a precarious and unreliable support of the new system. Colonial wealth encouraged the pretensions of some awkward components of the absolutist order while the problems of colonial trade fostered the opposition of the commercial and manufacturing bourgeoisie. The Duc d'Orléans, whose self-seeking demagogy caused much mischief to the royalist cause, drew large revenues from the Antilles and stimulated the intrigues of a planter faction there. The Parlement at Bordeaux, which did so much to obstruct royal plans for reform and rationalisation, numbered several important colonial interests in its ranks. Almost to the last some royal financiers believed that large revenues, or fabulous loans, could be raised on the basis of the colonial boom. The dimensions of the colonial trade had been increased by a decree of 1784 which relaxed the *exclusif*, permitting the colonists to buy a wider range of supplies from North America and ending the special status of Bordeaux and Nantes. Most French merchants also saw their interests threatened by the Anglo–French Trade Treaty of 1786–7, since this permitted the British to encroach on the colonial trade with their new manufactures and their growing demand for raw cotton. The measures modifying the *exclusif* were 'generally and violently criticised' by maritime centres in the *cahiers* they drew up for the Estates General.[3] If the problems of the monarchy were compounded by colonial prosperity, then the fault lay with the former not the latter. The *ancien régime* was a fortress of privilege and not a forum for articulating and reconciling opposed interests, such as those generated by the development of the colonies. Some of those enriched by the colonies enjoyed access to the privileges bestowed by the *ancien régime*, others resented the increasing difficulty of gaining entry to the charmed circle. Either way colonial interests added to 'the disparity, the disaccord, the incoherence of the different parts of the monarchy' about which Calonne wrote in his ministerial memorandum to the King of 1786.[4] As was only natural, those involved in American properties or trade tended to be deeply influenced by the institutions and example of the United States. The aristocrats with colonial estates lacked genuinely feudal roots or well-founded bourgeois stability, but they felt themselves to be part of a new world in the making. Those creoles who pursued a military career often enlisted in the artillery regiments. In politics many colonial proprietors wavered between British and North American models, admiring the oligarchic solidity of 'illegitimate monarchy' but tempted by the expansive republicanism of the Virginians. British occupation of Guadeloupe and Martinique during the Seven Years War had greatly benefited many planters and merchants, while the more recent alliance with the North American rebels had nourished further commercial contacts. Colonial proprietors subscribed to the political clubs set up in the metropolis in 1787–8. A youthful minority tended to an excited but inconstant radicalism: bearing ancient names they wished to be distinguished by enlightenment and political influence rather than inherited privileges. Among the noble young colonial proprietors whose volatile commitment was to mark the Revolution were Charles Lameth, Alexandre Beauharnais and Louis Philippe Ségur.[5]

Colonial proprietors resident in the Antilles were understandably more content with the relaxation of the *exclusif* than were the merchants of the metropolis. But the decrees of 1784 which had liberalised trade were accompanied by regulations requiring planters and their managers to give a stricter accounting of their financial transactions and of the treatment of their slaves; these regulations were very unpopular with the colonial proprietors. The colonists habitually complained of the tyranny exercised by royal officials though in practice the effectiveness of metropolitan rule was greatly reduced by corruption and by a rapid turnover in the higher posts. In the 1780s St Domingue had eleven different Governors and five different Intendants. The last pre-revolutionary Intendant, Barbé de Marbois, displayed an efficiency and reforming zeal which alarmed the planters and estate managers. Barbé de Marbois proposed a reform of the laws which guaranteed the planters' property against seizure for debt. He also suspended the *conseil* at Cap Francais after it had repeatedly refused to register metropolitan edicts. The planters were encouraged to channel their representations through newly created Chambers of Agriculture and Commerce, but these were granted weaker powers than the *Conseils Supérieurs*. The colonists of St Domingue further resented what they saw as official favouritism towards Martinique and Guadeloupe. On these two islands the colonists were granted newly established representative Assemblies. Though these Assemblies had little power the process of electing representatives to them proved a startling innovation; the vote was given to all properly registered male *habitans* of sixteen years or over, a surprisingly low age limit.[6]

Antoine Barnave, who was to be the most influential exponent of colonial policy in the early years of the Revolution, wrote that the tremendous growth of maritime commerce and of the manufacturing centres had upset the equilibrium of a feudal society, with its ruling order based on landholding: 'a new distribution of wealth involves a new distribution of power', he declared.[7] For the most part the maritime bourgeoisie did indeed support the growing challenge to royal authority. Arthur Young noted after his visit in 1788: 'Nantes is as *enflamée* in the cause of liberty as any town in France can be.' A recent historian of the port points out that a demonstration of its citizens raising the classic demands of the Third Estate was led by one Cottin, who owned valuable property in the colonies.[8] A recent historian of the Revolution in Bordeaux writes, 'the Third in Bordeaux showed a thrusting and persistent desire for representation'.[9] The subsequent spread of revolutionary clubs owed much to the commercial nexus spreading out from the major maritime ports; this was as true of the Jacobins, with their roots in a Breton society, as of the Girondins, with their links to Bordeaux. As the Revolution developed the maritime bourgeois of the metropolis would find themselves increasingly at logger heads with their clients in the colonies. The latter's unpaid debts and zest for smuggling aroused mercantile hostility. For the maritime bourgeoisie projects of colonial autonomy spelt a mortal threat to the *exclusif*. Yet in the early stages of the Revolution there were bonds of common interest uniting merchants and colonial proprietors. Both wished for political representation and both had a stake in the colonial system. Furthermore many merchants owned a share in a plantation, while many colonial proprietors, as absentees living in the metropolis, opposed the autonomism of the resident colonists.

According to one contemporary source there were no less than one hundred and fifty owners of colonial property amongst the thousand or so members of the Constituent Assembly of 1789. The numbers of those with interests linked to colonial commerce or administration would have been even larger. The observations of Barnave quoted above have seemed to some historians a striking anticipation of Marx's concept of 'bourgeois revolution'. Yet in fact the implications are rather different, since they highlight the economic vulnerability of the French bourgeoisie. The Constituent Assembly was indeed a predominantly bourgeois body, in the most literal sense of the term, with a significant proportion of its urban-based, property-owning members dependent on overseas trade.[10] But the French bourgeoisie lacked the broad base and security of its more developed British rival. The salience of commerce and colonies reflected the comparative weakness of the internal market and domestic circuits of accumulation.

The planters and merchants of the Antilles were split into two broad camps on the eve of the Revolution: those whose primary links were with the metropolis and those, often creoles, who aspired to autonomy or even separation. The pro-metropolitan complex included absentee proprietors and their representatives, the principals and agents of the French merchant houses, and the members of the civilian apparatus of colonial administration. Governors and senior military officers, while loyal to the Crown, often had ties to the large planters. It was not uncommon for those holding senior colonial posts to acquire plantations and other property: the membership list of the colonial proprietors club formed in 1789 – the Club Massiac – reads like a roll call of those responsible for French colonial administration, with such names as Choiseul, Bongars, Gallifet, Du Chilleau, and Malouet. The main Caribbean strongholds of the metropolitan complex were Cap Français, in St Domingue, and St Pierre, in Martinique. The former, with a population of 15,000 and the rich northern plain of St Domingue as its hinterland, was the most well-appointed of the French Caribbean ports: its theatre could seat 1,200 people. However, the administrative capital of St Domingue was Port au Prince in the West, a region where there were more medium-sized properties and a larger free coloured population. St Domingue's main smuggling centres were found in the South, where plantation development was still in an early phase.[11]

The French Governors commanded a formidable armed force; the regular garrisons included locally recruited troops, such as the coloured contingents of the *Légion de St Domingue* which had acquitted themselves well in North America. The whole apparatus of colonial government was a sub-branch of the Navy Ministry. The colonial establishments had swollen during the years of war with Britain (1777–83) and seemed more than adequate to maintain slave subordination and to deter invasion. Colonial administrators tended to distrust the white creoles and the white colonists were prone to envy the success of the free people of colour. While the great majority of St Domingue's 780 sugar estates were owned by whites about 2,000 coffee estates in the West and South were owned by people of colour; sugar estates were far more valuable though also more likely to be encumbered with debt. A tacit understanding often existed between colonial officialdom and the free coloured population since both distrusted the proclivities of the white colonists.

The white creole grouping in the French Antilles included most *cultivateurs*, or resident planters, together with merchants engaged in the legal or illegal trade with the United States or Britain. A high proportion of white creoles had some property or a profession while by extention this 'creole' grouping also included proprietors who, though born in France, had decided to settle permanently in the colonies. The *petits blancs* were, to begin with, not clearly aligned with either the metropolitan or the creole groupings; they included many recent immigrants who hoped to make money and return to France. While many *petits blancs* cherished links with France, they usually had little love for metropolitan officials, whom they associated with ministerial 'despotism' and favouritism towards mulattos. For the creoles memories of the clashes of the 1760s had been reactivated by confrontations of the 1780s. Commercial contacts with the British and North Americans stimulated the desire for free trade and political autonomy. Finally there were planters heavily indebted to French merchants, who dreamed of separation from the metropolis.

In St Domingue free people of colour were almost as numerous as white colonists, indeed possibly more numerous. The size of the free coloured population is not fully shown by official figures, which placed it at 25,000 because acquiring a proper certificate of manumission was a cumbersome and expensive business; in addition to those who held such certificates there were thousands of persons of colour who were free *de facto* rather than *de jure*; some of the former were known as the *libres de savane*, who were free to move within a given region but still beholden to a master who had not formally manumitted them. The *maréchaussée*, a force devoted to catching runaway slaves and supplementing plantation security, was recruited largely from the free people of colour. The free coloured population also included a layer of proprietors who in St Domingue between them owned about 100,000 slaves; nowhere else in the Americas did those of partly African descent figure so importantly in the ranks of the propertied classes. The *petits blancs* and white *cultivateurs* were prone to resent the success of the coloured proprietor or lawyer, and their rancour was not diminished if the latter, as often happened, bore the distinguished name of a French father. In the Lesser Antilles the free population of colour was proportionately not so large as in St Domingue and racial tensions amongst the free correspondingly less pronounced. But while racial rivalry was already a well-established theme of colonial society, especially in St Domingue, the free people of colour were still an integral component of the slave-owning class and of the apparatus of slave subjection.[12]

Thus clamped on top of the slave economy, there was a complex of interests, formed by the intersecting fields of force of a colonial and mercantile system, an aristocratic political order, a racial caste hierarchy, and a highly unequal distribution of private property within both the white and free coloured population. In the French Antilles of 1788 the social antagonisms rooted in slave exploitation and oppression were overlaid by conflicts stemming from this interlocking super-structure of control. The revolution weakened the grip of the metropolis and stimulated fierce factional strife, but this was a protracted and complex process. The colonial regime had survived repeated battering in the wars and commotions of the previous century; and it was so vastly profitable that it would not be abandoned until every resource and expedient had been exhausted.

There were no major slave uprisings in the French Antilles in the 1770s and 1780s. In St Domingue a stream of runaways took advantage of the colony's extensive and mountainous interior and common border with Spanish Santo Domingo. Maroon bands operated in the Artibonite in the North-east, in the area known as Plymouth in the South, and along the border. Smaller, but also more oppositional, than their Jamaican equivalents, the maroon bands of St Domingue still appeared to pose no threat to the slave order in 1789. Guadeloupe and Martinique are the largest of the islands of the Lesser Antilles; the former had a rugged interior zone where maroons held out while on Martinique there was a plantation uprising in 1789. But once again the formidable resources of the colonial social formation were quite sufficient to contain such challenges.[13]

In 1788, just as the pre-Revolution unfolded, an abolitionist society, the *Amis des Noirs*, was set up in Paris and began to circulate anti-slavery literature. Unlike the colonial factions the *Amis des Noirs* supposedly represented a general rather than particular interest. Not only did they declare themselves philanthropists, but if there was a 'hidden interest' animating their activities it was that of the integrity of the nation and

Empire as a whole, with these entities being understood in an inclusive rather than exclusive sense. Abolitionism was a cause that drew support from radical aristocrats impatient with caste distinctions, financial bureaucrats hostile to corporate obstruction, colonial officials worried by the security of the plantations and the loyalty of the planters, clerics concerned with the construction of a more humane social order, and members of the liberal professions committed to progress. The initial supporters of organised abolitionism inclined to be somewhat eccentric members of the ruling order, with several being of Protestant extraction, others linked to the world of high finance and many enjoying personal links with England or the United States. But while the the *Amis des Noirs* were sometimes accused of being English agents, they saw themselves as the most enlightened representatives of a truly national interest, extending civic belonging to all inhabitants of the Empire. In a social formation of rigidly separated orders and estates, each with their own privileges and exemptions, those sympathetic to abolitionism were also the champions of an overriding national authority, before which every citizen would have equal rights. Naturally the *Amis* laid claim to the French anti-slavery tradition.[14]

The tenor of French writing on slavery had often been more radical, if also more rhetorical, than that to be found in Britain or the United States, and less inclined to take the form of the systematic moral tract. Attacks on slavery had been launched in the best-known works of Montesquieu, Rousseau and Raynal. The Abbé Raynal saw himself as an exponent of France's true colonial interests. He claimed that slaves were treated better in the French than in the British colonies but he was nevertheless concerned that huge aggregations of plantation slaves endangered the colonial order. While he urged a relaxation of trade restrictions, he was not sympathetic to colonial independence. In a new edition of his *History* published in 1781 he added some proposals for achieving the gradual emancipation of slaves by freeing those born to slave mothers after a twenty-five-year apprenticeship period; Pechmeja's extreme anti-slavery passages were retained as a warning of what might happen if a moderate reform was not adopted. The measures proposed by Raynal would give the colonial state new power and authority in its dealing with the planters. Raynal was on good terms with senior officials of the Colonial Bureau and for a time in receipt of a subsidy from this quarter. The regulations of 1784 fell well short of Raynal's proposals, but planter opposition to them was provoked by the suspicion that they were simply the first instalment of a perilous official experiment in philanthropy.[15]

The practical bent of French abolitionism received more disinterested expression in the writings of Condorcet, and in particular in an essay first published in 1781 and subsequently reprinted by the *Amis des Noirs*, of which he was a founder member, in 1788. Condorcet united in his person the various strands which comprised French abolitionism in the early revolutionary period. He was an aristocrat of Protestant extraction and, prior to the Revolution, Secretary of the Academy, an associate of Turgot, briefly Director of the Mint, and an outstanding advocate of social and educational reform. One of the last of the *philosophes*, Condorcet lived to play an important part in the politics of the revolution, as a writer, as President of the Legislative Assembly, and as a constitutional and educational authority. Like other enlightened aristocrats he detested caste privileges, seeing in them trammels of the *ancien régime*. Condorcet's essay on slavery, though grounded in a humanist universalism, was far more concerned with the realities of social life in the colonies than the philosophical disquisitions of Millar and Beattie. He argued that slavery was an intolerable injury to human nature but that, for this very reason, emancipation should be approached with great circumspection. Slaves would need a lengthy tutelage before they were ready to exercise the responsibilities of freedom. Planters should be obliged to improve conditions for their slaves, freeing those born to slave mothers at twenty-five years of age, and laying the basis for a new agro-industrial pattern in which tenant or smallholding cultivators supplied sugar cane or unhusked coffee to planter-manufacturers. Condorcet insisted that it was social environment, not ethnicity, which shaped human potential. He concluded his pamphlet with a plea for the removal of the disabilities placed on Jews and Protestants as well as blacks.[16]

About a quarter of the original sponsors of the *Amis* were senior financial officials, including five Tax Farmers-General, two Under-Secretaries of the Finance Ministry, and five senior officials of the *Régie General*. Presumably these men, themselves under attack as social parasites, hoped to demonstrate their benevolence and public-spiritedness. More specifically they may have seen slavery and the slave trade as the unacceptable face of the old order, the perfect symbol of its infestation by special interests. As nobles most slave traders were only lightly taxed; indeed, under the *acquits de Guinée* bounty arrangement, they were in receipt of a substantial subsidy, rising from 1.5 million *livres* in 1786 to over 2.8 million in 1788. The *Amis* called for the immediate ending of this subsidy pending abolition of the slave trade itself by negotiation with Britain. Doubtless a more authoritative metropolis would also derive more revenue from the booming commerce of the colonies.[17]

If Condorcet was the most eminent intellectual sponsor of the *Amis*, its first organiser was the journalist Brissot de Warville, whose visits to

England and the United States had acquainted him with anti-slavery currents in those countries. He was also a close associate of Clavière, a financier of Protestant extraction. Brissot's links with the world of high finance did not inhibit him from composing an essay on property rights which stressed their arbitrary social character – indeed he got close to anticipating Proudhon's formula that 'property is theft'. Under the *ancien régime*, of course, legal property rights included seigneuries and public offices as well as human chattels.[18] Brissot aspired to be a visionary social philosopher and, beyond the convenience of the retainer he received from Clavière, may have felt that in this capacity he was a kindred spirit to the high financier, as the speculations of both vaulted over the awkward clumps of property built into the *ancien régime.*

With the calling of the Estates General the *Amis des Noirs* sent an anti-slavery circular to every *baillage* responsible for electing deputies. Partly as a result forty-nine out of about six hundred *cahiers de doléances* contained some proposal directed at the slave trade or favouring gradual emancipation. Perhaps significantly, twenty-eight of these attacks figured in *cahiers* submitted by the nobility or clergy and were rarer in the *cahiers* submitted by otherwise radical sections of the Third Estate. The maritime bourgeoisie had little inclination at this time towards abolitionism.[19]

These first representations were to be the high-water mark of the strictly anti-slavery work of the *Amis des Noirs*. While continuing to deplore the excesses of slave-traders and slave-owners, the members of the Society henceforth concentrated their main attacks on the cost of the slave trade subsidy, and on attempts to exclude free people of colour from political and social rights. In fact the *Amis* never became a campaigning body like its English counterpart. Its members were drawn from the salons of polite society and their chief activity was to lend their name to the Society's propaganda. In fact the Massiac Club, representing the colonial proprietors, was to be far more active as a campaigning force, sending out a stream of pamphlets and agents to the important political centres. Brissot, the Abbé Grégoire and other prominent members of the *Amis* advanced its aims in the course of their activity as leading protagonists of the revolution. Indeed part of the reason for the Society's low level of activity was certainly the wider pre-occupations of those who had founded it. If in the early months they saw in abolitionism a symbol of the struggle to purify the French monarchy, they were soon caught up in events in which the nature of the regime had to be addressed quite directly. Henceforth colonial controversies were important because they tested the scope of civic and suffrage rights rather than because slavery was at issue. In the years 1789–93 the British Parliament repeatedly debated the slave trade without taking any consequent action. During these same years the French assemblies discussed almost every aspect of the colonial regime other than slavery. Paradoxically by the time the Convention decreed the abolition of colonial slavery in 1794 the *Amis des Noirs* no longer functioned and most of its former members no longer played a role. It is almost as if enlightened abolitionism was as much part of the old order as the *exclusif* and the *acquits de Guinée*. Only once this whole super-structure was in ruins could slave emancipation be adopted in the metropolis. To explain why we must turn to the complex, multi-cornered contest of the intervening years.

The Governor of Guadeloupe was shocked at the insolence and assertiveness of the members of the colony's new Assembly in 1788. But the first colonists to seek a role in metropolitan politics were those from the north of St Domingue who, angered at the suspension of the *conseil supérieur* of Cap Français and the absence of any colony-wide assembly, petitioned in 1788 for colonial representation in the Estates General. The Marquis Gouy d'Arsy, an absentee proprietor linked to the Duc d'Orléans, formed a committee in Paris which associated itself with this demand; the Oriental Lodge of the Freemasons, of which Orléans was president, was heavily involved in this faction. The colonial ministry, headed by La Luzerne, formerly Governor of St Domingue (1786–7), successfully opposed this petition, anticipating that colonial representatives would simply undermine ministerial authority and put their own special interests above the need for rational reform – the former *conseil* at Le Cap had enjoyed a veto over fiscal innovations. Notwithstanding this opposition several thousand white colonists proceeded to elect deputies for St Domingue.[20]

When the Estates General met in May 1789 Gouy d'Arsy and other supporters of the proposal for colonial representation made a direct appeal, first to the Second Estate (many of the colonists were nobles), and then to the Third. The latter eventually accepted the principle of colonial representation largely because Gouy d'Arsy and his friends were prepared to support the Third in its battle with the King for majority representation; after declaring themselves ready to swear the tennis court oath the colonial deputies were admitted as *suppléants* and a report on colonial representation was commissioned from the Credentials Committee. Gouy d'Arsy requested that St Domingue be allowed twenty deputies to take into account the colony's commercial importance and total population. Mirabeau, who had endorsed the first statement put out by the *Amis*, made a response that echoed the debate in the US Constitutional Convention:

You claim representation proportionate to the number of inhabitants. The free blacks are proprietors and tax payers, and yet they have not been allowed to vote. And as for the slaves, either they are men or they are not; if the colonists consider them men, let them free them and make them electors and eligible for seats; if the contrary is the case, have we, in apportioning deputies according to the population of France, taken into consideration the number of our horses and mules?[21]

The Duc de la Rochefoucauld, another of those aristocrats who had been prepared both to support the *Amis des Noirs* and to join the Third Estate, attacked slavery without irony or qualification, but the generality of the deputies were alarmed at such talk. Eventually the Assembly voted to admit six colonial deputies as full members and the remainder as *suppléants*. In subsequent sessions deputies were also granted to Martinique, Guadeloupe and the other French slave colonies, until there were a total of seventeen colonial deputies. The deputies of St Domingue had triumphed not only over the objections of the Colonial Ministry and the *Amis des Noirs* but also over opposition from the more conservative Club Massiac.

The Massiac Club, formed at the Hôtel Massiac in July 1789 in the aftermath of the first debate on colonial representation, comprised a group of the largest colonial proprietors who distrusted Gouy d'Arsy's opportunism and penchant for anti-ministerial rhetoric. It opposed the call for colonial deputies on the ground that this would expose delicate colonial issues to the hazards of debate in the Assembly. Several members of the Club Massiac were themselves members of the Assembly or otherwise politically influential and felt quite competent to represent colonial issues in the metropolis themselves. These included Pierre-Victor Malouet and Moreau de Saint-Méry. Malouet was to emerge as a leader of the *monarchiens*, who accepted the destruction of feudal privilege and absolutism but thereafter rallied to the King as the essential guarantee of property and order. Moreau de Saint-Méry, an enlightened colonial magistrate and friend of the Abbé Raynal, was President of the Electors of Paris. In this latter capacity Saint-Méry formally received the keys of the Bastille after its seizure (these keys were shortly to be presented to another slaveholder, George Washington, through the good offices of Lafayette and Thomas Paine). Despite such liberal and revolutionary credentials Saint-Méry was to remain a determined defender of the slave system. Putting aside its reservations about the colonial deputies the Club Massiac decided that it must defend them when they came under attack from members of the *Amis des Noirs*. Some three or four hundred absentee proprietors adhered to the club and enabled it to finance a press campaign against the *Amis*.

Unlike the colonial deputies the Club Massiac rigorously abstained from criticism of the *exclusif* and strove to maintain a common position with deputies from the Atlantic ports.[22]

The events of 1789 aroused great enthusiasm among the colonists of the French Caribbean. The storming of the Bastille had an electric effect on the opponents of 'ministerial despotism' in the colonies. According to one account:

> Crowds of *petits blancs* gathered in the streets of [Cap Français] and discussed the Revolution and what it meant for the colony. The tri-coloured cockade was adopted amid wild transports of joy, and government officials who refused to wear it or to take the 'civic oath' were submitted to ill-treatment and violence. But, on the other hand, the mulattos were forbidden by the *petits blancs* to wear the sacred emblem.[23]

A group of patriot planters formed a National Guard under the captaincy of Bacon de Chevalrie. This 'turbulent nobleman' soon evinced autonomist inclinations. The National Guard arrested the Intendant, Barbé de Marbois, and put him on board a boat for France. By November 2nd a Colonial Assembly had been elected by the white *habitans* and vested itself with full powers of internal self-government. The Western and Southern provinces of St Domingue soon followed suit. These assemblies hesitated formally to abrogate the *exclusif*, but henceforth the colonial system became increasingly prone to leaks. The colonial assemblies invoked decrees which enabled them to import flour from North America in time of need; since the metropolitan Assembly had banned the export of wheat it was in a weak position to object. The real problem in the colonies was that of enforcement. The officials who remained were not prepared to offend colonists who still declared formal allegiance to monarch and metropolis. In Martinique the threat to the *exclusif* came to the surface in a bitter factional dispute between mercantile representatives from St Pierre and planter representatives from the rest of the island – in a bid to secure an overall majority the planters suggested that the parishes should be allotted representatives in proportion to their populations, with slaves counting, as in the United States, as three-fifths of a person. In this island an interim Governor who urged the mulattos to adopt the tricolour was also driven out after objections from the *petits blancs* of St Pierre. Reports of the work of the *Amis des Noirs* caused much consternation in the islands.[24]

The colonists tended to exaggerate greatly the impact of the propaganda produced by the *Amis*. The latter had lost the battle over colonial representation in the National Assembly and failed even to obtain a debate on slavery or the slave trade. Colonial issues were referred to specialist committees, on the grounds of their delicacy. Abolitionist advocates like the Abbé Grégoire had to content themselves with anti-slavery interjections in debates on other subjects, and were then shouted down for their pains by other deputies. The *Amis* were little more successful outside the Assembly, but their failure to make headway did not mean that they ceased to be a source of acute anxiety to the white colonists. The society did circulate a new edition of Condorcet's essay as well as translations of pamphlets by Cugoano and Clarkson.[25] Condorcet and Brissot were prominent contributors to the revolutionary press, where they were to publicise arguments that had been referred by the Assembly to consideration by its colonial committee. The white colonists were alarmed at the thought that copies of the abolitionist pamphlets, or of issues of the *Patriote Français*, might find their way to the Antilles.

The issue taken up most vigorously by the *Amis* was that of the civic rights of free people of colour. The colonial assemblies, representing the white colonists, were concerned because free mulattos were far more likely to read, and be influenced by, the statements of the *Amis* than slaves incarcerated on the plantations. The literary activity of the *Amis* was directed at metropolitan legislators and opinion rather than at inciting rebellion in the colonies; but the colonists were concerned at results not intentions.

The ineffectiveness of the *Amis* in the National Assembly chiefly reflected the strength of commercial and manufacturing interests with a stake in the prosperity of the slave colonies. Such interests had a veto power not only in the Assembly but also in the Revolutionary Clubs. A historian of the latter writes:

> In spite of their oft-expressed devotion for liberty and equality, the clubs long remained indifferent to the horrors of slavery and the slave trade . . . I have unearthed no evidence that any provincial Jacobin Circle corresponded with the *Amis des Noirs* prior to 1791. Indeed to have done so in a port city where the foundation and sustenance of the economy was colonial commerce would have alienated merchants and workers.[26]

The attitude of commercial deputies towards the colonies was one of watchful suspicion. The merchant houses were naturally well-informed about developments in the islands and were perfectly aware of the danger represented by autonomism and separatism. But there was some reason to believe that only a minority of planters and merchants based in the colonies were tempted to slip loose from the metropolis and that this minority could be restrained by the patriotic inclinations of the majority of colonists and officials. Abolitionist provocations were to be avoided since they would encourage the autonomist reflex. However, this willingness to defer to the white colonists was itself conditional on loyal observance of metropolitan regulations by the latter, failing which sanctions would be looked to.

The initial rapport between many white colonists and members of the metropolitan clubs reflected the appeal to both of revolutionary ideology as well as the link of colonial interest. Many *petits blancs* inclined to the more radical wing of the Revolution because they wished personal rather than property rights to be decisive for the exercise of political rights. In the colonies a property qualification would have the effect of enfranchising the stratum of well-to-do free men of colour while disenfranchising many white colonists. So far as many colonial Jacobins were concerned, the people of colour were a species of foreigner with no entitlement to political rights. Metropolitan Jacobins accepted this in a more or less unthinking way, at least to begin with. There were few blacks or mulattos in France; perhaps a few thousand, certainly less than England's *circa* 15,000. On the other hand, the fierce anti-ministerial radicalism of the colonial Jacobins made them welcome allies. The new sense of national identity that the Revolution helped to foster had a messianic quality, which oscillated between the inclusive and the exclusive depending on the conjuncture. When the Revolution was on the offensive citizenship was open to all mankind, at its limit even to women and blacks as well; but as the revolutionary tide receded 'ready-made' social identifications asserted themselves at the expense of the more generous new civic definitions.

The basic lines of colonial policy in the period from the autumn of 1789 to near the end of 1791 were set by the so-called 'triumvirate' which dominated the National Assembly. Adrien Duport, Alexandre Lameth and Antoine Barnave emerged as leaders by dint of a responsible patriotism and constitutional monarchism well attuned to the aspirations of the Third Estate and of the latter's supporters in the other two orders. These men were also sympathetic to the aims of enlightened American planters, so long as they did not challenge the *exclusif*. The Lameth family itself, of course, held large estates in St Domingue. Barnave attached himself to the Lameths, living at their Paris Hôtel. The leader of the patriots in St Domingue, Bacon de Chevalerie, was a cousin to Barnave, which may have given the triumvirate an inside perspective on colonial problems. Duport was a leading member of the Club of Thirty, whose propagation of American models and ideals had made its own contribution to the ideological crisis of the old regime.

The basic aim of the triumvirate's colonial policy was to foster the alliance between commercial and planting interests, as a bulwark against both King and populace. The Declaration of the Rights of Man gave ideal expression to the project of the triumvirate; it could not be openly repudiated without jeopardising the prospects for a stable post-absolutist order. While colonial policy was important, it was subordinate to the triumvirate's overriding preoccupation of conserving the gains of 1789 and the fragile new ruling bloc.

Barnave was prepared to adapt revolutionary principles to protect the 'internal regime' of the colonies but not to jeopardise the 'external regime' furnished by the *exclusif*, and the principle of metropolitan sovereignty over them. In October 1789 La Luzerne, the Colonial Minister, submitted a memorandum to the Assembly arguing for separate colonial constitutions, designed to safeguard their special property regimes. The triumvirate was prepared to entertain such a proposal so long as colonial powers were strictly limited to internal affairs. Alexandre Lameth supported a deputy from Guadeloupe, Louis de Curt, who proposed the setting up of a commission which would devise constitutions for the colonies which would guarantee the 'agricultural and commercial property' of the Antilles – a pleasing euphemism for slavery and colonialism. Some members of the Massiac Club would have preferred to see colonial policy left entirely in the hands of the Ministry but, with reports coming in of unrest in the colonies, they were unable to prevent the Assembly taking responsibility into its hands, at least to the extent of accepting Curt's proposal. The Colonial Commission established by the Assembly had twelve members, each elected by a simple majority vote of the whole Assembly. Those elected included Lameth and Barnave, together with two colonial deputies, two absentee colonial proprietors, four deputies from maritime centres, a naval officer and a deputy from Rennes. Barnave was selected as reporter for this committee; twenty-eight years of age he was already one of the Assembly's leading orators. The method of election had ensured that no supporter of the *Amis* had been elected to the new body. Colonial interests had scored a notable victory, though factional tension meant that not all appreciated this fact.[27]

The Committee on Colonies was established on March 4th 1790 and produced its constitutional recommendations within four days. News from the islands had prompted a sense of urgency. Petitions from the colonies and from the maritime centres demanded repudiation of the threat to slavery and the slave trade implied by the abolitionist sentiments of some deputies; the Assembly was warned that servile revolt and colonial secession would result if such repudiation was not forthcoming. Articles appeared in the Paris press warning that the overthrow of colonial slavery would lead to the break-up of estates and the distribution of property in France. It was said that Brissot would not be satisfied until five or six *enfants du Congo* sat as legislators of France.[28] Bordeaux dispatched a squadron of its Patriotic Army to the capital to demand assurances that the social order of the colonies be safe from any tampering by the Assembly. The colonial report introduced by Barnave contained a guarantee no less categorical for its studious avoidance of embarrassing references: 'the National Assembly does not intend to make any innovations in any of the branches of commerce between France and the colonies, whether direct or indirect; it puts colonists and their property under the special safeguard of the nation and declares guilty of treason whoever seeks to foment risings against them.'[29] The report granted internal self-government to the colonies, but insisted that they could make no permanent changes in commercial regulations without the sanction of the National Assembly and that the political process should be conducted under the tutelage of duly appointed colonial officials.

When presented to the Assembly the pledge given to the colonies' 'indirect trade' and to the colonists' 'property' was greeted with noisy enthusiasm by the deputies linked to colonial and commercial interests. Two supporters of the *Amis* tried to speak on the report but were shouted down with calls for an immediate vote. The report was forthwith adopted by acclamation. The Committee on Colonies now proceeded to draw up instructions concerning implementation of the decree. The most delicate question concerned the procedures to be adopted in the election of the colonial assemblies. The National Assembly had received a number of representations on behalf of the free people of colour, urging that they be given the right to 'active citizenship' on the same terms as white colonists. There was a small but well-established mulatto grouping in France which, with the help of the *Amis des Noirs*, ensured that the question of mulatto rights came before the Assembly. Among the leaders of this group were two lawyers: Julien Raimond and Vincent Ogé. These men were well educated and respectable – Raimond was the legitimate son of a marriage between a planter and a coloured woman – but nevertheless the services of a white advocate were engaged to place the petition before the Assembly and its Colonial Committee. It was couched in sufficiently moderate and persuasive terms to make an impact on both bodies. The free people of colour were evidently a crucial component of the colonial social order. The *maréchausée* and the *Légion* depended upon them, while in some parts of the south and west of St Domingue the majority of estates were in the hands of coloured proprietors. To exclude men of colour who met the financial criteria for 'active' citizenship (that is, voting and office-holding) would be a gratuitous provocation to a section of the colonial population with a reputation for loyalty to the metropolis. But as soon as this issue was raised the deputies from St Domingue and the Club Massiac argued that it should be referred to the colonial assemblies themselves and that the National Legislature should not try to adjudicate such sensitive questions. They warned that the good effect of the declaration on colonists' property would be entirely undone if mulatto rights were foisted on the colonies. The triumvirate wished to defer to colonial anxieties without sacrificing their authority. Barnave eventually produced a vague formula relating to the colonial franchise which, since it avoided direct reference to racial distinctions, did not positively endorse caste discrimination nor concede a free hand to the white colonists. The colonial assemblies were to be voted on by parishes: 'All persons aged twenty-five years and upwards, possessing real estate or, in default of such property, domiciled for two years in the parish and paying taxes, shall meet and form the parish assembly.'[30] The colonial officials and local notables could be left to exclude those who did not fit. Nevertheless some colonial deputies remained dissatisfied and warned that failure to be quite specific in excluding the *gens de couleur* from 'active citizenship' would have disastrous consequences. Neither Barnave nor the Assembly heeded these prophetic warnings. The full fury of the racial animosities of the colonial whites may not have been appreciated. The social formation of the metropolis did not generate this species of communal antagonism. As for the colonial proprietors, those who resided in France often sounded, as did Lameth, like members of the *Amis des Noirs*. Moreover the colonial deputies were not unanimous. Arthur Dillon from Martinique declared that mulatto rights would cause no problem in his colony.[31]

Barnave, in making his fateful decision on this matter, also had to consider the political cost of appearing to flout ideals, and practical arrangements, recently agreed for the metropolis. Giving direction and coherence to the deliberations of such a large and inexperienced body as the National Assembly was no easy task. The Declaration of the Rights of Man had been adopted as the Assembly's Charter. It conferred legitimacy on the new order and was central to the so-called 'national catechism' in which citizens were to be instructed.[32] With some difficulty the Assembly majority reconciled the Declaration of Rights to a franchise restricted to tax-payers and a rule whereby only property-owners, or those paying more than 52 *livres* yearly in taxes, could qualify as a deputy. The democratic objections of the Abbé Grégoire and of Robespierre were answered by the argument that 'active citizenship' could only be responsibly conceded to shareholders in the national enterprise and control of public funds could only be conceded to those who principally provided them. The triumvirate would have confused its followers and compromised its credibility if it had urged the Assembly openly to flout the 'national catechism' or if it had recommended constitutional principles for the colonies which explicitly replaced the property qualification by that of skin colour. By the same token many of the leaders of the democratic opposition – Grégoire, Robespierre, Reubel and others – were in a position to avenge their defeats on the definition of 'active citizenship' by their vigilant defence of mulatto rights. The sincerity of their commitment to 'the Rights of Man' only added to the zeal with which they assailed any equivocation or inconsistency in the formulas of the colonial committee. Barnave's compromise was eventually accepted by the Assembly after a considerable debate. Though its studied ambiguity was attacked by democrats and abolitionists it did not supply the white colonists with the clear-cut guide-lines they were seeking and was bound to stimulate conflict between rival colonial factions.

The planter faction in Martinique was skilfully led by the thirty-year-old Louis–Francois Du Buc. This man was a descendant of the leader of the Gaoulé – a famous colonial rebellion of 1717 – and the son of Jean–Baptiste Du Buc, a friend of Raynal and *premier commis* of the colonial department in Choiseul's Ministry in the 1760s. Louis–Francois Du Buc and other large planters on Martinique eventually succeeded in dominating the island's Assembly, in winning the support of the Governor and in decreeing, with the latter's support, temporary suspension of many of the provisions of the *exclusif*. This latter action provoked intense hostility from the merchants of St Pierre, who alleged that planters like Du Buc were seeking to evade their debts to French merchants, and opposition from the Intendant, Foullon d'Ecottier – the latter was son of the Comptroller General of Finances in the metropolis. When a detachment of the mulatto militia was massacred by the *petits blancs* in St Pierre, Du Buc was able to persuade the Governor to send in garrison troops to arrest those responsible. Sixty of the *petits blancs* were deported to France on the grounds that they were recent arrivals without a domicil in the colony. Though his departure was more dignified the Intendant was also persuaded to return to the metropolis. Du Buc's success was soon menaced, however, by a patriotic sedition amongst the garrison troops who were persuaded that the *petits blancs* had been dealt with in an unjust and arbitrary fashion by a Governor and Colonial Assembly that had little loyalty to France or its revolution. Following this mutiny the Patriots regained possession of St Pierre; the Colonial Assembly and the Governor were obliged to withdraw to the island's interior. On neighbouring Guadeloupe there were also tensions between *grands blancs* and Patriots but there was no powerful mercantile faction; St Pierre was, in effect, the commercial centre of the French Iles du Vent, serving Guadeloupe as well as Martinique (to the French at this time these were both Windward Islands, compared with the 'Leeward' St Domingue). The colonial establishment in Guadeloupe was also weaker: in any case the Governor, De Clugny, and the militia commander, De Gommier, were both themselves creoles. The arrival of the decree and instructions of March 1790 brought more comfort to Du Buc and the Colonial Assembly than to the mercantile faction since they had already won over the Governor, who would be responsible for applying the metropolitan measures. In the Iles du Vent the creole planter faction had no objection to conceding civic rights to a few wealthy mulattos and was quite prepared to use the free people of colour as a counter-weight to the patriotic *petits blancs*.[33]

In the French Windwards the March decree and instructions proved compatible with planter hegemony, some concessions to the free mulattos and a moderate autonomism because this suited the inclination of the main metropolitan officials there. But in St Domingue concessions, whether to the mulattos or to planter autonomism, had more explosive implications given the larger absolute and relative size of its free mulatto community and the vast commercial significance of its trade. In the French Windwards whites outnumbered free people of colour by two to one. The position of the mulattos of St Domingue, who were richer as well as more numerous, was strengthened by the return to the colony of several wealthy coloured proprietors – men such as Pierre Pinchinat, J.B. Lapointe and J.B. Villatte – who had been accustomed to respectful treatment in France. Vincent Ogé, the lawyer who had sought to vindicate mulatto rights before the National Assembly, also returned to the colony via London, where he raised money from Clarkson and the Abolition Society. Ogé also visited the United States where he purchased arms. These travels seem to have been facilitated by Masonic connections. Ogé arrived back in St Domingue in October 1790 demanding new elections based on the March decree, with full rights for qualified free people of colour. When this met with a predictable refusal from the Governor and Assembly of the North Ogé raised the standard of revolt, with support from a group of revolutionary Freemasons, both mulatto and white. Ogé's revolt was swiftly overwhelmed; he and his followers were subjected to summary trial, torture and execution in a display of 'exemplary' justice. This grim fate encouraged the leading mulattos of the South to make more effective preparations; the mulatto proprietors fortified their estates, arming and training their slaves, and conspiring with the mulatto veterans and under-officers of the Legion and *maréchaussée*. Villatte, one of the larger proprietors, had himself fought in North America. The potential strength of the mulatto community was based in the South and West; not in the North where Ogé had raised the standard of revolt.[34]

In St Domingue all factions amongst the white colonists distrusted the metropolis. They suspected it of radicalism with regard to the *régime intérieur* (slavery and the caste system) and of a rigid conservatism *vis-à-vis* the *régime extérieur* (the *exclusif* and its accompanying apparatus of administration and invigilation). A moderate planter faction came to dominate the provincial assembly of the North, meeting in Le Cap, while a radical faction dominated the first colony-wide General Assembly, which met in Saint Marc, on the West coast, in February 1790. In all provinces the resident planters, or *cultivateurs*, evinced hostility to absentees, to commercial restrictions and to colonial officialdom. Those with the strongest animus against ministerial despotism, or those with the heaviest debts to French merchants, were likely to be among the more politically active. The planter class of St Domingue, by comparision with that of Martinique or Guadeloupe, was weakened by divisions – there were different regional interests and a higher proportion of both absentee and mulatto proprietors. No single leader of the stature of Du Buc emerged in St Domingue and planter hegemony of the countryside was less secure. The relative weakness of the planters of St Domingue led them to make demagogic appeals and concessions to the *petits blancs*: given the volatility of the political passions of the latter this was a dangerous game. It also carried with it the danger of driving into open opposition the relatively large group of propertied mulattos. The political leaders in St Domingue were largely drawn from the planter class, but the support of the *petits blancs* was encouraged by granting voting rights to all male whites with one year's residence in the colony, regardless of whether they owned property or paid direct taxes. The General Assembly at St Marc organised new elections following receipt of the March decree and instruction but, while rigorously excluding mulattos, they retained the wide franchise for whites. Thus the peculiar *régime intérieur* of St Domingue led it to a swifter 'democratisation' of the political process among whites than was seen in the metropolis. The patriotic sentiments of the *petits blancs* were outraged that the National Assembly had passed a decree which clearly deprived many of them of voting rights while being ambiguous enough to enfranchise the propertied mulatto.

The radically autonomist and anti-ministerial planters who dominated the St Marc Assembly mobilised the prejudices of the *petits blancs* without necessarily feeling them so intensely. At earlier and later stages of the revolution the *cultivateurs* of the West and South showed themselves ready to make agreements with mulatto proprietors. The legislation and the *bases constitutionels* agreed by the St Marc Assembly were chiefly concerned with asserting far-reaching rights within the framework of the monarchy and not with racial questions. The Assembly acted as if it was a sovereign body entitled to negotiate directly with the monarch. The functions of the colonial magistrature and judiciary were entirely suspended and the Assembly arrogated to itself the right to propose commercial legislation and to reorganise the colonial garrison. By expressing a willingness to discuss the future scope of the *exclusif* the St Marc Assembly will have hoped to keep alive the possibility of achieving a *modus vivendi* with the metropolis. Some members of the Assembly may already have wished for complete separation, but this was not the outlook of the majority. However, their decrees went quite far enough to antagonise the Governor and the more cautious faction that dominated the Assembly of the North at Le Cap. In August 1790 the Governor denounced the acts of the St Marc Assembly as a virtual declaration of independence and dispatched troops against it. The forces assembled by the Governor mounted an effective blockade of St Marc, while the Assembly found that its patriotic rhetoric and programme for dispensing with the entirety of the former civil and religious administration had alienated an important stratum of *grands blancs* in the North and in Port au Prince. A number of the deputies slipped away to their plantations. The remainder, eighty-five out of more than two hundred, took advantage of a mutiny aboard the warship *Léopard*, then in St Marc's harbour, to make their escape. They persuaded the revolutionary sailors to take them to France where they could appeal directly to the National Assembly and to public opinion as victims of ministerial despotism and as the legitimate representatives of colonial Patriotism. When the *léopardins*, as they came to be called, landed at Brest, they were accepted as heroes of the Revolution. The arrival of their ship sparked off further mutinies on two ships of the line of the Brest squadron. But both the National Assembly and the triumvirate received these partisans of colonial liberty coolly and suspiciously. Despite the fact that his kinsman, Bacon de Chevalerie, was one of the *léopardins*, Barnave denounced the *bases constitutionels* adopted by the St Marc Assembly while praising the loyalty of the Assembly of the North. Eventually the St Marc deputies were permitted to appear before the Committee on Colonies; forty-five of them were persuaded to disavow the more extravagant claims of the St Marc Assembly.[35]

The events in both the Windward Islands and in St Domingue put the triumvirate in a very difficult position. The commercial and manufacturing interests involved in colonial trade knew that the colonists were exploiting the disturbed condition of colonies and metropolis to practise a large-scale contraband. North American, British and Dutch merchants were now making massive and brazen encroachments on the French colonial trade. Though Barnave and the triumvirate had repudiated the more extreme manifestations of planter patriotism they had not successfully defended the *exclusif*. This failure was the critical concern for the commercial interests of the metropolis. Towards the close of 1790 fresh forces and new Governors were dispatched to the Caribbean in an attempt to restore metropolitan authority. La Luzerne was replaced as Colonial Minister; his officials had been notably indulgent to *grands blancs* who had reciprocated by support for the *monarchiens*. The Committee on the Colonies now assumed more direct responsibility for colonial policy. The new Governor in Martinique swiftly came to terms with Du Buc, who had the island well under control. With the dispersal of the St Marc Assembly autonomism in St Domingue had acquired new sponsorship – this time from the Assembly of the North, with fulsome backing from Gouy d'Arsy in the National Assembly. Metropolitan authority in the colonies was represented by Governors and military commanders who lacked both the means and the desire to enforce the commercial regulations rigorously. The distinction insisted on by the Committee on the Colonies between an 'exterior regime' and an 'interior regime' proved quite artificial. The forced departure of the two crucial Intendants – Barbé de Marbois and Foullon d'Ecottier – had been accompanied by the disintegration of the system of metropolitan regulation of colonial commerce. Without 'interior' support the 'exterior' regime simply could not be enforced. The Governors and military commanders had always been drawn from the military aristocratic caste. They tended to sympathise with patrician *grands blancs* and not with the more uncouth Patriots of the towns; yet the latter included many of the clerks, notaries and petty officials upon whom an effective commercial system had to depend. The triumvirate in Paris was not suited to resolving this problem, since their own background and inclinations aligned them with the more respectable and enlightened planters rather than with Patriot enthusiasts prone to fomenting mutiny and insubordination.

By the early months of 1791 the triumvirate's conduct of colonial affairs came under attack in the Revolutionary Clubs and in the Constituent Assembly. Barnave and the Committee on the Colonies could be criticised for permitting Patriots to be persecuted in the colonies, for failing to enforce the *exclusif*, for giving a free hand to aristocratic royal officials and for failing to uphold mulatto rights. These criticisms might not be consistent with one another but were none the less damning for that. The collapse of the commercial system had a particularly damaging impact, uniting different constituencies against those who were seen as responsible for it. The political clubs reflected the anger of the port cities at lost trade and of the urban populace at rising prices for plantation produce, as sugar, coffee and cacao were diverted from the French entrepôts by the higher prices in New York, Amsterdam and London. Before the end of the year there had been several sugar riots in Paris. The commercial interests knew well that contraband was the explanation for most of the shortages. The Revolutionary Clubs, especially those in the maritime centres, began to denounce a criminal conspiracy of royal officials, aristocratic planters, and traitors to the national interest: they urged the dispatch of troops to the Antilles.[36]

Barnave and the Committee on Colonies were themselves anxious to assert metropolitan authority and the provisions of the *exclusif,* since their aim from the outset had been to reconcile the interests of planting and commerce, colonies and metropolis. In a report to the National Assembly of November 29th 1790, Barnave had admitted that: 'The administration of the colonies is going to pieces. The old laws are without force and the new are infinitely slow in being established.'[37] He pointed to the expulsion of the Intendants as a critical blow to the colonial system and attacked the attempt by colonial assemblies to usurp administrative functions. He recommended the drawing up of new Instructions to be enforced by specially selected Commissioners. Barnave knew that the parade of patriotism made by the colonists brought into question the legitimacy of metropolitan authority. The commissioners would be plenipotentiaries, entrusted with the power and prestige of the National Assembly itself in an effort to meet this problem. Moreover he intended that the Commissioners should themselves be prominent and respected individuals: thus Mercier de la Rivière, the eminent Physiocrat and former Intendant at Martinique, was nominated, though ill health prevented him from sailing. Barnave's desperate attempt to recoup the colonial situation had the initial disadvantage that the nature of the new Instructions would have to be agreed by the National Assembly as a whole. Up to this point the Committee on the Colonies had been able to avoid a general discussion within the Assembly on colonial affairs by presenting reports and moving that they be accepted without discussion. This tactic had worked because the Assembly contained a vociferous minority prepared to support the Committee and a majority which did not wish to be embarrassed by a detailed discussion of the colonies, with their peculiar 'internal' regime. Between January and May 1791 the Committee on the Colonies found it increasingly difficult to gain acceptance for its proposals without a discussion. Once again controversy centred on mulatto rights rather than on the commercial regime, or on slavery itself, or even on the precise powers to be allotted to the colonial assemblies. Indeed in the end controversy was to centre upon a very restricted aspect even of the issue of mulatto rights. Deputies sympathetic to the *Amis des Noirs*, supported by a number of Jacobins, proposed that the new Instructions should extend political rights to those free people of colour who were otherwise qualified to vote and *both of whose parents had themselves been free-born*. It was clear that there were very few free mulattos or blacks who met this criterion – as it transpired about four hundred in St Domingue.[38]

Evidently this battle over the rights of a handful of free people of colour reflected and symbolised other issues. It highlighted the principle of metropolitan responsibility and gave the revolutionary democrats an issue on which they could embarrass Barnave. The question of slavery was taboo for the great majority of deputies to the Constituent Assembly, while metropolitan sovereignty was a taboo question for most colonial representatives. The Constituent deputies wished to see the return of a profitable colonial system and did not believe that attacking slavery was the way to achieve this. The leading planters, on the other hand, desired self-government, but most of them still felt themselves to be French and to be subjects of the French King. They looked to the metropolis to maintain order in the colonies and they felt bound to it by personal ties. They generally avoided open attacks on the principle of metropolitan regulation of commerce and contented themselves with rendering it ineffective. Some planters may have felt that the *exclusif* was a price worth paying for the benefits of association with the wider French empire; others that it would be tactically unwise to provoke into opposition the entire commercial lobby of the metropolis. The mulatto issue had the advantage for both colonists and Constituent deputies of posing the question of the ultimate control of colonial policy without broaching the even more delicate questions raised by slavery or the commercial system. So far as the *petits blancs* were concerned the enfranchisement of even a small number of mulattos would be the thin end of the wedge. The *grands blancs* and *cultivateurs* did not see in mulatto rights a mortal threat to their position but they definitely did not want to see such rights imposed from the outside; given the opportunity the planter representatives always spoke of their great benevolence towards the mulattos, even when denying rights to them. So far as the Constituent was concerned the enforcement of mulatto rights, even the rights of a very small number of mulattos, would require the rehabilitation of an administrative structure responsible to the metropolis. Moreover it would undercut the moral and political credentials of the colonial Patriots without threatening slavery. French 'patriotism' was defined by civic virtue and love of country, just as it had been for British or North American Patriots; but what were the boundaries of the nation and who enjoyed civic rights? Narrowly bourgeois or racist conceptions could be denounced as the confection of a new aristocracy.

Thus the decision of the Jacobins and Constituent Left was not simply prompted by political calculation or economic interest. The issue of mulatto rights put to the test the principles enshrined in the Declaration of the Rights of Man and the Citizen. Of course the issue of slavery did as well but the abolitionist-minded deputy could persuade himself that conceding rights to mulattos, however modest these might be, was the first step towards improving the condition of the coloured people of the Antilles. Jacobins perceived in this question an opportunity to affirm the principles of 1789, expose the inconsistency of the triumvirate, assert the integrity of the nation and pursue a policy that had economic advantages as well as risks. The gruesome news of Ogé's martyrdom arrived in Paris at a time when popular distrust of the King was mounting; it was widely attacked as a barbarous example of caste revenge masquerading as royal justice. In the Revolutionary Clubs and newspapers denunciations of the 'aristocracy of the skin' in the colonies suggested parallels with the struggle against privilege in the metropolis.[39]

The Constituent Assembly debated the colonial Instructions for five days in May 1791. The colonial deputies, the Massiac Club and the *léopardins* united in warning of the dangers that would arise from even the smallest concession to the mulattos. Moreau de Saint Méry, now a deputy for Martinique, secured acceptance for a motion to the effect that no change could be made in the status of slaves (amended to 'persons not free') in the French West Indies that had not been formally and spontaneously demanded by the colonial assemblies themselves. But opinion among the mass of deputies was now seriously divided. A mulatto petition against white lynch law in the colonies was read to the Assembly on May 15th after Reubel, a Jacobin, proposed the motion that voting rights be given to qualified mulattos born of free parents. Despite Barnave's opposition this motion was passed by acclamation. Within days the directory of the department of the Gironde, and the Jacobins of Bordeaux, had congratulated the Assembly on its decision. But the radical Jacobins had no majority in the Constituent Assembly and no prospect of displacing the triumvirate. In an attempt to consolidate their temporary advantage the supporters of mulatto rights presented a 'declaration of motives' which was to accompany the decree to the colonies. Drafted by Dupont de Nemours and approved on May 29th this document theorised the compromising formula that had been adopted, declaring that the Constituent was not competent to accord civic rights to unfree persons, or freedmen, since these were members of a 'foreign nation'. Such concessions made little impact on the colonial representatives, who did all in their power to oppose and sabotage implementation of the May 15th decision. The Colonial Ministry and the Committee on Colonies were equally obstructive. The Governor of St Domingue sent a letter to the Constituent Assembly warning that introduction of the decree would provoke civil war, secession or even an invitation to the British fleet.

The extent of colonial resistance to the decree of May 15th began to undermine support for it in the maritime centres and in the Constituent Assembly. But the course of colonial policy was by no means determined solely by colonial events. The flight of the King in June, and the popular demonstration which escorted him back to Paris after his apprehension at Varennes, created a new political situation. The intrigues of the King created problems for the triumvirate, who were identified with the project of a constitutional monarchy. The latter was still the objective of the majority of the possessing classes since the monarch could serve as a rallying point for the disparate forces of property and commerce, for colonial planters and metropolitan merchants, for landowners and peasants, for regular officers and members of the burgeoning National Guard. But a constitutional monarchy required a constitutional monarch and this was a role which Louis XVI and the more ardent royalists were unprepared to play. The King's flight and the growing strength of the counter-revolution encouraged some leaders of democratic opinion, such as Condorcet, to canvass the republican alternative. But most members of the Constituent Assembly were more frightened of the populace and of the hazards of democratic experiment than they were of counter-revolution. Barnave and the 'Lamethists' formed a bloc with Malouet and many of the *monarchiens* in an effort to shore up the crumbling project of a constitutional monarchy. This new grouping, the *Feuillants*, had powerful backing from colonial interests, including those associated with the Massiac Club. The triumvirate had skilfully interpreted the mood of the Constituent Assembly, and of much of bourgeois opinion, even if not the true intentions of their sovereign. The *Feuillants* proceeded to repress democratic or republican agitation and to regain control of colonial policy. The failure to follow up the decree of May 15th with consequent Instructions had stalled its application, but it remained an embarrassment. On September 7th Barnave introduced a motion which referred the decree on mulatto rights for reconsideration by the Committee on the Colonies. Barnave presented this as a tactical withdrawal and had scathing words both for the social regime of the colonies and for ill-considered attempts to change it: 'This regime is absurd, but one cannot handle it roughly without unloosing the greatest disorder. This regime is oppressive, but it gives a livelihood to several million Frenchmen. This regime is barbarous but a still greater barbarity will result if you interfere with it without the necessary knowledge.'[40] But such rhetoric could scarcely disguise the craven capitulation to colonial interests that he was recommending. On September 24th the Constituent formally rescinded the decree on mulatto rights . C.L.R. James has underlined the moral and political significance of the failure to implement the decree of May 15th:

> It was the colonial question which demoralised the Constituent. Jaurès, so weak on colonial events, but so strong on Parliamentary assemblies, has traced this demoralisation with the profound insight of a great parliamentarian. Hitherto, says Jaurès, the revolutionary bourgeoisie had been reasonably honest (Jaurès, *Histoire Socialiste de la Revolution Francaise*, Vol. II, pp. 225–6). If they had limited the franchise at least they had done so openly. But to avoid giving the Mulattoes the Rights of Man they had to descend to low dodges and crooked negotiations which destroyed their revolutionary integrity. It was the guilty conscience of the Constituent on the colonial question that placed it at the mercy of the reactionaries when Louis fled. 'Undoubtedly but for the compromises of Barnave and all his party on the colonial question, the general attitude of the Assembly after the flight to Varennes would have been different.'[41]

While it is difficult to be certain which was cause and which effect there can be little doubt that colonial compromise cemented the ill-fated *Feuillant* bloc.

The rescinding of the decree of May 15th was almost the last act of the Constituent. In the newly elected Legislative Assembly, which met on October 1st, the *Feuillants* remained the largest grouping and retained nominal control of colonial policy through a new Committee on Colonies constructed along similar lines to its predecessor. But though a *Feuillant* ministry was to remain in office until March of 1792 it was already beginning to be overtaken by events. Barnave and his colleagues did not possess either the financial or the military resources to command the situation in the colonies. Their effort to appease the colonial establishment failed to bring calm. The vacillations on mulatto rights and the conspiracies of the royalist counter-revolution had intensified the struggle in St Domingue. In Le Cap and Port au Prince patriot bands, the *pompons rouges*, clashed with royalist gangs, the *pompons blancs*. In the summer of 1791 the patriot committees, supported by most resident planters, dominated new elections to a general colonial Assembly: despite the decree of May 15th mulatto proprietors were completely excluded from these elections. The officers of the garrison and of the royal squadron inclined to intransigent monarchism as did a number of the agents of metropolitan interests. The decree of May 15th encouraged the mulattos, who had already begun to mobilise, to assert their rights arms in hand. The Governor lacked either clear instructions or reinforcements of loyal troops.

These ragged conflicts, following nearly two years of uncertainty and revolutionary rhetoric, and accompanied by market pressures that made planters and managers avid for increased output, created the conditions for the most remarkable explosion of slave rebellion ever seen in the French Caribbean. Factional conflict had involved the fortification of some plantations and the arming of some slaves. The revolt took place in August, towards the close of the harvest season. White employees would, in many cases, have left the plantations, for recreation in the towns. Economic as well as political conditions had promoted a contradictory relaxation/intensification of the slave regime. Elite slaves circulated more freely, markets in slave produce flourished and the *maréchaussée* and police were distracted. Yet working conditions for the mass of slaves were no better, with overseers anxious to push their slave crews to the limit. On the one hand, the elaborate apparatus of slave subjection was weakened and divided. On the other, some slaves had unprecedented opportunities for meeting, for comparing experiences and for arming themselves.

The slave uprising began on the night of August 21st in the vicinity of Le Cap, the epicentre of struggles between colonial factions. A newly elected Assembly dominated by white Patriots was just about to meet in the northern capital. According to legend the outbreak was planned at a meeting of elite slaves held in the Bois-Caiman on the stormy night of August 14th. Boukman Dutty, a coach-driver, presided over the gathering and it was agreed that there would be a simultaneous revolt on a series of major plantations: Noé, Clement, Flaville, Gallifet, and others in the region of Limbé and Acul. At a voodoo ceremony the conspirators pledged themselves to one another and to victory over the whites and their evil God, crying out in *Kréyole*: 'Couté la Liberté dan coeur à nous', (Listen to the voice of Liberty which speaks in the hearts of all).[42]

The revolt spread rapidly across the northern plain, involving tens of thousands of slaves. The Colonial Assembly, now besieged in Le Cap, was to claim that 180 sugar estates and 900 coffee and indigo estates were engulfed by the revolt, with 100,000 slaves affected; though they probably exaggerated certainly nothing like this had been seen in

St Domingue before. Patriots insisted that royalist officials or rebellious mulattos were behind the revolt and had distributed arms to the slaves as part of a counter-revolutionary manoeuvre. The rebel leaders adopted the style and uniform of generals and some did claim that the King wanted to help the blacks. The rebels slaughtered hated overseers or whites who stood in their way. A few priests and doctors were said to have been spared; some even joined the black generals. The insurgents set fire to plantation buildings, and withdrew to refuge in the surrounding hills and forest; others remained, loath to abandon a place they thought of as home. Some rebels made common cause with the maroon bands, which mushroomed in number and in size. The garrison held Cap Français but was initially reluctant to venture far into the devastated Northern plain. One of the black leaders wrote to the Governor on September 4th saying that the only way in which peace could be secured was if the whites evacuated the entire region including Le Cap: 'They may take with them their gold and jewels. The only precious object we covet is liberty.' The Governor's forces gradually drove back the black columns from the main plantation zone. In November Boukman was killed by a regular column; the officer reporting this noted the presence of five cannon and a white man with Boukman's force of several hundred.[43] But there were now at least half a dozen large rebel and maroon forces active in the North and the borderlands. In parts of the South and West there were also disturbances; in these regions a free coloured militia assumed control. The Colonial Assembly appealed to the Governor of Jamaica for help. The seriousness of the slave revolt led white and mulatto proprietors to reach a 'concordat' in self-defence in a number of areas – but the mulattos were to remember their resentments when they heard that the May 15th decree had been rescinded. The Constituent Assembly had delivered this rebuff to the free mulattos in September 1791 before anyone in France was aware of the slave revolt in St Domingue. When the triumvirs withdrew rights from free people of colour they were appeasing white colonists and simply assuming the continued subordination of the slaves.

With hindsight we know that the rising of August 1791 was the beginning of the end of slavery in St Domingue. But this was not at all clear to contemporaries. The revolt had been far more widespread than any previously seen in the colony, but once the insurgents had retired to the hills and frontier zone a semblance of order returned to many plantations. While some rebels had achieved liberty, others remained to negotiate with the planters or overseers. In pitched battles the militia or regulars would usually prevail. The death of Boukman was believed to have dealt a crushing blow to the black insurgence. As yet it was not clear that a new power had been born; the rebels themselves issued no general programme or plan. When proper reports of the insurrection reached France at the beginning of November the most alarming aspect of the matter in the eyes of metropolitan observers was the planters' appeal to the Governor of Jamaica – an alarm that was increased by the fact that the London newspapers seemed much better informed about developments in St Domingue than the ministry in Paris. These metropolitan suspicions were, in fact, eminently justified, since a leading member of the Colonial Assembly, Cadusch, not only contacted the Governor of Jamaica but also sent a letter to Pitt inviting the British government to occupy St Domingue. A British warship arrived with supplies at Cap Français on September 22nd and was given an enthusiastic welcome by the white inhabitants. Reports of such ominous events as this reached France more or less at the same time as news of the insurrection itself. Those most interested in colonial affairs believed that colonists always exaggerated the extent of slave rebellions and that such outbreaks, even when serious, could always be contained sooner or later – separatist movements, as the North Americans had proved, were a graver threat to metropolitan interests.[44]

Following the insurrection in St Domingue about 20,000 former slaves left their estates and formed encampments in the foothills surrounding the Northern plain and at Ounaminthe near the border. The Northern capital at Le Cap remained in the hands of the Governor and the white Patriots of the Assembly. In some parts of the South and West there were smaller outbreaks of slave rebellion. Such outbreaks were not as extensive or as destructive of plantation property as the insurrection in the North.

Throughout the colony slaves who had family ties and garden plots were often reluctant to leave the plantation for the uncertain and rudimentary existence of the maroon. The planters or their managers acknowledged changed conditions by making concessions to their slaves – an extra free day per week, or more extensive cultivation rights – and in this way retained a work-force. In some parts of the country such concessions could be made because of high prices for sugar; in much of the North they might be made because the sugar mills were in no state to resume output in any case. The existence of rebel columns in the surrounding woods and hills was itself an inducement to plantation managers to be attentive to their crews. Most of the leaders of the slave risings, large or small, were prepared to negotiate with planters and political authorities to secure liberty for themselves, and their immediate followers, and better conditions for the mass of rebellious slaves. The leaders of the insurrectionary columns in the North – Biassou, Jean François, Toussaint Bréda – described themselves as soldiers of the King: it was sometimes claimed that the whites had concealed a royal decree granting the slaves an extra free day per week.

A Civil Commission dispatched by the National Assembly arrived in St Domingue at the end of November 1791 and soon opened negotiations with the leaders of the Northern revolt. The latter demanded not only freedom for themselves but also full political rights, pointing out that the metropolitan decrees had left this to the discretion of local authorities. The black leaders declared that so long as their own freedom, and those of some 400 followers, was formally guaranteed, and the mass of slaves allowed more time to work their plots, they would be prepared to enforce a return to the plantations. C.L.R. James describes this as an 'abominable betrayal', yet it would count as standard conduct for past maroon leaders, with, perhaps, a dimension of servile trade unionism. The leaders of the revolt were predominantly former elite slaves, or even *affranchis*. The elite slaves already enjoyed privileges and aspired to full freedom; the mass of slaves might be more willing to settle for improved conditions. The main black leaders spoke French. Jean François claimed that, by contrast, many of their followers were Africans who spoke only two words of French; by implication these followers were not bothered about French legal formulas, and could be satisfied by promises of more time to work their plots. While the black leaders did display an egoism and condescension which merits James's scorn it is probable that it was the uneven and incomplete development of slave resistance and revolt which made this possible.[45]

The Civil Commissioners were prepared to accept the terms offered by the black leaders, but prospects for a deal were sabotaged by the provincial assembly of the North, which refused to countenance it. The Civil Commissioners did not have the strength to impose their will on the mass of white colonists: the depleted forces of the garrison were outnumbered by the militia. In other parts of the colony slave outbreaks helped to bring about an uneasy truce or 'concordat' between whites and free people of colour. In the West a 'combined' force of whites and free mulattos defeated an attempt by patriot *pompons rouges* to seize control of Port au Prince; they were assisted in this by a young black named Hyacinth who had established a following among the rebel slaves. An official wrote of the West: 'there are really no insurgent slaves but those which have been armed by the two parties.' The South was divided into a patchwork of white-controlled and mulatto-controlled areas. But in the hills of Les Platons a stubborn slave revolt was only contained with difficulty and an official reported the following rebel reaction to peace feelers put out by the attackers:' "nous après tandé zaute", which is to say, we had expected you, and we will cut off your heads to the last man; and that this land is not for you it is for us.'[46] So long as the colonial power resisted civic concessions to mulatto proprietors and commanders, it was not well placed to regain its influence over the different regions of the colony.

Meanwhile, developments within the metropolis strengthened the position of those associated with the *Amis des Noirs* and further antagonised the white planters of the Antilles. Brissot and Condorcet were both members of the Legislative while all former members of the Constituent had been debarred from presenting themselves as candidates. In the clubs the influence of the *Amis des Noirs* was growing, as Barnave was discredited by his capitulations to arrogant and racist colonists.[47] Brissot now became the most effective opposition leader in the Legislative and the champion of a new forward policy which would take France to war in Europe and would reassert metropolitan authority in the Antilles. Both objectives required a rehabilitation and expansion of the nation's armed forces and administrative machine. Popular support for such aims could be aroused by proclaiming the need to end foreign encouragement of the counter-revolution and foil the plots of aristocratic emigrés and colonists. The King, foolishly devoted to a *politique du pire*, permitted the formation of a new ministry committed to the 'Brissotin' programme, led by Roland and Clavière, the latter, of course, a sponsor of the *Amis*. The 'Jacobin' ministry was formed on March 15th 1792. One of its first acts was to introduce a decree on April 4th conceding full civic and political rights to all free adult males in the colonies, regardless of colour.

Brissot did not trust the white colonial factions and looked to the *gens de couleur* to recoup the situation. In St Domingue support from the free people of colour would be essential to the restoration of authority and the rehabilitation of the colonial system. In much of the West the 'concordat' between white and coloured proprietors had already been based on recognition of the necessity to unite the free population, whatever their colour, in the face of slave insurgency. The slave revolts had created a new situation in which both metropolitan and creole interests recognised the advantage of enlisting the support of the free people of colour. The 'concordat' had been devised with the help of the Civil Commissioners but implemented by municipal authorities who increasingly acted for themselves without reference to a weakened and distant metropolis. So far as many proprietors were concerned, it was a step towards self-reliance and self-government; and these consorted happily with their practice of free trade. Several important mulatto proprietors and merchants decided that their interests would be best served by aligning themselves with creole autonomism and royalism. Thus in the West the royalist *pompons blancs* and the leaders of the 'combined force' acted together, led by the white planter Hanus de Jumécourt and the mulatto planter J.B. Lapointe. Some planters who favoured autonomism were prepared to work with the counter-revolutionary Princes, because the latter were in no position to impose ministerial despotism on the Antilles. Indeed it was now royalism rather than patriotism which could be used as a screen to defend the creole faction's aversion to metropolitan regulations. Such planter royalists saw British material support as the critical factor and were grateful for the help received from the Governor of Jamaica in the aftermath of the slave uprising. Spain might supply flanking support in St Domingue but it lacked Britain's commercial and maritime strength. Austria or Prussia might help to restore royal authority in France but had no purchase on the situation in the Caribbean.

The Brissotins did not control the state apparatus: within the Navy and its dependencies unreconstructed monarchism remained a powerful force and was strengthened by the adhesion of colonial *grands blancs* and *cultivateurs* who had earlier supported Barnave and Lameth. A more generous conception of citizenship would give Brissot the allies he needed to fashion a new colonial order. The Brissotin programme would, it was hoped, restore the flows of colonial commerce as well as promote plantation security; free mulattos and loyal whites would re-establish a functioning colonial administration and police. The now booming trade between the French colonies and the North American or British ports would be redirected back to Bordeaux and Nantes.

The planters' growing appetite for running their own affairs stopped just short of a desire for full independence. Under the impact of revolution and slave revolt the colony had fragmented into a score or so of separate municipalities and local assemblies, meeting in port towns such as St Marc, Jacmel, Jérémie and Léogane, as well as the provincial capitals of Le Cap, Port au Prince and Les Cayes. The planters and merchants who dominated the assemblies recognised that some sort of central authority was needed to check the activities of rebels and runaways. A constitutional monarchy or British protectorate might supply the back-up they required. To renounce France was not easy, but they did not wish to open up their ledgers and warehouses to the prying eyes of colonial tax inspectors and customs officials, whatever their colour. Many planters were disenchanted with the confusions of patriot democracy and thought these likely to be compounded by the admission of all free people of colour to citizenship. White proprietors were prepared to work with mulatto proprietors, but this did not mean that they accepted other men of colour as their equals; similarly the *grands blancs* had been prepared to exploit the racial resentments of the *petits blancs* but did not wish to see them occupying positions of influence. Up to this point the larger planters had dominated the colonial assemblies – though admittedly more securely in Martinique than St Domingue. *Petits blancs* had been allowed to vote but they had not stood as candidates; indeed not only *petits blancs* but also lawyers, priests and clerks had been largely absent from representation in the colonial assemblies. The Brissotin programme allowed these excluded layers of the white population to gain official posts at the risk of further alienating the richer planters and merchants, together with their hangers-on. It was hoped that the creole planters and merchants could be brought to accept the newly refurbished colonial state, since this would offer them a guarantee of slave subordination. Much as planters appreciated the profits of contraband it was hoped that security would be their overriding consideration.

The Legislative Assembly, aware that the colonial system could not be rebuilt without a much stronger metropolitan presence in St Domingue, dispatched a new Civil Commission and an expeditionary force of 6,000 men – 2,000 troops of the line and 4,000 National Guards – in July 1792; a smaller force was sent to the Windwards in the following month. The Civil Commissioners for St Domingue, of whom there were three, were entrusted with very wide powers by the Legislative Assembly enabling them to summon or dismiss the colonial assemblies and to investigate and restructure every branch of administration. The Commission comprised three members: Sonthonax, Polverel and Ailhaud.

Sonthonax, a twenty-nine-year-old lawyer and journalist, was a member of the Jacobin Club, a friend of Brissot and a supporter of the *Amis des Noirs*. He could generally count on the support of another, more cautious, Brissotin Commissioner, Polverel. Ailhaud was to return to France before revealing a distinctive political orientation. The expedition was accompanied by a new military commander and Governor, Desparbès, who was to be subordinate to the Commissioners. The expedition left France at an extraordinary moment. A Prussian general was poised at the head of a counter-revolutionary army to invade France. The intrigues of the King and court, underlined by the wholesale defection of royalist officers, had created an atmosphere of the greatest alarm and suspicion. Brissot had declared that '*La patrie est en danger*' and Robespierre had joined with him to call for a united patriotic mobilisation on June 28th. The *fédérés* who converged on Paris to celebrate the anniversary of the fall of the Bastille denounced the treason of the King and Queen. The Patriots of

Marseilles began their march on the capital and demands were raised
for the arming of all citizens, abolition of the distinction between active
and passive citizens, overthrow of the monarchy and election of a
National Convention on the basis of universal manhood suffrage. The
King's refusal to sanction a number of emergency measures further
inflamed the Patriots. Indeed the royal licence issued to the Civil
Commissioners for St Domingue was amongst the last official acts of
Louis XVI. The fact that an expedition of 6,000 troops was allowed to
leave France at this juncture was itself a tribute to the importance
attached to the colonies.

Notwithstanding their royal sanction the Commissioners had been
chosen for their loyalty to the Assembly and took with them to the
Antilles the spirit of patriotic vigilance and the fervour of a Jacobin
Club that had yet to split. But they also had to contend with an
incoherence at the heart of the Brissotin programme. Brissot wished to
rehabilitate the state administration yet, clinging to the dead formula of
constitutional monarchy, he failed to base his plans from the outset on
an authoritative new sovereign power. Having denounced the King in
June he was still prepared to negotiate with him in July. And even after
the arrest of the royal family and the triumph of the Republican
insurrection of August 10th Brissot and the Girondins seemed to be
leading the government of a Republic in which they only half-believed.
The Civil Commissioners acted with resolution, but they were dogged
by the problem of the ultimate legitimacy of their acts. The
Commissioners themselves had no difficulty in accepting the Republic
declared in September or accepting the authority of the Convention,
elected in the same month, which renewed their Commission. But the
overthow of the monarchy was the signal for a royalist *fronde*
throughout the French Antilles as creole planters and merchants seized
on a ready-made justification for their autonomist aspirations.

The Civil Commission arrived in St Domingue on September 17th
and was welcomed by the colonists of Cap Français because of the
strong forces they brought with them. The Commission was soon
plunged in a succession of difficult situations. The commander of the
regular troops, D'Esparbès, resented the powers conferred on the Civil
Commissioners and displayed little zeal for leading his troops in a
campaign against the insurgents holding out in the interior. From the
outset he revealed royalist sympathies, winning some planter support;
when news arrived in October that a Republic had been declared he
became bolder in his defiance of the Commissioners. Sonthonax
announced that the Commissioners fully respected the colonists
property and that they were determined to stamp out rebellion, whether
from the slaves or from the royalist counter-revolution. In a swift coup

the Commission managed to win over most of the metropolitan troops and colonial militia; D'Esparbès, together with his entire staff and twenty-five other officers, were arrested and sent to France. The Commissioners were assisted by the arrival of reinforcements and two ranking metropolitan commanders loyal to the Republic: Rochambeau, who stayed in St Domingue from November to January, and Etienne Laveaux, a *ci-devant* noble and participant in the recent Republican victories at Valmy and Jémappes. With this help the Commissioners began to reconstruct metropolitan authority in the colony along the lines embodied in their instructions. An appeal was made to the leaders of the black revolt, offering them their liberty in exchange for help in restoring order to the colony. But the black generals replied that those who had just overthrown their King were in no position to promise anyone freedom. The Commissioners, hoping to attract the support of slaveholders of all colours, ordered military operations against the rebel encampments. They were puzzled to discover that the blacks would often prefer to withdraw than to give battle.

Polverel and Ailhaud left for the West and South while Sonthonax took charge in the North. Because of the threat still posed by the black rebels in the North none of the metropolitan reinforcements could be subtracted from this province, leaving the Commissioners in the South and West at the mercy of local forces unsympathetic to the Republic. Ailhaud found such resistance to his authority in Port au Prince that he decided to return to France to warn of the colony's imminent defection. Polverel had more persistence and won support from coloured militia officers who welcomed the decree of April 4th. Fear of slave revolt and a desire not to antagonise the *gens de couleur* induced many planters and merchants to feign acceptance of the Republican authorities until there was a real prospect of replacing them.[48]

While wealthy mulatto proprietors continued to participate in the intrigues of the autonomist municipalities the majority of the free people of colour were attracted by the anti-racist policies of the Republican Commissioners. Because there had been a steady drain of white emigration the free mulattos and blacks now outnumbered the whites by perhaps two to one. In many places they already formed the largest militia units. Coloured officers and soldiers were impressed by the evident determination of Sonthonax and Polverel to dismantle racial discrimination. The Commissioners had no hesitation in promoting coloured veterans who had held commissions in the militia and in the *Légion de St Domingue*: important commands were given to Rigaud in the South, Chanlatte, Beauvais and Pinchinat in the West and Villatte in the North. The *Légion de St Domingue* became the *Légion d'Egalité*. Sonthonax defeated D'Esparbès with the help of the *pompons rouges* but he dispersed a club of radical white Patriots which committed outrages against 'citizens of April 4th'. He then proceeded to form *compagnies franches*, composed exclusively of *gens de couleur*. Making use of their wide powers the Commissioners dissolved all provincial assemblies and postponed new elections, pending a Republican education and reconstruction of the colony. The Civil Commissioners sponsored new revolutionary clubs, the *Amis de la Convention*, and intermediary commissions with executive powers. Whites and free *gens de couleur* were appointed to these bodies in equal numbers and charged with rooting out royalist suspects, investigating *émigré* estates and raising revenue. The Civil Commissioner spoke of liberating the true Third Estate of the colony. Despite the recognition extended to the free people of colour the Commissioners succeeded in retaining the support of a layer of white colonists – petty officials, notaries, constitutional priests, some merchants and even a few planters. While some Patriots, formerly vociferous in their racialism, rallied to the Republic, others, formerly sworn enemies of despotism, went over to the royalists.

The new Republican order was strongest in the North around Le Cap and Port de Paix, though the extreme North-west was in autonomist hands. In the West and South Polverel enjoyed the backing of the coloured commanders, but had to contend with municipal authorities with no commitment to the Republic and no desire to see the colonial system rehabilitated. In much of the West and South mulatto proprietors preferred 'royalist' autonomism to Republican 'equality'. The municipality of Port au Prince only abandoned its defiance after a full-scale siege and bombardment, but there were not enough troops to secure all outlying districts. Coloured commanders sometimes ignored the contraband activities of coloured proprietors. The local authorities in Môle St Nicolas, Jérémie and Jacmel openly defied the Republican authorities; even nominally Republican municipalities, like that of St Marc, traded and conspired with the British colonies where many émigrés were now to be found. The Civil Commissioners sent some special consignments of plantation produce to Bordeaux from Le Cap but their emergency administration was not adequate to enforcing the colonial regulation of commerce. Any move against suspected royalists and autonomists brought howls of anger from other planters. The Civil Commissioners' commitment to defend slavery left economic power, and control of the plantation militia forces, in the hands of their political enemies.

Republican emblem

News from Europe encouraged the planters and colonial establishment of the Windwards to declare for the King in September and October 1792. Significantly enough the assemblies of these two colonies, dominated as they were by the large planters, had meekly accepted the decree of April 4th when it arrived in June. In a fraught situation the planters realised that it would be folly to alienate a critical section of the free population. The news which precipitated planter rebellion in the Iles du Vent was that of the confrontation between the King and the patriot forces in July and August. Garbled reports relayed by neigbouring British colonies led many to believe that the King had re-established his authority and that the Duke of Brunswick, at the head of a victorious counter-revolutionary army, had crushed the democratic agitations of the Paris rabble. The naval and garrison commanders believed that the time had come to honour their oaths of loyalty to the King. The autonomist-inclined and planter-dominated assemblies were persuaded to form a Federation of the Iles du Vent and to hoist the white flag. The more astute leaders of the planters may have discounted the rumours of royalist victory but they clearly sensed that a moment had arrived in which, with royalist help, they could negotiate a deal with the British. Aware of the unpatriotic disposition of the planters of the Iles du Vent the Legislative Assembly had assembled an expedition of 2,000 men commanded by General Rochambeau to restore metropolitan authority there. This expedition left France on August 10th, apparently unaware of the Republican insurrection taking place in Paris on the same day. It arrived in the Windwards towards the end of September. The local authorities, and the commanders of the garrison and squadron, refused Rochambeau permission to land, informing him that his instructions had been revoked by order of the King. Rochambeau decided against attempting a contested landing and set sail for St Domingue. In a secret session on October 8th the Assembly of the Federation of Guadeloupe and Martinique dispatched Du Buc on a mission to Europe, with plenipotentiary powers to negotiate with the London government and the leaders of the counter-revolution. The émigré leaders themselves dispatched a commissioner of their own to the Antilles, one Cougnacq-Myon, a former member of the St Marc Assembly. Though the royalists had triumphed in the Iles du Vent they failed to consolidate their gains. Royalist warships were allowed to leave to join the British and persuade them of the advantages of backing the rebellion. On the islands themselves royalist officials suppressed the municipality of St Pierre and persecuted colonial Patriots, forcing a number of them to seek refuge on neighbouring Dutch or British islands or on Ste Lucie, an island with few plantations where the local commander had remained faithful to the metropolis.

The newly elected Convention despatched an envoy, Captain Lacrosse, to inform the colonists of the Iles du Vent of the proclamation of the Republic. Lacrosse arrived in early December aboard the frigate *Felicité*. Discovering that the royalists held the main French Windwards Lacrosse sailed on to Ste Lucie, from where he proceeded to engage in a pamphlet war against the royalists in Guadeloupe and Martinique. Lacrosse urged all Patriots to reject royalist treason and join forces with the *gens de couleur* as an insurance against both invasion and slave revolt.

Equality, liberty, these are the bases of our government. It is to you, citizens of all colours, that I address myself; we are one and the same family, our union will be our strength; and the slave, your property, must be attached to his labours by the example you give him. Are you not afraid that your crews will desert you at the first cannon shot fired against you by France? Attacked from without and menaced from within, what resistance would you be able to afford?[49]

The republican commander brought news of the consolidation of the new order in France and of impressive victories at Valmy and Jémappes. He assured the colonists that larger forces were on the way. The whites of St Pierre and the free people of colour of Guadeloupe proved sympathetic to the republican appeals. The patriot forces were swelled by victims of royalist persecution and by the return of refugees from nearby islands. Fearing the outcome of an armed clash the royalist planters and officials evacuated first Martinique and then Guadeloupe. To patriot cheers the *Felicité* sailed into St Pierre on January 7th with an enormous *bonnet rouge* on its mast; in a ceremony of welcome Lacrosse embraced a leading coloured citizen.

The patriot order in the Iles du Vent, based on the support of metropolitan merchants, a few *cultivateurs* and the majority of *petits blancs* and free people of colour, developed a vigorous Republican culture. There were at least a dozen Revolutionary Clubs dedicated to eradicating royalist treason. A number of *gens de couleur* were promoted to important military commands, among them Magloire Pélage and Louis Delgrès. Rochambeau returned to the islands in February and efforts were made to fortify them against the expedition which, with the outbreak of a wider war imminent, all expected. It was now the turn of patriots to persecute royalist collaborators. Up to this point the slaves of the Iles du Vent had remained quiet; but in March and August there were plantation revolts in Guadeloupe which were only suppressed with considerable loss of life.[50]

The precarious successes of republican colonial policy were jeopardised by the consequences of a war policy which put France on a collision course with Britain and Spain, thus furnishing the autonomist planters with the allies they sought. Brissot had declared that the defence of French liberty required the overthrow of Bourbons throughout Europe. The rhetoric of Danton simultaneously threatened the decrepit empires of the *anciens régimes* and the vigorous commercial interests of Britain's oligarchy. Republican advances, the opening of the Scheldt and plots to subvert Spanish America set the alarm bells ringing in London as well as Madrid. The trial of the King in November 1792, and his execution in January of the following year, was denounced by the British as well Spanish government. British ministers, shocked by the expansionism and commercial protectionism of the French Republic, and tempted by the prospect of Caribbean acquisitions, were ready to encourage counter-revolution in the Caribbean as well as Europe. The Republican decision to declare war on Britain and Spain in January and March 1793 was seen in part as a riposte to British and Spanish collusion with counter-revolution and colonial revolt.

When Du Buc arrived in London in early January he found that the royalist leaders lacked the resources to mount an independent expedition to the Antilles to regain the French colonies. The Princes had no funds for such ventures; indeed they were borrowing money themselves from de Curt, the wealthy planter who had represented Guadeloupe. The royalist commanders sought without success to extract a loan or supplies from the British government. Du Buc proceeded to negotiate directly with the British government, which itself found colonial royalists easier to deal with than prickly French ultras. As a historian of Martinique puts it: 'The chevalier Du Buc had inherited from his father that logical and realistic mind which had been the admiration of the Abbé Raynal. Together with MM. de Curt, de Clairefontaine, de Perpigna, de Charmilly and Malouet, he undertook negotiations based on the new situation and soon concluded an arrangement with the Ministers of George III whose execution would, he hoped, "satisfy all interests".'[51] The negotiating team was thus representative of the planters of Martinique (Du Buc and Perpigna), Guadeloupe (de Curt and Clairefontaine), St Domingue (Vernault de Charmilly, a former *léopardin*), and the Massiac Club (Malouet). The agreement formally signed with the British government on February 19th 1793 – the Republic had declared war on Britain on January 31st – placed the French Windward Islands 'into the possession and under the authority of His Britannic Majesty'. Britain undertook to restore them to France 'in the case that at the end of the present war, any of the princes of the French branch of the House of Bourbon (to the exclusion of Philippe Egalité and his race) regain the throne'.[52] So far as St Domingue was concerned no such royalist qualification was added. British possession was to continue until 'the allied powers' determined ultimate sovereignty over the colony; the final form of this agreement on St Domingue was not reached until April. These agreements, or propositions, were to be ratified by the colonial assemblies when circumstances permitted.

The invitation issued by the leading French colonists in London seemed to promise Britain easy and substantial gains as well as greater security for its own West Indian colonies. Long before the outbreak of hostilities British ministers were drawing up plans for new acquisitions in the Americas. The richest islands in the New World could be acquired, it seemed, with little trouble or expense; it was expected that British occupations would pay for themselves, through revenues and commerce, as had happened in 1757–63. St Domingue had the added interest that it had become a major supplier of cotton to Britain's manufacturers. While French colonial defences were undermined by disintegration and defection the British would be able to count on the support of the planters and their militias. Moreover there were plans for assembling auxiliary regiments of French émigré planters. In February

1793 there were said to be 2,000 colonial émigrés then serving with the Princes in Germany and eager to return to the Antilles. Montalembert, Bouillé and even Dumouriez were canvassed as possible commanders for these French forces. As hostilities between Britain and France commenced the British government laid plans for an expeditionary force to be sent to the Caribbean to capture the French islands; profitable in itself, the capture of the French colonies would also, it was hoped, place Britain in a good position to exploit the weakness of Spain, now its nominal ally. For their part the Spanish authorities intended themselves to have a hand in deciding the future of St Domingue.[53]

The revolutionary threat to the Bourbons had led to a state of undeclared war between French St Domingue and Spanish Santo Domingo even before the formal declaration of hostilities in March 1793. The military commander on Santo Domingo, the Marquis de Hermonas, was quite prepared to help black soldiers who were fighting the French Republicans. The rebel columns had been pushed back by a Republican offensive in the last months of 1792 and were desperately short of the supplies needed to maintain the struggle. While Candy, the mulatto leader of a maroon community, came to terms with the French the principal black commanders accepted supplies from Spain and eventually received commissions in July 1793. Jean François and Biassou, commanding several thousand soldiers each, became lieutenant-generals in the army of the Spanish King. One of the most effective black commanders was Toussaint Bréda, or Louverture, an *affranchi* who had joined the rebels shortly after the uprising of August 1791. A man of about forty-six years of age with knowledge of medicine and administration, he had become secretary and aide-de-camp to Biassou; he now commanded his own force of about six hundred men. In a separate negotiation Toussaint obtained a commission as a colonel. The Spanish had acquired invaluable auxiliaries and an influence over a potentially dangerous band of ex-slaves. Spanish officers and French royalists were assigned to advise the black troops. While the Spanish authorities were happy to recognise the freedom of black soldiers, they gave their new recruits strict instructions to respect the regime of slave subordination.[54]

Four wearing years of revolution had unravelled the complex skein of the French colonial regime. Royal power, the *exclusif*, the racial caste hierarchy had all disintegrated. Beginning in August 1791 the slaves in St Domingue had begun openly to contest their subjection. The intensity of the factional conflicts between Patriots and monarchists, whites and mulattos, creole autonomists and partisans of the *exclusif* had gravely weakened the slave order. The tenacity of the rebels and the sheer size, concentration and numerical preponderance of the slave population had made the revolt impossible to defeat. In the smaller Iles du Vent the free *gens de couleurs* had been much weaker and the different factions had not resorted to the arming of slaves; knowledge of what had happened in St Domingue probably contributed to the avoidance of bloodshed in the tussles between royalists and Republicans.

The slave risings in St Domingue were uneven in extent and duration, but the mass of blacks, whether in open revolt or not, sensed a new power. Like the first tremors of an earthquake the slave revolt had shaken every colonial institution, levelling a few structures but also weakening those which remained standing. The argument about mulatto rights had been transformed by the sight of smoke rising from burnt-out plantation buildings and cane fields. The autonomist inclinations of the French planters, and their willingness to appeal for help to Britain and Spain, had also been encouraged by the spectre of slave revolt. These two colonial slave powers seemed likely to be more consistent and effective defenders of slavery than the representatives of a metropolis mired in revolutionary turmoil. British and Spanish planters and officials on the spot had not waited for instructions before conspiring with French royalists.

As of the spring of 1793 all contenders for power in the French Caribbean were still committed to the defence of slavery: this was true of the British, despite the abolitionist protestations of Pitt and Wilberforce; of the Spanish, despite their bold alliance with black rebels; of the French Republicans, despite the fact that they were led by self-styled 'Friends of the Blacks'; of the colonial Patriots, despite their vaunted detestation of tyranny; of the free people of colour, despite the calls of racial solidarity; of the black generals, despite their resistance to their own enslavement.

In peacetime conditions it might just have been possible to reconstruct French colonial slavery without a monarch and without racial privilege. But could it be done with the black rebels still undefeated and in wartime conditions? In the early months of 1793 the Republican order in the French colonies appeared, against the odds, to have staved off complete disintegration. It had brought together a metropolitan-led alliance of *petits blancs* and free people of colour though not yet restored trade flows. The prospect of war probably helped the Republican authorities in the short run, feeding colonial patriotism and nourishing justified suspicion of the planters' plots. But British naval power meant blockades and the virtual certainty of invasion. Spain, with its new black allies, was poised in St Domingue to advance across the border. Sapped from within by planter treason and slave rebellion it seemed that only a miracle could save the Republicans.

Notes

1. Pierre Pluchon, 'Les Révolutions à l'Amérique', in P. Pluchon, ed., *Histoire des Antilles et de la Guyanne*, Paris 1982, pp. 265–328, p. 267. The value of colonial exports had risen from 136 million *livres* in 1776 to 217.5 million *livres* in 1789 according to the official valuations. Colonial trade was valued at metropolitan prices which were about twice as high as those obtained by planters selling their produce in the colonies: the gap between the two represented mercantile costs and profits, together with a small amount of sugar refining and the like. Gross mercantile profits in the region of 100 million *livres*, stemming from near-monopolistic privileges, gave the French Caribbean planters a strong motive to see the *exclusif* ended and the metropolis a correspondingly strong motive for defending it. French re-exports of Antillean produce in 1789 ran at 161 million *livres*, so that 72 per cent of French colonial imports were re-exported. Another striking fact is that French exports to the Antilles and to Africa paid for all imports from the Caribbean, leaving France to garner a huge surplus on its re-export trade. See Maurice Morineau, 'France', in C. Wilson and G. Parker, *An Introduction to the Sources in European Economic History, 1500–1800*, London 1977, pp. 174–5; and Jean Tarrade, *Le Commerce Coloniale de la France à la Fin de l'Ancien Régime*, Paris 1972, 2 vols, II, pp. 740–53.

2. French involvement in the American war cost the incredible sum, of 1,063 million *livres* over the period 1776–84, with service payments of 44 million in 1784, a sum slightly larger than the monarchy's *total* revenues in 1776. The ministry responsible for these expenses was that of the Navy and colonies, whose normal annual budget had been 27.9 million *livres*, of which 10.1 million came under the colonial department. While most historians stress that these expenditures bankrupted the regime it is also worth noting that they inflated the naval and colonial establishment, with its retinue of officers, clerks, contractors, financiers and merchants; while these interests did not act in concert they continued to make themselves felt well past the crisis of 1787–9, as we will see. At this time about 23 *livres* exchanged for £1 sterling; it has been estimated that the purchasing power of the *livre* in the 1770s was equivalent to the US$ of 1968. For all this see Jonathan Dull, *The French Navy and American Independence*, Princeton 1975, pp. xiv, 343–50.

3. Jacques Godechot, 'La France et les problèmes de l'Atlantique à la veille de la Révolution', *Regards sur l'Époque Révolutionaire*, Paris 1980, p. 80. For the colonial interests of the Bordeaux Parlement see William Doyle, *The Parlement of Bordeaux and the End of the Old Regime, 1771–1790*, London 1974, pp. 264–85.

4. William Doyle, *The Origins of the French Revolution*, Oxford 1980, pp. 43–52, 69–95, 132–3.

5. Patrice Higonnet, *Class, Ideology, and the Rights of Nobles during the French Revolution*, Oxford 1981, pp. 44–5; extensive noble involvement in the slave trade, colonial trade and plantations is summarised in Guy Chaussinand–Nogaret, *The French Nobility in the Eighteenth Century*, Cambridge 1985, pp. 56–7, 92–101. Indeed colonial development was the field, *par excellence*, of collaboration between nobles and merchants.

6. For St Domingue see the concise and well-judged account in David Geggus, *Slavery, War and Revolution: The British Occupation of Saint Domingue, 1793–8*, Oxford 1982, especially pp. 33–4; and Torcuato Di Tella, *La Rebelión de Esclavos de Haiti*, Buenos Aires 1984, pp. 21–55. For Martinique, Henry Lémery, *La Révolution Française à la Martinique*, Paris 1936, pp. 13–14 and Alfred Martineau and Louis Phillippe May, *Trois Siècles d'Histoire Antillaise*, Paris 1935, p. 90.

7. Antoine Barnave, *Introduction à la Révolution Française*, written in Paris in 1793,

quoted in Albert Soboul, *The French Revolution 1787–1799*, New York 1975, p. 51; see also Emmanuel Chill, *Power, Property and History: Joseph Barnave's Introduction to the French Revolution and Other Writings*, New York 1971, especially pp. 6–9.

8. Arthur Young, *Travels in France during the Years 1787–1788–1789*, I, pp. 104–5; Paul Bois, *Histoire de Nantes*, Paris 1977, p. 247. But the Nantes *cahiers* were mildly liberal and reformist rather than ultra-radical; see Robert Stein, *The French Slave Trade in the Eighteenth Century*, pp. 174–5.

9. Allan Forrest, *Society and Politics in Revolutionary Bordeaux*, Oxford 1975, p. 33.

10. For colonial proprietors in the Assembly see *Journal des Etats-Generaux*; Lehodey de Saultevreuil, XXXII, p. 159; quoted in M.B. Garrett, *The French Colonial Question, 1789–1791*, New York 1970, p. 2. For the French bourgeoisie on the eve of the Revolution see the discussion in Michele Vovelle, *La Chute de la Monarchie, 1787–1792*, Paris 1972, pp. 62–73; for Marxist assessments of recent debates on the social character of the Revolution see Gregor McLellan, *Marxism and the Methodologies of History*, London 1981, pp. 175–205, and George Comninel, 'The Political Context of the Popular Movement in the French Revolution', in Frederick Krantz, ed., *History from Below*, Montreal 1985, pp. 143–62.

11. Geggus, *Slavery, War and Revolution*, pp. 34–5, 405; J. Santoyant, *La Colonisation Française Pendant la Révolution, 1789–99*, Paris 1930, 2 vols, II, p. 425; Lémery, *La Révolution Française à Martinique*, pp. 41–2.

12. Yvan Debbasch, *Couleur et Liberté*, Paris 1967, pp. 82–3; François Girod, *La Vie Quotidienne de la Societé Creole: Saint Domingue au XVIIIe siècle*, Paris 1972, pp. 190–200. See also the contribution by Léo Elizabeth in D.W. Cohen and J.P. Greene, eds, *Neither Slave nor Free*, Baltimore 1972.

13. Jean Fouchard, *The Haitian Maroons: Liberty or Death*, New York 1981. Fouchard's information shows that slave escapes were common in the 1780s; but large-scale *maronnage* does not seem to have grown in consequence (see pp. 287–368), perhaps because the French military authorities achieved a high level of mobilisation in the colony during this decade as troops were withdrawn from North America. Individual runaways often led to *petits maronnages* or flight to the towns. Slaves practising the *petit maronnage* left the plantation but did not go far and often returned; since overseers and planters generally wanted their slaves back those who returned voluntarily, often after negotiation via some third party, might not be punished very harshly. The growth of the black population of the towns seems to have made it easier for runaways to hide in them. Fouchard's book celebrates in lyrical vein the spirit of resistance evident in large-scale *maronnage* and sometimes appears to discount *petit maronnage*; yet the latter would produce a layer of slaves with outside knowledge, experience and contacts, yet a continuing presence within the plantations, a combination that could, under the right conditions, lead to plantation revolts. Debien qualifies Fouchard's emphasis on the revolutionary significance of the maroons in St Domingue. See Gabriel Debien, *Les Esclaves aux Antilles françaises*, pp. 412–13, 424, 466–8. The Maniel maroons appear to have declined from a strength of 800 or so in the 1770s to some 133 in 1785 when they made a deal with the authorities. See Geggus, 'Slave Resistance Studies and the Saint Domingue Revolt', Florida International University, Winter 1983, p. 7.

14. Daniel P. Resnick, 'The *Société des Amis des Noir* and the Abolition of Slavery', *French Historical Studies*, vol. VII, no. 4, 1972, pp. 558–69.

15. See William Cohen, *The French Encounter with Africans: White Response to Blacks, 1530–1880*, Bloomington, Indiana 1980, pp. 132–52; and Michèle Duchet, *Anthropologie et Histoire au X Siècles des Lumières*, Paris 1971, pp. 151–60.

16. Antoine–Nicolas de Condorcet, 'Réflexions sur l'esclavage des nègres, 1781', in A. Condorcet O'Connor and M.F. Arago, *Oeuvres de Condorcet*, Paris 1847, VII, pp. 61–140 (with Condorcet's postscript, pp. 137–40).

17. Serge Daget, 'A Model of the French Abolitionist Movement', in Bolt and Drescher, *Anti-Slavery, Religion and Reform*, pp. 64–79, especially pp. 66–7.

18. Eloise Ellery, *Brissot de Warville*, Boston 1915, pp. 182–215; Brissot's questioning of accumulated property as theft is developed in *Recherches Philosophiques*

sur le Droit de Propriété et sur le Vol (1780). For an intellectual/biographical sketch see Norman Hampson, *Will and Circumstance*, London 1983, pp. 84–106, 171–92; the anti-capitalism of this bourgeois spokesman is noted on pp. 186–7.

19. Davis, *The Problem of Slavery in the Age of Revolution*, p. 97. For the limited scope of the activities of the *Amis des Noirs* after this early enthusiasm see Daniel P. Resnick, 'The *Societé des Amis des Noirs* and the Abolition of Slavery', *French Historical Studies*, vol. 7, no. 4, Fall 1972, pp. 529–43.

20. Gabriel Debien, *Les Colons de Saint-Domingue et la Révolution, Essai sur le Club Massiac*, Paris 1953, pp. 60–7. Gouy d'Arsy, sometimes spelt d'Arcy, was himself a man of considerable wealth, with estates in St Domingue worth 3 million *livres* according to Chaussinand–Nogaret (*French Nobility*, pp. 56–7). However, the Duc d'Orléans had an annual *income* of 3 million livres. His contribution to destabilising the regime in 1787–90 was very great, with the Palais Royal becoming the main centre of revolutionary agitation in Paris. While it is difficult to prove the role of the Freemasons in promoting revolutionary agitation in the colonies, it seems to have been considerable. For their role more generally see the unbalanced, but not totally mistaken, classic of counter-revolution and the 'conspiracy theory of history', John Robison, *Proofs of a Conspiracy against All the Religions and Governments of Europe*, London and New York 1798.

21. Quoted in C.L.R. James, *The Black Jacobins: Toussaint L'Ouverture and the San Domingo Revolution*, London 1980 (revised edn), p. 60.

22. Debien, *Les Colons de Saint-Domingue et la Révolution*, pp. 67–78.

23. Garrett, *The French Colonial Question*, p. 35. For similar scenes in Guadeloupe see Anne Pérotin–Dumon, *Etre Patriote sous les Tropiques*, Basse Terre 1985, pp. 107–36.

24. Geggus, *Slavery, War and Revolution*, pp. 34–5; J. Santoyant, *La Colonisation Française pendant la Révolution, 1789–1799*, Paris 1930, 2 vols, II, p. 425; Lémery, *La Révolution Française à la Martinique*, pp. 21–42.

25. Ottobah Cugoano, 'Réflexions sur la traite et l'esclavage' (1788), reprinted in EDHIS (Editions d'Histoire Social), *La Révolution Française et l'Abolition de l'Esclavage*, Paris 1968, 12 vols, X.

26. Michael L. Kennedy, *The Jacobin Clubs in the French Revolution: The First Years*, Princeton 1982, p. 202.

27. Garrett, *The French Colonial Question*, pp. 35–48; Debien, *Les Colons de Saint-Domingue et la Révolution*, pp. 187–9.

28. This racist jibe came from the pen of the patriot Loustalot in *Les Révolutions de Paris* and shows that it was not only colonial reactionaries who played the game of the Club Massiac; c.f. Debien, *Les Colons de Saint-Domingue et la Révolution*, p. 84. Another writer who compromised himself on this issue, though less blatantly, was Choderlos Laclos (p. 135).

29. Garrett, *The French Colonial Question*, p. 51.

30. Garrett, *The French Colonial Question*, p. 53.

31. Lémery, *La Révolution Française à la Martinique*, pp. 80–1.

32. Georges Lefebvre, *The French Revolution*, London 1962, p. 145. Lefebvre subsequently observes: 'The universalist claims of the Declaration of Rights indicated that men of colour – mulattoes and free Negroes – would lay claim to its benefits' (p. 172). Since property qualifications for the right to vote, with even stiffer qualifications for the right to be a representative, had already been accepted it was easier to overlook the civic rights of slaves. In fact some three million French men, and all women, were excluded from the franchise (c.f. Soboul, *The French Revolution, 1787–1799*, p. 180). Supporters of the *Amis des Noirs* tended to oppose property qualifications, but there were exceptions (for example, the Abbé Sièyes who invented the concept of 'active citizenship'), just as there were some democrats who did not sympathise with the *Amis* (for instance, Loustalot).

33. Lémery, *La Révolution Française à la Martinique*, pp. 67–86.

34. James, *The Black Jacobins*, pp. 73–4. Some of the Masonic Lodges in St Domingue, as in Philadelphia in the 1780s, had a racially mixed membership; whites took part in Ogé's revolt as well as *gens de couleur*. Ogé opposed a suggestion by a co-

conspirator, Chavannes, to invite slave support. See Jean–Philippe Garron–Coulon, *Rapport sur les troubles de Saint Domingue*, Paris 1797, vol. II, pp. 44–73.

35. Debien, *Les Colons de Saint Domingue et la Révolution*, pp. 210–34; Saintoyant, *La Colonisation Française pendant la Révolution*, II, pp. 22–32.

36. Kennedy, *The Jacobin Clubs in the French Revolution*, p. 82.

37. Quoted in Garrett, *The French Colonial Question*, p. 82.

38. Debien, *Les Colons de Saint-Domingue et la Révolution*, pp. 262–90; Garrett, *The French Colonial Question*, pp. 77–97.

39. James, *The Black Jacobins*, p. 75. Kennedy notes: 'Slavery was an economic issue; mulatto franchise was basically an humanitarian one. The provincial Jacobins could indulge their humanitarian proclivities and support this cause with little apparent danger to their pocket books or to those of their fellow townsmen' (*The Jacobin Clubs*, p. 205). The counter-position here of economic and humanitarian issues is too neat, since, as suggested above, the assertion of metropolitan authority in the colonies had economic advantages too, so far as maritime interests were concerned. Not only did 'humanitarianism' usefully embellish defence of the *exclusif* it also promised to secure allies for this, namely the mulattos themselves.

40. James, *The Black Jacobins*, p. 80.

41. James, *The Black Jacobins*, p. 81. As James himself comments: 'Slavery . . . had now corrupted the French bourgeoisie in the first flush of its political inheritance.' Debien entitles this section of his monograph: 'Le redressement – Avec Barnave vers le Roi (16 mai – octobre 1791)'. See also Vovelle, *La Chute de la Monarchie*, pp. 163–7. The triumvirate, to appease their consciences or their supporters, endorsed a decree suppressing the remnants of slavery in France a few days after their reversal on mulatto rights.

42. The traditional account is given in Fouchard, *The Haitian Maroons*, pp. 340–41, 358. Geggus cites evidence for a meeting which planned the uprising and concedes that a voodoo ceremony is quite plausible. He speculates that the uprising may have benefited from a royalist manoeuvre which backfired, though curiously concludes that, if true, 'the autonomy of the slave insurrection is considerably diminished' (*Slavery, War and Revolution*, p. 40). Fouchard also accepts that royalist intrigues to stimulate slave unrest were abroad at this time (p. 98), though in the end the slaves acted for themselves.

43. The letter to the Governor dated September 4th is cited in Pierre Pluchon, *Toussaint Louverture, de l'esclavage au pouvoir*, Paris 1979, p. 26. The report on the killing of Boukman is cited at length in Fouchard, *The Haitian Maroons*, pp. 342–3. The French official report on the revolt estimated that 12,000–15,000 slaves were involved by the end of August, Garran–Coulon, *Rapport sur les Troubles de Saint Domingue*, II, p. 214.

44. Geggus, *Slavery, War and Revolution*, pp. 52–3. Cadusch, a colonel of the *maréchaussée*, had helped to promote a 'concordat' between white and mulatto proprietors and was later to play a major part in engineering the British invasion. At this time his views were not yet shared by most planters.

45. James, *The Black Jacobins*, p. 106. Biassou and Jean François, though not Toussaint, were later involved as participants in a fairly active slave trade, thus richly meriting James's scorn. See David Geggus,'From His Most Catholic Majesty to the Godless Republique: The Volte Face of Toussaint Louverture and the Ending of Slavery in Saint Domingue', *Revue Française d'Histoire d'Outre Mer*, no. 241, 1978, pp. 481–99, p. 490.

46. Carolyn Fick, 'Black Peasants and Soldiers in the Saint Domingue Revolution', in Fredrick Krantz, *History From Below*, pp. 243–61, on pp. 245–6. This author reports that the rebel-held area was known to the blacks as the Kingdom of Platons.

47. Kennedy, *The Jacobin Clubs in the French Revolution*, p. 208.

48. For St Domingue at this period see Robert Stein, *Léger Felicité Sonthonax: The Lost Sentinel of the Republic*, Madison 1985, pp. 39–62; Di Tella, *La Rebelión de Esclavos de Haiti*, p. 83; and Geggus, *Slavery, War and Revolution*, pp. 46–67.

49. Quoted in Lémery, *La Révolution Française à la Martinique*, pp. 186–7.

50. Pérotin–Dumon, *Etre Patriote sous les Tropiques*, pp. 161–76.

51. Lémery, *La Révolution Française à la Martinique*, p. 225. In the light of the author's evident sympathy for those French planters who collaborated with the British to save slavery it is interesting to note that he became the Vichy government's first Minister of Colonies. For the agreements concluded see Lémery, *La Révolution Française à la Martinique*, p. 226, and Geggus, *Slavery, War and Revolution*, pp. 395–99.

52. Geggus, *Slavery, War and Revolution*, p. 100.

53. Saintoyant, *La Colonisation Française pendant la Révolution*, pp. 121–8.

54. José L. Franco, *Historia de la Revolución de Haiti*, Havana 1966, pp. 229, 238–4.

VI

Revolutionary Emancipationism and the Birth of Haiti

Que veut cette hordes d'esclaves
De traitres, de Rois conjurés?
Pour qui ces ignobles entravés,
Ces fers des longtemps preparés
Francais! pour nous, ah! quel outrage!
Quels transports il doit exciter?
C'est nous qu'on ose mediter
De rendre a l'antique esclavage
Aux Armes citoyens! formez vos bataillons; marchons, marchons,
Qu'un sang impur, abreuve nos sillons.

La Marseillaise (1792)

Dessalines sorti lan Nord,
Vini compté ça li porte,
Ça li porte.
Li porte fusils, li porte boulets
Ouanga nouveau!

(Dessalines is coming to the North
Come see what he is bringing.
He is bringing muskets, he is bringing bullets,
These are the new talismans.)

Haitian song (1803–4?)

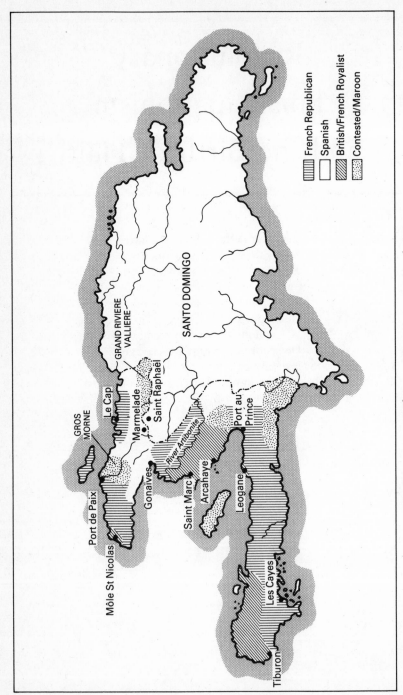

Legend:

- French Republican
- Spanish
- British/French Royalist
- Contested/Maroon

Map labels:
GROS MORNE, Le Cap, Marmelade, Saint Raphaël, GRAND RIVIERE VALLIERE, SANTO DOMINGO, Port de Paix, Môle St Nicolas, Gonaïves, Saint Marc, River Artibonite, Arcahaye, Port au Prince, Leogane, Tiburon, Les Cayes

St Domingue and Santo Domingo in April 1794

During the years 1793 and 1794 the French Antilles passed through the furnace of war and revolution to emerge with a radically new social order. British blockade soon made normal commerce and communication between France and its Caribbean possessions difficult and dangerous, but this did not prevent the sealing of a precarious but vital alliance between black liberation in the New World and the Jacobin Republic in the Old.

The position of the Republicans in St Domingue by the middle of 1793 was perilous. Only about 3,500 of the troops sent from the metropolis were still alive, and of these many were sick and others ready to desert. The Republican Commissioners exercised a precarious hold on the major centres thanks to this force and its major ally, the newly named units of coloured troops, the *Légion d'Egalité*, composed of 'Citizens of April 4th', that is free blacks and mulattos, often veterans of the *Légion de Saint Domingue*. But the Spanish, with their black commanders, were poised to advance across the border while pockets of royalist strength were to be found in many areas. The Republican authorities were further hampered by a dearth of resources. Metropolitan *assignats* had little currency in the Antilles, with the traditional colonial preference for gold and silver. The Commissioners decreed a property levy on urban and rural estates. This measure, often implemented by newly appointed coloured officials, provoked bitter hostility from white proprietors still within the Republican zone. The offensives undertaken against the black rebels proved indecisive, with the latter abandoning territory but regrouping in more remote areas. The Commissioners had successfully disposed of Desparbès but nearly six months later, with depleted forces and communications to France broken, they were to face another internal crisis.[1]

In May 1793 a new Governor, General Galbaud, arrived at Le Cap with a squadron that had evaded the British. Sonthonax was absent from the Northern capital at the time and Galbaud, who had inherited property in the colony, was turned against the Commissioner by white colonists who opposed his financial levies and promotion of the *gens de couleur*. Galbaud publicly insisted that he was not subordinate to the Commissioners and that they had been exceeding their authority. He assembled a large consignment of plantation produce which he proposed to sell to North American merchants in order to obtain military supplies. Sonthonax and Polverel rushed to Le Cap and issued a proclamation dismissing him from his post and ordering him to leave for France, charged with conspiring against the Republic. General Laveaux, commanding the Republican forces at Port de Paix, supported the Commissioners, but Galbaud refused to comply with the deportation order issued against him. In his defiance of the Commissioners he received support from most of the French naval squadron in the harbour at Le Cap together with most of the city's white militia forces. Le Cap at this time contained large numbers of dissident whites, royalists and autonomists, some having sought refuge there from areas of mulatto power in the West, others awaiting passage to the United States, and some sentenced to deportation to France. After clashes with Galbaud's supporters the Commissioners retired from Le Cap, with units of the *Légion d'Egalité*. The Republican enclaves in the South were too embattled to lend any assistance. However, in the hills around Le Cap there were rebel bands, led by such men as Macaya and Pierrot, who had stayed in the vicinity of the plantations while resisting the authority of the planters or managers. The Commissioners decided to appeal to these black partisans to help them regain control of Le Cap. Those who responded to their appeal would receive arms and liberty: 'We declare that the will of the French Republic, and that of its delegates, is to give liberty to all Negro warriors who will fight for the Republic under the orders of the Civil Commissioner.'[2] Several thousand black fighters responded to this appeal and descended on Le Cap on June 22nd and 23rd where they threw back the white rebels; Galbaud was persuaded to set sail, taking with him to Baltimore many thousands of white colonists. Much of Le Cap was destroyed during the fighting; in its aftermath the columns of Macaya and Pierrot returned to the countryside, leaving behind them the smouldering ruins of the once splendid provincial capital.

The Republican forces repossessed Le Cap, but their position throughout the North was critically weakened by the division that had erupted in their ranks. The black rebels had been ready to attack their former owners or managers in Le Cap, as an insurance against their return, as a way of acquiring muskets and perhaps with the prospect of plunder too; but afterwards, unwilling to accept Republican orders, they dispersed, taking their muskets with them. In July the Spanish forces advanced across a broad front in the North, with their black-commanded columns reaching deep into French territory. Spanish advances cut off the Republican garrisons in Le Cap and Port de Paix. Rumours of an imminent British invasion and of collusion by autonomist municipalities abounded. Polverel returned to Port au Prince, now Port Républicain, but in the South and West the writ of the Republic depended solely on the forces of the mulatto General Rigaud. In the North Laveaux and Sonthonax were bottled up in their coastal enclaves, seeking to enlist such black soldiers as they could. They urged the black generals fighting with Spain to join them, but to no avail.

With the Republican forces divided, Sonthonax was the supreme authority in the North. He sent a letter in early August to the National Convention urging that the time had come to proclaim the great principle of emancipation. The municipality of Le Cap submitted a petition to the Commissioner on August 25th 'in the name of the *cultivateurs* of Saint Domingue', saying that slavery must be ended. On August 29th 1793 Sonthonax took the fateful step of issuing a decree freeing all slaves in his jurisdiction. The decree was published in *Kréyole* to ensure that it could reach the mass of blacks.[3] In the North the slave order was already greatly weakened but in the North-west, South and West there were certainly still hundreds of thousands of slaves, perhaps as many as a quarter of a million. The Spanish occupying forces had strict instructions to uphold the slave regime. When the British occupied large tracts of the Centre and South in succeeding months, they found that planter militias had ensured the survival of the slave regime and of plantation production. The Spanish commanders used columns of black troops but they guaranteed slave property. Sonthonax's decree, following up the more limited appeal of June, was based on a judgement of the scope for building a Republican army from the mass of black slaves. Sporadic slave rebellions were reported from various parts in the summer of 1793 and this will have encouraged Sonthonax. But he also took the risk that mulatto proprietors would be alienated by his action, as indeed many were. Polverel, stationed in the South, had extended a promise of freedom to those fighting with four named maroon commanders – Armand, Martial, Formon and Bénnech – in late July. While the rebel chiefs were offered Republican commissions, and their followers obtained muskets and powder, they were expected to help maintain plantation discipline; Rigaud attacked Formon for his failure to comply with this order. Though planters or managers remained in control in many areas they faced widespread pressure for a five-day week, or for more far-reaching improvements in their labourers' working or living conditions. Polverel at first sought to limit emancipation offers to potential soldiers and slaves who were the property of émigrés. Despite reservations about Sonthonax's decree of August 29th, which he thought did not make adequate provision for an alternative labour regime, he decided to endorse it on September 21st. His willingness to defer to the mulatto proprietors was probably lessened by the knowledge that many of them were now colluding with the Republic's enemies. The decree of general emancipation allowed the Republican authorities to enlist some black soldiers and to present themselves as the champions of a new plantation regime which yielded to many of the most common demands of the slave crews. The previous policy of offering freedom only to individual blacks had forced potential recruits to abandon family and comrades which many had not been prepared to do. And so long as slavery remained legal newly freed blacks would still feel insecure. Under the pressure of the Spanish invasion Sonthonax had seen that it was essential to go further and make a collective appeal to the enslaved blacks. Sonthonax's decree, following up the more limited measure of June, extended the scope for recruiting blacks, allowed the Republicans to appeal to the good will of the black masses and conferred a moral advantage on the Republican cause.[4]

The Republican Commissioners and commanders urged the black generals fighting with Spain to rally to the Republic now that it offered general emancipation and civic equality. Toussaint Bréda, now commander at Marmelade in the West, replied to the effect that Republicans, having betrayed their King, were in no position to offer liberty to his subjects. While Toussaint rejected French appeals he now began to differentiate himself from the other Spanish commanders by finding ways to identify with black resistance to enslavement. Some time in the early months of 1793 Toussaint abandoned the name of Bréda, the plantation where he was born, and adopted that of 'Louverture', or more rarely 'L'Ouverture', he who makes an opening. Following the Spanish invasion in July Toussaint's forces had swelled in size and they had occupied much of the strategically important Artibonite, commanding the passage from the North to the West. Operating at this distance from his commanders Toussaint enjoyed considerable autonomy. Significantly enough, he was to issue an appeal to the oppressed population of the colony, given the same date as the decree issued by Sonthonax:

> Brothers and Friends. I am Toussaint L'Ouverture, my name is perhaps known to you. I have undertaken vengeance. I want liberty and equality to reign in San Domingo. I work to bring them into existence. Unite yourselves to us, brothers, and fight with us for the same cause etc. Your very humble and obedient servant. TOUSSAINT L'OUVERTURE, General of the Armies of the King, for the Public Good.[5]

Toussaint Louverture had reason to treat with reserve the approaches made by the French Republicans: it was far from clear whether the decrees of the Civil Commissioners would ever be endorsed by their home government. However, Toussaint did admit into his camp deserters and stragglers from the French military, using them to train his soldiers and to provide staff work; French *curés* were employed as secretaries. From the outset Toussaint's forces were distinguished by their discipline and mobility. Toussaint himself was an ex-slave of fifty who had worked successively as coachman and veterinarian. He had learned to read and write, acquired an estate by marriage, and been entrusted with considerable responsibilities by the manager of the Bréda plantation, who had manumitted him in the first place. Toussaint is reputed to have read Raynal's *History*, with its vigorous denunciation of slavery, in the library at Bréda. He enjoyed good relations with Bayou de Libertas, the plantation manager, and ensured his family's safety in the aftermath of August 1791. Toussaint's lieutenants included Moyse, a former slave at Bréda; and Dessalines, who had been the menial slave of a freedman. It was characteristic of Toussaint's force that many *nouveaux libres* held posts of command. As a former slave Toussaint could better understand the aspirations of the mass of blacks than did the mulatto commanders; as an *affranchi* he had more experience of administration and affairs than the other black generals. At the time of the Revolution he was already quite well off and his estate was worked by a dozen or more hired slaves. Joining the insurrection he risked more than others and perhaps for that reason expected more from it. He had acted as Biassou's secretary and aide-de-camp before acquiring an independent command and in the former capacities had participated in the dubious negotiations with the French authorities in the closing months of 1791. Not until he was installed in the remote and mountainous region of the Artibonite did he reveal any broader vision.

Toussaint Louverture and Sonthonax both understood that the slaves were the key to the future of the colony and that victory would belong to whoever was accepted by them as the bearer of their will to freedom. But both men were exceeding the authority given to them and directly flouting their instructions. Sonthonax could plead that the powers conferred on him allowed him to set aside the instructions he had received from the Navy Ministry but he realised that this was a precarious case to argue. In September he organised elections to fill St Domingue's quota of delegates in the National Convention and made sure that those elected were firm supporters of his emancipationist policy. Because of the blockade the delegates left for Philadelphia on their way to Paris. For his part Toussaint hoped to persuade the Spanish that they could only win control of St Domingue if they were prepared to match the Republican Commissioners' decree of general liberty. While the Marquis de Hermonas was prepared, as a military man, to consider such a proposal from one of his ablest black generals, the Spanish political authorities soon made clear that they would under no circumstances countenance any attacks on slavery. The Spanish authorities were hoping that, whatever happened in Europe, St Domingue and Santo Domingo would be reunited under the Spanish Crown as a flourishing slave colony.

In the last days of September a small British expedition – only 801 troops in the first instance – occupied Jérémie in the extreme South-west and Môle St Nicolas in the extreme North-west. St Marc and other Western ports were occupied by the end of the year, usually at the invitation of the municipality: the mulatto mayors of Arcahaie (Lapointe) and Léogane (Labissonnière) welcomed the British. In a pragmatic way the British were prepared to work with powerful mulatto proprietors though other free people of colour were promised no security in their rights and slavery was, of course, maintained. The main mulatto commanders in the South and West – Rigaud, Pinchinat and Beauvais – remained faithful to the Republic. Nevertheless the Republicans seemed caught in a pincer, with the Spanish free to move in across the Eastern border while the British could use naval power to land wherever they wished on the Western seaboard. With this cover French royalists acted with increasing boldness, visiting summary justice on any Republican they captured and making clear to all their determination to uphold the slave regime. Substantial British and royalist reinforcements were expected in the early months of 1794. While the main British expedition sailed to the Windward Islands the British occupying force in St Domingue grew to 3,600 men by April 1794; bridgeheads at half a dozen places enjoyed the protection of the Royal Navy. Republican St Domingue, by contrast, was almost completely cut off from its metropolis.[6]

The main British expedition, 7,000 men aboard eight ships of the line and a dozen lesser vessels, reached the Windwards in December 1793. The British first captured Trinidad and Ste Lucie while blockading Martinique and Guadeloupe. Martinique was captured in February, followed by Guadeloupe's small insular dependencies and, finally, Guadeloupe itself was taken on March 20th. Rochambeau and Lacrosse put up some resistance but, in the face of superior forces, surrendered the colony to the British. In the last weeks before the final British assault the Republicans of Guadeloupe decided to recruit a special black *chasseur* regiment from the colony's slaves; 300 out of a projected 500 were enrolled prior to the final invasion. Apparently both sides were prepared to leave the main body of 170,000 slaves in the Iles du Vent as spectators of the conflict. The British occupation was accompanied by the return of many planters who found their estates in reasonable working order. Once the British had secured the Windwards they could spare more forces for St Domingue, where they planned to capture Port au Prince.[7]

A crucial turning-point in the fortunes of Republican St Domingue came about between the end of April and the end of May 1794. On April 29th the British commander at St Marc learned that Toussaint, the commander at Gonaives forty miles up the coast, had broken with Spain and its royalist allies. On April 4th the planters at Gonaives had sent a petition to Toussaint's Spanish superior requesting his removal. They complained that Toussaint did not obey Biassou's orders and that the military posts that his forces controlled had become places of refuge for every type of black miscreant and runaway, including slaves who had stolen from, or even murdered, their masters. In the wake of the conflict Toussaint had clearly decided that his position as a Spanish officer was now untenable. Turning on Spain and its local allies he ordered his forces, which now numbered 4,000 seasoned fighters, to refuse further collaboration with the Spanish authorities and prepare to attack neighbouring Spanish strongpoints. Toussaint's forces apparently had no difficulty in accepting his volte-face. For some time it was unclear whether Toussaint intended to join the Republicans or to remain independent, as a number of black commanders had done in other parts of the colony. On May 24th 1794 Laveaux sent a message to Polverel reporting: 'Toussaint Louverture, one of the three chiefs of the African royalists, in coalition with the Spanish Government, has at last discovered his true interests and that of his brothers; he has realised that kings can never be the friends of liberty; he fights today for the Republic at the head of an armed force.'[8] Laveaux had yet to meet Toussaint and realise the full extent of the improvement in his situation.

In the conflict between the French Republicans and the invading forces the issue of slavery had surfaced irresistibly. Jean François and Biassou had shown themselves willing to maintain the slave regime, but Toussaint refused to do so. Military clashes and the competing appeals of Toussaint and Sonthonax had helped to set the scene for a new wave of slave resistance. The early months of 1794 had witnessed a fire-cracker chain of slave revolts in the North, spreading southwards to the West. Toussaint had orders to stamp out such insurrections but instead gave shelter to the rebels. It was this that had provoked the planter protests.[9]

Prior to May 1794 the Republic did have some capable black officers – they included Colonel Pierre Michel and Captain Henry Christophe, the latter now seconded to Toussaint's staff – but not the mainstream of those forces thrown up by the revolt. If Toussaint had not committed his by now well-trained and increasingly effective forces to the Republic the surge of slave resistance would not by itself have prevented the British and Spanish from completing their occupation of the colony. Toussaint's switch was soon followed by a lightning campaign in the course of which he recaptured most of the Northern plain from the Spanish occupiers. Between Toussaint's abandonment of the Spanish and his definitive adhesion to the Republicans had been a brief hiatus during which neither side knew for sure what he was doing. The timing of Toussaint's unequivocal declaration for the Republic may have been influenced by news received from Europe: on February 4th the French Convention decreed emancipation in all the French colonies. Whether or not Toussaint knew of this decree when he abandoned Spain it certainly cemented the basis for a fateful alliance and a new Republican order in St Domingue.[10]

The condition of the metropolis in 1793–4 was scarcely less troubled than that of the French colonies. The Brissotins had proved far more decisive in foreign and colonial policy than they were in the handling of the situation created by the disintegration of the *ancien régime* and the continuance of popular unrest. 1792 had witnessed a new *jacquerie* in the countryside. The disruption of colonial trade fuelled the far more serious revolt in the *Vendée*. The Brissotins had launched France on the path of war in the hope of nipping armed counter-revolution in the bud, restoring initiative to the executive and laying the basis for a new European order. But they proved unable to contain the forces unleashed by the war or to construct an authoritative political centre. Generals whom they had chosen defected, while military disaster provoked unprecedented popular mobilisations; the *grande levée* of 1793 put half a million men under arms. Eventually the more radical Jacobins of the Mountain gained ascendancy in the sections, amongst the soldiers, and in the Convention. The Committee of Public Safety was set up in April 1793. The Jacobins obtained the exclusion of the leading Girondins from the Convention in June 1793 and further consolidated their grip following the Federalist revolt which ensued. Under pressure from the popular movement and the needs of war the Jacobins began to construct a revolutionary administration and to elaborate a new Declaration of Rights which dispensed with the absolute guarantee to private property contained in the Declaration of 1789. The radical Jacobins were prepared to qualify the rights of the propertied, to curtail market forces and to sanction new social rights; but not to tolerate combinations of workers or to countenance the egalitarian doctrines that now emerged amongst the more extreme *sans-culottes* . It was at this time that the remaining non-capitalist forms of property were swept away. On July 17th, around the time Sonthonax was preparing to decree the extinction of slave property, the Convention finally abolished, without indemnification, all remaining feudal rights. In August the Abbé Grégoire, as President of the Convention, secured the abolition of the slave trade bounty. In October 1793 the revolutionary calendar was adopted, symbolising the aspiration to make the world anew.

The turbulence of revolution brought to the surface a subterranean current of rude popular egalitarianism and hostility to wealth and commerce. This underground tradition, reflecting the communal aspect of the outlook of peasants, labourers and artisans had been expressed better by communistic *curés* and 'contumacious Abbés' than by the mainstream of enlightenment thought, with its anti-slavery essays and exclamations. The *Testament* of Jean Meslier and the *Observations* of the Abbé Mably, with their attacks on large-scale property, on the false prosperity of the trading centres and the arrogance of the rich, articulated popular prejudices that undermined a crucial support of the colonial slave system, namely respect for the slaveholders' property rights. In 1793 Pierre Dolivier and other *curés rouges* attacked property in the name of *la justice primitive*, themes that were later to inspire the Conspiracy of the Equals. Chaumette, the Hébertiste prosecutor of the Paris Commune, declared that it was necessary to crush the rich before they starved the people. Where the social regime of the metropolis was concerned Babeuf was to be closer to giving political expression to this revolutionary undercurrent than were the Jacobins or even the Cordeliers. But Jacobin legislators still had to take account of it; in the case of colonial slavery they could do so with few inhibitions.[11]

The Jacobins were prepared to concede more to the popular movement than had the Brissotins, but were still far from satisfying it or from solving the crisis of the economy. The abolition of slavery by the Convention came at a point when the Jacobin Republic needed to overcome internal divisions and concentrate all energies on the revolution's fight for survival. It came at a peculiar moment of destiny and exaltation in the unfolding of the revolutionary drama, signalling the high-water mark of its social aspirations and of its preparedness to subordinate propertied interests to a higher end.

The troubles in the colonies continued to contribute to the disintegration of the metropolitan social order. The Brissotin policy of defending mulatto rights had helped momentarily to contain planter autonomism and royalism but not to restore the colonial system to proper working order. From June 1793 those scant supplies of plantation produce which French merchants could acquire in the Caribbean had to break the British blockade. Sugar and coffee became even harder to find – though by this time it was shortage of basic foodstuffs rather than sugar which sparked off riots. The political influence of the maritime bourgeoisie was destroyed by the fiasco of the Federalist revolt in the summer and by the collapse of the traditional commercial infrastructure linked to the colonies and foreign trade. The furore about the 'Foreign Plot' which permeated factional conflict from November 1793 was fed by reports of defections in the colonies;

slaveholding planters had placed themselves outside the national fold.[12]

In Paris there were few interests directly linked to colonial commerce, but a dubious attempt to refloat the Compagnie des Indes, exposed in January 1794, tainted those who had dabbled in colonial speculations and weakened the position of Danton's friends, the *indulgents*. By this time the *sans-culottes* were inclined to suspect all merchants of vicious and unpatriotic activities. Writing of February 1794 – Pluviôse An II – the very time when the Convention addressed itself to the question of colonial slavery, Soboul notes: 'Hostility towards merchants, a hostility so characteristic of the popular mentality, remained as strong as ever, despite the enforcement of various types of control over the economic life of the nation.'[13] The international situation, with the British playing a leading role in the counter-revolutionary coalition, remained menacing: but early victories and the success of the *grande levée* induced a definite revolutionary self-confidence.

The national Convention came to decide on colonial slavery just before the purge of the Hébertistes and Dantonistes but long after the flight, imprisonment or execution of most leading members of the *Amis des Noirs*. The *Amis* had never matched the public campaigns of the British Abolition Society; by the end of 1793 it was effectively defunct. Yet the *Amis* had helped to radicalise the revolution through their battle for mulatto rights; Sonthonax, one of their supporters, was instrumental in bringing the slavery question before the Convention. The three emancipationist delegates sent to the Convention at Sonthonax's initiative arrived in Paris in late January 1794. These new deputies – a black freedman, a mulatto and a white colon – were arrested on arrival at the instigation of colonial Jacobins critical of Sonthonax but they were soon released and presented themselves at the Convention. The black deputy, Jean–Baptiste Belley–Mars, formerly the military commander of Le Cap, was loudly applauded. Dufay, the white deputy, delivered a passionate speech on February 4th (Pluviôse 16, An II) defending the general liberty that had been decreed in St Domingue and urging that, as an act of both justice and military necessity, it be extended to the other French colonies. He pointed to the opportunities for a revolutionary counter-offensive in the Caribbean. It was common knowledge that a large British fleet had been dispatched to the West Indies. Dufay's declarations were met with rapturous applause. Levasseur of Sarthe proposed that the Convention move immediately to abolish slavery in the colonies: 'Citizen President, do not suffer the Convention to demean itself by a discussion.' The motion was thereupon carried by acclamation and embodied in a decree proposed by Lacroix of the Eure et Loire which ran as follows: 'The National Convention declares slavery abolished in all the colonies. In consequence it declares that all men, without distinction of colour, domiciled in the colonies, are French citizens and enjoy all the rights assured under the Constitution.'[14]

The decree came before the Convention for ratification without any report or recommendation from the Committee of Public Safety; on this occasion Danton spoke. In all probability the delegates from St Domingue had evoked a quite spontaneous and unexpected reaction. Danton declared:

> Representatives of the French people, until now we have decreed liberty as egotists for ourselves. But today we proclaim universal liberty . . . . Today the Englishman is dead! [Loud applause] Pitt and his plots are done for! France, until now cheated of her glory, repossesses it before the eyes of an astonished Europe and assumes the preponderance which must be assured her by her principles, her energy, her land and her population! Activity, energy, generosity, but generosity guided by the flame of reason, and regulated by the compass of principles, and thus assured forever of the recognition of posterity.[15]

Danton's overblown rhetoric of national messianism scarcely did justice to the Convention's decree which did indeed deserve, but has rarely received, the 'recognition of posterity'. It is usually relegated to little more than a footnote whether in histories of the French Revolution or in histories of New World slavery. The Convention was, it is true, confirming and generalising a decree which had already been issued locally by its Commissioner. The Convention's confirmation gave greater legal force and substance to the policy Sonthonax had already adopted and required that it should be spread to the other French colonies. In St Domingue it helped to convince a crucial section of the insurgent black forces that the Republic was their ally. At the time the Convention decreed the abolition of slavery a British expeditionary force was just completing its occupation of the French Windward islands, though of this the Convention was, as yet, unaware. In principle the decree of Pluviôse had struck down, without any compensation, the most important form of colonial property. The decree also had major foreign policy implications. If the execution of Louis XVI had outraged the monarchies of Europe, the decree of Pluviôse ranged the new Republic not only against all the European colonial powers but also against its one remaining potential ally, the United States. Awareness of this fact had induced a certain caution in the Committee of Public Safety, which was only overcome by the direct intercession of the St Domingue deputies and the general spirit of revolutionary audacity which had gripped the Convention.

The Commune of Paris celebrated the decree of Pluviôse in a special event held in the Temple of Reason, as Notre Dame was now called, with the participation of many coloured citizens.[16] Chaumette delivered a eulogy of the Convention's decree; together with other Hébertistes and sponsors of the Cult of Reason he had adopted the cause of emancipation with special fervour. Whatever reservations may have been entertained by the Committee of Public Safety concerning the decision of the Convention, these did not stop it immediately assembling an expedition to the New World, with instructions to undertake a revolutionary war for the liberation of the slaves. With the decree of Pluviôse anti-slavery had ceased to be an occasion for philanthropic gestures and sentimental declamation; united with the insurgent slaves of the Caribbean it became an active protagonist in the momentous conflicts of Europe and the New World. For a brief but vital period the programme of radical abolitionism was fuelled by slave rebellion and sponsored by a major power.

The expedition sent to the Caribbean successfully evaded the British blockade and arrived in the vicinity of the Windward Islands in April, a little over two months from the date of the decree. The expedition comprised 1,200 men aboard two frigates, five transports and one brigantine. It was under the command of two Commissioners appointed by the Convention: Victor Hugues and Pierre Chrétien, both supporters of the Mountain. They discovered on arrival that the French islands were entirely in the hands of the British, who had occupied them with the active complicity of royalists. Hugues effected a landing on Guadeloupe and by April 23rd had liberated a part of the island and defeated a 700-strong detachment of royalists. From this beach-head the Commissioner unleashed a revolutionary war upon the slave-owners and their British backers, freeing the slaves and forming them into units of the *Légion d'Egalité* and the newly created *Bataillon des Antilles*. Between April and December the Republicans ejected the British occupying force of between 3,000 and 4,000 troops, capturing 2,000 rifles and 38 guns. The Republican Commissioners brought with them a guillotine and a printing press, both of which machines were set busily to work. Victor Hugues, formerly the prosecutor at Rochefort during the Terror and with prior experience in the Antilles, soon established himself as the effective chief of the Republican forces. Captured royalists were summarily executed. Copies of the decree of Pluviôse, of the Rights of Man and of other revolutionary documents and addresses were translated into Spanish, Portuguese, Dutch and English and clandestinely introduced to all parts of the Caribbean. The main British forces on Martinique were too large and well entrenched to be tackled head-on, but expeditions from Guadeloupe liberated the islands of Ste Lucie and Desiderade from the British.[17]

Over the next two years Hugues organised a highly successful flotilla of corsairs which proceeded to prey upon British, Spanish and North American shipping. These corsairs – their ships had such names as *L'Incorruptible*, *La Tyrannicide*, *L'Ami du Peuple*, *Le Terroriste* and *La Bande Joyeuse* – continued to flaunt a species of buccaneering Jacobinism long after the overthrow of Robespierre in Paris. The Dutch colonies of St Eustatius and St Martin, which had been in British hands, were recaptured by the French Republicans on behalf of the newly declared Batavian Republic. Slave conspiracies and maroon rebellion erupted in several colonies, directly or indirectly inspired by the events in the French islands: Venezuela, Brazil, Jamaica and Cuba were all affected, as will be recounted in subsequent chapters.

The most sustained and impressive struggles erupted in two islands, Grenada and St Vincent, which Britain had acquired from France in the 1760s. Republican propaganda helped to create an extraordinary alliance in these colonies between a handful of *Kréyole*-speaking mulatto proprietors and the mass of slaves, most of whom also spoke the French colonial patois. On St Vincent the Republican forces were further strengthened by the adhesion of the 'black Caribs' who had resisted the British in the 1770s. The revolt in Grenada was led by Julien Fédon, a mulatto proprietor who freed his own slaves prior to raising the French Republican standard, inscribed with the words *Liberté, Egalité ou la Mort*, on March 1st 1795. Five hundred Republican reinforcements were landed on St Vincent in September 1795; with this help from Guadeloupe Fédon succeeded in confining the British garrison to a tiny enclave around the town of St George's by February 1796 after a series of hard-fought battles and skirmishes. Over this same period the British were also driven from most of St Vincent by a combined force of revolutionary Republicans and black Caribs, the latter led by their chief Joseph Chatoyer. The Republican regimes not only freed the slaves but armed them, thereby creating a formidable barrier to the predictable British attempt at reconquest.[18]

On Guadeloupe the French Republican forces were racially mixed with some liberated blacks, such as the celebrated Captain Vulcain, rising to posts of command. However, the experienced stratum of mulatto *anciens libres* predominated in the key commands. Most of the 90,000 or so former slaves on Guadeloupe itself remained on the plantations, where they were kept at work by regulations against vagabonds and rules which restricted access to the provision grounds to those working on the plantations. In principle the plantation labourers could not be beaten and were to receive a share of the proceeds after sale of the harvest – however, they may often have been cheated by the merchants, officials and former *commandeurs* to whom plantation administration was entrusted. Night-work in the sugar mills was suspended and the rigours of the new system were somewhat softened by Republican reliance on armed blacks. In a report to the Directory Victor Hugues blandly reported: 'These new citizens calmly enjoy their new status: although not paid they work, in truth a little slowly, but they work.' The Commissioner was also happy to note: 'At St Vincent we have renewed the ancient friendship which bound us to the Caribs; their chief is strongly attached to us.'[19] The more embattled Republican forces in Grenada and St Vincent had little possibility of maintaining plantation output but they did encourage an expansion of subsistence cultivation.

In St Domingue the Republicans' main gains in 1794–5 were at the expense of the Spanish. The British Navy, enjoying naval supremacy despite the corsairs, could bombard coastal strongpoints and concentrate forces at whichever point they chose. In St Domingue, with its long and heavily indented coastline, this was a considerable advantage. In June 1794 the British captured Port au Prince, capital of the South, together with some of its hinterland and a coastal strip, but thereafter their advance ground to a halt. The Republicans in St Domingue, strengthened by the adhesion of Toussaint and armed with the decree of Pluviôse, stoutly resisted the combined forces of the British, the royalists and the Spanish. The mulatto commanders Beauvais and Rigaud remained faithful to the Republic and checked British advances in the South and West. Rigaud's force numbered 5,000 infantry and 1,500 cavalry. Toussaint consolidated his hold on the Artibonite and much of the North: his forces grew from 4,000 to 10,000 infantry, with two cavalry regiments. Toussaint also managed to win to the Republican cause a few thousand maroons, led by Dieudonné. Laveaux in the North also won over new forces, the independent black rebels of the Gros Morne. From about this time Pierrot, who had helped to defeat Galbaud in 1793, aligned his forces with the Republic. The mulatto General Villatte, based on Le Cap, faced the Spanish in the North-east.[20]

Sonthonax, who had done so much to restore Republican fortunes, was recalled in June 1794 to answer criticisms that had been made of his conduct and administration. Had the Jacobins survived he might have become a victim of murderous factionalism since he could be accused of being the tool of Brissot, Danton or the Hébertistes. Jeanbon Saint–André, a member of the Committee of Public Safety linked to the colonial patriot milieu, had supported the charges against Sonthonax while Fouché was to defend the Commissioner. With the advent of the Directory Sonthonax's Brissotin past no longer counted against him and in the course of a lengthy inquiry he vindicated all his work in St Domingue; the last act of the revolutionary Convention of 1792–5 was to exonerate its Commissioner in St Domingue on all charges and to congratulate him on the success of his mission. Sonthonax's presence in Paris gave revolutionary St Domingue a well-informed and influential advocate; before long the new Colonial Minister, Admiral Truguet, was to nominate him to head another commission to the colony.[21]

In the summer of 1794 a Spanish invasion of France was driven back across the Pyrenees. Hoping to forestall attack by the Republic's formidable armies, Spain concluded peace with France in July 1795 and, by the terms of the Treaty of Basle, ceded Spanish Santo Domingo to France, though no effective French administration could be established there for some time. Biassou and Jean François still commanded several thousand troops when news of the treaty arrived; they withdrew to Santo Domingo, and were then evacuated to Cuba, leaving most of their followers behind. The Directory's diplomacy and victories in Europe thus reduced pressure on its still beleagured forces in St Domingue.

Republican resistance in St Domingue and the success of the revolutionary counter-offensive in the Windwards, against heavy odds, must have made a good impression in Paris. Admiral Truguet, the Directory's Minister of Marine during much of this time, was a professional of firm Republican convictions; he had been in Le Cap as a naval captain in June 1793 and had supported Sonthonax. The French Republicans in the Caribbean were spreading havoc amongst the enemy and forcing it to assemble a large new West Indian expedition. So far as the Directory itself was concerned the activities of the Antillean revolutionaries had the further advantage that they were not financially burdensome. The activities of the corsairs enabled Hugues to send back to France a stream of prize goods, captured treasure and plantation products. Hugues amassed a considerable fortune for himself and would not have been above maintaining his popularity in the metropolis by discreet pay-offs in the right quarters.

But over and above either strategic or financial calculations the Directory's commitment to revolutionary anti-slavery was highly congruent with its claims to Republican legitimacy. Jean François Reubel, one of the strongmen of the Directory, had been a leading supporter of the *Amis des Noirs* and the author of the decree of May 1791 on mulatto rights. Condorcet was declared the philosophical patron of the Directory and his works published in an official edition; these included both the essay on slavery, whose practical prescriptions found some echo in the new plantation regime, and his classic *Sketch for a Historical Picture of the Progress of the Human Mind*, written in prison in 1793 and alloting an important role to slave emancipation and the redemption of Africa in humanity's forward march. Historians have been prone to dwell on the seamy and chaotic side of the rule of the Directory. But, though not entirely free of such failings, its colonial policy drew strength from revolutionary virtue and coherence. In this area at least Thermidor stabilised rather than repressed the Jacobin impulse, and infused it with an internationalism which the Jacobins had lacked at the time of the paranoia about foreign plots.

If the Directory can be given credit for sustaining Republican emancipationism it is probable that without the radical Jacobin interlude such a sweeping measure of expropriation as the decree of Pluviôse would never have been enacted. It was at this point that the elemental upheaval of colony and metropolis coincided. The members of the Convention who were so overcome by Dufay's address had allowed political calculation to be subordinated to that spontaneous anti-slavery reflex found in such characteristic expressions of the popular mentality as the *Marseillaise*, with its denunciation of 'l'esclavage antique', and the common slogans 'Live Freely or Die', 'Rather Death than Slavery'.[22] The victory of 1792 for the rights of free blacks and mulattos had undermined the racialist justification for slavery, leaving only the mystique of private property. With the ousting of the Girondin bourgeoisie this remaining barrier to slave emancipation was flimsy enough to be swept away by the appearance of the delegation from St Domingue. The invention of black slavery in the Americas in a previous epoch has been called an 'unthinking decision' and the description might also be applied to the approval of the emancipation decree. Though sponsored by the apostles of Reason this decree had been an existential affirmation of the revolutionary project. Perhaps only those whose conception of human nature had been transformed by the revolutionary experience could see a general emancipation decree as a rational element of political strategy; at all events previous purely instrumental attempts to recruit slaves had never been thought to require a call for general emancipation.

The new revolutionary order in the Antilles faced a major British onslaught in 1796. The British policy of colonial aggression had backfired and the slave order of the whole region faced a desperately serious threat. The loss of Guadeloupe, St Vincent, Ste Lucie and most of Grenada, accompanied by the general instigation of servile revolt,

Jean-Baptiste Belley: deputy in the Assembly, 1797

sounded the alarm; an alarm compounded by the activities of revolutionary agents, rumours of slave or maroon conspiracies, throughout the Caribbean. Dundas declaimed against 'the extraordinary and unprecedented system now adopted by the Enemy for overturning all regular Government and subordination'.[23] With the help of his colleague Lord Hawkesbury, a West Indian proprietor, Dundas persuaded the British Cabinet to dispatch a veritable armada to the West Indian theatre: nearly 100 ships and 30,000 men were assembled for this purpose, equal in troop numbers alone to the Flanders expedition and one of the largest ever to have crossed the Atlantic. The objective was to regain the islands seized by the French and to complete the occupation of St Domingue. The priority was to recapture the British islands which had been largely lost – St Vincent and Grenada – and to retake Ste Lucie. A massive asssault on Ste Lucie in April of 1796 established a British presence on this island, but resistance did not collapse despite the overwhelming superiority of the invaders: 'the blacks', a British officer observed, are 'to a man our enemies'. The British commander, Brigadier General Moore, subsequently to become famous in the Peninsular War, noted that 'men after having been told they were free, and after carrying arms, did not easily return to slavery'.[24] While Moore placed much blame on 'white people attached to the Republic' for envenoming the situation, he also conceded that the

Republicans were 'joined by numbers of blacks from the plantations; all of that colour are attached to them'. He concluded regretfully: 'It was my wish to have governed the colony with mildness, but I have been forced to adopt the most violent measures from the perverseness and bad composition of those I have to deal with.'[25] The British press dubbed the conflict in the Lesser Antilles the 'Brigands' War' and reported Republican atrocities against non-combatants in lurid detail. In Grenada and St Vincent the British also encountered vigorous and widespread resistance. A force of 5,000 men landed at Grenada in March 1796 and forced Fédon into a guerrilla resistance in the woods and hills south of the Grand Etang. Fédon himself was probably killed in July but irregular warfare continued. There were further reports of atrocities committed by former slaves and their Republican instigators; in one case the slaves were said to have crushed a planter to death by feeding him through the rollers of his own mill. Aware that the Republican forces on the different islands were concerting their efforts the British descended on St Vincent with 4,000 men in June 1796. The veteran black Carib leader Chatoyer was killed in a clash in March 1795 but the black Caribs now fought with their French allies under a new chief Duvallé. While some slaves joined the Carib/Republican force, others remained on the estates and even helped the British.

Faced with heavy losses, many of them caused by illness, and needing large forces to patrol territory recaptured from the brigands, the British commanders called for reinforcements. Despite planter misgivings it was decided to raise black ranger batallions formed from specially purchased slaves who were promised pay and freedom. These West India regiments were to total 7,000 men, some based in Jamaica, others in the smaller islands. The black ranger forces were sent in small units to root out guerrillas in the hills. Anxious to end a draining conflict the British conceded terms to most of the 'brigand' forces, treating some as French soldiers surrendering with the honours of war and persuading others to break with their French allies. Thus on Ste Lucie those members of the *Armée française dans les bois* who were not native to Ste Lucie would be repatriated to French territory under a flag of truce; free natives of the island would be allowed to remain without any sanction; former slaves would be integrated into a free black batallion and sent to serve in Sierra Leone. By the close of 1797 the British forces had regained control of Ste Lucie by means of these concessions. Similar terms were offered to the 'brigands' on the other islands. Under duress the black Caribs of St Vincent eventually agreed to accept resettlement on the island of Rattan on the coast of Honduras. While the plantation regime survived on St Vincent the slaveholders of Grenada largely forsook sugar cultivation and devoted their lands and slaves to the less arduous and large-scale cultivation of cloves and other spices.

At least 40,000 British soldiers and sailors were lost in the campaigns in the Lesser Antilles in the years 1796–1800, some killed in action, many dying of disease and others discharged as unfit for service. Guadeloupe and its smaller dependencies were not regained. Events in St Domingue have tended to eclipse the memory of the war in the Lesser Antilles: yet the latter undoubtedly made a large contribution to British decisions concerning St Domingue, helping to draw off large British forces that could otherwise have been used there.[26]

The French Republic could not match the British expedition sent to the Caribbean, but nevertheless it sent sizeable forces. In the course of 1796 some 6,000 troops were sent to the Lesser Antilles and 3,000 to St Domingue. In St Domingue the emancipation policy meant that Republican forces required supplies rather than manpower; they were sent 30,000 muskets and 400,000 lb of powder in 1796.[27]

Following the departure of Sonthonax, Laveaux had continued the Commissioner's policy of promoting the growth of a black military power, seeing the former slaves as the foundation of Republican strength. A layer of mulattos who had previously supplied most of the commanding officers of the *Légion d'Egalité*, and many senior posts in the municipalities, resented the promotion of black commanders. In March 1796 Villatte and the municipality of Le Cap arrested Laveaux. However, this coup was foiled by the loyalty of some commanders – notably the black Pierre Michel and the mulatto B. Léveillé – and by Toussaint Louverture's dispatch of forces to quell the mulatto-led rebellion. This incident hastened and formalised the very growth of a black revolutionary power that it had been designed to thwart. Laveaux, as the ranking delegate of the Republic, appointed Toussaint to the post of Governor of the colony and promoted several black officers to the rank of general. At the ceremony of installation of the new Governor in April Laveaux hailed Toussaint as a saviour of the Republic and the redeemer of the slaves predicted by Raynal.

The new dispensation within the Republican zone was confirmed in May with the arrival of a new Civil Commission, headed once again by Sonthonax. The other members of the Commission were Raimond, who had championed mulatto rights in the National Assembly, and Roume, who in an earlier spell as Commissioner had helped to devise the Southern 'concordat' between whites and mulattos in 1791–2. On his arrival in Le Cap Sonthonax received the acclamation of the black population and was hailed by Toussaint as the 'fondateur de la liberté'. While the new Commission enjoyed similar powers to its predecessors local forces now greatly predominated over those sent from the metropolis.

The British presence in Port au Prince and the Centre still divided Republican St Domingue into two, precariously joined by a disputed neck of land. In the Southern area, under Rigaud's command, the mulattos conserved an influential position. In the North the blacks and *nouveaux libres* were the main power. The French reinforcements who arrived with the Commissioners at Le Cap were commanded by Rochambeau who became alarmed at the overturn that had taken place in the colony's structure of power and property. Sonthonax soon ordered him back to France where he later alleged that 'the war in St Domingue is that of the propertyless against the legitimate proprietors'.[28] Though denied by the Commissioners this charge had some substance.

Formally the Commission wished to rehabilitate the plantation economy with the help of patriotic planters and dutiful freedmen; in practice, at least in the North, it relied on armed former slaves to check the treason and contraband of unpatriotic estate owners and managers. Many 'legitimate proprietors' had left for the areas of British occupation, if not for Kingston, Philadelphia or London. Rochambeau probably spoke most directly for colonial proprietors in the metropolis, and for those mercantile interests with a lien on colonial properties, who believed that the time had come when they could publicly demand a return to order. However, within the Republican areas there were still some resident planters, above all mulattos, and a layer of administrators seeking to repossess estates. But in Sonthonax's view many of these were not true friends of the Republic; not only did they happily trade with the enemy but they also hankered for a return of slavery. As he explained in a letter to Truguet: 'The Revolution here has had the same phases as in France and Europe. The bourgeois fought the nobles in order to oppress the people; the men of colour wanted the humiliation and even the expulsion of the whites, but they abhored liberty.'[29]

The British presence shored up slavery in the occupied zone, so that the future of emancipation in St Domingue still seemed open. Many remaining proprietors and managers, including some *gens de couleur*, took shelter behind the British lines where plantations continued to function. Some 60,000 slaves still laboured in the plantations in the British zone. The British had received 4,000 reinforcements in 1795 and more than 10,000 in 1796. As auxiliaries there were large units of 'royalists': these comprised royalist officers, leading an assortment of whites fighting for pay and plunder, mulattos and former members of the *maréchaussé* similarly motivated, and blacks offered their freedom. The money, uniforms, food and supplies which the British could offer were a magnet for recruits in an increasingly war-devastated land. With their sea-power, artillery and reinforcements the British and their royalist allies were in a strong position. Disease was to take its toll in the British ranks but, even before it did so, the British regime's hope of extending the area of occupation was rendered vain by its defence of slavery. No doubt only a minority of blacks in the Republican zone really enjoyed full civic rights but the ending of slavery there did formalise and guarantee the end of planter control over the life of the direct producers.

Official Republican efforts to rehabilitate plantation production, using regulations similar to those in force in Guadeloupe, met with indifferent results. According to the original decree of emancipation issued by Sonthonax, those former slaves not enrolled in the army were required to remain on their plantation for a period of at least a year; the value of the harvest was to be divided between the owners and the cultivators in the proportion of one to two or three. The estates of *émigrés* and royalists were seized and leased out to administrators under a system of *fermage* devised by the Civil Commission. Field hands were urged to remain ready for labour and their attempts to claim larger plots of land were denied. But in many areas there was, in effect, a stand-off between the Republican regime and the former slaves, with the latter beginning to construct an autonomous existence for themselves and working only fitfully on the plantations. On the estates let under the system of *fermage* the harvest was to be divided up between the cultivators, the administrators and the state. A regulation of 1796 created a rural gendarmerie whose task was to enforce labour discipline and to suppress vagabondage. Those without labour contracts binding them to work on an estate would, in theory, be denied access to provision grounds. Finding administrators for the estates was very difficult, since there were few with the necessary technical competence, and most of those who did possess such competence were former overseers or *commandeurs* who would be distrusted by the mass of labourers. The year 1796 witnessed repeated conflicts over the attempts to impose the new labour regulations. Two years earlier Sonthonax had encouraged the former slaves of the North to defy the authority of their owners and managers arms in hand. It was now impossible simply to dragoon the field hands back to the plantations. In one Southern version of the labour regulations the labourers were told that they must work a six-day week if they wished to claim their full share of the sale of the crop. But many preferred a half share for five days' work, or even no share for four days' work; in the latter case their access to a plot of land would be their sole 'payment' for four days' labour.

Government officials or army officers would take on responsibility for an estate, but even they had difficulty in containing the resistance of the producers. Sugar output dropped sharply, with destruction of plantation equipment, and of irrigation works, explaining part of the fall. Coffee output suffered less of a decline. This crop could be grown on a small scale, with the Republican authorities or their appointees claiming a share of the harvest. In a number of areas women cultivators refused to take part in the sugar or coffee harvest unless they were promised the same pay-out as male cultivators; the original decrees of emancipation had offered them only two-thirds of a male workers' share.[30]

Between 1796 and 1798 the military capacity of the Republican forces was considerably enhanced. While there were still many black irregulars of indeterminate allegiance the regiments commanded by Toussaint were no longer a guerrilla force but highly disciplined contingents capable of strategic deployment to any part of the colony. British officers paid tribute to the military capacity and tactics of Toussaint's *demi-brigades*.[31] The social order of Republican St Domingue reflected the half-peasant, half-proletarian character of the former slaves, without whose support, however grudging, it could not have survived. Sidney Mintz has written of the 'proto-peasant' aspirations of slaves in the Caribbean and there can be little doubt that many of St Domingue's former slaves saw emancipation principally in terms of their opportunity to cultivate a plot of land, and raise a family, unmolested by their former overseers.[32] On the other hand, the regime of plantation slavery had developed a disciplined and deracinated labour force; some former slaves had been themselves organisers, and indeed task-masters; many had not yet developed strong local attachments. Localistic, 'proto-peasant' resistance largely thwarted attempts to recreate a plantation regime. But paradoxically those who had been formed by the plantations played a major part in sustaining the new Republican political order. Ultimately it was the discipline and coherence of the army, echoing that of the plantations, which defeated the partisans of re-enslavement.[33] Black resistance to the British and to slavery drew on a variety of sources. The majority of adult blacks had been born in Africa; a synthesis of African religious and political ideas encouraged them to shake off enslavement. Some of those who led maroon bands and practised voodoo were prepared, like Hyacinth, to collaborate with the British. But however egotistical particular chiefs might be they discovered that alignment with the defenders of slavery was liable to alienate the mass of blacks. Behind the British lines the fate of particular plantations greatly depended upon the attitude of the slave elite; if they decided to leave so would the rest of the crew. As the conflict dragged on security could not be guaranteed on 'loyal' plantations. Having intervened to defend slavery the British occupation actually provoked a more systematic and deeply rooted resistance to it. The

Republicans prospered to the extent that they allied themselves with, and lent coherence to, this elemental social force.

The last stages of the war against the British witnessed an assertion of Toussaint's independent power and a certain *rapprochement* between the black general and his mulatto counterpart in the South, Rigaud. In the South and West liberated slaves also supplied the rank and file of the Republican forces, but in this zone most officers were mulattos or *ancien libres*. The Republican generals succeeded in confining the British to increasingly beleaguered enclaves. A pressing problem for both commanders was that of obtaining resources with which to supply their troops. In this situation both Toussaint and Rigaud rediscovered the advantages of that commercial autonomy at which the planters of the Antilles had so often aimed. Their control of the countryside gave them access to at least some coffee, sugar and cotton. North American merchants were prepared to pay for these with military supplies or good coin; the remaining mercantile agents of the metropolis, impeded by the British blockade, had little to offer. Sonthonax and Laveaux inclined to a different solution to the problem of supplies and revenue; like Hugues in Guadeloupe they began to organise a revolutionary *guerre de corse*; there was now a 'Quasi-War' between France and the United States, as President Adams had aligned his country with Britain. But neither Commissioner nor general were any longer in a position to determine policy.

In March 1797 elections were held for a new French Assembly; probably at Toussaint's instigation both Laveaux and Sonthonax were chosen as deputies for St Domingue. Laveaux accepted this new assignment with good grace; he transferred overall command to Toussaint and on his return to Paris continued to defend the new order in St Domingue. Sonthonax refused to leave. Tension mounted between the Civil Commissioner and the black Commander in Chief until in September Toussaint obliged Sonthonax to comply with a recall order from Paris. Toussaint claimed that Sonthonax was plotting to make St Domingue independent and to slaughter the whites. In reality it was Toussaint who was taking a step towards independence while covering his tracks with these distortions.

The departure of Laveaux and Sonthonax came at a time when Toussaint and Rigaud were poised to roll back British control of the occupied territories. But given the strength of British sea-power and the fortification of the occupied enclaves this promised to be a difficult operation. Via intermediaries the British commander intimated that he would be willing to negotiate a withdrawal with Toussaint and Rigaud. The British were beginning to realise that there was no way they could win in St Domingue; the occupation was costly and ineffective. The

London government sent a new commander with secret instructions to explore terms for a partial or wholesale withdrawal; it was hoped to persuade the coloured commanders to withdraw support from the policy of revolutionary offensive outside St Domingue. Toussaint and Rigaud were to be offered an orderly evacuation that would enable them to take possession of the plantations, port facilities and military installations in the British occupied zone. In return for this the British insisted that the activities of the Republican corsairs and revolutionary agents should cease, that traders should be free to visit St Domingue's ports and that those French planters who wished to remain should be permitted to do so. Toussaint was prepared to accept, and honour, these terms; Rigaud agreed with some hesitation. Neither Laveaux nor Sonthonax would have been offered, or been prepared to consider, such a deal with the British.[34]

A menacing turn of events in France complicated the clash between Toussaint and Sonthonax. The elections of March 1797 brought many covert royalists, and former members of the colonial establishment, back into the mainstream of French political life. Barbé Marbois, the former Intendant of St Domingue, became the president of the Five Hundred. In the opening sessions of this body calls were made for the restoration of order in the colonies and for a disavowal of the extremism of Sonthonax. Rochambeau's reflections on the subject of colonial anarchy were extensively quoted by Viennot Vaublanc, who emerged as chief spokesman for the planter interest. There also seemed a prospect of peace between the contending powers in Europe. The French royalist promoters of the British occupation of St Domingue, Malouet and de Charmilly, believed that a royalist restoration and an end to the war were now in prospect. Sonthonax and Toussaint were both greatly alarmed by reports and rumours of developments in Europe. Sonthonax was thoroughly committed to both the Republic and to the new revolutionary order in the colonies. Toussaint was more narrowly concerned to defend the new order in St Domingue. If Sonthonax did plan independence for St Domingue, as alleged, this would have been in the event of a royalist restoration in France; and his alleged plan to slaughter the whites probably referred to retribution for those planters who had collaborated with the British. Toussaint was less committed to any particular regime in the metropolis, saw some potential advantages in the return of planters and managers, and wished to keep open the possibility of negotiating with the British. Consequently Toussaint broke with Sonthonax and, in James's phrase, 'threw him to the wolves'.[35] (Once more the Jacobin Commissioner's luck held; by the time he arrived back in France the intrigues of royalists and colonial proprietors had been foiled by the coup of Fructidor.)

Toussaint was prepared to disembarrass himself of Sonthonax, whom he compared to other extremists like Robespierre and Marat, but he simultaneously dispatched to Paris an eloquent and vigorous riposte to Vaublanc and Rochambeau. He warned that the former slaves would know how to fight 'should General Rochambeau . . . reappear at the head of an army in order to return the blacks to slavery'.[36]

The British position began to collapse in the early months of 1798. Some 20,000 British troopers had died or deserted or been discharged as unfit for service by this date; total British losses in the Caribbean theatre were soon to reach 60,000. Disease had taken a heavy toll and military operations in St Domingue had yielded very meagre results. At no point had the occupiers succeeded in mounting major offensives against the Republicans, nor had they extended the occupation beyond the boundaries that it had reached in its first months, thanks to the French planter militias. The casualties of the British forces fighting in the Lesser Antilles were about twice as great as those in St Domingue; if the British had not suffered this distraction and depletion they might even have succeeded in stifling the revolt in the larger colony. The poor results and heavy casualties of Britain's West Indian operations encouraged anti-war sentiment and gave openings to the Foxite opposition in Parliament.[37] Following the departure of Sonthonax, Toussaint and Rigaud kept up the pressure on the British forces. For a time the British hoped to retain control of the naval base at Môle St Nicolas, or of some other enclave. Not until July–August 1798 was an agreement struck with Toussaint and Rigaud for a complete British withdrawal. It was agreed that St Domingue would no longer be used as a base for attacks on British shipping or on the British slave colonies. Those French planters who wished to do so could remain. The British had themselves recruited black auxiliary forces for the defence of the occupied zone; some of these forces were now integrated into Toussaint's army.

Toussaint and Rigaud undertook these negotiations without proper sanction from the Directory and several of the more delicate accords were kept as secret clauses when the Treaty was signed. The British entertained Toussaint lavishly at the Môle St Nicolas prior to their departure and invited him to establish an independent kingdom – though gratified by these attentions he declined the invitation. Reports in the British press hinted at the agreements reached – indeed they mischievously encouraged the view that Toussaint was about to desert France. The metropolitan authorities were by now thoroughly suspicious of their Governor in St Domingue. Raimond and Roume remained as titular Commissioners but had no power other than as advisers. In April 1798 another Commissioner, Hédouville, was sent by

Paris but he arrived unaccompanied by troops. The new Commissioner had little alternative but to approve an expurgated version of the Treaty with the British. Hédouville suspected Toussaint of having compromised the Republic by a series of concessions – to the British, to former *émigrés*, whom he had allowed to return, and to the mass of blacks in the North, who were fitful in their attention to the cash crops. The Commissioner announced that labourers would henceforth be obliged to sign labour contracts for three years instead of one year. This provoked revolt in the North and persuaded Hédouville that he should retire to France. Before going he promised Rigaud full support if he should challenge Toussaint's power. This parting shot played upon already existing antagonisms and rivalry between the two generals, and more generally between blacks and *mulâtres*. After a period of tension open civil war broke out in March 1799. It took the black general a little over a year to establish full control and to eject Rigaud and other leading mulattos from the island. While the latter sought refuge in France, Toussaint's advance on the South was facilitated by United States naval cover; the Adams administration followed the British government in regarding Toussaint as less menacing to Caribbean commerce and order than those who were more faithful to the French Republic. However, Toussaint tried to give his regime some shreds of Republican legitimacy by attributing the title of Commissioner successively to Raimond and Roume. In December 1800 his forces invaded the still Spanish-administered half of the island, and decreed the emancipation of the colony's 15,000 slaves. This action had no metropolitan sanction and was undertaken in order to prevent Santo Domingo being used as a staging post for a French expedition. Toussaint had attentively followed Napoleon Bonaparte's rise to power and saw some parallel between himself and the First Consul. He still sent occasional letters to Paris justifying his conduct; one of them, destined to remain unanswered, began, 'From the First of the Blacks to the First of the Whites'.[38]

Toussaint was ruler of St Domingue until the arrival of a large French expeditionary force in February 1802. He supervised a certain recovery of the economy and the introduction of a new constitution. According to figures assembled by the treasury of St Domingue exports in 1800 ran at only one-fifth of the volume achieved in 1789; because of higher prices, and higher charges, customs revenue was almost the same. The export volume figure may have been understated to conceal the extent of trade with the United States or Britain. Nevertheless there is no doubt that revolution and war had produced a major slump in plantation output.

Table 2 Exports of St Domingue, 1789 and 1800–1801

lb '000	1789	1800–1801
White sugar	47,516	17
Raw sugar	93,573	18,519
Coffee	76,835	43,220
Cotton	7,004	2,480
Indigo	759	1

Source: Pluchon, *Toussaint Louverture*, p. 275.

The irrigation systems for which St Domingue was famous had been badly damaged and much equipment destroyed. The population of the French part had dropped to under 400,000, roughly two-thirds of its previous level. Population decline resulted from the cessation of slave imports and the historically low proportion of children in the slave population as well as the devastation of war. The new peasantry was more interested in subsistence cultivation than producing cash crops. This held out hope of demographic recovery in the future but undermined the plantation economy. In the peasant saying '*Moin pas esclave, moin pas travaye*' (I'm not a slave I don't have to work), the work referred to was essentially that performed for others. About two-thirds of the surviving plantations were held by the state, which had confiscated the estates of *émigrés* and counter-revolutionaries; though Toussaint allowed those willing to do so to return to reclaim their land. The *domaines nationaux* were leased out to private individuals or to army officers. The Commissioners Raimond and Roume had each acquired, or leased, a string of estates; General Dessalines controlled thirty-three sugar estates, while General Christophe was reported to be worth more than $250,000 in 1799.[39] Under the system of *fermage* the leaseholders of *domaines nationaux* were expected to pay out a quarter of the value of the harvest to the labourers and to hand over a half of all produce to the state. A state budget for 33 million *livres* was drawn up for 1801. It was common for the fiscal authorities to make a levy of produce rather than cash; British or North American traders would then exchange arms, ammunition, textiles and equipment for coffee or sugar. According to the official financial balance the sale or exchange of produce of *domaines nationaux* raised more revenue than the customs.[40]

Army officers or officials operated estates because they were more likely to have access to disciplined labour. The direct producers were only permitted to work their garden plots so long as they contributed labour to the estates. A decree of October 1800 placed all those in agriculture – labourers, overseers, managers and proprietors – under military discipline. Every adult had to be able to give proof of 'useful employment', while managers and proprietors had to submit accounts to the military commander of their district. A special rural guard, based on units fifty-five men strong, was organised to enforce this decree.

Juridically the new labour regime resembled a species of serfdom in that labourers were supposed to be bound to their estates, and obliged to labour, in return for which they had access to means of subsistence, an autonomous family life and a notional share in plantation proceeds. In practice the direct producers must sometimes have been in a position to check or challenge the full severity of the labour decrees. Bands of maroons still existed in many parts of St Domingue owing no defined allegiance to the state and linked instead to particular localities. The maroons still tended to comprise mainly younger men. Women made a large economic contribution in the settled areas, working in the fields and organising local markets. To conserve its labour force an estate had to offer some incentives and rights to the producer beyond the formal ban on whipping. Labourers on the estates often had to be armed while the army itself was recruited in large measure from the ranks of the peasantry. The real relations of force in the countryside, where many former slaves had been armed, virtually precluded the full reinstitution of slavery. On the other hand, the soldiery often assessed and collected tribute in a rough and ready manner, without regard to the producers' formal rights.

Toussaint's style of rule echoed that of an autocratic and independent-minded colonial Governor – with the difference that he had no Intendant or metropolitan minister to dispute his authority. The old Governor's Palace at Port au Prince, now Port Républicain, served as his offical residence and headquarters, from which he set out on repeated tours of inspection. Toussaint's personal staff included four or five secretaries (usually whites) who took down a stream of orders, decrees, letters and proclamations. His entourage included several long-standing white and mulatto advisers or administrators. Among these were five 'constitutional' priests, radical *curés* who appear to have identified with slave revolt from the outset. Other important members of Toussaint staff included the mulattos Raimond and Pascal; Nathan, the *juif interprète*; Bunel, a former colonial administrator; and Vincent, a French colonel of engineers. Many of these men, despite French nationality, loyally served Toussaint in his negotiations with the British or Americans. Most of the officers in the army were blacks and former slaves; men like Dessalines, Christophe and Moyse. Among the few

Toussaint Louverture

white or mulatto officers were Agé, the white chief of staff, and Clairveaux, the mulatto commander in the East. In the course of the war with Rigaud the number of mulatto officers dropped considerably. Suzanne Simon, Toussaint's wife, and Claire Heureuse, the wife of Dessalines, also played some part in public affairs, appealing for clemency in the bloody caste feuds which rent St Domingue.

Grand receptions were held at the Governor's Palace, attended by officers of the new order, foreign traders and planters who had returned to their estates. Toussaint would dress simply but was usually accompanied by a splendid honour guard. Toussaint imposed himself on his collaborators by his force of personality and by his control of the army. He spoke a vigorous but ungrammatical French, and had read widely. In the Governor's Palace and other public buildings were to be found busts and portraits of Raynal, who, rather than Rousseau or Condorcet, was adopted as the prophet of the new order. Just as Raynal's work reflected the aspirations of enlightened planters as well as championing slave emancipation, so there was a double quality to Toussaint's new regime. It rested on the forces unleashed by slave revolt and slave emancipation; at the same time it reflected or recreated the ideals of the autonomist planters and enlightened administrators. Toussaint was a former slave; he was also a former slaveholder.[41]

In July 1801 a new constitution was drawn up by a Central

Assembly whose ten members had been nominated by Toussaint. It proclaimed him Governor for life. The Assembly comprised three whites, three mulattos and four inhabitants of the former Spanish colony. The text of the Constitution had been drafted, in consultation with Toussaint, by Raimond, the Assembly's Secretary, and Bertrand Borghella, its President. Borghella was a large planter and a former member of the notoriously autonomist *Conseil Supérieur* of Port au Prince. The constitution declared St Domingue to be a self-governing colony of France enjoying freedom of commerce. Toussaint had the right to nominate his successor from amongst the army generals. Freedom and French nationality were the prerogative of every inhabitant. Catholicism was to be the official religion. Toussaint himself always displayed a great respect for the religion in which he had been brought up; *Te Deums* would be offered for his victories and the general would himself enter the pulpit to deliver admonitions to the congregation. The Constitution only allowed for a notional link between metropolis and colony; no resident agent of the metropolis was envisaged, simply correspondence between the Governor and the French head of state. However, the Louverturian Constitution did stop short of declaring outright independence and, as a placatory gesture, a copy was sent to the First Consul for his endorsement.[42]

The new order over which Toussaint presided made massive and prudent provision for defence. The prospective enemy was no longer Britain but the metropolis itself. While war continued between Britain and France the metropolis was in no position to send an expedition to the Antilles. But by 1799 it was clear that peace would soon be made. The replacement of President Adams by Jefferson in the election of 1799 was a further ominous development for St Domingue, since it was likely to result in the ending of the so-called 'Quasi-War' between France and the United States. Adams had favoured trade with St Domingue and his Agent there had played an important part in the negotiations with the British. Jefferson was not only pro-French but a Virginian slave-owner and, as such, likely to be particularly hostile to an adjacent black power in the Americas. Toussaint had been willing to end anti-slavery activity directed at other American territories, which had pleased Adams; it was thought that to his successor the very existence of an emancipationist black state would be anathema. Calculating that this would be welcome news the First Consul conveyed a message to the new President that insubordination in St Domingue would not be tolerated. From a mixture of motives to be explored in the next chapter Jefferson did nothing to discourage the French.

The militarisation of the Louverturian order in St Domingue is stressed by Pierre Pluchon, who argues that it was both tyrannical and burdensome. Toussaint's army was maintained at a regular strength of 20,000, with a similar number organised in the militia and *gendarmerie*. Certainly armed forces totalling more than a tenth of the total population constituted a heavy charge upon available resources. The legacy of disorder bequeathed by a decade of civil war, revolution and foreign intervention severely tested the new power and impelled it along the path of centralisation and militarisation. Toussaint often found it easier to incorporate free-lance military groups or defeated enemies than to seek to disband them, leading to a further growth of the military establishment. The manifest danger of new interventions helped to justify such a policy.[43]

The French expedition feared by Toussaint duly appeared at the beginning of February 1802. It initially comprised some 16,000 men commanded by Leclerc, a noted Republican general and brother-in-law to Bonaparte. Leclerc carried with him an appointment as Governor General and a proclamation to the effect that France would always respect the liberty of its new citizens. The size of the expeditionary force and its simultaneous descent upon the island's principal ports made it clear that Bonaparte's intention was to break the power of Toussaint's army and to reintegrate the colony. Leclerc's second in command was Rochambeau; he was also accompanied by the mulatto commanders Rigaud and Pétion.

Bonaparte was intent on creating a new French empire in the Americas. The preliminary accord for a peace treaty with Britain had been reached in September 1801. Under its terms Martinique and other colonies occupied by Britain were to be returned to France or its allies – only Trinidad was retained by Britain, though the First Consul regretted even this. At about the same time France acquired Louisiana from Spain by a secret clause of the Treaty of San Ildefonso. The reconquest of St Domingue was to be the centre-point of this strategy. With some success Bonaparte sought to persuade the British and American governments that the 'annihilation of black government' in St Domingue was in their interest; he urged the 'necessity of stifling in every part of the world every kind of disquiet and trouble'. In France itself there was an influential lobby of colonial proprietors or merchants who wished to recoup their old prosperity. The First Consul's wife, Josephine Beauharnais, owned property in St Domingue and Martinique. Barbé Marbois was now a member of the Council of State, as was Moreau de Saint Méry, the former representative of Martinique and member of the Club Massiac. Talleyrand seems to have felt that the Caribbean venture was a convenient outlet for the First Consul's ambitions. Later Napoleon was to blame 'the Council of State and his ministers' for having promoted the expedition to St Domingue; they were, he thought, 'hurried along by the clamours of the colonists, who formed a considerable party at Paris, and were, besides . . . nearly all royalists, or in the pay of the English faction'.[44] Napoleon's attempt to disclaim responsibility should not be accepted at face value; nevertheless the colonial lobby and merchants anxious to supply a large continental market with tropical produce generally favoured the expedition, as did those who wished for good relations with Britain and the United States. The destruction of 'black government' in St Domingue would have earned Napoleon the gratitude of slaveholders throughout the New World.

Toussaint had consolidated the revolution in St Domingue by playing off the major Atlantic powers against one another. Now this was no longer possible. At the time of the arrival of the Leclerc expedition Toussaint was also vulnerable domestically. Some four months prior to Leclerc's arrival Toussaint had carried out a wholesale purge of the army, involving the execution of Moyse, commander of the North. The precise reasons for this purge are difficult to establish but it was linked to unrest among the cultivators caused by the implementation of the labour decrees. Moyse had failed to suppress this unrest, or even positively supported it, while his followers had charged that Toussaint intended to reduce the field labourers to being little more than slaves or serfs of their former owners or, perhaps even worse, of jumped-up *petits blancs* or army officers. According to a report made by the US Consul at Le Cap, Moyse had revealed a readiness to overthrow Toussaint and to establish better relations with France. The summary execution of Moyse, and some 2,000 real or supposed supporters, was followed by the adoption of a draconian decree on internal security. All citizens were required to possess an official identity card and an elaborate series of controls was established over the movements of labourers and soldiers. Idleness was to be punished with forced labour, sedition with death and suspect foreigners were to be deported. This decree did not simply tighten up the plantation regime; it desperately sought to stave off political disintegration.[45]

Leclerc's landing on the island was carried through with surprising success in its first stages. In many places Leclerc's authority was accepted by army commanders, including Paul Louverture and Clairveaux, who seemed to lack clear instructions from their commander-in-chief. Toussaint had first demoralised his supporters by a purge and then left his generals unprepared for an invasion which everyone knew was coming. Perhaps Toussaint expected Bonaparte to offer him a deal. There was also the difficulty, ignored by some, that loyalty to the Republic was still a powerful force, among people of colour no less than with most whites. The only effective resistance to Leclerc came from the forces commanded by Toussaint and Christophe in the North and Dessalines in the West. Toussaint now rediscovered his vocation as a revolutionary. He urged the destruction of all that could help the French and warned that they had come to restore slavery. He appealed directly to the cultivators of the North, arming them and advocating a guerrilla strategy. Toussaint's principal lieutenants, however, insisted on fighting a more conventional campaign and suffered a number of reverses. In the last days of April Christophe and Dessalines offered to come to terms with Leclerc on condition that they would retain their ranks and commands. Leclerc accepted this offer. In early May Toussaint also indicated a readiness to make peace with the new Governor General, on condition that he could retire to his estates with his personal guard and that his troops would be integrated with the Republican forces. Once again Leclerc was happy to agree, though he distrusted Toussaint's intentions. Despite these capitulations irregular warfare continued, led by the chiefs of maroon bands and of militia or army units who had no faith in the French commander or no prospect of striking a deal with him. Leclerc's aim was to disarm and disband as many of the black troops as possible and to leave no black officers in the army with a rank above that of captain. The continuation of resistance made it impossible for him to implement this plan. Probably with good reason he suspected Toussaint and other black generals of plotting insurrection. On June 6th Toussaint was arrested and transported to France.

On July Ist Napoleon wrote to Leclerc urging him to arrest all the black generals and deport them to France before the end of September: 'without this we will have done nothing, and an immense and beautiful colony will be poised on a volcano and fail to inspire any confidence in capitalists, colonists or commerce.'[46] Leclerc explained that he was now far too weak to take any such measure and that the colony could only be held with the assistance of the loyal black generals. Though Leclerc had received some reinforcements, his troops had suffered heavy casualties: the seige and capture of the fort at Crête à Pierrot, held by Dessalines's troops, had alone cost the lives of more than 1,500 French troops. With the onset of summer, yellow fever began to take its toll. Meanwhile the black resistance continued and Leclerc complained that the arrest of Toussaint counted for nothing, since there were 2,000 black chiefs whom it would be necessary to arrest. Leclerc himself succumbed to the fever in October and died on November 2nd. In his last letters to Napoleon he complained that his position was being fatally undermined. The white *colons* who had returned with him, many intent on reclaiming their former property, longed for the day when the full rigour of the old regime could again be enforced, including both slavery and the caste system. The provocative behaviour of these white *colons*, and of the National Guards recruited from them, caused endless trouble with the mulatto and black troops. The French troops, drawn mainly from the Army of the Rhine, often displayed little sympathy for the colonial whites and sided with the coloured commanders. The memoirs of one Republican general recall the troubled silence that descended upon his troops when they heard the defenders of Crête à Pierrot singing French patriotic and revolutionary songs: 'In spite of the indignation that the black atrocities excited, these airs generally produced a painful feeling. Our soldiers looked at each other questioningly; they seemed to say: "Are our barbaric enemies in the right? Are we really the only soldiers of the Republic? Have we became servile political instruments?"'[47]

Leclerc repeatedly insisted that the French Republic would have scrupulous regard for the freedom of the former slaves in St Domingue, and to begin with he had been believed. In the summer of 1802 the arrest of Toussaint, and the arrival of news from France and the Windward Islands, began to destroy Leclerc's credibility on this key issue. The reincorporation of Martinique, where the slave plantations were intact, obliged the Consular regime to clarify the status of slavery in the French colonies. The result was the decree of Floréal An X (May 19th 1802), presented to the Tribunat with the preamble that it was necessary 'to ensure the good security of our neighbours'. The decree restored the legality of slavery and the slave trade in the French colonies; though no specific reference was made to St Domingue or Guadeloupe, it was explained that the competent colonial authorities would make provision for those who had been freed by revolutionary laws. The decree of Floréal was approved by 54 votes to 27 in the Tribunate and 211 votes to 63 in the Senate. The Legion of Honour was established on the same day by the Tribunate; in the previous week branding for criminals had been restored. Floréal effectively brought the first French Republic to an end: the plan for a plebiscite making Napoleon Consul for life was also devised at this time.[48]

The French attempt to reimpose slavery was first made in Guadeloupe. Victor Hugues had been replaced as Governor in February 1798 and forced to leave the colony in 1799. The regime he had established was preserved in its essentials by his immediate successors, who included Laveaux; the latter was arrested in March 1800. There were said to be over 1,000 estates farmed out to black cultivators; after the dismissal of Hugues an attempt was made to introduce a somewhat less regimented system of share-cropping (*colonat partiare*). The mass of black labourers of Guadeloupe did not acquire the robust independence of the ex-slaves of St Domingue; this was both because emancipation 'from above' had predominated and because the relatively small size of the island gave less scope to peasant cultivation and *maronnage*, two vital supports of black freedom in the larger colony. The Republican military establishment in Guadeloupe incorporated *gens de couleur* in the most senior positions, the mulatto General Magloire Pélage and the black general Louis Delgrès being notable amongst them. In 1801 Bonaparte sent Lacrosse, who had saved the Iles du Vent for the Republic in 1792, to prepare Guadeloupe for the Consulate's special colonial regime. Magloire Pélage quickly divined this threat and arrested Lacrosse on October 24th. Bonaparte thereupon dispatched a large force to the colony commanded by General Richepanse. Magloire Pélage came to terms with Richepanse in May, but Louis Delgrès opted for armed resistance. After a heroic last stand in the crater of the volcano Matouba Delgrès was killed and most of his followers overwhelmed. As soon as Richepanse received the decree of Floréal he decided to reintroduce slavery. No attempt was made to re-enslave black soldiers or *anciens libres* proprietors but labourers on the estates were generally returned to their former condition.[49]

To Leclerc's consternation news of the restoration of slavery in Guadeloupe reached St Domingue in July, demolishing the idea that the decree of Floréal was only applicable to Martinique and other territories where slavery had never been abolished. Leclerc complained to Paris that fear of the restoration of slavery was having a disastrous effect, stimulating the black revolt and undermining the loyalty of his black and mulatto commanders. Dessalines and Christophe had pitilessly repressed the rebels in the areas entrusted to them by the French Captain General. In August and September they began to hedge their bets, covertly assisting some rebel groups while vigorously eliminating potential rivals. In an effort to retain the loyalty of his black generals Leclerc sent Rigaud back to France. But the racism of the white colonial establishment had recreated the alliance between black and mulatto which had disappeared in the civil war of 1799. The black commanders, slighted by the French, were also profoundly aware of the depth of popular resistance to slavery and the caste regime. A decade of struggles had fused the pragmatic and the ideological dimensions of anti-slavery in the popular mentality. Intelligence of the restoration of slavery thus triggered the defence of quite specific rights and possessions; as for the *anciens libres* they sensed that their own civic status would be similarly degraded if black slavery was restored.

On October 13th–14th 1802 the most outstanding black and mulatto generals – Dessalines, Christophe, Clerveau and Pétion – simultaneously turned on the French, with regiments comprising some 6,000 disciplined and well-armed troops. Leclerc only just escaped capture and the loss of Le Cap, where he lay on his death-bed. In November Rochambeau took over command of the French forces while a conference of the rebel generals appointed Dessalines as their commander-in-chief. Rochambeau now faced not only popular revolt but experienced and capable military formations. While the rebel bands had made the colony impossible to conquer their new alignment with the black demi-brigades meant that the French could be defeated. Relations between France and Britain were deteriorating rapidly as Napoleon threatened British positions in India and the Near East while the British refused to give up their bases in the Mediterranean, as had been agreed at Amiens. France's acquisition of Louisiana had aroused North American suspicions. The black rebels in St Domingue found it somewhat easier to acquire supplies from British or North American traders. In May 1803 war broke out again between Britain and France; good relations between France and the United States were rescued when Napoleon made over Louisiana to the American Republic. However, Napoleon had no intention of abandoning St Domingue and succeeded in sending 15,000 reinforcements to Rochambeau prior to the imposition of a British blockade on the island. The desperate French attempt to recover St Domingue involved the wholesale massacre of non-combatants and reached an exterminist pitch that foreshadowed the colonial wars of a later epoch. The wars that ravaged St Domingue had often been marked by the most atrocious blood-letting. The various conflicts that ranged royalists against Republicans, masters against slaves, whites against coloured, mulattos against blacks, invaders against invaded had rarely admitted the observance of any 'rules of war'. Toussaint, animated by a more constructive ideal, had been one of the few generals to give quarter to his enemies, though he did permit occasional atrocities against mulatto opponents. In one of his last letters to Napoleon Leclerc warned: 'Here is my opinion. You will have to exterminate all the blacks in the mountains, women as well as men, except for children under twelve. Wipe out half the population of the lowlands and do not leave in the colony a single black who has worn an epaulette.'[50] If Rochambeau, despite reinforcements, found execution of this baleful testament beyond him, it was not for want of trying.

The need at all costs to prevent escape by Toussaint, 'the man who has fanaticised this island', was another refrain of Leclerc's last letters. On April 17th 1803 Toussaint Louverture died in the icy dungeons of the Fortress of Joux in the Jura Mountains, after months of brutal and humiliating treatment. At a conference of the rebel generals held at about this time, it was decided no longer to fight under the tricolour. According to legend Dessalines held up the flag of the Republic and tore from it the white band; henceforth the rebels fought under a red and blue standard on which the initials R.F. had been replaced by the motto 'Liberty or Death'. The French expedition and its avid retinue of white colonists managed to hold out a few months longer and even retained the collaboration of some black and mulatto soldiers. But the threat they represented of a full dress restoration of the colonial *ancien régime* reforged the alliance between the coloured army and the black cultivators, between *nouveaux libres* and *anciens libres*, between the blacks and the mulattos. The twin project of restoring slavery and destroying 'black government' foundered. On November 29th the British agreed to evacuate Rochambeau and his forces as prisoners of war; some 4,000 troops and as many civilians embarked at Le Cap for Jamaica. A French presence remained in the former Spanish half of the island but St Domingue was now entirely in rebel hands. Not until January 1st 1804, at the conclusion of another conference of rebel commanders, was the Republic of Haiti proclaimed. The name chosen for the new Republic was Amerindian rather than African or European. Dessalines was named as 'Governor General', a title chosen, perhaps, for its Louverturian echoes.

The French defeat in St Domingue made a powerful impact on contemporary opinion – especially in Britain as it again faced the prospect of a French invasion. Napoleon had sent some 35,000 French troops to St Domingue; about 20,000 had died of various sicknesses while 8,000 perished on the field of battle. Among those lost were Leclerc and eighteen other white generals. The losses amongst white and coloured auxiliaries at least doubled total losses on the French side, though sickness was not nearly so important a cause of death for the local forces.[51] The impact of the French defeat was all the greater since Napoleon had been free of other military distractions in the first eighteen months of the attempted reconquest. The costly lesson which had been learned by first the British and then the French was noted by all colonial and slaveholding powers. The British had sought to secure and extend their slaveholdings in the West Indies; instead they had lost some 60,000 men, expended sorely needed resources and consolidated the power of the emancipated slaves they had set out to crush. Napoleon's war against black government, and ignominious attempt to re-establish slavery, had provoked an unprecedented liberation struggle and had given birth to the new state of Haiti.

The defeat of the French made it easier for the British to register the significance of their own débâcle in St Domingue. The example and martyrdom of Toussaint was to become a source of inspiration to radical abolitionists, first in Britain, subsequently in France and the United States. The British press, which would have been happy to celebrate his execution in 1796, gave harrowing accounts of his imprisonment and death. On February 3rd 1803 the *Morning Post* published Wordsworth's sonnet to Toussaint which ended:

> Though fallen thyself, never to rise again,
> Live and take comfort. Thou hast left behind
> Powers that will work for thee; air, earth, skies;
> There's not a breath of the common wind
> That will forget thee; thou hast great allies;
> Thy friends are exultations, agonies,
> And Love, and man's unconquerable mind.

If Wordsworth's tribute is taken to refer to the resistance of anonymous black masses, who fought on even when deserted by their leaders, then his invocation of their elemental and essential strength was very apt. Around the same time James Stephen, who was brother-in-law to Wilberforce, published a pamphlet entitled *The Opportunity or Reasons for an Immediate Alliance with St Domingo*, in which he urged the advantages of helping the rebels. Stephen was to be a leading light in the second wave of British abolitionism, which dates from this time: abolition of the slave trade regained a House of Commons majority in May 1804, leading, in circumstances to be considered in chapter 8, to the Act of 1807. But long before this the London government had rediscovered the advantages of discreet accommodation to the Revolution in St Domingue/Haiti.[52]

During the early stages of the war between France and Britain there were no engagements in Europe and a large French fleet was dispatched to Martinique. The British proved most unwilling to allow the West Indies to become a zone of hostilities, and long postponed any attacks on the remaining French islands. The West India regiment, formed from specially purchased Africans, played an important part in the defence of the British Caribbean. Neither the anti-French forces in St Domingue nor the new Republic of Haiti were accorded official recognition but both received some military supplies and some naval cover from the British. Without any necessity for a formal treaty of alliance Dessalines's *demi-brigades* were a formidable barrier to any new attempt to reconstruct the French Antilles.[53]

In the short run the defeat in St Domingue had little impact in France itself, where Napoleon had broken his opponents and was soon planning larger adventures. The *Amis des Noirs* had briefly flickered into existence in 1797–8 only to expire again. The elevation of Abbé Grégoire to the Senate in 1801 had been one of the last acts of independence by the legislature; he was to vote both against the decree of Floréal and against the establishment of the Empire, but to equally little effect. Laveaux and Sonthonax had moved into opposition to Bonaparte as First Consul, but both were suspect as Jacobins; Laveaux had been arrested for a time in December 1801 following the explosion of the 'infernal machine'. Colonel Vincent had been arrested after bringing Toussaint's Constitution to the First Consul; he warned of the dangers of invading St Domingue and was later exiled to Elba, where he was on hand to greet the Emperor in 1814. Victor Hugues secured appointment as Governor of French Guiana where he implemented the decree restoring slavery. Many of the French who remained in Haiti were slaughtered in a massacre on the aftermath of the declaration of independence. The only prominent French Republican to find refuge in Haiti was the Jacobin Terrorist Billaud–Varenne, Hugues's sponsor in 1794, who ended his days there in 1815–18. Malouet, the veteran *monarchien* who had helped to organise the British occupation of the French Antilles, became Louis XVIII's first Colonial Minister. Du Buc also became an ornament of the Restoration.

The Republic of Haiti set up in 1804 preserved a vital element of continuity with the St Domingue of Toussaint Louverture. Both outlawed slavery by express constitutional provision, both were led by an insecure new ruling class that united economic and military functions, and both expressed an aspiration to effective independence.

The death of slavery had been confirmed by the defeat of the French, as had the new status of the mass of Haitians who had made that defeat possible. All successor regimes sought to find ways of obliging the country dwellers to work. Many have been tempted to equate the stringent rural codes enacted by Toussaint, Dessalines and Henry Christophe with the slave condition under the old regime. Yet when offered the choice of a return to full chattel slavery, the labourers had always preferred to ally with their new masters against their old. Under the new labour regime the overseer's whip was banned; though other forms of coercion may have taken its place, this ban does seem to have been generally observed and generally welcomed. The fact that the new masters were black or brown while most of the old had been white does not adequately explain the seeming preferences of the mass of *nouveaux libres*. In the *ancien régime* the condition of the slave of a free black had never been regarded as enviable.

The new condition of the mass of labourers was freer than that of the slave in certain decisive respects. In the first place the writ of governments and landowners was from the outset very much less effective and complete, scarcely reaching to the mountain districts and often ignored even in the plains. The scale of the peasant rebellions and 'peasant republics' in nineteenth-century Haiti was to be qualitatively greater than that of their eighteenth-century precursors, the maroons. Thus from 1807 to 1819 large areas of the South-west constituted an autonomous farmers' Republic led by the African former slave and maroon, Jean–Baptiste Duperrier, commonly known as Goman. Even within the regions of more settled administration the new authorities found it prudent to limit exploitation of the direct producers: too much pressure on them would undermine the basis of political power. Ultimately the army and police were recruited from the mass of peasants and labourers, whose disaffection would encourage military revolts, conspiracies and coups. Free-lance groups of armed peasants and labourers, known as *picquets* or *cacos*, were to play an important part in Haitian history.[54]

Militarism itself was certainly to be the bane of Haitian society, with armed forces totalling as many as 40,000 absorbing much of the social surplus and discouraging the diversification of commodity production. The Haitian peasants preferred subsistence cultivation to meet their own needs rather than cash crop cultivation, since the proceeds of the latter could be more readily appropriated by grasping landlords or military administrators. In the days of slavery the producers had been super-exploited to produce a vast export surplus; under the burdens of militarism and landlordism the Haitain peasant produced a far more modest surplus, but enjoyed a more autonomous existence. While the export trade languished, local markets, in which women played a major role, were quite vigorous.[55]

A significant index of the new condition of the mass of the population was to be a strong recovery in population levels during the first decades of independence. According to one contemporary estimate the population grew from 375,000 in 1800 to 935,000 in 1822.[56] While the precise figures may be questioned there was undoubtedly a sizeable increase in population over these decades. Haitian governments claimed to promote family life. While there was much diversity in family form, with polygamy being quite common, this offered qualitatively greater opportunities for child-rearing than the old slave order.

Despite the ambivalent role they had played in the struggle against France Toussaint's generals became the leaders of the new state, in uneasy collaboration with the mulatto leaders of the South and West. Dessalines declared himself Emperor in 1804, but this emulation of Napoleon was accompanied by a strongly anti-French orientation. The French, but not the British, were attacked for fostering slavery in the Caribbean. The massacre of remaining Frenchmen was followed in 1805 by an unsuccessful invasion of the still French-controlled Eastern half of the island. The British authorities did not officially condone

Dessalines's bloodthirsty vendetta against the French, but it may have aimed to impress them as well as to exact vengeance. Many mulattos and *anciens libres* were not as hostile as Dessalines towards the French and were more suspicious of the British. Dessalines took over French estates as *domaines nationaux* and announced a plan to distribute small plots of land to veterans. Mulatto proprietors were alarmed at plans to confiscate estates which they claimed had been bequeathed to them by white kinsmen. Despite decrees imposing labour duties on the cultivators, the economy of the new state, weakened by war, official neglect and the slaughter of administrators, yielded few cash crops. A profligate and disorganised imperial Court absorbed what tax revenues were available, leaving the army unpaid. Following a Southern rebellion in 1806 the Emperor was assassinated.

After Dessalines's death Haiti was divided roughly in two, with Henry Christophe ruling the North and Alexandre Pétion the South. Christophe, who had been born in Grenada, pursued a pro-British policy. Alignment with Britain was undertaken as an insurance against the return of the French and in the hope of economic concessions. In 1808–9 Christophe backed a successful Spanish revolt against the French who still occupied the Eastern half of the island. While the North relied mainly on British traders, the South had its own merchants and hoped for good relations with the United States. In 1811 Christophe had himself crowned as King Henry I of Haiti, with court etiquette and regalia based on that of St James; apart from gratifying his own vanity the option for a kingdom was intended to demonstrate soundness to the British. Pétion in the South remained ostentatiously faithful to Republican forms, but he too was obliged to accommodate to Britain. Both states, in deference to British pressure, lowered duties on imports from Britain.

Under the terms of the Treaty of Paris in 1814 France was permitted to recover its New World colonies. Martinique and Guadeloupe were to be handed back with their plantations in quite a flourishing condition after years of British occupation. Since neither government in Haiti had been recognised by any power, there was an implication that France could reclaim 'St Domingue'. The negotiators were persuaded by Talleyrand that colonial concessions to France would make the restored monarchy more palatable to French opinion while tying up French energies at a safe distance from Europe. Plans laid for suborning and threatening the new leaders of Haiti, as a prelude to some new expedition, came to nothing. French overtures were indignantly rejected; King Henry arrested the envoy sent to him, published the secret instructions he carried and offered a joint resistance pact to Pétion. Though the French government retained a formal claim to

St Domingue, in 1815 it was recognised that recovering it *manu militari* would meet implacable and united opposition from the Haitian leaders and expose France to hostile opinion.

Neither Haitian state was recognised by any foreign government. Lacking any diplomatic recognition both the kingdom and the Republic were to cultivate relations with the leaders of anti-slavery in Europe. The French threat of 1814–15 had been thwarted in part because of an upsurge of abolitionist sentiment in Europe; in France itself the 'Hundred Days' had seen a decree against the slave trade while in Britain, as will be seen in chapter 8, this episode occasioned massive abolitionist protest. Subsequently King Henry engaged in a lengthy correspondence with Wilberforce and Clarkson, requesting their advice and help on diplomatic, economic and educational policy. President Pétion, and his successor Boyer, turned to the Abbé Grégoire for counsel and support.[57]

Both kingdom and Republic publicly renounced interference with the slave order elsewhere in the Americas. Nevertheless both found ways of lending some practical assistance to the struggle against colonial slavery. Christophe followed Dessalines in welcoming freedmen from North America, especially when they had skills that could assist the reconstruction of the country. Christophe's navy, built up as a weapon against the Southern Republic, was also used against slave-traders breaking the various bi-lateral treaties devised in the aftermath of the Congress of Vienna. Pétion in the South was to encourage Bolivar to adopt an emancipationist policy (about which more in chapter 9).

In the North King Henry maintained some enclaves of plantation production, using the *fermage* system and imposing stern labour regulations. The daily routine of the labourers on the large estates was, in principle, minutely regulated: after rising at 3 a.m. there were prayers and breakfast, followed by a morning stint in the fields from 4.30 to 8 a.m., a second stint from 9 a.m. to midday, a lunch-break until 2 p.m., followed by an afternoon shift until sundown, around 6 p.m., when they returned to their *cailles*. On Saturday's they would cultivate their garden plots; Sundays were a day of rest and, supposedly, worship. (Like Toussaint before him Christophe was a devout Christian and disapproved of voodoo.) The good discipline of Christophe's army and the high price of plantation produce allowed this policy to achieve some success and helped to finance the construction of a remarkable series of fortifications and palaces. Christophe's commanders were issued with telescopes; supposedly to be used both to spot invading fleets and to ensure that work proceeded in the fields. The economic successes of the royal state probably owed as much to state coordination of the economy as to intensive exploitation on the plantations. A number of schools were founded and some attention was paid to agricultural improvement. The foreign exchange earned by sales of sugar and coffee was also used to buy male slaves of military age from Dahomey; kept at a strength of 4,000 the royal *Dahomets* helped to maintain the labour regime and the rule of King Henry. Henry was eventually overthrown by an internal revolt in 1820. Henry was in bad health and his regime weakened by Republican propaganda and a decline in the price of sugar and coffee; but the severity of the plantation regime he established must have contributed to his isolation.[58]

The Republic of the South and West was less integrated and disciplined than the Northern kingdom. At different times both Rigaud and Jérome Borghella, the mulatto son of the French merchant who had collaborated with Toussaint, set up break-away statelets. Pétion, as president, showed great skill at containing such challenges, usually without resort to armed force. In the South and West there was a larger independent proprietory class, many of them *anciens libres*. In 1809 Pétion sought to strengthen the republican regime by dividing up confiscated estates, and other public lands, among soldiers and public officials. In this way a medium and small-holding peasantry was created. Retired soldiers received 5 *carreaux* of land (about 6.5 hectares or 17 acres), colonels 25 *carreaux*. During the presidency of Pétion (1807–18) over 150,000 hectares of land were granted or sold to more than 10,000 persons. However, large estates survived and were worked by tenant farmers. Following the overthrow of King Henry the North was invaded by the South, now under the leadership of President Boyer; the royal treasury was found to contain 13 million *livres*, roughly £500,000. Sugar output collapsed, but coffee exports remained important at around 20,000 tons annually; enough to make Haiti a major producer. The plantation system in the North did not survive the overthrow of King Henry, so that the agricultural system of the Republic as a whole was now based on a combination of peasant minifundia and tenant-worked latifundia.[59]

The precarious survival of Haitian independence was a thorn in the flesh of the slave order throughout the western hemisphere. The overturn in St Domingue and the consolidation of black power in Haiti had a terrible message for the slave order throughout the Americas. Black rebels in Cuba in 1812 , in the United States in 1820, in Jamaica and Brazil in the 1820s, found inspiration in Haiti. British, French and North American abolitionists all wrote books about Toussaint Louverture and the drama of the Haitian revolution. The example of St Domingue lived on in the fears of planters and colonial authorities. As we will see British emancipation, the options of the Cuban and Brazilian planters, the waning of the slave systems on the smaller

Caribbean islands and the growth of more secure systems on the mainland and in Cuba, were all to reflect the impact of the first liberation in St Domingue.

The chain of colonial slavery in the Americas had broken at what had been, in 1789, its strongest link. The Revolution had succeeded in St Domingue/Haiti for a combination of reasons: the massive numerical preponderance of slaves, some of them 'raw Africans' unused to American slavery, others creoles with new capacities formed by the plantation regime itself; the emergence of a slave elite, with some freedom of movement; the presence of a large free coloured community, with property and military experience; the disintegration of the mechanisms of slave control, as the metropolitan Revolution spilled back into the colonies, and as different factions of the free population fought with one another and armed slaves to further their own ends; the willingness of the metropolis to defend colonialism by jettisoning caste discrimination; the remarkable explosion of slave revolt in August 1791; the size and situation of the colony, facilitating the survival and spread of slave resistance and rebellion; the tenacity of the mass of blacks in pushing back planter power and defending their newly won freedom; the decision of the Jacobin Commissioners to ally with the slave resistance and build an emancipationist power; the diplomatic and military help of the Directory in resistance to royalist planters and the British occupation; the interplay of imperial and commercial rivalries opening up space for an emancipationist black state; two expeditions, mounted by the leading powers of the age, radicalising the Revolution they had been designed to crush.

In 1794 the message of revolutionary slave emancipation in St Domingue had been carried to France and from France it had been carried back across the Atlantic to the Lesser Antilles. The Iles du Vent lacked some of the crucial circumstances that favoured revolution in St Domingue. In these islands even quite intense factional struggles between Patriots and royalists had not involved the slaves. The free people of colour were less numerous. Planter hegemony had proved resilient, helped by the more manageable size of the islands, the skilful tactics of Du Buc, the intervention of the British and the deficient revolutionary initiative of the French representatives there. Prior to the arrival of Hugues in April 1794 neither intense Republican celebration of liberty and equality, nor the threat of British occupation, had produced any major challenge to slavery. The Jacobin expedition overthrew slavery and repulsed the British in Guadeloupe and stimulated Republican emancipationism in many parts of the Lesser Antilles and wider Caribbean. But both the manner of liberation in

Guadeloupe and the size of the colony made this achievement more vulnerable than in St Domingue. Just as struggles in the Lesser Antilles distracted the British in the mid-1790s, to the advantage of the St Domingue revolution, so in 1802 the resistance of Delgrès helped to alert coloured officers in the larger colony as to Napoleon's real intentions.

Sometimes historians have written as if the collapse of the colonial regime by itself propelled the slaves to freedom, or they have suggested that the revolutionary agents in the Caribbean had no choice but to decree emancipation. The conduct of Rochambeau and Lacrosse in the Lesser Antilles in February 1794 showed otherwise. The overthrow of slavery required conscious and dedicated protagonists as well as favourable conditions. Without the emergence of 'Black Jacobins' in 1793–4, and their alliance with revolutionary France, a generalised emancipation would not have been consolidated in St Domingue. The aspiration of the black masses for autonomy and living space required a generalising politics and programme, or what Napoleon was contemptuously to refer to as 'ideology'. The revolutionary emancipationism and egalitarianism of the 1790s was adopted for that reason and proved an enduring ideology. One of Napoleon's gravest miscalculations, when he set out to reconquer St Domingue and re-enslave the blacks, was to underestimate the extent to which liberty and equality had become the religion of the formerly enslaved, and even most of the *anciens libres*. Part of the grandeur of the great French Revolution is that it came to sponsor slave emancipation in the Americas; and part of the grandeur of the great Revolution in St Domingue/Haiti is that it successfully defended the gains of the French Revolution against France itself.[60]

But to say this is not to argue for some self-sufficient realm of discourse, revolutionary or otherwise, within which the drama of liberation unfolded. The message of black autonomy might be conveyed in a variety of idioms – French, or *Kréyole* or some African language – and with a variety of political or religious inflexions – royalist, Republican, Catholic, voodoo – so long as slaveholder power was broken. At a number of crucial junctures the meaning of the action of the black fighters was constituted not by what they had to say but by their physical impact on the structures of oppression and exploitation, enabling the mass of slaves to discover and assert a new collective identity *vis-à-vis* their oppressors and exploiters. From the outset the essential message of black autonomy was sustained by a myriad of local partisans, of diverse allegiance and formation, who resisted any return to the old order, whether justified in terms of republicanism or monarchy, patriotism or personal advantage. In 1802 all the famous leaders had collaborated with Leclerc yet he had still been opposed. It might be thought that Haitian resistance to Napoleon was sustained by nationalism, just as Spanish or Russian nationalism helped to inspire resistance to French occupation. Yet the very name of Haiti was not thought of until the French were already defeated – and no sooner had the new state been founded than it splintered. So it does seem reasonable to postulate some prior, more basic identity emerging from, and defined by, resistance to the slave condition and articulated by a multitude of local associations and popular memories. After all the Haitian Revolution had involved more profound upheavals and mobilisations than even the French Revolution itself. Black emancipationism was a product of the whole extraordinary experience of the decade and a half following the revolt of 1791. In the case of St Domingue the break with slavery furnished the indispensable basis for the break with colonialism. Black emancipationism was something deeper and more constant than a febrile tropical patriotism. It thus long pre-dated the declaration of independence and ensured that independence had an emancipationist content. Haiti was not the first independent American state but it was the first to guarantee civic liberty to all inhabitants.

Notes

1. For the situation of the Republicans in mid-1793 see Geggus, *Slavery, War and Revolution*, pp. 64, 100–101.

2. Stein, *Léger Félicité Sonthonax*, pp. 75, 95. Sonthonax's original instructions, while giving him extensive powers, expressly stated: 'It is unnecessary to remind you that the equality of rights extended to the men of colour and the blacks must not suffer any extention.' Monge, Minister for the Colonies, August 25th 1792, quoted in Saintoyant, *La Colonisation Française pendant la Révolution*, II, p. 118. Stein's account makes it clear that Sonthonax was writing to Paris urging general emancipation from February 1793. From this date he granted many piecemeal manumissions; from May he ordered the protective clauses of the regulations of 1784 to be read out every Sunday in the churches. Following the June decree he extended freedom to the womenfolk of the black warriors, so long as they were prepared to go through a Republican marriage ceremony. The Navy Minister and the Convention widened the powers available to the Commission in March 1793 and were probably aware of the use that might be made of them.

3. Stein, *Léger Félicité Sonthonax*, pp. 76–106; Thomas Ott, *The Haitian Revolution, 1789–1803*, Knoxville 1973, p. 71.

4. Pluchon, *Toussaint Louverture*, pp. 17–19. While the course of events in the North was to prove decisive, both Toussaint and Sonthonax were aware of smouldering rebellions elsewhere and of forms of resistance short of outright rebellion: see Carolyn Fick, 'Black Peasants and Soldiers in the Saint Domingue Revolution: Initial Reactions to Freedom in the South Province (1793–4)', in Frederick Krantz, ed., *History from Below*, Montréal 1985, pp. 243–60.

5. Quoted in James, *The Black Jacobins*, p. 125. Toussaint was responding to Sonthonax's action in freeing slaves since he had issued a proclamation to the slaves dated August 25th which declared: 'Having been the first to champion your cause, it is my duty to continue to labour for it. I cannot permit another to rob me of the initiative. Since I have begun I will know how to conclude. Join me and you will enjoy the rights of

freedmen sooner than any other way.' Quoted in *Toussaint L'Ouverture*, ed. George Tyson, Jr., Englewood Cliffs, NJ 1973, p. 27. As a Spanish officer Toussaint could at most offer freedom to those who enlisted with him, though evidently he sought to press this authority to its limit.

6. Geggus, *Slavery, War and Revolution*, pp. 105–14.

7. Pérotin–Dumon, *Etre Patriote sous les Tropiques*, pp. 216–20.

8. Polverel's summary quoted in Pluchon, *Toussaint Louverture*, p. 44.

9. Geggus, *Slavery, War and Revolution*, pp. 116, 304.

10. David Geggus , 'From His Most Catholic Majesty to the Godless Republique: The Volte Face of Toussaint Louverture and the Ending of Slavery in Saint Domingue', *Revue Française d'Histoire d'Outre Mer*, 241, 1978, pp. 481–99. The possibility that Toussaint had early news of the National Convention's decree on emancipation is increased by the fact that he was in the vicinity of the port of Gonaives in April and May.

11. For social pressures on the Jacobins see D.M.G. Sutherland, *France 1789–1815: Revolution and Counter-Revolution*, London 1985, pp. 129–44; George Rudé, *Revolutionary Europe, 1783–1815*, London 1970, pp. 139–54; Soboul, *The French Revolution*, pp. 313–34. Rousseau's writings came closest to articulating the radical undercurrent of popular egalitarianism. The writings of the Abbé Bonnot de Mably also tended in this direction: for example his *Doutes Proposés aux Philosophes Economistes* of 1768 and his *Observations on the Government and Laws of the United States* (London 1790). The celebration of equality and natural liberty in *Le Testament* of Jean Meslier, written in the early eighteenth century but not fully published until the nineteenth, is said to have circulated in manuscript; the point is not so much that Meslier exercised 'influence' as that he reflected in heightened form a radical tradition to be found amongst the lower clergy and other 'organic intellectuals' of the peasantry and small producers. By the revolutionary period the proto-socialist current begins to assume secular forms as in Sylvain Maréchal's *Manifeste des Égaux*; this secularisation ot popular politics may have assisted the generalisation of egalitarian principles to those, such as African slaves, who were not necessarily members of the Christian religious community.

12. Forrest, *Society and Politics in Revolutionary Bordeaux*, pp. 28–9, 42, 57.

13. Soboul, *The French Revolution*, pp. 369–70. For rival interpretations of the critical moment through which the Revolution and Republic was passing see Jaurès, *Histoire Socialiste de la Révolution Française*, I, p. 247; Claude Mazauric, 'Quelques voies nouvelles pour l'histoire politique de la Revolution française', *Annales Historiques de la Révolution Française*, vol. 47, no. 219, January–March 1975, p. 157; Higonnet, *Class Ideology and the Rights of the Nobles during the French Revolution*, pp. 170–218. Like all fundamental political crises that of the Jacobin Republic concentrated and condensed a wide range of social issues and conflicts; colonial slavery was simultaneously a real issue at stake and an unparalleled source of symbolic representations. While Higonnet stresses anti-nobilism, a contrasting emphasis on anti-capitalist elements in the Revolution is found in Immanuel Wallerstein's forthcoming third volume in his study of the emergence of a world system. In fact French anti-slavery was made possible by the *confluence* of anti-nobilism, anti-absolutism and anti-capitalism. However, Higonnet and Wallerstein neglect anti-absolutism, with its aspiration to a new and more far-reaching concept of sovereignty, since they deny that the *ancien régime* was at root a feudal power apparatus.

14. Augustin Cochin, *L'Abolition de l'Esclavage*, Paris 1861, 2 vols, I, pp. 13–15; Stein, *Légér Félicité Sonthonax*, pp. 110–11; see also *Decret de la Convention Nationale*, in *La Révolution Française et l'Abolition de l'Esclavage*, Paris 1968, XVII. Cochin, with the reflexes of a moderate nineteenth-century abolitionist, comments: 'The Assembly dared nothing, the Legislative could do nothing, the Convention risked everything' (p. 7).

15. *Le Moniteur Universel*, 17, 18 Pluviôse, An II, nos. 137, 138, February 1794. Danton's role in promoting emancipation was to bring down on him the charges of irresponsibility and treachery. The factional purpose of such charges was revealed when the emancipation was, nevertheless, pursued.

16. P.G. Chaumette, 'Discours sur l'abolition de l'esclavage', *La Révolution Française et l'Abolition de l'Esclavage*, XII. For a strategic and principled defence of the Pluviôse

decree see also the article from the *Creole Patriote* published in Paris on Pluviôse 28 and reprinted in Yves Benot, *La Révolution et la fin des colonies*, Paris 1987, pp. 249–52. Yves Benot points out that Sonthonax, Chaumette and Sylvain Maréchal all wrote for *Les Révolutions de Paris* in 1791–2 (pp. 125–7).

17. Oruno Lara, *La Guadeloupe dans l'Histoire*, pp. 94–107. This work by an early twentieth-century historian from Guadeloupe gives a rather positive assessment of the emancipationist regime in the colony; a longer and more hostile account will be found in the biography by a French naval historian: Ste Croix de la Roncière, *Victor Hughes, le Conventionnel*, Paris 1932, p. 111–70. (The title here gives a variant spelling of Hughes's name.) The prior Republican education of Guadeloupe did something to prepare the way for Hughes's revolutionary war, despite its pro-slavery commitment, Pérotin–Dumon, *Êtres Patriotes sous les Tropiques*, pp. 231–46. The exploits of Victor Hughes are the subject of Alejo Carpentier's novel, *El Siglo de las Luces*; however, the latter relied on Roncière and should not be taken as historically accurate on all points: see the contribution by Françoise Treil–Labarre in J. Baldran *et al.*, *Quinze Études au Tour de 'El Siglo de las Luces' de Alejo Carpentier*, Paris 1983. The impact of Hughes's expedition on the British is recounted in Michael Duffy, *Soldiers, Sugar and Seapower*, Oxford 1987, pp. 115–36.

18. For the revolts in Grenada and St Vincent see Michael Craton, *Testing the Chains*, pp. 180–94; and Duffy, *Soldiers, Sugar and Seapower*, pp. 137–56.

19. *Rapport fait, au nom de comité de salut public, sur la Guadeloupe et autres Iles de Vent*, Defermond, Paris An III, p. 5. Given the considerable military significance and social interest of Republican emancipation in Guadeloupe it is surprising that it has not attracted more attention. See, for example, the surprising mistake in Cohen, *The French Encounter with Africans*, p. 118, who appears to believe that emancipation never reached Guadeloupe. The abolition of night-work in the mills, a major gain for the labourers, is confirmed by the otherwise hostile account of M.A. Lacour for whom the Republican regime embodied 'neither slavery nor freedom but disorder' in which 'insolent' blacks abused official tolerance; Lacour, *Histoire de la Guadeloupe*, Basse Terre 1858, pp. 384–9.

20. James, *The Black Jacobins*, pp. 163–73; Pluchon, *Toussaint Louverture*, pp. 56–64; Geggus, *Slavery, War and Revolution*, p. 185.

21. Stein, *Léger Félicité Sonthonax*, pp. 107–20.

22. Marc Bouloiseau, *La République Jacobine, 10 Août 1792–9 Thermidor An II*, Paris 1972, p. 78.

23. Quoted in Geggus, *Slavery, War and Revolution*, p. 191.

24. The British officer is quoted by R.G. Buckley, *Slaves in Red Coats: the British West India Regiments, 1795–1815*, New Haven and London 1979, p. 90.

25. General Moore is quoted by Craton, *Testing the Chains*, p. 198.

26. Buckley, *Slaves in Red Coats*, pp. 25–8, 82–105; Craton, *Testing the Chains*, pp. 211–23.

27. Oruno Lara, *La Guadeloupe dans l'Histoire*, p. 100; Geggus, *Slavery, War and Revolution*, p. 196.

28. Pluchon, *Toussaint Louverture*, p. 75.

29. Stein, *Léger Félicité Sonthonax*, p. 135.

30. For the new social order in the colony and the policies of the Commissioners see Stein, *Léger Félicité Sonthonax*, pp. 123–55; Carolyn Fick, 'Black Peasants and Soldiers in Saint Domingue', in Krantz, *History from Below*, pp. 243–61; James, *The Black Jacobins*, pp. 155–6, 174–6, 218–20; Pluchon, *Toussaint Louverture*, pp. 72–5; Ott, *The Haitian Revolution*, pp. 129–31; Fouchard, *The Haitian Maroons*, pp. 358–9.

31. Roger Norman Buckley, ed., *The Haitian Journal of Lieutenant Howard*, Knoxville 1985, pp. xvii–xviii.

32. Sidney Mintz, *Caribbean Transformations*, Chicago 1974, pp. 146–56.

33. See James's observations on this topic, *The Black Jacobins*, pp. 85–6.

34. See the remarks of the British Agent in Tyson, *Toussaint L'Ouverture*, p. 91; Geggus, *Slavery, War and Revolution*, p. 287.

35. James, *The Black Jacobins*, p. 193.

36. Toussaint's letter is given in Tyson, *Toussaint L'Ouverture*, pp. 36–43. Toussaint was here replying to Rochambeau's statement, which he quoted, that 'one day it will be necessary to fight to make them (that is the blacks) return to work'. Toussaint's replies to his French critics, and warning to the Directory, has a vigour and directness entirely lacking from his laboured attempt to justify his attacks on Sonthonax, given by Tyson on pp. 46–9. For an account sympathetic to Sonthonax see Stein, *Léger Félicité Sonthonax*, pp. 156–73.

37. Geggus, *Slavery, War and Revolution*, pp. 212–13, 383; David Geggus, 'The Cost of Pitt's Caribbean Campaigns, 1793–1798', *Historical Journal*, vol. 26, no. 3, 1983, pp. 699–706. The figure given above includes as casualties those who died, deserted or were discharged as unfit for service; it includes sailors as well as soldiers. Geggus calculates that British casualties so defined totalled 55,670, to which must be added a further 3,500 or so losses among foreign auxiliary forces, probably French royalists. The campaigns cost the enormous sum of £16–20 million (p. 705). For the longer period 1793–1801 Duffy calculates much higher British casualties – 87,000–97,000, with at least 64,000 dead in the Caribbean, Duffy, *Soldiers, Sugar and Seapower*, pp. 333–4.

38. Robert Debs Heinl Jr. and Nancy Gordon Heinl, *Written in Blood: The Story of the Haitian People*, Boston 1978, p. 96.

39. Heinl and Heinl, *Written in Blood*, p. 95.

40. Ott, *The Haitian Revolution*, pp. 127–38; Pluchon, *Toussaint Louverture*, p. 279; Mats Lundhall, 'Toussaint L'Ouverture and the War Economy of Saint Domingue', *Slavery and Abolition*, vol. 6, no. 4, 1985, pp. 122–38.

41. Pluchon, *Toussaint Louverture*, pp. 18–9, 220–50.

42. Heinl and Heinl, *Written in Blood*, pp. 96–7.

43. Pluchon, *Toussaint Louverture*, pp. 292–9.

44. Tyson, ed., *Toussaint L'Ouverture*, p. 88; Henry Adams, *History of the United States of America during the First Administration of Thomas Jefferson*, New York 1962, pp. 391–2.

45. The text of the decree is printed in Tyson, *Toussaint L'Ouverture*, pp. 59–64; see also the discussion in James, *The Black Jacobins*, p. 279 *et seq*. It is interesting to note that around this time *livrets* were being introduced in France too as a security device and a check to vagabonds.

46. Quoted in Pluchon, *Toussaint Louverture*, p. 346. Leclerc's original instructions from Bonaparte were to proceed in three stages: 'In the first phase you will not be exacting: negotiate with Toussaint, offer him anything he asks. . . . This done you will become more exacting. . . . In the first phase confirm them in their rank and position. In the last phase send them all to France . . . ship out all black generals, regardless of their conduct, patriotism or past services. . . . No matter what happens, during the third phase disarm all *noirs*. . .' (quoted in Heinl and Heinl, *Written in Blood*, pp. 100–101).

47. Pamphile de Lacroix, *Memoires*, vol. II, p. 164; quoted in Ott, *The Haitian Revolution*, p. 257.

48. Cochin, *L'Abolition de l'Esclavage*, pp. 22–3; M.J. Sydenham, *The First French Republic, 1792–1804*, London 1974, p. 280.

49. Oruno Lara, *La Guadeloupe dans l'Histoire*, pp. 109–30.

50. Quoted in Heinl and Heinl, *Written in Blood*, p. 113.

51. A further 8,000 French sailors also lost their life from the fighting or from disease. Pamphile Lacroix estimated that there had been 62,481 fatalities among the pro-French forces, black and white, military and civilian (Pluchon, *Toussaint Louverture*, p. 385). Both the British and the French lost more soldiers in St Domingue than they did at Waterloo.

52. David Geggus, 'British Opinion and the Emergence of Haiti', in Walvin, *Slavery and British Society*, especially pp. 140–49.

53 Heinl and Heinl, *Written in Blood*, p. 123–37.

54. David Nicholls, 'Rural protest and Peasant Revolt', in *Haiti in Caribbean Context: Ethnicity, Economy and Revolt*, London 1985, pp. 167–84, especially pp. 170–74.

55. For the formation of a Haitian peasantry in the early independence period see

Paul Moral, *Le Paysan Haïtien*, Paris 1961, pp. 34–45.

56. James Franklin, *The Present State of Hayti*, London 1828, p. 331. A recent writer estimates that the population of Haiti grew from circa 400,000 in 1804 to circa 600,000 in 1824. See Mats Lundhal, *Peasants and Poverty: A Study of Haiti*, London 1979, p. 190.

57. Ruth Necheles, *The Abbé Grégoire, 1787–1831*, Westport, Conn. 1971, pp. 253–89.

58. Hubert Cole, *Christophe, King of Haiti*, London 1967.

59. Nicholls, 'Economic Dependence and Political Autonomy, 1804–1915', in *Haiti in Caribbean Context*, pp. 83–120, especially p. 93. For a socio-political sketch of both monarchy and Republic see also David Nicholls, *From Dessalines to Duvalier: Race, Colour and National Independence in Haiti*, Cambridge 1979, pp. 35–60. More material on the kingdom will be found in Cole, *Christophe, King of Haiti*, and on the Republic in Hennock Trouillot, 'La République de Pétion et le Peuple Haïtien', *Revue de la Societé Haïtienne d'Histoire*, vol. 31, no. 107, January–April 1960, pp. 96–115.

60. These points are underlined by the survival of slavery in the French Indian Ocean island of Réunion and also in the Dutch colonies. The government in Paris had very little contact with its representatives in Réunion, who deferred to the local slaveholders. On the other hand there was no slave uprising in Réunion sufficient to force emancipation onto the agenda, as happened in Saint Domingue. In the Dutch colony of Curaçao there was a slave revolt in 1795, inspired by the events in the French Caribbean, but the colonial authorities succeeded in crushing it. Note that the Dutch Patriots did not control the Netherlands in February 1794 at the time of the French emancipation decree. Even once the Patriot Batavian Republic was consolidated in Europe it had little purchase on events in the colonies. See Claude Wanquet, 'Révolution française et identité réunionnaise', and Francois J. L. Souty, 'La Révolution française, la République batave et le premier repli colonial néerlandais (1784–1814)', in Jean Tarrale, ed., *La Révolution française et les colonies*, Paris 1989. Another informative study brings out the importance of the historic convergence of black insurgency and French Jacobinism in 1794. See Florence Gauthier, *Triomphe et mort du droit naturel en Révolution*, Paris 1992.

VII

Abolition and Empire: The United States

What in short is the whole system of Europe toward America?
One hemisphere of the earth, separated from the other by wide
seas on both sides, having a different system of interests flowing
from different climates, different soils, different productions,
different modes of existence and its own local relations and duties,
is made subservient to all the petty interests of the other, to their
laws, their regulations, their passions and wars.

Thomas Jefferson, 1811

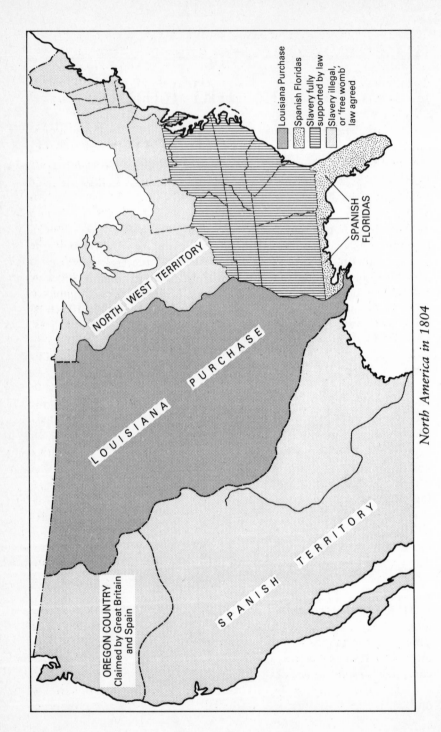

Louisiana Purchase
Spanish Floridas
Slavery fully supported by law
Slavery illegal, or 'free womb' law agreed

SPANISH FLORIDAS

NORTH WEST TERRITORY

LOUISIANA PURCHASE

SPANISH TERRITORY

OREGON COUNTRY
Claimed by Great Britain and Spain

North America in 1804

While the American Revolution had furnished inspiration to the French, the Jacobin policy of expropriatory slave emancipation went far beyond anything envisaged in 1776 or achieved in the 1780s in North America. The contrast between a social and a political revolution can be clearly seen if the North American, French and Haitian Revolutions are compared.

In North America revolutionary transformations had been almost wholly concentrated in the political domain; rejecting colonial rule, rejecting the oligarchic structures of 'illegitimate monarchy' and laying the basis for a white man's democratic republic. Changes in the underlying property regime and in social relations had been modest. Prior to 1776 capitalist farming, mercantile capital and plantation slavery had already constituted the dominant pattern of colonial economy and the Revolution had only given them freer reign. In the Northern workshops, ports and dock yards free wage labour also predominated prior to 1776. Even the Emancipation Laws adopted by some states had been limited in scope, emancipating only the unborn and leaving large numbers of blacks in slavery. Yet, modest as it was, the constraint placed on slavery by these Laws, and by the North-west Ordinance of 1787, did at least confirm that wage labourers and independent small producers would not have to compete with slave labour in large areas of the North.

The significance of this gain was itself qualified by the failure of emancipation in New York and New Jersey. With all their limitations the political changes in North America did have a genuinely revolutionary character and brought new social forces to the helm. In eighteenth-century Britain political power was in the hands of a landed and mercantile oligarchy. In the United States government was accountable not only to planters and merchants but also to the mass of farmers and artisans. While the Briton was a subject the North American was a citizen. According to the 1790 Naturalisation Law citizenship was open to 'all free white persons' who had resided for more than a year in the United States and who wished to apply for it.[1] The different states still had residual property as well as residence and ethnic qualifications but the principle of popular sovereignty had been resoundingly established.

The social transformations produced by the French Revolution were qualitatively greater, and nowhere more so than in the Antilles; not simply expropriations and property transfers on a far larger scale than in North America but the abolition of old types of property and the consolidation of new social relations. In North America there had been a revolt of civil society against the state; in France a revolutionary dictatorship arose on the ruins of feudal absolutism actively promoting a new distribution of property, a new pattern of economic activity and a vision of life transformed. In the French Antilles the world had been turned upside down; in Haiti colonialism, monarchy and slavery had all been destroyed. Neither in France, nor still less in the Francophone Antilles, did these transformations involve a simple transfer of power to a new bourgeois ruling class within a purely capitalist order; artisans, petty functionaries, smallholders, peasants and labourers had to be accommodated in the new political structures and social regime. The Jacobin Republic, the Directory and the Napoleonic regime all embodied different concessions to these various social strata just as in Haiti the post-revolutionary regimes had to negotiate a relationship with the post-emancipation peasantry.

While American leaders were able to greet the opening stages of the French Revolution as an echo of their own recent experience the advent of the Jacobin phase created deep divisions and found the government of the United States aligned with Britain rather than France. As the French Revolution subsided, and most particularly as the French government reversed its commitment to revolutionary slave emancipation, so relations improved between the governments of the United States and France, in the years after 1799. But it would be misleading to concentrate solely on official interstate relations and to miss the considerable popular impact of French republicanism even during the period of the 'Quasi-War'. The drama of the French Revolution and its memorable proclamation of the Republican ideals of 'liberty, equality, fraternity' could not fail to have an impact in the United States and to inspire many with the idea that there should be a democratic revision and extention of the achievements of America's own recent Revolution. The North American 'democratic republicanism' of the 1790s was not a species of American Jacobinism, as it opponents liked to allege, but the 'Revolution of 1800' did check tendencies towards bourgeois oligarchy in the young Republic. And as a by-product of the political strife it occasioned there was a modest 'second wind' for US abolitionism, which encompassed emancipation laws in the two Northern states where slavery had remained legal – New York (1799) and New Jersey (1804) – passage of a law ending the slave trade to the United States (1807), and confirmation that slavery would be barred from the Northwest. As it turned out these belated doses of abolition, together with the impact of events in St Domingue, did not prevent the United States establishing itself as a new and more expansive type of slaveholding empire during these very same years.

Both in conception and execution the French revolutionary emancipationism of 1794–5 seems to belong to a different political universe to the mainstream of Anglo–American abolitionism. Yet the anti-slavery achievements of the former did abash the latter. Wilberforce's decision to put forward annual resolutions to Parliament on the slave trade made it easier for him to support a government which sent an armada to the Caribbean to defend slavery.

In January 1794 the various North American Abolition Societies came together for the first time in Philadelphia to discuss co-ordinated activity. The calling of this convention reflected a belief amongst North American abolitionists that anti-slavery had made great strides in the Old World and that it was high time to mount new initiatives in the United States. It was decided to meet annually. Speakers questioned Federal complicity with slave-owning and urged an extension of emancipation legislation in the North. It was argued that an international agreement to end the slave traffic would be a welcome contribution to a more general pacification of the oceanic trade routes. For a time the arguments of the idealistic anti-slavery minority were again publicly aired in the North and became a rare point of coincidence between radical democrats and conservatives.

Though emancipation was not a directly partisan issue in New York or New Jersey fierce party strife between Federalists and Democratic Republicans, in which both sides sought to outdo the other in protestations of patriotism, was to make it more difficult to postpone or fudge emancipation once again on procedural grounds. The Federalists would not countenance anything that looked like an assault on the rich; but many Federalists had supported a decorous anti-slavery on the grounds that property would be more easy to defend if disassociated from personal bondage. The main concern of Democratic Republicans was scarcely abolition, since they received important backing from southern slaveholders. But they articulated their opposition to the Federalism of Hamilton and Adams in terms of a radical democratic rhetoric that could acquire anti-slavery connotations where the institution was already weak. Paradoxically the very same political mobilisation that delivered the *coup de grace* to slavery in New York and New Jersey overthrew the mildly abolitionist President Adams and ensured that he would be succeeded by a long line of slaveholders.

The mid-1790s witnessed rapprochment between the government of Britain and the United States, but the political culture and class relations of the young Republic made wholesale oligarchic recidivism untenable. The example of revolutionary France, and an economic boom stimulated by the recovery of Caribbean trade, emboldened American artisans and farmers, and a layer of merchants and manufacturers. Politicians in search of a popular following began to challenge the conservative features of the constitutional settlements of the 1780s and Federalist schemes for funding the public debt; they knew their countrymen were allergic to new taxes, to the speculations of government-favoured financiers and to the growth of public patronage. The Federalist programme of national development seemed to be bringing back the hated instruments of Hanoverian tyranny. There were diplomatic concessions to Britain and plans for a standing army. A Philadelphia paper warned : 'A funding system is to the United States what a nobility is to a monarchy. It has a separate representation, for, as it forms a phalanx of support, so it has the countenance or sympathy of government. It is a machine which sustains administration at all times and under all circumstances, and like action and reaction, administration sustains it.'[2] In a climate of economic recovery farmers, artisans and labourers were unwilling to see a mercantile and financial oligarchy establish untrammelled power in the young Republic.

Many Virginian planters were equally suspicious of, and hostile to, Federalist plans, as they found their taxes being used to finance an expansion of government that brought them no direct benefit; Virginia's state debt had already been discharged in the 1780s, yet the state was expected to contribute to paying off the consolidated debt of the Federal government. James Madison's assurance that the Federal structure would prevent obnoxious factions from seizing the state machinery had evidently not reckoned with the power of finance.

Congressional debates on taxation and citizenship were alarming to southern slaveholding opinion for another reason. In order to finance the 'Quasi-War' against France the Adams administration proposed a scheme for direct taxation in 1797–8. Southern slaveholders did not welcome new taxes being laid upon them – but worse than this was the spectacle of Congress publicly deliberating the best way of taxing land and slaves. If land alone was taxed then the planters, with their broad acres, would be penalised. But taxation of slave property was no more welcome. Some feared that the power to tax and the power to abolish were impossible to separate, since taxes could always be raised to punitive levels. Southern anxieties could be somewhat allayed by apportioning direct taxes according to the 'Federal ratio'. But the Congressional debates and resolutions of the summer of 1798 were nevertheless deeply disturbing to the more far-seeing southern Republican. Congress debated in detail whether taxes should fall on all slaves or only on the economically active, and what methods of assessment and collection should be adopted; worst of all the votes on such questions divided southerners and revealed the scope for northern manoeuvring that could sow discord in the South. Northern representatives were usually happy to ignore the slaveholding that prevailed in the southern states, but circumstances might arise in which they would attack the southern states on their most vulnerable point. A small incident in 1793 revealed the scope for northern demagogy. A southern Republican put an amendment to a new Naturalisation Bill stipulating that foreigners wishing to claim American citizenship should renounce all claim to aristocratic titles. A Congressman from Massachusetts riposted to this by putting an amendment that slaveholding foreigners must renounce their slaves before being admitted to citizenship. Southern representatives had been stunned by the insult implied to their own civic worth; the amendment was eventually voted down with northern help but this unpleasant incident was not easily forgotten. It showed the danger of allowing Congress powers to interfere in the domestic affairs of the slave states.[3]

Jefferson and other Democratic Republicans contested the very principle of a Federal power to levy direct taxes. Jefferson believed that the best defence of the integrity of the southern social formation was strict adherence to the constitutional principle that the Federal government had been established for limited and specific purposes and that the several states retained all powers not specifically made over to the Federal authorities. Jefferson had not been involved in the Constitutional Settlement of 1787 and was not satisfied that it incorporated all necessary safeguards. His campaign for a 'strict construction' of the constitution was therefore accompanied by a stress on the need to strengthen the authority and the representativity of the state governments, fortifying them as bulwarks against Federal misrule. His approach was strategic rather than defensive, reaching out for allies against the Federalists and being happy to offer democratic measures to the mass of white citizens; protection of civil liberties and the removal of property qualifications to the franchise. Jefferson will have been well aware that no popular coalition could be built around the unattractive plank of defence of slaveholding. The nearest he came to striking this note was in a statement he allowed to go forward in his name in South Carolina prior to the election of 1800 which simply stated: 'That the Constitution has not empowered the federal legislature to touch in the remotest degree the question respecting the condition of property of slaves in any of the states, and that any attempt of that sort would be unconstitutional and a usurpation of rights Congress do not possess.'[4] For Jefferson to make such explicit reference to the awkward issue of slavery was unusual and no doubt reflected the particular circumstances of a state where slaveholding was most extensive. In the Kentucky and Virginia Resolutions prepared by Jefferson and Madison as a counter-blast to the Federalists in 1798 states' rights and civil rights were vigorously defended without any reference to slaveholding. The sole ostensible object of the 'Resolutions' was the unconstitutionality of the

Alien and Sedition Laws introduced at the behest of the Adams administration in 1798. While there is no reason to doubt the sincerity of southern Republican opposition to this law, such opposition was expressed in terms of 'strict construction' and states' rights.[5] Moreover Jefferson and his fellow revolutionary slaveholders based their Republican politics on an alliance between planters and the common man – whether farmer or artisan – in which the latter would be assured every consideration and respect. Intransigent defence of popular liberties and of states' rights could and would isolate the Federalists; references to southern property rights in human beings would not. Jefferson and the other main southern Republican leaders understood that such an alliance would have to entail respect for the prejudices of their potential northern allies, the farmers and artisans opposed to the budding Federalist oligarchy. The latter might not be pro-black, but they were certainly hostile to competing with slaves and slaveholders. Jefferson not only supported the extension of political rights to all citizens but he also saw no need to require northern Republicans to support slavery in their own states. His attachment to a generous measure of sovereignty residing in the states, and a correspondingly limited competence for Federal government, meant that each state could adopt the policies appropiate to its circumstances. Since slavery was a sad necessity, not a positive good, in Jefferson's view, he may even have welcomed a moderate and responsible emancipation process where there were few slaves.

Events in St Domingue can only have confirmed Jefferson's commitment to avoiding any outside meddling in the affairs of the slave states. The fate of St Domingue had demonstrated the perils of outside interference long before the Jacobin adoption of emancipation: royalist *agents provocateurs*, the decree on mulatto rights, Republican Commissioners attempting to enforce the *exclusif*, all had a share of the blame for the ruin of the slave system. Southern planters had been keen on self-determination prior to the troubles in St Domingue, but the terrible spectre of the latter underlined that vague understandings and compromise formulae would not do. The southern Republican alternative was to build a coalition under southern planter leadership that would guarantee states' rights and ensure the responsible and limited exercise of Federal powers.

Abolition in New York was assisted by the sharp polarisation between Federalists and Democratic Republicans that had arisen from the early 1790s as the latter pressed home their attack on the allegedly aristocratic and oligarchic features of national and state government during the Presidencies of Washington and Adams. Alexander Hamilton and John Jay were founding members of the New York Manumission

Society and like Adams were sensitive to the rise of abolitionism in Britain. Jay was elected Governor of New York in 1795, and however moderate his abolitionist beliefs, some initiative on the issue was expected of him. On the other hand, politicians appealing to a radical constituency such as Melancton Smith had also supported emancipation. There were Republicans who believed in a white man's democracy; they simultaneously abhorred slaveholders, slaves and blacks. Yet there was a more generous strain in Republicanism. The urban radical milieu was perceived, at least by its opponents, as embracing coloured radicals: a Federalist lampoon shows Jefferson improbably presiding over a democratic republican audience composed of Tom Paine, a tavern-keeper, a black man, a pirate, a French Jacobin, a school-teacher, a surly artisan and other supposedly typical members of the dangerous classes.[6]

When the partisans of abolitionism in New York eventually achieved the victory that had eluded them for so long in 1799 the numbers of slaves in the state had dropped to about 12,000, partly through manumissions and partly because slaveholders had deemed it wise to dispose of their human chattels via the internal slave trade. The final battle over slavery in New York occurred at a time when the Federalists needed to prove that, notwithstanding the Alien and Sedition Laws, they were genuine friends of liberty. In this climate the Emancipation Law helped Federalist leaders to re-establish their concern for civic freedom. On the other hand, the New York *Argus*, a leading Republican newspaper, had published articles by authors signing themselves 'A Consistent Democrat' and 'An Invariable Friend to the Equal Rights of Man' which supported emancipation and warned that votes would be withheld from Republicans who failed to do so. The Republican camp included refugee British radicals who strongly supported abolition. Defenders of slavery used a battery of arguments, some with a Federalist flavour, others calculated to appeal to Republicans. It was urged that the measure was 'class legislation' unfairly aimed at the established Dutch community of rural New York amongst whom there were many slaveholders; Federalists might be expected to be sensitive to this charge. Alternatively it was argued that the 'poor man' was more dependent on his slave domestic than the rich, 'wallowing in luxury' and with armies of servants; this approach had a Republican ring to it. And the conscience of both Federalists and Republicans could be pricked by the thought that emancipation would rob widows and orphans of slaves that were their only means of support. As in the 1780s the defenders of slavery warned that slaveholders would see little benefit in raising slave children only to see them freed as soon as they became adults; they would consequently abandon such children who would become a burden on the community. It was also urged on both Federalists and Republicans that emancipation would promote the notion that there should be a community of goods and an equal sharing of property. Such arguments could no longer stop emancipation but still had some influence on its terms. A moderate Emancipation Law was adopted by a large majority – it freed male children of slave mothers at twenty-eight years of age and female children at twenty-five years. At a time when Federalists and Republicans loved to oppose one another emancipation attracted almost equal support from representatives of the two groupings. The extent of Republican support is remarkable, since New York abolitionism had hitherto been a Federalist cause. The strengthening of democratic opinion in New York in the late 1790s evidently extended to the slavery question. In one important respect the New York law did reflect a radical democratic approach: it conferred full civic rights on freedmen, allowing them to vote and bear arms. In this respect New York showed greater respect for Republican equality than Massachusetts or Rhode Island where blacks suffered legal discriminations.[7]

The passage of the New York Emancipation Law encouraged new attempts to commit New Jersey to emancipation. This state also had well-established Dutch farmers who found slaveholding convenient and profitable. When defenders of slavery urged that blacks needed to be kept in bondage otherwise they would be a danger both to others and themselves, an abolitionist riposted that the real motive of such pro-slavery advocates was that blacks 'make excellent slaves, and in that capacity are very valuable'. The absence of a large urban conurbation like Philadelphia or New York had delayed the rise of radical politics in New Jersey, but around the turn of the century the Democratic Republicans acquired a majority in the state. The Emancipation Law passed by the legislature in 1803–4 received the support of twenty-nine Republicans and fifteen Federalists against four Federalists and one Republican. The law which achieved such support was more generous to slaveholders than any previous emancipation measure while virtually ignoring black rights. The age at which children of slave mothers would be freed was quite high – twenty-five for men and twenty-one for women – but in addition slaveholders were offered the possibility of obtaining a subsidy from the Overseer of the Poor if they claimed that they could not support the infants concerned. This was the nearest approach to financial compensation of expropriated slaveholders in any northern emancipation law. It proved very expensive and was abandoned within a few years but not before the New Jersey slaveholders had derived great advantage from it. [8]

Slavery had been vulnerable in New York and New Jersey because it was a marginal and declining institution. If the dynamics of party rivalry in New York weakened slaveholding, this was not at all the case in the Union as a whole where cross-sectional alliances were essential to political success. Jefferson and Madison had good reason to assume leading roles in national politics despite their insistence that the Federal state should have very limited powers. Even partisans of strict construction conceded that slavery questions could impinge on national politics if they concerned foreign trade (after 1807), the disposition of conquered territory or the conduct of Federal appointed officials. Restricted though these questions were, slaveholders were still nervous enough to expect not only that Federal powers and policy should be as little intrusive as possible but also, to make assurance doubly sure, that they should be in the hands of persons in whom slaveholders could have confidence. The Democratic Republican cause was eventually represented at the highest level by Jefferson, Madison and Monroe, three Virginian slaveholders.

Jefferson remained enough of a revolutionary to resent Federalist subservience to Britain and, as he saw it, Federalist preparedness to put financial interests ahead of the well-being of artisans and labourers, up-country farmers and western pioneers. Moreover by placing himself at the head of the popular anti-Federalist movement he could ensure that it did not fall into the hands of dangerous demagogues. Jefferson detested the Federalists because he thought they were dragging his country away from its pastoral virtues and creating in its place a society with avid bankers and contractors, on the one hand, and desperate *canaille* and proletarians, on the other. In the fierce political battles of the 1790s Jefferson was careful to keep the question of slavery in the background so far as possible.

The triumph of the Democratic Republicans in the Presidential election of 1800 showed that North American politics had escaped sectional polarisation. Jeffersonian Republicanism succeeded in finding followers in the south, north and west. Despite his attacks on the constitution Jefferson found as President that it could be made to serve the purpose dearest to him; a national expansion that would draw on the healthy energies of all sections. The Virginian leaders who dominated the Presidency for the next two decades were not particularly proud of slavery. The revolution in St Domingue redoubled their conviction of the need for a prudential ban on the importation of African or foreign slaves; in 1798 even Georgia fell into line so that, for a time, slave imports from abroad were allowed in no American state. On the other hand, the North American slave system was as vigorous as ever. The numbers of slaves in the United States were growing rapidly. In 1790 there were 698,000 and by the close of the century the number had grown to 893,000. At this latter date there were still 35,900 slaves in the north because the Emancipation Laws had usually freed the children of slaves rather than slaves themselves.[9]

While slavery was gently declining in the north, in the South it had a new vigour that was not simply demographic. Southern planters were beginning to respond to the growing demand for cotton. In the first instance most cotton was grown in the coastal south but the invention of Whitney's cotton gin in 1793 meant that it could be cultivated and processed far inland as well. US exports of raw cotton grew from 0.5 million lb in 1793 to 18 million lb in 1800 and 83 million lb by 1815. In the years 1801–5 40 per cent of British cotton imports came from the United States. This was, of course, just a beginning. Up to the early 1790s slavery in North America, as throughout the continent, had been overwhelmingly concentrated in coastal regions. Whitney's gin removed a major technical obstacle to westwards migration.[10]

Jefferson's Republican success had brought white American men closer to their government, but by securing the cross-sectional alliance it riveted more securely the chains of southern blacks. The very Republicans who had voted for emancipation in the north helped to elect a slaveholder President. In the South the Federalists were almost as zealous as the Republicans when it came to tightening up the slave regime, but the Federalist alliance was hegemonised by the north-east while Virginians played the leading role in the democratic republican camp. Jefferson's hostility to the Federalists was animated by the view that they had allowed the United States to become a sort of commercial and maritime dependency of Britain. He believed that the British wished to recolonise North America through commercial and financial instruments and to bind its future to them. He had attacked the treaty with Britain negotiated by John Jay as the work of 'the vile aristocratic few who have too long governed America, and who are enemies of the equality of man'.[11] In his view the British would encourage the unhealthy growth of the eastern commercial ports while preventing the young Republic from spreading out to control its own continent. The national and international issues raised by the contest with the Federalists quite over-shadowed the slave question, or even put it in a new light.

In private communications Jefferson maintained that, however unwise it was to have enslaved so many blacks, it could not be undone without even greater danger. Towards the end of his life he was to sum up his view like this: 'We have the wolf by the ears; and we can neither hold him nor let him go. Justice is in the one scale, and self-preservation in the other.'[12] Jefferson believed that the threat from American-born blacks might be containable and could best be tackled at some remote future date when the United States would have grown in strength and maturity, and when the mass of its (white) citizens were smallholding farmers spread out across the whole continent. In the meantime slaves were more adaptable and reliable than degraded whites who had been deprived of their natural birthright – the ownership of a plot of land. He believed farmers to be more naturally virtuous than slaveholders, but he did not despair of encouraging the latter to the path of wisdom and self-restraint. He demonstrated the versatility of slave labour by himself becoming one of the largest nail manufacturers in the country. He was particularly anxious that the South should not lose out to the northern commercial states in the race for development; events in the Caribbean and Europe were to help him secure extra living room for southern slavery, as will be seen below.

James Madison, who was to follow Jefferson as President, likewise did not allow private reservations about slavery to cloud his public defence of slaveholder interests or to prevent him from grasping the reasons for its economic vitality. His lucid intelligence furnished a clear explanation of why it was so difficult to give up holding slaves. Writing to a critic he concurred 'as to the evil, moral, political and economical' of slavery. But he urged that there could be 'much improvement' in slave culture as he had discovered from 'proofs annually taking place within my own sphere of observation; particularly where slaves are held in small numbers, by good masters and managers'. He urged his correspondent to consider that the risks of running a plantation might actually be less than those of a speculation in stocks or bonds: 'look at the wrecks everywhere giving warning of the danger'. But perhaps his decisive argument was that slave plantations were the most convenient and rapid path to agricultural expansion in American conditions. If his correspondent invested in land then he would need labour: 'Will you cultivate it yourself? Then beware of the difficulty of procuring faithful or complying labourers. Will you dispose of it in leases? Ask those who have made the experiment what sort of tenants are to be found where an ownership of the soil is so attainable.'[13]

With men like Jefferson and Madison at the helm slavery was in safe hands. Following the passage of emancipation in New York and New Jersey the northern abolitionists were caught in a compartmentalised political structure that had been specifically designed to frustrate them. The southern abolitionist societies urged more generous manumission laws while those in the North spoke of the need to educate the free black in the duties of citizenship and freedom. Many abolitionists supported the 'colonisation' of freedmen outside US borders; there were few opportunities for raising the question of emancipation in the main slaveholding states. Southern abolitionism had not entirely disappeared but it was certainly embattled. In the South there were now much larger numbers of free blacks than there had ever been in the pre-revolutionary epoch, but freedmen and women were subjected to draconian invigilation and in several cases slaveholders or their heirs challenged previous manumissions and legalised re-enslavement. The vigour of the slave economy and the racial panic induced by reports from St Domingue led southern Methodists and the Baptists to retreat from their earlier disapproval of slaveholding. The *cri de coeur* of a southern Methodist bishop in 1798 still expresses the defeated abolitionist impulse of some southern professionals, artisans and farmers:

> O! to be dependent on slaveholders is in part to be a slave, and I was free born. I am brought to conclude that slavery will exist in Virginia perhaps for ages; there is not a sufficient sense of religion nor of liberty to destroy it; Methodists, Baptists, Presbyterians, in the highest flights of rapturous piety, still maintain and defend it. I judge in after ages it will be so that poor men and free men will not live among slaveholders, but will go to new lands; they only who are concerned in, and dependent on them will continue to live in Old Virginia.[14]

By this time even attempts to encourage individual manumission and to educate the manumitted as useful and responsible citizens attracted the odium of slaveholders.

So far as North America's planter statesmen were concerned the St Domingue Revolution was replete with lessons for them and for all citizens of the Republic. Even those who hoped for the eventual disappearance of slavery, they argued, must wish to avoid the chaos and bloodshed that had been seen in St Domingue. It showed the necessity for taking new precautions to safeguard the good order of the slave states. As often happens 'the revolution revolutionised the counter-revolution'. Not only should the slave states be protected from outside interference, but they should also prevent slave majorities building up via an unchecked slave trade, as was happening in Georgia prior to the 1798 ban, and they should make sure that the free coloured population was as small and as tightly controlled as possible.

The aim of sealing off the United States from contagious notions of servile liberation became an obsession of the North American slaveholder. The 'Gabriel conspiracy' uncovered in the vicinity of Richmond in 1800 received considerable publicity and did reveal a potential for black revolt. The conspirators formed an ambitious plan for seizing the capital of Virginia and had supposedly been encouraged by the example of St Domingue. The prime movers of the conspiracy were slave artisans and watermen, who had involved a few hundred in their seditious meetings and plans. Their message was conveyed in the ritualised catechisms of a secret society: 'Are you a true man?' 'I am a true hearted man.' 'Can you keep a *proper* and *important* secret?' 'Yes.' 'The Negroes are about to rise and fight the white people for their freedom.' One said that the plan was to kill all whites except Frenchmen, Methodists and Quakers.[15] The conspirators believed that they could obtain French help once they had started the insurrection and counted on spontaneous support from the country blacks, though they had no contacts with the former and few with the latter. Preparations for a rising had been talked about for some four months when the authorities learned of the conspiracy and made large numbers of arrests, soon executing about twenty of the leading suspects. Gabriel Prosser himself escaped from Richmond aboard a ship captained by a white anti-slavery Methodist, but was denounced by another slave when the ship was boarded. A visitor to Richmond noted: 'Military service is performed night and day, Richmond resembles a town besieged . . . the negroes . . . will not venture to communicate with one another for fear of punishment.'[16]

Monroe, the Governor of Virginia, reported the exceptional measures taken to expose and suppress the conspiracy. At the behest of the state legislature he asked Jefferson to consider ways in which all free blacks and rebellious slaves might be deported to a colony outside the United States, arguing that this would be the humane alternative to further executions. Although there was no evidence of involvement by free blacks it was widely felt by the whites that their presence had encouraged the conspiracy. A law of 1793 had required all free blacks to place themselves on a register; a supplementary law of 1801 stipulated that they could only change their place of residence with the permission of the county authorities. Legally any black was to be assumed a slave unless he or she could prove otherwise; thus any black or coloured person not carrying proof of their free status could be detained until such proof was forthcoming.[17]

There was also concern to exclude slaves from sensitive or strategic occupations. The frame of mind of Jefferson's Cabinet is conveyed by a letter sent by the Postmaster General in 1802 to a Senator from Georgia, a member of a committee investigating the work of his department. It is worth quoting also since it still manages to convey a shamefaced awareness of revolutionary ideals, albeit in the form of a belief in their subversive potential:

Sir, An objection exists against employing negroes, or people of colour, in transporting the public mails, of a nature too delicate to engraft into a report that might become public, yet too important to be omitted or passed over without full consideration. I therefore take the liberty of making the committee, through you, a private representation on the subject. After the scenes which St Domingo has exhibited to the world, we cannot be too cautious in attempting to prevent similar evils in the four southern states, where there are, particularly in the settled eastern part of them, so great a proportion of blacks as to hazard the tranquility and happiness of free citizens. Indeed in Virginia and South Carolina (as I have been informed) – plans and conspiracies have already been concerted by them more than once to rise up and subjugate their masters. Everything which tends to increase their knowledge of natural rights, of men and things, or that affords them an opportunity of associating, acquiring and communicating sentiments, and of establishing a chain and line of intelligence, must increase your hazard, because it increases their means of effecting their object. The most active and intelligent are employed as post riders. These are the most ready to learn and the most able to execute. By travelling from day to day, and hourly mixing with people, they must, they will acquire information. They will learn that a man's rights do not depend on his colour. They will, in time, become teachers to their brethren. They become acquainted with each other on the line. Whenever the body, or a portion of them, wish to act, they are an organised corps, circulating our intelligence openly, their own privately. Their travelling creates no suspicion, excites no alarm. One able man among them, perceiving the value of this machine, might lay a plan which would be communicated by your post riders from town to town, and produce a general and united opinion against you. It is easier to prevent this evil than to cure it. The hazard may be small, and the prospect remote, but it does not follow that at some day the event would not be certain. With respect and esteem, Gideon Granger (Postmaster General).[18]

In 1803 further alarm was caused by the arrival of free blacks and mulattos from Guadeloupe, escaping from the reimposition of slavery there. Responding to a petition from North Carolina, Congress passed an act barring the entry of free blacks from other American territories. In 1806 the state of Virginia closed its borders to slave imports even from other states of the Union. And in the same year it repealed the major provisions of the Manumission Law of 1782. Henceforth slave manumission would be more difficult and those manumitted would not be allowed to remain in the state for more than one year; the latter provision was calculated to make manumission less attractive to master and slave alike and made it most unlikely that manumitted slaves would be given land. The free black population of Virginia had grown from 3,000 in 1780 to 30,000 in 1806; thereafter it was to stagnate as a proportion of the total population. The slave population of Virginia had grown over the same period from 250,000 to 400,000 and soon it was well established as a supplier of slaves to the South and west. The

Virginian legislation of 1806 also made it an offence for free blacks to own a firearm; previous official toleration for schools for free black children was also withdrawn. The years 1800–1806 witnessed a similar wave of repressive legislation against free blacks in other North American states. The 'black codes' of the slave states were uniformly and systematically discriminatory; many of the northern states followed suit in the first two decades of the century.[19]

While North American slaveholders were keen to take every necessary domestic precaution the principal Virginian leaders did not allow a fear of black revolutionaries to dictate foreign policy. Jefferson, in particular, saw the Haitian Revolution as an opportunity to further specifically American interests at the expense of all the powers of the Old World.

Shortly after the foundation of Haiti Dessalines ordered a massacre of some of the remaining French. When it was reported to him that one of his colleagues thought that this would jeopardise good commercial relations with the other white powers Dessalines observed: 'Such a person does not know the whites. Hang a white man below one of the pans in the scales of the customs house, and put a sack of coffee in the other pan; the other whites will buy the coffee without paying attention to the body of their fellow white.'[20] Dessalines's own bloodthirsty conduct did not strengthen Haiti, but his observation was acute: it drew attention to a disassociated, instrumentalist sensibility that was now gaining ground in the western world. The calculations of imperial statesmen added cynicism to the merchant's heedless rapacity. Pitt's invasion of St Domingue, Napoleon's attempt to restore slavery there, are spectacular instances of failed *realpolitik*. The conduct of President Jefferson towards the Revolution in Haiti was no less cynical but it was to yield a resounding and historic success, for himself and for the slaveholders of the United States. It enabled him to double the size of the United States and greatly to extend the area open to the further expansion of North American slavery.

Following his election to the Presidency Jefferson still privately assured abolitionists that he would act against slavery with 'promptitude and zeal' should 'an occasion ever occur in which I can interpose with decisive effect.'[21] As it happened the situation in which Jefferson did interpose with 'decisive effect' brought no comfort to the abolitionists. In his campaign against Adams and Jay the Virginian had attacked them for their capitulation to the British. He did not want to see the United States swamped by British loans and cheap British manufactures. He also believed that British statesman would block the young Republic's natural path of continental expansion and that the

Federalist leaders of the north-east were complicit with the British. North-eastern Federalists had little enthusiasm for acquiring territory in the south-west or for securing the Mississippi's outlet to the Gulf since such developments could only detract from the trade of the eastern ports. Jefferson's strategic opposition to the pro-British policy of Adams and Jay had been animated by the belief that the United States had a vital interest in securing the south-west – to deny it to any hostile power, to provide an outlet for western cultivators and to open an area of settlement for the buoyant white population of the east. His endorsement for this prospect had helped to strengthen the cross-sectional democratic republican alliance. Jefferson's foreign policy stance of hostility to Britain and friendly neutrality to France could be represented as a natural extension of Republican politics at home; it had the further advantage that France was more likely than Britain to fall in with plans for US continental aggrandisement.

Given that he was himself a slaveholder Jefferson's pro-French policy, which he maintained throughout the later 1790s, argues strong nerves. Many southern slaveholders regarded the policy and conduct of the British and French as being almost equally dangerous and demagogic so far as slavery was concerned. The abolitionist oratory of the House of Commons impressed American slaveholders not at all; but of course the rise of Toussaint and black power were even worse. The British deal with Toussaint had been seconded by the Adams administration. One of President Adams's last acts was to sponsor a bill which facilitated trade between the United States and St Domingue, exempting the latter from the commercial sanctions which had been invoked against France. Jeffersonian Republicans lambasted this as a pact with cannibal chiefs. Adams and the Federalists, with their links to mercantile interests, were more scandalised by the activities of Hugues and the corsairs than by the regime of Toussaint; indeed growing acceptance of Toussaint as a respectable leader and valued business partner may have helped to enhance the chances of emancipation in New York in 1799. Southern planter politicians, by contrast, had little inclination to become reconciled to Toussaint but were less bothered by Hugues and the corsairs. While they granted that French privateering was a menace Democratic Republicans argued that the 1794 treaty with Britain had been entered into under duress, since Britain's Royal Navy had seized over 300 US ships in 1793–4. Democratic Republicans saw in the whole course of British policy a refusal fully to accept US independence and sovereignty.

The pro-French stance of Jeffersonian Republicanism answered to strategic options as much as ideological sympathies. In fact Jefferson himself had no time for Jacobinism and little trust in either the

Directory or Bonaparte. Jefferson's eyes were on the Floridas and Louisiana, the vast swathe of territory stretching from the Gulf to Canada and bottling up the Republic in the West and the South, just as Canada did in the north. The Democratic Republican ideal of a farmer's and planter's republic could best be realised if Louisiana and the Floridas could be acquired. Britain would certainly not favour such a development, while the French might be induced to. From 1795 it was clear that France could influence the vulnerable regime in Madrid, from which it had already acquired Santo Domingo. In 1800 at the Treaty of San Ildefonso, as noted in the last chapter, France re-acquired its old colony of Louisiana, though this provision was for a time kept secret. It is unclear how much Jefferson knew of this when he became President in March 1801. But he did know that France had leverage in Madrid and that Bonaparte would be willing to pay a price for re-establishing friendly relations with the United States. Jefferson was prepared to endorse French designs in the Caribbean if this might promote US acquisitions on the mainland.[22]

Bonaparte and Talleyrand no doubt believed that Jefferson welcomed their expedition against Toussaint in the hope that it would, as they had promised, extirpate 'black government'. Jefferson would have applauded such an outcome, but it seems he did not rate French chances very highly. The Virginian did not allow racial animosities to blind him to the probable effectiveness of black resistance. He had, after all, himself led a war of resistance to a European attempt at recolonising American territory. Whatever the outcome he saw that an expedition to recapture St Domingue would make Bonaparte anxious for American friendship and would very probably weaken the French ability to sustain imperial ambitions elsewhere in the New World. Jefferson spoke favourably of the prospects of such an expedition to the French *chargé d'affaires* in Washington. But when Jefferson learned that a French fleet was about to sail to Louisiana to possess that territory for France he abruptly changed tack. Instead of supplying Leclerc's forces, as had been promised, US merchants continued to do business with the black rebels. Even the capture of Toussaint failed to convince Jefferson that Napoleon's plans for St Domingue were succeeding: 'Some other black leader will arise and a war of extermination [of the whites] will ensue for no second capitulation will ever be trusted by the blacks.'[23]

From the outset Jefferson had instructed US envoys to sound out the French government on its willingness to allow the United States to acquire the Floridas and Louisiana. The losses suffered by Leclerc, and the prospect of renewed war with Britain, made Napoleon willing to respond at last to these overtures. The First Consul clearly understood that this was the surest way to regain alliance with Jefferson's United

States. Barbé Marbois, now Finance Minister, was instructed to draw up a treaty for the sale of Louisiana. One clause of the sale implied that the United States might be able to claim western Florida as well as Louisiana. When Talleyrand was pressed by the US delegation to accept this construction he replied that the United States had made a 'noble bargain and I suppose you will make the most of it'.[24] Louisiana was to be sold for $15 million (£3 million) not a negligible sum but, as Napoleon well understood, utterly incommensurate with the true value of the vast territory in question.

Louisiana was purchased two weeks before the resumption of war between Britain and France in 1803. Jefferson, the Republican scourge of the monarchical powers of the Presidency, used his executive authority to make the bargain, which was then referred to Congress for ratification. Though Louisiana was little developed there were some 12,000 slaves out of a total population of 60,000; the slaves were mainly concentrated in Lower Louisiana in the vicinity of New Orleans. The acquisition of Louisiana was a tremendous coup for Jefferson and did much to ensure his re-election in 1804. Jefferson did not intervene publicly in the disputes surrounding the organisation of the new territory, though on this as on other matters his influence behind the scenes was considerable whenever he chose to exercise it. It was widely accepted that the northern reaches of the purchase, adjacent to the north-west territory, should be reserved for Indians and free settlers. The southern Republicans, focusing on the prospects for slavery expansion in the south-west, did not seek to dispute this. However many southerners were determined not only that slavery should continue to be legal in Lower Louisiana, or the Territory of Louisiana as it was now called, but that it should also be legal to introduce slaves there from other parts of the United States. If this was not permitted then North American slaveholders would have been unable to exploit the Territory's potential for sugar and cotton cultivation. However, the Senate, by a large majority, voted to exclude all new slaves from Louisiana. If Jefferson had been waiting for an opportunity to weaken slavery then he could have given Presidential backing to this veto. Instead he permitted lobbying and horse trading to overturn the Senate majority and permit Louisiana to draw slaves from other states, though not to import them from abroad. This resolution had Jefferson's consent because it gave a natural outlet to southern settlers. He still shrank from avowing himself a partisan of the consolidation and extension of slavery. Rather he persuaded himself that opening the western territories to slavery would weaken the institution by spreading the slaves more thinly over the available territory. It must have been hard for Jefferson to convince himself that slavery would not flourish in a land where there was already a sugar industry and where there were prospects for cotton cultivation. Jefferson displayed a keen interest in the progress of Eli Witney's gin for processing inland cotton and should not have been much surprised at the subsequent westwards march of the cotton planters.

The Louisiana purchase confirmed that the United States was an empire as well as a republic and it confirmed that slaveholders would have their own reserved space within that empire. Because he was President, because of his historic role and because he was a Virginian Jefferson was the only man who could have prevented this development; though certainly this would have made his re-election more difficult. Instead the slave population of Louisiana tripled to 35,000 by 1810 and reached 69,000 by 1820.

With Louisiana incorporated in the North American Republic the next obvious potential acquisition was Spanish Florida and here too Napoleon's good offices could be decisive. In his second Presidency Jefferson sought to add the Floridas to Louisiana, by means of further concessions to France. In 1805 the President asked Congress for a ban on trade with Haiti; while some slaveholders thought this necessary to defend their own interests the French had asked for the move. Even after the French withdrawal from St Domingue in 1804 France for a while retained control of the eastern half of the island, Santo Domingo. Talleyrand urged the North Americans to support French efforts to isolate the black Republic. In July 1805 he urged his envoy in Washington to appeal for US support: 'The existence of a negro people in arms, occupying a country which it has soiled by the most criminal acts, is a horrible spectacle for all white nations.'[25] Jefferson's recommendation to Congress to suspend trade with Haiti was ostensibly aimed at isolating the contagion of black insubordination; it was also designed to regain the goodwill of Napoleon in the hope of acquiring Florida. Many Congressmen will have supported this action because they feared any contact with Haiti; it passed by a large majority but was never rigorously enforced, since New England merchants were loath to lose business.

In the years 1803–8 developments in the north-western territory of Indiana subjected the pact between the slave and non-slave states to a significant test. Some wealthy southern emigrants to the Territory wished to bring slaves with them. As a way to get round the ban on introducing slaves they confected 'indenture' agreements with their bondsmen, which would subject them to perpetual labour and permit their masters to return them to a state where slavery was fully legal. Governor Harrison, a man of southern extraction, connived at these arrangements and even urged the assembly to legalise slavery. But pioneers and settlers rallied against the proposal and in 1808 voted down the Governor. During this controversy leading southern Republicans made it clear that they did not favour any attempt to undo the north-west Ordinance; with the fertile lands of the south-west beckoning to slaveholders this was unnecessary as well as provocative.[26]

Jefferson's contribution to a stronger and more expansive North American slave system in no way reduced his commitment to the ending of slave imports. Indeed this was manifestly more urgent than ever. In December 1806 he urged Congress to end the import of slaves as soon as this was constitutionally proper. But the abolition he sponsored was studiously disassociated from emancipationist or pro-black sentiment. Indeed the abolition of the US slave trade was to be a remarkably downbeat affair, no doubt because it was conceived of as a measure for strengthening the new nation and its slaveholding social formation. South Carolina had shocked every other state and embarrassed its own representatives by re-opening the slave trade in 1804. Tens of thousands of slaves were rushed in to beat the ban confidently expected for 1808. The decision of South Carolina created a climate in which Congress was eager to prevent further imports as soon as possible.

The first bill on the topic was introduced in December 1805 and was postponed for one year on the grounds that it was premature. Jefferson's message of December 1806 was followed by the preparation and passage of a bill which he was able to sign into law in the first days of March 1807, to come into effect on January 1st 1808. The act laid down that any person found importing slaves would be liable to a fine of $20,000 and that his ship and cargo would be forfeit, the latter to be sold off by the state where the offender was apprehended. In the Committee of the Whole the bill received 113 votes with only 5 against; most of those voting against wanted stiffer penalties, and opposed sale of the confiscated slaves.[27] However, passage of the bill was not treated as a famous anti-slavery victory. Jefferson's biographer notes that the nation's four leading papers greeted the first day of the slave trade ban with a 'discreet silence'.[28] While other abolitionist acts prompted the most extravagant self-congratulation this was truly the Quiet Abolition. Those guiding the destinies of the imperial Republic sincerely wished to avoid the dishonour, the violence, the complications and instability of continuing participation in the Atlantic slave traffic. Jefferson had no wish to swell the size of the black population; he was well aware that it doubled every twenty five years without slave imports. Like most North American slaveholders Jefferson believed that native-born slaves were more amenable and reliable than those from other parts. But to have attributed anti-slavery significance to the suppression of the slave trade, or to have made any great fuss about it, would only have embarrassed southern politicians and slaveholders.

It is possible, or even probable, that the United States would have ended the slave trade, acquired Louisiana and fortified slaveholding even if there had been no revolution in St Domingue. But certainly the latter event supplied propitious circumstances for the achievement of these aims and a reminder of the inherent strength of the New World in its contests with the Old. In shaking Louisiana loose from the European empires Jefferson had boldly finessed the leaders of the Old World. But he knew that this vital acquisition still had to be secured. Naturally the British refused to recognise the bargain that had been made with Napoleon while the Spanish government, even before Napoleon's invasion in 1808, was disposed to challenge the US interpretation of the treaties involved. Jefferson's reversion to a consistently pro-French stance in his second term (1805–9) was part of a larger Americanist policy that should not be reduced to the twin concerns of securing Louisiana and gaining the Floridas, important as these were.

The example of the Haitian independence struggle was not entirely lost on the slaveholders of North and South America, whatever their fears and prejudices. It had been a signal demonstration of the vulnerability of the European powers in the New World. If the miserable slaves of St Domingue could repulse the French as well as the British, why should any part of America allow itself to remain the victim of European domination?

Jefferson's policy in his second Presidency was at least as much anti-British as pro-French. He was outraged at Britain's arrogant naval policy and alarmed at the implications of its maritime predominance. British Orders in Council in 1805–6 claimed the right to prevent neutral shipping from trading freely with Napoleonic Europe. British war ships would not only detain and search US ships but also seize sailors from them who they claimed to be British deserters; 3,800 US sailors were kidnapped in this way arousing memories of the depredations of the press-gangs in the 1760s and 1770s. Jefferson was loath to embark on war with Britain because he knew that the Republic's defences were not in good shape and because he distrusted the political consequences of creating a stronger army and navy. He persuaded Congress to adopt as an alternative a complete embargo on foreign trade in December 1807. Though this stimulated manufacturing in both north and south it caused so much commercial dislocation and political disaffection that it was suspended within fourteen months. Jefferson's successor Madison eventually declared war on Britain in June 1812.

Britain had furnished US opinion with ample provocation, yet many in New England and the Middle Atlantic states now opposed war believing that it would only exacerbate their commercial and maritime problems. Madison had been forced to act if he was to retain the confidence and support of Republican opinion in the South and West; southerners and westerners saw the British as barring the road to expansion in the Floridas, in Canada and on the western frontier, where British intrigues were encouraging the resistance of the Indian nations. Even before war was declared free-lance forces had occupied portions of the Floridas.

In 1813 and 1814 the British targeted the southern states for a series of coastal raids. The British commanders, Admirals Cochrane and Cockburn, seized the opportunity to offer freedom to all slaves who would join them; about three hundred did so and according to a British report they conducted themselves very well and 'were uniformly volunteers for the Station where they might expect to meet their former masters'.[29] In August of 1814 a British raiding party led by Cockburn, and including some of these black recruits, seized Washington and burned the White House and other public buildings. The President and his wife took refuge in the Virginia woods. While British incendiarism was widely denounced by North American opinion, so was the nervelessness of the American commanders and administration. The United States now had a population of 7 million, and could supposedly field over half a million armed men, yet was apparently unable to defend its capital from capture by enemy forces operating thousands of miles from their home base. The British recourse to military slave emancipation provoked unease as well as outrage.

The war had caused commercial losses and much disaffection in the north whose representatives had voted against it. It was learned after the outbreak of hostilities that Britain's 'Orders in Council' had in any case been repealed, making it seem as if Madison had been manipulated by Napoleon's diplomacy and carried away by young Republican 'war hawks' bent on Indian-fighting and land grabbing. In New York Republicans, led by De Witt Clinton, had joined with the Federalists in 1812 to oppose the war; in December of that year Federalists had backed the renegade Republican against Madison in the Presidential election, but the latter had won by mobilising support in the south and west. By 1814 the sorry succession of British incursions and US reverses emboldened the New England Federalists to meet to discuss withdrawal from the war and revision of the constitution. At the Hartford Convention in December 1814 the Federalists drew back from open treason, but they did call for abandonment of the 'Federal ratio', which inflated the national representation of the slave states and without which Madison might not have defeated De Witt Clinton in the 1812 election. Since the south would never accept abrogation of the 'Federal ratio' this call hinted at secession. However, the resolutions of the Hartford Convention were soon to be discredited by the military course of the war, by a burgeoning and wounded sense of nationhood, and by the rapid conclusion of a peace treaty.[30]

The British forces had aimed a blow at New Orleans and offered support to the insurgent blacks and Seminole Indians of Florida. Some believed that Britain would insist on retaining those portions of Louisiana its forces had captured at the time peace was made. However, the British thrust in the south was convincingly and comprehensively defeated by General Andrew Jackson at the battle of New Orleans in January 1815. As it happened peace terms had already been agreed in Europe in December 1814 by a delegation which included a leading Federalist. It did not involve cession of Louisiana by the United States. Nevertheless this war and Jackson's famous victory resoundly confirmed both the independence and sovereignty of the United States and its possession of Louisiana.

The victory at New Orleans redeemed the dishonour of the sacking of Washington and gave a needed boost to US self-esteem. National unity had been saved and a continental destiny beckoned. The composition of the 'Star-Spangled Banner' after the British bombardment of Baltimore in September 1814, though only much later adopted as a national anthem, signalled the birth of a new national consciousness:

> And where is the band who so vauntingly swore,
> That the havoc of war and the battle's confusion
> A home and a country should leave us no more?
> Their blood has washed out their foul footsteps' pollution
> No refuge could save the hireling and slave
> From the terror of flight or the gloom of the grave
> And the star-spangled banner in triumph doth wave
> O'er the land of the free and the home of the brave.
> O thus be it ever when free men shall stand
> Between their loved home and the war's desolation.
> Blest with vict'ry and peace may the heav'n rescued land
> Praise the power that hath made and preserv'd us a nation.

Republican leadership had been vindicated and those Federalists who had attended the Hartford Convention now speedily withdrew from the positions they had adopted there. Federalism never recovered from its flirtation with secession. The whole course of the conflict with Britain strengthened the grip of the Virginian leaders and the character of the United States as an expansionist and slaveholding power. Since at least 1806 abolitionism had become feeble and subordinate, incapable of raising issues in public life; the Abolitionist National Convention decided to cease meeting annually in that year. But the fact that anti-slavery had little or no national presence did not cancel the original compact according to which there would be major areas of the United States free of slavery. The last year of the war with Britain produced a further crumb of anti-slavery in the North-east. The New York Emancipation Law had still left thousands of adult slaves in the state. In 1813 the Clintonian People's Party had won state elections with the help of black votes; in the following year they urged in the state legislature that slaves should be freed of all remaining obligations to their masters. The necessary legislation did not reach the statute book until 1817 when it was enacted that all slaves born before July 4th 1799 would be declared free as of July 4th 1827. By the latter date no slaves would be left in New York.[31]

The further career of the United States as a slaveholding power, and the tensions this engendered, form the subject of a subsequent work. But the War of 1812, or the Second War of American Independence as it is sometimes called, has a further significance for the struggle against the colonial form of slavery with which the present volume is concerned. North American merchants had always practised contra-band with the Spanish and Portuguese territories. Britain's alliance with the legitimate imperial authorities of Spain and Portugal, following Napoleon's invasion of the Peninsula in 1808, meant the United States was more or less openly at war with all European empires in the Americas. Because of the weakness of its regular armed forces the United States encouraged its own variant of the *guerre de la corse* in the years 1812–15 and sponsored the rise of irregular French and Spanish–American privateers throughout the Caribbean. Already in 1808 US authorities were willing to recognise letters of marque issued by the remaining French authorities in the Caribbean; they were also willing to accord belligerent rights to the colonies which rejected Spanish rule after 1810. About 1,500 British and Spanish ships were seized; in many cases they were brought as prizes to the United States where their cargoes would be sold. Whatever the motives for which it was adopted, this use of the privateers against Britain and Spain gave an impetus to the Republican cause in South America. In an indirect way it even weakened colonial slavery. Many of the privateer crews were black or mulatto and not a few of them had sailed with the French revolutionary corsairs of the 1790s. In 1810 General André Rigaud returned from France to Haiti, possibly with Napoleon's blessing; he established the short-lived *Republique du Sud* around Les Cayes, declared a desire for normal relations with the United States and gave succour to the privateers. A characteristic figure of the time was Renato

Beluche, a resident of Louisiana of Spanish and Italian extraction who operated as a privateer with a largely black crew and a letter of marque from the French authorities in Guadeloupe in the years 1807–9. Subsequently he obtained a letter of marque from Cartagena (Colombia) following its rejection of allegiance to Spain in 1811; Bolivar's alliance with these privateers and long association with Beluche will be considered in chapter 9. In 1815 General Jackson commissioned Beluche as commander of the artillery forces defending New Orleans. Jackson also mobilised 200 coloured militia from Louisiana; this militia, reflecting French and Spanish traditions, had coloured officers. Once New Orleans was safe Jackson was to turn his attention to the Floridas, where the British had encouraged resistance to US incursions by a combined force of blacks, Indians and Spanish royalists.[32]

Before considering the character and course of revolution in other American lands, and their implications for slavery, it is necessary to return to the Old World to account for Britain's adoption of abolitionism in 1807 at a crucial juncture of its crusade against Napoleon, a variation on the theme of 'abolition and empire', and an option with its own large implications for the future of colonial slavery in the Americas.

Notes

1. Robinson, *Slavery in the Structure of American Politics*, p. 253.
2. Quoted in Lance Branning, *The Jeffersonian Persuasion*, Ithaca 1978, p. 225. For the Democratic Republican appeal to the dynamic forces of small-scale accumulation in US society see Joyce Appleby, *Capitalism and a New Social Order*, New York 1984.
3. Robinson, *Slavery in the Structure of American Politics*, pp. 254–64.
4. Cooper, *Liberty and Slavery*, pp. 97–8.
5. Thomas Jefferson, *Writings*, New York 1984, pp. 449–56.
6. The Federalist lampoon, dated 1793, is reproduced in Sean Wilentz, *Chants Democratic*, New York 1985, illustration no. 5 between pp. 216–17.
7. Zilversmit, *The First Emancipation*, pp. 176–82; McManus, *Black Bondage in the North*, pp. 171–8.
8. Zilversmit, *The First Emancipation*, pp. 192–9.
9. Robert McColley, *Slavery in Jeffersonian Virginia*, 2nd edn, Urbana 1978, pp. 163–8; Berlin, *Slaves without Masters*, pp. 396–7.
10. For British cotton imports see Seymour Drescher, *Econocide*, pp. 84–5. For the impact of the gin see W.W. Rostow, *How It All Began*, p. 160.
11. Miller, *The Wolf by the Ears*, p. 118.
12. Miller, *The Wolf by the Ears*, epigraph, p. ix.
13. McColley, *Slavery in Jeffersonian Virgina*, p. 184.
14. McColley, *Slavery in Jeffersonian Virginia*, p. 186.
15. Gerald W. Mullin, *Flight and Rebellion: Slave Resistance in Eighteenth Century Virginia*, London 1972, p. 146.
16. M. Mullin, ed., *American Negro Slavery*, Columbia, South Carolina 1976, p. 123.
17. John H. Russell, *The Free Negro in Virginia*, 2nd edn, New York 1979, pp. 98, 101.

18. Quoted by Alexander Cockburn, 'Ashes and Diamonds', *Anderson Valley Advertiser*, Boonville, California, May 13, 1987. The letter was discovered in the US National Archive by Stan Weir of the AFSCME.

19. Russell, *The Free Negro in Virginia*, pp. 96, 107, 121, 140–41, 167. Virginia and Maryland had many more free blacks than any of the other southern states. For a survey of the comprehensive tightening of discriminatory legislation against free blacks in the south, much of it enacted between 1793 and 1806, and the simultaneous retreat from abolitionism in this section, see Berlin, *Slaves without Masters*, pp. 79–107.

20. Quoted in Nicholls, *From Dessalines to Duvalier*, p. 37.

21. Miller, *The Wolf by the Ears*, p. 131. This was written in a letter declining sponsorship of an anti-slavery poem.

22. See Walter La Feber, 'Foreign Policies of a New Nation', in W.A. Williams, *From Colony to Empire*, New York 1972, pp. 9–38; John Mayfield, *The New Nation, 1800–45*, New York 1982, pp. 3–21; Tyson, *Toussaint L'Ouverture*, pp. 93–105.

23. Quoted in Miller, *The Wolf by the Ears*, p. 139. Jefferson's previous encouragement of the French *chargé d'affaires* is cited on p. 133.

24. Quoted in Dumas Malone, *Jefferson the President: First Term 1801–1805*, Boston 1970, p. 306. For the Louisiana purchase and its immediate consequences see pp. 311–63 of this work; also Henry Adams, *The History of the United States during the First Administration of Thomas Jefferson*, Boston 1931, vol. 2, pp. 377 *et seq*.

25. Nichols, *From Dessalines to Duvalier*, p. 36.

26. Henry Adams, *History of the United States of America during the Second Administration of Thomas Jefferson*, New York 1931, vol. 2, pp. 75–7; Eugene Berwanger, *The Frontier Against Slavery*, Urbana 1967, p.12. Berwanger notes that in the same year the territorial assembly also denied free blacks the vote or the right to testify and excluded them from the militia.

27. W.E.B. Dubois, *The Suppression of the Atlantic Slave Trade*, New York 1896, pp. 94–108.

28. Dumas Malone, *Jefferson the President: Second Term 1805–9*, Boston 1974, pp. 541–7.

29. Reginald Horsman, *The War of 1812*, London 1969, p. 78.

30. Robinson, *Slavery in the Structure of American Politics*, pp. 278–82, 404.

31. Zilversmit, *The First Emancipation*, p. 182; Roi Ottley and William J. Weatherby, eds, *The Negro in New York*, New York 1967, p. 62. The Democratic Republican Van Buren, a demagogic critic of the 'aristocratic' Federalists, privately branded the philosophy of the Clintonite 'People's Party' of New York state in 1817 as 'Jacobinism' (Donald C. Cole, *Martin Van Buren*, Princeton 1984, p. 52).

32. Jane Lucas de Grummond, *Renato Beluche: Smuggler, Privateer and Patriot 1780–1860*, Baton Rouge 1983, pp. 26–130.

VIII

British Slave Trade
Abolition: 1803–14

Oh me good friend Mr Wilberforce mek me free
God Almighty thank ye! God Almighty thank ye!
God Almighty mek me free!

Buckra in dis country no mek we free!
Wa negro fe do? Wa negro fe do?
Tek force wid force
Tek force wid force!

West Indian Song (1816)

What art thou, Freedom, O! Could slaves
Answer from their living graves
This demand, tyrants would flee
Like a dream's imagery;
Thou art not, as impostors say,
A shadow soon to pass away,
A superstition and a name
Echoing from the cave of fame.

To the rich art thou a check,
When his foot is on the neck,
Of his victim, thou dost make
That he treads upon a snake.

The Mask of Anarchy (1819), P.B. Shelley

The revival and progress of anti-slavery in Britain is impossible to understand if it is abstracted from the momentous international, imperial and domestic challenges confronting Britain's rulers in the first decade of the nineteenth century. After the revolutionary drama of emancipationism in the French Antilles, it is well to remember that anti-slavery themes and a critique of the Atlantic slave trade had emerged in the discourse of moral philosophy, jurisprudence, social reform and political economy in late eighteenth-century Britain because they corresponded so well to middle-class anxieties and aspirations. Anti-slavery promised to tame and reshape the rampant force of commercialism and industrialism, the arrogance of the ruling class and perhaps even the waywardness of the labouring classes. In the years 1788–93 British anti-slavery had also attracted a radical following which stressed the rights of free labour and the iniquities of a slave-trading mercantile and financial oligarchy. The ambivalence of abolitionism meant that it had momentarily established an alliance between the reform-minded middle classes, the radical democrats and a popular following. The anti-slavery critique could respond to the need to develop new norms of social reproduction and cohesion, and recommend itself to politically alert members of the ruling order. But despite the variety of ways in which the anti-slavery cause might appeal to different constituencies, it still remains to be explained how it recovered strength after 1803 and imposed itself on Britain's narrow governing oligarchy at a time when the latter confronted a multitude of seemingly more urgent issues. The abolitionist advance of 1788–92 had been stopped in its tracks by a change in the political conjuncture: the anti-Jacobin mobilisation at home and abroad, reinforced by the perceived necessities of imperial defence and competition. The second phase of abolitionist advance, covering the years 1803–14, saw a dismantling of these obstacles to abolitionism; in a deeply conservative political system abolition of the slave trade became not so much the most urgent, as the least controversial, reform that could be undertaken. In Britain as in France a seemingly peripheral issue raised by colonial slavery acted as a lightning conductor for struggles over peace and war, empire, national destiny, the formation of class blocs and the nature of the domestic political regime.

Abolition edged back onto the agenda of ruling-class politics in 1803–4 following the breakdown of the Peace of Amiens. It reflected alarm at the state of imperial security and concern with the wider purposes of the conflict with France. During the first bout of hostilities with France

(1793–1801) Britain's ramshackle oligarchy and 'illegitimate monarchy' had come perilously close to disaster in the mortal struggle with its rejuvenated historic foe. The overthrow of the French *ancien régime* had released prodigious furies upon the established order in both the Old World and the New. Britain's rulers, who had been battling French monarchy since time immemorial, suddenly discovered unsuspected virtues in it; the execution of Louis XVI had been regarded as an important *casus belli*. Revolutionary France inspired animus more as the agency of subversion than as a capitalist rival. Two counter-revolutionary coalitions sponsored and subsidised by Britain had crumbled before the revolutionary armies. Britain's problems in the Americas were no less serious. British forces had been forced to withdraw from St Domingue and had only regained and pacified Britain's own Windward Islands at a terrible cost and after arming thousands of blacks. The security of the Empire had been threatened at the centre as well as the periphery, with mutiny rife in the home fleets and a French-assisted rebellion in Ireland.

The emergency of 1797–8 and the fear of French invasion at least stilled the disaffection of the middle classes. The strength of the British economy, with its far-flung commercial Empire, and of British bourgeois society, with its protection of corporate and propertied interests, ensured basic loyalty to a still quite unreformed political system. But when the direct threat of revolution or invasion receded the bulk of the middle class lacked enthusiasm for the war. The outbreak of hostilities had occurred just as the Anglo–French trade treaty was proving highly advantageous to British manufacturers and merchants; paying for the war meant higher taxation, culminating in the fateful innovation of income tax. Charles James Fox and the oppositional Whigs urged, in and out of season, that no more should be sacrificed to defend the continental monarchies and that peace should be sought with the Paris government. Even Wilberforce, despite his abhorrence of Jacobinism, favoured peace with France. British war-weariness eventually led to the conclusion of the Treaty of Amiens in 1802 which conceded much to the French, setting a strict limit on British trade and political influence. The British were to evacuate all wartime conquests, save Trinidad. This in itself might have been acceptable had it not immediately become clear that Bonaparte would use military leverage to wage a continuing commercial war against British merchants in Europe and the Americas. There was to be no renewal of the Anglo–French trade treaty; French influence was applied to exclude Britain from continental markets. The American colonies of Spain and Portugal were to become privileged and protected French trading zones; together with the resumption of friendly relations with the United States and the reconquest of

'Chasing a maroon', by William Blake, published in
J.G. Stedman's 'Narrative'

St Domingue France seemed set to hegemonise the New World almost as completely as it already did the continent of Europe.

The advantageous terms extracted by Bonaparte at Amiens, and his evident intention to exploit them to the hilt, educated British public opinion in the logic of imperialist rivalry. The threat of French invasion in 1804–5 brought about a fervent, even unprecedented, climate of national unity. Against this backdrop there was a new wave of patriotic enthusiasm, unclouded by the divisions of the 1790s. In its train came a revival of hopes for political and social reform. The decade 1793–1802 had been marked by both political repression and a feverish prosperity. Military mobilisation and anti-Jacobin panic had increased the weight of the state while the erratic advance of industrialisation and rural enclosure revealed the woeful inadequacy of the Poor Law system. Britain was the richest country in the world yet bad harvests, as in 1800–1, meant widespread distress, even starvation, for the labouring classes; a commercial downturn, such as that of 1805–6, brought desperate petitions from the manufacturing districts. Wartime conditions meant fat rent rolls and farming profits as food prices climbed, but spelled hardship for the mass of the underlying population. Social discontent threw into relief the arbitrary and unrepresentative pattern of oligarchic power. Once the mortal peril was past the question of the purpose and shape of government gradually re-entered the area of permitted discussion.

Pitt and Wilberforce had argued in the 1790s that political reform must await a return to calmer times. But even they had acknowledged the need for an 'economical reform' in which the numbers of government-appointed sinecures would be drastically pruned: no less than a thousand such posts were abolished in the years 1782–1800, often by the device of allowing the sinecure to expire on the death of its holder. (This relatively painless approach to divesting office-holders of property bears comparison with Pennsylvania's slave emancipation, freeing those yet to be born.) But while administrative abuses could be quietly removed, and sinecures wound up, the central apparatus of government and representation had remained stubbornly resistant to even the most limited reform. Indeed the abolition of sinecures, by reducing government patronage, reduced the government's ability to press through other innovations. The interests organised by the new Tory coalition and the entrenched institutions of 'illegitimate monarchy' were animated by lingering fear of Jacobinism and a lively determination not to yield up the privileges of political hegemony. One major political change had been undertaken – the Union with Ireland – but with the eminently conservative aim of consolidating British rule. Pitt had hoped both to end the vexation of a separate Irish Parliament and to admit a layer of Catholic proprietors to the exercise of some political rights so long as they swore to uphold the British monarchy and constitution, including the privileges of the established Church. However this aspect of Pitt's scheme was unacceptable to the King, to powerful vested interests and to the Protestant reflexes of many English patriots. Pitt was forced into opposition in 1801. Lord Grenville, the veteran Foreign Secretary, was also driven into opposition where he became a fierce critic of the terms of the Peace of Amiens.

The Foxite Whigs, excluded from power since 1784, posed as champions of democratic sentiment, and had even flirted with republicanism, but remained rather vague on the detail of the reforms that would satisfy them. They were prepared to support the defence of national interests in 1803–5, though they still believed in the possibility of some future *modus vivendi* with Bonaparte if he should abandon his plans for aggression. The spectre of revolutionary republicanism had been exorcised by Bonaparte himself in the interests of rationalised and expansionary French capitalism and militarism. The French threat no longer inspired the same divisive hopes and fears within the middle-class public. The renewal of the struggle against France on new terms allowed old patriot themes to be revived. The repression of former Jacobins abated and it could be argued publicly that the threat from the new France could best be met by an overhaul of British institutions. In the Commons Windham, who had been Secretary for War in Pitt's government, appealed to English Jacobins to show themselves true lovers of liberty by rallying to the defence of their country. Evidence of a new popular mood was supplied when an advocate of parliamentary reform, Sir Francis Burdett, won Middlesex in 1804 – a victory celebrated by a London crowd estimated at half a million strong, with cries of 'Burdett and No Bastille' and an assortment of songs redolent of patriot radicalism, the strains of 'Rule Britannia' mingling with those of '*Ca Ira*'. In 1807 Burdett scored another popular electoral victory at Westminster, fighting the seat with Lord Cochrane, a naval hero. Burdett, a radical baronet, and Cochrane, a patriot naval commander, were, of course, far more reassuring standard bearers of popular hopes than the plebeian democrats of the 1790s.[1]

The reawakening of the anti-slave trade movement in Britain was favoured by radical revival and by the shake-up within the ruling oligarchy. Abolitionism's return was signalled by two interlinked events: reactivation of the Abolition Committee in April 1804 and three convincing votes for a general Abolition Bill in the House of Commons in May and June of the same year. Thomas Clarkson again became active in the abolitionist cause and the committee was strengthened by the adhesion of men who widened its contacts and experience. Among the new members were James Stephen, Zachary Macaulay and Henry Brougham. They were to integrate the case for suppressing the slave trade within detailed conceptions of national and imperial strategy. Stephen was a rising barrister with a West Indian background and evangelical leanings who had married Wilberforce's sister. He had worked as a lawyer in the West Indies and retained links with many merchants and planters. His reputation as an expert on legal aspects of commercial and naval policy had led to an appointment with the Prize Appeals Court of the Privy Council. Zachary Macaulay had also worked in the West Indies and had links to the Colonial Office; he had just returned from a stint as Governor of Sierra Leone, the British-sponsored settlement for free blacks on the West African coast. Both Stephen and Macaulay were well placed to encourage official doubts about the wisdom of further extending colonial slavery in the Caribbean; they were also both members of the so-called Clapham Sect, a group of Anglican evangelicals. By recruiting Henry Brougham the committee was further extending its range, in this case outside the ranks of religious enthusiasts. He was at this time an up-and-coming lawyer, with Whig connections and an education in Scottish political economy. He had just published a comprehensive two-volume work on the colonial policy of the European powers and was a leading contributor to *The Edinburgh Review*; this latter journal, founded in 1802 and with a circulation rising to 7,000, rapidly established itself as the most authoritative voice of responsible reform.

The new Abolition Committee decided that its cause would not best be served by moving immediately to promote a new extra-parliamentary campaign of meetings and petitions. Though there had been some relaxation of the climate of repression a popular clamour for abolition would have risked reawakening the fears of conservative parliamentarians. But this did not mean that the Abolition Committee made no appeal to a wider public, since it could avail itself of such newspapers as the *Leeds Mercury*, newly-established to cater to the prosperous and growing middle class in the north and the Midlands.[2]

James Stephen and Henry Brougham were both accomplished pamphleteers. Most of their work was aimed at a select readership, which included the country's legislators and senior administrators. James Stephen had established his reputation as an expert on colonial affairs with the publication of a lengthy study of *The Crisis of the Sugar Colonies* (1802) in which he wrote that the Revolution in St Domingue showed the inherent fragility of the slave systems of the West Indies and predicted that Napoleon would be defeated by black insurgency. He argued that a black victory was in the interest of 'the British Empire as a whole' since it would prevent the reconstruction of a new and menacing French colonial system in the Americas. Victory for the rebels posed a danger of a different sort to the British islands; this could be met by reforms that would remove the motive for slave insurrection. Henry Brougham reached similar conclusions from a different starting point in his *Inquiry into the Colonial Policy of the European Powers* (1803). This work did not harp on anti-French themes, as Stephen was prone to do, nor did it express any sympathy with the black cause in St Domingue. It combined advocacy of Anglo–French co-operation, wherever this might be possible, with an emphasis on the need for an imperial reform that would end the slave trade and relax the system of colonial tariff preference. While deploring the slave trade Brougham happily appealed to derogatory stereotypes of Africans, arguing that it made no sense to fill up Britain's colonies with a mass of resentful savages. Brougham devoted a chapter to the slave trade which was reissued as a pamphlet by the Abolition Committee in 1804 and circulated to every Member of Parliament. The argument of the pamphlet is worth considering in some detail since it had a considerable impact on the Commons vote of 1804.

Brougham's critique of the slave trade, while tossing in both racist and humanitarian arguments for good measure, devoted most attention to marshalling the argument from 'sound policy'; Brougham was ambitious to be a politician not a 'Saint'. He urged that abolition would do no harm to British West Indian interests, if properly understood: 'The experience of the United States has distinctly proved that the rapid multiplication of the Blacks in a natural way, will inevitably be occasioned by prohibiting their importation.' Brougham looked forward to the time when 'the structure of West Indian society will more and more resemble that of the compact, firm, and respectable communities which compose the North American states'. Lest the security aspect touched on here be overlooked he added:

> When fire is raging to windward, is it the proper time for stirring up everything that is combustible in your warehouse, and throwing into them new loads of material still more prone to explosion? Surely, surely, these most obvious considerations only have to be hinted at, to demonstrate, that independent of any other consideration against the negro traffic, the present state of the French West Indies renders the idea of continuing its existence for another hour worse than infamy.[3]

The question of imperial security was a complex one but Brougham's arguments had a direct purchase on recent British experience. In

1795–6, with tiny forces and in a space of months, the French Republic had succeeded in overturning two British sugar islands, with a combined slave population of 50,000; the subsequent 'War of the Brigands' had cost forty or fifty thousand British casualties and had only been successfully concluded by raising eight black regiments; the British War Office made special purchases of Africans suitable to be enrolled in these regiments. As a short-term expedient this had worked well, but doubts as to its long-run viability were aroused when the Fourth West Indian Regiment, stationed on Dominica, mutinied in 1802; an official report argued that those involved in the mutiny were exclusively African.[4] The years 1795–1804 witnessed the publication of several accounts of war and revolt in the Caribbean, most of which stressed the dangerous mixture represented by spontaneous African rebelliousness and creole trouble-making; even Bryan Edwards, the planters' spokesman, did not deny that the French Revolution had had an extraordinary impact on the Caribbean, requiring a quite new attention to colonial security and defence. In Brougham's view the survival of a 'negro commonwealth' in the Caribbean meant that it would be folly to overlook the possibility of new insurrections. While Brougham's work did not have the authority of first-hand accounts of the West Indies, it did plausibly link the new awareness of the vulnerability of the slave colonies with the critique of the slave trade.[5]

Brougham also outlined an economic case against supposing that the slave trade was vital to the well-being of either metropolis or colonies. He calculated that the Africa trade accounted for no more than a twentieth part of British exports and that, because of the distances involved, returns were slow. He summarised his conclusions thus: 'the trade does not occupy any considerable part of the national capital – that the profits are of the description least beneficial to the country, and that the same capital, if excluded from this employment, would immediately and easily find a more advantageous vent.' He did not deny the past profitability of the trade, nor question the present value of West Indian commerce: 'the fruit of our iniquity has been a great and rich empire in America. Let us be satisfied with our gains, and being rich, let us try to become righteous – not indeed by giving up a single sugar cane of what we have acquired, but by continuing in our present state of overflowing opulence, and preventing the further importation of slaves.' Brougham did not claim that any purely economic advantage would accrue from abolition, merely that it would enhance security and cost little: 'Surely it is abundantly sufficient to have proved that the termination of by far the most criminal traffic which humanity has ever carried on, will be attended by no injury to interests already in existence, although it should be admitted that the prospects of a few individuals will be disappointed.'[6]

In the 1790s abolition had been associated with opposition to the war with France and had suffered in Parliament and elsewhere as a result. Following Napoleon's attempt to restore slavery abolitionism was to become quite compatible with patriot hostility to the French. Stephen published, anonymously, a three-part pamphlet, entitled *Buonaparte in the West Indies, or the history of Toussaint L'Ouverture, the African Hero*, appealing to radical sentiment and priced at only 3*d* each part: 'What! Are [Bonaparte] and his ruffians to stab and drown all the poor labourers of St Domingo because they chuse to work as men for wages, and not like horses under the driver's lash; and must Englishmen be kept in the dark about it?' 'It will be seen who are the true friends of the common people. . . . Those who hate, oppress and murder the labouring poor in one part of the world [cannot] really wish to make them free and happy in another.'[7] This work went through four printings in a year, suggesting that it did find the popular readership at which it aimed. In the 1790s Wilberforce had been militant in his domestic anti-Jacobinism but not in his recommendations for imperial and foreign policy. In their most considered publications Brougham and Stephen openly canvassed the best ways of capturing markets and advancing imperial interests. While Brougham clung for a while to the radical Whig belief that a global settlement and division could be reached with Napoleon, James Stephen was an unabashed and accomplished advocate of commercial and naval aggression.

The Abolition Committee's appeal for a strategic reappraisal of the slave trade, and Stephen's efforts to present anti-slavery as a patriot cause, helped abolitionism to regain the initiative but they failed to press home victory in 1804. The Commons votes were solid enough: the bill passed in three votes: 124 to 49, 100 against 42, and 99 against 33. Many of the new Irish members, representing the Protestant ascendancy, swung behind abolition, seeking thereby to advertise their high-mindedness and generosity; they were also, no doubt, gratified to learn that Wilberforce supported the regime of Anglican privilege in Ireland. Pitt, brought back as Prime Minister to direct the war effort, re-iterated his support for abolition; in one debate he spoke with a copy of Brougham's pamphlet in his hand. But he still refused to make the Abolition Bill a government measure. The bill was tabled by the House of Lords on the grounds that there was not sufficient time left in the session for it to be considered. When a new Abolition Bill was presented early in 1805 Pitt's personal endorsement did not prevent a defeat: the bill was voted down on its second Commons reading by 77 votes to 70.[8] The case of abolition at this time was overshadowed by the looming naval contest between Britain and the combined fleets of France and Spain. Moreover Pitt was now more dependent than ever on the 'King's Friends' and the imperial lobby. The Irish members switched their votes against abolition, having been persuaded that its victory would encourage reform initiatives elsewhere in the Empire. The abolitionists were keenly disappointed, the more so since Denmark was, in compliance with the decree of the previous decade, thought to be ending its slave trade, putting Britain's slave trading role into harsher prominence. Pitt consoled the abolitionists with the hope that the slave trade could be substantially reduced by non-legislative means.

Even prior to the setback of 1805 James Stephen and the Abolition Committee were at work on a new approach to their campaign against the slave trade, the aim of which was to split or neutralise the West India lobby and gain acceptance of abolitionist measures aimed exclusively at the supply of slaves by foreign traders or to newly acquired territories. Pitt encouraged this approach and promised it his support. The established British planting interest had good reason to prevent the supply of slaves to new territories which would be competing with its own products. Though there were not more than about thirty 'West Indian' MPs in the House of Commons, with a similar number of 'West Indian' peers, other members tended to defer to the judgement of West Indian proprietors when it came to adjudicating the abolition question. The slave-traders themselves had far fewer friends than the West Indian proprietors. Stephen was well aware that some planters and merchants had always seen merit in selective abolition. Between a half and two-thirds of the British slave trade of the 1790s and early 1800s represented an effort to build up plantations in foreign colonies or in newly acquired territories. British traders were far and away the most important suppliers of the entire Caribbean zone; the only competition they faced was from Cuban or North American traders, the latter usually flying the Spanish flag. When Martinique was handed back to France at the Peace of Amiens its plantations were in a flourishing state thanks to the efforts of the British traders. The retention of Trinidad at the Peace posed an even worse threat to the planters of the 'old colonies' since, as British territory, its products would have privileged entry to the British market. In 1802 George Canning introduced a motion in the Commons limiting the future supply of slaves to Trinidad. C.R. Ellis, an MP with substantial West Indian holdings, lent his support to this measure, allowing Canning to recommend it to the House in the following terms: 'It is not the slave trade *and*, but the slave trade *or*, the old West India interest that you must support – slave trade in all its naked charms without the cloak of the pretended West India interest to hide them.'[9] It gave

Canning much satisfaction to combine the argument from interest with the appeal to humanity and the potency of this mixture was duly noted. However, the tactical gain on Trinidad proved quite modest as some 15,000–30,000 slaves annually were being supplied to other, more dangerous, rivals such as Cuba and Dutch Guiana. The return of war soon led to new British conquests; Guiana, the most important, imported over 7,000 slaves annually in the years 1803–1805. Of course the older colonies could also replenish their slave crews and Jamaica opened up new territory, mainly for coffee cultivation. But as each year passed the position of the older colonies was being steadily eroded and the profits boom of the 1790s began to ebb. Within the British Parliament the old established West India interest was naturally better represented than that of the new speculators investing in the foreign slave trade or the development of Guiana.

In 1805 James Stephen published a major new study of the threat posed by foreign competition in wartime conditions, entitled *War in Disguise or the Fraud of the Neutral Flags*. Drawing on evidence he had acquired in the Prize Appeal Court, Stephen advocated a new wartime commercial strategy which barely hinted at any abolitionist motivation. He demonstrated that the West Indian colonies of the enemy powers – notably France and Spain – were supplying vast quantities of sugar, coffee and cotton to continental markets by the simple device of using neutral carriers – most of the latter being North American vessels sailing via New York or Philadelphia. Britain's re-export trade was undermined far more effectively by such competition than by Napoleon's decrees. Most of the 36,000 tons of sugar exported from the French and Spanish colonies, and of the 46,600 tons exported from Brazil, was shipped to Europe in 1805–6 under neutral flags, thus securing it from seizure by the British blockades. The British colonies exported just over 170,000 tons of sugar but were saddled with extra freight charges because of the need for protection against French privateers. British re-exports of sugar dropped from 93,000 tons in 1802 to 47,000 in 1804 and 1805. In his pamphlet Stephen singled out the growth of Cuban plantation output as the greatest danger:

> The gigantic infancy of agriculture in Cuba, far from being checked, is greatly aided in its portentous growth during the war, by the boundless liberty of trade, and the perfect security of carriage (in neutral ships). Even slaves from Africa are copiously imported there, and doubtless also into the French islands, under American colours ... so wide has been our complaisance to the depredation of our belligerent right, that even the slave trading smuggler has been able to take part of the spoil.

Stephen also argued that the interests of manufacturing exporters were harmed since the neutral traders brought European manufactures for sale in the Americas: 'They supplant even the manufacturers of Manchester, Birmingham and York; for the looms and forges of Germany are put into action by the colonial produce of our enemies.'[10] Stephen's conclusion was that neutral ships should be prevented from carrying on in wartime any trade with enemy colonies which had not been available to them in peacetime. The British Navy should revert to its tactics in the Seven Years War and institute a blockade that would apply to most neutral, as well as enemy, shipping. The export trade of the enemy colonies would be cut off and their demand for slave imports would cease.

Stephen's analysis and recommendations, so far as they went, were soundly based; beyond conjunctural considerations they also moved Britain closer to claiming a wider maritime hegemony. But they did neglect the danger of provoking a conflict with the United States. His advice proved highly influential and was incorporated in 'Orders in Council' issued in 1805, which he had a hand in drafting. Pitt agreed to include in the Orders a clause preventing any further slave imports to Guiana, on similar grounds to those which restricted the Trinidad import trade.[11] Thus, without the need for a parliamentary vote, the strategists of abolition had considerably reduced the scope of the slave trade and had committed Britain to an aggressive naval policy that deployed the full might of the British Navy in defence of the interests of the older British colonies. The neutral slave trade to foreign colonies such as Cuba had been virtually destroyed, but the British slave trade to foreign colonies remained and was to be the next target of abolitionist attack. There was, however, a danger in the 'line of least resistance' approach that Stephen, Wilberforce and other parliamentary abolitionists had adopted. The Orders in Council were temporary wartime measures with no permanent legislative effect; to the extent that they removed interested objections to the foreign slave trade they might simply reinforce the slave traffic that remained. Finally, the association of abolition with the restrictive and provocative features of the Orders could alienate those traders and manufacturers with interests in neutral trade. Britain was now importing large quantities of cotton from the United States, and exporting to it large quantities of manufactures. Indeed the 'abolitionist' clauses of the Orders in Council may have driven some American traders to become last-ditch supporters of the Africa trade.

Pitt had held together the bloc of forces which had pressed for war with France; some of the same forces had helped to frustrate a general abolition – men such as Henry Dundas, now the Earl of Melville, and Lord Hawkesbury, who had accepted the title Earl of Liverpool in recognition of his efforts to promote that city's trade. These men had tolerated pragmatic measures against the foreign slave trade, but they thought that a principled and general ban on the slave traffic was a needless hostage to fortune, since Britain's slave colonies, with their hugely important commerce, might prove unable to sustain themselves without fresh slave imports.

The last months of 1805 and the first months of 1806 witnessed a transformation in Britain's international situation and a reorientation of the ruling oligarchy. Events large and small conspired to make abolition acceptable to the British government, ranging from the impeachment of Melville following a Commons censure motion in 1805 to the death of Pitt in January 1806, from Britain's victory at Trafalgar in October 1805 to the defeat of its European allies at Austerlitz in December of the same year. The impeachment of Melville, on charges of condoning corruption at the Admiralty, was a minor event but certainly one favourable to a new approach to abolition and a broader conception of imperial policy. Wilberforce, who had never publicly attacked the man he saw as Pitt's evil genius, now gravely added his authority to those clamouring for his downfall. The removal of Melville from the Cabinet led to the appointment of Sir Charles Middleton, a veteran supporter of abolition, as First Lord of the Admiralty. The Earl of Liverpool had retired from political life; his son, the new Lord Hawkesbury, also defended the West India interest and served in Pitt's administration, but he did not yet wield his father's influence. These shifts permitted Pitt to include a bolder anti-slavery dimension in the Orders in Council, consecrating selective abolition as 'sound policy' and securing royal approval for measures which aroused the King's gravest suspicions.[12]

With Pitt's death abolitionism was to advance more openly and on a broader front. None of Pitt's younger followers had the stature to lead a new government so the King was obliged to call upon the veteran Lord Grenville to form an administration. Grenville refused to do so unless it included Fox, the leader of the Whig Opposition. As Pitt's Foreign Secretary through much of the 1790s he knew how volatile public opinion was in wartime and how dangerous it would be to allow Fox to remain in opposition once the immediate danger of invasion was past. There was no one left in the Commons who could match Fox's oratory. Trafalgar made a parliamentary consensus both more difficult and more necessary, if there was to be public support for continued struggle against France now that the immediate danger was past. In these circumstances the King consented to Grenville bringing Fox into the

Cabinet as Foreign Secretary and leader of the administration in the House of Commons. Fox was to be allowed to put out peace feelers to Napoleon, though Grenville anticipated that little would come of this. The formation of the Grenville–Fox coalition was smoothed by a diminution in the personal power of the monarch. The recurrent illnesses of the King had reached a point where he could no longer refuse to admit the Prince of Wales to a share in the exercise of the royal powers; Fox and his followers had always cultivated the 'reversionary interest' of the heir to the throne.

Both Grenville and Fox had long been declared supporters of abolition. They were to find that it was the most promising reform measure they could propose to Parliament with any hope of success. The Grenville–Fox government was formed at a time when popular expectations were still high, though the obstacles to fundamental change remained as formidable as ever. William Cobbett, the leading radical journalist, wrote in March, 1806, as follows: 'of one thing all reasonable men seem to be thoroughly convinced, namely that some great change is absolutely necessary; some great change; something new and something great; something capable of producing a powerful effect upon the minds of the people. . . . We are now arrived at that point where a mere hired army will no longer suffice.'[13] Cobbett was himself no friend of abolitionism and certainly had other 'great changes' in mind when he wrote this. Yet he was right about the need to motivate popular support for the war. As it turned out abolition of the slave trade was the only reform measure which was simultaneously widely popular, agreed between leading members of the government and within the realm of the 'art of the possible'. Fox was a partisan of parliamentary reform, but this was not an issue which enthused Grenville, controller of one of the most extensive networks of 'rotten boroughs'; and both men knew that while those favoured by the oligarchic system would instantly unite in its defence it would be extraordinarily difficult to reach agreement amongst the partisans of reform. Fox and Grenville both supported alleviating the civic disabilities of loyal Irish Catholics, but this question of imperial security and liberal principles had little popular support and would be sure to antagonise the royal family. Abolition was a popular cause; the spade work of the Abolition Committee had helped to make it look more like 'sound policy'. However the royal family remained a problem and had shown itself quite capable of frustrating 'sound policy' on issues, such as Catholic relief in Ireland, where a principle was thought to be at stake. The Prince of Wales was amenable to the political managers, since he was at this time looking to the government both to pay off his debts and to pursue his vendetta against his wife (the so-called 'Delicate

Investigation' of Princess Caroline's infidelities was about to be concluded). The Prince himself advised ministers that his father was less disposed to contest abolition than Catholic emancipation, probably because he felt more isolated on the former than the latter issue.[14] Nevertheless the monarch's antipathy to abolition remained a major preoccupation.

When the King had been informed of the ban on the supply of slaves to Guiana in the Orders in Council of 1805, great care was taken to assure him that it had the support of West Indian proprietors and that in no way was this a partial step to general abolition. The King had assented to the Orders only after himself minuting these various assurances.[15] When contemplating parliamentary strategy for the session of 1806 Wilberforce noted 'the great point would be to get if possible the royal family to give up their opposition'. Wilberforce was very gratified when Grenville and Fox showed themselves keen to bring forward the abolition question; though he had always distrusted these two men on the ground of their lack of religion he was to find them more reliable than Pitt. Memories of past frustration doubtless coloured a diary entry made by Wilberforce in March: 'Consulting about Abolition, Fox and Lord Henry Petty talked as if we might certainly carry our question in the House of Commons, but should certainly lose it in the House of Lords. This looks but ill, as if they wished to please us, and yet not forfeit Prince of Wales favour, and that of G.R. and other anti-abolitionists.'[16] As this note suggests the danger was not so much that the King would refuse royal assent to a measure which had passed both Houses as that he would assert his influence to ensure defeat in the Lords. Both the abolitionists and the government adopted an approach that would minimise the danger of a royal veto. In the first instance they proposed a partial measure – the Foreign Slave Trade Bill – which could be justified without recourse to general abolitionist arguments. The Foreign Slave Trade Bill, introduced in April 1806, aimed to suppress the sale of slaves by British traders to foreign colonies, including foreign territories occupied by the British – following Trafalgar there was, of course, every prospect of new overseas conquests. This bill was a legislative extension of the approach already embodied in the Orders in Council of 1805. Abolitionists adopted a low profile in the debate on this measure, though James Stephen had helped to draft it. After a briefing from Stephen, Grenville introduced the bill in the Lords, urging support for it on grounds of imperial interest now that Britain really did rule the waves. He argued that 'it was clear and obvious policy that we should not give advantages to our enemies'. He pointed out that 'if we gave up the trade it was not possible for any other state, without our permission, to take it up'. Grenville continued:

'Did we not ride everywhere unrivalled on the ocean? Could any power pretend to engross this trade, where we commanded from the shores of Africa to the western extremities of the Atlantic? America had been presented as likely to succeed us in the trade; but were not the noble Lords aware that there was a majority of the United States decidely hostile to this traffic?'[17] In fact British West Indian planters now had as good a reason as their cousins in Virginia to stem the inflow of slave labourers to their competitors. And Grenville's peroration also shows that the victory at Trafalgar had not only persuaded the Hanoverian oligarchy to readmit a dissident faction. In giving Britain mastery of the high seas it also presented all problems of imperial, naval and commercial strategy in a new light. Britain was now the arbiter of all oceanic exchanges and could regulate the terms of colonial competition. The vision of a pacified global system of commerce, so often proclaimed by abolitionists, had become the realisable objective of a single power.

Stephen had constructed a tangible imperial interest and had devised the Foreign Slave Trade Bill to serve it. But Grenville saw that abolition could elevate both his administration and Britain's war effort. He was attacked in the Lords' debate for seeking to introduce 'abolition in disguise'. He replied: 'Were this true he should be glad indeed, not of the disguise but of the abolition.' In fact the favourable impact made by the bill on public opinion encouraged him to go further in the second reading, as is clear from the report of his speech: 'It would be an event most grateful to his feelings to witness the abolition of a traffic that trampled upon the rights of mankind. But he could see no reason for disguise upon that subject. He had heard of fraud in disguise, of injustice and oppression in disguise; but justice and humanity required no disguise. Those who felt those virtues would be proud to acknowledge them.'[18] The bill passed in the Lords by forty-three votes to eighteen. Shortly thereafter Grenville wrote to Wilberforce: 'I saw our strength and thought the occasion was favourable for launching out a little beyond what the measure itself actually required. I really think a foundation is laid for doing more and sooner than I have for a long time allowed myself to hope.'[19]

The leaders of both the government and the Abolition Committee were disposed to follow up quickly the advantage they had gained. The new administration needed to call for a General Election fairly soon to strengthen its parliamentary position. On May 19th Stephen composed a memorandum in which he argued that 'an early dissolution of Parliament will strongly influence in our favour many Members of the House of Commons who have been instructed by large bodies of their Constituents to vote for an Abolition of the Slave Trade'.[20] In the following month Grenville and Fox themselves introduced a general abolitionist resolution which, though possessed of no legislative force, would serve as a marker for any new administration: 'That this House, considering the African Slave Trade to be contrary to the principles of justice, humanity and sound policy, will, with all practical expedition, take effectual measures for the abolition of the said trade, in such manner, and at such period, as may be deemed advisable.' After powerful speeches from Fox and Grenville the resolution passed both Houses. In the Commons debate two West Indian proprietors who had supported the Foreign Slave Trade Bill spoke against the resolution, but overall voting showed little slippage of support. Fox pointed out in the Commons that the United States was likely to end its participation in the slave trade in 1808 while Grenville argued in the Lords that supporters of gradual abolition could vote for the resolution. Most of the Irish members voted for abolition, aware that Catholic relief was the most likely alternative reform to which the government might commit itself. In July Parliament also agreed without a division on a 'Humble Address' to the King to the effect that joint undertakings to suppress the slave trade should be included in any treaty it might be possible to reach with France or the United States. The unanimity of the British Parliament on this proposal suggests that it was acceptable even to the Members for Bristol and Liverpool, men like Tarleton with large investments in the West Indies. The inclusion of the proposal for a joint ban on slave-trading in no way improved the prospects of a peace with Napoleon. For Napoleon to have accepted the British proposal would have meant accepting Europe's long-run dependence on Britain in the supply of plantation products. In 1805 the slave population of the French-controlled Caribbean stood at 175,000, the slave population of Spanish Cuba about the same, while that of the British-controlled Caribbean stood at 715,000. A mutual agreement to end the slave trade would only perpetuate British preponderance.[21] When the British envoys put this proposal Talleyrand politely insisted that it should not even be considered until a peace agreement had been reached. The *pour-parlers* soon foundered on Napoleon's insistence that only a return to the terms of the Peace of Amiens furnished a basis for a new agreement. Britain would have to renounce hope of entering the markets of Europe and in the overseas dependencies of the continental powers just when its merchants and manufacturers were casting greedy eyes on Spanish America. In September 1806 Fox died and in the following month the *pour-parlers* were broken off. On October 14th Britain's only useful European ally, Prussia, suffered a crushing defeat at Jena.

The cause of abolition had appeared to carry all before it in the summer of 1806, yet the 'main question' had still to be decided. Many parliamentarians who had voted for the resolution or subscribed to the 'Humble Address' might only have been supporters of a gradual and 'multilateral' ban on the slave trade and have remained sternly opposed to any unilateral action. The opponents of any immediate British action on the slave trade still included such influential personages as the Duke of Clarence, Robert Peel, Lord Castlereagh (one of the ablest young Pittites), and Lord Sidmouth, a former Prime Minister who had been prevailed on to join the government coalition and who controlled a considerable following in the House of Commons. Grenville at first proposed that they might achieve their objective by a prohibitive tax on slave imports to the British West Indies. But this plan was soon abandoned and it was agreed to give priority to a general Abolition Bill in the next parliamentary session. Because of Sidmouth's opposition this bill could not formally be presented as a government measure, but Grenville's own commitment to it was to be highly consequential. In October 1806 Grenville called for a General Election in the hope of strengthening his administration. The death of Fox was a heavy blow, leaving the government, despite its vaunted title as 'the ministry of all the talents', very short of effective spokesmen in the Commons. Grenville and the abolitionists made a *de facto* alliance for the purposes of the election. Brougham orchestrated a press campaign in favour of the government candidates and Stephen obtained a winnable seat. Grenville extended help to Wilberforce who faced a stiff challenge in Yorkshire; the followers of Sidmouth were allotted the most difficult seats. The government emerged strengthened from the election and Grenville almost immediately moved to introduce a slave trade bill. To minimise the dangers of obstruction and royal influence the bill was introduced first in the Lords and only subsequently in the Commons.

Britain's rulers were being asked to decide the abolition question at an extraordinary moment. The issues at stake included but also transcended those which have preoccupied so many historians of British anti-slavery – issues such as whether there was or was not over-production of sugar in the early months of 1807 or the precise degree to which British abolitionists were motivated by Christian evangelism. Britain's oligarchy had a world to win if they could pull through – and a kingdom to lose if they did not. Resolving the predicament of the oligarchy was a test of political leadership. While neither the counting house nor the pulpit could be ignored nor could they decide important questions of state; there were in any case merchants and clerics on opposing sides of most questions, including abolition. In Britain in 1806–7 every political issue was either borne aloft or dashed down by the gale force of the wider conflict then engaged. The political conjuncture to be negotiated by the oligarchy was one of growing danger and isolation, with Britain soon ranged in conflict against almost every significant power in the world – Spain, Russia, Turkey, Sweden, the United States as well as France. Austerlitz and Jena not only eliminated Britain's allies and persuaded Russia to change sides, but also led directly to the Berlin decrees of November 1806, extending the scope of Napoleon's blockade of Britain through the Continental System. At home there was a palpable danger of war-weariness, middle-class pacifism and even explosive social discontent, as taxes and prices rose to intolerable heights. Hundreds of thousands of young men were to be dragooned into the armed forces. They and the country had to be given some more inspiring goal than that of placing a Bourbon on the French throne. Anti-slavery, chiming in as it did with patriotic conceptions of English liberty and a new sense of global trusteeship, furnished at least part of the answer. It also offered a ray of hope to middle-class reformers who were asked once again to postpone their hopes for domestic advance for their cause.

During the election of 1806 and prior to the parliamentary session of 1807 the Abolition Committee fostered a campaign aimed directly at voters and legislators. The best tribute to its success was to be paid in the Commons by a Liverpool MP, General Gascoygne, who was strongly opposed to abolition. He complained that

> every measure that invention or art could devise to create a popular clamour was resorted to on this occasion. The Church, the theatre, the press, had laboured to create a prejudice against the slave trade. It had even been maintained from the pulpit that 'England could never expect to be victorious in war while she persisted in such an abominable traffic'. . . . The attempts to make a popular clamour against the trade were never so conspicuous as during the last election, when the public newspapers had teemed with abuse of this trade, and when promises were required from different candidates that they would oppose its continuance. There had never been any question agitated since that of Parliamentary reform, in which so much industry had been exerted to raise a popular clamour, and to make the trade an object of universal detestation. In every manufacturing town and borough in the kingdom all those arts had been tried.[22]

Introducing the bill in the Lords Grenville declared that its passage would be ' one of the most glorious acts that had ever been undertaken by any assembly of any nation in the world'.[23] The bill passed its second reading in the House of Lords by one hundred votes to thirty-six. Those favouring the bill often cited the statistics and arguments contained in the writings of Brougham and Stephen. As it became clear that the bill was destined to pass, Grenville's invitation to patriotic self-congratulation was to be reiterated by speaker after speaker. In distinctively English terms they echoed Danton's satisfaction with the French National Convention's emancipation decree – though of course this precedent was mentioned by no one. In the Commons George Walpole, an MP who had acquired great respect for the Maroons in Jamaica when commanding the campaign against them in 1795–6, lent the authority of his experience to the argument from imperial security. The Solicitor General drew an extended parallel between the troubled conscience of the French Emperor and the serenity of Wilberforce retiring after the vote that night 'into the bosom of his happy and delighted family', knowing that he had preserved the life of so many millions of his fellow creatures. This peroration brought a packed House to its feet as, contrary to parliamentary custom, the Members roared their acclaim and gave three cheers to the veteran abolitionist. The bill passed in the Commons by 283 votes to 16. Its passage meant that it would be unlawful for any British ship to participate in the Atlantic slave trade as from January 1st 1808.[24]

The government fell shortly after passage of abolition, as if its work had been done. Grenville half-heartedly introduced a bill allowing Irish Catholics to serve as officers in the militia in England as well as Ireland; the King opposed this and dismissed the ministry. Grenville himself knew that there was no further reform measure that he could offer his followers and was content to allow Tory politicians to assume responsibility for prosecuting the war. The fall of the ministry led to no diminution of the national commitment to abolition, despite the fact that Grenville's successor, the Duke of Portland, had opposed it. Canning, who supported abolition, became Foreign Secretary. Both the King and Lord Sidmouth had been glad to see Grenville go, in part because they resented the way they had been out-manoeuvred on the slave trade question. But there could be no question of a reversal of the verdict, partly because the arguments from 'sound policy' were, indeed, sound, and partly because the measure had been greeted with such tumultuous self-congratulation. Previous positions on the slave trade no longer counted: even former opponents of abolition now recognised that it would be in Britain's interest to secure an international convention against any renewal of the slave traffic as part of any peace settlement. A species of abolitionism became part of the reigning consensus. The parting gift of Fox and Grenville to their Tory opponents had been a cause which dignified and elevated Britain's resistance to Napoleon and bid for global hegemony. The self-confidence of the ruling class was boosted and at least some of the ground-swell of democratic patriotism evident in 1804–6 harnessed to the war effort. Official support for abolition enabled Britain's rulers to identify themselves with a universal goal. The members of the British

Parliament were for the most part bluff, hard-hearted men who showed little tenderness for the plight of rack-rented Irish peasants or English pauper apprentices, and who tolerated impressment and merciless floggings in the Royal Navy. But, once convinced that abolition did not contradict 'sound policy', and knowing it to be dear to the heart of the middle-class reformers, they allowed themselves to be shocked by the appalling brutalities of the Atlantic slave trade. Wilberforce, Fox and Grenville persuaded them that the traffic was an unprecedented and unnecessary evil, and that by acting against it the British Parliament would raise its character in the eyes of the entire world.

In the short run, abolition, though essentially a middle-class issue in the years 1804–7, did nothing to promote middle-class representation within ruling institutions. The passage of abolition offered symbolic satisfaction to middle-class reform while preserving unchanged the substance of oligarchic power. Romilly, the former Solicitor General, was privately outraged when the Royal Jubilee in 1809 was made the occasion to credit George III with passage of the Abolition Bill. While Britain's stance on the slave trade demonstrably improved the morale of Britain's governing classes, its impact on actual or potential opponents is more difficult to estimate. It was certainly no talisman to ward off the discontent of desperate labourers or merchants faced by ruinous exclusion from European or North American markets. In fact British governments in the years 1807–14 faced greater domestic opposition than in previous years when they had stonewalled abolition. The dislocation and misery caused by the war led both to a campaign against it by the largely middle-class 'Friends of Peace', as well as to militant working-class resistance from General Ludd and his 'army of redressers'.[25] The government was obliged to build a network of barracks in the north of England and to station 12,000 troops there, more than had been sent to fight in the Peninsula. A number of the main centres of support for anti-slavery in Yorkshire and the Midlands were also centres of Luddite activity and of working-class combination against employers. Just as abolitionist legislation helped the oligarchy to assert its right to rule and deflect middle-class agitation for reform, so in the industrial districts middle-class abolitionism helped manufacturers to outface menacing combinations, cement ties with other respectable persons and assert their social conscience. The Luddites sought to halt or deflect capitalist industrialisation by threats of violence; the abolitionists proclaimed the need to pacify market relations and base them on a minimum respect for personal inviolability and autonomy. Abolition did not solve the problems of either government or employers, but it lent a more hopeful aspect to national sacrifice and discipline.

The grave wartime difficulties faced by British trade led to a movement against the 1807–8 'Orders in Council' in the years 1810–12. The Orders in Council had set the scene for an escalating conflict with the main 'neutral' power at which they had been aimed, the United States. New openings in Spanish and Portuguese America failed to compensate for the closure of the US market, following the retaliatory boycott decreed in 1808. Brougham, now an MP, played a leading role in the agitation against the Orders. So intense were the resentments of the merchants and manufacturers affected that eventually the government felt obliged to rescind the Orders, though this action was taken too late to avert the outbreak of war with the United States. The anti-slave trade consensus survived the conflict over the Orders in Council, because British merchants knew that their problems stemmed from the loss of the North American and European trade and not from the decline of the much smaller African trade; indeed the plantation trade itself was also suffering from the closure of European and North American markets. Instead of producing a setback for the abolitionist cause, the campaign against the Orders in Council furnished the occasion for Brougham to introduce a bill which applied stiffer penalties for any British trader caught participating in the Atlantic slave trade. The opponents of the Orders were happy to demonstrate in this way that they were not aiming at a return of the slave trade.[26]

An international ban to prevent the revival of the Atlantic slave trade accorded with both the material interests of the British colonies and British conceptions of a new international order. The slave traffic to the Caribbean had virtually ceased following the 1807 Act but, depending on the terms of the Peace, the ending of the war would create a quite new test. The British government's abolitionist zeal, and anxiety to protect the interests of West Indian proprietors, had to be measured against other war aims and the interests of its allies. While 'diplomatic abolitionism' nicely symbolised Britain's aspiration to global tutelage, it was to create its own problems both at home and abroad. Of course the passage of abolition in no way troubled Britain's chief potential allies: Prussia, Austria and Russia. But following Napoleon's invasion of the Iberian Peninsula Britain entered the lists to defend the legitimist governments of Spain and Portugal, with their large interest in colonial slavery. Since the Spanish and Portuguese governments were heavily dependent on British support they were obliged to treat British proposals for a ban on the slave trade with at least formal respect. But the Iberian monarchies lacked either the will or the ability to take efficacious measures against the traffic. The British thirst for free trade with Spanish and Portuguese America itself contributed to this situation. The plantation economies of Cuba and Brazil had been boosted by the decline of St Domingue and had prodigious prospects of expansion, if fed by a continuing slave trade. The Portuguese government and monarchy, now installed in Brazil, could scarcely ignore Brazilian interests. Cuba's prosperity held out the promise of future revenues and its *hacendados* demonstrated loyalty in difficult times; however pressing the demands of the British government, the interests of Cuban planters and merchants could not easily be ignored. The British had adopted abolition when Spain was an enemy power and there seemed an excellent prospect of separating it from its American possessions. Spanish resistance to Napoleon offered the British government the opportunity of a European alliance at a time of almost complete isolation. Though British ministers continued informal discussions with South American leaders such as Miranda and Bolivar, their main interest was now to strengthen Spanish resistance to the French. The rivalry between Spanish American juntas of loyalist or autonomist inclination gave some leverage to the British, but not in the case of Cuba where the Spanish connection remained unquestioned.

In 1810 the British government negotiated an agreement with the Portuguese authorities which promised gradual abolition of the slave trade in the South Atlantic. If the Portuguese commitment was a little vague, the British also gained important commercial concessions in the direct trade with Brazil.[27] In Spanish America the creole oligarchy displayed its own resistance to the Atlantic slave traffic, its motives resembling those of the Virginian plantocracy. The import of African slaves was seen as derogatory to creole interests and identity, even by partisans of autonomy or independence who were themselves slave-holders. The revolutionary Junta at Caracas issued a decree suspending the slave trade, while the leaders of the Mexican insurrection went further and called for slave emancipation. These Spanish American declarations emerged from a highly fluid and unstable political conjuncture; perhaps deliberately, they were an embarrassment to the British government, with its determination to shore up the Spanish Bourbons. The convocation of the Cortes at Cadiz in 1811 afforded some hope to British abolitionists, since the Liberal leader Arguelles proposed a ban on the slave trade – this motion bracketed slavery with judicial torture as an abuse to be suppressed. However, the Cuban delegates objected and the Havana municipality submitted a lengthy and well-informed memorandum making such points as the following: the British Parliament had deliberated on abolition for twenty years before finding the best time and method for effecting it; the British colonies were well stocked with slaves in 1807, whereas Cuba's plantations suffered a labour shortage and a heavy gender imbalance; the Portuguese abolition agreement was 'vague and indeterminate', envisaging only a gradual termination of the traffic; though the lot of the Cuban slave was perhaps unfortunate, Spanish laws offered much better protection than did those of the British colonies.[28] These and other arguments were embellished with supporting references to the pronouncements of British and North American statesmen; they were accompanied by detailed tables and annexes on comparative slave populations and the text of relevant decrees and international agreements. The 'worthy and indefatigable' Wilberforce was commended as respectfully as the cautious pronouncements of the Duke of Clarence or Lord Hawkesbury. The case for abolition presented to the Spanish Cortes by Arguelles had been in certain vital respects more radical in its anti-slavery objectives than the measures pursued by British abolitionists. Arguelles argued that suppression of the slave trade should be followed by emancipationist measures, such as the freeing of those born to slave mothers. The Cuban memorial countered such proposals by pointing to the fate of St Domingue once attempts were made to tamper with its internal regime. The Cuban memorialist, the *hacendado* Francisco Arango y Parreño, argued that emancipation would have to come eventually but it should be left to the colonists to devise it. The Spanish Cortes evidently heeded the Havana memorial since the Arguelles motion failed; the cogency of the municipality's arguments was doubtless enhanced by the knowledge that the Cuban customs revenue remained one of the Spanish government's few remaining sources of finance. The Liberal leaders persisted in demanding an end to the slave trade in the following year but, with the suppression of the Cortes in 1814, and the restitution of full power to Ferdinand VII, no more was heard of the matter and Francisco Arango y Parreño became a member of a restored Council of the Indies. So long as the war lasted few slaves reached Cuba but the London government had been given a taste of troubles in store.

British forces captured Curaçao and the Danish West Indies in 1807, Mariegalante and Desiderade in 1808, Martinique and Cayenne in 1809, Guadeloupe in 1810. The British also extended their position in West Africa by converting Sierra Leone into a Crown Colony in 1807 and capturing French Senegal in 1809. British control of the Caribbean had a depressive effect on the prices of plantation products, since European markets were difficult to enter; the captured territories were mainly held as bargaining counters for future negotiations. From 1813 the continental blockade began to disintegrate and plantation product prices rose. Britain had by this time seized control of all European colonies in Asia and Africa, save those belonging to Spain or Portugal. The overriding goal of the London government was to restore a semblance of the old order, and the old balance of power in Europe, while retaining its global predominance. But this did not mean clinging on to all the colonial territory it had taken. Apart from any other consideration a limit had to be set to the acquisition of plantation colonies in the interests of British colonial proprietors themselves. The London government also had to consider the stability and repute of the new governments it was hoping would bury the memory of Jacobinism and Bonapartism. Their credibility would certainly be weakened if deprived of all overseas possessions. The British Cabinet knew that it would have to return some of the French colonies that it had occupied. Yet to do so would compound the problems already experienced with the Portuguese and Spanish governments.

Britain's rulers all agreed that monarchy should be restored in France and the majority opted for installation of the legitimist candidate, Louis XVIII. The French royalists – some of them, like Malouet, closely linked to colonial interests – naturally insisted that French sovereignty over all former colonial possessions, including 'St Domingue', should be restored. The British Foreign Secretary, Castlereagh, sought to extract agreement to a ban on the slave trade as a quid pro quo for the return to France of occupied territories. The Netherlands received back Surinam, Curacao and Java on condition that there would be no renewed slave traffic; the Dutch Netherlands were also reunited with the Austrian Netherlands and disposed to accept that there would be no renewal of the long-defunct Dutch slave trade. However, the restored Bourbon in France proved more prickly and independent. Castlereagh felt that some concession was in order. The first draft of the Treaty of Paris stipulated that Martinique and Guadeloupe would be returned to France and that French sovereignty over St Domingue would be recognised. For a five-year period the French colonies were to be permitted to restock their plantations by importing Africans, after which the traffic would cease.

Publication of the terms of the Treaty of Paris provoked a storm of protest in Britain. The Abolition Committee had been wound up in 1807, transferring responsibility for monitoring implementation of abolition to a new organisation, the African Institution. The new body was conceived of as little more than an auxiliary to the Colonial Office and was ill-equipped to wage a campaign against the peace terms. However, the local abolitionist networks were still sufficiently vigorous to mount highly vociferous opposition to ratification of the treaty. Convinced abolitionists were joined by several important sectors of opinion. The British West Indian lobby favoured the return of occupied colonies to France, but saw no reason why they should be permitted to import slaves. Parliament certainly felt some obligation not to impose unequal competition on the British planters. Abolitionist opposition to the Treaty of Paris was also broadly supported by all those who objected to the government's conduct of the war and indulgence to the defeated enemy in the peace negotiations. The use of British power and British tax-payers' money to restore the French monarchy was itself questioned by a number of middle-class reformers. Even less agreeable was the evident intention of the restored European regimes to continue to raise obstacles to British merchandise. Neither Louis XVIII in France nor Ferdinand VII in Spain displayed any regard for liberal sensibilities. The clauses of the Paris Treaty which envisaged a continuing slave trade helped to focus general antagonism to the strategy of peace-making.

The British ministers justified the colonial and slave-trading clauses of the Paris Treaty on the grounds that they were calculated 'fully to open to France the means of peaceful occupation, and to transform her from a conquering and military to a commercial and pacific nation'. Conceding to France's rulers their former boundaries and possessions would help to reconcile the French to the end of the Empire and to the return of the Bourbons. But these arguments failed to make headway against the abolitionist outcry. Wilberforce declared that Castlereagh had brought back the angel of destruction under the wings of victory; the treaty would prove 'the death warrant of a multitude of innocent victims'.[29] He estimated that nearly half a million slaves would be needed just to rebuild the plantations of St Domingue (Haiti), quite apart from the preceding massacre of former slaves that would be needed to recapture it. It was urged that once the French slave trade had been brought back it would be foolish to suppose that it would then disappear in the time specified. The parliamentary abolitionists received the support of a massive extra-parliamentary movement. Within two months 774 petitions had been received denouncing the relevant clauses of the Paris Treaty – the previous peak of abolitionist petitions had been 509 in 1792. An abolitionist delegation was dispatched to Paris with the object of persuading the French government itself to renounce the slave trade. It met a curt response from Malouet, the new Colonial Minister, who inquired: 'Do you English mean to bind the world?'[30] Napoleon's escape from Elba effected a change in the position of the French government. During the Hundred Days the Imperial Senate itself decreed the formal abolition of the French slave trade, possibly hoping to influence British public opinion. When Louis XVIII found himself once more back on the French throne he deemed it no longer advisable to ignore the anti-slave trade representations of the British Foreign Secretary. At the Congress of Vienna the French representatives agreed that the slave trade to the French colonies would not be legalised.

The British ministers also brought back from Vienna an international declaration against the slave trade, to which all the powers had subscribed. The Tsar Alexander had already agreed to a British proposal on the matter; though vague as to implementation, the declaration against the slave trade helped to confer moral prestige on the actions of the authors of the treaty. Spain, Portugal, Sweden and France all subscribed to the declaration but took no effective measures to prevent their nationals engaging in the traffic. Neverthess the British abolitionists appeared to have achieved a notable victory. For its part the British government undertook to continue bi-lateral discussions with the Portuguese, Spanish and French authorities with a view to making a reality of the Vienna Declaration. Indeed diplomatic initiatives against the Atlantic slave trade became a staple feature of British diplomacy. Successive Foreign Secretaries found that their correspondence on this topic exceeded that on any other question; a special 'Slave Trade Department' was created within the Foreign Office to negotiate and monitor bi-lateral treaties suppressing the Atlantic slave trade. However, the will to press these to an effective conclusion was very uneven. In 1817 the British government signed a treaty with Portugal which prohibited the trade north of the equator but left the flourishing Luso–Brazilian slave trade in the South Atlantic unscathed. A treaty with Spain in 1817 provided for complete cessation of the Spanish slave trade by 1820, with Britain furnishing compensation payments to the Madrid government. The Spanish and Portuguese governments had little inclination to enforce these treaties, especially at a time when they feared colonial insubordination, but the terms of the treaties gave British warships the right to search suspect Portuguese or Spanish vessels. Enforcement of these treaties was to give employment to two sizeable squadrons of the British Navy, one stationed on the African coast, the other in the Caribbean. Spanish ships accused of slave-trading would be seized and taken to be judged by 'mixed courts' presided over by a British judge and a Spanish judge. Slaves found on board such vessels were to be delivered up to the British authorities in Sierra Leone or the Spanish authorities in Cuba.[31]

From the outset British slave trade diplomacy aroused the resentment of the governments at which it was directed. For a sovereign state to bow to foreign pressure on an issue of this sort was wounding to national pride, especially when it meant yielding exceptional powers to the Royal Navy. Abolition gave the British government a good excuse for meddling in the affairs of other Atlantic states of which it often availed itself. But direct financial, commercial and naval pressures might have underwritten British influence without creating the complications involved in slave trade diplomacy. Castlereagh and his successors were anxious not to provoke abolitionist opinion. But their efforts to appease it led them to bully and discredit monarchical regimes in France, Spain and Portugal which they had no wish to weaken. The rulers of these countries were, in fact, doubly discredited; first for allowing the British to impose anti-slave trade treaties upon them and secondly for failing to enforce them. The US government was strong enough both to resist British pressure for 'a right of search' and to take effective measures to prevent substantial importation of slaves into its territory. The stance of the US government did, however, indirectly contribute to a continuation of the slave trade, since ships flying the US colours could not be seized by the British Navy's patrols.[32]

International agreements against the slave trade were so riddled with loopholes, and bedevilled by bad faith, that they completely failed to stem a strong recovery in the cross Atlantic traffic in the years 1815–30. The numbers of slaves sold in the Americas during this period rose to equal or exceed those introduced in the last two decades of the eighteenth century. The remaining colonies controlled by France were restocked, while the slave economies of Cuba and Brazil underwent a rapid expansion. Direct British participation virtually disappeared, though British manufacturers still sold to slave traders while British merchants purchased slave-grown produce.

During the years 1815–23 British abolitionism was a dormant force. During its second wave, 1804–15, it had concentrated on the slave trade, explicitly disavowing any intention of pressing for slave emancipation in the British colonies. Amidst the enthusiasm of the passage of the 1807 Act one young MP had proposed gradual emancipation; this was opposed by Wilberforce himself who declared that, though he looked forward 'with anxious expectation to the period when the negroes might with safety be liberated', he did not feel that they were yet 'fit . . . to bear emancipation'.[33] Together with most other abolitionists Wilberforce hoped that the ending of the slave trade would itself bring about an amelioration of the slaves' condition. Brougham, with his concern for 'sound policy', was even more categorical on the imprudence of moving to a 'free negro' system until the slaves had been thoroughly exposed to civilising influences. Most abolitionists hoped that the ending of the slave trade would itself encourage an improvement in slave conditions, obliging slave-owners to foster the natural reproduction of their plantation labour force. Wilberforce was a leading light in the movement to recruit missionaries for the work of Christianising the inhabitants of the Empire; he believed that religious instruction would be particularly beneficial for the black population of the West Indian colonies. A combination of market pressures and Christian principle would improve the slave condition, encouraging family life and hard work.

The parliamentary abolitionists, favoured by the mass campaign of 1814–15, did press for one legislative measure, a register of the slave populations of the West Indian colonies. The aim of such a register would be to ensure that slaves were not smuggled into the British colonies and to monitor the pattern of births and deaths. An inter-island slave trade was still legal; a registration system would ensure that this was not used as a cover for introducing slaves from Africa. The Colonial Office had already introduced a register of the slave population of the Crown Colony of Trinidad in 1812, but elsewhere in the West Indies an Act of Parliament would be needed to establish one. When Wilberforce introduced such a bill in 1815 there was a storm of protest from the colonial assemblies. They feared that the compilation of a slave register would licence official interference and might reveal patterns of mortality and fertility that could be used against them. While the West Indian interest in Parliament supported diplomacy to suppress foreign slave trades, it vigorously opposed registration. Since 1812 the government had been led by the second Lord Liverpool; he declined to support registration on the grounds that there was no evidence of smuggling. However, Wilberforce attracted enough support to induce the colonial assemblies to declare that they would institute local registers under their own control.

Wilberforce abandoned the proposal for a Central Register, administered by the metropolis, after news was received of a major slave outbreak in Barbados in 1816; this Easter rising, known as 'Bussa's rebellion', erupting in Britain's oldest West Indian slave colony, put the parliamentary abolitionists on the defensive. They had argued that it was raw Africans who constituted the danger, yet there were fewer Africans in Barbados than any other British colony; the rise of natural reproduction rates had long diminished the slave trade to this island and creoles comprised 93 per cent of the slave population by 1816. The parliamentary supporters of registration were even more discomforted to learn that the debate on their proposal had quite probably contributed to slave unrest, encouraging the belief that the British Parliament wanted to improve slave conditions and was being prevented from doing so by the local plantocracy. The Barbados rebels acted with restraint and deliberation, some convinced that the Governor was bringing a 'free paper' for the slaves, others that sufficiently determined action would break the authority of the planters, as had happened in 'Mingo (Santo Domingo). While a dozen or more plantations were damaged, with buildings set alight, only one white civilian and one black were killed by the rebels. The rebellion was suppressed with much bloodshed by the local forces of law and order; 50 rebels were killed in the fighting, 70 were executed after capture or surrender, 144 were executed after summary trial and 132 were deported. The rear admiral commanding the naval squadron stationed at Barbados commented: 'The Militia, who could not be restrained by the same discipline as the Troops, put Many Men, Women and Children to Death, I fear without much discrimination.'[34]

Reports of the uprising, which naturally dwelt on the violence of the rebels, led Wilberforce not only to withdraw the Registration Bill but also himself to sponsor a Parliamentary Address to the Prince Regent, which formally declared that there existed no plan for introducing emancipation into the West Indies. In this way the leading champion of 'abolition' seemed to confirm the indefinite continuation of slavery in the British colonies, though the address also expressed the view that improvements in the slave condition were to be hoped for. Wilberforce acted on the advice of Lord Castlereagh in these matters and accepted an assurance from the government that it would itself introduce a registration measure, after having first secured the consent of the colonial assemblies.[35]

The retreat, indeed capitulation, of the parliamentary abolitionists was occasioned not only by the Barbados revolt but also by a harsh polarisation of opinion on all political questions, which found Wilberforce, once again, lending his support to the forces of reaction. The advent of peace had brought further social unrest as demobilisation swelled the ranks of the unemployed and the decline of military spending accentuated an economic downturn. Prices dropped but so did wages, and both movements claimed victims and stimulated discontent. The national debt had swollen to vast proportions, with heavy annual interest charges, yet Parliament had greeted the peace by voting down the income tax, loading the extra burden on indirect taxation and introducing new protectionist Corn Laws which helped to keep up the price of bread. In these circumstances there were clashes between labourers and employers or magistrates, and vigorous attacks were made in the radical press on a vicious and exploitative aristocracy. Government and Parliament were horrified by events such as the Spa Fields meeting of December 1816, at which plans were openly discussed for an armed uprising and the expropriation of all landowners. In 1817 the government introduced the Coercion Acts, suspending habeas corpus and giving the government power to ban meetings, followed by the Six Gag Acts of 1819, which further curtailed civic rights. Wilberforce stood by the government, despite its unpopularity, from conviction; he also hoped thereby to maintain Cabinet support for

The Peterloo Medal

abolitionist diplomacy and for the promised new bill for slave registration. Even in the 'Humble Address' Wilberforce had not renounced interest in the fate of the slaves, nor categorically rejected some future scheme of gradual emancipation. In 1818 the government did introduce a Registration Act, which had been cleared with the most influential colonial interests. However, Wilberforce judged the political climate unsuitable for any public ventilation of slavery questions.

Though there was no organised abolitionist activity for several years after 1815, it is interesting to note that anti-slavery ideas still had resonance in the radical milieu. The Society of Spencean Philanthropists, an early socialist grouping inspired by the doctrines of Thomas Spence, had played a leading role in the Spa Fields affair. The Spenceans advocated support for slave rebellion and slave emancipation; one of the leading Spenceans, Robert Wedderburn, a tailor, was of African descent and the son of a slave. In 1818 he published *The Axe Laid to the Root*, which called for slave emancipation and universal suffrage. The Spenceans were amongst those to be persecuted under the Coercion Acts and Six Gag Acts. In 1818 Wedderburn was prosecuted for advocating the right of slaves to kill their masters at a meeting of the Spencean grouping which he led. According to a government spy Wedderburn's contention was approved at a meeting where the question was 'decided in favour of the Slave without a dissenting Voice, by a numerous and enlightened Assembly, who exultingly expressed their Desire of hearing of another sable Nation freeing itself by the Dagger from the base Tyranny of their Christian masters. . . . *Several gentlemen declared their readiness to assist them*.'[36] Wedderburn was eventually convicted and jailed not for incitement but for blasphemy. A similar revolutionary emancipation was proclaimed in the pages of the radical newspaper, *The Black Dwarf* (1819–28). The support given to the government by Wilberforce and other parliamentary abolitionists also led radicals to make satirical use of anti-slavery themes. When a dozen or so were killed by militia at a peaceful demonstration in Peterloo, Manchester, in 1819, a radical paper proposed the making of a 'Peterloo Medal' from the melted down bugle of the officer commanding, depicting a kneeling demonstrator being cut down, with underneath the following exchange: 'Am I not a Man and a Brother?' 'No! – you are a poor weaver.'

Wilberforce was not disposed to yield up the anti-slavery cause to revolutionaries or democratic agitators. He was privately troubled by the concessions which he and his associates had made to the planters and more convinced than ever of the need to increase the number of missionaries in the colonies. Together with other pillars of the African Institution Wilberforce found a vicarious outlet for his abolitionist convictions in official and unofficial diplomatic activity. He urged the government to press ahead with bi-lateral treaties against the slave trade. Anxious that Haiti should be a showcase for anti-slavery, he engaged in lengthy correspondence with King Henry and arranged for the dispatch there of missionaries and teachers. Henry was aware that British abolitionism had opposed French plans against his country in 1814 and Wilberforce was gratified by Henry's emphasis on religion, hard work, family life and monarchism. Henry sagely considered the advantages of converting his country to protestantism. Wilberforce also urged the importance of Sabbath obervance and 'Female Improvement'. He solemnly informed King Henry: 'We boast in this country [that is, Britain], not without reason, that, speaking of the higher circles, our women are much more generally faithful to their husbands than the ladies of any other country in Europe; Switzerland and Holland perhaps excepted.'[37] He was pleased to inform the Haitian monarch of the 'unpolluted purity' of the court of Britain's royal family. Wilberforce could muster no enthusiasm for Haiti's Republicans though, as will be seen in the next chapter, it was they who were to assist the next anti-slavery advance in the Americas.

Notes

1. The reawakened radical mood is evoked in Edward Thompson, *The Making of the English Working Class*, Harmondsworth 1968, pp. 491–507. For an informative account of Britain's social and political structure at this time – of the oligarchy, the middle classes and the labouring classes – see A.D. Harvey, *Britain in the Early Nineteenth Century*, London 1978, especially pp. 6–39 for the composition and workings of the 'oligarchy', pp. 39–49 for the distribution of the vote and the formation of 'public opinion', pp. 64–78 for the impact of religious controversies, and pp. 220–29 for the rebirth of reform.

2. For an account of the northern middle-class reform milieu see J.E. Cookson, *The Friends of Peace*, Cambridge 1982; for the 'Liberal Press' see pp. 84–114.

3. Henry Brougham, *A Concise Statement of the Question Regarding the Abolition of the Slave Trade*, London 1804, pp. 61, 62, 77.

4. Buckley, *Slaves in Red Coats*, pp. 76–7.

5. The security situation in the West Indies occupies much of the third volume of the 1801 edition of *The History Civil and Commercial of the British Colonies* by Bryan Edwards. Craton, *Testing the Chains*, p. 365, n. 5 cites some of the numerous contemporary reports. One of the most influential and affecting accounts of war in the Caribbean published in these years was J.G. Stedman, *Narrative of a Five Years Expedition against the Revolted Negroes of Surinam*, London 1796 (1st edn), 1801 (2nd edn), 1813 (3rd edn); it described campaigns of the 1770s with some sympathy for the black rebels and fine illustrations by William Blake; little imagination was needed to see its relevance to the later period. Brougham's argument that the Caribbean would be safer if Napoleon crushed independent St Domingue is found on p. 119 on the second volume of his *Inquiry*. The pamphlet version of Brougham's argument did not include this passage or the more egregious racial slurs to be found in the larger work. While his new abolitionist allies would have objected to them, they would not have diminished Brougham's reputation as a colonial expert. In later years defenders of slavery republished Brougham's views as *Opinions of Henry Brougham Esq. on Negro Slavery with Remarks*, London 1826.

6. Brougham, *A Concise Statement of the Question regarding the Slave Trade*, pp. 43, 48–9. This pamphlet undoubtedly had a major impact on parliamentarians but does not usually receive its due from historians of abolition; see Chester New, *The Life of Henry Brougham to 1830*, Oxford 1961, pp. 21–31.

7. Stephen's pamphlet is quoted and discussed in David Geggus, 'British Opinion and the Emergence of Haiti', in James Walvin, ed., *Slavery and British Society*, London 1982, p. 141.

8. Anstey, *The Atlantic Slave Trade and British Abolition*, pp. 344–6.

9. Quoted in Anstey, *The Atlantic Slave Trade and British Abolition*, p. 337.

10. James Stephen, *War in Disguise or the Frauds of the Neutral Flags*, London 1805, pp. 62–3, 70. Large estimates of the size of the foreign slave trade were made without challenge in parliamentary debates; see Anstey, *The Atlantic Slave Trade and British Abolition*, p. 375, n. 36, and p. 376, n. 39. For a modern estimate and the dimensions of the Atlantic sugar trade see Drescher, *Econocide*, pp. 78, 95.

11. Anstey, *The Atlantic Slave Trade and British Abolition*, pp. 353–6, 358–9.

12. Coupland, *Wilberforce*, p. 596; Christopher Hibbert, *George IV, Prince of Wales*, London 1972, pp. 185–200.

13. William Cobbett, 'A Plan for the forming of an Efficient and Permanent Army', *Cobbett's Political Register*, March 22nd, 1806, vol. IX, no. 12, col. 391. Motivating the need for a large army was not the least of the government's problems, since soon one in seven adult males was enrolled.

14. Hibbert, *George IV, Prince of Wales*, pp. 220–24.

15. See A. Aspinal, ed., *The Later Correspondence of George III*, Cambridge 1968, p. 322.

16. Wilberforce is quoted in R.I. and S. Wilberforce, *Life of Wilberforce*, London 1838, 5 vols, III, pp. 257, 259.

17. Quoted in Anstey, *The Atlantic Slave Trade and British Abolition*, pp. 373–4.

18. Quoted in Anstey, *The Atlantic Slave Trade and British Abolition*, p. 374.

19. Quoted in R.I. and S. Wilberforce, *Life of Wilberforce*, III, p. 261.

20. Quoted in Drescher, *Econocide*, p. 218.

21. Drescher, *Econocide*, p. 34.

22. *Hansard's Parliamentary Debates*, vol. VIII, December 15th 1806–March 4th 1807, col. 718–19.

23. *Hansard's Parliamentary Debates*, VIII, col. 955. For the geo-military plight of Britain at this juncture see Jones, *Britain and the World*, pp. 287–91, and for the domestic conjuncture see Harvey, 'The Ministry of All the Talents', *Britain in the Early Nineteenth Century*, pp. 170–96, and Cookson, *Friends of Peace*, p. 182.

24. *Hansard's Parliamentary Debates*, VII, col. 999. Cf. Samuel (Wilberforce), Bishop of Winchester, *The Life of William Wilberforce*, London 1872, p. 279.

25. For these two very different reactions see Thompson, *The Making of the English Working Class*, pp. 515–659, and Cookson, *The Friends of Peace*. The condition of the labouring classes was often so desperate that it would be absurd to claim that respect for the abolitionist policy of the government would have stayed their hand – even supposing, that is, that they were aware of it at all. The middle-class 'Friends of Peace' were another matter and may have been somewhat abashed that abolitionism had been made into a war aim. Wilberforce continued to be returned for Yorkshire, despite his general support for the war. Of course his constituents would have included many farmers, who were doing well from the high agricultural prices which reigned during the war years. While oligarchic sponsorship of abolition did not produce generalised consensus, it did, other things being equal, redound to its credit with the mass of the population and do so at a time when its need for ideological mobilisation was great and its resources limited.

26. Clive Emsley, *British Society and the French Wars, 1793–1815*, London 1979, p. 160; Arthur Aspinall, *Lord Brougham and the Whig Party*, London 1927, pp. 10–13.

27. Leslie Bethell, *The Abolition of the Brazilian Slave Trade*, Cambridge 1970, p. 8. The treaties between Britain and Portugal respecting the slave trade and respecting other commercial matters were formally separate, but they were negotiated jointly and signed on the same day. Under article 9 of the commercial treaty Brazilian tariffs on British goods could be no greater than 15 per cent *ad valorem*, while under article 10 the British government could appoint special judges to deal with cases involving British citizens who came into conflict with local laws.

28. 'Representacion de la Cuidad de la Habana a las Cortes', July 20th 1811, in Hortensia Pichardo, ed., *Documentos para la Historia de Cuba*, vol. I, Havana 1971, pp. 219–52. For the background to this see David Murray, *The Odious Commerce*, Cambridge 1980, pp. 50–71. The progress of anti-slavery in the mainland revolutions will be considered in the next chapter.

29. Quoted in Drescher, *Econocide*, pp. 152–3; see also Drescher, 'Two Variants of Anti-Slavery', in Bolt and Drescher, eds, *Anti-Slavery, Religion and Reform*, p. 47.

30. Quoted in Coupland, *Wilberforce*, pp. 396–7. See also Betty Fladeland, 'Abolitionist Pressures on the Concert of Europe', *Journal of Modern History*, XXXVII, 1966, pp. 355–73.

31. Bethell, *The Abolition of the Brazilian Slave Trade*, pp. 18–20; Murray, *The Odious Commerce*, pp. 72–92.

32. The failure of Anglo–US negotiations is traced in Betty Fladeland, *Men and Brothers, Anglo–American Anti-Slavery Co-operation*, Chicago 1972, pp. 112, 117–24. The dimensions of the continuing slave trade are explored by David Eltis, 'The British Contribution to the Nineteenth Century Slave Trade', *Economic History Review*, 2nd series, vol. XXXII, no. 2, 1979, pp. 11–27.

33. Quoted in Gratus, *The Great White Lie*, pp. 127–8.

34. Craton, *Testing the Chains*, pp. 261–2; see also Hilary Beckles, *Black Rebellion in Barbados*, Bridgetown 1984, pp. 86–8.

35. Michael Craton, 'Proto-Peasant Revolts? The Late Slave Rebellions in the British

West Indies', *Past and Present*, no. 85, November 1979, pp. 99–125, p. 108; Coupland suggests that Wilberforce's willingness to defer to the government reflected anxiety at the domestic situation, *Wilberforce*, pp. 406, 459.

36. Quoted in Fryer, *Staying Power*, p. 223. For Wedderburn see Iain McCalman, 'Anti-Slavery and Ultra Radicalism in Early Nineteenth Century England', *Slavery and Abolition*, vol. 7, no. 2, September 1986, pp. 99–117. Thomas Spence's lecture of 1775, mentioned in ch. 1, was republished in 1793 as *The Real Rights of Man* and again in 1796 in *The Meridian Sun of Liberty*.

37. Quoted in Gratus, *The Great White Lie*, pp. 133–4.

IX

Spanish America: Independence and Emancipation

The sansculottes of France
Have made the world tremble
But the shirtless ones of America
Will not be far behind.

The American Carmagnole (1810)

Among us there are no sansculottes

El Patriota de Venezuela (1810)

Hear, oh mortals! the sacred cry:
Freedom, freedom, freedom!
Hear the noise of broken chains;
See the throne of Equality the noble.

Argentine national anthem (1813)

For a long time the Peruvian, oppressed,
dragged the ominous chain;
condemned to cruel serfdom,
For a long time he moaned in silence.
But as soon as the sacred cry of
Freedom! was heard on his coasts
he shakes the indolence of the slave,
he raises his humiliated head.

Peruvian national anthem (1821)

HAITI
1816

VENEZUELA
1811, 1813, 1816

COLOMBIA
1819

EQUADOR
1822

PERU
1824

BOLIVIA
1825

1821

ARGENTINA
1811

CHILE
1818

0   500   1000 miles

The Independence Struggle in Spanish South America

Despite the abolitionist proclamation agreed upon at the Congress of Vienna in 1815 the programme of monarchical and colonial rehabilitation, which formed the substantive part of the Congress's work, returned to Spain, France, Denmark and the Netherlands those American slave colonies over which they had lost control as a direct or indirect consequence of the Napoleonic Wars. Colonial slavery was recognised and upheld by the Congress as were the restored rights of the various metropolitan monarchies of Spain, Portugal, France and the Netherlands. All these powers consented to a formal ban on the Atlantic slave trade, but Spain and Portugal were permitted a few years to restock their plantation colonies before the ban came into force; subsequently neither the Iberian powers nor France took the steps necessary to suppress a continuing illegal traffic. The United States implemented its own ban on slave imports but failed to concert measures with Britain for the ending of the clandestine traffic to other territories. The ending of the wartime commercial blockades reopened the European and North American markets for plantation produce; the elimination of St Domingue, recently the largest supplier, gave extra scope to planters elsewhere.

But the prospects for the restored colonial slavery of 1815 were clouded by memories of the revolutionary epoch, by doubts concerning the viability of the regimes of monarchical reaction and, most immediately, by the challenge of the liberation movements in Spanish America. The Spanish Empire had been shattered by Napoleon's invasion of the Peninsula and the subsequent war. Prior to 1808 the Spanish American colonies had been unresponsive to the revolutionary appeals of the age. The imperial authorities and their local allies had been strong enough to contain internal unrest and to keep contraband down to an acceptable level. The imperial authorities had been forced to suppress Indian uprisings, such as that of Tupac Amarú in 1780–82, or slave conspiracies, such as those in Venezuela in the 1790s, or popular resistance to new taxes, such as in the revolt of parts of New Granada in the 1780s, but prior to 1808 the structure of empire itself had been almost unchallenged. The Venezuelan patriot Miranda led an invasion in 1806 but attracted little support even in a province with a tradition of contraband and political defiance. On the one hand, the revenues from the silver mines of Upper Peru and Mexico supported a strong apparatus of metropolitan control; on the other the creole elite had been unwilling to move because of its dependence on the imperial infrastructure and its fear of the mass of Amerindians, mestizos, mulattos and blacks.

The relaxation of commercial restrictions and the interruptions of war had allowed Spanish American planters and ranchers to buy slaves and expand their operations. The slave proprietors of late colonial Spanish America were not absentees, unlike so many in the British or French West Indies, and were thus in some respects better placed to defend their slaveholdings. Slavery was, it is true, marginal in Mexico and Central America and still a secondary presence in most of Spanish South America in 1810, but in a number of regions there were nearly as many free people of African descent as slaves; outside the mountainous Andean region free and enslaved blacks and people of colour often possessed strategic significance in the social formation. Large-scale plantation slavery now flourished in Cuba, where the cultivation of sugar and coffee helped to employ around 200,000 slaves by the second decade of the nineteenth century; the smaller island of Puerto Rico had 17,500 slaves, about half of whom worked on plantations. The two island colonies were traditionally Spanish strongpoints on the route back to Spain; their fate is considered in the next chapter. Mainland Spanish America contained about 225,000 slaves, but slavery was a diffuse and secondary form of property or labour. Outside the plantation enclaves in Venezuela and Peru the great landowners did not, like Caribbean planters, have their principal wealth invested in slave crews. But many of them did own a few slaves, whom they valued as servants, craftsmen or even trusted agents. Slaves had always been prized possessions in Spanish America; the *dueño de esclavos* had status as well as a valuable piece of property. Any man with a white or pale complexion in Spanish America could aspire to be a gentleman (*hidalgo*); a man who owned a slave was a *señor*, a lord and master.

In Mexico and Central America there may have been between 10,000 and 20,000 slaves; these slaves, and the more numerous free descendants of slaves, were found as port-workers, artisans, or domestics in the principal towns, or as foremen and labourers on the plantations or in the mines. Slaves were expensive both to buy and to maintain, since the cost of living was high. In Mexico as in other parts of Spanish America slaves were sometimes placed in positions of trust and responsibility. The great majority of those who worked the silver mines were free labourers earning quite high wages. In the major urban centres there were many more free blacks, mulattos and mestizos than slaves. In New Granada, roughly the future Colombia, there were 45,000 slaves in 1778, concentrated in the port towns or the gold workings of the Choco and Cauca. Slaves comprised about 5 per cent of the total population of the Viceroyalty at this time, though their numbers may have declined as the gold workings became less profitable; a number of the 368,000 *mestizos* in New Granada, though in the main ethnically Indo–European, would have had some African ancestry. There were about 5,000 slaves in the Presidency of Quito (Ecuador) – principally concentrated, like the free blacks, on the coast around Guayaquil. In the Captaincy General of Venezuela there were as many as 87,000 slaves out of a total population of 900,000 in 1800; moreover there were thought to be 24,000 fugitive slaves and 407,000 *pardos* of partly African descent in this latter province. The Venezuelan slaves were concentrated in the cacao groves of the central coastal region and constituted the largest enclave of plantation economy in Spanish South America. In Chile in 1812 there were said to be 10,000–12,000 slaves, while the free blacks, numbering 25,000–32,000, comprised a little over 3 per cent of the population. In Peru there were some 40,000 slaves working in the towns and plantations of the coastal region, where they comprised at least a quarter of the population, with free blacks and mulattos being equally numerous: those of African descent were believed to be better adapted to the more humid lowlands. Few free or enslaved blacks were to be found in the Andean region, where most of Peru's population of over a million was to be found. The Presidency of Charcas in Upper Peru (Bolivia) contained 4,700 slaves working mainly as domestics or artisans or on estates in the vicinity of La Paz. In the region of Rio de la Plata and its hinterland at least 30,000 slaves comprised about a tenth of the sparse population; the population of free blacks and mulattos was of the same size. The slavery of the La Plata region derived from its historic role as an entrepôt in the traffic between Africa and Spanish South America, notably Charcas with its mines; the slaves were employed as domestics, artisans, porters, muleteers and estate workers.[1]

In the last decades of the Spanish empire the imperial authorities sometimes looked to the free black or mulatto population of the New World as a potential counterweight to the white Spanish Americans with their autonomist aspirations. When the British seized Havana in 1762 the creole elite had put up only a feeble resistance and had soon settled down to trading briskly with the occupiers. This episode had delivered a shock to the colonial authorities and encouraged them to look increasingly to free blacks and mulattos as recruits to the militia. The newly created or expanded coloured militia units were subordinate to the metropolitan regulars, with some men of colour appointed as junior officers. All free blacks were required to register with the *caja de negros*, which would draw up a roster of militia service. In 1789 Madrid issued a new code governing the condition of slaves and bearing on the racial caste system. New World planters disliked this metropolitan attempt to regulate slavery, even though it was accompanied by no effective invigilation or sanction. The system of racial caste privileges, which governed tax exemptions, office-holding and legal rights, was also relaxed in favour of those free blacks and mulattos who could afford to purchase certificates suspending their disabilities. In law those of mixed blood were barred even from wearing Spanish dress. The native white *criollos* of Caracas complained in 1795 when the instrument known as *gracias al sacar* allowed *pardos* (free mulattos) to purchase the privileges of whiteness. In a number of strategically vital imperial centres – Havana, Mexico City, Lima, Buenos Aires – free mulattos and blacks comprised a third or more of the militia forces available to the colonial authorities by the turn of the century.[2]

The favours bestowed by the imperial authorities on some *pardos* and free blacks did not threaten slavery and were quite compatible with a modified caste system; indeed the value of the concessions made to individuals depended on a context in which people of colour did not, as of right, enjoy full citizenship. Nor did such assumptions dent the traditional view that Indian ancestry, especially if noble and distant, was more acceptable than black ancestry. Some Indian *caciques* had received titles of nobility and could claim legal immunities. For a white to marry a black or mulatto involved loss of caste, and in some instances was legally prohibited; on the other hand, in the early days of the Conquest Spaniards had been happy to marry the daughter of a *cacique*. Most 'pure' Indians kept to themselves; blacks and mulattos, whether free or enslaved, lived side by side with the whites, usually performing the more menial tasks disdained by the latter. Caste divisions helped to constitute the imperial order; they were matched by a complex set of corporate privileges and exemptions, extended to municipalities, professional bodies, militia units and ecclesiastical institutions. The more 'enlightened' Spanish officials, impatient of creole privileges and particularism, were willing selectively to relax caste discrimination.

Spain had allowed African slaves to be introduced to the New World to strengthen its hold on newly conquered territories and to plug gaps in the fabric of empire; on the eve of the liberation struggles this was still the role of some slaves and free blacks in Spanish America, who were found in the towns, and along the lines of communication, working as artisans, labourers and domestics. The last decades of the eighteenth century, and the first years of the nineteenth, witnessed a new rise of silver output, mined by free waged workers, supplemented in Peru by the *mita* system of communal forced labour. However, in Mexico a significant proportion of the free workers of the mining zone were of partly African descent, since African slaves had in former times comprised a quarter or a third of the mining work-force. Only in New Granada were slaves engaged in mining – in this case panning for gold in the river valleys of the South-east. The numbers still employed in the gold workings had dropped by the end of the eighteenth century, with mine owners finding that the deposits were not sufficiently good to justify the trouble and expense of maintaining a large slave labour force. In this part of New Granada slaves, former slaves, or their descendants, often clung on as tenants or squatters to the land allotted to them for their subsistence.

In most parts of Spanish America agriculture was organised by haciendas or ranches where few or no slaves were employed. In the regions of settled agriculture the subjugated Indians furnished the bulk of the dependent labour force; free mestizo or *pardo* cattlemen worked the ranches. In most provinces there were a few sugar plantations mainly catering to the local market – such as those found in Tucuman (Argentina), coastal Peru, or the basin of Cuernavaca (central Mexico) – but by the late colonial period the proportion of slaves in these patriarchical establishments had declined and the main labour force were dependant *peones* of partly African descent.

The historic strongpoints of the Empire were established in the major mining zones of Mexico and the Andes, and in the Caribbean along the lines of communication with the metropolis. In these areas the impulse to independence was stifled. The independence movements were to be more vigorous in areas where slaveholding ranchers and planters were to be found: the River Plate, Venezuela, New Granada and the Pacific coast lowlands. In the backlands of South America there was a sizeable fugitive slave and free black or mulatto population, engaged in ranching and subsistence agriculture. These were areas where there were few Indians but many partly Hispanicised people of mixed blood, *mestizos* (usually meaning a mixture of Indian and white), *pardos* (black and white), and *zambos* (Indian and black).

The vast interior of the continent had always beckoned to slave runaways and rebels. Survival in the South American backlands was not easy but probably not as difficult as in North America, whose Western grasslands were dominated by powerful and warlike Indian nations. In Venezuela slave-based development was concentrated in the province of Caracas and even there it was limited and modified by the possibility of escape to the interior; slaves in the commercial agricultural zone did not work in gangs under supervision but were assigned quotas and required to deliver given quantities of the cash crop to their owner. Venezuelan agricultural slavery conceded significant work autonomy to the slave, though *mayorales* would severely punish those who failed to make the required deliveries. Some slaves even grew cacao on their *conucos* or garden plots. While some slaves became estate administrators other slave cultivators might convert themselves by degrees into manumitted tenants. These arrangements lent an extra resilience to slavery in Venezuela and possibly encouraged in slave-owners a boldness reminiscent of the Virginian planters of the 1770s. The 1795 slave rebellion in the western province of Coro was a rare instance of open and organised contestation of slavery, and had been quite swiftly defeated, with some three hundred rebels, free men of colour as well as slaves, losing their lives. While Coro itself was to be a centre of royalist strength in the independence period the central zone around Caracas, where most plantation development was concentrated, produced the first republican attempts.[3]

In most parts of Spanish South America slave resistance and flight, and the availability of others forms of dependent labour, had checked the emergence of large-scale slavery; together with the relative frequency of manumission, slave escapes had helped to produce the growth of a free or fugitive black or *pardo* population. The last quarter of the eighteenth century had witnessed a multiplication of the number of *palenques*, or fugitive slave settlements, in mainland South America, especially in Venezuela and New Granada; in Peru and Rio de la Plata there had been slave revolts on the former Jesuit estates in the 1760s and 1770s when these had been sold off to new owners. Insecure conditions in the backlands were inimical to large-scale slavery but they were quite compatible with surviving pockets of personal bondage, as vulnerable individuals sought the protection of powerful *hacendados* or caudillos. In the more central regions the urban rich and large landowners or ranchers would own some slaves whom they would employ as domestics or managers (*mayordomos*).

The creole aristocracy and middle class resented metropolitan patronage and trade restrictions. *Peninsulares* received a disproportionate share of the most lucrative or influential posts; in law Spanish office-holders were barred from marrying creoles in their regions of jurisdiction. While some aristocratic creoles were co-opted into the structures of imperial government, or enjoyed membership of municipal bodies with real powers, the policies and personnel imposed by Madrid easily offended an increasingly self-confident local elite. *Comercio libre* allowed any Spanish merchants to trade with the colonies but left in place a metropolitan monopoly, raising the prices of all manufactured imports for Spanish colonists. The white creoles found even the less privileged *gachupines* to be grasping and officious. By the late colonial period the traditional caste structure was unable to absorb without strain the growth of large intermediary layers between the Peninsular

Spaniards and white creoles on the one hand and the subjugated Indians or blacks on the other. The so-called *castas*, those of mixed Indian, European and African ancestry, comprised an ever larger proportion of the population. The mestizos and mulattos were partly Hispanicised in culture and those with skills or education would be in competition for jobs and privileges with local whites; since *pardos* were prone to be somewhat more Hispanicised the competition they offered to white creoles was that much stronger. The latter were still known as *españoles* but increasingly thought of themselves as Americans; the term *criollos* was less popular with them since it could imply mixed blood.

At the beginning of the nineteenth century there were only about 160,000 *Peninsulares* and 3 million native whites out of a total population of about 14 million in Spanish America. While there were 6–7 million living in Indian communities the diverse but semi-Hispanicised *castas*, numbering 4–5 million, were more numerous than the whites and were growing steadily as a proportion of the population as a result of inter-marriage and acculturation.[4] Spanish power and the imperial society of orders more easily controlled, contained and accommodated the Indian village communities, with their recognised *caciques*, than the free-floating population of *castas* found both in newer commercial centres and in the backlands. When the imperial authorities were challenged by the creole aristocracy they would appeal both to *pardos* and to the loyal Indian communities, with their privileged *caciques*, but in doing so they themselves put at risk the ultimate coherence of the imperial order.

The first tentative steps towards autonomy or independence were not made until the metropolis was paralysed by the Napoleonic invasion. The empire did not encounter serious internal opposition until its metropolis was already occupied and impotent. The creole aristocracy of Spanish America waited for more than a generation after 1776, partly because it was restrained by fear of the Indians and the *castas* beneath them and partly because mining, the most dynamic economic sector, both depended upon and could sustain an imperial bureaucracy and military establishment.

Prior to the French invasion of Spain in 1808 Napoleon captured the Spanish monarch and persuaded him to abdicate in favour of Joseph Bonaparte. For a time resistance to the invaders was co-ordinated by a central junta which refused to recognise the Bourbon abdication and accepted alliance with Britain. French advances in 1809–10 dispersed the junta and forced it to appeal to all parts of the kingdom to organise their own resistance. Loyalist forces retreated to the enclave around Cadiz; the council based on Cadiz, which continued to claim jurisdiction over Spanish America, was naturally attentive to the interests of this historic monopoly entrepôt. Liberals gained the upper hand in Cadiz – they established a constitutional regency, convoked the Cortes and elaborated the constitution of 1812. Spanish America was given representation but not in proportion to population; resident *peninsulares* were to vote but not those with African blood. Some Mexican delegates opposed these arrangements, which aimed to keep creole representations in a permanent minority. These same delegates advocated the ending of slavery; some Spanish liberals responded by proposing abolition of the slave trade. All such proposals failed, but created a stir none the less.

News of the events in Spain encouraged the municipalities of the American provinces to take their fate into their own hands. The Spanish American juntas had nothing to fear from the French and were not disposed to defer to the Liberals in Cadiz. To begin with the Spanish American juntas declared that their aim was simply to uphold the legitimate rights of Fernando VII, pending his restoration. These juntas were based in the first instance on existing institutions, though those which aspired to self-government or freer trade usually convoked a *cabildo abierto* or meeting open to leading men in the province. In some cases the juntas were dominated by creole interests with autonomist pretensions; in others members of the colonial establishment concerned to defend metropolitan interests predominated.

The defence of the rights of the Bourbon dynasty was, in itself, an eminently conservative cause. The imperial establishment in Havana, Peru and Mexico proved sufficiently strong to contain the autonomist impulse of the colonial population, though not without a stiff struggle in Mexico and significant concessions in the case of Cuba. In Peru and Upper Peru there were still lively memories of the great Indian uprising of Tupac Amaru in the 1780s and this helps to explain the ease with which Spanish officials retained control there. In Havana a pro-independence conspiracy led by Juan Aponte, a free Negro, was swiftly suppressed; on the other hand, the flouting of trade restrictions by Cuban merchants and *hacendados* was ignored by Spanish officials.[5]

Gran Colombia

Venezuela, with the largest concentration of slaves in mainland Spanish America, was to be the principal battle ground in the first phase of the independence struggle. The news of developments in Spain led to the emergence of a creole-dominated junta in Caracas in April 1810. Venezuela became the first province to declare its independence in July 1811. This declaration reflected the growing influence in Caracas of a

Patriot Club, drawing support from the younger generation of creole
letrados and aristocrats; this was patronised by Francisco de Miranda,
the pioneer of Spanish American independence who, after winning fame
as a French revolutionary general in 1792, had conspired with Pitt
against Spain and urged Wilberforce to use his influence to support
American independence. The imperial establishment in Caracas was
weaker than in Mexico and Peru while the creole aristocracy had long
enriched itself by the practice of contraband and the defiance of
imperial authority. Even if the project of independence did not
command universal assent within the creole oligarchy, the new
Venezuelan Republic strove to make itself acceptable to it. Republican
leaders sought to offer a new freedom and security to the large
landowners and new opportunities to frustrated members of the creole
middle class. They decreed that a National Guard would patrol the
plantation zone and ensure the continuing subordination of the slaves
and *pardos*. A projected franchise based on property holdings
recognised the wealthy proprietors as the true rulers of the country.
Members of Venezuela's leading landowning families – the Bolivars,
Tavars, Toros, Blancos and Machados – lent their support to the
Republic. The Republic's social conservatism was coupled with attacks
on clerical privilege and the announcement of a ban on the slave trade.
Royalist opposition to the Caracas junta was organised to the West,
South and East in the provinces of Coro, Maracaibo and Guayana. The
royalist counter-offensive mobilised the *pardo* militia and evoked
support from all those who distrusted the creole aristocracy; royalist
commanders encouraged slave resistance to patriot slave-owners. The
Republicans fell back on an enclave around Caracas and appointed
Francisco de Miranda as Dictator. Miranda issued a decree ordering
that 2,000 slaves should be enrolled to fight for the Republic, while the
state would compensate their owners; after ten years' military service
these slaves would be manumitted. Moderate as it was this decree still
encountered opposition within the republican ranks; it was itself soon
overtaken by royalist counter-measures. Spanish priests and colonial
officials were prepared to back *pardo* resistance to the pretensions of
the creole aristocracy and even to denounce the mistreatment of slaves
by patriot proprietors; the threat of servile insurrection was designed to
show vacillating creole proprietors the folly of republican indepen-
dance. Royalist commanders were happy to enroll slaves fleeing from
patriot slave-owners. The Spanish Archbishop of Caracas, Coll y Prat,
declared that the republican authorities and the planters who supported
them should be resisted; he later claimed that his statements sparked a
royalist slave revolt. The Archbishop doubtless exaggerated, but it was
indeed the case that several thousand blacks in the coastal zone

acquired arms; they acted in concert with the royalist forces converging on Caracas, without necessarily sharing their objective of restoring metropolitan authority. Besieged by a motley coalition of opponents, failing to establish a sufficiently broad social base and weakened by a terrible earthquake, the first Venezuelan Republic collapsed after only a year. Republican determination was also sapped by news of the proclamation of the liberal 1812 constitution by the Cortes in Cadiz. The Republicans capitulated on condition that the persons and property of their supporters would be respected. The restored colonial regime itself lacked authority or unity of purpose and the terms of the capitulation proved difficult to observe. Bands of *pardos* and escaping slaves refused to lay down their arms and return to their previous condition. Republican forces continued to hold out in some areas, including along the border with New Granada.[6]

In 1813 Simon Bolivar, one of the younger republican partisans, led a daring new republican advance from Cartagena to Caracas. The Second Republic was proclaimed in January 1814. Bolivar urged that a 'terrible power' was needed to crush the Spaniards and overcome republican disunity. Bolivar offered more vigorous leadership, based on accentuating the potential conflict of Americans against the Peninsular Spanish, and diminishing all sources of division amongst the creoles themselves. Bolivar met the often arbitrary and cruel repression of the colonial authorities with the declaration of a 'war to death' against Spaniards based on an explicit double standard: any Spaniard who refused to give positive support was liable to execution while creoles would be treated leniently, even if they had colluded with the Spanish authorities. Bolivar was himself a leading member of the creole aristocracy, but he was willing to proclaim a sweeping civic equality for all those of free American birth. But egalitarian proclamations could not immediately dispel the identification of the republican cause with the white creole elite, nor save the Second Republic from the fate of the First. Bolivar did not have the military or political apparatus to give reality to his social programmes and proclamations; the column with which he had reconquered Caracas was less than a thousand strong. The clash between Republicans and royalists allowed the bands of fugitive slaves and free-lance *pardos* to act on their own account, making *ad hoc* alliances where necessary. The creole aristocracy failed to throw its united weight behind the Republic but its strength was sufficiently imposing to deter the republican forces from appealing to the slaves or *pardos* against it.

The royalists had also attracted the support of some of the military chiefs of the plains cattlemen, the *llaneros*; the republican cause was doomed unless it could win the support of the formidable horsemen of the *llano*. The First Republic had unwisely issued decrees, the *ordenanzas del llano*, which sought to impose tidy juridical concepts of private property on the grasslands and cattle herds of the interior. The *llaneros*, many of whom were men of colour, felt little in common with the status and property-conscious *mantuanos*, as the white *criollo* proprietors of Caracas were called. Some of the *llanero* columns were led by plebeian Spanish immigrants, such as the legendary royalist commanders Tomás Boves and Tomás Morales; Boves was a petty merchant from Andalucia who established himself as the chief of a large force drawn from both *llaneros* of the interior and *pardos* of the coastal region; Morales, a Canary Islander, became one of Boves's principal lieutenants. Yet royalist influence among the *llaneros* was not deep-rooted and many Southern *caudillos* had no wish to see a strong imperial authority. The eruption of slave resistance further complicated the picture. Some slave-owners had the resources to retain authority in the main zone of plantation agriculture; there were slaves who thought life safer if they stuck to the cacao groves, or who were unwilling to abandon family attachments, but those who wished to escape had more opportunities to do so. Columns of *pardos* or fugitive slaves roamed throughout the countryside and would happily plunder the towns and the rich, even if they did not always see the need to generalise slave insurrections. A veritable social explosion sent the republican forces reeling in 1814 and favoured an anomalous victory for the royalist cause. An irregular armed force of 19,000 men, mainly *llaneros* and *pardos*, returned Venezuela to loyalism just at the moment when an effective monarchist regime was restored in the Peninsula.[7]

With the ending of hostilities in the Peninsula Fernando VII suppressed the constitution and despatched veteran troops to bolster imperial authority in the Americas. Bolivar had withdrawn to New Granada (Colombia) towards the end of 1814 and in the following year sailed for Jamaica in order to rethink the strategy of liberation and re-group the republican forces. Other partisans of independence retreated to the backlands. Pablo Morillo, a Spanish general who had distinguished himself in the war against the French, arrived in Venezuela with 10,500 troops to reinforce the restored monarchical and colonial regime. Morillo was disconcerted by the extent of destruction and by the 'loyalist' forces from whom he was to take over. One Spanish official observed that the war against the Republicans had transformed the *pardos*: he noted that this experience had produced 'even in the loyal ones (*pardos*) a very mistaken idea of the subordination and duties of the good vassal'. Another wrote: 'the very army of Boves, and of Morales, is in rebellion against the white class; its total force of negroes and mulattos refuses to obey; they have pursued several white officers and killed others . . . so that one can say that the idea of a war of colours has become widespread.'[8] Morillo's force was large enough to overawe the irregulars. The death of Boves in one of the last engagements with the Republicans probably made it easier for Morillo to establish his authority. While he speedily reconquered most of New Granada his administration always confronted severe problems in Venezuela itself. Some of the 19,000 irregular troops were sent to New Granada, while most of the remainder were ordered to disband. Many former royalist partisans found that it made sense to team up with the remnants of the patriot resistance.

The restoration of the old order meant the restoration of official caste discriminations and attempts to rehabilitate the power of masters over their slaves. This might have gratified white creole proprietors but many of them also felt the heavy hand of Spanish repression, often administrated by despised plebian officials or immigrants from the Canary Islands or the Basque country. Morillo, acutely short of finances and supplies, resorted to a policy of wholesale sequestration of estates owned by patriots; amongst the 205 haciendas seized from 101 families were 110 cacao groves, 41 sugar plantations and 29 coffee plantations.[9] These estates yielded 912,000 *pesos* to the royal treasury in 1815–16 – a considerable sum though by no means large enough to cover the needs of Morillo's army. The running or leasing of these estates gave the colonial regime and military a quite direct stake in slavery. The Spanish authorities in Venezuela also imposed forced loans and sent urgent requests for money to the Intendancy in Cuba. Though imperial authority was successfully restored in Mexico, and had not been strongly challenged in Peru, the events of 1808–14 had completely disrupted the mining economy and the flow of silver across the Atlantic. The complex arrangements for the extraction, transport and taxation of specie were difficult to reassemble; security whether on land or at sea was appallingly bad. In the meantime the empire was afflicted by severe fiscal crisis and Spanish commanders were driven to extortionate levies which could only narrow the basis of their local support. The Captaincy General of Cuba, with its flourishing plantation economy and absence of armed conflict, was in a more fortunate position. It served as a place of refuge for royalist *émigrés* and a base for the resupply of the forces on the mainland. The loyalty of the Cuban oligarchy was encouraged in 1817 and 1818 by suspension of the tobacco monopoly; plantation development was favoured by the import of 10,000–20,000 slaves a year and by a decree which converted traditional *encomiendas* into freely alienable landed property. The Havana authorities began remitting large sums of cash to the Spanish authorities on the mainland; with the rapid advance of Cuba plantation slavery acquired a new importance in the pattern of Spanish American empire and could not be tampered with.[10] When their backs were to the wall Spanish commanders were still prepared to arm slaves and offer them eventual manumission. But they knew that the empire could not afford any general policy of slave emancipation. And of course the ultra-monarchists in Madrid were not attracted to abolitionism as an ideology, though they might be proud of Spain's humane slave code. After their two defeats the Republicans of *Tierra Firme* received support from a very different Caribbean source.

The reverses of 1811–15 persuaded Bolivar that a more radical and coherent social programme, as well as more decisive military measures, were needed if the liberation struggle was to be re-engaged with success. The British authorities he approached in Jamaica were not prepared to see the colony used as the launching-pad for an invasion of the mainland and so Bolivar moved to the Republic of Haiti. This significant option itself reflected the support the republican cause had attracted from a cosmopolitan layer of free-lance traders and corsairs, many of them with contacts in Haiti. Patriot privateers based on Cartagena, the island of Margerita and La Guaira, had caused great damage to Spanish sea communications. The corsair captains included Louis Brion, Renato Beluche, Louis Aury and Jean–Baptiste Bideau, formerly an adjutant to Victor Hugues. While these men cultivated contacts in republican Haiti their crews, with a high proportion of blacks or *pardos*, kept alive the rough and ready egalitarianism of the 'brethren of the coast'. This was a milieu with its own political weaknesses but it was not one deeply respectful of any type of private property, let alone slavery. Through the good offices of Brion, Bolivar appealed to President Pétion for help in relaunching the independence struggle in Venezuela.

In appealing for support to the Republicans of Haiti Bolivar was rejecting the deep-seated prejudices and taboos of his class. On arrival in Haiti Bolivar was given immediate access to the President. Bolivar outlined to Pétion his plans to roll back the royalist offensive and liberate the continent. Pétion was prepared to give substantial help to Bolivar but only if the Venezuelan would undertake to free the slaves in all the lands he liberated. Bolivar agreed. Slave emancipation would help to assert a new Spanish American identity; it would facilitate recruitment and give free blacks and mulattos the reassurance that the taint of slavery would be removed from people of colour. The expedition assembled by Bolivar represented a major effort to revive the republican cause: it comprised seven ships, arms and ammunition for 6,000 men, a printing press, and a number of Haitian military men, *los franceses* as they were called. This was the first of several expeditions from Haiti bringing men and supplies to the coast and islands of Venezuela.[11]

Bolivar henceforth adopted a policy of military manumission and urged a more general emancipation policy on his civilian and military colleagues. For their part the Spanish authorities still had *pardo* militias and as many as 2,000 slaves, or former slaves, fought in the regular units. But the Spanish commanders were obliged not only to respect the rights of law-abiding slave-owners but were at least formally bound by the imperial system of racial privilege; Morillo unsuccessfully asked the King for permission to annul all caste discrimination. The republican commitment to civic equality gradually acquired a degree of substance and credibility as mestizos and *pardos* were confirmed in positions of responsibility and command. On the other hand, many republican leaders, while prepared to welcome into their columns the fugitive slaves of royalist proprietors, did not feel that they could simply expropriate the property of patriot slave-owners. Concern for the rights of the patriot slaveholder was to prove a major restraint, though one which could be partially neutralised, in the case of adult male slaves, by appeal to the republican principle of universal liability to military service.

At a time when the property and persons of all able-bodied male citizens were liable to conscription, it was difficult to argue that Patriot-owned male slaves should remain apart in some purely private sphere. If every able-bodied citizen was expected to contribute to the liberation effort, why should slaves be exempt? And if a man's horse or cattle could be commandeered, why not his slave? The needs of the struggle against the occupying army frequently dictated obligatory recruitment. The republican authorities sometimes allowed proprietors to offer a slave as a substitute, just as others might be allowed to buy themselves out of military service. If such procedures failed to produce enough recruits then republican chiefs proceeded simply to impress those who had failed to enlist and to demand a levy from slave-owners of one in five or one in ten of their slave crews. Masters whose slaves had been commandeered in this way could claim compensation from the republican authorities – the latter was usually given in the form of public bonds or title to public lands. As may be imagined these proceedings were rarely as elevated as the rhetoric with which Republicans celebrated their commitment to anti-slavery; nevertheless they did have anti-slavery consequences. The slaves enrolled were promised manumission; perhaps only a minority survived the dangerous career of the patriot soldier, but some escaped and very few were ever re-enslaved.

In Bolivar's absence republican resistance had developed in many parts of Venezuela's huge territory, under the leadership of local *caudillos* strongly committed to regional interests and regional autonomy; they ignored or flouted schemes or decrees they found elaborate or inconvenient, whether these were favourable or unfavourable to slave proprietors. The arrival of Bolivar's expedition helped to focus revolt and furnish it with a leadership and strategy; however, the strength of the Spanish garrison in the coastal region eventually led Bolivar and the main republican forces to withdraw to the interior where contact was made with sympathetic *llanero* commanders. Bolivar used his military authority to decree the liberty of slaves in Carúpano and some other coastal districts; some slaves were recruited but the decrees could subsequently be countermanded by patriot planters of the region. The allies and supporters Bolivar was to find along the upper reaches of the Orinoco, Apure and Meta were quite disposed to challenge the property rights of slaveholders, indeed some of them were fugitive slaves. Bolivar decreed that all the slaves of Guayana and Apure were free; in the *llanos* there were not enough slaveholders to contradict him.

Bolivar saw dangers as well as advantages in the new balance of social forces within the republican camp. He opposed what he saw as tendencies favouring *pardocrácia*, supposedly a regime in which rule by the *castas* would displace rule by whites. General Piar, a prominent republican *pardo*, was tried and executed, charged with insubordination and encouraging people of colour to organise separately and against the whites; however, equally insubordinate white generals, such as Mariño, were not so severely dealt with.[12] Though Piar had promoted people of colour, he does not seem to have urged a more radical anti-slavery policy than did Bolivar. Bolivar's hostility to *pardocrácia* was no doubt reassuring to white creoles; like his abolitionism, it also can be seen to reflect his determination to promote nation-building against any sectional interest, and to stress the antagonism to *peninsulares* over and against other social antagonisms.

In the years 1818–19 Bolivar's continental vision was joined to the *élan* of the republican *llanero*, General José Antonio Páez, and they proceeded to deal hard blows to the occupying power. At the first Congress held by the republican forces, at Angostura in February 1819, Bolivar delivered an address that included a passionate appeal for the abolition of slavery; he also promised land to the landless. He urged a 'balanced' constitution, supposedly on the British model, in which an elected legislature would be checked by a hereditary senate, an independent judiciary and the *poder moral* of the executive. The Liberator undoubtedly hoped that his anti-slavery commitments would favourably impress the British government; he had visited London in

1810 and been introduced to Wilberforce by Miranda. The Congress of Angostura elected Bolivar as President but was unenthusiastic about the Liberator's espousal of abolition and of British constitutional forms. The Congress gave Bolivar the authority he needed to drive out the Spanish; as commander he could continue with a sweeping policy of military manumission. But Venezuela's political leaders refused to declare any immediate or general emancipation of the slaves: such a policy, they feared, would push slave-owners into the royalist camp, unleash the uncontrollable forces of servile and racial revolt, and bring few more recruits to the revolutionary armies than a policy of selective and controlled manumission. The freeing of royalist-owned slaves who had fought in the forces of liberation was confirmed, but patriot planters were entitled to compensation and often held positions which enabled them to block, or limit, the conscription of slaves.

In the year following Angostura Bolivar and Páez pushed back Spanish power in Venezuela and undertook major operations in New Granada. Bolivar's forces were not large and prevailed by virtue of swift and bold moves across vast distances: the layer of *pardos* and former slaves in the liberation army sometimes proved more willing to undertake such operations than localistic white creoles. After crossing the Andes Bolivar defeated the Spanish at the battle of Boyacá (August 1819), opening the path to the viceregal capital of Bogotá and enabling him to unite the free territories of Venezuela and New Granada in the Republic of Gran Colombia. The patriot forces in New Granada had maintained a stubborn resistance to Spain without achieving even the degree of coherence and unity which first Miranda and then Bolivar had imposed on Venezuela. Cartagena had established its own semi-autonomous coastal Republic with the help of the privateers. A patriot government had been established in the mining region of Antioquia in 1813–14 and one of the patriot leaders, J.F. Restrepo, had promulgated a 'free womb' decree. But divisions within the patriot ranks and sporadic advances by the Spanish forces seem to have deprived this decree of other than symbolic significance. The Patriots of New Granada found it easier to unite in support of Bolivar than to recognise one of their own number as chief of the revolution. The arrival of Bolivar's forces in 1819 was generally acclaimed, though there was some resistance to the policy of military manumission. When the columns of Bolivar's Granadan lieutenant, Francisco de Paula Santander, reached the gold mining region of the Cauca, Bolivar urged on him sweeping military manumission, but Santander was anxious not to alienate the proprietors of the region. Bolivar pointed out that the slaves made reliable and hardy soldiers and if manumitted would identify their own fate with the *causa pública*. Making use of bad as well as good arguments he argued that if slaves were not allowed to die for their country then the African element would loom larger in the population when the war was over – as was happening, he suggested, in Venezuela. However, the slave-owners resisted the conscription of their chattels and Santander remained unwilling to use the necessity of war to impose manumission. Bolivar himself sought to encourage patriot slave-owners by freeing all the remaining slaves on his own estates, to the number of about a hundred, in 1820.[13]

Spanish resistance in South America was greatly weakened in 1820 when a large expeditionary force gathered at Cadiz refused to embark for the New World and instead demanded the return of the constitution of 1812. Liberal politicians and military dominated the Madrid government until the French intervention of 1823, which restored full power to Fernando VII. The Spanish Liberals had little grasp of the nature of the conflict in America. They gave Spanish Americans representation in the Cortes and offered an armistice to those fighting for independence. Their ambition was to restore imperial unity. General Morillo was still in command of the Spanish forces in Venezuela and New Granada. Short of men, Morillo offered Spanish citizenship to all blacks and *pardos* who would fight in his army. As ordered he negotiated a truce with the Republicans. These actions provoked disarray and outrage in the Spanish camp. The truce allowed Republicans openly to canvass their views. In Maracaibo, still nominally controlled by Spain, local authorities persecuted a group of *pardos* who had demonstrated support for Spain and its King.

Once it became clear that the Spanish Liberals were unwilling to concede independence hostilities resumed. The patriot army inflicted a decisive defeat on the Spanish forces in June 1821 at Carabobo. A largely British-recruited Foreign Legion made a contribution to the patriot victory. Spanish control of the northern littoral had been destroyed.

The Republic of Gran Colombia formally adopted a Manumission Law at the Congress of Cúcuta in 1821. It also adopted a Constitution in which full citizenship was reserved to literate men with property worth 100 *pesos*. In an address to the Congress Bolivar implored it to endorse slave emancipation as a 'reward for Carabobo'. The Manumission Law stipulated that henceforth children born to slave mothers should be free. However, the emancipationist content of this legislation was deferred by clauses which required the *emancipados* to work for their mother's owner until the age of eighteen, to reimburse the latter for the supposed costs of their maintenance. Bolivar urged the Congress not to confine itself to freeing only future generations while allowing the living to languish in bondage. In deference to this plea the law also set up Manumission Boards, financed by locally administered inheritance taxes, with the power to buy the freedom of slaves from their owners.[14]

While it remained to be seen whether the local proprietors would make effective use of this legislation the Manumission Law enacted at Cúcuta certainly associated the South American cause with anti-slavery. By contrast the Liberal authorities in Madrid continued to uphold slavery as a strategic imperial interest. Though they made concessions in many areas they could not afford to endorse any measures against slavery – Cuban remittances ran at $3.2 million in the years 1820–23. In 1822 Madrid could even appear more solicitious of slaveholder interests than Fernando VII had been in 1814; it sent its American representatives a warning that the delicate institution of slavery should be respected at all costs. This warning was the more necessary since some Liberals did sympathise with abolitionism. A Manumission Law was vainly proposed to the Cortes by, ironically enough, a Cuban delegate elected by the radical *menu peuple* of Havana; the same man unsuccessfuly pleaded for colonial self-government.[15]

The patriot victory at Carabobo had confined Spain's forces in New Granada and Venezuela to a few coastal strongpoints. But most of Peru, Upper Peru and Ecuador remained in Spanish hands. Republican action against slavery tended to be associated with military operations, creating, as they did, a pressure for manumission. In mobilising for the liberation of Ecuador Bolivar was forced to order particularly heavy levies of the slave population of Colombia, since many *llaneros* were unwilling to follow him so far from their native habitat; as always desertions and illness had taken a far higher toll of the patriot ranks than battle casualties. In José Antonio de Sucre Bolivar found a lieutenant willing to brush aside the complaints of the slave-owners.

Revolution in the Southern Cone

The independence movements of the River Plate region faced a less formidable Spanish power than had the liberation forces in Venezuela but encountered grave problems by virtue of their own disparity. The impulse to creole self-assertion had been revealed in 1806–7 when the militia, including *pardo* detachments, had acquitted itself well in defeating the expedition of the British Admiral Popham. In May 1810 a creole-dominated Assembly in Buenos Aires established an autonomous junta there. After a fierce struggle the junta was taken over by a radical faction led by Rivadavia. One of the ways in which Rivadavia's group signalled its ascendancy was to publish a decree against the slave trade; the conservative and monarchist forces enjoyed the support of the large merchants of Buenos Aires, many of whom had some involvement in the slave trade. In February 1813 a Constituent Assembly enacted *libertad de vientres*, namely freedom for the children of slave mothers. The sixth article stipulated that 'the children of *castas* who are born free must remain in the house of their masters (*patrones*) until they reach the age of twenty'. Until the age of fifteen the *liberto* was to work without payment and should be paid one *peso* a month during the next five years. Subsequent decrees made provision for the education of slaves and *libertos*. The Assembly also decreed that any slaves introduced to the territory of the United Provinces would be free, a provision that angered the Brazilians and some of the *caudillos* of the interior. This Assembly did not declare for complete independence but it was certainly concerned to establish the authority that would underpin far-reaching self-government. The anti-slavery decrees were endorsed at a time when it was known that anti-slave trade measures had been proposed to the Cortes at Cadiz. The Assembly wished to establish its own credentials in this field and, as a Buenos Aires newspaper put it, to immortalise the 'first instants of its moral existence ... without offending against property rights.'[16]

This cautious method of enacting abolition meant that the condition of the 15,000 or so slaves of Buenos Aires had not been altered; patriots urged the slaves to blame Spaniards for having reduced them to a legal state from which no decree could really free them, since they had become another's personal property. Military necessity led the Assembly to adopt one further measure with some anti-slavery implications, namely the conscription of slaves and free blacks for service with the revolutionary armies.[17] Masters were obliged to sell a proportion of their male slaves of military age to the state; on completion of five years' military service these involuntary recruits would be legally free. In May 1813 the Assembly established Battalions 7 and 8, comprised of over a thousand slaves conscripted in Buenos Aires; in 1816 the coloured battalions were reinforced by the compulsory purchase of 576 slaves of Spanish masters. Slave-owners could avoid military service by contributing a slave recruit; the proprietor might then be enrolled in a militia or guard unit, with only light, local police duties. The regiments destined for the front lines were hard to fill and not infrequently vagabonds or criminals would be drafted into them. Unless they had some powerful protector, free blacks were vulnerable to arbitrary military impressment. That slaves were regarded as particularly acceptable recruits is suggested by a penalty imposed on non-slave-owning Spaniards; they were required either to buy a slave for the army or to pay $200.[18]

The provinces of the interior were eager to shake off colonial rule but were anxious that Buenos Aires should not replace Spain as the new metropolis and arbiter of their commerce. These provinces wished to regulate their own trade with the outside world and not suffer dictation from the merchants and officials of Buenos Aires. The resistance of the interior provinces was both geographically and politically hetero-geneous; some caudillos resented the anti-slavery measures of the Assembly of 1813, others, more responsive to the large *pardo* population, proved willing to go further. The gaucho leader Artigas first urged the need for a federation of autonomous states and then led armed defiance of both Spain and of the *porteños*. Artigas and his followers in the *Banda Oriental* (nucleus of the future Uruguay) maintained their independence with great difficulty; in 1817 they reached a separate commercial agreement with British consular officials. Artigas was himself a *caudillo* who originally enjoyed the support of fellow *estancieros*, the large cattle-ranchers. But in the course of sustaining his challenge he proposed swingeing taxation of the wealthy and a more radical approach to slave emancipation than that adopted by the Congress of 1813.

The *Reglamento provisorio* issued by Artigas in 1815 proclaimed the confiscation of royalist property and the distribution of land to all those willing to work it, specifically including the mulattos and former slaves. A contemporary noted:

> There is no doubt a considerable fermentation has been excited amongst the slaves by his proclamations, and it is extremely probable very many of them will escape and join his army. . . . The general feeling amongst people of property, not only on this side of the River Plate but also on the opposite one, is against Artigas, whose popularity, although considerable, is entirely confined to the lower orders of the community.[19]

The radical approach pursued by Artigas led the Portuguese authorities in Brazil to combine with the forces of Buenos Aires against him. Other *caudillos* of the interior failed to support him and he was eventually obliged to withdraw, defeated, to Paraguay in 1820.

However, the vigour with which Artigas had fought nourished a sense of American independence and impressed the military in Buenos Aires, whose leaders had repeatedly failed to extend the revolution to Upper Peru and who had given ground to the Portuguese in the struggle to maintain the misnamed 'United Provinces' of the River Plate. The United Provinces had not declared their independence until 1816 and were subsequently stuck in a mainly defensive posture, resisting royalist expeditions from Upper Peru. So long as Spanish power remained entrenched in the Andes the independence of the fractious provinces of the River Plate could not be secure, nor could they have much hope of recovering land lost to royalist Brazil.

The forces and strategy needed to consolidate American independence in the south, and to advance upon the Spanish forces in Peru, were assembled by General José San Martín, leader of the Army of the Andes based in the eastern province of Cuyo. San Martín planned to liberate Chile and advance up the coast to Lima, outflanking the Spanish forces which had repulsed several direct attacks from the United Provinces. At least a half of San Martín's soldiers were to be *pardos* or blacks, and many of them former slaves, including the Eighth Battalion. General Miller, the British second-in-command of the Eighth Battalion, wrote that these soldiers, mostly former house slaves, were 'distinguished throughout the war for their valour, consistency and patriotism. . . . Many of them rose to be good non-commissioned officers.'[20] While General Belgrano had expressed low regard for the blacks, San Martín saw them as a crucial resource in extending the revolution. As Governor and commander of Cuyo he made vigorous use of the manumission powers latent in the decree of 1813. In the province of Cuyo there were 4,200 slaves, 13,000 Indians and mestizos, and 8,500 free blacks out of a total population of 43,000. San Martín enrolled 780 slaves in the province compared with 1,500 free men; slaves of military age not recruited to the Army of the Andes were enrolled in auxiliary detachments. Masters whose slaves were conscripted were compensated by receiving land allocations; in a number of cases Spanish prisoners replaced slaves in the workshops or on the estates. San Martín was later to display little sympathy for democracy but, perhaps in an effort to consolidate his base, the Mendoza electoral regulations of 1817 stipulated that all free men over twenty-one years old, including manumitted ex-slaves and free *pardos*, were entitled to vote.[21]

Crossing the Andes with 5,000 men San Martín joined forces with the Chilean forces led by Bernardo O'Higgins. In an address to former slaves before the battle of Chacabuco in February 1817 San Martín pointed out that they were now full citizens and warned them that the Spanish already had offers from merchants in Santiago to buy captured blacks and return them to slavery. San Martín eventually defeated the Spanish at a decisive engagement, the battle of Maipú, in 1818.

Neither slavery nor the imperial establishment were very strong in Chile. The fact that there were only 10,000 slaves in Chile had encouraged the Chilean autonomists to adopt anti-slavery measures, albeit moderate ones, at an early period. A junta led by creole officials had set about organising self-government in 1810. Without ever formally declaring independence it had convoked a Congress dedicated to elaborating a new constitution in 1811. Following a factional struggle, the more conservative deputies were purged. Manuel de Salas, Secretary of the Congress, then presented to it a law which banned the slave trade, freed the children of slave mothers and freed slaves brought to Chile for more than six months; slavery was denounced as contrary to the spirit of Christianity and humanity; slave-owners were urged to treat their slaves kindly.[22] This law was approved and made Chile the first Spanish American territory to adopt the *libertad de vientres*. The passage of the law had a considerable impact on the slave population of Santiago. Some 300 slaves, some it was later claimed carrying knives, came forward to demand their liberty and to offer themselves as soldiers for the *patria*. This caused some alarm and seven of the leading members of the *liga de esclavos* were arrested. The junta had enacted a measure in August 1811, two months before the 'free womb' decree, allowing the military recruitment of slaves – half their pay was to go as compensation to their former owners and they were only to be enlisted with the latter's consent. In Chile as elsewhere in South America there was often a gap between law and reality; a supplementary decree of May 1813, noting with distress that the term *esclavo* still appeared in parish registers for new-born infants, made this an offence.[23] As royalists advanced into Chile in the following year the radical patriot commander Carrera, who had already liberated his own slaves, secured agreement for raising a regiment of *Ingenuos*, or manumitted slaves; their masters were compensated, as before, but did not have to consent. However, this measure was soon overtaken by events, as a royalist restoration suspended all patriot legislation.

The victories of the Army of the Andes in 1817 and 1818 led to the resuscitation of earlier laws relating to slavery. Slaves were enrolled in the patriot forces and the coloured militia and police of Santiago distinguished itself at the battle of Maipú. The *libertad de vientres* was reasserted but no further steps taken to promote military manumission. For five years after 1818 nothing further was done for Chile's three or four thousand remaining slaves. They were themselves too few to constitute much of a social or political force, though the persistence of slavery remained a symbolically charged issue. The young Republic's energies were drained by the continuing struggle against Spain. O'Higgins, as *Director Supremo*, put the resources of the Chilean government at the service of San Martín.

In 1820 San Martín used Chile as the springboard for an attack on Peru, where Spain's Viceroy, administrators and garrison still held undisputed sway. Peru had a population of a little over a million, some

600,000 of whom were Indians, living in communities subject to the labour levy of the *mita*; some 300,000 mestizos were mainly concentrated in the mining regions and urban centres of the Andes, or in regions of subsistence agriculture adjacent to them; about 40,000 slaves and 40,000 free blacks and mulattos furnished the principal menial labour force in Lima and the coastal lowlands. Though creoles greatly predominated among the 140,000 or so whites, fear of the Indians and mestizos made them hesitant to support the independence movement. Following the great convulsion of 1780, led by Tupuc Amarú, there had been further more localised outbreaks of Indian revolt. Tupac Amarú had declared an end to personal bondage, though slaves were rare in the Andean region – there were said to be 300 blacks in Cuzco some of whom joined Tupac Amarú. When the 'free Indians' of Lacamarca rose in rebellion in 1806 they attacked the landowners project to turn them into *mitayos* and *yanaconas* – the latter being the Inca term for slave. However, the landowners of Peru had no real prospect of turning Indian villagers into chattel slaves – their true aim was to subordinate them to periodic forced labour and to reduce all Indians to a uniform degree of dependence, cancelling out all concessions extended to particular communities in the course of past conflicts.[24]

With the aid of a Chilean fleet commanded by Lord Cochrane, San Martín established an expeditionary force on the southern coast of Peru in September 1820 and, joining forces with a contingent of Peruvian patriots, began a slow advance on Lima. A high proportion of the liberating army were men of colour. By February 1821 4,180 slaves belonging to royalists had been conscripted. However, San Martín made no general appeal to the 'lower orders' since, as he explained to the British commodore Bowles, there was a danger that these would obtain 'an undue preponderance' and manifest 'a revolutionary disposition dangerous in any country but more particularly in this . . . where the unenlightened portion of the community are so numerous (particularly the slaves and Indians) and at the same time so formidable'.[25]

San Martín's strategy was to use military pressure to induce the Peruvian oligarchy to desert the Spanish cause. The news of the successful *pronunciamento* at Cadiz in favour of a Liberal constitutional regime strengthened San Martín's hand in negotiating for the support of the Peruvian aristocracy. The Spanish military commanders, believing that the empire could only be saved by emergency measures, removed the duly appointed Viceroy, Pezuela, on the grounds that he was not acting decisively enough; they replaced him with one of their own number, General José de la Serna. Peru and Upper Peru were now the only sizeable territories controlled by Spain in South America and their defence was vital to the empire's prospects of survival. Amongst the measures taken by the new Viceroy was the conscription of 1,500 slaves to strengthen the depleted royalist garrison; the owners of the slaves were promised compensation while the slaves themselves were promised manumission at the end of six years' service.

Despite the promises given by La Serna, his action in conscripting slaves was disturbing to the *hacendados* of the region and was a factor in encouraging some of them to side with San Martín's expeditionary force. San Martín's forces entered Lima in July 1821 and several thousand citizens signed a declaration of independence for Peru a few days later. San Martín was declared Protector of the new state. In the following month the new authorities issued a decree establishing *libertad de vientres* and banning the slave trade. But they hesitated to offer manumission to all slaves prepared to fight against Spain. The restraint of San Martín and the revolutionary junta reflected the continuing importance they attached to winning the support of the Peruvian oligarchy. The junta was somewhat bolder in its declarations concerning the Indian tribute, announcing its abolition in August 1821; the Indian levy was a fiscal instrument whose suppression created a problem for the treasury rather than property-holders.[26]

The Spanish garrison successfully held out in Callao, Lima's port, and prevented the liberation army from consolidating their coastal bridgehead. San Martín's forces suffered illness and demoralisation. In November 1821 the revolutionary authorities offered freedom to the slaves of Spaniards who were willing to fight for the new nation, but not to similarly disposed slaves belonging to Patriots. Threatened with a royalist advance on Lima, the Republicans organised a slave militia; San Martín declared that twenty-five members of this force, chosen by lot, would be manumitted after payment of compensation to their owners. But despite such restraint the ragged conflict between Spanish and republican forces promoted the disintegration of the slave regime. Slaves were recruited on an *ad hoc* basis by commanders whose columns had been thinned by illness; and, of course, the disruption of war allowed slaves to escape.

In a number of the early Republics the quickly changing political conflict led to the successive enactment of laws or constitutions which contradicted one another. In none did the somersaults follow one another so swiftly as in Peru, at least so far as slavery was concerned. Threatened by royalist successes the conservative Peruvian leader the Marquis of Torre Tagle, a member of San Martín's administration and himself a large landowner, at last consented on April 11th 1822 to decree a general levy of slaves, taking one-fifth of those in the towns and one-tenth of those on rural estates. Elaborate procedures for verifying the fitness of the slave recruits, for compensating their masters and for conceding manumission after lengthy terms of service were drawn up. Two weeks later, on April 25th, the same official decreed a *Retracción de manumisiones*; the military situation had improved and doubtless the *hacendados* had made their opposition clear. A similar comedy was repeated the next year, with a sweeping manumission decree issued in January being revoked on March 1st. Nevertheless, more than three-quarters of the members of the liberation army were men of colour, many of them former slaves. The numbers of white *criollos* volunteering to liberate Peru was very disappointing. The free blacks, formed into a *Batallón de Civicos Pardos*, were more responsive. The Indian populations of the *altiplano* remained both geographically and politically beyond the range of the liberation movement. Free-lance *montoneros* infiltrated the Andean provinces from Argentina as well as the Peruvian coast; but the Indian communities were as likely to harass as to welcome these guerrillas, some of whom acted as predators rather than liberators. The Spanish eventually evacuated Callao but no progress was made against La Serna's main forces, which continued to hold the interior where the bulk of Peru's population lived.[27]

The cautious Peruvian strategy of liberation contrasted with the victories of Bolivar and Sucre in Colombia and Ecuador. Colombian forces occupied Quito, following Sucre's victory at Pichincha in May 1822. Bolivar enjoyed executive power in Ecuador and was able to enrol and manumit those slaves he deemed suitable for his army. San Martín sought to persuade Bolivar to assume leadership of the revolution in Peru at the celebrated conference of Guayaquil in July 1822; failing to do so he withdrew, leaving the way clear for the Northern Liberator. In March and April 1823 Bolivar assigned a large army, commanded by Sucre, to march to the assistance of the disintegrating forces of liberation in Peru. Bolivar himself arrived in Lima in September. By a decree of February 1824 the Peruvian Congress appointed Bolivar dictator.

After great efforts Bolivar and Sucre brought an army of nearly 8,000 men to the sierra; about half of them were *pardos* or blacks. La Serna was strongly entrenched with a larger Spanish force and many Indian auxiliaries, though somewhat distracted by the disaffection of an ultra-royalist faction. In December 1824 Sucre inflicted a crushing defeat on La Serna at the Battle of Ayacucho. This was the death-knell of Spain's South American empire. The quasi-independent royalist regime in Upper Peru was brought down in April 1825 and the remaining outposts of Spanish resistance surrendered within the year.

In the meantime the Republic of Chile had moved to suppress slavery, though not under the leadership of O'Higgins. Chile's first *Director Supremo* was forced to resign in 1823. He had committed the country's scant resources to the Peruvian conflict without achieving any decisive result. Indeed the manifest deterioration of the position of the liberation forces in Peru in 1822–3 greatly alarmed patriot opinion. O'Higgins was also opposed by members of the landed aristocracy who had been alienated by his suppression of titles and attempt to abolish *mayorazgo* (entail). The more liberal patriots were opposed to O'Higgins's dictatorial style and to his refusal to sanction the military manumission of slaves. However, the motley coalition of urban Liberals and provincial *caudillos* who ejected O'Higgins found difficulty in constructing a successor regime. A Constitutional Convention was held at which a call was made to emancipate all slaves; the chief author of this decree was a lawyer and veteran patriot leader, José Miguel Infante. The Chilean Emancipation Law, more radical than any adopted in North America, was unanimously endorsed by the Senate at a time when it was at loggerheads with the new *Director Supremo* or chief of state, General Ramón Freire. Doubtless the Senate, and the Liberal politicians who now controlled it, saw the slave question as one which would embarrass Freire and his Minister of Government, Mariano de Egaña, a Liberal who had always proclaimed abolitionist convictions. Freire and Egaña informed the Senate that they could not accept an emancipation decree that did not indemnify slave-owners for the loss of their property. But the Senate, aware of the strength of patriotic and popular opinion on which it could count, maintained that emancipation should be accompanied by no compensation. In July 1823 the new *Director Supremo* and his Government Minister gave way, though the latter issued 'regulations' which stipulated that slaves could only obtain their freedom by registering with the police, when they would have to prove that they had a job or were properly married. The office of the Supreme Director received two protests against the abolition of slavery: one from a group of respectable women complaining that the law would cause unhappiness and insubordination amongst domestic slaves; the other supposedly from 200 slaves arguing that they did not want to lose the protection and welfare afforded to them by their masters. However, these were the last attempts to defend slavery in Chile.

Both because of the small number of slaves affected and because of the lack of compensation, Chilean abolition might be compared to emancipation in Massachusetts; but the fact that it was openly legislated by the government, rather than smuggled in the back-door by judicial decision, gave it a more radical and clear-cut character. The

Chilean treasury was exhausted and in no position to fund compensation for the slave-owners. Expropriation of the latter was widely accepted both because many other proprietors had been taxed for the war effort and because Chile's few thousand slaves worked as domestics; unless they were conscripted into the armed forces – admittedly a probable fate for those of military age – they were likely to remain in the service of their masters who would suffer no real loss. Slavery lacked economic weight and slaveholding was a minor source of wealth even for most slaveholders. Nevertheless, Chilean emancipation was a striking patriotic gesture and facilitated recruitment to the army and navy of those who had been protected from conscription by their slave status.[28]

Some *de facto* slaveholding may have survived in Chile for a few years after 1823; certainly it survived for over two years in the Spanish-controlled parts of the national territory, notably the off-shore island of Chiloé, whose surrender completed the liberation of South America in January 1826. The republican commitment to abolition was to be reiterated in all basic documents over the next decade. Even the authoritarian and paternalist constitution proposed by Juan Egaña, son of the previous government Minister, in December 1823 confirmed that there could be no slaves in Chile. For a few years Chilean political life was dominated by struggles within the oligarchy. The diverse factions of Liberal *pipiolos* (novices), Conservative *pelucones* (bigwigs) and Liberal–Conservative *estanqueros* (state contractors) or *o'higginistas* were agreed in upholding both the formal freedom of all citizens and the real subordination of the mass of exploited peasantry. While the landed oligarchy was largely white the peasant *inquilinos* and *peones* were mostly coloured. But no faction supported the restoration of a formal caste system or the reinstitution of slavery. A mulatto officer who had distinguished himself at Maipú, José Romero, was promoted to the Captaincy of the *Batallón Cívico* in 1830 and was subsequently nominated to an honorary post with the Chamber of Deputies. The Liberal Constitution of 1828 and the Conservative Constitution of 1833 both reiterated that there were no slaves in Chile. The Liberal/patriotic interlude of 1823–9 had legislatively discredited and destroyed slaveholding; with the succeeding Conservative regime the country's compact size permitted the creation of a government of greater competence, integration and authority than was to be found in the other succession states of South America. The suppression of slavery became a fact as well as a law. The decree of 1823 and its subsequent reaffirmations made Chile the first properly constituted Spanish American Republic to abolish slavery outright.[29]

The Chilean example encouraged Bolivar to capitalise on his

triumphs by proposing new anti-slavery measures in neighboroughing Peru and Bolivia. The Liberator's objective was to establish authoritative government not to embark on some universal crusade against slavery; indeed prior to the Congress of Panama in 1826 Bolivar made it quite clear that consolidation in South America would take priority over attempts to spread the revolution to Spain's slave colonies in the Caribbean.[30]

The Post-Independence Settlement in South America

The victories of Bolivar and Sucre gave them enormous prestige and appeared to make them the arbiters of the nations they had liberated. Bolivar recommended a constitution for Peru and laws for Bolivia that would inaugurate a programme of extensive slave manumission. He saw the survival of slavery as a derogation of proper sovereignty, a mark of primitiveness and parochialism. Abolitionist measures would help to assert a new American civic ideal based on the rejection of caste distinctions and odious discriminations. While he did not favour immediate, outright emancipation, he did urge the new states to fund manumission boards which would arrange for the systematic freeing of slaves. In the aftermath of war there were still some thousands of slaves in Peru and a general shortage of labour made *hacendados* very unwilling to lose those that remained to them. Bolivar proposed that the Peruvian Constitution of 1826 should include a clause committing the state to the emancipation of the slaves; this was removed by the delegates on the grounds that it would be inimical to agricultural recovery in coastal Peru. The new Peruvian government also restored the tribute levied from the Indian communities, since the government suffered a chronic lack of funds. The recalcitrance of the Peruvian proprietors was born of a failing rather than thriving plantation agriculture.[31]

An attempt was made to restore slave discipline in the Peruvian plantation zone in 1825, with new controls over slave movements and prohibitions against allowing slaves access to arms. But even the influential coastal *hacendados* knew that they could not return to slavery those who had fought in the liberation armies. The Peruvian plantations were left with slave crews containing disproportionate numbers of women, children and old people. The slave population overall had dropped to perhaps a half its former size, if the *libertos* owing labour to their mothers' owners are included. The purchase tax on slaves was eliminated in 1825 and it is possible that some may have been brought to the country, perhaps from Brazil, despite the previous bans. However, the plantation economy of the coastal zone did not prosper; it lacked either a well-balanced or skilled work-force, or a prosperous internal market, while freight charges to Europe were exorbitant. The dismal fate of O'Higgins, the former dictator of Chile who had been given a Peruvian sugar plantation by San Martín, illustrates some of the problems. In an attempt to modernise his estate he bought an English steam-engine to grind the cane; the slaves and *libertos* were housed in barracks named after his victories or fellow Liberators. But try as he might O'Higgins failed to restore the estate to viability and was obliged to devote more land to subsistence cultivation. He lacked the sort of skilled workers hired or trained by the Cuban planters and his work-force was desultory and disorderly. When invited to review the passing-out parade of the Peruvian military academy in 1828, O'Higgins had to decline since his old uniform was in tatters and he could not afford a new one.[32]

With several disappointing experiences behind him Bolivar sought to establish in the new Republic of Bolivia a more effective and imposing system of government. Strong government powers, conferred on a President-for-life, were to be balanced by guarantees for the liberty of the individual, including a provision which outlawed slavery. In Bolivar's view the state should be the embodiment of a 'moral power' and not the plaything either of special interests or of the populace. The General Assembly of the new state voted to give Bolivar a million dollars in recognition of his services. He would only accept the money on condition that it was used to purchase the freedom of 1,000 slaves. The money was never paid. Bolivar's draft of the constitution declared that 'all those who until now have been slaves are Bolivian citizens; and they are thereby freed by the publication of this constitution; a special law shall determine the amount to be paid as indemnity to their former owners'. Bolivar's text was amended by the delegates to read that the slaves were now citizens 'but they cannot abandon the house of their former masters except in the form which a special law shall determine'.[33] There were very few slaves in Bolivia – they were thought to number 4,700 – but those there were owned by the white creoles who dominated the new state. The latter were prepared to envisage an end to slavery as a juridical status but only if their former chattels remained servile dependants. Unlike Chile in 1823 there was now no military pressure for manumission or concessions to a more expansive patriotism; moreover some of the Bolivian slaves were concentrated on estates near La Paz, giving slavery somewhat greater economic weight. But perhaps the decisive reason for the recalcitrance of the Bolivian delegates was simply that they had tired of Colombian tutelage, with its large ambitions and concern for abstract issues. Bolivar and Sucre, who could only count on their own increasingly unpopular Colombian or Venezuelan troops, had no choice but to give way to the Bolivian oligarchy. When Sucre withdrew from La Paz in 1828 the question of slavery in Bolivia had not been clearly resolved; in 1831 and on later occasions slavery was declared at an end. But the real situation of the former slaves remains unclear, since Bolivia's political classes, though possessed of a definite sense of national identity, lacked the will or capacity to sustain a proper government or state despite the Liberator's hopes.

In the last years of his life Bolivar grandiosely planned to recover from the setbacks he had encountered by leading a Union of the Andes, encompassing Venezuela, Colombia, Ecuador, Peru and Bolivia. But by 1830 his plan was in ruins and he was himself obliged to step down as President of Colombia; he died in December of that year. The Liberator had returned to Gran Colombia in 1826 in the hope of bringing order and purpose to this disunited Republic. The Venezuelans resented the government in Bogotá, which had been entrusted to Santander, the executive Vice-President. Colombia itself resembled a congerie of mini-republics, or rather an incongruous juxtaposition of latifundist fiefdoms and rural communes of former slaves and Indians hostile to republican authority. The Bogotá authorities had raised large loans in Europe which had been eaten up by salaries or frittered away in half-complete development projects. Attempts to introduce regular steam services along the River Magdalena proved abortive.

The Liberator was angered to discover that only 300 slaves had been manumitted by the boards established for that purpose in 1821. In a decree of 1827 he attempted to strengthen the *Juntas de Manumisión* and ordered that their funds should be spent within one year on manumissions, starting with the oldest and most deserving slaves. The failure of the juntas was rooted in the fact that they were beholden to the local possessing classes who had no interest in liquidating slave property. In unscrupulous hands the Manumission Boards could devise ways of prolonging the servitude of the *manumisos* by alleging that they would otherwise become vagabonds. The reform of the Manumission Boards obliged them to levy the inheritance tax more systematically and to render a proper accounting to the central government. However, Bolivar was not prepared for a confrontation with the slave-owning *hacendados*. Bolivar's aim was to restore the unity and integrity of Gran Colombia by accommodating prevailing interests and concentrating on the main enemy – Santander's Liberalism, with its legalistic attachment to the federal principles of the 1821 constitution and policy of saddling Colombia with expensive foreign loans and allowing monied interests a free rein. Bolivar also opposed the localism of the landed proprietors and of the military *caudillos* thrown up by the liberation struggle, but he saw Santander's liberalism as the greater threat. Bolivar was painfully aware that the new race of *caudillos* were interested in the state as a source of land titles and salaries rather than *poder moral*. But he believed he could make use of his old ties to the military to defeat the prostitution of the state to financial interests and deploy his prestige to discipline localistic landowers.[34]

In a fateful move Bolivar endorsed the claim of Páez to be the military and political chief of Venezuela; the veteran *llanero* now owned huge estates, including plantations worked in part by slave labour. Bolivar hoped that Páez would help him to check Santander. The aftermath of the independence struggle had left several competing leadership factions and continuing struggles over the precise social content of the new order. Blacks and *pardos* were involved in several attempted revolts in the years 1824–8, initially against Santander, subsequently against Bolivar. Soldiers who had been discharged without pay were particularly restless, while others could not see why white *letrados* should enjoy the lion's share of public posts. Páez, as an uneducated mestizo, could appeal demagogically to such resentments despite being one of the largest latifundists in Venezuela. As a result of republican legislation the collective property of Indian communities had been made alienable, thus exposing them to the risk of dispossession; mestizo peasants had little possibility of buying land which was sold in large lots or conferred on military or political leaders. A commitment to the market and private property inclined Liberals like Santander to endorse such developments. Santander's Liberals defended the 1821 Manumission Law both on principle and in the hope that it would release labour on to the market. Bolivar could see no solution to Colombia's social problems except the construction of a custodial political monopoly based on virtuous veterans of the liberation struggle. The assassination of Sucre in 1830 on a visit to the south-east was a heavy blow to him.

Bolivar's reintegration into the Bogotá regime made him the target of the revolt of Admiral Padilla, a *pardo* or *zambo* corsair who rallied to the Liberal opposition and received backing from the people of Cartagena and the coast, including many people of colour. Like Piar before him Padilla was executed. Bolivar had sided with Páez, and crushed Padilla, largely because the former was Santander's opponent, the latter his ally. Despite Padilla's colour and vaunted Liberalism it is unclear that, even if successful, he would have been either more willing or more able to promote slave emancipation than Bolivar.[35]

Páez proclaimed the Venezuelan Republic in 1830; by the time of Bolivar's death in December Gran Colombia was no more. The new state modified the Manumission Law; *libertad de vientre* remained, but the *libertos'* period of obligatory service was extended from eighteen to twenty-one years and they were obliged to prove subsequent gainful employment to the Manumission Boards. On the other hand the new government confirmed Bolivar's wartime decrees freeing all the slaves in the provinces of Apure and Guayana; to have done otherwise would have provoked a rebellion amongst the *llaneros* of these provinces.[36]

The population of slaves and *libertos* was surprisingly large. Despite the devastation of war and civil war, despite slave uprisings and escapes, despite royalist support for *insurrección de otra especie* and republican abolitionism, slavery remained quite widespread in the new state. The census of 1834 revealed that Venezuela contained just under 36,000 slaves and *libertos* (children of slaves still obligated to serve their mother's master), with Caracas accounting for 20,600 of this total.[37] At the outbreak of the independence struggle there had been over 80,000 slaves. Venezuela's population had suffered greatly during the fighting, dropping by as much as a third between 1811 and 1821. Thus the decline in the number of slaves was somewhat heavier than that of the population as a whole, but the residual slave population still sizeable. The plantation economy had been hit by the war and Venezuela's exports of cacao also fell by a half; the prices of all plantation products dropped by a half or more as Brazil, Cuba and the United States expanded their output. The survival of slavery did not correspond to a particularly vigorous plantation sector. The plantations which had employed slaves – cacao groves and sugar estates – became of greatly reduced importance. In the 1820s and 1830s coffee replaced cacao as Venezuela's most important export crop; the coffee estates were worked predominantly by wage labourers or tied peasants, with only a few slaves.[38]

The persistence of slavery in Venezuela can be explained in a number of ways. The *conucos* given to the slaves encouraged them not to leave the plantation/hacienda; during the war slaves had sometimes extracted further concessions from their masters. Military manumission had only been offered to adult male slaves of military age; though some relatives might also have gained freedom, slave women and children in principle remained in servitude. Moreover slaves who distrusted the Patriots, or who saw no advantage in exchanging a military for a civilian master, tried to evade military manumission. The survival of slavery in Venezuela, as in some other parts of South America, will have reflected the very insecure conditions that prevailed during and after the independence struggle. With rival armed columns roaming the country, not to speak of simple bandits, the slave could easily find the master's household a place of refuge that it would be unwise to forsake, or to which it would be wise to return. The pressure of political instability was compounded by that of economic insecurity. Independence exposed Venezuela and other parts of the South America to the withering blast of economic competition at a time of recession in many parts of the Atlantic world. The growth of the coffee economy was neither strong enough nor secure enough to compensate for this. The conditions of life for the mass of poorer Venezuelans, even if free, were undoubtedly very precarious. The police were urged to round up all vagabonds and the courts were empowered to condemn them to penal labour. The hoary special pleading of the slave-owner that he furnished the slave with protection and welfare could have had some substance in the immediate post-independence period in Spanish America.[39]

However, the strongest reason for the survival of slavery was probably economic – the value of slaves not as labourers but as property and as collateral. The Manumission Boards posted slave prices which then acted as a guaranteed minimum. As late as the early 1850s, when there were only 12,000 slaves left in Venezuela, their capital value was still greater than that of the year's coffee crop.[40] Páez, who dominated Venezuelan politics for most of the period 1830–48, was to be closely associated with the interests of latifundists and large merchants; the latter advanced credit to slave-owners against the value of their slave property and were consequently disposed to defend slavery.

For a similar mixture of reasons slavery survived in Colombia, though no challenge was made to the principle of the Manumission Law of 1821. Endemic conflict between Liberals and Conservatives created conditions in which government and law lacked authority and effectivity; but such conflict did not favour the growth of large-scale slaveholding. In mid-century there were still claimed to be 20,000 slaves and *libertos* in Colombia, though this figure may have been inflated. In this Republic, as elsewhere in Spanish South America, *libertos* were often pressured to enlist in the army to ensure their freedom.[41] Military service was widely unpopular because of poor pay and arbitrary discipline. The recruitment of *libertos* suited the mass of citizens by reducing their own liability to military service; it also suited the new rulers, since *libertos* were generally more reliable than Indian recruits, with their ties to the major exploited community. However, it did seem that, with whatever delays, slavery was on the way out. The position of the *liberto* was unenviable, but it was not the same as that of a chattel slave. Even a 'free womb' law that was tampered with, or half-ignored, deprived slave-owners of the positive legal framework that they required. The fact that Manumission Boards set slave prices and maintained a register did promise an eventual end to outright slavery, as it became impossible to claim that some fit young man or woman was really forty years old.

Ecuador rejected Gran Colombia in April 1830, its dominant classes believing that Bogotá's free trade and *laissez-faire* policies were inimical to their commercial and agricultural interests. The new Republic was contested by the Liberals of Guayaquil but temporarily welcomed by the proprietors of the Cauca, formerly part of New Granada; some of the latter were attracted by the possibility that the new Republic would be more indulgent to slaveholders. But in 1832 Ecuador was forced to return the Cauca to Colombia. The adhesion of Guayaquil, with its *pardo* and free black population, and a compact between the Liberal and Conservative factions led to agreement that the classic Manumission Law was still in force. The military administration of Sucre and Bolivar had left few slaves and *libertos* in Ecuador, though some were still to be found in the interior.[42]

The Buenos Aires constitution of 1819, a document reflecting *porteño* interests, stated that there were no slaves in the United Provinces of the River Plate. When Buenos Aires' claims were challenged by the Federalists of the interior both sides recruited slaves to their armies. During the years 1821–4 the pioneer patriot Rivadavia regained influence and sought to impose a doctrinaire Liberalism and utilitarianism on those parts of the country controlled by the government in Buenos Aires. Rivadavia's ambitious plans for the United Provinces, inspired by his correspondence with Bentham, included the introduction of modern industry, the eradication of slavery, a public educational system and the elaboration of a stringent new labour code, fiercely penalising laziness and vagabondage. These schemes proved hopelessly to over-estimate the administrative and financial resources at the disposal of the government and Rivadavia was forced out. In practice Argentinian manumission did not go beyond the decree of 1813; it meant that female slaves and their children were to be found as domestics in the house of their owners; male *libertos* reaching the age of eighteen were conscripted to the army and often did not become free citizens until they finished lengthy service in it. In 1826 a corsair landed in Patagonia with a hundred slaves; these were declared to be *libertos* simply by virtue of having landed on the soil of the United Provinces – and were then promptly impressed into the army.[43]

In the years 1825–8 the United Provinces had need of soldiers because of its efforts to free the *banda oriental* from Brazilian occupation. The war against the Brazilian Imperialists led to the establishment of Uruguay in 1830, a Republic in which there were very few slaves, though still a sizeable population of *pardos* and blacks; the early anti-slavery of Artigas and military manumission during the later liberation struggle help to explain this, though doubtless some slave-owners sold their slaves to Brazilians while they could. When the Uruguayan constitution of 1830 declared slavery at an end, it may have exaggerated but only a little; the constitution was otherwise a document of moderate liberalism conferring political rights only on property-holders. The British favoured the independence of Uruguay, both because it opened its markets to British merchants and because it banned the slave trade. Uruguay's independence was menaced by both Argentina and Brazil; this led some Uruguayan leaders to appeal for British and French support. The country was convenient both to Brazilian slave smugglers and as a place of refuge for Brazilian slaves fleeing their masters. When parts of the country were occupied by Argentina some slaves were reintroduced. In 1842 and again in 1846 the Uruguayan government decreed that there could be no slavery in the country; on the first occasion there were said to be 300 slaves on Uruguayan soil. The Brazilian government continued to demand the return of escaping slaves and sometimes Brazilian masters would send slave-catching teams into Uruguay to recover them.[44]

In the mid-1820s there were still some 6,000 slaves left in Buenos Aires. The shortage of labour in the whole region of the Rio de la Plata encouraged slaveholders to retain as many slaves as they could. A certain amount of slave trading as well as slaveholding took place in Argentina during the 1820s. It was tolerated for a while by the truculent Federalist *caudillo* Juan Manuel de Rosas, who ruled Buenos Aires from 1829. Proximity to Brazil and conflicts with the Unitarians in Uruguay gave opportunities to the Brazilian slave-traders. But Rosas, whose dictatorship was to last until 1852, did not renounce the Manumission Laws. Moreover, he made a point of cultivating a following amongst the urban blacks, whose fraternities and festivals he patronised. The numbers of slaves and *libertos* steadily declined as a consequence of military manumission and the working out of the 1813 law. Rosas saw his mission as being to re-establish order, discipline and respect for the landed proprietors. He was both ruthless and effective in pursuing this goal. Slaveholding was eventually limited by the consequent check to rampant localism and preparedness to enforce legal contracts. Slave-holders were at least obliged to respect the letter, if not the spirit, of the Manumission Laws; in Mendoza a surprisingly large number of the few remaining slaves in 1853 were listed as being forty years old, so that they just escaped being *libertos*.[45]

Slavery probably survived more vigorously than elsewhere in the Spanish River Plate region in Paraguay, within the isolationist and patriarchal regime of the dictator José Gaspar Rodríguez de Francia.

Artigas found refuge in Paraguay and land was made available to his ex-slave soldiers. But the Paraguayan leader was a foe not of slavery but of those who claimed to control the River Plate. He responded to the blockade of Paraguay with a complete embargo on trade with the riverine Spanish American states. In this way he protected Paraguay's traditional economy, with its haciendas and *obrajes*, from foreign competition and the disruptive effects of free trade. By the 1830s there were some 25,000 slaves in Paraguay, as many or more as there had been in the last days of Spanish rule. Thousands of these slaves worked in state-owned workshops and estates set up either because *émigrés* had abandoned them or because they filled a national need. However, this was not the intensive slavery of the Caribbean plantations. The Hispanic slave codes, limiting hours of work and strokes of the lash or stipulating a minimum diet, may have been more rigorously enforced in independent Paraguay than they had ever been in the Spanish American empire. Both the medieval *Siete Partidas* and the Code of 1789 were incorporated into Paraguayan law. The commercial isolation of the Republic meant that the remorseless pressure of production for an unquenchable market was replaced by the more fitful pressure of production for local needs. On the death of Francia in 1840 his own slaves were freed. In 1842 the independence of Paraguay was reaffirmed, the suppression of the slave trade reiterated and a law of the 'free womb' adopted. The only country with which Francia's Paraguay had normal trading relationships had been Brazil; the cautious abolitionist decree of 1842 was partly designed to remove the country from the cross-fire between the participants and antagonists of the Brazilian slave trade.[46]

With Paraguay's acceptance of the 'free womb' all of Spanish America had committed itself to an eventual rejection of chattel slavery; a more radical conclusion had already been reached in Mexico.

Mexico and Central America

Mexico achieved independence from Spain not as the result of a protracted but ultimately victorious struggle, as in most parts of South America, but rather through the exhaustion of the imperial power and the growing self-confidence of a largely counter-revolutionary creole elite. The only genuine struggle for independence in Mexico, that led by Hidalgo and Morelos in 1810–15, was defeated, though in ways which weakened both Spanish rule and slavery.

In Mexico the established colonial order was already in disarray prior to Napoleon's invasion. The government in Madrid had attempted to sequester the rich holdings of the Church to help finance war against Britain, but in so doing had menaced the colony's entire system of credit. The disturbances in the Peninsula encouraged the Viceroy to express sympathy with the creole proprietors whose mortgages had been called in by the Church. The autonomist leanings of the Viceroy provoked the *Peninsulares* to organise his removal; this coup was led by the Spanish owner of a sugar plantation in central Mexico. The seizure of power by the ultra-Spanish faction provoked a middle-class creole conspiracy against Spanish rule, which in turn detonated a popular uprising in the Bajío, a region of dynamic commercial agriculture and manufacture adjacent to the mining zone north-west of Mexico City.

The conspirators had realised that they needed to mobilise Indian support and had turned to Miguel Hidalgo, a rural priest who spoke Indian languages and was himself perhaps of mixed blood. Few of the labourers and small proprietors of the Bajío were incorporated in traditional Indian communities; the mining boom and its associated prosperity had been interrupted by international uncertainties, conflicts over sequestration and the struggles between rival factions. Food prices had risen sharply; large latifundists and merchants, many of them Spaniards, made a killing. Urging that the *castas* and Indians were victims of fraud, monopoly and extortion, Hidalgo attacked Spanish property and power, soon attracting a ragged armed force 80,000 strong, whose roaming bands would destroy mining buildings and equipment. Guanajuato was sacked in September 1810 and Guadalajara seized shortly thereafter. A movement that invoked the protection of the Virgin of Guadaloupe, and that claimed to be acting as the custodian of Mexico while its monarch was in captivity, mobilised *campesinos* and miners against wealthy *Peninsulares*, generally sparing the lives of rich creoles but not their property. Hidalgo proclaimed the end of the Indian communal tribute system and the suppression of all types of personal bondage. In December 1810 Hidalgo declared from the Palace of Government in Guadalajara that slavery was ended in Mexico. No more than a handful of slaves are likely to have directly benefited from this proclamation, but the rich did own some slaves, while significant numbers of the population of the region would have been of partly African descent; in 1792 the mines of Guanajato recorded a work-force of 3,176 whites, 2,389 mestizos (part Indian) and 2,469 mulattos (part African).[47] While some miners rallied to Hidalgo he also received support from the predominantly Indian *campesinos*.

In January 1811 Hidalgo's ill-organised forces were defeated outside Mexico City by Spanish regulars and creole militia; the radicalism of Hidalgo's movement had rallied most white creoles behind the Spanish administration and had prompted the mine-owners to create a permanent military force of their own. The Liberals in Cadiz made an effort to accommodate creole reformism by giving Mexico a score of representatives in the Cortes; though some creoles demanded representation based on Mexico's total population. In March 1811 Hidalgo himself was captured and executed. But this was not the end of the uprising. Small guerrilla groups continued the struggle for independence and liberty. José Maria Morelos, another rural priest of mixed descent, assumed leadership of the rebellion and created a small but effective and disciplined armed force. Morelos argued: 'When kings are absent, sovereignty resides solely in the nation; and every nation is free and entitled to form the type of government which it pleases, and not to remain the slave of another.'[48] Morelos declared that all should be equal and that henceforth no distinction should be made between whites, Indians and *castas*. Blacks and mulattos enlisted in his column, some of them former slaves. A radical group amongst his followers, the *Guadalupes*, advocated the distribution of land to the cultivators and the creation of collectively owned agencies for buying and selling agricultural produce. Morelos seems to have endorsed these proposals, at least as a war measure, in the *medidas politicas*. At the Congress of Chilpancingo in 1813 Morelos sponsored a formal Declaration of Independence and the issuing of a decree which confirmed the suppression of slavery in the new nation. Doubtless because of the small number of slaves in Mexico Morelos had little difficulty persuading other leaders of the revolt to accept abolition; in contrast his plans for breaking up landed estates were controversial, even within the ranks of his own movement. In 1815 Morelos was captured and executed by Spanish forces. By 1816 the revolt was extinguished everywhere but in the south, where a small column of independence fighters led by Vicente Guerrero, a follower of Morelos, still held out.

Fearful of the popular rebellion the great majority of whites and of the propertied, whether creole or Spanish, had united behind the imperial power. By so doing the creole militia and military had won some influence within the system of government. The *Cabildo* of Mexico City espoused a moderate autonomism from the beginning of the imperial crisis. A key member of the *Cabildo*, José Miguel Guridi y Alcocer, had represented Mexico in the Cortes at Cadiz in 1811; he had there unsuccessfully urged colonial self-government, the distribution of unoccupied land and the abolition of slavery. He had argued that unless serious reforms were adopted the popular revolt would prevail. Guridi returned to become treasurer of the *Cabildo* of Mexico City and one of those waiting for an occasion to reopen the question of institutional reforms.[49]

The 1820 revolt in Spain had a deeply disruptive effect on the Spanish regime in Mexico. Control of the press was lifted and elections were held for deputies to the Cortes. The stream of decrees and pronouncements which issued from the Liberals in the Cortes alarmed landowners and the Church without offering any substantive concession to creole autonomism. In this confused situation the royalist commander in southern Mexico, a first-generation creole named Agustín Itúrbide, issued the *Plan de Iguala*, establishing an autonomous Mexican monarchy: 'All inhabitants of New Spain, without any distinction between Europeans, Africans and Indians, are citizens of this monarchy, with access to all positions according to their merits and virtues.'[50] Itúrbide enlisted the support of the Church, and his record as a soldier during the insurgency of Morelos earned him the respect of all conservative interests. However, the official armistice had allowed him to enter negotiations with Vicente Guerrero, who supported the *Plan de Iguala*, calculating that it would at least destroy Spanish rule. Itúrbide also gained the support of the Liberals in Mexico City; Guridi y Alcocer was appointed to the sovereign council of the new monarchy. Many of the Spanish royalist troops went over to Itúrbide, while even the representative of the regime in Madrid, a liberal general whose action was subsequently disavowed, signed a treaty recognising Mexican self-determination. In September 1821 Mexican independence was declared, with Itúrbide as President of the Regency Council while a suitable monarch was found. A Commission on Slavery had been established by the sovereign council; it reported that there were just under 3,000 slaves left in Mexico and that they were employed mainly in the ports, notably Vera Cruz. On October 13th 1821, two weeks after the Declaration of Independence, the sovereign council issued a decree banning the import of slaves and declaring the freedom of all those born on Mexican soil. This decree sounded abolitionist, though it left Africans in slavery. Extra pressure to endorse anti-slavery may have been provided by the military situation; the fort of San Juan de Ulúa, just outside Vera Cruz, where there were many free blacks as well as slaves, was one of the few places still in the hands of troops loyal to Spain.[51]

After defeating a Bourbon monarchist faction, Itúrbide declared himself Emperor Agustín I in May 1822. His supposed commitment to abolition did not prevent him from plotting, albeit unsuccessfully, to add to his dominions Cuba, with its rich slave plantations. However, Iturbide was forced out by Federal Republicans in March 1823. While the Republic reaffirmed the suppression of the slave trade, the exact status of slaves or former slaves under the terms of the 1824 constitution devolved upon the constituent states of the Federation. In a number of states the movement of Hidalgo and Morelos had popularised radical social programmes which now reappeared; these included state purchasing agencies and the abolition of slavery. Between 1825 and 1827 a number of states suppressed slavery outright until there was enough support for a Federal measure. In 1829 Vicente Guerrero was able to mark his brief occupancy of the Presidential Palace by decreeing the suppression of slavery throughout Mexican territory.[52]

Mexican emancipation directly affected only a few thousand slaves. In some ways it may be compared to the suppression of slavery in Chile at about the same time. But it encouraged the enemies of slavery elsewhere and angered the slave-owners, or would-be slave-owners, of the Mexican state of Texas – these being mainly North American interlopers who were moved to set up their own Republic of Texas (1836) in which slavery was again legalised. In contrast to the early Chilean Republic, Mexico in the 1830s was a huge, sprawling and diverse state some parts of which were effectively beyond the reach of the writ of the Federal government. Forms of personal bondage may have survived in the Yucatan or in the wilder reaches of California. But, as the reaction of the Texan slaveholders suggests, the Mexican government at least had an authority worth challenging; silver output had dropped off considerably but it still gave Mexico greater resources than the other Spanish American states.

The creole oligarchy of Central America avoided any major confrontation until 1821–2 when it declared the adhesion of the Captaincy General of Guatemala to the Mexican Empire. In so doing it also adopted, at least formally, the abolitionist decree of October 1821. With the fall of Itúrbide the United Provinces of Central America declared their independence from Mexico. At a meeting of the Constituent Assembly held in 1824 José Simeón Cañas y Villacorta, a deputy from El Salvador, pleaded that without further delay it should be made clear that 'our enslaved brothers should be declared free citizens'.[53] The measure actually adopted decreed that slaves could no longer be born in Central America and established a fund to promote slave manumission. Over the next two decades the United Provinces broke up into the separate states of Guatemala, Nicaragua, Honduras, El Salvador and Costa Rica. None of the successor states sought to challenge the abolitionist provisions of 1824 and the subsequent development of a modest cash crop sector in agriculture did not depend on slave labour.

The struggle for independence in Spanish America had engaged extraordinary energies. Slaves and former slaves had comprised between a quarter and a half of those who had risked their lives against the

Spaniards. The liberty and equality of the citizen had been proclaimed in countless manifestos and constitutions; manumission and the 'free womb' had been enshrined in many laws. A few mestizos like Páez or Vicente Guerrero could now hold the highest positions but the social pyramid continued to be light-skinned at the top, dark-skinned at the bottom. Slavery had been lamed and the formal caste system largely dismantled. The subjugation of Indian and mestizo peasants survived virtually unscathed; indeed *laissez-faire* principles left some more exposed to dispossession and exploitation than before.

Slavery was a doomed institution and yet it stubbornly lingered on in a number of the new Republics. It had been entirely suppressed only in Mexico and Chile, where the slaves comprised 1 per cent or less of the population. It had shrivelled to insignificance in Bolivia and Central America, where there had likewise been very few slaves to start with and where the main 'social question' related to large Indian communities. The successor states of Gran Colombia retained sizeable slave populations as did parts of the River Plate region. On the one hand, slavery was part of the traditional Hispanic American order and perfectly congruent with the continuation of social relations of direct personal dependence. On the other, new social relations, encouraged by greater involvement with Atlantic markets, demanded the utmost respect for private property. Even though slaveholdings in the new Republics were only a third or a quarter as large as they had been in 1810, in some cases much less, it would still require a substantial capital sum to buy out their proprietors.

The new governments, desperately short of cash as they were, saw no possibility of funding a compensated programme of slave emancipation. Most of the new states borrowed in the early years from foreign banks and found it impossible to maintain interest payments or the value of their public bonds – hence the latter could not be offered in compensation. The British government encouraged the new Republics to commit themselves to a ban on slave imports, but it also urged them to adopt free trade and low tariffs. British influence, favouring priority to paying off foreign loans, itself helped to deprive Spanish American governments of the resources they would have needed to finance the sort of emancipation acceptable to Britain.

The setting up of Manumission Boards prepared to buy the freedom of slaves led to a most paradoxical and unexpected result in the successor states of Gran Colombia. Slaves became one of the best possible forms of collateral, since they were backed by a guaranteed reserved price. The Manumission Boards thus helped to sustain a pyramid of credit in countries where financial institutions were notoriously unstable and public bonds of doubtful value.

The compromise measure of *libertad de vientre* had been adopted in in Chile in 1811, in the Río de la Plata in 1813, in Gran Colombia and Peru in 1821 because it respected both patrimonial authority and private property. It freed the unborn and conferred only a conditional freedom on the *libertos*, who could be pressured to perform further service for their master or the state. Its effects had been somewhat anticipated by military manumission, though many freed in this way will have perished in the wars.

In Spanish America as elsewhere a racial caste spirit survived even more tenaciously than the residual black slavery. The old caste system had in its own way regulated racial competition and conflict. It had usually combined small privileges as well as large disabilities. The new system of racial relations would take time to consolidate itself. The greater intrusion of market relations entailed novel, and sometimes virulent, antagonisms which could cluster around colour and inherited ethnic identifications. In Venezuela and Colombia *pardos* had acquired formal equality and some held municipal office or commands in the army. In the Spanish American Republics the free black or mulatto enjoyed more rights and a somewhat better position in society than did the free Negro in the Northern United States, a relevant but not demanding standard of comparison.

Beyond the compromise abolitionism usually implemented the Spanish American liberation struggle had also thrown up a more radical anti-slavery current, notably in the movements led by Hidalgo and Artigas, but their impact had been reduced by defeat. Significantly these movements had been prepared, at the limit, to expropriate landowners as well as slave-owners; in the parlance of the epoch they were 'agrarians', willing to challenge large-scale private property in all its forms. Radical anti-slavery currents had not gained the upper hand, nor had blacks and *pardos* themselves possessed the social weight to destroy slavery outright. But they had inflected the course of the liberation struggle to which they contributed so much and persuaded a number of the Patriots and Liberators, including Bolivar in his better moments, to satisfy some of their demands.

In 1810 Spanish American slavery had been a secondary, perhaps declining, force. However, the mainland did contain nearly quarter of a million slaves and they constituted a major component of the labour force in the vicinity of Caracas and Lima, in some of the valleys of New Granada and such provinces as Córdoba in Río de la Plata. But for the anti-slavery consequences of the liberation struggle these elements of a slave system could have been stimulated and redeployed, much as happened to slavery in Virginia in the period after 1815. Thus coffee cultivation developed apace in the hills bordering the Caribbean in the

1820s and 1830s – and largely because of the advances of anti-slavery this did not take place on the basis of slave labour. In 1810 the enclaves of slave labour in mainland Spanish America had been suspended within a wider economy of commodity-producing haciendas, some frustrated by imperial regulation, others protected by it. With independence commercial agriculture could develop along new paths. The pre-independence arrangements between masters and slaves were often already in transition, partly in response to the pressure of slave resistance and revolt. Following independence *hacendados* in the commercially dynamic sector found they had to pay wages or grant the usufruct of land to a semi-autonomous peasant if they wished to undertake systematic cultivation. Slavery had become more of a residual and decaying status than an element in a mode of production; slaves survived as retainers of the *hacendados* in the declining cacao sector, but even here their cultivation rights made them seem more like *peones*. Life was still hard for peasants and labourers, but the ferocious discipline maintained by the *mayorales* of the *grandes cacaos* had disintegrated.

Around the year 1830 the new states of Spanish America, with the obscure exception of Paraguay, possessed more advanced anti-slavery legislation than any of the remaining European colonies in the New World. Indeed British and French abolitionism were to be encouraged by reports from independent Spanish America. Unlike the United States, the South American Republics had put slavery on the road to extinction throughout their national territory. Whatever the ultimate fate of the slaves left in Spanish America there was no question – barring foreign intervention or some dramatic domestic counter-revolution – of a new slave system arising in these lands, as manifestly was happening in the cotton states of North America. In this important sense Spanish American independence marked a major advance over North American independence.

Notes

1. For information on the slave populations of the Spanish American provinces see, for New Granada, Chile, Buenos Aires and Puerto Rico, Hebe Clementi, *La abolición de la esclavitud en América Latina*, Buenos Aires 1974, pp. 45, 63–4, 89, 93–4, 188; for Cuba, Fernando Ortiz, *Los negros esclavos*, Havana 1914, p. 23; for Peru, Núria Sales de Bohigas, *Sobre esclavos, reclutas y mercaderes de quintos*, Barcelona 1974, p. 105; for Venezuela, Miguel Acosta Saignes, *Vida de los negros esclavos en Venezuela*, Havana 1978, p. 164, and Federico Brito Figueroa, *Historia económica y social de Venezuela*, 2 vols, I, Caracas 1966, p. 160; for Bolivia, R.A. Humphreys, ed., *British Consular Reports on the Trade and Politics of Latin America*, London 1940, p. 208; for Ecuador, Enrique Ayala, *Lucha política y origen de los partidos en Ecuador*, Quito 1982, p. 39; for Mexico, Hugh Hamill, *The Hidalgo Revolt*, Gainesville, Florida 1966, p. 195.

2. Jorge Domínguez, *Insurrection or Loyalty; The Breakdown of the Spanish American Empire*, Cambridge, Mass. 1980, p. 79.

3. The peculiarities of Venezuela plantation slavery in the late colonial epoch are examined in Gastón Carvallo and Josefina Ríos de Hernández, 'Notas para el Estudio del Binomio Plantación–Conuco en la Hacienda Agrícola Venezolana', in *Agricultura y sociedad: tres ensayos historicos*, Equipo Sociohistorico, Centro de Estudios del Desarrollo, Universidad Central de Venezuela, Caracas, June 1979, pp. 4–14, 23–35.

4. James Lockhart and Stuart B. Schwartz, *Early Latin America: History of Colonial Spanish America and Brazil*, Cambridge 1983, pp. 316–20, 338.

5. José Luciano Franco, 'La Conspiración de Aponte, 1812', *Ensayos históricos*, Havana 1974, pp. 125–90. For official indulgence towards Cuba's plantation economy and export trade see Roland T. Ely, *Cuando reinaba su majestad el azucar*, Buenos Aires 1963, pp. 60–77.

6. John Lynch, *The Spanish American Revolutions*, London 1974, pp. 184–206. For the Republic, see also Manuel Vicente Magallanes, *Historia política de Venezuela*, I, Caracas 1975, pp. 173–94; and for the Spanish counter-mobilisation see Stephen K. Sloan, *Pablo Morillo and Venezuela, 1815–1820*, Columbus, Ohio 1974, pp. 29–42, and Germán Carrera Damas, *Tres temas de historia*, Caracas 1961, pp. 207 *et seq.*

7. See Gerhard Masur, *Simon Bolivar*, Albuquerque, New Mexico 1948, for a powerful evocation of Bolivar's campaign (pp. 155–200), of the Venezuelan plains with their cattle, rivers, seasonal lakes and wild inhabitants (pp. 201–13), and of the collapse of the Second Republic (pp. 214–32).

8. These observations are quoted in Sloan, *Pablo Morillo and Venezuela*, p. 71.

9. Sloan, *Pablo Morillo and Venezuela*, pp. 158, 162. Carvallo and Rios de Hernandez quote regulations of 1817 and 1818 aimed at restoring plantation discipline in their paper, 'Notas para el estudio del binomio plantación–conuco', *Tres ensayos*, pp. 29–31.

10. The texts of the decrees on Cuban economic reforms are printed in Pichardo, *Documentos para la historia de Cuba*, pp. 261–7. Spain's fiscal crisis was so acute that the royal government sold Florida to the United States for $5 million in 1819, thus also permitting General Jackson to complete his ruthless campaign against the Seminoles and blacks of the region. In the previous year Fernando VII accepted $2 million from Britain in return for endorsing an anti-slave trade treaty which his officials thereafter ignored; the money was used to buy a war fleet from the Tsar.

11. Paul Verna, *Pétion y Bolívar*, Caracas 1980, pp. 150–72. This work sheds much light on the Caribbean revolutionary milieu of the epoch and on the subsequent vicissitudes of the relationship between Haiti and republican Colombia/Venezuela. In 1816 Pétion probably wished to check monarchist and colonialist reaction as well as to convert the Venezuelan Republicans to an anti-slavery policy.

12. Masur, *Simon Bolivar*, pp. 290–320. At this period, as later, Bolivar managed to combine willingness to challenge slavery, and a commitment to civic equality, with racial fears which led him to be very hostile to any hint of *pardo* separatism. His anti-slavery record is documented and stressed in J.L. Salcedo–Bastardo, *Bolivar: A Continent and Its Destiny*, Richmond, Surrey 1977, pp. 103–12. Bolivar's hostility to 'black power' is dwelt on by Leslie Rout, *The African Experience in Spanish America*, Cambridge 1976, pp. 176–9.

13. Bolivar's letter to Santander is quoted in Núria Sales, *Sobre esclavos reclutas*, pp. 93–4. The slaves freed by Bolivar in 1820 probably belonged to estates administered by the Spanish authorities since 1814.

14. John Lombardi, *The Decline and Abolition of Negro Slavery in Venezuela*, Westport, Conn. 1971, pp. 46–50; Núria Sales, *Sobre esclavos reclutas*, p. 99. The Manumission Law was presented at Cúcuta by delegates from Antioquia who knew exactly how far the proprietors of the region could be pushed on this question. By this time the slavery of western Colombia appears to have been in transition towards a species of *peonaje* and the former *cuadrillas* were rare. James Parson, *Antioqueño Colonization in Western Colombia*, Berkeley 1949, pp. 50–53, and David Bushnell, *The Santander Regime in Gran Colombia*, Westport, Conn. 1970, p. 168.

15. For Cuban remittances see Jacobo de la Pezuela, *Diccionario geográfico, estadístico, histórico, de la Isla de Cuba*, Madrid 1859, 4 vols, I, pp. 389–90. For Madrid's instructions to American representatives see Timothy Anna, *Spain and the Loss of America*, Lincoln, Nebraska 1983, pp. 145 (in 1814), pp. 274–5 (in 1822). The Cuban delegate to the Cortes, Padre Félix Varela, argued that constitutional liberty could only be stabilised if slavery was abolished; he advocated a manumission policy that would not deprive slave-owners of their capital. The political freedom he advocated for Cuba was thinly disguised independence. The text of his proposals will be found in Pichardo, *Documentos para la historia de Cuba*, pp. 269–75.

16. *El redactor*, February 1813, quoted in Clementi, *La abolición de la esclavitud en América Latina*, p. 54.

17. G.A. Andrews, *The Afro-Argentines of Buenos Aires*, Madison 1980, pp. 113–37.

18. Núria Sales, *Sobre esclavos reclutas*, pp. 59–76. The dependence of Buenos Aires on black and *pardo* regiments did offer some guarantees that manumission would not be an empty gesture; see Tulio Halperin–Donghi, *Politics, Economics and Society in Argentina in the Revolutionary Period*, London 1975, pp. 193–5.

19. Quoted in John Lynch, *The Spanish American Revolutions*, London 1973, p. 78.

20. Quoted in Lynch, *The Spanish American Revolutions*, p. 86.

21. José Luis Masini, *La esclavitud negra en Mendoza, epoca independiente*, Mendoza 1962, pp. 13, 25, 43–50.

22. Guillermo Feliú Cruz, *La abolición de la esclavitud en Chile*, Santiago de Chile 1973, pp. 38–9.

23. Feliú Cruz, *La abolición de la esclavitud en Chile*, pp. 50–52.

24. Lynch, *The Spanish American Revolutions*, p. 165. Pumacahua, one of the Indian *caciques* who had fought against Tupac Amarú, was drawn into creole resistance to the royalist restoration of 1814; the spectacle of armed Indian columns soon caused most whites to rally to the royalists.

25. Quoted in Lynch, *The Spanish American Revolutions*, pp. 174–5; for republican and royalist slave recruitment policies see Timothy A. Anna, *The Fall of the Royal Government in Peru*, Lincoln, Nebraska 1979, pp. 172–4.

26. Núria Sales, *Sobre esclavos reclutas*, p. 103.

27. Anna, *The Fall of Royal Government in Peru*, pp. 196–7; the contradictory decrees are reprinted in Núria Sales, *Sobre esclavos reclutas*, pp. 110–19.

28. Feliú Cruz, *La abolición de la esclavitud en Chile*, pp. 60–97.

29. Feliú Cruz, *La abolición de la esclavitud en Chile*, pp. 98–107, pp. 120–52. The ranks and honours bestowed upon Romero were of the second rather than first class; that he should achieve recognition in the 1830s, at the hands of a government of conservative *pelucones*, may have been related to the rebirth of anti-slavery in Europe at this time.

30. *Selected Writings of Bolivar*, compiled by Vicente Lecuna, ed. by H.E. Bierk, New York 1951, II, p. 499.

31. Lynch, *The Spanish American Revolutions*, pp. 275–6; Núria Sales, *Sobre esclavos reclutas*, pp. 120–27.

32. Stephen Clissold, *Bernardo O'Higgins and the Independence of Chile*, London 1968, p. 225; Humphreys, ed., *British Consular Reports*, p. 177.

33. Lynch, *The Spanish American Revolutions*, p. 289. This admirable general history of Spanish American independence struggles systematically notes their record on slavery; in this it reflects the prominence given by the Liberators themselves to declarations and actions concerning the status of slaves.

34. Masur, *Simon Bolivar*, pp. 597–623. Santander for his part was antagonistic to the plans of some of Bolivar's supporters to turn Colombia into a monarchy or empire. Because the Liberals supported republican legality and a wider franchise, they tended to be aligned with a *pardo* constituency. (C. Parra–Perez, *La monarquía en Gran Colombia*, Madrid 1957, pp. 106–10.) The differences between Santander and Bolivar did not concern slavery; neither man proposed simply ending slavery but equally neither would contemplate renunciation or enfeeblement of the 1821 law – something which cannot be said of all of their successors.

35. Masur, *Simon Bolivar*, pp. 633–4; Lynch, *The Spanish American Revolutions*, pp.

263–4. Padilla's alignment with Santander reflected both support for Liberalism and gratitude towards a man who had built up the Colombian Navy. Santander spent most of the money received from the foreign loans acquiring war *matériel*, including a dozen *pailebots* and two splendid frigates; when plans to invade Cuba were shelved this left the Colombian Navy rather over-equipped. (David Bushnell, *The Santander Regime in Gran Colombia*, p. 264, and Enrique Uribe White, *Padilla*, Bogotá 1973.)

36. Lombardi, *The Decline and Abolition of Negro Slavery in Venezuela*, pp. 61–94. This is the best study I know of slavery and abolition in independent Spanish America. Altogether less than a thousand slaves were to be freed by purchase under the Manumission Laws (p. 154). In 1839 the period of obligatory service for *manumisos* was further extended from twenty-one to twenty-five years. Up until the point where the first *manumisos* would be freed the total number of slaves and *manumisos* grew; one source quoted by Lombardi suggests that there were nearly 50,000 slaves and *manumisos* in 1844, over a year before *manumisos* born in 1821 could claim freedom (p. 162).

37. Brito Figueroa, *Historia económica y social*, I, p. 247. The figures in this count may have been somewhat inflated, since slave-owners had an interest in boosting the numbers of slaves they declared, with a view both to enhancing their credit-worthiness and to future compensation in the event of emancipation.

38. The price of cacao in Venezuela dropped from $45 a *fanega* in 1810 to $20 a *fanega* in 1820 and was still at $20 in 1830; cotton dropped from $15 a quintal in 1810, to $10 in 1820 and $8 in 1830; coffee dropped somewhat less drastically from $12 a quintal in 1810 to $8 in 1820 and $8 in 1830. (Brito Figueroa, *Historia económica y social*, p. 224.) Debt peonage is a complex topic, but for an argument that it bound small producers to merchants in the coffee economy, see William Roseberry, *Coffee and Capitalism in the Venezuelan Andes*, Austin (Texas) 1983, pp. 89–96.

39. This suggested source of persisting enslavement might be compared to the forms of self-sale found in early modern Russia, with its destitute and vulnerable poor and insecure borderlands; see Richard Hellie, *Slavery in Russia: 1450–1725*, Chicago 1982, especially pp. 333–5. Statistics on the actual extent of slavery in independent Venezuela are difficult to have confidence in; nevertheless they do sometimes suggest an increase in the population of slaves and *libertos* which could relate to 'voluntary' re-enslavement. It is likely that the reproduction rates of slaves and *manumisos* were higher than those for freedmen or other propertyless Venezuelans.

40. Lombardi, 'The Abolition of Slavery in Venezuela', in Robert Brent Toplin, ed., *Slavery and Race Relations in Latin America*, Westport, Conn. 1974, p. 242. The crucial role of slaves in the credit structure is also brought out by Lombardi, *The Decline and Abolition of Negro Slavery in Venezuela*, pp. 110–11. The implications for the financial system of collateral whose value would begin to contract as *manumisos* approached freedom had already been pointed out by Venezuelan 'Liberals' hostile to the Manumission Law in the days of Gran Colombia. (See Bushnell, *The Santander Regime in Gran Colombia*, p. 169.)

41. Núria Sales, *Sobre esclavos reclutas*, p. 89.

42. Bushnell, *The Santander Regime in Gran Colombia*, p. 291; Lynch, *The Spanish American Revolutions*, p. 256; Ayala, *Lucha Politica*, pp. 37–51.

43. Clementi, *La abolición de esclavitud en América Latina*, p. 57; for Uruguay see Ema Isola, *La esclavitud en el Uruguay*, Montevideo 1975, pp. 293–323.

44. John Lynch, *Argentine Dictator: Juan Manuel de Rosas, 1829–1852*, London 1982, pp. 119–23; Masini, *La esclavitud negra en Mendoza*, p. 52. According to Lynch free blacks in the Argentine in the 1820s had a mortality rate nearly three times as high as that of slaves; this tends to support the thesis suggested in the discussion of the persistence of slavery in Venezuela that it could reflect the very insecure and vulnerable situation of poor free blacks and *pardos* (see note 39 above).

45. Josefina Pla, *Hermano negro: la esclavitud en Paraguay*, Madrid 1972, especially pp. 55–111.

46. Enrique Florescano, *Origen y desarrollo de los problemas agrarios de México, 1500–1821*, Mexico 1971, pp. 152–5.

47. Hugh M. Hamill, *The Hidalgo Revolt*, Gainesville, Florida 1966, p. 136.

Clementi, *La abolicion de la esclavitud en América Latina*, p. 109.

48. Quoted in Lynch, *The Revolutions of Spanish America*, p. 313. The sentiments expressed here were not unusual and the use of the term 'slavery' to describe the condition from which Americans were seeking to escape was very widespread. Hidalgo and Morelos also warned of the danger of a 'war of races' in terms similar to those used in South America; see, for example, the remarks of Hidalgo quoted by Clementi, *La abolición*, p. 111. For the use of emancipationism to mobilise those of partly African descent see Hamill, *The Hidalgo Revolt*, p. 195.

49. Elsa Gracida and Esperanza Fujigaki, 'La revolución de independencia', in Enrique Semo, ed., *México: un pueblo en la historia*, Mexico City 1983, pp. 11–89, especially pp. 37–8; see also T.E. Anna, *The Fall of the Royal Government in Mexico City*, Lincoln, Nebraska 1978, pp. 107, 195–6; and Dominguez, *Insurrection or Loyalty*, pp. 163, 181–95.

50. Lynch, *The Spanish American Revolutions*, p. 320.

51. Lynch, *The Spanish American Revolutions*, pp. 323, 332.

52. Clementi, *La abolición de la esclavitud en América Latina*, p. 112.

53. Clementi, *La abolición de la eslavitud en América Latina*, p. 125. For Costa Rica see C.F.S. Cardoso, 'La formación de hacienda cafetalera en el siglo XIX', in E. Florescano, *Haciendas, latifundios y plantaciones en América Latina*, pp. 635–66.

X

Cuba and Brazil:
the Abolitionist Impasse

The ridge of that mountain, whose fastnesses wild
The fugitives seek, I beheld, and around
Plantations were scattered of late where they toiled,
And the graves of their comrades are now to be found
The mill-house was there and its turmoil of old . . .
I sought my dear brother, embraced him again,
But found him a slave as I left him before.
To my bosom I clasped him and winging once more
My flight in the air, I ascend with my charge,
The sultan I seem of the winds as I soar,
A monarch whose will sets the prisoner at large.
Like Icarus boldly ascending on high,
I laugh at the anger of Minos, and see
A haven of freedom aloft, where I fly,
And the place where the slave from his master is free.
'Twas then Oh my God! That a thunder clap came,
And the noise of its crash broke the slumbers so light,
That stole o'er my senses and fettered my frame,
And the dream was soon over, of freedom's first flight.

The Dream (1838), Juan Manzano

While the independence struggles on the Spanish America mainland resulted in difficult victories for republicanism and abolitionism, in Cuba and Brazil monarchism and slavery continued to reign. Beneath the apparent contrast between Spain's 'ever-faithful island', as Cuba came to be called in the 1820s, and the independent Empire of Brazil, declared by a Braganza Prince in 1823, there were striking parallels. Cuba and Brazil both largely avoided the disruptive and dangerous conflicts and mobilisations that attended the birth of the new Republics; nevertheless in both there were also far-reaching changes in the state and the social formation favourable to export agriculture.

The planters and merchants of Cuba and Brazil knew that they could ill afford revolutionary disturbances, though they did wish to see fundamental changes – above all most hoped for a lifting of commercial restrictions on the plantation economy and a dismantling of the regime of special interests incorporated in the absolutist structures of the metropolitan state. Their fear of the slaves prompted caution rather than paralysis; inhibited from democratic appeals to a partly coloured free population, they instead redoubled their intrigues and pressures within the established order, seeking to secure commercial freedom and a regime of independent property. Afraid of revolution from below, they still pursued a 'passive revolution' from above. The Napoleonic invasion of 1808 followed by the saga of the Spanish American liberation struggle created conditions which favoured such a strategy by making concessions seem unavoidable to the imperial governments.

The planters of Cuba and Brazil were, of course, far more dependent on slave labour and slave subordination than were the possessing classes of mainland Spanish America, or even most of English North America. There were roughly as many slaves in the Spanish Caribbean as on the whole of the mainland taken together in 1810; they comprised about 40 per cent of Cuba's population compared with 10 per cent or less for the provinces of the mainland. Brazil contained at least a million slaves in 1810 and they too comprised 40 per cent or more of the population. The slave population of Virginia in 1776 had been of similar proportions and yet had not stilled the historic revolutionary energies of the Virginian planters. However, the slave-owners of Brazil and Cuba, a category wider than that of planters, had two good reasons to be wary of emulating the Virginian Patriots: first, the intervening revolution in St Domingue, and secondly the fact that, unlike Virginia, Cuba and Brazil lacked a sizeable white majority. In Cuba black slaves and free people of colour together constituted a majority; there were some 217,000 slaves and 109,000 free people of colour compared with 274,000 whites in 1810. In Brazil they comprised about two-thirds of the population of about 2.5 million in 1808. In Virginia in 1776 there had been very few free blacks or mulattos. The revolution in St Domingue had shown that free people of colour would be prone to assert their own rights in any situation of flux and, in some circumstances, even to throw in their lot with the slaves. In Cuba and Brazil free blacks, mulattos or *pardos* comprised, respectively, roughly a fifth and a third of the population and had long traditions of semi-autonomous organisation in self-help brotherhoods and associations; free people of colour were, in fact, more numerous and better-established in these two territories than anywhere else in the New World – with the possible, but ominous, exception of Venezuela. Moreover such towns as Havana and Rio contained large numbers of urban slaves, in communication with the free people of colour and notoriously more troublesome than slaves incarcerated on plantations.[1]

The slave revolt of 1791 in St Domingue was as much a watershed in Brazil as in nearby Cuba. In 1789 disgruntled members of the oligarchy in Minas Gerais plotted an independence modelled on that of the United States and one leader even envisaged freedom for Brazilian-born slaves. But by 1792 most slave proprietors and whites were gripped by fear of the consequences of any revolutionary challenge to the metropolis. An English traveller in Rio in 1792 noted a sense of what he called 'black power': 'The secret spell, that caused the negro to tremble at the presence of the white man, is in great degree dissolved.'[2] This judgement would have reflected the condition of the urban slave and would not apply to field slaves kept in isolation on the estates. Nevertheless fear of incipient desubordination led Brazilian planters and merchants to behave with great circumspection and to avoid opening up any rift between the colonial regime and the slave regime. The pride of free blacks and mulattos could itself be channelled into the black and mulatto regiments; these had coloured officers as well as coloured non-commissioned officers.

There were enough disturbances within Brazil itself to prevent dissipation of the social fears of the white proprietors and their consequent loyalty to the established order. 'French principles' inspired a demonstration and conspiracy in Bahia in 1798, chiefly supported by people of colour and with a programme that was both republican and emancipationist. On August 12th manifestos appeared on walls throughout the city calling for the removal of the 'detestable Portuguese yoke' and declaring: 'The happy time of our liberty is about to arrive; the time when all will be brothers, all will be equal.' 'All black and brown slaves are to be free, so that there will be no slaves whatever.' 'All citizens, especially mulattos and blacks, are equal, all are equal, there will be no differences, there will be freedom, equality and fraternity.' Soldiers were promised an increase in their wages and it was said that a government that was 'democratic, free and independent' would open the port to all nations, and most particularly to French ships. In fact France was at this time the final destination of much of the produce of Bahia, though the trade was still formally controlled by Portuguese merchants. Within two weeks the Governor had arrested forty-seven people in connection with the conspiracy, most of them mulatto artisans, at least one soldier and nearly a dozen slaves. The 'Tailors' Conspiracy', as it came to be known, was crushed by hanging three leaders and sentencing most of the others to the lash and banishment. The Governor reported to Lisbon that respectable proprietors (*homens de bem*) were not involved and that the conspiracy was the work of malcontents drawn from the 'lower orders' (*baixa esfera*).[3]

In contrast to this highly programmatic urban conspiracy Brazil also witnessed a succession of elemental revolts against captivity by African slaves, inspired by Muslim beliefs or the solidarity of particular African nations. A Hausa conspiracy was discovered in Salvador in 1807, while around Christmas 1808 several hundred slaves in the southern Recôncavo broke out of their plantations, burned the cane fields and attacked the town of Nazaré; about 400 slaves escaped from Salvador to join the revolt. On January 6th 1809 a threat to Nazaré was repulsed; government troops took 95 rebels prisoner while others withdrew to the backlands. The Governor issued a decree imposing curfews and others measures of control and denouncing 'slaves principally of the Hausa nation who with total disregard and resistance to the laws of slavery have become revolutionaries and disloyal'.[4]

These revolts and conspiracies set a pattern of African rebellion that was to punctuate Brazil's history for nearly three decades. A number of the rebels gained their liberty, either by retreating to the *quilombos* of the interior or by finding refuge amongst the black population of the towns. Had there been any violent clash between Brazilian proprietors and the imperial power, then such rebellions could well have contributed to the birth of a black power and an anti-slavery force. But in part for this very reason no such violent clash occurred. The preservation of the essential integrity of the englobing political and social order meant that slave contestation of it did not become politicised and remained at the level of struggles for freedom by individual groups of rebels. The particular ethnic and religious identifications often invoked by the rebels could cut them off from other slaves and people of colour; and in this sense they made it easier for the authorities to deploy black and mulatto troops and militia against these rebellions, as frequently happened.

In the period between 1789 and the declaration of independence there was to be only one republican attempt to challenge Braganza rule, the Pernambuco revolt of 1817. This revolt centred on the twin cities of Recife and Olinda in the north-eastern sugar province of Pernambuco. Leading citizens of the port, Olinda, resented the fact that tariffs and port duties levied on their trade were absorbed by the royal bureaucracy at Rio; a bureaucracy which imposed many cumbersome regulations upon the merchants of the north-east, without supplying any valued services in return. The merchants of Recife–Olinda were particularly desirous of easier trade with the United States but had been prevented from enjoying this by a royal government that gave preferential treatment to the British. Among those involved in the revolt were graduates of the local seminary, established by Bishop Azeredo Coutinho in 1804. Supporters also included Freemasons and young Brazilian officers who resented a military hierarchy dominated by the Portuguese nobility. The commanders of the local garrison were swiftly overpowered and imprisoned in February 1817 with the aid of an urban mob that had little love for Portuguese royal bureaucrats. The royal Governor of the province abandoned it to the rebels. The 'Republic of Pernambuco' committed itself to free trade and abolished titles of aristocracy and all privileged monopolies. It modelled itself chiefly on the United States and dispatched an envoy to Washington in search of arms and recognition: the envoy did meet the US Secretary of State 'unofficially', but the arms he purchased privately arrived too late to affect the outcome. To begin with, the leaders of the revolt abstained from any appeal to the slaves and were alarmed by the mobilisation of the people of colour. In a clumsy attempt to reassure the planters it was said that, though slavery was unjust, property of all sorts would be scrupulously respected. The merchants, clerks and professionals of Recife–Olinda did not themselves directly depend on slave labour and the more radical spirits amongst them still felt the attraction of 'French principles'. The revolt failed to attract support from the *senhores de engenho* or the *lavradores de cana* of the north-east; in its last desperate days an appeal was made by some republican commanders for slaves to enroll in the ranks, but to very little effect. As if yearning for magical deliverance some young officers proposed freeing Napoleon from St Helena and persuading him to accept command of the republican forces; however, this could not be attempted since the Royal Navy retained control of the sea and blockaded Olinda. The Republic was crushed with little difficulty, after a little over two months of existence. Evidently the mass of Brazilian slave-owners felt that even a moderate republican challenge was too risky to attempt.[5]

There were fewer revolts and conspiracies in Cuba but the proximity of St Domingue and Venezuela was sufficient to alert Cuban proprietors to the menace of revolutionary and republican politics. A stream of refugees, bringing tales of terrible destruction, brought this message with them. Cuba received 20,000–30,000 refugees from St Domingue.

In 1795 Nicolas Morales, a mulatto smallholder of Bayamo at the extreme east of the island, within sight of St Domingue, was charged with fomenting unrest among people of his class; he claimed that the royal decree of *gracias al sacar* of 1795 offered equality to all *castas* and that its implementation had been frustrated by white creoles and corrupt officials. Morales and his fellow conspirators, who included some whites, also discussed abolition of the sales tax and confiscation of land from *hacendados* who had not made proper use of their *mercedes* (royal land grants). Some of the conspirators believed that Cuba was about to be handed over to France, as Spanish Santo Domingo was at this time. Morales had enough support to alarm the authorities, but the limits of the conspiracy are suggested by the fact that it was broken up, and Morales himself arrested, largely by local militia. The late 1790s witnessed a number of isolated plantation outbreaks in Cuba; these probably reflected poor security in new plantations filled with recently arrived African captives, though rumours of revolution may have played some part. The colonial government of Cuba strengthened its position in eastern Cuba by reaching an agreement with the descendants of the *esclavos del rey* near the copper mines of Prado in Oriente. The freedom of these blacks was recognised over a century after their forebears had rejected the slave condition. At an imposing ceremony held on March 19th 1801 in Santiago de Cuba, in the presence of its Governor and the massed ranks of white and coloured militia, a royal decree was proclaimed recognising the liberty of the *cobreros*, guaranteeing them against re-enslavement and recognising their right to continue cultivating their lands.[6]

The first pro-independence conspiracy in Cuba was that led by Ramon de la Luz, a Freemason and member of the creole elite, in 1810; the aim of these conspirators was to establish an independent American Republic, enjoying freedom of commerce with the United States. A draft constitution for Cuba later published by one of the participants declared that slavery would be upheld so long as it was necessary to agriculture. Despite some mulatto support the conspirators did not even commit themselves to the abolition of all caste discrimination. Havana was the centre of the conspiracy, whose participants included a handful of white creoles and a number of free mulattos. Despite some support from members of the Havana militia the conspiracy was nipped in the bud and the ringleaders sent to the Spanish prisons on the African coast.[7]

Following the invasion of the Peninsula the leading merchants and planters in Cuba knew themselves to be in a difficult, fluid and vulnerable situation. The trade war between Britain, France and the United States had seriously damaged their commerce. The Captain General, Someruelos, worked closely with the Havana municipality, ignoring any inconvenient instructions. The core of the creole oligarchy was determined not to commit itself too strongly to any side, to avoid civil commotions of any sort and to do business with the victors. When news had arrived of Napoleon's invasion of Spain a mob had taken to the streets of Havana shouting 'Death to the French', 'Long Live Fernando VII'; evidently the presence of French *émigrés* had aroused some popular antagonism.[8] The Havana municipality was determined to clamp down on any expression of popular politics and otherwise to await developments. When Arango y Parreño suggested forming a junta this proposal was rejected, undoubtedly because it was thought that any *cabildo abierto* could get out of control. Members of the Cuban oligarchy were to be found on both sides of the struggle in Spain itself. Casa Calvo, former Governor of Spanish Santo Domingo, supported Joseph Bonaparte as did Ricardo O'Farrill, member of another important planter family, who became his Minister of Defence.

The Havana municipality remained outwardly loyal to the Bourbons, and was well aware that Cuba was in no position to defy the British. The loyalty of the Cuban oligarchy was strained by the first reports of the Cortes debate on slavery and the slave trade in 1811; after a two-day emergency session it engaged in discussions with William Shaler, the US Consul in Havana, concerning the possibility of annexation to the United States, an eventuality which interested both Madison and Jefferson. Many Cuban planters and some merchants would not have been dismayed by a Bonapartist victory in Europe and a US victory in the Americas. France and the United States seemed the natural outlets for Cuban produce. A victory for Britain raised complications of two sorts: first, the preferential treatment given by Britain to its own sugar islands and, secondly, its policy of suppressing the Atlantic slave trade. During the years 1808–12 many Cuban vessels were seized by the British on the grounds that they were engaged in the slave trade or were intent on violating Britain's Orders in Council; the legality of such seizures was often dubious even in the eyes of James Stephen though certainly, as the Cubans were well aware, Cuban losses were quite acceptable to the British West Indian sugar planters. However, annexation to the United States would also have meant accepting a ban on the slave trade; the *ayuntamiento* had only been prepared to contemplate this because misleading early reports implied that the Cortes was favourable to a motion of Guridi y Alcócer which envisaged an end to slavery, not simply the slave trade. Once this rumour had been dispelled the oligarchy had recovered its nerve. The *Real Consulado* dispatched a stiff memorial to the Cortes attacking all the abolitionist proposals. It pointed out that Cuba was not like St Domingue because slaves were not in a majority in any town or province and that in fact wartime disruption meant that the plantations were all understocked. It also made pointed reference to the economic contribution which Cuban slavery could now make to Spanish imperial finances. According to its calculations Cuba had imported 100,000 slaves since the ending of the *Asiento* in 1789; these had cost Cuban planters $33 million (£6 million) and had helped to produce sugar worth $73 million 'without taking into account the other branches of agricultural production and an infinite variety of smaller industries which slave labour had been instrumental in assisting to grow and prosper'.[9] Apart from delivering a vigorous but polished counter-blast to the abolitionists and to the British (see chapter 8), the municipality also took steps to encourage a Cuban lobby in Spanish politics. Martínez Pinillos, the son of a prominent Spanish merchant in Cuba, remained in the service of the Bourbon government and learned how to influence prominent Spanish politicians and military men during these years. The former *intendente* in Cuba, Juan Pablo Valiente, also returned to the Peninsula around this time. The Liberal leader Arguëlles found his proposed slave trade ban blocked by the Cortes. The matter was referred to a small commission, including a Cuban planter, which failed to deliver a report prior to the suppression of the Constitutionalist regime. Cuban mercantile and slave-owning interests were nonetheless gratified to learn the news of the restoration of full power to Fernando VII. The new Spanish government was still obliged to discuss suppression of the slave trade with the British, but it was likely to be far less compliant in its dealings with London than had been the Constitutionalists.

The unsettled years 1808–14 witnessed at least one major Cuban conspiracy which was bound to alarm the slaveholders. Between January and March 1812 the police authorities unearthed what they saw as a plot to overthrow the colony's entire political and social system. The key figure in this conspiracy, or at least the leading spirit of the most important subversive network, was José Antonio Aponte, a free black woodworker of African birth who had been an NCO in the militia; now in his fifties, he had been first mobilised in the 1780s to defend Spanish possessions from the British. He was retired from his militia duties following the conspiracy of 1810 because he was

389

suspected of involvement. Aponte was a leading member of one of the African societies which existed in Havana, offering companionship and self-help to free blacks and urban slaves. These societies usually adopted a Catholic patron saint, though their ritual would have a strong African content. Aponte's society was commonly known as the Shangó-Teddum and Aponte probably claimed descent from the West African God Shangó. On the other hand, the official banner of the society was a white flag with the image of Nuestra Señora de los Remedios embossed in green. Aponte had contacts in different parts of Cuba, though not, perhaps, as many as claimed either by himself, when encouraging his followers, or the authorities, when bringing charges against him. He impressed his followers with the example of black power in Haiti and hoped to gain the support of the recently crowned King Henry; portraits of the Haitian monarch in full regalia were found among the possessions of several of Aponte's followers and contacts. Aponte also sought to gain the support of a black Spanish officer from Santo Domingo then resident in Havana; this man, Gil Narciso, was a former lieutenant of Jean François and had achieved the rank of brigadier in the *Tropas Auxiliares Negras* in the 1790s. Some believed that Jean François himself would arrive to aid the plot though in fact he died in 1811 in Spain. The expectations of some Cuban blacks had been raised by reports of the Cortes debates on slavery and some believed that the captive Spanish King wished to free the slaves and honour his coloured subjects. Beginning on January 6th, the *dia de los reyes*, the early months of 1812 were marked by a number of urban disturbances and plantation outbreaks in different parts of Cuba, some inspired by Aponte, others perhaps spontaneous. The *hacendados* usually found that the local militia, drawn from employees, tenants and smallholders of the region, would mobilise against insurgent slaves, though in some parts of Eastern Cuba this did not happen and regular troops had to be used. The standard claim of the *hacendados* was that the slaves wished to kill all white men and seize their women. This racial and sexual fear was no doubt prompted by the fact that young males were heavily predominant on the plantations. If the Havana municipality had committed itself either to independence or to the United States, then there could even have been a junction of loyalism and black revolt such as erupted in Venezuela at this time. Instead the municipal and colonial authorities stood together as the Aponte conspiracy, and all signs of unrest, were stamped out. Aponte himself was executed and his head displayed, together with those of some of his followers, on one of the main Havana streets. Dozens of lesser suspects were tortured, whipped and condemned to forced labour. This incident encouraged the conviction of Spanish colonial officials that fear of the slaves and blacks was a powerful incentive to white Cuban loyalty and a major reason why Havana abstained from gestures of independence – or, in reality the more serious threat, treasonous agreements with the North Americans. The unfolding of the struggle in Venezuela during the years 1810–14 could only underline the dangers in a colony with a much larger slave population.[10]

Both at this time and later the Cuban oligarchy was also restrained by fear of the British Navy. They were reminded of its strength when it used Cuba as a base during the campaigns against the United States in the War of 1812; in return for this facility the British were bound to uphold the authority of the Spanish government. The last thing the Cuban planters wished for was a British blockade or occupation. But the Cuban oligarchy's loyalty to Spain was not solely determined by negative sentiments. Once again there is a parallel here between Cuban loyalism and Brazilian royalism, and it will be helpful to compare the situation of Brazilian and Cuban planters with that of their counter-parts in the British and French West Indies. Having evoked the justified fear of revolution entertained by the majority of planters it is now necessary to add that they proved able to achieve most of their goals by non-revolutionary means.

The social composition of Cuba and Brazil dictated caution but it by no means condemned the class of *hacendados* and *fazendeiros* to impotence or passivity. They displayed a self-confidence and autonomy which contrasts with the stance of the British West Indian planters in the 1770s and 1780s. The Brazilian proprietors had long been aware that their country was overtaking its metropolis; the Cuban proprietors knew that their plantation wealth and potential gave them great leverage in Spain. By contrast the British planters were almost abjectly dependent on the metropolis for privileged access to the British market, for protection against other powers and, last but not least, for supplying the military force which ultimately guaranteed slave subordination. The reactions of the British West Indian planters, whether in the 1770s or later, were profoundly conditioned by two crucial circumstances: first, a large proportion of them were absentees, secondly, slaves comprised 80 per cent or more of the population, twice as much as the proportion in Cuba or Brazil. The planters of the French West Indies in the 1790s had acted with more boldness and initiative than their British counterparts. This was partly because more of them were resident in the colonies but mainly because the political situation was more threatening to them, and the economic situation correspondingly more promising. The outbreak of the Revolution in 1789 and the subsequent dissolution of tariff controls allowed French planters, who had constructed the most productive slave system in the Americas, to reach out for unfettered access to the markets of Europe and North America. If the result in St Domingue was disaster, at least the planters of Martinique, their interests adroitly defended by Du Buc, had enjoyed considerable good fortune. The slave-owning oligarchies of Brazil and Cuba were dealt a stronger hand than the British or French planters and, from their own class perspective, played it to considerable effect. They did not aim at the revolutionary laurels earnt by the Virginians, but they found a path to making Brazil and Cuba respectively the second and third slave powers of the nineteenth century.

During the period 1790–1840 a new and more dynamic system of plantation slavery was to be consolidated in these two territories. While slavery had existed in Cuba and Brazil almost from the dawn of Iberian conquest its subsequent development had been conditioned by the colonialist mercantilism of absolutist states with a thirst for specie. The Iberian Empires expected their colonies to return a profit and viewed gold or silver as the most acceptable and necessary products of imperial enterprise, with plantation products allotted a secondary position. In Brazil gold output declined steeply after about 1760; Spain continued to receive a flow of silver from Mexico until 1807 but not thereafter. A new breed of 'enlightened' colonial official understood that plantation slavery could produce profits as large, or larger, than those derived from silver or gold mines, so long as the right conditions prevailed. The revolutions in North America and in St Domingue created a new situation and gave vast new openings to the planter class of those territories where sugar and coffee could be produced. The North Americans had a large and efficient merchant marine. The United States could supply the manufactures and provisions needed to sustain a plantation economy and bought ever-larger quantities of plantation products, either for domestic consumption or for trans-shipment to Europe. In the period 1793–1807 there was increasingly cordial co-operation between metropolitan officials and colonial planters in both Cuba and Brazil because the colonial state and the landed oligarchy had a common interest in realising the large profits to be made in the new situation.

Prior to 1808 the ministers of Spain and Portugal still felt constrained to limit and control colonial commerce; but this became impossible with the Napoleonic invasion of the Peninsula. Well before 1807 the governments in Madrid and Lisbon had recognised the need to modify the old formula of conferring monopolies on particular individuals, companies or ports. The cumbersome fleet systems had been abandoned in the 1760s and the colonial companies wound up in the early 1780s. However, the subsequent process of dismantling remaining restrictions and monopolies could be slow. The first concession made to creole interests was to confer such privileges on a member of the local oligarchy; the 'enlightened' Cuban planter Arango y Parreño became a flour monopolist for a time in the 1790s. But both the logic of reform and the international situation demanded further moves to freeing trade.

In the first instance *comercio libre* in the Spanish Empire had simply meant permitting colonists to trade with any Spanish port and with one another. In a second phase of reform, it meant a transition from trade regulated by prohibitions to trade regulated by tariff differentials. The slave trade *Asiento* had been temporarily suspended in 1789, allowing for the participation of Cuban merchants and planters, among them Arango y Parreño himself. Fernando Po, a Spanish island off the coast of Africa, was to become a dependency of the Cuban treasury. Cuban merchants, with North American help, became major carriers in the Atlantic slave trade for the first time.

During the French wars further prohibitions were lifted from time to time in a more or less *ad hoc* fashion. Because of its greater proximity to the zones of conflict Cuba was more affected by this *de facto* relaxation than Brazil. In the years 1795–1805 Cuba became an emporium of the Americas; over a thousand merchant ships called at Havana in the year 1801. Regulations were not so much counter-manded as ignored: the Captain General, the Intendant and other senior officials were thanked and rewarded by the planters and such bodies as the municipality, the *Real Consulado* and the *Sociedad Económica de Amigos del País*. With the return of peace in 1815 Madrid conceded to Cuba the right to trade with all nations, using tariffs to raise revenue and protect Spanish exports. Arango y Parreño became a member of the Council of the Indies and an *Intendente* was appointed, Alejandro Ramirez, who enjoyed the confidence of the planters. Successive decrees issued between 1816 and 1819 abolished the tobacco monopoly (*estanco*), instituted absolute property rights in land and removed protection from the forests, hitherto reserved for the exclusive use of the naval construction yards. The abolition of the tobacco *estanco* released the *vegueros* from an oppressive monopoly. The owners of the tobacco *vegas* were smallholders rather than planters, working their highly productive farms with the aid of family labour and perhaps a few slaves. In the longer run the introduction of a free market in land did not favour those *vegueros* who stood in the way of sugar expansion, but this was not immediately clear. *Hacendados* who held royal *mercedes* were dispensed from the duty to supply local towns with food, could freely alienate their land and could acquire the *realengos*, or royal land attached to each of the *mercedes* (land grants). In this way as many as 10,000 landholders were given property rights. The abolition of the naval monopoly over woodlands gave the sugar *hacendados* access to a highly useful resource – and one they consumed with even greater voracity as they installed steam power in their mills.[11]

Residual attempts to regulate the slave trade were abandoned as the Madrid government took up a formal stance of disapproval towards it. The resulting 'illegal' traffic was indeed more vigorous and unlimited than the old *Asientos*. In 1817 the Spanish government agreed to a treaty with Britain designed to end the trade within four years. Madrid asked for and received substantial 'compensation', but did nothing to ensure that the treaty would be implemented; Spanish officials in Cuba showed no zeal in tracking down the slave-traders and some entered their pay. The British complained at slow progress but Madrid and its colonial representatives played the part of a baffle between British official abolitionism and the slaving interests of its Caribbean colony.[12]

The outbreak of the Constitutionalist Revolution in Cadiz in 1820 did little to disrupt the harmonious relations between Spain and Cuba's oligarchy. The British envoy in Madrid sought to have tougher anti-slave trade legislation introduced into the Cortes in 1821; a majority favoured this but the Minister of the Indies intervened and made sure it came to nothing. The military leaders, however anxious to curb royal power, had already discovered the reliability of the Cuban treasury. In Cuba itself the Constitutionalist interlude did witness the beginnings of free political discussion in Havana and a few other centres. Some members of the creole population welcomed the right to be represented in the Cortes and had high hopes of Spanish liberalism. The decrees of the Constitutionalists did help to sweep away certain remaining absolutist cobwebs. There were bitter factional conflicts between creole Liberals, including younger members of the planting oligarchy such as the Conde de O'Reilly, and a sizeable ultra-royalist and ultra-loyalist faction, swelled by *émigrés* from the mainland. A sector of creole public opinion was prone to resent the actions of the Spanish military and of Spanish officialdom, a resentment that did not abate because the latter enjoyed cordial relations with planters and slave-traders. The election of Padre Félix Varela to the Cortes in 1822 expressed the incipient radicalisation of a layer of the Cuban creoles, especially the youth and *menu peuple* of Havana. Varela was known to be a man of advanced views from his teaching of political economy and moral philosophy at a seminary in Havana. However, once in Madrid he went beyond the mandate given to him. The Cuban delegates were instructed to call for the repudiation of the slave trade treaty with Britain, but instead Varela presented to the Cortes a resolution strengthening the ban on the slave trade and even envisioning the gradual abolition of slavery. These abolitionist representations were soon lost without trace as the Cortes was suppressed by a French-backed royalist coup.[13]

The cause of opposition to the slave trade won a more surprising recruit about this time in the person of Arango y Parreño, a man who could claim to be the founder of the Cuban slave trade. Arango had decided that Cuba now had enough slaves; they had been arriving at the rate of 10,000–20,000 a year. Arango himself had taken care to purchase a large number of women slaves for his own plantation in the hope of boosting the natural reproduction rate. His preparedness to envisage an end to the slave trade reflected a view that Cuba should not allow itself to be swamped by Africans; and like many 'enlightened' planters he was suspicious of the slave-traders, with their dubious links to Spanish officials. Arango's approach reflected concerns similar to those of the nation-building protagonists of republican independence in other parts of the Americas. While he thought either republicanism or independence to be excluded from Cuba he distrusted the instability of Madrid and privately entertained the prospect of Cuba becoming some sort of British protectorate, with a status similar to that of the Ionian Islands.

However, there was really no such thing as abolitionism in Spain or Cuba in the early 1820s, even when constitutional liberty was at its height. There was no equivalent to the *Amis des Noirs* or Abolition Society in either metropolis or colony. Varela lamented how difficult it was to arouse the interest of Habaneros in questions of political principle; he declared that the citizens of this city were obsessed with the counting house and the wharf. Arango y Parreño was capable of taking the long view, but he had no intention of launching a campaign on the slave trade. Cuba's professional or middle classes and artisans were not impressed by Britain's hostility to the slave trade since they saw it simply as a dishonest way of retarding the country's plantation development. Even Varela attacked the British for hypocrisy. Investment in the slave trade was not confined to the very rich, since shares in slave trading expeditions could be bought for $100 or less. The British judge attached to the Anglo–Spanish Mixed Commission in Havana reported his puzzlement at the large numbers of 'honourable slave dealers and liberal minded slave owners' that he met.[14]

In 1822 Spanish rule was overthrown in one part of the Spanish Caribbean. Santo Domingo, which had been returned to Spain in 1810, was swiftly overrun by the troops of President Boyer and incorporated into the Republic of Haiti; several thousand slaves were emancipated and land titles conferred on smallholders. While white Cubans would generally have abhorred invasion by Haiti, there were Patriots who looked forward to the mounting of an expedition of liberation from the mainland. However, the geographical situation of Cuba and Puerto Rico certainly made any project of liberation from the outside a most formidable undertaking. In 1823–4 Cuban partisans of independence approached Santander and Bolivar for help in the liberation of their island but instead found themselves invited to fight in Peru. The latter was seen as both a more important and a more vulnerable Spanish outpost than Cuba or Puerto Rico. Spanish power was inherently stronger in the Caribbean; the islands were strongly fortified and garrisoned way-stations on the imperial sea lane between Spain and America. Puerto Rico was less given over to a slave plantation economy than Cuba, but its small size and close links with Spain made it particularly difficult to envisage its separation from the metropolis. At different times Iturbide and Santander did contemplate such an expedition but never succeeded in bringing it to fruition. Greater Colombia did have a navy and in Peru the liberation forces did demonstrate the capacity to mount combined naval and land operations. But Spanish forces were so well entrenched in the Caribbean islands that no proper effort was made to dislodge them. The considerations which restrained the Cuban oligarchy – fear of black revolt and of international complications – also had weight with the South American revolutionaries.

The strategic situation of Cuba and Puerto Rico meant that their fate preoccupied the United States, Britain and France; it also enabled these powers to play a more direct role in preventing outcomes of which they disapproved. The South American leaders were anxious not to antagonise the United States; US leaders did not disguise their view that they saw Cuba and Puerto Rico, like Florida, as natural extensions of the North American Empire. In 1819 Spain, desperately short of cash, sold Florida to the US for $5 million; Cuba was next on the list for North American expansionists. The US Secretary of War, Calhoun, told his Cabinet colleagues that he had two fears relating to Cuba which could be allayed by annexation: 'one that the island should fall into the hands of Great Britain; two that it should be revolutionised by Negroes.'[15] But the British were not prepared to see the United States aggrandised in this way or commanding the entrances of the Caribbean. Canning explained this candidly to the US envoy in London in 1825; 'You cannot allow that *we* should have Cuba; we cannot allow that you should have it; and we can neither of us allow that it should fall into the hands of France.'[16]

Fernando VII was restored to full power in Spain in 1823 with the aid of 100,000 French troops; the following year a large French fleet was sent to Caribbean waters, partly to reassert French interests in the

New World and partly to provide cover for the Spanish forces. Following Ayacucho, Bolivar and Santander turned their attention to the possibility of now moving against the remaining Spanish outposts, but they were impressed by the great difficulty of the undertaking. On May 25th Bolivar wrote to Santander on the necessity for caution:

> Never forget the three political admonitions that I gave you; first it will not be to our advantage to admit La Plata to the League; second, or the United States; third do not attempt to liberate Havana. I believe that our League can maintain itself perfectly well without embracing the extremes of North and South and without creating another Republic of Haiti; Respecting Havana we should tell Spain that if she does not make peace she will lose her two large islands.[17]

If there was a threat in this last sentence it never materialised. The size of the French fleet that had by this time arrived in the Caribbean certainly represented a daunting obstacle and made some think that France itself would like to buy Cuba from Spain. President Monroe's famous declaration directed at European interference in the New World, made in December 1823, was prompted by distrust of French intentions. Yet paradoxically enough, it served to underline the international understanding that Cuba should remain Spanish. Without its mainland Empire Spain would be weak and unthreatening to the other powers, and could be allowed to retain Cuba and Puerto Rico.

External geo-political considerations thus reinforced an internal relationship of forces inimical to independence within the insular social formations. During the years 1820–23 Cuban Liberals looked to Spain for reform confident that their island's importance would ensure important concessions. It was only after 1823 that Varela came out in support of independence and not until 1824–5 that a significant pro-independence conspiracy stirred in Cuba, the *Soles y Rayos de Bolívar*. But by this time it was too late. The Spanish garrison in Cuba was built up to a strength of 15,000–20,000 troops during these years as forces from the mainland were evacuated; and the naval strength of the rival powers also steadily increased during these years. In 1825 Madrid conferred enlarged powers, *facultades omnimodas*, on a new Captain General, Vives. For many years Cuba was to be under martial administration and to be ruled by 'special laws' decreed by the Captain General.[18]

However, at least a section of the Cuban oligarchy gained something from the events of the early 1820s. As if in some new colonial pact, every encouragement was given to Cuba's export economy and the chief of the island's economic administration, the *Intendente*, was for many years to be a Cuban. For a brief period Arango y Parreño was awarded this post, but he was replaced by Martínez Pinillos in 1825. While Arango articulated the outlook of the more far-sighted creole planters, Pinillos organised the interests of the slave-traders and of those planters most closely linked to them or to the Spanish mercantile complex. Martínez Pinillos, soon to become Conde de Villanueva and a grandee of Spain, held the post of *Intendente*, with a brief interruption, until the 1850s. He became a powerful force behind the scenes in Spanish politics. Following the death of Fernando VII in 1833 he backed the cause of the moderate Liberals. The ultra-monarchist Carlists were seen as a threat to Cuba's new socio-economic regime as were, in a quite different way, the radical Liberal *exaltados*. Consequently the influence of Havana's treasury was thrown behind the moderate Liberals and the cause of Maria Cristina as Regent and Isabella II as Queen. Villanueva became a member of the Council of the Indies and was well placed to make sure that Madrid did not interfere in the business affairs of the Cuban slave-traders and slave-owners. For many years the Cuban treasury was able to supply Madrid with a cash subvention of several million *pesos* annually as well as to cover the costs of a large garrison and Atlantic squadron. In the years 1823–35 the Cuban treasury had revenues of around $5 million annually, of which some $500,000 would be remitted to Madrid each year, while the remainder sustained the local Spanish-recruited establishment. Between 1835 and 1845 remittances from Cuba grew sharply to an average of just over $3 million annually; during much of this time the Madrid regime was involved in an expensive civil war against the Carlist legitimists. Thus for a considerable price the Cuban oligarchy acquired a 'protector'.[19]

The Cuban oligarchy did not only require protection against the possibility of a slave uprising. It also needed to be shielded from the instability of native American republicanism and from the international pressure to end the slave trade. Every Spanish official, from the Captain General downwards, received a rake-off from the slave-traders in return for non-compliance with the Treaties against the slave trade. Indeed by the 1840s those making investments for Queen Isabella herself were heavily implicated in the slave trade to Cuba. Against this background Cuba steadily climbed to become the world's largest sugar producer.[20]

Brazil's plantation output also bounded forward during this period. The Pombaline companies of the 1770s had already allowed Brazil to take some advantage of the drop in North American supplies of indigo, tobacco and rice. In the aftermath of the St Domingue revolt royal officials recognised the new opportunities opening up – though they remained obsessed with schemes to resuscitate mining. From 1795 to

1796 a new team of metropolitan officials gave greater attention to general economic conditions and to plantation agriculture, while still trying to reserve all commerce to Portuguese merchants. The key figure in a developing *rapprochement* between the royal government and the Brazilian oligarchy was D. Rodrigo de Sousa Coutinho, a godson of Pombal who had family connections and property in Brazil. Rodrigo was appointed as permanent overseas secretary in 1796 by Dom João, the Prince Regent. Irksome monopolies, such as that over salt, were abolished while members of the Brazilian elite were solicited for their advice as to the best path of development for the colony. Thus Bishop Azeredo Coutinho, who had himself run a sugar estate, pointed to the huge potential for reviving this branch of plantation agriculture, if only it could be freed from prevailing restrictions. Thus planters were obliged to sell at fixed prices and *lavradores de cana* were obliged to devote a proportion of their land to subsistence crops. These restrictions were not immediately abolished, but at least a more propitious climate was created in which economic reforms could be canvassed. Those members of the creole elite still imprisoned for their participation in the Minas conspiracy, despite its sympathy for American independence, were released. On the other hand there was no clemency for the free blacks and mulattos implicated in the republican conspiracy of Bahia in 1798.

The greater attention shown to Brazilian interests by Rodrigo and his colleagues was still unduly focused on hopes of reviving the mining economy and might have had few really substantial results but for the shock of the Napoleonic invasion. Rodrigo, like others, had seen the invasion coming and had been asked to prepare plans against this eventuality. He had observed that Portugal itself was neither 'the best nor the most essential part of the monarchy'.[21] If the Prince Regent was forced to choose, then he should leave Portugal and establish his court in Brazil. This advice was taken in 1807–8 and produced the remarkable spectacle of the political establishment of an entire regime – some 8,000 ministers, judges, nobles, merchants and ecclesiastics – embarking on board a flotilla of ships and being carried across the Atlantic to the soil of Brazil. The British Navy had encouraged this option but it also echoed previous contingency plans drawn up for Portugal's rulers at times of special danger, such as 1762 when Spanish invasion threatened. Indeed the translation of the court from Portugal to Brazil demonstrated the exceptional autonomy of Brazil's 'maritime absolutism'.

On January 28th 1808 the Prince Regent issued a decree suspending the Portuguese monopoly over Brazil's trade. Ships of all friendly nations were now to be free to enter Brazilian ports; imports were taxed at 24 per cent *ad valorem* and export taxes were fixed within each captaincy. In 1810 the London government extracted a reduction of the import tax on British goods to 15 per cent, consolidating their already strong position and squeezing out the United States which had already declared itself a friendly nation. Based in Rio de Janeiro, the royal government now imposed a more effective centralisation on Brazil than the colony had ever previously experienced. The various captaincies, often known as 'the Brazils', had each enjoyed separate lines of communication and authority with the metropolis. Now the captaincies were governed from Rio as a unified Kingdom. Indeed the capital of Brazil itself became the metropolis for other Portuguese colonies in Africa and Asia. Troops commanded and financed by the Rio government took part in operations against France – Brazil ejected Victor Hugues, Governor of French Cayenne, in 1809 – and later undertook forward operations in the River Plate zone. The slave-owners of the Brazilian south were pleased to see royal troops sent against the incendiary Uruguayan Patriot, Artigas, and to have the *Banda Oriental* annexed to Brazil.[22]

Brazil's commerce responded vigorously to its new-found freedom. Sugar and cotton, with some coffee, sustained a trade which grew from £1.2 million in 1812 to £2.3 million in 1816 and reached £4 million by 1822. Dom João, now King João VI, decided to stay in Brazil at the conclusion of hostilities in Europe and in 1815 he raised his Kingdom of Brazil to equal stature with that of Portugal itself within the framework of the Empire. Portuguese ships and merchants were given tariff advantages but this was insufficient to enable them to recapture their former position in the Brazil trade. The court at Rio assumed some of the trappings of a 'tropical Versailles', but the economic policies of the exiled monarchy began more and more to reflect the interests of commercial agriculture. In a major programme of public works the docks were enlarged, warehouses, an arsenal and a prison built, and roads improved. Those with cash found little difficulty in gaining huge royal land grants (*sesmarías*). The size and cost of the royal establishment and retinue remained a problem; three palaces were built for members of the royal family. Titles, offices and contracts were distributed to Brazilians as well as Portuguese, but proprietors in areas distant from the court – especially the north-east – shouldered the burden of export taxes without receiving commensurate benefits. While individual Brazilians gained from the presence of the court, the Brazilian treasury had to underwrite a royal establishment and military operations on a scale it had not known before.[23]

Portugal, much damaged by the war and confronted by a colony that had become a rival metropolis, saw less of the profits of Empire and discovered the inconvenience of being ruled by a distant goverment. In

August–September 1820 a revolt spread from Oporto to the rest of Portugal calling for the King's return and for the elaboration of a constitution. Many of those who backed this revolt looked forward to reconstructing a more effective colonial system, with watertight guarantees for Portuguese manufacturers and merchants in the Brazilian market. Ideologically the revolt was influenced by Spanish Constitutionalism and the rising in Cadiz. There was much talk of the need to abolish feudal restrictions. Nevertheless the Portuguese revolt was not republican, partly in deference to the European powers and partly because the monarchy was the essential link with Empire. The Portuguese Constitutionalists demanded the return of the King to assert their authority over him, and with the hope of reconstructing an imperial centre in Portugal.

In Brazil there was also support for the idea of a constitution, since many Brazilians were weary of the expensive, top-heavy court, with its arbitrary powers and over-representation of Portuguese. Many Brazilians thought it a good idea for the King and his Portuguese courtiers to return to Portugal. Juntas were formed in Rio, São Paulo and other centres urging João to respond to the demand for a convention and to promise to respect its conclusions. Pressed on both sides, João did leave for Portugal in April 1821, and some 4,000 courtiers, administrators and lawyers accompanied or followed him. He left his son Pedro as Regent of the Brazilian Kingdom, commanding a less overweight bureaucracy. Aware that Portuguese power in Brazil was now much weakened, João advised his son that, in the event of Brazil seeking to separate itself from the metropolis, Pedro should himself take leadership of the movement rather than allow 'the Crown to be seized by some adventurer'.[24]

Brazil's population had now grown to 4 million, a little ahead of that of the metropolis. The Portuguese Constitutionalists devised a system of representation which, while formally based on population, gave the smaller kingdom a majority of delegates; Brazil's slaves, now numbering at least 1.5 million, were simply omitted from consideration. Brazil was allotted 75 delegates in a convention of 205; only 50 Brazilians arrived in time to participate in the proceedings. The Portuguese delegates insisted that Portugal should be the administrative and legislative hub of the Empire. A Cortes meeting in Lisbon would be responsible for imperial trade regulations and a budget; administration and justice would also be centred on Lisbon. Brazil would no longer count as a unified kingdom but its separate provinces would each enjoy some local powers and be represented in the Lisbon Cortes. The Brazilian delegates did not like the substance of these proposals at all, but matters were aggravated by the condescending manner adopted by some Portuguese delegates. Thus the white Brazilians would entertain their own racial conceit but did not like Portuguese referring to their country in terms derogatory to its racial mixture. When one Portuguese delegate insisted that Brazil needed Portuguese tutelage and protection because of the threat of slave revolt, he drew the tart riposte that Brazilian slave-owners could manage their slaves very well by themselves and that, even were this in doubt, Portugal was in no state to help them.

The Brazilian delegates opposed the idea of a unified empire with a single Cortes meeting in Lisbon; they pointed to the extreme inconvenience of journeying so far from their estates and families. The delegates chosen included declared opponents of the royal power such as Manuel Tavares, a priest who had been a leading supporter of the Republic of Pernambuco in 1817. Many of the Brazilian delegates argued for a loose dual monarchy with two assemblies, one in Portugal, the other in Brazil. They argued that Brazilian conditions were quite different from those prevailing in Portugal – and therefore required different laws. Slavery was cited as a salient example. Interestingly enough the São Paulo delegation, who arrived with a well-worked-out brief elaborating the proposal for a dual monarchy, also called for reduced reliance on slavery and encouragement for European immigration. But this mild abolitionism was accompanied by insistence that Brazil had its own special problems and must govern itself. It soon became clear that the Brazilian proposals were completely unacceptable to the Portuguese Constitutionalists; one suggestion made by the Brazilians was that Portugal's overseas colonies could choose in which Cortes they wished to be represented, that of Lisbon or that of Rio. Alarmed by the spectre of Brazilian autonomy the Cortes demanded the return of Pedro, the Prince Regent, to Portugal.[25]

Opinion in Brazil itself reacted sharply when it was learned that the Cortes intended to eliminate Brazil's administrative autonomy and divide it into separate provinces. Brazilians were also angered by the order given to their Regent. The advent of the constitutional epoch had permitted the emergence of an independent press which reported the deliberations of the Cortes in detail, including real or supposed slights on Brazil made by Portugese delegates. These papers had very small circulations but, at least in the towns, they contributed to a developing political culture, still dominated by the rich and powerful but often articulated by journalists, doctors, lawyers or priests and drawing behind it many kinds of artisan and petty bourgeois. Rio, with 50,000 inhabitants in 1808 was now a city of 100,000 inhabitants. As the crisis in relations with Portugal developed remaining Portuguese merchants or officials became the target of popular anger.

Petitions were drawn up by leading citizens in many parts of Brazil urging the Prince to stay. On January 9th 1822, in reply to an address from the Municipal Council of Rio de Janeiro, Pedro announced that he would not return to Portugal. He appointed as First Minister José Bonifácio de Andrade e Silva, a veteran royal official of 'enlightened' views and at the time a member of the municipal council in São Paulo. José Bonifácio had attracted attention as one of the authors of the plan taken by the São Paulo delegation to the Cortes in Portugal. While José Bonifácio continued for a while to speak of a dual monarchy, as chief of Pedro's Cabinet he pursued a policy of almost unqualified Brazilian autonomy. In February, acting on the advice of José Bonifácio, Pedro refused to permit the Portuguese squadron sent to collect him to land at Rio and later ordered all Portuguese troops who were unhappy at the situation in Brazil to return to Portugal. The Prince Regent and his minister used their powers and authority to win over or isolate the Portuguese commanders; some of the latter had little sympathy for the Portuguese Cortes while all of them depended on the Rio Treasury to pay and supply their troops. In June 1822 the Prince called for a Brazilian Constituent Assembly, with delegates to be elected by all men receiving a certain minimum income from property or a profession. From Lisbon came news that the Cortes was preparing a military expedition against Brazil. On September 22nd 1822 Pedro declared Brazil's independence; two weeks later that Brazil would be a constitutional empire, the constitution to be drawn up by the Constituent Assembly. Pedro's coronation as Emperor, a splendid affair, followed in December. The fact that Brazilian independence had been declared by the Prince Regent and royal heir allowed for an exceptionally smooth transition to independent statehood, with great continuity at the levels of both symbolic authority and personnel. In the euphoria of independence it was little noticed that Pedro had not clearly repudiated the right of succession to the Portuguese throne for his children. Brazilian independence was, of course, challenged by the Portuguese government. The overthrow of the constitutional order in Portugal in the latter part of 1823 made this predictable Portuguese opposition more rather than less urgent.

In the south of Brazil the Portuguese commander left peacefully after receiving assurances, and perhaps money, from the imperial government. The threat of an expedition from Portugal never materialised – the British, who stood to lose from any closing of the Brazilian market, urged that it would be folly to attempt any reconquest. José Bonifácio found a French officer who had fought in Colombia to train the Brazilian forces; he also secured the services of Lord Cochrane, whose squadron subdued a recalcitrant Portuguese garrison in the north.

Within less than a year, and with very little bloodshed, Brazil ejected the remaining Portuguese loyalists. In most cases what was required was a show of force, sufficient to allow the Portuguese commanders an honourable withdrawal. In one incident a Portuguese commander was suspected of having fomented slave rebellion; Labatut, the French military expert retained by Pedro, ordered fifty black insurgents to be shot. But in general the Portuguese loyalists were whites while the Brazilian militia units reflected the former colony's racial mixture. The black troops of the historic *Batalhão dos Henriques* rallied to the Emperor; to boost the size of the imperial forces a new *Batalhão dos Libertos* was formed, comprised of former slaves – their masters receiving full compensation. The Constitutional Assembly approved this latter measure and pursued its debates against a background of continuing confrontation with Portuguese garrisons loyal to Lisbon.[26]

The Assembly deliberated on the proper scope of Brazilian citizenship and, in a special closed session, the advisability of ending slavery and banning the slave trade. José Bonifácio opposed what he saw as the demagogy of liberal democrats and was quite prepared to use police powers against them as well as against Portuguese sympathisers. But he urged a catholic concept of citizenship that would ignore the old caste barriers. Some delegates, including former participants in the Pernambuco revolt of 1817, argued that free Africans, or even all former slaves, were not entitled to citizenship rights. But the Assembly eventually came down in favour of giving citizenship to all free men of colour; stiff income qualifications for voters and office-holders sufficed to exclude the majority from direct political participation in any case.

At the closed session of the Assembly Jose Bonifácio secured support for easier manumission laws and a ban on the slave trade. The Assembly was meeting in the aftermath of Cúcuta, which may have encouraged the view that something should be done about slavery. Many delegates deplored Brazil's reliance on a huge influx of African slaves; however, they would not commit the Empire to a 'free womb' law. Slave imports at this time were running at 20,000–30,000 a year, leading to the danger of a slave majority that could not be contained. Even delegates who felt the time had not yet arrived for a total or immediate ban knew that there were good reasons to appease British abolitionism. The British could not be relied on to restrain Portugal's plans for reconquest unless the slave trade was officially denounced; in theory Portugal had itself banned the trade, though many Portuguese were still involved in every phase of the traffic.

José Bonifácio's opposition to the slave traffic was quite genuine. Though a scourge of the Liberals he favoured steps to end slavery, encourage European immigration, establish a university and force the large landowners to hand back land grants which they had not brought into cultivation. His enlightened social ideas earned him the emnity of the conservative interests just as his zeal for public order had earnt him the hostility of the Liberals. Few yet shared the nation-building vision of José Bonifácio and his abolitionist proposals helped to isolate him, despite his outstanding role in the moves to independence. In many ways his outlook and position came to parallel that of Arango in Cuba.[27]

Pedro became uneasy at the powers the Assembly arrogated to itself and at its willingness to arbitrate anything and everything, leaving him with an empty ceremonial role. He was particularly concerned when the Assembly refused, by a narrow majority, to make the Emperor's sanction necessary to the passage of legislation. In November 1823 Pedro dissolved the Assembly and suspended its constitution; José Bonifácio and leaders of the Assembly were sent into exile. Pedro's actions were endorsed by the municipal authorities in the various centres and met with the consent of the great proprietors. The Assembly had contained quite a large number of lawyers, priests, military men and public officials. Though these men were not exactly firebrands – most of them were over fifty years of age and had spent long years in the service of the monarchy – it probably seemed sensible to the large proprietors, who did not themselves intend to spend all their time in Rio, to safe-guard continuity and stability by allowing the Emperor a veto. The Assembly's deliberations on slavery and the slave trade were never mentioned as a reason for disbanding it but may have made the Emperor's action more acceptable to the large slave-owners and slave-traders.

To begin with the Emperor had no difficulty in finding moderate Liberals who would work with him. In March 1824 he decreed a new constitution which guaranteed prevailing institutions; slavery was not mentioned in the declamatory sections of the document, though references to masters and slaves crept into minor clauses. Under the terms of the constitution there was an Assembly from which governments were to be drawn; but the Emperor had the power to appoint ministers, to veto legislation and to dismiss the Assembly. Citizenship was extended, as before, to freedmen. The right to vote and hold office was limited to those with a qualifying income from property; this might well be slave property but the allocation of representation did not, as in the United States, reflect slave numbers. While the 'moderating power' of the Emperor was considerable, the workings of the constitution allowed the large proprietors considerable latitude in their own regions.[28]

The imperial decree against the slave trade remained a dead letter. Britain extended *de facto* recognition to the Empire in 1825 despite the fact that no agreement on co-operation in enforcing the ban had been reached. A Slave Trade Treaty was eventually signed between the Empire and Britain in 1827 which allowed for a continuing traffic for a further three years; inevitably the effectiveness of this treaty would depend on the attitude of the imperial authorities, both at the centre and in the localities; the latter would be drawn from, or appointed by, the large slave-owning proprietors. Canning knew that he had been lenient with Brazil, but he was anxious to give support to Pedro and the imperial regime. Pedro was willing to accept the continuing validity of previous agreements made between the London and Portuguese governments, including those which gave the British favourable access to the Brazilian market. Canning also liked the fact that at least one of the new South American states, indeed the largest of them, had a monarchical regime. British diplomatic pressure also paved the way for Portuguese recognition of Brazilian independence – in return for Brazil paying out massive compensation to Portugal, £2 million, for its loss of public property in its former colony. London banks advanced Brazil the money to pay this, saddling the new Empire with heavy commitments to foreign rentiers.[29]

The relative social conservatism of Brazilian proprietors was again revealed by the one republican challenge which the empire had to face. Following the suspension of the Constituent Assembly some Liberals of the north and north-east mounted a short-lived Confederation of the Equator in 1824, loosely modelled on Greater Colombia. The leaders of the rebellion failed either to win the support of the large landowners of the region or to make a revolutionary appeal to the slaves. Recife–Olinda was once again the main support of the challenge to the authorities in Rio. Some radical Liberals participated in the rebellion, such as the doctor Cipriano José Barata, a man with a considerable political past by this time: he was thought to have been the 'intellectual author' of the 1798 conspiracy in Bahia, he had played some role in the Republic of 1817 and he had been elected to the Cortes in 1820. The free coloured population of Recife–Olinda played a somewhat confused part in the uprising. The companies of both *pardos* and blacks rallied to the revolt but a *pardo* commander, Major Emiliano Mundurucu, had to be restrained from leading his men in the pillage and destruction of all houses in the city belonging to imperial sympathisers. As his men sacked the palaces of the rich merchants and planters they sang a song popular with the free people of colour:

Let us imitate Christophe,
The immortal Haitian,
Eia! Imitate his deeds,
O my sovereign people!

Mundurucu and his men were brought under control by the commander of the company of black troops. The Pernambuco revolt reflected the inchoate political radicalism of the free urban population and never developed a social programme. Militarily it was quickly isolated. The navy, under Cochrane's command, first blockaded the rebels and then, in concert with land forces, obliged them to surrender. The conservative sugar planters and mill-owners of the region contributed their own private forces to the final assault; a *senhor de engenho* could normally mobilise a dozen or more retainers, including employees and tenants.[30]

That slavery survived the independence period almost entirely unscathed reflected not only the particular methods whereby it was won but also the very diffuse nature of slavery in the Brazilian social formation. In Bahia the most important slave-owners were the *senhores de engenho*, who had an average of just over sixty-five slaves each in a count of 1816–17; however, together they only held 7.7 per cent of all slaves. The *lavradores de cana* held just over ten slaves each and these holdings accounted for 22 per cent of all slaves. Tobacco farmers held an average of just over thirteen slaves each but only accounted for 0.2 per cent of all slaves. Smallholders, tenants, fisherman, and employees who owned slaves held an average of between one and six each; they accounted for just under 18 per cent of all slaves between them. Priests, small businessmen, government officials and other urban dwellers each owned a few slaves on average. In this count 824 individuals for whom no occupation was listed held an average of 3.4 slaves each and accounted for 38 per cent of all slaves in the count. Altogether about 70 per cent of all slaves were owned by small proprietors. And a contemporary observed of Bahia: 'It is proof of extreme poverty to not own a slave; they may lack every domestic convenience but a slave at any cost.'[31]

There were, of course, many very poor free people, amongst them many *pardos*, who were dependent on the larger proprietors. Nevertheless slaveholding was sufficiently common to create a distinctive species of slaveholding 'middle class' and 'lower middle class'. Possession of a few slaves eased the burdens of daily life for the owners; such slaves worked at household tasks, subsistence cultivation, or could be hired out – very profitably if they had a skill. If it is further borne in mind that there was a dense web of real and fictive kin relations, and of patronage, between rich and poor, it becomes easier to understand why there was so little disposition to question slavery.

Property-ownership had become the key to power and influence in Brazil considerably before the provisions of the constitution of 1824. This is clearly suggested by the lapidary formulation of a contemporary Brazilian writer who observed:

> Political society is divided into proprietors and those who own no property; the former are infinitely fewer than the latter, as is well known. The proprietor tries to buy as cheaply as possible the only possession of the propertyless or wage-earner, his labour. The latter in turn tries to sell it as dearly as possible. In this struggle the weaker contestant, although greater in numbers usually succumbs to the stronger.[32]

In the export sector of the economy the slaves were the basic labour force. But poor free men were still important to the *fazendeiro* as overseers, henchmen, tenants, share-croppers and so forth. Despite slavery this was, in its own way, a social formation thoroughly penetrated by commercial relationships. The main surplus was extracted by extra-economic pressure, but the apparatus of coercion itself was assembled and held in place to a significant extent by economic forces.

Brazil had moved far away from the customs of a traditional estate order. A foreign visitor in 1805 remarked:

> It is astonishing to see how little subordination of rank is known in this country; France in its completest state of revolution and citizenship never excelled it in that respect. You see here the white servant converse with his master in the most equal and friendly terms, despite his commands, and wrangle about them if contrary to *his better opinion* – which the superior receives in good part and frequently acquiesces in. The system does not rest here but extends to the mulattos and even to the negroes.[33]

Both the passage to independence and its aftermath can be seen as giving some expression to a particular, heavily qualified, sense of freedom and civic equality, excluding the mass of slaves but including the mass of the free urban population and a layer of free people in the countryside. In the early days of independence Pedro won a following amongst the free people of colour and the urban unemployed since he appeared more disposed to recognise them and protect them than the Liberal ideologues.

Despite the ballast of slavery the Empire did not quickly achieve political stability. The Brazilian oligarchy found that it was overly dependent on an Emperor who had not entirely renounced his claims as a Braganza. Following Portuguese recognition of Brazil Pedro had allowed his father to call himself 'Emperor of Brazil' as a courtesy title. When his father died in 1826 Pedro claimed the Portuguese throne for his daughter Maria, and proceeded to devote himself to vindicating her cause against that of his brother Miguel. Many Brazilians resented the agreement to pay £2 million to Portugal and suspected that Pedro had been the more willing to do this because of his residual links and involvement with the old metropolis. The agreement with Portugal had also required Brazil to recognise that Angola was a Portuguese colony, thus ending the Brazilian dream of a transatlantic empire. Pedro retained many Portuguese in his entourage, which made him vulnerable to nativist criticisms. The concessions made to the British, whether on tariffs or the slave trade, weakened the Emperor's support. Pedro often ignored the Assembly and ruled by imperial fiat; loans were contracted, foreign troops hired and treaties entered into without the assent of the legislature.

In the years 1825–8 the imperial army became bogged down in an expensive and unsuccessful war to retain control of the *Banda Oriental*, ending with the evacuation of Brazilian forces and recognition of the new state of Uruguay in 1830. The imperial army included a number of mercenary foreign detachments which became unruly in defeat or when their pay was not forthcoming. Economic difficulties compounded the problems of the Empire and the Bank of Brazil was obliged first to suspend payments and then to dissolve itself. The Brazilian press – there were now over forty newspapers in the country – gave their readers pointed accounts of the overthrow of the French King Charles X in 1830. In March 1831 Pedro conceded to pressure by appointing a Cabinet of semi-oppositional Liberal politicians. Disliking their first actions as a government, he tried to dismiss them but found the greatest difficulty in assembling a workable administration. In April 1831 he abdicated in favour of his five-year-old son, Pedro II. José Bonifácio was persuaded to become tutor to Pedro II while a conservative politician and landowner, the Marquis of Caravellas, was sworn in as Regent. The ex-Emperor went to Portugal where he died in 1834, after leading an expedition which, with British help, defeated the ultra-monarchist Miguelists and regained the throne of Portugal for his daughter Maria.

One of the first acts of the Regency was an edict of June 1831 which declared that foreign treaties were only valid if ratified by the Assembly. In appearance a triumph for parliamentarianism and constitutional government, this edict was a gift to the slave-traders; it put in question the Slave Trade Treaty with Britain, which gave British judges and naval officers powers to seize Brazilian vessels suspected of involvement in the slave trade. The treaty had come into effect in March 1831 and there were signs of a pause in the Atlantic traffic as slave-traders waited to see whether the Brazilian government would comply with its side of the treaty. However, the broader political and ideological climate of the early Regency was hostile to the slave-traders. The overthrow of Pedro I had expressed a nativist and Liberal reaction against what was seen as a conservative, Portuguese-influenced regime. Many of the slave-traders in Brazil were Portuguese, since it was the Portuguese traders who had the contacts in Africa. Moreover the business of the slave-trader was introducing Africans, an activity unwelcome to nativist sentiment. If the slave-traders gained from the Regency, it was not because they were popular but rather because, on the one hand, they had the resources to influence government and, on the other, the popular classes failed to find a programme or organisation which could impose itself on the rulers. For a decade or so central government was weak.

The Brazilian Empire survived the turbulent period of the Regency (1831–40), though plantation development was uncertain. Attempts by the radicals in the Assembly to introduce Liberal reforms and a more federal structure plunged areas of the country into civil war. The Liberal leaders disbanded parts of the army and in August 1831 set up the National Guard, an armed militia commanded by the richer citizens. Despite vociferous appeals to Liberal principles it was tacitly agreed that slaves should not be involved in the quarrels of free men. These years saw the last of the large scale, African-inspired revolts in the Brazilian north-east; warriors captured in the Muslim *jihads* of West Africa were particularly prone to rebellion on arrival in Brazil. There was little communication between the unstable radicalism of the urban *menu peuple* and the recently arrived African rebels. The chief form taken by anti-slavery was opposition to the slave trade; though there was no organised abolitionism the more radical Liberals did take up the need for Brazilian legislation against the slave trade. In November 1831 a law was passed which its sponsors claimed would end the import of Africans. But its effects proved nugatory since it relied on local magistrates and juries to impose penalties on the slave-traders; the latter found no difficulty in locating pliant authorities. The now 'illegal' slave trade soon regained something very like its former scale.[34]

For nearly ten years Brazil lacked a strong central government; the worst strife erupted in the outlying provinces. In the plantation zone order was maintained by the National Guard, which was given more resources and power in 1834. Against the expectations of many, Brazil remained a united Empire governed in essentials by the constitution of 1824. When Pedro II's majority was declared and the Regency ended in 1840, a more coherent central authority emerged. The young Emperor came to rule in the manner of Louis Philippe or of one of the Hanoverian 'illegitimate monarchs'. The Emperor worked with and through the leaders of the Conservative or Liberal factions of the oligarchy. The Assembly was treated with respect, though the Emperor could use his 'moderating power' to make and unmake governments. Once the Emperor had appointed a Cabinet it was responsible for the budget and for directing an increasingly effective civil administration. A more disciplined and unified army was created, with beneficial effects for orderly commerce. The great landowners lived on their estates, ruling their slaves and tenants, and taking little account of central government. The latter derived its revenues from tariffs and other taxes levied on the sphere of circulation. In the course of the 1840s and 1850s coffee cultivation, based on slave labour, spread in the hinterlands of Rio and Santos and inland around São Paulo, making Brazil into the world's largest producer.[35]

There was still no public questioning of slavery; the presence of a large, probably growing, number of slaves and their vital contribution to the export economy remained a powerful inhibiting factor. On the other hand, the continuing slave trade was a latent source of controversy just below the surface of political life; abolitionist sentiment, such as it was, concentrated on this and not on slavery as such. A number of imperial statesmen, and Pedro II himself, contrived to present themselves as friendly to a moderate and judicious abolitionism, designed to end the import of Africans, though the slave trade continued to thrive down to the early 1850s.[36]

The survival of slavery in Cuba and Brazil in the epoch of South American independence reflected the deliberate but not ineffectual caution of their slave-owners. They saw no reason for hazardous experiments in republicanism, when the prevailing regime could give them so much of what they wanted. Just as sharp breaks in regime gave an opening to abolitionism so the comparatively smooth transition in Cuba and Brazil meant that the social order was less vulnerable to conspiracies and revolts. There were certainly difficult moments for the slave-owners in Cuba and Brazil, especially at times of political tension, but they found a way to survive and flourish. Since they were not challenging an established order, the Cuban and Brazilian leaders had no need to mobilise slaves in the manner of a Bolivar or San Martín.

The Cuban and Brazilian planters had the advantage that they confronted a metropolitan authority that had been greatly weakened, above all by the Napoleonic invasion and its consequences. This made it far easier to dismantle those structures of colonialism and absolutism that stifled commercial agriculture. In the Cuban case the metropolis had great need for the colony, while in the Brazilian case the colony had actually outgrown the metropolis. The slave-owners of the British and French Caribbean after 1815 faced a far more difficult situation; a large slave majority and metropolitan powers that could not so easily be defied, as in Brazil's case, or ignored and manipulated, as in Cuba's case.[37]

The new relationship between planters and the metropolis was a function not simply of the latter's size but also of changes in the inner character and organisation of the metropolitan state. The absolutism of the imperial states, and the autonomy of their dynastic ruling houses, had been destroyed. Napoleon's invasion had not only broken up the former state apparatus and snapped the imperial link. It had also permitted new social forces to assert themselves: on both sides of the Atlantic there emerged a strange mixture of popular nationalism, programmatic liberalism and forms of military organisation no longer structured from above. The new state forms which emerged in the aftermath no longer had the capacity to impose themselves on the social formation but were obliged to adapt to it, and especially to independent economic property. In Spain and Portugal successive coups and civil wars weakened the imperial state and undid restorationist attempts; the loss of Empire removed both a source of revenue and the pedestal for an important sector of the state apparatus. Portugal retained an Empire in Africa, just as Spain retained Cuba, but the articulation of these new empires was quite different from their absolutist predecessors. Nobody could doubt that the Madrid government controlled the apparatus of Bourbon administration in America in the eighteenth century; indeed the impulse to independence had been called forth precisely because of the effectivenesss of the system of centralised colonial administration, with its short terms of office, regular inspections and rendering of accounts. In the shrunken Portuguese and Spanish Empires of the period after 1824 colonial officials became far more autonomous from the centre and far more reliant on local sponsorship from traders, especially slave-traders, and landowners, especially those in command of slave-worked estates. The Captain General of Cuba or Angola was henceforth not so much a representative of the metropolis in the colony as a conduit through which the slavers and slave-owners influenced the course of metropolitan politics.[38] The Brazilian Empire came to acquire a somewhat greater degree of coherence and integrity but could not be other than attentive to the demands and interests of the notables who inhabited it.

Britain had played a large role in shaping the new pattern of state forms and socio-economic development on both sides of the Atlantic. Its traders had eagerly penetrated the imperial markets, its soldiers of fortune had helped to undermine the old structures, its statesmen and diplomats had promoted the new regimes, extending sponsorship and recognition in return for advantageous commercial agreements. By the 1820s Latin America accounted for over a quarter of Britain's manufacturing export trade, with Brazil and Cuba being the best customers. The regimes established with British blessing – indeed usually with the aid of British arms and money – increasingly resembled, as in a sort of caricature, British 'illegitimate monarchy'. The Spain of Maria Cristina and Isabella II, the Brazil of the two Pedros, the Portugal of Maria had each symbolically flouted the rules of succession. These were now regimes representing a new type of notable, not the feudal magnate, but independent landed proprietors and military men, planters and merchants. State revenues were drawn from the sphere of circulation (taxes on trade and consumption) and from the sale of Church property; feudal property forms were deprived of legal sanction. While feudal jurisdictions were suppressed the military claimed their own special exemptions from civil law. The new landed notables were involved in realising surplus through the sale of agricultural commodities, but in Spain or Portugal capital and wage labour were not yet as developed as in Hanoverian Britain. On the other hand, the planters of Cuba and Brazil revealed an entrepreneurial commitment and vigour that had been lacking in Britain's West Indian absentees. The new notables were fair-weather Liberals but emphatically not democrats. At local level they exercised juridical and political authority as well as economic power as landlords and employers. Monarchy gave them a title to rule, while parliamentary forms and Liberal rhetoric allowed them to feel in the mainstream of progress.[39]

British opinion might be flattered by imitation, and gratified by the vigorous sale of textiles in the new states, but there was at least one highly embarrassing aspect of the newly emerging Atlantic order. British statesmen had trumpeted the cause of slave trade abolition at every international gathering, yet Britain's client states were the principal participants in it. International agreements to suppress the slave traffic had come to symbolise the new aspiration to a *Pax Britannica* yet proved utterly ineffective. By contrast the United States, with its republican principles and refusal to agree to British conditions, had more effectively stopped the inflow of slaves. Many of those British manufactures sent to Havana or Recife were simply *en route* to the African coast where they would be exchanged for human cargoes.[40]

If the liberation of Spanish America had encouraged anti-slavery in the Old World by means of positive example, then the continuance of the slave traffic to Cuba and Brazil did so by straining credibility in Britain's official abolitionism. Britain was meant to be the strongest naval power in the world, yet its squadrons had little success in catching the slave-traders. This failure was particularly glaring in the Caribbean, where the squadron was far less zealous and effective than was the case on the African coast. Thus in the years 1820–23 not a single slave-trader was caught in Caribbean waters by the British. By contrast several slavers were seized by Colombian or Haitian warships; a paradox which was the more pointed in that one of Boyer's most effective cruisers was the *Wilberforce*.[41]

The momentum of Atlantic commerce had raised slave prices on the African coast and encouraged a trade in the years after 1815 which frequently equalled, or even exceeded, the annual averages of the 1780s. Nearly 100,000 slaves were carried across the Atlantic in 1828, destined for Brazil, Cuba and the restored French colonies; this was very close to the record years of the pre-abolitionist era. British statesmen were uneasily aware of the conflicting objectives which they were seeking to reconcile: Britain as trading power and Britain as arbiter of a new Atlantic order. At the time he was negotiating Brazilian independence Canning warned Wilberforce that it would be necessary to satisfy 'the commercial as well as the moral feelings of the country'. In 1828, when Prime Minister, the Duke of Wellington explained to his Foreign Minister with soldierly directness: 'The whole question is one of impression. We shall never succeed in abolishing the foreign slave trade. But we must take care to avoid to take any step which may induce the people of England to believe that we do not do everything in our power to discourage and to put it down as soon as possible.'[42] Whether pessimistic, cynical or merely candid the Iron Duke's judgement in this matter, as in others, was comprehensible enough coming from someone who made little parade of abolitionist zeal. The stance of the British government became the more awkward in the 1830s and 1840s when vaunted champions of abolitionism like Palmerston were responsible for British policy.

Notes

1. The free and slave populations of Cuba and Brazil were not reliably counted until later in the century. The Cuban figures given in the text come from a contemporary estimate cited in Fernando Ortiz, *Los Negros Esclavos*, Havana 1916, pp. 22–3. Ortiz cites an estimate for 1825 which gives a total population of 715,000, with 325,000 whites, 100,000 free people of colour and 290,000 slaves, making 390,000 people of colour. For Brazil's population breakdown around 1800 see Lockhart and Schwartz,

Early Latin America, pp. 398–401. Brazil's total population grew from 2.5 million in 1808 to nearly 4 million, probably larger than that of Portugal, by the time of independence, with the slave proportion rising, because of heavy imports, from roughly 34 per cent to over 40 per cent.

2. Kenneth R. Maxwell, *Conflicts and Conspiracies: Brazil and Portugal, 1750–1808*, p. 218.

3. Maxwell, *Conflicts and Conspiracies*, pp. 219–20, 222.

4. Stuart Schwartz, *Sugar Plantations in the Formation of Brazilian Society: Bahia, 1550–1835*, Cambridge 1985, p. 482. The timing of this revolt and the attack on Nazaré on the 'day of kings' suggest either a religious element in the rising or an attempt to exploit the distraction of the masters' festivals, or both.

5. Glacyra L. Leite, *A Insurreicão Pernambucana de 1817*, São Paulo 1984.

6. José Luciano Franco, 'La conspiración de Morales', *Ensayos históricos*, Havana 1974, pp. 93–100; José Luciano Franco, *Las minas de Santiago del Prado y la rebelión de los cobreros*, Havana 1975, pp. 126–31.

7. José Luciano Franco, *Las conspiraciones de 1810 y 1812*, Havana 1977; 'Proyecto de constitutión para la isla de Cuba', Pichardo, *Documentos para la historia de Cuba*, I, pp. 253–60.

8. José Luciano Franco, 'La conspiración de Aponte', *Ensayos historicós*, pp. 127–90, p. 139. The wider context is sketched in Anne Pérotin–Dumon, 'Aux origines de l'impérialisme insulaire nord-américain: *corsarios insurgentes* et "fidelité" cubaine (1810–30)', in *Cuba: les étapes d'une libération*, Toulouse–Mirail 1979.

9. David Murray, *Odious Commerce*, p. 32. The *Consulado* was an official body representing the leading merchants and planters.

10. José Luciano Franco, 'La conspiración de Aponte', *Ensayos históricos*, pp. 127–90.

11. Manuel Moreno Fraginals, *El ingenio: complejo económico social Cubano del Azúcar*, pp. 105–11. As Fraginals's classic work makes clear the 'superstructural' changes followed rather than preceded the first Cuban sugar boom, the 'dance of the millions' in 1800–1802. Measures such as the abolition of the *estanco* had a political as much as economic rationale; that of retaining the loyalty of the tobacco farmers. Some of the relevant decrees are found in Pichardo, *Documentos para la historia de Cuba*, I, pp. 261–3.

12. Murray, *Odious Commerce*, pp. 50–71.

13. Félix Varela, 'Memorias que demuestra la necesidad de extinguir la esclavitud de los negros en la Isla de Cuba, atendiendo a los intereses de sus proprietarios', *Documentos para la historia de Cuba*, I, pp. 276–88.

14. Robert Francis Jameson, *Letters from Havana during the Year 1820*, London 1821, p. 8. The 'Mixed Commission' comprised British and Spanish appointed judges who tried suspected slave-traders brought to Havana by the naval forces of either state and handed over those slaves seized to the local authorities.

15. Quoted in Herminio Portell Vilá, *Historia de Cuba en sus relaciones con los Estados Unidos y España*, Havana 1938, 5 vols, I, p. 141. This rather old-fashioned exercise in diplomatic history gives copious and enlightening quotations from all the leading statesmen involved in the 'Cuban question' at the time.

16. George Canning to Rufus King, August 7th 1825, C.K. Webster, ed., *Britain and the Independence of Latin America 1812–30: Selected Documents from the Foreign Office Archives*, London 1953, p. 521.

17. Vicente Lecúna, compiler, *Selected Writings of Bolivar*, edited by H.E. Bierke, New York 1951, p. 499.

18. Jorge Ibarra, Direción política de las FAR, *Historia de Cuba*, pp. 93–103. Support for independence came chiefly from regions outside the central zone of plantation development. The Captain General reported to Spain that the pro-independence conspiracy was only supported by a few 'irresponsible youths' and 'angry and heedless *campesinos*'; he regretted that mixed up in it were 'decent people with mulattos and blacks' (p. 99). As this remark implies the racial caste system still reigned in Cuba though for some time yet there were *pardo* and black militias.

19. During the latter period the Havana treasury expended a further $4 million annually on maintenance of the garrision and squadron. (Raimundo P. Garrich, *Estado de los ingresos y erogaciones de la tesoreria general de Ejército de Habana en los años 1823 à 1849 ambos inclusive, formado del órden del Exmo. Conde de Villaneuva*, Havana 1850.) The Spanish state was acutely short of funds during this whole period . See Josep Fontana, *La Quiebra de la monárquía absoluta*, Barcelona 1971, and *Hacienda y estado en la crisis final del antiguo régimen español*, Madrid 1973. For an account of the importance of Cuba to Spain see Tuñón de Lara, *Estudios sobre el siglo XIX español*, Madrid 1978.

20. Hugh Thomas, *Cuba: The Pursuit of Freedom*, London 1970, pp. 156–67, 193–9.

21. Quoted in James Lang, *Portugese Brazil: The King's Plantation*, New York 1979, p. 193.

22. Sérgio Buarque de Holanda, *História geral da civilizacão Brasileira*, Tomo II, O *Brasil monárquico*, vol. 1, O *processo de emancipacão*, São Paulo 1965, pp. 278–99. The former 'Robespierre of the islands' was defeated ingloriously. As a military measure the invaders offered freedom and arms to the slaves who joined in the final assault; a 'model estate' belonging to the Governor was among the first to be captured. Under the terms of the treaty of capitulation, it was agreed that liberated former slaves would not remain in the colony, since this was thought a threat to public order, and their former owners were to receive compensation. Hugues returned to France where he was briefly imprisoned; during the 'hundred days' he was again active in the entourage of Fouché, evidently still his patron.

23. Mariá Odila Silva Diaz, 'The Establishment of the Royal Court in Brazil', in A.J.R. Russell–Wood, ed., *From Colony to Nation*, Baltimore 1975, pp. 89–108, p. 98.

24. This advice was recalled by Pedro in a letter to his father which is reprinted in António Vianna, *A emancipacião do Brasil*, Lisbon 1922, pp. 503–7, on p. 504.

25. Oliveira Lima, *O movimento da independência*, São Paulo 1972, pp. 101–12.

26. José Honório Rodrigues, *Independência: revolucão e contra–revolucão*, 5 vols, II, pp. 112–37; III, pp. 121–48; IV, pp. 126–30.

27. For an excellent portrait of this complex man see Emilia Viotto da Costa, *The Brazilian Empire: Myths and Histories*, Chicago 1985, pp. 24–52. This volume also contains a helpful summary of the independence movement (pp. 1–23) and an incisive sketch of Brazilian liberalism (pp. 53–78).

28. C.H. Haring, *Empire in Brazil: A New World Experiment in Monarchy*, Cambridge 1965, pp. 28–30.

29. Vianna, *A Emancipacão do Brazil*, 444–67.

30. Sérgio Buarque de Holandia, *História geral da civilizacão Brasileira*, Tomo II, O *Brasil monárchico*, vol. 1, pp. 227–37.

31. Schwartz, *Sugar Plantations in the Formation of Brazilian Society*, p. 439.

32. Santos Vilhena, *A Bahia, no século xviii*, quoted in Schwartz, *Sugar Plantations in the Formation of Brazilian Society*, p. 435. Schwartz also cites a newspaper editorial of 1834 to the following effect: 'the class of masters concentrates all political power in Brazil . . . if the proletariat as a class has little importance they are (at least) free men, and have no grounds for complaint because they possess all the constitutional rights and privileges without bias whatever of caste, colour or custom. . . . Two great interests tend to reunite and join all members of a society so constituted . . . the sentiment of nationality and the necessity of conserving dominion over the slaves' (p. 437).

33. Thomas Lindly, quoted in Stuart Schwartz, 'Elite Politics and the Growth of a Peasantry in Late Colonial Brazil', in Russell–Wood, *From Colony to Nation*, pp. 133–54, pp. 151–2. See also Stuart Schwartz, 'Late Colonial Brazil', *Cambridge History of Latin America*, II, pp. 601–60.

34. Clovis Moura, *Rebeliões das senzalas*, São Paulo 1959; Mauricio Goulart, *Escravidão Africana no Brasil*, São Paulo 1949, pp. 243–62, 272.

35. A systematic account of the Brazilian slave system under the Empire is attempted in a companion volume, *Nemesis of the Slave Power*, which is a sequel to the present work.

36. For an account of controversies over slavery in the Empire see Brasil Gerson, *Escravidão no império*, Rio de Janeiro 1975.

37. For a thoughtful comparative discussion see Fernando A. Novais, 'Passagens para a Novo Mundo', *Novos estudos*, CEBRAP, July 1984, pp. 2–8.

38. Valentim Alexandre, *Origens do colonialismo Português moderno, 1822–1891*, Lisbon 1979, pp. 5–70.

39. The above is only a preliminary sketch of these regimes; it is amplified in *Nemesis of the Slave Power*.

40. David Eltis, 'The Export of Slaves from Africa, 1821–1843', *Journal of Economic History*, vol. 37, 1977, pp. 409–33.

41. Murray, *Odious Commerce*, p. 78.

42. Bethell, *The Abolition of the Brazilian Slave Trade*, p. 66.

XI

The Struggle for British Slave Emancipation: 1823–38

And that slaughter to the nation
Shall steam up like inspiration,
Eloquent, oracular;
A volcano heard afar.
And these words shall then become
Like oppression's thundered doom
Ringing through each heart and brain.
Heard again – again – again.

'Rise like Lions after slumber
In unvanquishable number –
Shake your chains to earth like dew
Which in sleep hath fallen on you –
Ye are many – they are few.'

The Mask of Anarchy (written 1819, published 1832), P.B. Shelley

The lull in abolitionist activity in Britain after 1815 was brought to an end by a gradual relaxation of the political climate in the early 1820s. The oligarchy could weather a crisis with strong measures, but factional conflict within it ensured that new champions of reform would appear. The government was widely blamed for heavy taxation and continuing economic difficulties. The death of George III in 1820 and the succeeding conflict between the new King and Queen gave a field day to advocates of reform like Brougham, who acted as legal adviser to Queen Caroline. Lord Liverpool's administration had consented to George IV's request for a parliamentary bill to divorce him from his wife. That the spectacularly dissolute and adulterous George should seek to set aside the Queen on the ground of her impurity led to a widespread public campaign in her defence, replete with meetings and petitions of the sort which had not been seen since 1815. Wilberforce was approached in an attempt to reach a compromise settlement but to no avail. The Divorce Bill was defeated in the Commons. The oligarchic regime of 'illegitimate monarchy' was plunged in disarray. From this time on the Liverpool administration no longer had the political strength to smother Opposition demands: Catholic relief, slave emancipation, repeal of the Test and Corporation Acts, and parliamentary reform began to be advanced in and out of Parliament. Oligarchic government was sustained neither by economic success nor by fear and was obliged progressively to justify itself in the very terms of the challenge made to it by middle-class reformers.[1]

Wilberforce, Stephen and Macaulay had always privately intended to press for the removal or mitigation of slavery. In the 1820s they each published critical surveys of conditions in the British colonies pointing to evidence that the slave populations were declining, that mortality was high, family life difficult and religion lacking. They argued that the time had come to consider gradual emancipation. Reports of the emancipationist proclamations made by Bolivar and other leaders of the Spanish American liberation movements helped to put British abolitionists on their mettle; these developments were closely followed by the press because of British interest in Spanish American markets and because thousands of British volunteers, including Lord Cochrane, were fighting with the Spanish Americans.

In 1823 a number of the veteran abolitionists, including Wilberforce and Brougham, established the Society for Mitigating and Gradually Abolishing the State of Slavery throughout the British Dominions. Once again Quakers were active in support. Among new recruits were Stephen Lushington, an MP and advocate of prison reform; and Thomas Fowell Buxton, an MP and a brewer with many Quaker and evangelical connections. Wilberforce invited Buxton to take over the work of leading the anti-slavery forces in Parliament. As its title implied the new Society started out with modest aims: these included easier manumission laws, the ending of Sunday labour, the promotion of religious instruction on the plantations, legal recognition of slave marriages, legal recognition of slave property, and the admissibility of slave evidence in courts of law. The society also mooted the possibility that the children of slave mothers should be freed.[2]

This cautious rebirth of organised abolitionism soon aroused a significant popular response, accompanied by the emergence of fresh forces and far more radical perspectives. The ameliorative legislation proposed by the parliamentary leaders of the new society was supported by a new petition campaign and by the formation of local societies. The first Annual Report of the society was able to identify 220 local societies and to record that 825 petitions had been presented to Parliament; in the following session there were a further 674 petitions, those from four major cities – London, Manchester, Glasgow and Edinburgh – contained no less than 168,000 signatures.[3] That abolitionist themes were strategically lodged within British political culture was confirmed not only by the rapid build-up of the campaign but also by the government's response. Once again reformers found it easy to make a concerted attack on this issue and once again the government deemed it advisable to bring forward its own plans for giving some protection to the slaves. Canning introduced a series of motions that envisaged a ban on the whipping of female slaves, the admission of slave testimony in courts of law, and a programme of religious instruction; however, the society's proposals for emancipating the children of slave mothers were rejected on the grounds that the white populations of the West Indies were generally too small and vulnerable to cope with a large population of free blacks. The government's response had been cleared with at least some of the colonial proprietors; an Order in Council embodied some of the ameliorative proposals, but it was left up to the colonial assemblies themselves to interpret the Orders and to enact their own schemes for improving conditions on the plantations.[4]

If the new abolitionist movement had been limited to the objectives set out by the parliamentary leaders, then it might have been simply prepared to press for implementation of the government's compromise proposals. But instead a radical anti-slavery current developed which distrusted the timid proposals of the parliamentarians as well as the deceptively accommodating response of the government. In 1825 the society commenced publication of the *The Anti-Slavery Reporter* which furnished it with a means for debating the proper objectives of abolitionism as well as for conducting its own propaganda. This journal was initially edited by Zachary Macaulay, with assistance from his son, Thomas Babington Macaulay. It published detailed information on the continuing Atlantic slave trade and on the workings of the various American slave systems.

Among the veteran abolitionist leaders Thomas Clarkson and James Stephen insisted that no trust or hope should be invested in voluntary action by the colonial legislatures. James Stephen published a compendious and documented account of the inhumanity of the slave system, *The Slavery of the British West Indian Colonies Delineated*, published in two volumes in 1824 and 1830. Stephen's eldest son, also called James, had been engaged as legal counsel to the Colonial Office and could supplement from offical sources his father's account of the workings of the slave systems. However, both Clarkson and Stephen remained proponents of gradual emancipation. The most novel element in the new wave of the 1820s was that some within the respectable ranks of organised abolitionism took up the call for immediate emancipation, without compensation to the slave-owners. An anonymous pamphlet entitled *Immediate Not Gradual Emancipation*, first published in 1824, had great success with the local abolitionist groups. This pamphlet was followed by a stream of anti-slavery writings imbued with a vehemence and intransigence lacking in parliamentary abolitionism. Interestingly much of the new 'immediatist' anti-slavery writing was the work of women, including the pamphlet *Immediate Not Gradual Abolition* whose author was Mrs Elizabeth Heyricke. Among the local societies were a number of women's groups, a development of which Wilberforce disapproved. The chairwoman of one of these societies responded vigorously to news of Wilberforce's disapprobation: 'men may propose only *gradually* to abolish the worst of crimes, and only to *mitigate* the most evil bondage. . . . I trust no Ladies Association will ever be found with such words attached to it.'[5]

As it turned out the timing and content of emancipation were not matters which would be solely decided by British reformers or the British Parliament, a circumstance which was to lend extra force to Mrs Heyricke's protest.

In the aftermath of the French wars and of the suppression of the Atlantic slave trade new social and demographic patterns became visible in the British West Indies. Between 1807 and 1834 the total slave population of the West Indian colonies, including occupied territories formally acquired in 1815, dropped from 775,000 to 665,000, a decline of about 14 per cent overall. The decline was much sharper in the new colonies, notably Demerara–Essequibo, where the plantation development had been rapid and the build-up of population recent. The slave population in the older colonies, better established and more balanced, declined only slightly and in the case of Barbados there was to be overall growth, apart from a brief dip between 1809–12, with the slave population of this island rising from 75,000 to 85,000 between 1808 and the early 1830s. The overall British West Indian annual rate of population change at −0.4 per cent in fact represented an improvement on the appalling negative growth rates of the slave colonies in the previous century.[6] Cessation of the slave trade reduced the risk of imported epidemics, while the passage of time itself enlarged the core of American-born slaves with their increased adjustment to American conditions. Nevertheless anti-slavery advocates were able to cite population decline, reflecting both low fertility and high mortality, as an index that planters and managers were misusing their slaves. In so far as there was a clear link between negative or low growth and intensified slave-driving regimes on the plantations the anti-slavery advocates were perfectly justified.

However, the decline in the size of the slave population was also associated with a growth in the size of the free population. Free people of colour comprised only 2–3 per cent of the total population of the British West Indies in the 1770s. In the aftermath of the American war some blacks who had claimed freedom from the British settled in Jamaica or other islands. The revolution in St Domingue and the French Windwards also led to an influx of people of colour who had, or soon acquired, their freedom. It was common practice in the British West Indies for overseers or managers to take slave mistresses; sometimes they would make arrangements for the manumission of their offspring, thus further expanding the size of the free coloured population. Because the free coloured population was inured to the local disease environment and spared the rigours of forced labour it exhibited a positive natural growth rate. A further, though modest, factor favouring the rise of the free coloured population was new legislation, enacted in response to metropolitan pressure, which made manumission cheaper and easier to obtain. Between 1810 and 1830 the free people of colour grew from 6.6 per cent to 12.2 per cent of the population of the British West Indies. This compares with an overall drop in the size of the white population from 7.2 per cent to 6.6 per cent. In Barbados, with its well-established white population, free people of colour still comprised only 5.2 per cent of the population in 1830; in Jamaica the free people of colour comprised 7.4 per cent of the population in 1810, rising to 10.6 per cent in 1830 while the white population of the colony dropped from 6.9 to 5.0 per cent.[7] Absenteeism amongst the large proprietors was at record levels.

These demographic shifts would have put considerable pressure on the traditional racial caste system even if egalitarian and democratic ideas had not been in the air. The British abolitionists were much less concerned with 'mulatto rights' than their French counterparts had been; Wilberforce was at least consistent in that he placed quite a low value on civic rights for white Englishmen at home too. Nevertheless the abolitionists did urge that black freedmen should not suffer blatant social discrimination. In 1813 it was decreed that the testimony of free people of colour would be acceptable in courts of law and it was recognised that they were competent to transmit and inherit property. The formation of the six West Indian regiments brought an armed black force around 7,000 men strong into existence; from 1807 the black privates and NCOs were manumitted and enjoyed similar rights to their white equivalents. Most members of this force were recruited by purchase or impressment in Africa but a minority were West Indian born; when some of the regiments were disbanded in 1815 the government acceded to pressure to return many of the soldiers to Africa. Once enrolled the black soldiers received elementary education and religious instruction. During and after the wars the sight of well-accoutred black NCOs commanding dispirited squads of white deserters or miscreants was common. Apart from minor incidents the black soldiers were loyal and disciplined, in some ways more so than white soldiers, yet they were perceived by local whites as a threat to the racial hierarchy.[8]

In 1815 a group of free people of colour in Kingston, Jamaica, petitioned for removal of the ban on their admission to the local theatre, and in the following year they asked for representation as taxpayers in the Colonial Assembly. From 1823 there were regular meetings of free coloured people in Kingston at which they demanded equal social and political rights. A submission from the Jamaican free people of colour in 1825 estimated that 400 of their number could be considered rich, possessing property worth more than £5,000; a further 5,500 owned property worth more than £1,000; altogether propertied mulattos owned about 50,000 slaves, out of a total slave population of 310,000.[9] The free coloured population of Jamaica was not as wealthy as its counterpart in St Domingue in 1790, but whereas the latter had been roughly equal in numbers to the local whites Jamaica's 45,000 free blacks in 1834 faced only about 15,000 whites. The Colonial Office and some of the larger planters favoured extending citizenship rights, including the vote, to the better-off coloured freeholders in the hope of ensuring their loyalty. The distinction between different freeholders, or between freeholders and leaseholders, was no less arbitrary for the free coloured population than it was for the white electorates in both metropolis and colonies; consequently it left many unsatisfied. In 1825 the Jamaican Assembly deported two free men of colour who had organised petitions, alleging that they were agents of Haiti and were plotting a slave insurrection. The men chosen were of partly French extraction, had commercial links to Haiti and were also involved in a *Société de Bienfaisance* set up by immigrants from the black Republic. Though the allegations against them were far-fetched, the example of Haiti no doubt encouraged their demand for civic equality. Following their deportation the two men travelled to London to present their case to the British Parliament and courts. With backing from Stephen Lushington and other abolitionists they won the right to return to Jamaica. British opinion was impressed by the moderate and respectable appeals of the two men. Henceforth the free coloured community in Jamaica retained the services of an 'Agent' in London, to represent their interests, just as the various island assemblies had done for so long.[10]

Because of its size the free coloured community in Jamaica made the running in the campaign for civic rights. They demanded to be allowed to hold office, as well as to vote, if otherwise qualified. Their leaders talked of the need to explore a gradual emancipation, so long as it was accompanied by compensation. In July 1830 a radically minded coloured bookseller, Edward Jordan, commenced publication of a twice-weekly newspaper, *The Watchman*, which soon established a reputation for itself with lively and documented exposés of the corruption and abuses practised or tolerated by the planter class. *The Watchman* declared that the days of slavery were numbered and quoted copiously from British anti-slavery literature. *The Watchman* reached only a few thousand readers but nevertheless it contributed both directly and indirectly to weakening the slave system; directly by siding with the critics of slavery, indirectly by attacking the caste system which had always been a prop of black enslavement in the British West Indies.[11]

The spread of Nonconformist religion among the black population, both free and enslaved, was a further factor undermining the slave system, despite the fact that all white missionaries, and most black deacons, called for slaves to be hard-working and obedient. There had been some Moravian missionaries since 1754, but the real expansion of churches with a black membership did not occur until the 1790s. In the aftermath of the American war a small number of black Baptists found refuge in Jamaica and began forming congregations. Wesleyan Methodists became active in Jamaica from 1789; by 1822 they had about 8,000 in their congregations. The British authorities had generally favoured the sending of missionaries, who were strictly enjoined to preach submission at all times. By 1834 there were 150 missionaries in the

British West Indies – 63 Moravians, 58 Methodists, 17 Baptists and sundry others – with a total of 47,000 attached to their chapels and a further 86,000 'hearers or enquirers'. Apart from the missionaries very few whites were involved; free blacks gave strong backing to the Nonconformist Churches, which welcomed their presence in the front pew rather than obliging them to stand at the back, as would happen in the Anglican places of worship. Free blacks, or even slaves, were enrolled as deacons, taught to read and encouraged to hold Bible classes. The religious needs of the white population were largely met by the services of one hundred or so Anglican priests; the latter had nominal duties towards the slaves but very few followers. There were also independent black preachers, such as the Baptist Moses Baker, who had a following of around 3,000; but planters and managers would not allow slaves to attend their meetings, so they were mainly supported by free people of colour and urban slaves. The Assemblies were little impressed by the piety supposedly inculcated by the missionaries, seeing the chapels simply as a threat to the authority system of the plantation. The Jamaican Assembly was reported as declaring:

> The preaching and teaching of the sects called Baptist, Wesleyan Methodist, and Moravians (but more especially the sect called Baptist) had the effect of producing in the minds of the slaves, a belief that they could not serve both a temporal and a spiritual master, thereby occasioning them to resist the lawful authority of their temporal, under the delusion of rendering themselves more acceptable to a spiritual master.[12]

Services in the chapels and classes would naturally often be conducted in patois, and African beliefs appear in Christian guise. Black aspirations to respect and freedom would be articulated in terms of the only permitted ideology, a system of Christian beliefs and symbols that was simply convenient for some, a matter of conviction for others, and a mixture of both attitudes for many. The black deacons found in the Scriptures the story of the release from bondage of the Ancient Israelites; they also found in the New Testament an offer of personal salvation that may well have been attractive to those who had been uprooted by the workings of the slave system.

The ending of the slave trade meant that the creole proportion of the slave population thereafter steadily grew. In Jamaica the proportion of African-born slaves in the total slave population dropped from 45 per cent in 1807 to 25 per cent in 1832. This change, together with the fact that the remaining Africans had long been resident in the West Indies, produced a culturally more homogenous slave population. Purely African sources of solidarity, such as had helped to fuel slave revolts in the mid-eighteenth century and before in Jamaica, became less important. Virtually the totality of slaves could now communicate with one another in the local patois and all would share an outlook shaped by colonial society. A continuing slave traffic between plantations and islands spread rather than weakened this more unified basis for slave community and solidarity.

The years following the Napoleonic Wars witnessed an intensification of slave exploitation as planters and managers strove to increase output from a static or declining work-force. A decline in the prices of plantation products encouraged planters to maintain their revenue by expanding output. The price of sugar halved between 1815–19 and 1830–34, but there was no alternative crop for those aiming at large returns. In the new territories land reclamation and steam power were used to extend cultivation and to boost processing capacity. But these developments in no way lightened the load of the slave labour force. Overall production of sugar in the British West Indies rose from 168,000 tons in 1815 to 202,000 tons in 1828. The decline in the slave labour force was even larger than the decline in the total slave population during these years, since the proportion of the old and the young grew as a more normal population structure developed. Rising sugar output was the result of the transfer of slaves to sugar cultivation and relentless pressure on those already on the sugar estates. Since conditions on the sugar estates were widely recognised as being harsher than those on other estates, a view very much born out by vital statistics, these years must have witnessed deteriorating conditions for many. The slave registers show not only that the slave population was declining between 1818 and 1830 but that the rate of decline was increasing in Jamaica from −0.25 per cent in 1818 to −1 per cent in 1830. The ending of slave imports meant that field slaves could no longer be promoted to lighter tasks; indeed some craft slaves were probably obliged to work in the fields instead. With gross revenues declining, the rations received by the slaves are likely to have been more meagre. While the 'head people' were aware of controversies surrounding slavery, local markets and the growth of black congregations encouraged a black information network.

In August 1823 about a thousand rebel slaves from plantations east of the Demerara river in the Guyanas moved against their managers and the colonial authorities to demand better conditions, as they believed to be their due. The revolt in Demerara was encouraged by the news that the London government had proposed measures of amelioration of the slave condition, following the formation of the new abolitionist society in January 1823. The slaves in this colony inherited something of the long tradition of maroon resistance which had marked the former

Dutch possession. In the area affected by the rebellion large numbers of slaves had recently been switched to sugar cultivation; this occasioned the breaking of personal ties between slaves as well as harsher labour conditions, both of these being traditional sources of unrest. In the outbreak of 1823 the goal was to transform the colonial regime rather than to opt out of it. The government's amelioration measures were modest enough but still sufficient to arouse rumours that more fundamental changes were in prospect. Those who were to lead the slave action knew the amelioration measures were limited but also that they aroused planter hostility. The concern of many British abolitionists that Sunday should be kept as a day when the slaves should be released from labour, and able to attend a place of worship, raised the question of an extra free day to allow the slaves to cultivate their garden plots. The 1823 amelioration measures banned the holding of markets on Sundays, requiring them to be held on a different day. Sunday observance also offered opportunities to the slaves which were social and political as well as religious. They could meet and talk with slaves from neighbouring plantations.

The failure of most planters themselves to organise religious services meant that many slaves had attended the Nonconformist chapels set up by missionaries from England. The first English missionary had arrived in Demerara in 1808; after initial planter resistance he had eventually persuaded many masters that chapel attendance would make the slaves more industrious and obedient. By 1817 the Bethel chapel, now under the supervision of the Reverend John Smith, was attended by about 800 slaves every Sunday with about 2,000 in receipt of religious instruction. A number of the leading deacons of this chapel were responsible for the resistance movement of August 1823 in Demarara. The movement began when the slaves on half a dozen plantations on Demerara's east coast took over their plantations, placed white overseers and managers in the stocks, and demanded talks with the Governor. The Governor arrived with a militia detachment to parley with a crowd of about several hundred rebels, some of them armed with pikes, machetes or fowling pieces. After the slaves had agreed to lay down their arms the Governor asked them what they wanted, to which they replied 'Our right'. The Governor explained the limited nature of the amelioration measures proposed by the Colonial Secretary but the slave spokesmen made it clear that they wanted more: 'These things they said were no comfort to them. God had made them of the same flesh and blood as the whites, and that they were tired of being Slaves to them, that their good King had sent orders they should be free and they would not work any more.' After a musket shot had been fired the Governor broke off the discussions and returned to

Georgetown. Meanwhile the revolt spread to embrace most of the east shore as far as Berbice. The Governor called out well-armed troops and militia, including a detachment of one of the West India Regiments. At the Adventure plantation the Governor's force encountered about 2,000 rebels.

An eyewitness report of the confrontation noted: 'Some of the insurgents called out that they wanted lands and three days in the week for themselves, besides Sunday, and they would not give up their arms till they were satisfied.' The British commander noted: 'At first there was more demand for freedom and three days than anything else, but latterly when I came out again they were all for freedom, and all of them dwelt considerably on going to Church on Sunday.'[14] The commanding officer was handed a written series of demands by Jack Gladstone, one of the rebel leaders. The commander declared that he was unable to meet the rebels' conditions and ordered them to disperse. When they refused to do so the troops were ordered to fire on the assembly; about 100–150 rebels were killed outright, at a cost to the Governor's forces of one casualty. Fleeing rebels were hunted down and executed on the spot; slave suspects were mercilessly flogged. The terror unleashed against the slaves aimed at restoring a system of hierarchy and subordination that had been badly damaged by the resistance movement. Quamina Gladstone, an older deacon who some had proposed be elected King, was eventually tracked down about a month after the beginning of the rebellion; his bullet-riddled body was displayed in chains in front of the plantation where the action first began. Over the next four months 72 slaves were brought to trial; 51 of these were sentenced to death, 16 sentenced to receive 1,000 lashes and others to lengthy prison terms. Others were tried at a later date, with about 250 slaves in all losing their life. The victims were strung on gibbets in front of the dwelling quarters on the affected plantations.

In the furore that followed these events the Reverend John Smith was brought to trial on a charge of having incited the slaves to rebellion. Smith himself did sympathise with the slaves, writing in letters to the Missionary Society that sponsored him of the way in which pregnant women were forced to work long hours in the field, the common neglect of sick slaves, the pervasive use of the whip, and the difficulties married slaves had in seeing their partners. But it is most unlikely that Smith knew what the slaves intended, and virtually excluded that he incited their action. On the other hand, his presence, and the existence of his chapel, represented a fissure in the ideological universe of the slave system; together with other more familiar sources of revolt, the missionary presence did have a destabilising effect, irrespective of the pacific intentions of Pastor Smith himself. The prosecution persuaded one of the main leaders of the revolt, Jack Gladstone, son of Quamina, to testify against Smith; in return Gladstone was exempted from the death sentence passed on all others seriously connected with the uprising. Smith's position was further weakened by a note he had written to another member of his congregation on the eve of the uprising:

> To Jacky Reed, I am ignorant of the affair you allude to, and your note is too late to make an enquiry. I learnt yesterday that some schemes were in agitation; without asking any questions on the subject I begged them to be quiet. I trust they will; hasty, violent, and concerted measures are quite foreign to the religion we profess, and I hope you will have nothing to do with them. Yours, for Christ's sake. J.S.

The local jury found Smith guilty and he received the death sentence; the Governor submitted this sentence to London, as he was obliged to do, and added a recommendation for mercy to be shown. The London authorities agreed to commute Smith's sentence but he died in prison before this news was received; Smith died of consumption following incarceration in a dark and damp cell. Abolitionists in Britain were horrified by Smith's fate and by the conditions described in his letters. Many British abolitionists were, of course, themselves Nonconformists and had suffered some harassment for their convictions; the martyrdom of John Smith filled them with outrage. News was also received from Barbados that the Demerara events had led 'a party of respectable gentlemen' to burn a Methodist chapel to the ground in retaliation for what they described as 'unmerited and unprovoked attacks, which have frequently been made on the community by Methodist missionaries'.[15] When the House of Commons debated the events in Demerara Wilberforce delivered his last parliamentary speech while Brougham, speaking for three hours, threw the planters' representatives onto the defensive in what was acclaimed as one of his most powerful speeches; Sir John Gladstone, owner of Quamina and Jacky and father of the Liberal statesman, spoke up in defence of colonial justice. The abolitionists lost the vote in the Commons but helped to build anti-slavery sentiment in the country at large.

Following the events in Demerara local colonial authorities went to great lengths to still rumours that slavery was about to end. Baptists and Methodist missionaries were willing to spread the message and to urge obedience on the slaves whenever they were allowed to. But there was a new restiveness amongst the slave populations of the British Caribbean. Even without echoes of metropolitan controversies British West Indian slaves would have been likely to respond to new opportunities and harsher conditions. Beginning on Christmas Day 1831 Jamaica was the scene of a resistance movement of unprecedented scope, involving between 20,000 and 30,000 slaves, which swept through the west of the island. The outbreak had been preceded by many attacks by planters and managers on new regulations imposed on them by the Colonial Office; these regulations derived, in fact, from the amelioration proposals of 1823 whose application to Jamaica had long been obstructed by the local Assembly. Once again the idea had spread that masters were concealing an emancipation decree – an idea possibly encouraged by an executive order freeing Crown slaves. The revolt centred on an area of western Jamaica where the Baptists had many followers. The Baptists permitted or encouraged freedmen and slaves to run their own services and organise membership drives. Samuel Sharpe, a black slave deacon, travelled widely through the area affected by the revolt. A witness at a later trial hearing was to report that Sharpe

> referred to the manifold evils and injustices of slavery; asserted the natural equality of man with regard to freedom. . . . He concluded by observing that because the King had made them free, or resolved upon doing it, the 'whites and Grignon' (a militia commander) were holding secret meetings with the doors shut close . . . and had determined . . . to kill all the black men, and save all the women and children and keep them in slavery.[16]

Many slaves involved in the revolt were persuaded that they would gain their ends if they simply stopped work, resorting to force only if attacked. In the year 1831 Christmas day fell on a Sunday; refusal to grant the slaves an extra day of rest probably sparked the action by them. The revolt spread with great rapidity and soon passed out of the control of Sharpe and his Baptist congregation. As militia forces were assembled to crush the slaves some of the rebels formed a Black Regiment, under a commander known as Colonel Jackson, but this was exceptional. It took the troops and militia, with the advantage of fire power and training, two weeks to reassert control of the areas affected by the revolt. Fourteen whites had been killed and property valued at £1,132,440 was destroyed. The destruction and loss of life would have been much greater if that had been the rebels' main object. Thus on the Georgia estate, Trelawny, the slaves led by the head driver, Edward Grant, had simply refused to work. A militia detachment armed with a field piece attacked them at dawn, dragging slaves from their cabins and shooting one as an example. As was always the case, the repression was far more bloody than the original uprising. Some 200 rebels were killed in the course of suppressing the revolt; a further 312 were executed subsequently. Those killed judicially came from the estates affected by the uprising and were those accused by the overseers or managers of being involved, or simply because they were known trouble-makers, 'great rascals', 'notorious runaways' and 'liars'.[17]

When news of the 'Baptist War' reached Britain it at first threw abolitionist advocates on the defensive. West Indian planters and their friends could argue that missionary work, and government concessions to the abolitionists, were to blame for the havoc and destruction. In Jamaica itself the white colonists had no doubt who was responsible for stirring up the slaves: in the aftermath of the revolt nine Baptist chapels and six Methodist chapels were burned by an organisation describing itself as the 'Colonial Church Union'. One missionary was tarred and feathered, another expelled from the colony. A number of Baptist missionaries were jailed, supposedly for their own protection since there was no evidence against them. The Methodist and Baptist missions decided to send several of their number back to Britain to explain what was happening to them. The returning missionaries disassociated themselves from Samuel Sharpe and the leaders of the revolt, while arguing that the slave system was bound to generate more violent outbursts. Their testimony took time to reach a broader public in Britain, but when it did so it shone a spotlight on the brutality and bloodshed of the repression. Those who left at this time included two missionaries, Knibb and Burchell, who proved themselves powerful and radical advocates in the anti-slavery cause and a businessman, Henry Whiteley, who wrote his own account of the slaveholders' attempt to terrorise slaves and missionaries alike.[18]

The colonial assemblies protested vigorously at government toleration of missionary activity and attempts to impose ameliorative regulations on the plantations. When invited to introduce its own ameliorative measures the Jamaican assembly debated for four hours whether to agree to a ban on the 'indecent' flogging of the female slaves – that is the flogging of women in a state of undress – before finally deciding that such flogging should be allowed. As the largest colony Jamaica was crucial to any prospect of planter resistance to abolitionism. The Jamaica Assembly issued brave proclamations reminiscent of 1776 and produced fine denunciations of the atrocious conditions in Britain's factory districts. Yet the Colonial Office and government knew that the white colonists were utterly dependent on the British garrison and that they did not enjoy the backing either of the free population of colour or of many of the absentee proprietors. In Jamaica the colonial authorities tolerated and protected Jordan's *Watchman* in part because they saw the free coloured as a check on the white colonists. Some white proprietors sought to make overtures to their coloured counterparts but most white colonists were not interested in a joint defence of slavery if it meant diluting their racial privileges. The *Watchman* found the following sufficiently acute to reprint it from an English paper:

> The cry which resounds from the West Indies is raised by men who are trembling less for their property than for their caste: these are the persons who love slavery for its own sake . . . they may have no possessions but they have white faces. Should compensation be given few of them will receive a Sixpence; but they will lose the power of oppressing, with impunity, every man who has a black skin.[19]

The new assertiveness of the free people of colour, and the eruption of large-scale slave resistance, took place at a time when the weight of the slave colonies within the Empire was declining sharply. Patrick Coloquhoun estimated the value of the annual production of the British West Indies at 4.8 per cent of that of the empire as a whole in 1812; over the next two decades it slipped to between 2–3 per cent.[20] In fact by the 1820s and 1830s a thoroughgoing reorientation of Britain's imperial interests was already well underway. The West Indian slave plantations were still quite profitable so long as they were outside the area of Jamaica affected by rebellion. But such troubles combined with increasingly stiff Cuban competition could persuade the individual owners, especially the absentees, to switch resources out of the plantations and into other areas. From the imperial standpoint the relative decline of the West Indies was now unmistakable.

The contrast between wartime prosperity and postwar recession was quite sharp as the metropolis exploited peacetime conditions to find new markets and new sources of supply. In 1804–6 the West Indies took no less than 21 per cent of British domestic exports; this trade dropped to 11 per cent of the total by 1824–6. By contrast British exports to Asia had been 7 per cent in 1804–6 and rose to 34 per cent in 1824–6, while those to Latin America grew from 3 per cent to 11 per cent.[21] The British re-export trade in plantation produce disappeared with the end of wartime conditions. British importers looked to the United States as their main supplier of cotton and began to purchase small quantities of Cuban and Brazilian sugar despite having to pay sugar duties on it. Because of the protection afforded by the colonial system the British West Indies remained the largest supplier of sugar to the metropolis, but once again, as in the years before 1790, it was easy to argue that British consumers were subsidising the West Indian planters, or even saving them from commercial extinction. Because of tariff protection and reductions in the cost of plantation supplies the

British West Indian planters could still make profits, but the profit rate had declined and so had the scope for reinvesting in the plantation economy. J.R. Ward's sample of Jamaican plantations witnessed a drop in annual profitability from 9.6 per cent in the years 1799–1819 to 5.3 per cent in the years 1820–34; in the Leeward Islands the annual profit rate dropped from 9.1 per cent to 3.9 per cent over the same period. Profits were still high in the newly developing colonies of Trinidad and British Guiana where annual rates of return of 16.0 per cent in 1799–1819 dipped to 13.3 per cent in 1820–34.[22] If exception is made of the 'new colonies' then plantation ownership was becoming a dwindling asset. In the context of a larger crisis of colonial slavery lower profitability, and declining estate values, made West Indian proprietors more willing to look for a way out.

The Abolition Act of 1808 had itself restricted the future growth of the British slave plantations to that which could be achieved within the demographic momentum of the given slave population. Yet the decline in the relative commercial importance of the British West Indies was not principally caused by the prior metropolitan decision to suppress further imports of African slaves. Britain's traders were bound to make efforts to diversify their trading outlets once wartime conditions were over; the expansion of British rule in India and the conquest of independence by the new Latin American states gave them major new openings. Likewise the wartime re-export trade in plantation products would have been very difficult to maintain even if the British planters had still been able to buy new slaves from Africa. Brazil, Cuba and the United States were all well placed to supply European markets and to offer stiff competition to the British planters. The US planters, who were to supply Britain with most of the cotton it needed, were also cut off from Atlantic slave imports. The British Caribbean islands had not been able to sustain much of a re-export trade prior to the French wars and did not have the vast reserves of well-watered and accessible land, suitable for plantation development, that underpinned the post-1815 expansion of the mainland slave systems. The so-called 'new colonies', and in particular Demerara–Essequibo (Guyana) and Trinidad, did have scope for expansion, but then they did continue to expand. Until 1825 the estates in the new colonies could still buy slaves from other British Caribbean colonies, though such transfers required a licence; between 1815 and 1825 about 20,000 slaves were imported in this way by the new colonies.[23] The transfer of slaves from old to new areas was, of course, normal and unrestricted within each colony. While the London-imposed ban on African slave imports was a handicap for British planters, it was offset by the tariff protection the metropolis offered to their principal export, sugar. Cuban, Brazilian and US planters largely supplied markets in which they had no tariff advantage. And although the Brazilian and Cuban planters still imported African slaves the activities of British diplomats and naval squadrons obliged them to pay steadily rising prices for them.[24]

The advance of British anti-slavery agitation was to be broadly congruent with imperial reorientation in the period 1823–38; without this fact emancipation would have been less likely to obtain parliamentary sanction. But this does not mean either that the new imperial priorities dictated parliamentary emancipation or that the latter would have occurred if there had not been other powerful reasons for heeding the anti-slavery movement. Oligarchic interests would have been quite capable of supporting the continuation of British colonial slavery, and would have done so but for the great pressure they felt under to act differently. Other European colonial powers – France, the Netherlands and Denmark – also retained slave colonies of declining importance and yet slavery was to survive in them somewhat longer than it did in the British West Indies. The scale of slave resistance and revolt was growing in the British colonies, but by itself this too was not a decisive consideration. The French clung on to their slave colonies despite their defeat in St Domingue/Haiti. In purely military terms the British colonial authorities had contained the outbreaks with very low casualties compared with those suffered by either France or Britain in the revolutionary period; the size of the garrison could have been increased had there been a prospect of fostering a new growth in the planting economy and had it been possible to contain the domestic political opposition that this would surely have aroused. In practice the West Indian decline meant that governments were less inclined to pay the considerable political and financial costs of continuing to defend slavery in the West Indies and the squeeze on planting profits also made planters more willing to consider a compensated abolition of slavery.

As a topic of political controversy anti-slavery was second only to reform in the years 1830–32. The Anti-Slavery Society, as it was henceforth to be known, was effectively re-founded in May 1830, at a meeting attended by 2,000 supporters; a further 1,500 had to be turned away as there was no room. The new Anti-Slavery Society was dedicated from the outset to immediate freedom for the slaves in the colonies. The platform, which included Wilberforce, Brougham and Buxton, was surprised when an 'immediatist' motion proposed from the floor had been overwhelmingly carried. The new rise of anti-slavery activity, which this meeting heralded, must be seen against the background of a deepening crisis of the oligarchic regime.

The issues of reform and abolition were bound up together in many ways. There was little hope that the unreformed Parliament could be brought to accept slave emancipation. The West Indian interest was still strongly represented within it. The wartime colonial planting boom had helped to promote the West Indian proprietory interest to an even stronger position within the oligarchy. In the 1790s there had been about thirty 'West Indian' MPs in the House of Commons; in the years 1828–32 the number rose as high as fifty-six.[25] Proportionately West Indian interests were even stronger in the Lords. The colonial proprietors could also rely on large majorities in both Houses to oppose any tampering with private property. Not only was this a Parliament of property-holders but it was one built around a far-reaching, yet rigid, concept of property in which office-holding and the right to choose MPs were themselves deemed to be property rights acquired by purchase. Finally, the unreformed Parliament did not enjoy sufficient public confidence to undertake a measure as large in its implications, and in its probable demand on resources, as slave emancipation. Financially, even administratively, slave emancipation seemed beyond the capacity of 'illegitimate monarchy', even supposing the will to have been there. On the other hand, the intimate links and affinities between slaveholding and 'Old Corruption' meant that anti-slavery could damage or discredit the established order, even while appearing to be non-political. Lastly anti-slavery agitation attacked the oligarchic regime in the name of abolitionist values to which it had been officially attached ever since 1807. Wilberforce was now too old to play much of an active part, but his patronage helped to demonstrate this line of continuity. Wellington's government in 1828–30 stood four-square with the planting interest; but it still could not disavow a formal commitment to ending the Atlantic slave trade and improving the lot of the slaves.

The Tory governments of the mid- and late 1820s had striven to grapple with a new panorama of economic and social problems by adopting measures that half-heartedly acknowledged the pressure for reform from the growing middle-class public. A free trade policy was announced but the resultant tinkering with the schedule of corn and sugar duties did not remove the protection they afforded nor the pressure they exerted on the cost of living. At last the antique system of religious discrimination was modified. The Test Act was repealed in 1828 after a campaign against it by English Dissenters and Irish Catholics. While the English Dissenters petitioned, the Irish, led by Daniel O'Connell, were prepared to threaten rebellion. The Irish movement was sufficiently menacing to persuade the London government to enact Catholic emancipation, as it was called, in 1829; this permitted Catholic freeholders to vote and hold public office so long as they swore loyalty to the Protestant succession and denied the right of the Pope to interfere in British affairs. Neither the Nonconformists nor the Catholics were satisfied with these concessions, which left many Anglican privileges and monopolies in place. But they did succeed in dividing and demoralising the upholders of the status quo. In this sense they were similar in effect to the proposals to 'ameliorate' slavery in the colonies.

With the accession of a new King, William IV, in June 1830, and the consequent holding of an election, the question of parliamentary reform came to the fore. The Whigs committed themselves to bringing in a reform bill and in November 1830, following the collapse of the Wellington government, the King was obliged to ask the Whig leader, Lord Grey, to form a government. The aim of the reform was to remove the worst abuses and to admit the middle classes to a share of political representation. While the very wealthy could buy their way into the political system those of middling wealth, and resident in new manufacturing or commercial regions, were deprived of voice or vote in national affairs – and often local affairs as well. In the whole of Scotland there were less than 5,000 voters. Because of the tiny size of many constituencies about 170 landlords, often themselves members of the House of Lords, were in a position to select 355 members of the House of Commons. Beyond the problem of oligarchic control of the state was that of its structure and competence. The abolition of many sinecures, and successive campaigns to reduce public expenditure, meant that the great Departments of State operated with tiny staffs; usually a few dozen quill-pushers in Whitehall. The apparatus of public administration needed by an urbanising and industrialising society was almost entirely lacking.[26]

The years 1824–32 witnessed serious economic dislocation and social distress in Britain; governments beholden to landed and moneyed interests were widely blamed for these conditions. The most widely held radical doctrines focused quite narrowly on the oligarchical state, its protectionism and its fiscality as the explanation for popular miseries. The anti-slavery movement occupied a different terrain, though its campaigns often shadowed or paralleled the surges of radical politics. Many of its leaders saw it as standing above politics and the quarrel of interests. Yet every prominent anti-slavery advocate in fact held to a middle ground, eschewing either support of the unreformed Parliament or radical republican opposition to it. There were, of course, different ways of taking up this middle ground. Buxton and Brougham, despite their moment of discomforture at the 1830 meeting of the Anti-Slavery Society, remained its outstanding parliamentary advocates. Buxton concentrated on anti-slavery and other social reform issues, while Brougham mixed it in with vigorous advocacy of political reform.

Brougham won a Yorkshire seat in the election of 1830 with the help of his anti-slavery reputation and used it to campaign flamboyantly for parliamentary reform.

The anti-slavery cause challenged the oligarchy where it was weakest, and did so in an indirect and selective way. It supplied a social and moral dimension to the reform programme. While political and institutional reform might simply whet the popular appetite for more far-reaching measures, the abolition of slavery could strengthen the authority of the government and the state. The various reform proposals abolished privileges and abuses, while leaving others in place, and they each extended the franchise to an arbitrary boundary, much short of manhood or even household suffrage. By comparison the freeing of the slaves, though not without its practical difficulties, was a self-contained measure. It turned attention outwards to the responsibilities of Empire, not inwards to the structure of oligarchic power. And it lent a certain spiritual or moral dimension to politics. The leaders of Nonconformity looked benignly upon anti-slavery. Jabez Bunting, the Wesleyan Methodist leader, joined the Abolition Committee in the 1820s; the Methodists, who now numbered more than a quarter of a million, gave strong backing to the anti-slavery societies and petitions.

In 1831 the work of the national Anti-Slavery Society was greatly extended by the creation of an 'Agency Committee' devoted to building an anti-slavery movement in the country. The Agency Committee had a staff of five 'stipendiary agents', travelling round the country and setting up local societies. The Agency Committee soon built up 1,200 local societies. Its petitions attracted hundreds of thousands of signatures.[27] The money needed to launch the work of the 'stipendiary agents' was furnished by a few Quaker businessmen, notably James Cropper, an East India merchant from Liverpool, and Joseph Sturge, a wheat merchant from Birmingham. Cropper and Sturge were themselves drawn from precisely those social groups which were pressing for reform: but their abolitionist zeal reflected a deep conviction that political tinkering was by itself a quite inadequate programme. Cropper had a devout belief that political economy, based on free labour and free trade, would reveal God's plan; Sturge was animated by a belief that the new patterns of society had to demonstrate that they ensured social justice as well as freedom. The anti-slavery cause attracted radical young men and women, many of whom were impatient with the caution of their parliamentary champions.[28]

In acutely troubled times anti-slavery helped middle-class reformers to highlight their socio–economic ideals. Anti-slavery thought had a bearing on the overall conduct of policy and on the pattern of the economy. It furnished a model of legislation dictated by general policy rather than particular interests. It justified state intervention in regulating the workings of economic contract, while sanctifying contract itself. The advocates of emancipation presented it as furnishing an economic stimulus via market expansion. The free worker was also a consumer. An abolitionist pamphlet published in Liverpool in 1828 pointed out that India had overtaken the West Indies as a market for British cotton manufactures and argued that a fillip would be given to West Indian demand by emancipation: 'The slaves in our West India islands, by being made free would not only raise more produce, but also consume much more of our manufactures.'[29]

The argument that emancipation would help to revive the West Indian market for British manufactures had a common-sense appeal to workers as well as their employers at a time of commercial recession. Such assertions were also born of confidence in the superior productivity of free labour. Many abolitionists believed that economic arrangements pivoted around two competing methods for motivating the direct producer – *Wages or the Whip*, as the title of one anti-slavery pamphlet put it.[30] In popularising works of political economy Harriet Martineau rehearsed the Smithian arguments against slave labour. On the other hand, the 'economists' who loomed increasingly large in public discussions in the post-Napoleonic period were little concerned with slavery. For its part the Agency Committee refused to make a purely or predominantly economic argument against colonial slavery and its lecturers were instructed to make clear that the central objection to slavery was humanitarian and religious. Abolitionism as a movement derived strength from its association with the critique of the operation of pure market forces, rather than their celebration. West Indian planters were attacked for working their slaves to death and making profits from an inhuman, immoral and irreligious system.

Both radicals and reactionaries could find something to endorse in anti-slavery themes. The radicals inclined to argue that social conditions in England itself were perilously close to slavery. The more conservative trends in anti-slavery, which predominated in its national leadership, tended to a rosy view of wage labour. They also argued that economic, legal and moral restraints should be constructed to replace the harsh physical restraints of the state of slavery. Abolitionist thought was generally quite congruent with the elaboration in public policy of the coercive constraints needed to make a system of 'free labour' broadly coincident with a system of 'wage labour'. But this was not the only way anti-slavery themes could be articulated. Those who favoured independent production by petty producers, or trade union combinations, or factory legislation, also invoked anti-slavery themes at this time. In 1830 Richard Oastler, an evangelical Tory who had been

involved in anti-slavery agitation, published an attack on what he called
'Yorkshire Slavery', namely the pitiless overworking of children and
women by the Yorkshire mill-owners. This article initiated a vigorous
campaign for legislation to limit child labour and the hours of the
working day which made copious use of anti-slavery imagery and
became a major challenge to the employers. While the analogy was a
loose one, there were indeed striking parallels between the regular
demographic deficit of slave plantations in Guyana and the manufacturing districts in Leeds.[31] Some of the offending manufacturers, or of
those who sided with them, supported slave emancipation; but if they
hoped thereby to distract attention from their own system of
exploitation they made a mistake. Anti-slavery, by itself, did not
encourage any fundamental critique of capitalism or industrialism but it
did imply that, where they conflicted, humanitarian and familistic
values should prevail over business and property interests, and that
capitalism and industrialism should be obliged to adjust to a self-
reproducing human order.

Whatever the ultimate implications of abolitionist ideology, in the
pre-emancipation period the main champions of parliamentary anti-
slavery, and their supporters within the government machine, went out
of their way to reassure planters that emancipation would be
accomplished in such a way as to ensure to the West Indian estates a
continuing supply of labour. They acknowledged that emancipated
slaves might choose subsistence cultivation, supplemented by occasional
labour for cash or production for the market; were this to happen
markets would not have been widened and wage labour sufficient to
plantation production would have been lacking. The officials of the
Colonial Office, though favourable to abolition, were exercised by these
possibilities. A memorandum drawn up prior to emancipation argued:
'A state of things in which the negro escaped the necessity for . . .
labour would be as bad for him as for his owner. He would be cut off
from civilising influences, would have no incentive to better his
condition or to impose any but the slightest degree of discipline on
himself. Thus he might well become a more degraded being than his
ancestors in Africa.' Schemes for emancipation thus included discussion
of ways in which former slaves could be barred from significant land
ownership while vagrancy laws penalised attempts to leave the
plantations. Buxton, for the parliamentary wing of abolitionism,
conceded that 'it may be extremely necessary for the state to introduce
laws for protecting persons from living in idleness to the detriment of
the state'.[32] He argued that former slaves convicted of vagrancy could
be obliged to make a labour contract with an estate; former slaves
might gain possession of their garden plots only on the same basis.

Buxton compared these proposed arrangements with his own practice of allotting company houses to the workers in his brewery. Buxton agreed that the post-slavery labour regime would need its own new disciplines and sanctions, including a strong police force, an independent body of magistrates and a prison system. Since he also believed in reforming and strengthening the metropolitan counterparts of these institutions, there was consistency in his approach. On the other hand, the popular anti-slavery campaigns of the Agency Committee did not dwell on such matters and rather stressed the need for protective legislation – legislation restraining the wealthy rather than the direct producers. The most popular single anti-slavery pamphlet was to be Henry Whiteley's *Three Months in Jamaica*, in which he urged the need for laws to limit the hours of work in British factories, especially those of children, as a domestic counterpart to colonial emancipation.[33]

The anti-slavery of this period acquired a greater moral radicalism by a new openess to the experience of the slave. The *Anti Slavery Reporter* ran regular and detailed accounts of the abuse of slaves in the Caribbean and encouraged those who had managed to escape from slavery to tell their story. One of the most affecting narratives to emerge in this way was *The History of Mary Prince, A West Indian Slave, Related by Herself* (1831), which went through three editions in its first year of publication. Mary Prince had accompanied her owners to Britain in 1828, but left their household after ill treatment; she wished to rejoin her husband in Barbados but feared to return because her owners refused to manumit her. The plight of Mary Prince exposed the limitation of Mansfield's decision of 1772, the more so since it appeared that she still owed service to her owners. The editor of the *Anti-Slavery Reporter* persuaded Mary Prince to tell her life story and published it as a book, together with correspondence with her owner and his own account of her predicament. The concluding paragraph of Mary Prince's *History* is worth quoting extensively since it is one of the few documents available of the slave's experience of colonial slavery and since it directly nourished the radicalisation of British abolitionism. The editor notes that 'the whole of this paragraph especially, is given as nearly as was possible in Mary's own words':

I am often vexed, and I feel great sorrow when I hear some people in this country say, that the slaves do not need better usage, and do not want to be free ... I say, Not so. How can slaves be happy when they have the halter round their neck and the whip upon their back? and are disgraced and thought no more of than beasts? – and are separated from their mothers, and husbands, and children, and sisters, just as cattle are sold and separated. Is it happiness for a driver in the field to take down his wife or sister or child, and strip them, and whip them in such a disgraceful manner? – women that have had children exposed in the open field to shame! There is no modesty or decency shown by the owner to his slaves: men, women and children are exposed alike. Since I have been here I have often wondered how English people can go out into the West Indies and act in such a beastly manner. But when they go to the West Indies they forget God and all feeling of shame, I think, since they can see and do such things. They tie up slaves like hogs – moor them up like cattle, and they lick them, so as hogs, or cattle, or horses never were flogged; and yet they come home and say, and make some good people believe, that slaves don't want to get out of slavery. But they put a cloak about the truth. It is not so. I will say the truth to English people who may read this history that my good friend, Miss S—, is now writing down for me. I have been a slave myself – I know what slaves feel – I can tell by myself what other slaves feel, and by what they told me. The man that says that slaves be quite happy in slavery – and that they don't want to be free – that man is either ignorant or a lying person. I never heard a slave say so. I never heard a Buckra man say so, till I heard tell of it in England. Such people ought to be ashamed of themselves. They can't do without slaves, they say. What's the reason they can't do without slaves as well as in England? No slaves here – no whips – no punishments, except for wicked people. . . . Let them work ever so hard in England, they are far better off than slaves. If they get a bad master, they give warning and go hire to another. They have their liberty. That's what *we* want. We don't mind hard work, if we had proper treatment, and proper wages like English servants, and proper time given in the week to keep us from breaking the Sabbath. But they won't give it; they will have work – work – work, night and day, sick and well, till we are quite done up; and we must not speak up nor look amiss, however much we be abused. And then when we are quite done up, who cares for us, more than for a lame horse? This is slavery. I tell it to let English people know the truth; and I hope they will never leave off to pray to God, and call loud to the great King of England, till all the poor blacks be given free, and slavery done up for evermore.[34]

This passage does evoke the superior position of the English wage worker. But its force derives from the picture it presents of the slave condition; those moved by it would not thereby become enthusiasts for English child labour, or of the employers' right to a fourteen hour working day. Indeed the argument of the editor in his afterword encouraged a general view that unequal power structures were liable to yield abuse, however decent the individual power-holder.

Anti-slavery assembled an unstable class coalition. It elicited some support from that section of the oligarchy prepared to make major concessions to the new middle-class public and to the popular pressure for a less arbitrary and corrupt political system. But anti-slavery had an appeal for all classes. In its organized form it was sustained principally by the middle-class public but at the height of its influence it was endorsed by tradesmen, artisans, domestics and labourers; it attracted support in villages and rural towns usually uninvolved in politics. It allowed bourgeois and petty bourgeois reformers to project a social ideal in which there was a place for the fair-minded employer, the salaried employee, the free waged labourer or responsible tenant, and the ministrations of a clergyman. The more popular version idealised the independent small producer and used anti-slavery themes to justify regulation of the hours of labour. Domestics and women, and others not well placed to contest the prevailing structures of power directly, found in abolitionism and in works like those of Mary Prince and Whiteley a means of asserting principles of fair and decent treatment. There were now forty ladies' anti-slavery societies and one of the most influential – the Birmingham Ladies Negro's Friend Society – led the way in demanding immediate emancipation in 1831.

Anti-slavery tapped deep-seated social aspirations and fears but in this period it was also put to the political test. The last years of the unreformed Parliament, and of colonial slavery, were marked by a complex class struggle. The anti-slavery cause was interwoven with that of parliamentary reform, at one moment serving to illustrate the noble measures being blocked by the regime of vested interests, at another becoming an awkward and expensive commitment which, if not implemented, would expose the reform Parliament to radical attack. Ultimately colonial slavery was menaced not by a specific, capitalist interest but rather by the social struggles which capitalism had unleashed, in both colony and metropolis. The contestation of the prevailing regime reached an intensity in the 1830s that had not been seen before and required a stronger and more legitimate state to contain it.

The popular demand for reform was spearheaded by Political Unions which were committed, as a minimum, to the elimination of parliamentary seats filled by aristocratic nomination, the extension of the vote to every head of household, or even to every adult male, and the institution of a secret ballot. The parliamentary champions of reform demanded bold measures in public, but themselves had difficulty in retaining the confidence of impatient middle-class followers and a growing working-class movement. The leaders of the Whig government, in particular Lords Grey and Althorp, were acutely aware that the final package must be acceptable, *in extremis*, to the King and the Lords. Popular pressure was salutary so long as it showed the latter the necessity for reform. Of course a number of the most prominent advocates of reform were also supporters of anti-slavery – notably

Brougham and T.B. Macaulay. The Whig leader Lord Grey had been responsible as Viscount Howick in 1807 for steering the Abolition Bill through the Commons; he was to be more robust in his initiatives on reform than on slave emancipation but knew that large concessions were needed on both questions if the loyalty of the reform-minded middle-classes was to be secured. The opponents of reform were, on the whole, also opponents of slave emancipation. The Duke of Wellington was no friend to emancipation, while Lord Harewood and Viscount Chandos, two of the most vociferous defenders of the unreformed Parliament, were also linked to the West Indian interest. General Gascoyn, who had supported the slave trade down to 1807, was to be one of the most irreconcilable foes of reform.

In 1830–31 the agitation against colonial slavery had helped to build up steam for reform generally. However, following the election of April 1831, the battle over specific Reform Bills overshadowed, without entirely displacing, the anti-slavery question. Even Buxton, with his belief in divine providence, could not be optimistic concerning the prospects for the abolition of slavery in the unreformed Parliament. Without a victory for parliamentary reform the anti-slavery forces could not hope to win.

The Hanoverian regime was gripped by something approaching a pre-revolutionary crisis in the years 1831–2, a crisis whose de-stabilising effects were not overcome until 1835 and after. The triumph of the July Revolution in Paris in 1830 showed that political revolutions did not have to entail large-scale blood-letting. The regime of Louis Philippe bore a certain resemblance to Britain's own 'illegitimate monarchy', which had indeed been the model for those who helped to devise it. But the French monarch was answerable to an Assembly in which middle-class wealth was more fairly represented; among the first steps taken by the new French government was that of stopping the clandestine slave trade and announcing plans to alleviate the slave condition. These developments encouraged reform sentiment and somehow made revolution seem a less remote possibility.

Peacetime British governments were quite vulnerable at this time. The National Debt consumed the bulk of public revenue and governments lacked the support to re-establish the income tax that had been dropped in 1815. By 1832 the public exchequer was paying £28.3 million in service payments on the National Debt, compared with only £14.4 million for the armed forces and £5 million for all civil expenditure. Austerity measures and the needs of imperial security left a greatly reduced garrison in Britain. Unrest in Ireland required a large force to be stationed there. Around the year 1831 there were only 11,000 troops in the whole of Britain and of these 7,000 were needed to safeguard the capital.[35] From 1828 a police force had been established in London but other parts of the country were less well prepared against civil unrest. In the years 1830–32 the forces of law and order had the greatest difficulty in holding the line against a varied assortment of antagonists. These included the widespread 'Captain Swing' riots in the countryside; the marches and meetings of the new working-class organisations, with tens of thousands of supporters, in the capital and in mining or manufacturing districts; and, most ominous of all, the marches and drilling of Political Unions demanding parliamentary reform, and drawing support from the middle-class as well as artisans, craftsmen and labourers.

A wave of revolts in about a dozen English counties in 1831 was provoked by the deteriorating condition of the labourers; they strangely paralleled the uprisings in the West Indies. Crowds of labourers demanded higher wages and destroyed machinery and property; while landlords and magistrates were besieged and threatened only one life was taken by the rioters, that of a yeoman in Wiltshire. Repression of the movement was extensive with 200 sentenced to death. Because of a public outcry only three rioters were actually executed but 450 were transported to Australia. There was panic and excess in the response of the magistrates because they confronted a new type of class struggle which traditional mechanisms of social control had failed to contain.[36]

The emergence of new working-class organisations and the danger that radical Political Unions might ally them with the reform-minded middle classes represented an even graver threat than rural disorder. The Union of the Working Classes in London held meetings at the Rotunda and elsewhere; a demonstration in October 1831 was attended by 70,000 supporters, many of them artisans, craftsmen and labourers. Demands for the 'abolition of the wages system' were raised, but the main object of attack was the oligarchic regime, with its corruption and fiscal exactions. In many parts of the country middle-class and working-class radicals were jointly organised in Political Unions which demanded sweeping measures of parliamentary reform, aimed at dismantling 'Old Corruption' and establishing universal manhood suffrage; in Blackburn there was a Ladies' Reform Association and some radicals, like William Thompson and Anna Wheeler, demanded votes for women. The radical democrats claimed support in 102 towns and cities. In Birmingham Thomas Attwood's Political Union was prepared to accept a fairly limited Reform Bill but was also prepared to go to the brink of civil war when the King and the Lords sought to block it. The Political Union's thousands of supporters, uniting both the middle and working class, met in open air meetings at which they would march with a military drill. The Birmingham Union, which had counterparts in other towns, impressed because it was 'at once moral, orderly and enthusiastic'.[37]

The successive Reform Bills were designed to head off the burgeoning radical movement and in particular to detach the middle-class reformers from the democratic agitators. All or most of the 'rotten boroughs' and 'pocket boroughs' were to be eliminated and distributed to towns like Manchester and Birmingham which lacked representation. But all the proposed reform measures left nine-tenths of the adult population unenfranchised, since the vote would only be granted to men meeting the necessary property qualification. But any reform which did away with the 'rotten boroughs' and 'pocket boroughs' was bound to meet unyielding opposition from vested interests in the Commons, Lords and at Court. The 'borough-mongers' would be expropriated and the monarch and nobility would have to contend with a more representative and legitimate Lower House. If reform was defeated then there was a real danger that the moderate radicals would opt for an extra-parliamentary confrontation, joining forces with the extreme democrats and radicals. In the event the First Reform Bill gained a majority of only one vote in the Commons in March 1831 and was subsequently defeated in committee. The Whig leader, Lord Grey, called an election in which supporters of the Reform Bill did well in all popular contests. The Second Reform Bill was presented in September and passed by a large majority in the Commons. The House of Lords defeated the bill on its second reading. The extra-parliamentary movement for reform was outraged; in Bristol a rioting mob took over the town for several days, and elsewhere there were more disciplined, and in some sense more threatening, outbreaks. For once the middle-class champions of reform did not back down; they could point out that the riots had been worst where the Political Unions were weak and spontaneous popular feeling, spurred by democratic agitation, had taken control. They urged the mobilisation, and even arming, of their members in the interests of law and order. In the House of Commons Macaulay warned:

> I know of only two ways in which societies can permanently be governed – by public opinion, or by the sword. I understand how the peace is kept in New York. It is by the assent and support of the people. I understand also how the peace is kept at Milan. It is by the bayonets of the Austrian soldiers. But how the peace is to be kept when you have neither popular assent nor the military force – how the peace is to be kept in England by a Government acting on the principles of the present opposition, I do not understand.[38]

Parliamentarians with an abolitionist background played a key role in presenting the case for reform to the Houses of Parliament. The terms in which they did so help to establish the nature of the crisis and the reason for the continued significance of anti-slavery. In the Commons Macaulay summarised the issues at stake in the following way:

All history is full of revolutions, produced by causes similar to those which are now operating in England. A portion of the community which had been of no account expands and becomes strong. It demands a place in the system, suited, not to its former weakness, but to its present power. If this is granted all is well. If this is refused then comes the struggle between the young energy of one class and the ancient privileges of another. . . . Such was the struggle of our North American colonies against the mother country. . . . Such was the struggle which the Third Estate of France maintained against the aristocracy of birth. . . . Such is the struggle which the free people of Jamaica are now maintaining against the aristocracy of skin. Such, finally, is the struggle which the middle-classes in England are waging against an aristocracy of mere locality, against an aristocracy the principle of which is to invest a hundred drunken pot-wallopers in one place, or the owner of a ruined hovel in another, with powers which are withheld from cities renowned to the furthest ends of the earth for the marvels of their wealth and industry. The question of Parliamentary reform is still behind. But signs, of which it is impossible to misconceive the import, do most clearly indicate that, unless that question also be speedily settled, property, and order, and all the institutions of this great monarchy, will be exposed to fearful peril.[39]

Macaulay's advice was 'reform that you may preserve'. In the Lords Brougham made a similar plea in which he urged the necessity of accommodating 'those middle classes who are genuine depositories of sober, rational and intelligent English feeling . . . Rouse not, I beseech you, a resolute people.'[40] The approach adopted by Brougham and Macaulay rested on an understanding of an absence of fundamental conflicts within the possessing classes which opened the way for compromise. The obtrusiveness of the references to class corresponded to a corporatist ideology in which the middle classes, while insisting on a larger place within ruling institutions, did not aspire to seize and re-model them. Macaulay declared that property was 'divided against itself' and that reform would heal the breach. Instead of setting out to 'rouse a resolute people' the parliamentary champions of reform offered a compromise in which the middle classes would respect the venerable structures of the British constitutional monarchy, with its powerful hereditary and oligarchical element. The landed aristocracy was not to be swept away, but rather its representation brought closer to its real economic and social weight. All the proposed measures of reform not only preserved the House of Lords and the royal prerogative but also over-represented landed property in the House of Commons. No parliamentary advocate rose to echo the slogan that the Third Estate was nothing but must be everything. The middle classes knew their place – in the middle. Despite this modest and corporatist goal the campaign for parliamentary reform attracted vast popular support. The leaders of radical opinion like William Cobbett and Francis Place saw the proposed reform as an essential preliminary that would open the path to further extensions of the franchise and further inroads on aristocratic control of the state. The resistance put up to reform by the King and the Lords further encouraged the view that a fundamental change was in prospect and that for the time being all efforts should be concentrated on securing its passage.

With mounting popular pressure Lord Grey presented a Third Reform Bill to the House of Commons. This bill was radical in so far as it completely eliminated the 'rotten boroughs', and did so without compensation; moderate in that it only enfranchised £10 freeholders and actually disenfranchised many in Westminster and some other formerly popular constituencies who could not meet the property qualification. The Third Reform Bill received a large majority in the Commons, with even Members for boroughs scheduled for abolition voting for it. The Lords proceeded to block the bill by amendment and the King dismissed the Grey ministry in May 1833 after refusing its request to create enough peers to ensure passage of the bill in the Upper House. The King and the Duke of Wellington, who was invited to form the government, intended to introduce a reform measure little different from Grey's but to make it clear that this was their own gracious decision. Before they could do so the country moved to the brink of civil war. The Birmingham Political Union, led by Thomas Attwood, armed 1,500 of its members warning of the danger of an anti-reform coup; they faced only 150 troopers of doubtful loyalty. The reform leaders called on their followers to demand gold payment for their banknotes and refuse to pay taxes. During these 'Days of May' the Political Unions openly declared for 'hostile defence', yeomen made it clear that they would not obey orders to disperse the unions, and a far-reaching financial, commercial and industrial stoppage was evidently under way. In Scotland, where the old system of representation was particularly narrow and the demand for reform particularly strong, the very absence of riots made the civic determination all the more impressive. The opposition to the Wellington government was such a 'persuasive and terrifying expression of the national will' that the King decided to recall Grey and to agree that if necessary enough peers would be created to ensure the passage of reform. William IV is usually regarded as one of the more insignificant of British monarchs, notable only for his liking for the sea. Yet if the 'sailor King' had clung to

Wellington the reform crisis could easily have taken a violent turn and the monarchy itself might not have survived. Instead the newly appointed Grey government reintroduced the Reform Bill which passed both Houses, with many Tories abstaining, in June.[41]

It is scarcely surprising that support for reform and support for slave emancipation had been strongly correlated. Those who were most zealous for slave emancipation were aware that their cause stood no chance of being approved by the unreformed Parliament, given the strength of the West India interest in the Commons, the veto power of the Lords, the hostile attitude of the King and the oligarchic disposition to protect private property of all types. And, as suggested above, the affinity between reform and abolitionism was by no means simply a product of parliamentary calculation. Both movements questioned what they saw as aberrant types of property. Abolitionism was the perfect complement to the campaign for reform, reassuring those who saw it offering either too much or too little. The Dissenters and Methodists still had important quarrels with the Anglican establishment, with its many educational and fiscal privileges. They supported the secular cause of reform but with some apprehension at involvement in the hurly-burly of political agitation. The anti-slavery cause helped to dignify the concern with a limited extention of the franchise. In a similar way anti-slavery helped to lend a more generous aspect to the comparatively modest step towards representative government embodied in the reform proposals. The reform measures, with their limited and exclusive clauses, offered little by way of spiritual nourishment or moral inspiration. Yet the struggle to achieve reform, and to use it, was sufficiently hard-fought to require sustenance of this sort. A pure class corporatism and a nakedly bourgeois reformism would not even have aroused the middle classes themselves to a sense of their political destiny. Anti-slavery helped to mobilise the middle classes, and a popular following, without the danger that the movement would capsize into revolution. It added a humanistic appeal to a class whose other creeds – Dissent, utilitarianism and *laissez faire* – were notably lacking in this 'existential' ingredient. It raised middle-class morale and gave reformers an issue which could be taken to the people.

The leaders of the reform movement needed to mobilise their own constituency if they were to impose 'middle-class' terms on both the 'upper' and 'lower' classes. To some extent the more moderate Political Unions were able to perform this task, but they were generally assisted in doing so by the existence of Anti-Slavery Societies. The Political Unions were open to radical and democratic influence and could not be relied upon to follow the lead of the parliamentary spokesmen. Abolitionism provided the latter with a connective tissue, bringing them into communication with layers of the population beyond the reach of the Political Unions.

While Brougham was centrally involved in the reform crisis Buxton tended to remain aloof from too direct an engagement in political strife. His diary registers both his own unease at the threatening political climate and the consolation he found in pressing the anti-slavery cause. His entry for October 26th 1831 records his anguished discussions with Samuel Hoare concerning 'the dangers from reform or the rejection of reform' and the 'perils of the Church and the State':

> We now stand in a peculiar Crisis. . . . Last week the Bristol riots prevailed, and the same spirit may spread through the country. In this neighbourhood the incendiary has been briskly at work. Last week the news arrived that the cholera had really commenced its ravages in England; and tomorrow a meeting of the working classes is to take place in London. Storms seem gathering in every direction, and the tempest may soon brake upon my own house.

Buxton was comforted by the thought that the Almighty had ordained that he was to labour to free the slave: 'It has pleased God to place some duties upon me with regard to the poor slaves, and those duties I must not abandon. Oppression, cruelty, and persecution, and, what is worse, absence of religion, must not continue to grind that race through my neglect.'[42] He was soon to learn of events that prompted guilt at his own distraction.

The arrival of the first news of the slave insurrection in Jamaica in December 1831 contributed to the national sense of conflict and uncertainty without at all favouring parliamentary abolitionism. Reports of rampaging blacks at first led MPs to sympathise with the planters. In April and May 1832, just as the reform crisis itself was coming to a head, the British public learnt of the persecution of the Methodist and Baptist missionaries. Moderate abolitionists who had been alarmed at black insurgence began to see the white colonists as the problem. Outrage in the abolitionist ranks was stimulated by the eye-witness reports of those missionaries who had been expelled. As it happened the annual meeting of the Anti-Slavery Society coincided both with the 'Days of May' in 1832 and with growing abolitionist awareness of the atrocities in the West Indies. Indeed the House of Lords had provocatively established its own committee to examine colonial questions not long before it had thrown out the Reform Bill. The Anti-Slavery Convention demanded that there should be an immediate riposte by its parliamentary supporters. Buxton responded to these pressures by a dramatic new anti-slavery initiative. Even before the reform issue was settled he introduced a resolution committing Parliament to immediate slave emancipation. This was voted out on the grounds that there was no time to consider it, but Buxton picked up an unexpected degree of support. As a compromise the government agreed to establish a parliamentary committee to consider the most practical way of freeing the slaves. In moving his own resolution Buxton warned that Britain might not retain the colonies if slavery was upheld and asked what the government would do if faced with 'a general insurrection of the negroes'.[43]

From this point anti-slavery agitation once again went into high gear, equalling or exceeding the mobilisation of 1830–31. The question of reform had now been settled and the Whig government had agreed in principle to investigate slave emancipation. The events in Jamaica, and reports of disturbances in other islands, made it clear to abolitionists that there must be no more postponement or equivocation from Parliament. The calling of the first election held under the Reform Act furnished a further stimulus to abolitionist activity. For their part the leaders of the reform movement and of the Whig government also needed to choose the platform on which they would fight with great care. In seeking to explain the progress of emancipation it is necessary to take into account both the impulse of the popular movement and the calculations of the rulers; emancipation would not be embodied in a parliamentary act unless it made sense to the managers of the government and the Members of Parliament.

Once the King and the Lords had given in over reform the limitations of the measure became easier to see. The electorate was enlarged from 4–500,000 to 6–800,000. Only a seventh of adult males possessed the vote, a proportion very similar to that which had prevailed in 1714. There was no secret ballot and the number of rural county seats, often dominated by powerful landlord connections, was actually increased from 188 to 253. The £10 franchise that prevailed in the 'borough' seats admitted most of the middle class; in certain areas some craftsmen or artisans also qualified, though in Middlesex or Westminster many were disenfranchised. The House of Lords, with its hereditary peers and Anglican bishops, retained all its formal powers, as did the monarch; in practice they had learnt to be circumspect in using them. The Great Reform Act had appeared to open up Parliament, as Grey put it, to 'the real and efficient mass of public opinion . . . without whom the power of the gentry is as nothing'.[44] But the whole edifice of the state remained oligarchic in character. Macaulay, introducing a moderate reform of the East India Company, justified it in terms that might have been applied to the Reform Act as well: 'The very meaning of compromise is that each party gives up his chance of complete success in order to be able to be secured against the chance of utter failure. . . . The Company is an anomaly, but it is part of a system where everything is an anomaly. . . . I will not, therefore, in a case in which I have neither principle nor precedent to guide me, pull down the existing system. . . . which is sanctioned by experience.'[45] The proud rhetoric of 1831 had subsided to a mumble.

Macaulay was himself inclined to approach the question of slave emancipation in a similar spirit of compromise and expressed his private annoyance at the single-minded fanaticism of the anti-slavery campaign. But in the conditions of 1832–3 the anti-slavery cause was taken up not only by the advocates of parliamentary compromise but by a broad and radical extra-parliamentary movement, without which little or nothing might have been done. The extra-parliamentary Agency Committee had always been a little suspicious of the caution of the parliamentary abolitionists; following the reform it had new scope for pressing its case on the government. It also found new allies, in the shape of previously sceptical radicals and democrats.

The anti-slavery societies exerted themselves in the unprecedented electoral campaign of 1832 to commit candidates to the support of immediate slave emancipation. In the event 104 of the new Members had subscribed to a pledge supporting slave emancipation drawn up by the Anti-Slavery Society. The unprecedented nature of the election, and the throng of issues brought forward for the attention of the new Parliament, meant that the anti-slavery question had to jostle for priority with many other urgent issues, such as the need for a reform of the Poor Laws, the need to reform municipal corporations, the need for factory legislation, the future of the East India Company, the repeal of the Corn Laws, and a host of others. A speech by Edward Baines, the editor of the *Leeds Mercury*, gives some idea of the problem. 'The fruits of reform are to be gathered. Vast commercial and agricultural monopolies are to be abolished, the Church is to be reformed. . . . Closed corporations are to be thrown open. Retrenchment and economy are to be enforced. The shackles of the Slave are to be broken.'[46]

Emancipation is left until last but gives a needed flourish to this litany of middle-class reform objectives. As we have seen middle-class reformers had always solidly supported anti-slavery. But radicals and democrats had been more circumspect, tending to regard abolitionism as a potential diversion from domestic ills. The link with middle-class reform had itself made abolitionism suspect to some of the leading radical journalists; thus they would pass racist comments on the happy condition of the 'sleek and stupid negro' in the West Indies, which they contrasted with the famished state of English labourers.[47] But such attitudes were far less common in the 1832 election and its aftermath. In a number of contests radical candidates linked the call for slave emancipation to demands for a bill to limit factory hours, or to attacks on the remaining political influence and privileges of members of the oligarchy with colonial holdings. Radicals knew that the Reform Bill had qualified rather than abolished the political rule of the landed and financial aristocracy. No longer seeing anti-slavery as a diversion, radicals and democrats now recognised slave emancipation as a way in which they could renew the assault on the oligarchy. William Cobbett, who had always disdained anti-slavery, had a West Indian proprietor as an opponent in the contest at Oldham; his announced conversion to the cause of slave emancipation probably helped him to victory and certainly gave him a new stick with which to belabour both Tories and Whigs.[48]

When the new Whig Cabinet drew up the programme of measures to be outlined in the first 'King's speech' to the reformed Parliament it did not include emancipation of the slaves. The members of the government were aware that some new initiative on colonial slavery would have to be taken but felt it unwise to commit themselves to freeing the slaves until they had resolved the enormous practical problems which it posed. Of these the most awkward was the huge expense that would be involved in compensating the slaveholders for the loss of their property. The reform movement had just imposed a swingeing act of expropriation on Parliament. It had succeeded in doing so because a wing of the parliamentary oligarchy had judged such a concession to be necessary; in the end even most Members for 'rotten boroughs' had voted for the extinction of their own seats. The Whig Cabinet judged that the abolition of slave property would have to be accompanied by compensation; only in this way could it be justified to a propertyholders' Parliament. Emancipation could strengthen the legitimacy of large-scale private property at a time when it was under attack from the new working-class socialism – but it could only do so if the principle of economic property was respected by the payment of compensation.

The deliberations of the parliamentary committee on the colonies and private soundings had already revealed that some West Indian proprietors were prepared to endorse emancipation so long as sufficient compensation was available. T.B. Macaulay wrote to his father in August 1832 that 'Lord Harewood, Lord St Vincent, and Lord Howard de Walden [three influential West Indian proprietors] ... have all ... declared themselves decidedly for emancipation as necessary for the safety of their property'.[49] The Jamaican uprising, and reports of disturbances in many of the smaller sugar islands, thus had a visible impact on planter calculations. The West Indian proprietors least reconciled to any plan of emancipation were those with a stake in the new colonies, where there were still good prospects of expansion.

Some Ministers thought the planters should be compensated by a loan, others by entitlement to continuing forced labour for a lengthy period, others by concessions on taxation or the sugar duties. The West India Committee insisted that nothing short of an outright grant to the full value of the slaves would be acceptable. Both the King and the Lords could be relied on to support the West Indians. Yet emancipation on these terms would alienate all those calling for lower taxes and economical government, and might be opposed by radical abolitionists who saw no reason to give any compensation to former slaveholders. The silence on slavery of the King's Speech, delivered in February 1833, reflected the intractability of these problems.

The failure of the new administration to come forward with an emancipation proposal provoked the most far-reaching abolitionist campaign that had ever been seen. Meetings attended by several thousand persons each were held in most major towns and cities. In Glasgow the Ladies' Anti-Slavery Society held meetings attended by 1,800 women; a petition eventually signed by 350,000 women was drawn up. Altogether more than five thousand petitions were presented to Parliament; they were said to contain the signatures of nearly one and a half million people. Professional strongmen were hired to carry them to the bar of the House. The King's Secretary noted in his diary: 'Of all the political feelings, and passions and such, this rage for emancipation is rather more than a matter of interest – it has always struck me as the most extraordinary and remarkable.'[50] The climax of this campaign came in an Anti-Slavery Society Convention at Exeter Hall in April. The assembled delegates of the Anti-Slavery Society declared that the emancipation of the slave must be integral; 'No scheme that would leave him half a slave and half a freeman would be beneficial.' However, they were prepared to consider some compensation to the expropriated slave-owner or, as they put it, 'reasonable measures for the relief of the planter'.[51] The decisions of the convention were conveyed by a 330-strong delegation to the Prime Minister and Colonial Secretary.

This upsurge of anti-slavery reflected in part the impact of the news, still coming in, of the repression in Jamaica. Henry Whiteley's pamphlet was published at this time; it sold 200,000 copies within a month of publication. British Nonconformists were particularly incensed at the treatment of their missionaries or their co-religionists. More generally the anti-slavery issue allowed the Nonconformist Churches to assert themselves in a seemly way in the aftermath of reform. Of the petitions presented to Parliament no less than 1,900 were directly organised by Methodist congregations and another 800 by other Dissenting Churches.[52] The large delegation sent to Grey and Stanley after the Exeter Hall Convention included many clergymen, parading to Downing Street in full canonicals.

The Whig government was intensely aware of the brittle state of popular opinion in the aftermath of reform and of the probability that many expectations would be disappointed. The new House of Commons was very difficult to handle, one half of the Members being new to Parliament and the majority refusing a distinct party affiliation. The MPs sought to display great respect for their constituents' wishes. The old aristocratic political families were still well represented but no less attentive to constituency opinion. The new Members exhibited an unlovely streak of class egoism: their first concerns being to open up municipal corporations to the middle-class electorate, to reduce the rates by ending outdoor poor relief, to prevent any irksome limitation on the length of the working day, and so forth.

Lord Holland, a member of the Whig Cabinet, noted his own sense of government isolation and of the difficulty of maintaining the prestige of the reform Parliament: 'Although we have the prospect of steering through this very formidable and difficult pass, it is too manifest that our hold on the country is less firm than when the Reform Parliament met.' Holland knew that slave emancipation was the single issue that commanded most support in the country, but he felt that its parliamentary advocates had been irresponsible in pressing it without spelling out the precise measures of compensation that would be necessary: 'After working the people to a state of madness on the topick of immediate and unconditional emancipation, he [Brougham], like other abolitionists, had no plan for carrying their object into execution.'[53]

The Prime Minister, Earl Grey, was worried that if the Whig government fell at a time when the Tories were weakened and discredited then the radical democrats might seize their opportunity, and unleash the pent-up discontents of the populace on the oligarchic system. There could be no doubt that emancipation would help to take the wind out of the sails of those demagogues who traduced the work of Parliament. The public outcry for emancipation also helped to surmount the compensation problem. Having demanded emancipation so noisily even parsimonious middle-class liberals could scarcely complain at financing it. The Colonial Secretary, Edward Stanley, introduced an Abolition of Slavery Bill in May 1833, which envisaged compensating the colonial proprietors by giving them a public loan of

£15 million plus the right to the continuing labour of their slaves, now dubbed 'apprentices', for a period of twelve years. In the course of three months of debate and negotiation these terms were to be modified. The West Indian proprietors succeeded in changing the monetary clauses of the bill from a loan to an outright grant of £20 million. Subsequently the anti-slavery MPs succeeded in reducing the period of 'apprenticeship' from twelve to six years. Buxton had difficulty in persuading some anti-slavery MPs to accept the bill, which he supported on the grounds that no other measure had a hope of appearing on the statute book. O'Connell, the Irish leader, voted against the bill because his abolitionist convictions would not let him accept its compensation and apprenticeship provisions. Only two out of thirty-one MPs who were West Indian proprietors voted against the emancipation bill; of these two, one objected to compensation on economical grounds, the other on abolitionist grounds. Some 'economists' and some 'East Indians' grumbled at the size of compensation. But in the end the Abolition of Slavery Bill passed with large majorities in both Houses and received the royal assent at the end of August 1833.[54]

The size of the sum granted to the planters surprised even those who agreed it. There was a fit of nervous hilarity when an MP pointed out, following passage of the compensation clause, that the House usually haggled for hours before agreeing to the creation of a new post with a salary of £500 a year. At the close of the lengthy Cabinet session at which the precise compensation terms were hammered out the Prime Minister fell asleep where he sat; his colleagues tiptoed out in order not to wake him. The Whig government and the Reform Parliament had commemorated their existence in a most signal way and could enjoy the satisfaction of the wealthy philanthropist who has made a large public donation to charity. The compensation offered to the planters came close to representing the full value of their slaves. The slaves themselves were to cover a significant proportion of the cost of compensation since during the 'apprenticeship' period they were obliged to remain on the plantations and work a ten-hour day. The £20 million grant was paid in the form of government bonds, at a standard rate for each slave age and sex category. Cobbett complained that the West Indian slaves were being freed at the expense of Britain's own already-burdened 'tax-paying slaves'.[55] Since interest on the compensation bonds was paid from general taxation, mainly Customs and Excise, Cobbett had a point. But the monetary element in the compensation was absorbed by Britain's system of public finance in ways that obscured who was footing the bill. Planters could sell the bonds if they wished, while the new bond issue only added marginally to the already huge national debt; others things being equal it would have risen by 3 per cent, though in fact service payments remained steady as the Chancellor found other ways of reducing government liabilities. Slaveholder compensation in the British colonies was thus facilitated by the relatively modest size of slaveholder wealth by comparison with imperial wealth and the size of the National Debt; it also demonstrated the mobile character of economic property in a capitalist economy and *rentier* state. Of course the mysteries of public credit did not detract from either the real gains of the planters or the perceived generosity of Parliament. Shortly thereafter Parliament proceeded to approve a reform of the Poor Law which set up workhouses and stopped payment of outdoor relief from the local rates which had been running at £7 million in 1832.[56] While this contrasts most instructively with the treatment of the slaveholders, and reflected within Parliament as a whole a broad consensus on the need for a market in labour disciplined by penal disincentives to 'idleness', it is only fair to add that several abolitionist MPs were to be found among the minority which voted against the harsher provisions of the Poor Law, notably those involving incarceration in workhouses and the break-up of families.[57]

Much anti-slavery opinion outside Parliament objected to the payment of compensation and almost every abolitionist objected to the proposed term of 'apprenticeship'. But overall the organised anti-slavery movement was greatly pleased by its success. The 1833 Abolition of Slavery Act, to take effect in the colonies in August 1834, had, after all, been a government measure and was thus not the direct responsibility of the abolitionists. De Tocqueville was later to write that slave emancipation in Britain had been 'the act of the nation and not of its rulers'. In that the decisive impulse came from the surge in public opinion this near-contemporary judgement is correct. But the terms of emancipation were the work of the rulers, and neither the abolitionists nor the wider movement fully supported them. It was the rulers, also, who appropriated to themselves a large share of the credit for the passage of emancipation. Grey, content that government and Parliament had confirmed and consolidated a difficult transition, retired in July 1834, handing over the Premiership to the safe hands of Lord Melbourne. The latter gave his private opinion in a candid avowal to the English Primate: 'I say, Archbishop, what do you think I would have done about this slavery business if I had my way? I would have done nothing at all. It is all a pack of nonsense. There have always been slaves in most civilised countries, the Greeks, the Romans. However they *would* have their own way and we have abolished slavery. But it is all great folly.'[58]

The Tory opposition, having consented to both reform and emancipation, relaunched itself with the Tamworth Manifesto in

December 1834. Those who had played a forward part in reform, even appearing to threaten revolution in its support, found themselves relegated from the centre of political life. Brougham was dropped from the Melbourne Cabinet, never to hold office again, while Macaulay was dispatched to India, and subsequently left politics and devoted himself to writing and history. Edward Stanley, author of the Abolition Act and later the fourteenth Earl of Derby, was able to take the credit both for emancipation and for the generous treatment of the planters; he went on to lead four administrations as Prime Minister. Melbourne's Whig–Liberal government survived two brief challenges to last until 1841, but so far as the radicals were concerned it never fulfilled its promise. Only the more narrowly conceived middle-class reforms ever made it on to the statute book; significant public spending on education and infrastructure was still far in the future.

To the great relief of the abolitionists Emancipation Day passed off rather quietly in the West Indies. The Nonconformist Churches organised decorous thanksgiving services and urged continued hard work. The colonial authorities strengthened security arrangements and began to enlist special officers and 'stipendiary magistrates' to invigilate the apprenticeship scheme. The mass of slaves continued to labour, glad for any slight amelioration and aware that the physical guarantees of their enslavement had not yet been removed. Plantation output in 1834–6 was comparable with previous years. But as the 'stipendiary magistrates' arrived and the local assemblies passed local regulations to accompany 'apprenticeship' controversy began to stir again.

The abolitionists believed, with reason, that the planters and managers would do all in their power to ensure that apprenticeship was simply slavery by another name. Thus, contrary to the act, female apprentices would still be whipped. New prisons, equipped with treadmills, were built for apprentices who absented themselves from the fields. The badly constructed treadmills were little better than instruments of torture. New colonial laws savagely penalised recalcitrant apprentices while ignoring the derelictions of overseers and planters. The Colonial Office, whose officials had favoured emancipation, dispatched 132 stipendiary magistrates to invigilate its workings. Some of these men were overawed by the white colonists but a number displayed some scruple in reporting conditions on the plantations, or in deciding such cases as were referred to them. The internal life of the plantations was difficult to penetrate but in Jamaica and some other islands the Nonconformist missionaries wrote to abolitionists in Britain drawing attention to abuses. William Knibb reported that apprentices were still being flogged and urged that a British abolitionist delegation should be sent to observe what 'apprenticeship' meant in practice. However, in some of the smaller islands the assemblies encouraged a less provocative approach than did the Jamaica Assembly. In Antigua the Colonial Assembly decided that the conflicts that apprenticeship was likely to produce were too great; on this small island the planters had an effective monopoly of all cultivable land and the field labourers thus found that they had to work on the plantations if they were to eat. The island Assembly thus ended apprenticeship of its own accord, granting full freedom to all.[59]

British abolitionists were alert to the abuses of apprenticeship. In April 1835 a protest meeting was held in Exeter Hall, addressed amongst others by the recently dismissed Brougham. In autumn of 1835 the Birmingham Anti-Slavery Society launched a national campaign for the ending of apprenticeship at a rally attended by several thousand supporters. Joseph Sturge, the wealthy backer of the Agency Committee and now an MP, was to be a leading light in this campaign. In 1836–7 he made a tour of inspection of the West Indian colonies, reporting the abuses which he saw flourishing under the regime of 'apprenticeship'. In November 1837 Sturge addressed a large rally at Exeter Hall which set up a Central Emancipation Committee. Sturge wrote up as a pamphlet the 'Narrative of James Williams', an apprentice, showing the abuse to which the former slaves were still subject. New petitions were organised and bills ending apprenticeship were submitted to Parliament. Though the Lords turned down such a bill the beginnings of a new popular campaign on the issue were already evident. The new Emancipation Committee launched a journal, *The Emancipator*, and published Sturge's report on his tour of the West Indies in January 1838.[60]

The West Indian proprietors became highly alarmed at developments both in the colonies and in the metropolis. Continuation of the campaign against 'apprenticeship', and of the activity of the missionaries and of newly formed abolitionist societies in the colonies, threatened an unending prospect of insecurity, with official reports, government concessions and the risk of black revolt. In deference to the abolitionists the government had already announced that male apprentices could not be flogged after August 1838. Some planters were encouraged by the example of Antigua. At all events between March and July 1838 the various colonial assemblies introduced legislation ending apprenticeship. By doing so they averted another exercise in metropolitan intervention, with its unwelcome and unsettling publicity. The West Indian proprietors also hoped to secure abolitionist support for their attempt to retain a protected status for colonial 'free grown' sugar in the face of the already menacing trend to free trade.

The Melbourne government and the Colonial Office had made clear their support for the ending of apprenticeship, pointing out to the planters that they could not expect favourable treatment unless they assisted in the removal of this embarrassment. There was to be continuing controversy over the stern laws against vagrancy and squatting introduced by the colonial assemblies. In the long run the abolitionists were on weaker ground in attacking these laws, since they so often merely echoed metropolitan legislation. Once apprenticeship was ended Fowell Buxton was prepared to allow the planters some latitude, but Joseph Sturge and the Birmingham Anti-Slavery Society propounded a radical abolitionism that was vigilant in defence of the freedmen and prepared to defend the rights of labourers in Britain as well as in the colonies. The government thought it prudent to pay attention to abolitionist representations, though it became increasingly concerned to ensure good order and good labour discipline in the colonies and saw no other way of doing this than to support the planters. So long as the Melbourne government survived – that is, until 1841 – the abolitionists had some political leverage. There was also a general metropolitan disposition to distrust the planter assemblies, especially that of Jamaica; in 1839 the London government first suspended the Jamaica Assembly and then secured parliamentary legislation limiting its powers. Coloured proprietors and professionals, including Jordan, obtained representation within the Assembly; however, such representatives were often to align themselves with the white planters when it came to legislation against squatters and vagrants. In the 1840s the Colonial Office in London became a much less effective or concerned restraint on proprietors or employers in the colonies.

The freedmen and women played a large part, wherever conditions permitted, in shaping the new colonial order. Thus the former slaves sometimes succeeded in asserting possession of their provision grounds and used income from the sale of provisions to buy formal title to their land. The provision grounds were usually situated in the plantation hinterland, perhaps in the hills, and might not be covered by the planters' title deeds. In some colonies there was extensive Crown land which was successfully invaded by the freedmen. In Dominica the comparatively large size of the pre-emancipation free population of colour allowed coloured proprietors to became the major influence in the island Assembly; Dominica was the largest of the Windward Islands and it was difficult for planters to stop freedmen claiming and farming their old provision grounds in the mountains. At the time of the ending of apprenticeship there was only one policeman on Dominica and the colonial authorities had no wish to send troops there. After all, the British Parliament had enacted the abolition of slavery in part because it wished to reduce, not increase, outlays on West Indian security.[61]

The precise outcome of emancipation differed from island to island, with the planters still in a strong position in some of the smaller islands where land was scarce. The planters of Barbados, like those of Antigua, managed to preserve the plantation regime and to dominate the island Assembly, since many of them were residents and could count on the support of the relatively numerous white population. In these islands plantation output was increased and most blacks excluded from the electoral register by property and tax-paying qualifications; partly under pressure from the freedmen and women and partly for its own reasons the plantocracy permitted the growth of Church of England schools. In Grenada, on the other hand, large-scale plantation production had never properly recovered from the so-called 'Brigands' War' of the 1790s and in the aftermath of emancipation small-scale proprietorship developed further as Grenada produced provisions for other colonies. Overall there was a considerable decline in the plantation economy of the British West Indies and even where it survived it did so by accepting a new relationship with the work-force. Annual sugar output declined by 36 per cent if the average production of 1824–33 is compared with that for 1839–46.[62] Women, who had played an important part in the slave gangs, were now more rarely seen in the cane fields. Wherever the former slaves were dependent on planters' land for their subsistence the planters could exact a labour rent. The planters feared declining prices for their sugar and were generally unwilling to undertake new investments in plant and equipment. Wages of 6d.–8d. a day for cane cutting were offered to begin with in Jamaica; the planters felt they could pay no more yet insufficient labour was forthcoming at this wage. William Knibb, the missionary, campaigned in Jamaica against the terms on which the Colonial Assembly had ended apprenticeship. The Jamaican planters had set a general rate of 6d. a day and threatened their labourers with eviction from their garden plots and huts if they refused to agree. Knibb attacked the 'sixpenny plot' at meetings attended by thousands of apprentices. He urged that mass eviction could not be permitted by the colonial government. In the event planters did pay somewhat higher wages, often over 1s. a day, and found eviction difficult. The suspension of the Jamaican Assembly in 1839, and the subsequent limitation of its powers, gave a respite to the freedmen. The London price of sugar rose in the years 1837–42 as colonial output sagged and the protectionist regime prevented the large-scale import of foreign sugars. About half the plantations of Jamaica successfully adjusted to a wage labour regime, the remainder going out of production, squeezed by a sharp drop in prices from 1842.[63]

Material conditions probably improved for the freedmen up to the middle of the 1840s. The wages for male labourers rose in most colonies to over 1s. a day, though they were a little lower than this in Grenada where there were few plantations. Women rarely received much over 1s. a day and few belonged to the better paid or more permanent work-force. The overall numbers of women working for the planters contracted sharply and freedwomen devoted most of their time to domestic labour, subsistence cultivation and petty trading. Plantation wages were probably highest in Guyana, at between 1s.8d. and 2s. a day; several thousand immigrants from Jamaica and the Windwards were drawn to Guyana by the hope of more advantageous employment. Throughout the British West Indies artisan freedmen were able to secure wages of between 2s. and 4s. a day, or even as much as 6s. a day. In 1844 there were 12,000 artisans recorded in Barbados, 17,500 in Jamaica, 6,000 in Guyana and 2,500 in Antigua. The Nonconformist Churches established schools in the colonies and received a small government subsidy to assist them. The missionaries might occasionally side with the freedmen in disputes with their employers, but they encouraged former slaves to become smallholders rather than trade unionists. In Jamaica and elsewhere such missionaries as Knibb, Bleby, Phillippo, Clerk and Burchell helped to sponsor 'model villages'. More generally freedmen found that they could build houses and buy land titles, saving money from wages and selling provisions from their plots. The number of black or coloured smallholders grew steadily, though the typical holding would be very small; in Jamaica there were found to be 2,114 smallholders in 1838, rising to 27,379 in 1845 and as many as 50,000 by 1861, with the great majority of new smallholders being former slaves. Most smallholdings were only a few acres in size; with only 4,000 in Jamaica in 1861 being between ten and fifty acres. In Guyana there was also a considerable growth in the extent of black smallholding, with some 40,000 former slaves living on 11,000 small farms by 1851. Even on the smaller islands there was a growth of black petty proprietorship in the post-emancipation period. In Grenada there were 1,943 smallholdings in 1845 rising to 3,571 in 1853; in St Lucia there were 1,345 freeholders in 1845 rising to 2,343 in 1853. In Trinidad there were 7,000 smallholders by 1849 and in Tobago 2,367 by 1853. On St Kitts there were 2,800 freeholders and 2,300 leaseholders in 1845. The previous civic status of these freeholders and leaseholders is not clear, but the majority of new proprietors would have formerly been slaves. In all the British colonies there was a wave of house-building by former slaves and in most a considerable increase in school attendance. By the 1850s visitors remarked on the absence of paupers, the low level of crime, high church and chapel attendance, high levels of illegitimate births and the appearance of a moderately prosperous coloured peasantry.[64] The spread of coloured land ownership also led to an increase in coloured representation in some of the colonial assemblies. Thus while emancipation weakened the plantation economy it brought tangible benefit for many former slaves; the end of super-exploitation, a measure of personal freedom, the possibility of a more stable family life and the growth of smallholding, based on production for local use rather than for international markets.

The populations of the British West Indies had, with the exception of Barbados, declined in the last years of slavery, though at a slower rate than previously. In the decades after emancipation population levels began a slow recovery, recording positive growth rates in every colony during the rest of the century. This achievement is the more remarkable in that the numbers of doctors in the islands declined considerably as the sugar estates cut costs or closed down. Jamaica's total population was around 376,000 in 1834, though no precise count is available; the first census after emancipation, held in 1844, recorded a population of 377,000; despite the ravages of a cholera epidemic at mid-century population rose to 441,000 in 1861 and to 506,000 in 1871. In the last years of slavery Jamaica's slave population had a crude birth rate of 32 per 1,000; by 1881–5 this had risen to 37.4 per 1,000. Jamaican infant mortality rates in 1881 seem to have been little different from those in the last days of slavery; on the other hand, the death rate for those aged five years and over was considerably lower. Thus the ending of slavery was good for the slaves in the elementary sense that it allowed them to live longer.[65]

In British Guyana and Trinidad, where there were still good prospects for plantation expansion, the planters faced continuing resistance from their former slaves, including a number of hard-fought strikes. With the permission of the Colonial Office the British Guyanese planters turned to another part of the empire for an alternative supply of plantation labour. In the 1840s poverty-stricken Indians were signed up and brought to the Caribbean by contractors for sale to the planters, for whom they were then legally obliged to work for three, five or seven years. When it was discovered that contract labourers were being flogged like slaves on the Gladstone estates, there was an abolitionist outcry in Britain. The import of contract labourers was suspended in 1839, but resumed a few years later when abolitionist influence was in retreat and after the planters had agreed that the indentured labourers possessed certain minimum personal rights. Altogether between 1834 and 1865 96,580 Asian contract labourers were imported by West Indian proprietors for work on the plantations. The sugar output of the British West Indies lagged behind its most dynamic competitors, but from around mid-century there was some recovery. In 1834–6 they had produced 184,000 tons; in 1839–46 output dropped to 131,000 tons; by 1857–66 output had risen again to 191,000 tons.[66]

The triumphs of British abolitionism had been both signal and substantive. It has been suggested that they were made possible by:

(a) the pressure of slave revolt (in the French Caribbean in the 1790s and the British Caribbean in 1815–32);
(b) the modest or declining relative economic importance of first the slave trade and then colonial slavery;
(c) the congruence of abolitionism with the ideal image of a reformed bourgeois order and global British role;
(d) the need of British governments to reinforce their legitimacy and to maximise popular support at times of imperial and national political crisis;
(e) a qualification of (c) and concomitant of (d), massive popular mobilisations against colonial slavery, reflecting the ability of anti-slavery themes to extend traditional conceptions of 'English liberty' and to articulate fears aroused by the industrial capitalist order.

The abolitionist successes of 1806–14 and of 1832–8 were the product of the conjunction of these various considerations and conditions. While factors (b) and (c) were permissive conditions, slave resistance and popular contestation, threatening a vulnerable ruling order, imposed emancipation in the 1830s.

Emancipation had triumphed first in St Domingue because of the depth of the political crisis of the French monarchy and the tensions generated by plantation slavery in the full flood of development, the centrifugal impulse of colonial wealth, the insubordination of the planters, the explosion of slave resistance, the vulnerability of the French commercial bourgeoisie, the impact of imperial rivalry and the ascendance of revolutionary egalitarianism. The British Empire and social formation was riven by less extreme conflicts. But as the Hanoverian regime of 'illegitimate monarchy' was overtaken by its own success, abolitionism helped its rulers to grapple with the challenge of global pre-eminence, a prodigious growth in the numbers and wealth of the 'middle classes', and the emergence of a working-class movement animated by democratic and semi-socialist or anti-capitalist doctrines.

These conclusions do not mean that anti-slavery had allowed the British 'middle classes' to achieve hegemony in society. The abolitionist mobilisations had been most important in 'the making of the middle classes' – that is, in forging an alliance between middling manufacturers and merchants, professional men, shopkeepers, newspaper proprietors, salaried clerks, and farmers. In the great struggles that led to the Reform Act, and during the crucial test of the first reform Parliament, the anti-slavery campaigns helped these middle classes to assert themselves and supplied a certain ideological safety-catch, mobilising popular sentiment in ways that did not constitute a fundamental threat to the oligarchy or to the new bourgeois order. But it fell short of establishing middle-class hegemony in at least two decisive respects. To begin with, because anti-slavery was eventually, at the moment of decision, taken up by the more far-sighted section of the oligarchy itself. Of course Wilberforce, Buxton and Brougham were themselves, in their own eccentric ways, each members of the oligarchy. But even more significant was the sponsorship extended to abolition by three belted earls, outstanding members of the Whig faction of the oligarchy. The remarkable contribution to abolitionist success of Lords Grenville, Grey and Derby is too often overlooked: it was they who ensured the parliamentary acceptance of the acts of 1807 and 1833. And, as suggested above, the passage of these abolitionist measures conferred such prestige on Parliament that it reduced pressure on it for more far-reaching changes, including changes which would have permitted a more thoroughgoing middle-class victory. Anti-slavery never identified oligarchic rule as a fundamental obstacle, and its mainstream inclined to see abolitionism as integral to a reformed and moralised version of the established order.

However, a second caveat must be entered concerning the impact of anti-slavery. If abolitionism was something less than a formula for middle-class political hegemony it was also, in an important sense, something more than an ideology of undiluted capitalism. Anti-slavery doctrines were, of course, compatible with wage labour and capitalist social relations. But they corresponded to the ideals of small producers and artisans as well as larger capitalists; the antithesis of slavery could be independent production or employment rather than wage labour. They could also serve to justify trade unionism. In fact in the years after 1834 anti-slavery themes were drawn upon by domestic radicals, by trade unionists and later by Chartists; Sturge and many of his associates were to declare sympathy and support for Chartism. In the West Indies they inclined to sympathise with the freedman and to attack the recourse to indentured labour. The growth of a free black or coloured artisanate and smallholding class in the West Indies testified to a 'fit' between the more radical dimensions of anti-slavery and the aspirations of many former slaves. And despite the many problems faced by the newly free population of the West Indies their new position in society both reflected and reinforced a restraint that had been applied to the untrammelled rule of white colonists and large-scale capital. So far as the British anti-slavery radicals of the 1830s were concerned, many went on to become political and social radicals on domestic questions just as anti-slavery moderates, such as Bright and Cobden, used techniques pioneered by the anti-slavery movement to attack the Corn Laws in the name of free-market capitalism. However, when the free trading liberals came to attack the sugar duties and to advocate the free import of 'slave-grown sugar' they met resistance from the main bodies of organised abolitionism. British anti-slavery bequeathed a contested legacy. As a passively received tradition it allowed Britain's rulers truthfully to claim to have struck down colonial slavery. But the world order which British governments and British capital now increasingly shaped and dominated was to witness an expansion of slavery and of others forms of servile labour; there was even to be a continuing slave trade. In this context consequent anti-slavery was often to conflict with the logic of British capitalism and of its 'empire of free trade'. British governments found themselves on the one hand committed to anti-slavery policy in deference to public opinion; on the other entangled with governments beholden to slave-owners and even slave-traders. The 'illegitimate monarchy' aimed to legitimate and 'bourgeoisify' itself by accepting the abolitionist programme. But it did not thereby succeed in doing so. The abolitionist initiatives of 1807 and 1833 gave a welcome temporary boost to governments that were in difficulty, symbolically prefiguring later sources of legitimacy, and helping to make possible a gradual transition to a new formula of bourgeois rule. During the long reign of Victoria the extension of the suffrage and the growth of the British Empire made possible a new basis for the legitimacy of the state: democracy and imperialism. If abolitionism looked forward it also looked back and gave a new twist to the moral economy of 'illegitimate monarchy' and in particular to the notion that the subject was offered a guarantee of social freedom as a compensation for permitting the ruling oligarchy to rule.

With the ending of British colonial slavery a species of abolitionism was deemed to have anointed Britain's oligarchy. In 1839 Sir Thomas Fowell Buxton established the Society for the Extinction of the Slave Trade and the Civilisation of Africa, presided over by none other than Prince Albert, consort of the new Queen. The heavy respectability of this organisation is suggested by the fact that its Vice-Presidents included five Dukes, four archbishops, eight marquises, fifteen earls and eighteen bishops.[67] In this same year the picture which commanded all attention at the Royal Academy show was Turner's *The Slave Ship*,

originally entitled *Slavers Throwing Overboard the Dead and Dying –
Typhoon Coming On.* Turner's own early career had been sponsored
by commissions from a 'West Indian' MP. The terrible deeds depicted in
his multi-coloured 'Guernica', and its sense of impending apocalypse,
are redeemed by bravura composition and the 'tinted steam' of spray
and sky. It is not, perhaps, too far-fetched to suggest that Britain's
rulers could have seen in this painting not simply the slave-trader
jettisoning his cargo but also a symbolic representation of their own
sacrifice of slavery, in order to render the ship of state more seaworthy
in a storm.

Notes

1. Elie Halévy, *The Liberal Awakening: 1815–1830*, London 1949, pp. 80–154,
214–18.
2. Fladeland, *Men and Brothers*, pp. 168–72.
3. Fladeland, *Men and Brothers*, p. 177.
4. Reginald Coupland, *The British Anti-Slavery Movement*, London 1964, pp.
125–6.
5. Quoted in Gratus, *The Great White Lie*, p. 197.
6. B.W. Higman, *Slave Populations of the British Caribbean, 1807–1834*, London
1984, p. 72. These bare facts of continuing population decline were well established,
partly because of registration, and were used by abolitionists as the ultimate indictment of
the slave systems. Buxton declared that this evidence was particularly telling since it did
not rely on any 'excitement of feeling' and since planters themselves would judge the
stewardship of a manager in part by his success in maintaining or increasing slave
numbers. Cf. Higman, *Slave Populations*, p. 303. However, this was to oversimplify the
problem, since the ending of the Atlantic slave trade did have some effects which would
temporarily reduce population reproduction rates, notably a decline in the proportion of
women of child-bearing age in the population as a more normal age distribution
developed within it. On a colony by colony basis the pattern was complex, yet Higman's
figures do show that the main sugar producers – Jamaica and Demerara–Essequibo – had
the worst demographic record: as an old colony Jamaica had a low negative rate of
growth but this worsened in the 1820s, while the new colony of Guyana (Demerara–
Essequibo) had a heavy, but erratic, negative growth rate. Not only Barbados, but also
some of the other smaller islands, especially those where large-scale plantation production
was less pronounced, showed convincing improvements in the rate of natural increase
after 1815 (Higman, *Slave Populations*, pp. 307–13).
7. Higman, *Slave Populations*, p. 77.
8. Buckley, *Slaves in Red Coats*, p. 143.
9. E. Braithwaite, *The Development of Creole Society in Jamaica, 1770–1820*,
Oxford 1971, especially pp. 152–65, 194–8.
10. W.A. Green, *British Slave Emancipation, the Sugar Colonies and the Great
Experiment, 1830–1865*, Oxford 1976, pp. 12–15; Mavis C. Campbell, *The Dynamics of
Change in a Slave Society: A Socio-political History of the Free Coloureds of Jamaica,
1800–1865*, Madison and London 1976, p. 62.
11. Campbell, *The Dynamics of Change in a Slave Society*, pp. 160–63. Jordan was a
long-standing Wesleyan; cf. Turner, *Slaves and Missionaries: The Disintegration of
Jamaican Slave Society, 1797–1834*, Urbana 1982, p. 198.
12. Campbell, *Dynamics of Change in a Slave Society*, pp. 102–17; Mary Turner,
Slaves and Missionaries, pp. 1–64. Mary Turner links the disintegrative effect of black

Christianity to the ways in which the latter reflected and strengthened the petty producing and trading complex among slaves; she also stresses African survivals in slave culture and in the colonial patois. The ultimately disruptive impact of Nonconformist religion among Jamaican blacks must be seen in relation to the size of this colony, the large number of free blacks and the tensions of the Jamaican slave system. The small island of Antigua furnishes an interesting case. Observers claimed that Methodist influence promoted an orderly transition from slavery on this island and there was even a Methodist militia. Yet there were disturbances on Antigua in Easter 1831, caused by the planters attempt to impose Sunday working. See Goveia, *Slave Society in the British Leeward Islands*, p. 297, and Craton, *Testing the Chains*, p. 291.

13. B.W. Higman, *Slave Population and Economy in Jamaica, 1807–1834*, Cambridge 1976, pp. 76, 231–3, 223–4.

14. Quoted in Michael Craton, 'Slave Culture, Resistance and the Achievement of Emancipation in the British West Indies', in Walvin, ed., *Slavery and British Society*, pp. 100–122, on p. 120. For the course of the Demerara revolt see also Craton, *Testing the Chains*, pp. 267–90.

15. Deerr, *A History of Sugar*, II, pp. 324–5.

16. Quoted in Craton, *Testing the Chains*, p. 300.

17. Turner, *Slaves and Missionaries*, pp. 148–78; Craton, *Testing the Chains*, pp. 291–321. As so often, the rebels included drivers and skilled slaves.

18. Turner, *Slaves and Missionaries*, pp. 168–73; Craton, *Testing the Chains*, 316–21; Gratus, *The Great White Lie*, pp. 223–4. Sharpe was executed on May 23rd 1832. One of the missionaries who visited him in his cell wrote: 'I heard him two or three times deliver a brief extemporaneous address to his fellow prisoners on religious topics, many of them being confined together in the same cell, and I was amazed both at the power and freedom with which he spoke, and at the effect which was produced upon his auditory. He appeared to have the feelings and passions of his hearers completely at his command; but when I listened to him once, I ceased to be surprised at what Gardner had said to me, "that when Sharpe spoke to him and others on the subject of slavery", he, Gardner, was "wrought up almost to a state of madness".' Henry Bleby, *Death Struggles of Slavery*, London 1853, p. 116.

19. Campbell, *The Dynamics of Slave Society in Jamaica*, p. 160.

20. Patrick Coloquhon, *A Treatise on the Wealth, Power and Resources of the British Empire*, London 1815, pp. 97–8; while the value of British GNP nearly doubled in the period 1811–31, rising from £169 to £303 million in constant prices, that of the British West Indies remained static or even declined. For UK national income see Deane and Cole, *British Economic Growth*, pp. 8, 166. The value of Jamaica's exports, also at constant prices, dropped from £4.6 million in 1805–9 to £3.4 million in 1830–34. Cf. Higman, *Slave Population and Economy in Jamaica*, p. 213. The growth of Guyana and Trinidad partially compensated for Jamaican decline, but the overall picture was still one of stagnation if the value, rather than volume, of output is considered.

21. Calculated from R. Davis, *The Industrial Revolution and British Overseas Trade*, p. 88.

22. J.R. Ward, 'The Profitability of Sugar Planting in the British West Indies, 1650–1834', *Economic History Review*, 2nd series, XXXI, 1978. The generally deflationary condition of the British economy after the Napoleonic wars prevents this uneven decline in profitability being anything like a compelling reason for abandoning slave investments. The average rate of return on British West Indian plantation investments, even though running at only a half of its wartime level, was still double the rate offered by government bonds. In an unpublished paper Ward himself has insisted that the slave plantations were still a viable business proposition on the eve of emancipation: J.R. Ward, 'The Profitability and Viability of British West Indian Plantation Slavery, 1807–1834', paper presented at the Institute of Commonwealth Studies, London University, February 28th 1979.

23. For the reasons adduced above it is not possible to accept the implication of Seymour Drescher's book *Econocide*, namely that British West Indian decline was a consequence of the 1807 act; however, it should be said that Drescher's most informative

study concentrates on showing the very considerable value of the British West Indies prior to 1814 and does not pursue its analysis much beyond this point.

The new colony slave import figure given in the text is from Higman, *Slave Populations of the British Caribbean*, p. 81. The inter-colonial slave traffic effectively ceased in 1828. Slave prices came to reflect the differences in productivity/profitability between the 'old' and the 'new' colonies, with the price in Guyana of a field labourer being twice that in Jamaica by the early 1830s (compare Higman, *Slave Populations*, p. 79). The rise of other competitors to the British West Indian plantations reflected similar differances in productivity and profits as steam-age technology enabled extensive inland cultivation in Cuba, Brazil and the United States. See 'Slavery in the Steam Age', in the present author's companion volume, *The Nemesis of the Slave Power*.

24. E. Phillip Le Veen, *British Slave Trade Suppression Policies, 1821–1865*, New York 1977.

25. Roger Anstey, 'The pattern of British Abolitionism in the Eighteenth and Nineteenth Centuries', in Bolt and Drescher, *Anti-Slavery, Religion and Reform*, pp. 19–42, on p. 24. The salience of colonial wealth in Britain's oligarchy is drawn attention to in Halévy's classic studies. Cf. Elie Halévy, *The Triumph of Reform*, London 1950, p. 80–81. This work gives an excellent account of the alliance between reform and anti-slavery.

26. Walter Bagehot, 'Lord Althorp and the Reform Bill of 1832', *Biographical Essays*, London 1895, pp. 305–46, on p. 334. Norman Gash, *Aristocracy and People: Britain 1815–1865*, London 1982, pp. 43–51. About three-quarters of the MPs over the whole period 1734 and 1832 were connected with the land according to G.P. Judd, *Members of Parliament, 1734–1832*, New Haven 1955, p. 71; in 1826 one-quarter of the 658 MPs were businessmen of some description, but only eight of these were manufacturers, compared with forty-two bankers and forty-four East Indian traders. Cf. B. Gordon, *Economic Doctrine and Tory Liberalism, 1824–1830*, London 1979, p. 5.

27. James Walvin, 'The Propaganda of Anti-Slavery', in Walvin, ed., *Slavery and British Society*, pp. 49–68, on pp. 53–6; see also Edith Hurwitz, *Politics and Public Conscience: Slave Emancipation and the Abolitionist Movement in Britain*, London 1973, pp. 1–24; Howard Temperley, *British Anti-Slavery, 1833–1870*, London 1972, pp. 12–18.

28. David Brion Davis, *Slavery and Human Progress*, Oxford 1984, pp. 182–6.

29. *West India Sugar*, Liverpool, printed by George Smith, 1827. It is likely that Cropper wrote or inspired this pamphlet, given its place of publication and strong free trade orientation.

30. Josiah Conder, *Wages or the Whip*, London 1833. This pamphlet was to be cited by MPs as justification for supporting abolition. Compare Patricia Hollis, 'Anti-Slavery and British Working Class Radicalism', in Bolt and Drescher, *Anti-Slavery, Religion and Reform*, pp. 294–315, on pp. 305–6. Conder's argument was based in part on the approach of Harriet Martineau's *Tale of Demerara: Illustrations of Political Economy*, London 1832.

31. Cecil Driver, *Tory Radical: The Life of Richard Oastler*, New York 1946, pp. 36–57. See also Seymour Drescher, 'Cart Whip and Billy Roller; or Anti-Slavery and Reform Symbolism in Industrial Britain', *Journal of Social History*, vol. 15, Fall 1981, pp. 3–24; and Drescher, *Capitalism and Anti-Slavery*, pp. 144–9.

32, David Eltis, 'Abolitionist Perceptions of Society after Slavery', in Walvin, *Slavery and British Society*, pp. 195–213, p. 199, 201. It was, of course, this period which gave rise to Edward Gibbon Wakefield's famous theory of slavery and colonisation in which he argued that in colonies where land was freely available only slavery would secure a permanent labour force; this observation was used to argue the need for restrictions or taxes on land use in new colonies, thus obliging new settlers to work for wages. Cf. Edward Gibbon Wakefield, *England and America*, London 1834.

33. Henry Whiteley, *Three Months in Jamaica*, London 1833. While Whiteley did look forward to the passage of a Ten Hours Bill regulating factory work, he found slavery more objectionable than the conditions in the industrial districts; child labour is 'very bad' but outright slavery in the West Indies is 'infinitely worse' (p. 16).

34. *The History of Mary Prince, A West Indian Slave, Related by Herself*, edited with

an introduction by Moira Ferguson, London 1987, pp. 83–4.

35. For a recent estimate of the (un)preparedness of the state at this time see Malcolm Thomis and Peter Holt, *Threats of Revolution in Britain, 1789–1848*, London 1977, pp. 87–9. The persistence of the localistic ideal within 'illegitimate monarchy', with its minimal central state, is remarkable. Lord Liverpool explained in 1819: 'We must have an army in peace to protect the metropolis [i.e.London], including as it does, the King, the Parliament and the Bank. We must have a regular force likewise for the protection of our Dock Yards, and other great public depots – but the Property of the Country must be taught to protect itself.' Quoted in Hilton, *Corn, Cash and Commerce*, London 1977, p. 81. For the onset of the Reform crisis see Michael Brock, *The Great Reform Act*, London 1973, pp. 186–9.

36. Eric Hobsbawm and George Rudé, *Captain Swing*, London 1976, p. 47.

37. G.M. Trevelyan, *Lord Grey of the Reform Bill*, London 1920, p. 287.

38. Quoted in Trevelyan, *Grey of the Reform Bill*, p. 311.

39. Thomas Babington Macaulay, *Miscellaneous Writings and Speeches*, London 1889, pp. 483–92.

40. Quoted in Thompson, *The Making of the English Working Class*, p. 889. Thompson stresses Brougham's demagogic role as false friend to the radicals. For a splendidly malicious portrait of Brougham, revealing that his demagogy also earned him solid bourgeois foes, see Bagehot's essay on him in *Biographical Essays*.

41. Trevelyan, *Grey of the Reform Bill*, p. 261. The perils of the 'Days of May' are questioned by John Cannon, *Parliamentary Reform, 1640–1832*, Cambridge 1973, pp. 242–63, but even in his account the peace of the realm turns on the political sagacity of the King. Under the regime of 'illegitimate monarchy', now on its way out, the monarch could still play a decisive role; see also B.W. Hill, 'Executive Monarchy and the Challenge of Parties', *Historical Journal*, XIII, 1970, pp. 379–401.

42. Quoted in Hurwitz, *Politics and the Public Conscience*, pp. 121–2.

43. Mary Turner, 'The Baptist War and Abolition', *Jamaica Historical Review*, vol. XIII, 1982. See also M. Craton, 'Emancipation from Below?' in J. Hayward, *Out of Slavery*, London 1985, pp. 110–31.

44. Gash, *Aristocracy and the People*, p. 147.

45. C.H. Phillips, *The East India Company, 1784–1834*, Manchester 1968, p. 294.

46. Thompson, *The Making of the English Working Class*, p. 901.

47. For this and many other expressions of radical hostility to abolitionism see Patricia Hollis, 'Anti-Slavery and British Working Class Radicalism in the Years of Reform', in Bolt and Drescher, *Anti-Slavery, Religion and Reform*, pp. 294–315, especially pp. 296, 299–30. William Cobbett and Bronterre O'Brien, the two most outstanding popular journalists of the day, embellished with racist epithets the argument that black slaves were far better off than English agricultural labourers or mill-hands. Undoubtedly some of their animus is to be explained by the very fact that anti-slavery had, as suggested above, enabled middle-class reform to win a popular following. While there was no doubt popular racial prejudice there is very little evidence of popular pro-slavery feeling. The West India Committee did organise meetings with a large attendance, but these were mainly of those with a direct stake in the colonies.

48. Drescher, 'Cart Whip or Billy Roller', *Journal of Social History*, pp. 7–11. The Methodist leader Jabez Bunting, despite his long adherence to the abolitionist movement, voted for a 'West Indian', and against a radical anti-slavery candidate in the 1832 election, because of his opposition to radical politics. Drescher, 'Public Opinion and the Destruction of Slavery', in Walvin, *Slavery and British Society*, p. 30.

49. Higman, *Slave Population and Economy in Jamaica*, p. 231.

50. Charles Greville, *A Journal of the Reigns of King George IV and King William IV*, ed. Henry Reeve, New York 1886, II, p. 139.

51. Hurwitz, *Politics and Public Conscience*, p. 81. As a sign of his new interest in anti-slavery Cobbett published the full text of this statement in the *Political Register*, vol. 80, May 18th 1833, p. 433.

52. Drescher, *Capitalism and Antislavery*, pp. 120–34; Drescher points out that at this time artisans were heavily over-represented in Nonconformist ranks. They comprised 23.5 per cent of English society yet 62.7 per cent of all Wesleyans and 63 per cent of the

Baptists and Congregationalists. By the same token nearly every other social category – except miners – was under-represented in Nonconformist ranks. Since nearly every adult Wesleyan Methodist in Britain signed an abolitionist petition in 1833, this information certainly establishes that support for anti-slavery reached far outside the middle class in this year.

53. Abraham D. Kriegel, ed., *The Holland House Diaries, 1831–40*, London 1977, p. 208, 212–13. In fact the younger James Stephen had elaborated an emancipation plan but it was not used. The various emancipation schemes are discussed in Green, *British Slave Emancipation*, pp. 114–20.

54. Izhak Gross, 'The Abolition of Negro Slavery and British Parliamentary Politics, 1832–3', *Historical Journal*, vol. 23, no. I, (1980), pp. 63–85.

55. *Poor Man's Guardian*, July 1833. For the value represented by compensation see Fogel and Engerman, 'Philanthropy at Bargain Prices', *Journal of Legal Studies*, no. 3, 1974. These authors estimate that the monetary element in the compensation amounted to 49 per cent of the value of slave property on the basis of current values, while the prospective six-year 'apprenticeship' would have been worth a further 47 per cent, giving a total compensation of 96 per cent. Ward has argued that these estimates overstate the value of the prospective six-year 'apprenticeship' and that the compensation was worth only 77 per cent of previous slave values. Indeed, taking into account the decline in plantation valuations subsequent to emancipation, he suggests that the real compensation rate was nearer to 60 per cent. He also insists that most proprietors in no way welcomed emancipation which they saw as imposed on them by Parliament and public opinion. Cf. Ward, 'The Profitability and Viability of British West Indian Plantation Slavery, 1807–1834'. While it is worth noting that the planters did oppose emancipation so long as they were able, and only settled for compensation out of fear that worse might befall them, the level of compensation that they received was still very impressive. The grant of £20 million compares with total British government revenue of only £54.5 million in 1831. See Chris Cook and Brandan Keith, *British Political Facts, 1830–1900*, London 1985, p. 239.

56. Introduction, *The Poor Law Report of 1834*, S.G. and E.O. Checkland, eds, London 1974, p. 41.

57. Davis, *Slavery and Human Progress*, p. 340, n. 26.

58. Lord David Cecil, *Lord M.*, London 1954, pp. 9–10. Melbourne was a Whig grandee with a distaste for humbug who no doubt took some glee in shocking the archbishop. He had no particular animus against the West Indian blacks; the governments he was to lead were to intervene in favour of the freedmen and women, under pressure from the latter and the abolitionists.

59. W.L. Burn, *Emancipation and Apprenticeship in the British West Indies*, London 1937, pp. 196–266; Temperley, *British Anti-Slavery*, pp. 30–36.

60. Mathiesen, *British Slave Emancipation*, pp. 35–49.

61. Temperley, *British Anti-Slavery*, pp. 36–41.

62. Mathiesen, *British Slave Emancipation*, p. 82.

63. Green, *British Slave Emancipation*, pp. 165–70.

64. For a well-documented contemporary survey see W.G. Sewell, *The Ordeal of Free Labor in the British West Indies*, London 1968 (original edition New York 1862), especially pp. 45, 71, 75, 79–80, 87, 245, 247–55. Sewell was a moderate bourgeois abolitionist; his naively expressed class and racial prejudices make the book's tribute to the freedmen and women all the more impressive. See also Douglas Hall, *Free Jamaica, 1838–1865*, New Haven 1959, p. 193; and for an informative survey, J.R. Ward, *Poverty and Progress in the Caribbean, 1800–1960*, London 1985, pp. 31–45.

65. G.W. Roberts, *The Population of Jamaica*, Cambridge 1957, pp. 49–51, 65. For lower mortality rates after emancipation see p. 309 and for higher fertility rates p. 247.

66. Green, *British Slave Emancipation*, pp. 191–229; Craton, *Searching for the Invisible Man*, pp. 48, 116–7. Craton's reconstruction of the Worthy Park records shows that it was the fall of sugar prices which was most destructive of the plantation pattern, since this drop made it hopelessly uneconomic to engage as many labourers as had been employed during the days of slavery (pp. 275–93).

67. Temperley, *British Anti-Slavery*, p. 55.

XII

French Restoration Slavery and 1848

'This period lasted about six years, from 1810 to 1816 . . . It was fashionable then to ape royalty, just as today one apes Parliament by forming all sorts of committees complete with chairmen, vice-chairmen and secretaries; societies of flax-growers, silk-growers, agricultural and industrial societies. We have even got to the point of discovering social evils in order to form societies to cure them.'

Cousin Pons (1847), Honoré de Balzac

'You're deluding yourself, dear angel, if you imagine that its King Louis-Philippe that we're ruled by, and he has no illusions on that score himself. He knows, as we all do, that above the Charter there stands the holy, venerable, solid, adored, gracious, beautiful, noble, ever young, almighty franc.'

Cousin Bette (1847), Honoré de Balzac

Following the second Bourbon restoration it seemed that the government of Louis XVIII was reconciled to a ban on the slave trade and to
the failure of its intrigue to return Haiti ('St Domingue') to French rule.
Louis gave a personal undertaking to the British Prince Regent
disavowing the slave trade. Yet the pressure on the French King to be
seen to vindicate French colonial interests was as strong, or stronger,
than ever. Colonial proprietors, past and present, remained reliable
supporters of the Restoration; after the experience of the 'Hundred
Days' this was an important consideration. It was also generally
believed that the prestige of France and of the monarchy required
flourishing colonies. Before the Revolution the French sugar islands had
been the most dynamic and successful in the Caribbean; the value of
Britain's colonies had been shown during the conflict with Napoleon.
Municipal delegations were soon at hand to remind the royalist
ministers of the need to restore the prosperity of the Atlantic ports. The
publication in 1819 of Comte Chaptal's 'Balance' of French commerce
underlined the colonial and mercantile achievements of the past, while
the surveys of Morreau de Jonnès (*Prosperité des Colonies*, 1822, and
Le Commerce au Dix-neuvième Siècle, 1825) drew attention to present
competition and future prospects.

Despite its solemn undertakings the French government made only a
show of banning the slave trade. A royal ordinance of January 1817, reinforced by the Law of April 1818, declared that the captains of slave-
trading vessels, if apprehended, would be deprived of their licences and
their cargoes would be liable to seizure. A cruiser was sent to the West
African coast in search of slave-traders in 1818, but to little effect.
These were probably the minimum steps required if France was to
ensure its readmittance to the European concert and regain possession
of all its lost colonies (Senegal was not handed back by the British until
1817, Guyane not until 1818). The Governors of the French Caribbean
simply turned a blind eye to a continuing clandestine traffic. The
relatively small size of the islands of Guadeloupe and Martinique meant
that enforcement of a slave trade ban posed no practical difficulties. The
real obstacle was that French planters were clamouring for slaves to restock their plantation after a decade in which no new supplies of slaves
had reached them. The French *armateurs* were keen to meet this
demand; in doing so they also helped to restore the French presence in
West Africa. The fact that a legal Atlantic slave trade persisted to the
Spanish colonies (until 1820), and to Brazil (until 1830), and that
British planters in the 'new' colonies could buy slaves from Britain's
older Caribbean possessions, made it seem that the slave trade ban had
been imposed on France's colonies as an act of revenge and as an unfair
measure of competition; the misdeeds of Napoleon were being visited

on French planters who had been staunch members of the royalist opposition. The intellectual and political climate of the newly restored monarchy encouraged few qualms about slavery or the the slave trade. Chateaubriand, who made Europe weep for the fate of the Natchez, coldly inquired 'Who will now plead the cause of the blacks, after the crimes they have committed?'[1] The most prominent surviving member of the former *Amis des Noirs* was the Abbé Grégoire; as a constitutional priest and regicide his continuing association with abolitionism scarcely recommended it to Legitimists. Madame de Stael and her circle also opposed the slave trade but since they were open to attack as Protestants, Anglophiles or Liberals their endorsement did not help abolitionism either. In the long run the failure of France's royal government to implement its commitment to stamp out the slave trade was bound to reflect either on its competence or on its integrity. But the overriding priority of the legitimist regime was to show its zeal in the pursuit of French interest and power. The Navy Ministry also had an institutional stake in colonial rehabilitation, since its own establishment could be partially underwritten by colonial revenues.

The first French slave-trading vessels were sent out in 1814; between that year and 1831 about 125,000 new slaves were introduced to the Caribbean by French traders in the course of about 700 voyages.[2] High prices for sugar and coffee made planters eager to buy slaves, if possible on credit, and encouraged merchants to supply this demand. Slave prices had roughly doubled since the 1780s but pent-up metropolitan demand for plantation produce drove forward a new colonial boom. Colonial commerce was accorded significant protection and rose to account for just under 10 per cent of total French trade. In the early 1820s French colonial sugar production was running at 50,000 tons a year and by 1828 it had reached over 80,000 tons, equivalent to the quantity produced in all French colonies, including St Domingue, in the mid-1770s; this was enough to supply a greatly expanded domestic market and a modest re-export trade. Colonial sugar, though itself protected, had to pay a stiff revenue tariff; by the late 1820s duties on colonial imports raised 36–40 million francs annually, equivalent to two-thirds of the entire budget of the Navy Ministry.[3] This contribution was appreciated the more since the Bourbons were obsessed with the need to balance the government's books and to avoid at all costs the sort of financial crises which had precipitated the events of 1788. Tariffs on colonial imports were easy to collect, with colonial trade limited to a few ports; as in the past, merchants could recover the tariff paid on re-exported sugar.

The colonial administration and navy were restaffed with prominent members of the mercantile and planting interests. Following the death of Malouet in 1815 Baron Portal, an *armateur* from Bordeaux, became head of the Colonial Bureau (1815–18) and then replaced Molé as Navy Minister (1818–21). Portal reappointed Du Buc as Governor of Martinique and Foullon d'Ecotier to the Intendancy in Guadeloupe. Portal's successor at the Colonial Bureau was Mauduit, a *ci-devant* royalist official in St Domingue. The longest-serving Prime Minister of the Legitimist Restoration, Villèle, whose administrations spanned the years 1821–8, was himself a planter from Ile de Bourbon (Réunion); this Indian Ocean colony developed a slave plantation economy very similar to those prevailing in the Caribbean and furnished about a quarter of France's colonial commerce. Villèle's colonial background not only made him familiar with the planters' problems but also gave him a certain experience as an administrator and financial manager. From 1826 the Colonial Bureau was administered by Filleau de Saint Hilaire, who was to win the confidence of the planters and direct this department until 1842.[4]

The regime that was restored in the colonies was a scaled-down replica of that which had been swept away in the course of the Revolution. Not only was the *Exclusif* restored but colonial trade was limited to just a few ports, amongst them Nantes and Bordeaux. While these towns did not quite recover their former splendour they did stage a comeback; Nantes, partly thanks to the activities of the slave-traders, became a major manufacturing centre. In the colonies themselves Governors and Intendants once more discharged their functions while the slaves were again subject to the *Code Noir* of Louis XIV. Napoleon and the British had combined to stamp out the embers of black resistance; the resumption of the slave trade had the incidental benefit of furnishing the plantations with labourers who had no memories of the Caribbean in the 1790s. Those blacks and mulattos whose freedom had been recognised by the Bonapartist or British authorities in principle retained their status; this included some slaves who had been manumitted at government expense to serve in the militia in the years 1801–10. Those who could not prove their title to freedom were vulnerable to re-enslavement or were impressed by the colonial authorities for service in special battalions of sappers. The reimposition of the old colonial regime encountered some opposition. In 1822 there was a slave outbreak at Carbet in Martinique; its suppression was followed by the execution of seven participants and suspects. The security measures subsequently enforced by the authorities provoked resistance from free people of colour whose dwellings were searched for anti-slavery materials. An educated free mulatto, Cyril Bissette, and two of his friends were arrested for possession of a pamphlet which attacked the denial of civic rights to free people of colour. The sentence passed on these men by the colonial magistrature in 1824 involved confiscation of their property and a life sentence to the galleys – they were branded GAL in consequence. Metropolitan liberals were shocked at this savage display of *ancien régime* justice and the matter became something of a *cause célèbre.*[5]

Despite such serious incidents the subjugation of the mass of slaves was successfully maintained and good profits were to be made by colonial planters and merchants. The regime of slave labour on Guadeloupe differed in one significant respect from that in Martinique or that which had existed before 1789 in Guadeloupe itself. The notorious night-shift system, by which field slaves worked a shift in the mill as well on alternate nights, was not reinstituted. The night-shift had been suppressed during the 1790s and not restored with slavery in 1802, presumably because it was anticipated that this would provoke too much unrest to be worthwhile. The planters of Guadeloupe received good prices for their sugar because of colonial protection which made it easier for them to live with this concession; they may also have discovered that suppression of the extra night-shift had raised fertility, since a high proportion of the field slaves involved would be women. On both Guadeloupe and Martinique the standard slave working day on the cash crop would be sun-up to sun-down, excluding meal breaks betwen nine and eleven hours; they would have to cultivate the provision grounds in the evenings and on their 'free day' if they were to have enough to eat.[6]

The successfully rehabilitated colonial system of the Restoration created problems of a new and unexpected sort. Under the *ancien régime* the *exclusif* had been designed to reserve the colonial market for French manufacturers. In the 1820s its effect was rather to reserve the metropolitan market for French planters. Of course the *Exclusif* had always involved some reciprocity but in the eighteenth century St Domingue had become the largest and cheapest producer of sugar in the Americas, with much of its output being clayed rather than raw sugar. The tariff system of the Restoration kept out foreign sugars but encouraged the growth of metropolitan refineries by extending protection only to raw sugar. The tariff preference favouring French colonial suppliers kept the metropolitan sugar price rather high. In turn this created conditions in the 1820s for the re-emergence of a sugar beet industry in the metropolis. Methods for extracting sugar from beets had been introduced to France from Prussia in the last years of the Empire, but most of these sugar factories had collapsed in the first years of the peace. However, while colonial sugar had to pay a revenue tax sugar beet produced in the metropolis was ignored. By the late 1820s about 5,000 tons a year were being produced by the beet refiners, not yet enough to bring down sugar prices or to deprive colonial producers of a market, but troubling to the latter all the same. There was controversy in ruling circles over the extent of tariff protection of French sugar and over the remission of duty that was granted to merchants who re-exported colonial produce. This device was costly for the Treasury and drew off supplies which would otherwise have forced down metro-politan sugar prices. The price of sugar was, of course, a significant element in the cost of living. Some Atlantic merchants would have liked to meet the competition of beet sugar by importing the cheaper cane sugar from Brazil or Cuba. The planters argued that protection and a tax on beet sugar were essential for the maintenance of the imperial and naval establishment. The whole issue was publicly ventilated but not resolved by a commission of inquiry set up by the government in 1828.

The virtual exclusion of foreign sugars from France's growing internal market made this by far the most profitable product that the Caribbean planters could cultivate. In the 1780s sugar accounted for about 50 per cent by value of French Caribbean exports while cotton, cacao, indigo and coffee made up the remainder. In the 1820s and 1830s the planters of Guadeloupe abandoned these 'secondary' crops and concentrated on sugar until such crops supplied less than 10 per cent of the colony's exports. The long occupation of Martinique by the British had encouraged a switch from coffee to sugar cultivation since there was a better British market for the latter crop. Martinique's exports of coffee had reached 3,400 tons in 1788 but were 3,700 tons in 1820 and under 1,000 tons in 1835. While the colonies supplied virtually 100 per cent of France's sugar imports in 1821 they only supplied 49 per cent of its coffee and 3.9 per cent of its cotton. French textile manufacturers did not wish to be burdened with high-priced colonial cotton and looked rather to the United States for supplies of the raw material they needed. So far as coffee was concerned colonial supplies accounted for a steadily dwindling proportion of French imports; they did not receive the strong tariff protection accorded to sugar. Sugar had always been regarded by colonial planters as the prime crop and, given its great profitability in the 1820s, they were easily persuaded to devote themselves to it. The sugar plantations had been able to buy English processing equipment in the years of occupation; there were about a dozen steam engines installed in Martinique in 1815. The slave plantations in Guadeloupe had an average crew size of seventy-nine in the 1820s; this was on the low side for sugar plantations but in the given conditions this did not prevent their operation being very lucrative.[7] The willingness of the French colonial planters to concentrate on sugar made it easier for France to reach a new commercial relationship with Haiti, under the terms of which France admitted Haitian coffee and Haiti promised to compensate expropriated French planters. This arrangement was a by-product of wider diplomatic and military dispositions.

France was accepted back into the European concert of powers at the Congress of Aix-la-Chapelle in 1818 and was able to play an important part in the 1820s in arbitrating the affairs of Spain and its remaining American possessions. Following the Congress of Verona in 1822 France had the backing of the Holy Alliance for an French invasion of Spain in April 1823, leading to the restoration of Ferdinand's absolutist regime by September of that year. A French fleet was dispatched to the Caribbean with the aim of preventing the spread of revolution there. It could not change the outcome of the conflict on the Spanish American mainland but it did help to deter the Republicans from mounting an expedition for the liberation of Cuba or Puerto Rico.

Paying a 'courtesy' visit to Haiti, now united under President Boyer, the French fleet pressed the Haitian government to accept the obligation to pay compensation to the former proprietors of St Domingue. The royalist government knew that the reconquest of Haiti was out of the question but it needed to come up with something for the St Domingue planters; the more so since *émigrés* who had lost property in France itself during the Revolution received handsome compensation in the years 1823–4. For its part the Haitian government was prepared to come to an arrangement if this included French diplomatic recognition and a commercial agreement – up to this point Haiti was not recognised by any power. Eventually Boyer agreed to pay an indemnity of 150 million francs – about £6 million – to the former French proprietors. Since this sum was beyond Haiti's means – total exports were worth about £1.25 million annually at this time – an arrangement was made to float a loan in Paris to finance the compensation payments. The loan proved a crippling burden for the Haitian treasury, though for many years service payments were made. The Haitian government also agreed to a commercial treaty with France which lowered tariffs on French imports; this agreement did promote Franco–Haitian trade but it limited the ability of the Haitian government to raise revenue from tariffs. On the other hand, the agreement did permit Haiti to become one of France's largest suppliers of coffee. The government of Charles X was one of the most reactionary in Europe in an epoch of general reaction. Yet in its zeal to reward its old colonial supporters it became the first, and for a long time the only, government to recognise the black Republic.[8]

The successes of the restoration in the diplomatic, military and colonial fields meant that France was again undeniably a great power and for that reason itself less vulnerable to the sort of intervention it had mounted in Spain. This gain for France was not so reassuring to the dynasty, since the latter aroused only tepid loyalty amongst its own soldiers and had failed to root itself anew in a social formation which had been transformed by the Great Revolution. Foreign bayonets had restored the Legitimists to the throne in 1814 and 1815, but as the 1820s progressed it appeared increasingly unlikely that this could happen again – though admittedly proclamation of a Republic might have provoked some new intervention. The Legitimists had been given an opportunity in which to re-establish the dynasty and failed to develop a political formula of rule which could reconcile the different factions of the possessing classes. Louis XVIII had been persuaded by Talleyrand to endorse a constitutional charter, with a Chamber of Deputies elected on a narrow property-holders' franchise and guarantees for an independent press. While the ultras pressed the King to satisfy the material and symbolic demands of royalist reaction, some also defended constitutional liberties and an uncensored press – the press laws of 1817 and 1818 lifted censorship, though publishers had to put up a bond which would be lost if they were found guilty of irresponsibility or alarmism. The regime lacked either the authority or the social basis of absolutism, while unwisely electing to clothe itself in the latter's unloved vestments. The coronation of Charles X in 1825 was an orgy of medieval clerico-monarchist ritual; the King prostrated himself before the archbishop, prior to the traditional gesture of touching the prelate's scrofular, while the archbishop himself delivered a sermon in which he denounced the charter as a blasphemous infringement of Divine Right.

The governments of Charles X (1825–30) confronted a sharply deteriorating domestic economy, with poor harvests, multiplying bankruptcies and rising unemployment. The Legitimists were not responsible for the economic conjuncture but their fear of debt led them to raise taxes and retrench on public expenditure. Government distrust of the middle classes led to disbandment of the National Guard in 1827. When Charles opted to rely on the ultra-royalist faction, the *Journal des Débats* declared:

> Thus it is broken once again, that bond of love and trust that tied the people to the monarch! Here they are again, the court with its old grudges, the emigration with its prejudices, the priesthood with its hatred of freedom, throwing themselves between France and the King. . . . Koblenz, Waterloo, 1815! These are the three principles, the three protagonists of our new government![9]

When the new administration was defeated in the Chamber of Deputies in June 1830 Charles X called for new elections. Despite the limitations of the franchise these strengthened the opposition. Charles X issued an ordinance in July again dissolving the Chamber but this time also drastically revising the method of election and clamping down on the press. The barricades went up and in a matter of days Charles X was in exile. Before matters could get out of hand the opposition deputies and the moderate liberal bourgeois of the Hotel de Ville offered the Crown to Louis Philippe, Duke of Orleans, after he promised to respect and strengthen the constitutional provisions of the charter. Lafayette was appointed Commander-in-Chief of a reformed National Guard and the tricolour replaced the fleur-de-lys as the national flag.

Colonial and slavery issues played only a minor part in the popular effervescence that overthrew the Legitimist regime. At a secondary level there was a popular perception, also borne out by colonial policy, that the Legitimist government was chiefly concerned to advance the interests of faithful monarchists whatever the consequences for the mass of the French people. The rehabilitation of the French plantations had been achieved thanks to the exclusion of cheap sugars from elsewhere; the price of sugar in Paris in the mid-1820s remained very high. Bordeaux was the only provincial city to have a revolutionary *journée* in July 1830. In part this was an expression of the longstanding civic liberalism of the Bordelais in the face of ultra-royalist provocation. However, rioters in the city attacked the excise station and plantation produce entered free of duty. The new regime could not afford to dispense with customs or taxes on consumption so the excise officers were soon back at work – though disputes about sugar were to loom large in the affairs of the July Monarchy.

While the overthrow of Charles X would no doubt have occurred irrespective of colonial policy, the re-emergence of a species of abolitionism in the 1820s did make a discreet contribution to assembling an alternative monarchist formula. The colonial successes of the Restoration had been brought, as we have seen, at the cost of flouting the ban on the slave trade. By the 1820s this was seen by a widening circle of respectable opinion as derogatory to the dignity of France as well as contrary to morality. If the Legitimist governments had openly rejected the slave trade ban then at least they could have adopted a consistent posture. But to publish decrees against the slave traffic and then fail to enforce them disturbed *bien pensants* concerned at the integrity of the monarchy. Liberal monarchists took up the issue of the clandestine slave traffic, aware that here was an issue of international as well as national significance. Criticism of the slave trade was orchestrated by the *Societé de la Morale Chrétienne*, founded in 1821 and sponsored by highly respectable and moderate liberals. This organisation exhibited many of the preoccupations which agitated

Wilberforce and his milieu – the reform of morals, promotion of family life, religious education as well as abolition of the slave trade. The society had a select male membership drawn from the *haute bourgeoisie* and liberal professions, with an over-representation of Protestants. It had only 255 members in 1823, rising to 338 in 1827, yet their names read like a roll-call of the ministers and notables of the July Monarchy. Louis Philippe was himself a member of the society. Others included the Duc de Broglie, the Comte d'Argout, Charles de Remusat, Sébastiani, and Guizot together with, from the world of finance, Casimir Périer and the André brothers. The writer Benjamin Constant was Secretary to the society's slave trade committee; he campaigned, together with F.A. Isambert, against the savage sentences passed on Bissette and his colleagues in Martinique.[10]

In France in the 1820s as in Britain in earlier years the critique of the slave trade was not couched in purely moral and humanitarian terms. The liberal economists Sismondi and J.–B. Say published attacks on the slave traffic, emphasising its connection with a wasteful and inefficient labour regime which could only flourish in the artificial climate created by tariff protection. Abolitionism became linked to advocacy of free trade and attracted the support of bankers and merchants who found irksome the protectionism of the governments of Charles X.

Sismondi and Say also rehearsed the arguments of the Scottish political economists to the effect that free labour was more productive and profitable than slave labour. The slave trade committee of the *Société de la Morale Chrétienne* organised a petition from French merchants against the trade, arguing that it was inimical to commercial growth; the petition was signed by 150 merchants from the leading sea-ports – with the exception of Nantes where only the Protestant shipbuilder Thomas Dobrée would come out against the slave traffic.

This new French abolitionism did not engage in the campaigning activity which marked the high-tide of its British counterpart. When the society presented a petition from Paris against the trade in 1825 it was happy to announce that it had secured the support of 130 of 'the foremost citizens'.[11] It held private meetings, published reports and urged representations to be made in the press, in the Chamber and in memoranda to government ministers and to the King. The considerable support it received from British abolitionists and from French Protestants limited its broad appeal without removing its political value to liberal monarchists. The failure of the executive to implement the Chamber's law of 1818 encouraged liberal suspicion of the regime's absolutist inclinations. In 1828 a new law with stiffer penalties against slave-traders was debated and passed, but the dynasty was overthrown before it could be clear whether this was to be enforced any more effectively than its predecessor.

The Legitimist governments maintained to the end that action against the slave trade did not require acceptance of the British demand for a mutual right of search; the British demand was seen as arrogant and demeaning, indeed little more than a cloak for Britain's traditional maritime claims. The abolitionists took a different view and advocated co-operation with London. Guizot, de Broglie and the others would have been aware that their more accommodating approach was likely to win sympathy from a power whose consent and recognition would facilitate any change of regime and deter any intervention by the Holy Alliance.

The governments of the July Monarchy brought a speedy end to the clandestine slave traffic to the French colonies. The Comte d'Argout, as Navy Minister, introduced a new law against the slave trade in 1831. Sébastiani, as Foreign Minister, negotiated an agreement with the London government to co-operate in stamping out the Atlantic slave trade; each state conceded a right of search to the other in the case of suspect vessels. The French navy and mercantile marine was the more willing to concede this, since the British squadrons had regularly seized French suspects without benefit of a treaty; between 1817 and 1831 the British had seized 108 French slave ships.[12] The French authorities had been poorly placed to protest and in no position to recover the slaves who were generally returned to the African coast or settled in the British islands. The agreement of 1831 put an end to these unseemly incidents and the legal tangles they occasioned. In 1833, with the Duc de Broglie as Foreign Minister, the Anglo–French right of search agreement was extended and reinforced. Slave-trading vessels continued to make for the Caribbean, but they did not fly the French flag nor call at Guadeloupe or Martinique. Controversy over the 'right of search' was to flare up again in the late 1830s and early 1840s, but the specifically French slave trade had been brought to an end.

The governments of the July Monarchy were willing to reform the colonial system in so far as this could be done cheaply and without endangering property rights. The bounty system for re-exports was abolished and the *Exclusif* modified. The racial code in the colonies was speedily dismantled. French abolitionists of the 1820s had taken up questions of civic equality somewhat in the spirit of their Girondin forebears. The campaign against the sentences passed on Bissette and his colleagues had drawn attention to the persecution of free people of colour and eventually resulted in Bissette's release from prison. In 1829 free people of colour in Martinique and Guadeloupe petitioned the Chamber of Deputies for alleviation of their condition and received some support from liberal deputies. A ministerial directive of November 1830 ordered French colonial officials to disregard all laws which imposed extra handicaps on free people of colour. A royal ordinance of 1832 set out a new framework conferring on all free citizens an equality of legal rights. In 1833 there were serious clashes in Martinique when local whites sought to intimidate free people of colour, garrotting some black prisoners and wounding seven coloured members of the militia. Bissette, who remained in France, founded the *Journal des Colonies* in which he monitored developments in the Antilles and publicised the incidents in Martinique. Though those responsible for the outrages in Martinique were not brought to book the colonial administration henceforth kept the white *colons* on a tighter rein. As ministers were themselves fully aware concessions to the free people of colour actually strengthened the colonial slave regime. The two French Antilles had a garrison of 6,000 troops, backed up by 5,000–6,000 members of the militia; free people of colour were recruited to both the regular and the militia units.[13]

In 1829 the abolitionists of the *Société* had published a pamphlet advocating the gradual emancipation of the slaves. But in general the French abolitionists still approached this question very gingerly, displaying lively concern for the property rights of slaveholders and the need to ensure continuing good order and subordination. An *ordinance* of 1831 had suppressed the prohibitive tax formerly required to register manumission; a licence to manumit had cost 4,200 francs, or more than the price of a slave. This measure enabled recognition of the freedom of many thousands of *libérés* whose position had previously been doubtful. But like other reforms it did not encroach on the slave system as such. However, in 1834 the Duc de Broglie and other members of the *Société de la Morale Chrétienne* decided to set up a *Société Francaise pour l'Abolition de l'Esclavage*. This decision may well have been prompted by the dramatic advances of British anti-slavery. And since the Orleans dynasty had been linked to abolitionism it is likely to have been seen as necessary to the prestige of the regime. The political conjuncture in France, which remained unsettled and menacing for several years after the *coup d'état*, also encouraged prominent Orleanists to reaffirm the liberal bourgeois values of which the regime was the custodian. The change of regime was followed by a further twist in the economic crisis and by republican attacks on the narrow electorate conceded by the new constitution. The new doctrine of socialism made thousands of converts. It promised to save society from unceasing conflict by imposing a collective discipline on private property – a cure that was worse than the disease in the eyes of the Orleanist bourgeoisie. In 1834, following an insurrection in Lyons, stringent measures were taken to outlaw worker's combinations. This was a political and social climate where some Orleanist notables felt the need to reassert the regime's liberal promise and in which bourgeois philanthropists felt the need to extol the virtues of free labour.

The Abolition Society attracted the endorsement of many leading politicians, including Guizot, Hyppolite Passy and Odilon Barrot. Yet it was to prove remarkably ineffective. For many years it eschewed any appeal to a wider public and concentrated on decorous statements issued by the notables who belonged to it. In 1837 Passy introduced a bill for gradual emancipation of the slaves, to be achieved by a 'free birth' clause and easier manumission arrangements; however, before the Chamber could decide on this Passy, who joined the government as Finance Minister, was persuaded to remit his bill for further consideration. In 1839 de Tocqueville, another sponsor of the Abolition Society, submitted a different emancipation proposal to the Chamber; this followed the British legislation in freeing all slaves after a six-year 'apprenticeship' with compensation of 150 million francs for the owners of the quarter of a million or so slaves now to be found in the French colonies (nearly 200,000 of them in the French Caribbean). However, the government managers also tabled de Tocqueville's bill for further consideration. A committee on colonial slavery was set up, presided over by the Duc de Broglie and including several representatives of the colonial interest, notably Filleau de Saint Hilaire, head of the Colonial Bureau. While this commission undertook lengthy hearings an immediate palliative measure was agreed – 650,000 francs was voted to promote the moral education of slaves in the colonies.[14]

After several years' deliberations the de Broglie committee produced a report in 1843 which marshalled many eloquent arguments for emancipation – it also skilfully summarised objections to each and every method of accomplishing it. The commission approached its work with a cautious and practical spirit, refusing to allow itself to be carried away by emotion or rhetoric. While short-term emancipation schemes were bound to be expensive, because of the compensation payments that would have to be made, long-run solutions, freeing future generations through the 'free womb', would at a certain point reduce the slave crews below the threshold at which they could sustain the impetus of gang labour. The Spanish American and North American states which had adopted the 'free womb' did not rely on slave labour to anything like the extent that was characteristic of the French sugar islands. The de Broglie Commission recommended a ten year programme of emancipation in which the slaves would underwrite the cost of their own liberation; their right to a peculium and to rewards for working on their free day would encourage thrift and labour.[15]

Despite their moderation the commission proposals provoked fierce opposition and the government backed down. In default of this Baron Mackau, the Navy Minister and a former governor of Martinique, introduced a law of April 1845 which incorporated a series of amelioration measures and supposedly facilitated manumissions. It confirmed a ban on the whipping of female slaves. It stipulated that families should have their own separate dwelling units and that slaves should have possession of a garden and a free day to cultivate it. If applied this *Loi Mackau* alleviated the slave lot without cancelling the slave condition. One advantage of which both minister and deputies would have been most sensible is that it cost very little. The more radical abolitionists argued that little was to be expected of such legislation, which would be frustrated thanks to the combined efforts of the planters and the administrators. Only twelve slaves had been enrolled by 1845 in the schools set up by the money voted in 1839. The new law led to few prosecutions or manumissions. The *Procureur Général* in Guadeloupe soon drily noted that 'the magistrates are satisfied with the colonists and the colonists are satisfied with the magistrates. This reciprocity is certainly significant.'[16] Nevertheless the planters attacked the law because it recognised slave rights and because it had been introduced as an abolitionist measure.

The various reforms undertaken by the Orleanist regime led to some decline in slave numbers and a corresponding increase in the size of the free population. Slave numbers fell in Guadeloupe from 97,000 in 1831 to 93,000 in 1838 and reached 88,000 in 1848; in Martinique the number of slaves dropped from 86,500 in 1831 to 76,500 in 1838 and 75,000 in 1848. With the ending of the slave trade some dip in slave numbers was likely. However, the strength of the field gangs probably suffered less than the fall in numbers might suggest. The official encouragement given to manumission led to the freeing of domestic slaves, while field slaves remained in bondage. The free population of Martinique rose from 23,000 in 1831 to over 40,000 in 1838, that of Guadeloupe from 22,000 in 1831 to 35,000 in 1838. The free people of colour now outnumbered the white *colons* as they had not in the 1790s. In Martinique the free people of colour owned about a ninth of the land in 1838 and about a third of the urban dwellings.[17]

The tariff protection afforded to colonial sugar was reduced but not abolished by the governments of the July Monarchy. A 33.3 per cent differential duty helped to bring down sugar prices a bit but only admitted a few thousand tons of foreign sugar a year. The real threat to the colonial sugar plantations came from the development of the domestic beet sugar industry. Output rose from 7,000 tons annually in the early 1830s to 64,000 tons in 1848.[18] The planters persuaded the

Paris government to tax beet sugar in 1837 but only opened up fierce polemics between partisans of the two sugars. Representatives of the beet cultivators, concentrated in northern France, were naturally inclined to question colonial slavery. On the other hand, the dignitaries of the Abolition Society did not always reciprocate. The Duc de Broglie made it quite clear in his report of 1843 that he supported continuing favourable treatment of the planters. Perhaps this was said partly to placate them, but in fact the whole conduct of the moderate abolitionists displayed consideration towards, and fellow feeling with, the colonial planters. The sugar beet refiners and the smallholders of northern France who supplied them were angry that their product had been forced to pay a tax in the interests of protecting planters in the Antilles.

The disposition of Orleanist politicians to defend the interests of Antillean planters, whether over emancipation or protection from the beet interests, is puzzling, because of the political price they would have to pay. Indulgence to Caribbean slave-owners undermined the July Monarchy's ideological coherence and its ability to appeal to a layer of the peasantry. It can partly be explained by the regime's even greater concern to defend those powerful institutions with a vested interest either in sugar taxation or in colonial slavery; the Treasury found sugar taxation very convenient while the armed forces saw colonies as an honourable outlet for martial energies. The equalisation of sugar duties was calculated to raise 17 million francs. This measure would also enable the customs to continue collecting large revenues from colonial sugar. The taxes placed on cane sugar and other colonial products made a major contribution to fiscal returns; in 1844 colonial trade only accounted for 5 per cent of all trade but it yielded 27 per cent of customs receipts. It was calculated that the average annual output of a slave on a plantation was 850 kilos of sugar; at the going rate of duty each slave thus contributed 420 francs to the Treasury per annum, enough to entitle them to vote or stand for the Chamber had they been free citizens of France.[19]

The sugar colonies were administered by the Navy Minister and provided justification for a naval establishment. Several senior military men such as Clauzel, the General appointed to be Governor of Algeria after the July Revolution, had experience of and contacts in the colonies. To dispel the uncertainty which plagued the first Orleanist governments Marshal Soult was brought in as nominal head of government in 1832 and this imperial veteran was to adorn the regime, with a few short breaks, down to 1847. Military men saw colonial expansion as an opportunity to win fame and fortune; they would not be happy with a policy which ruined France's plantation colonies, with their military establishments, for the sake of some half-baked philanthropic ideology.

If France's domestic sugar beet producers had been left untaxed while colonial sugar still had to pay 33.3 per cent, then many colonial planters would certainly have gone to the wall. The excessively moderate abolitionists who filled the Cabinets of the July Monarchy realised that this would bankrupt the sugar plantations and deprive the French Antilles and Réunion of most of their economic *raison d'être*. Planning some day to move against slavery they deemed it only fair to equalise the duties paid on the two types of sugar. As it was the sugar planters ran into severe problems from 1830 onwards as the metropolitan price tumbled; beet sugar competition as well as the generalised economic downturn and the reduction in tariff protection produced this fall. The 1837 decision to equalise the sugar taxes did not satisfy the planters who asked for the beet refineries to be closed in the interests of colonial Frenchmen. Indeed the planters' representatives advocated expropriation with indemnification (of the beet refineries) rather more vigorously than the parliamentary abolitionists demanded equivalent measures to eliminate slavery.

The bourgeoisie of Bordeaux, Nantes and Le Havre had no relish for slave emancipation for a very traditional reason. The Antillean planters owed them large sums of money, often secured on the value of their properties. The drop in prices in the 1830s had greatly aggravated the perennial indebtedness of the planters; without having intended it, metropolitan merchants found short-term credit converted into long-term mortgages. In Guadeloupe the planters' accumulated debt rose from 70 million francs in 1836 to 94 million francs in 1842. Those holding these debts thus looked to compensation arrangements in case of emancipation that would enable them to be discharged. The whole question of planters' debts was further complicated by the fact that they traditionally enjoyed protection from seizure in case of default. The aim of this protection was to preserve the integrity of the plantation as a productive ensemble; it prevented local creditors from seizing slaves or equipment to the detriment not only of the planter but of his other creditors. The provisions of the *Loi Mackau* further reinforced the immobility of the factors of production since they gave slaves more rights in a given plantation and prevented the break-up of slave families.[20]

The bourgeoisie of the Atlantic ports was not positively pro-slavery and preferred simply to advocate the most cautious measures in the handling of colonial slavery. The regime of Louis Philippe was strongly supported in Bordeaux as were the various compromises on colonial slavery approved by the Chamber of Deputies. The *Courier de la*

Gironde thought that the *Loi Mackau* was most judicious: 'We will see whether *liberal* slavery, which tempers beings brutalised by the most rude barbarism in order to make them laborious, intelligent and Christian, will not better achieve the emancipatory end towards which the world moves than wild liberty which tends to keep them at the bottom of the ladder where they have fallen.'[21]

The task of positively justifying the slave regime was left to a busy and well-funded clique maintained by the colonial proprietors themselves. Adolphe Granier de Cassagnac defended the planters in the Paris press and in pamphlets that were sent to all peers and deputies. The larger colonial proprietors were at least assured of a respectful hearing in the official circles. Many maintained establishments in Paris: 'the large Antillean planters, the great creole families, were integrated into the world of the notables, their sons often attending the same Parisian schools.'[22]

The more far-sighted leaders of the regime understood the need to tackle the thorny question of colonial slavery. Without decisive action it could only rob the Orleanist bourgeoisie of its *amour-propre*. The half-way measures actually adopted had the further disadvantage of depriving the most efficient colonial producers of the labour they needed to take proper advantage of steam power and more industrial processing methods. Undoubtedly the property interests of the slave-owners were the heart of the problem. On the one hand, they could not simply be expropriated without compensation; on the other, the cost of compensating them was found excessive. This problem was very much accentuated by the very nature of the regime.

Previous forms of government in France had run into problems for being insufficiently representative of the possessing classes. The July Monarchy was, by contrast, too representative of propertied interests. It represented them, as it were, indiscriminately and without sufficient provision for mediating institutions which would assert general class interests. In a discussion of the nature of the Orleanist regime Jardin and Tudesq cite the paralysis over slavery and sugar as textbook examples of the regime's failings:

> The effectiveness of the central power was neutralised by opposing pressure groups representing either material interests (as in the case of the two kinds of sugar, the very symbol of a hopeless predicament) or moral interests. The Guizot government was favourable to the abolition of slavery in the colonies, and so was public opinion ... but since no agreement about its methods could be reached, the status quo continued.[23]

Private property was sacrosanct for the July Monarchy, furnishing the basis and principle of its political system. Its Finance Ministers were keen to avoid taxes on property or income since these were seen as infringements of the rights of the individual and harbingers of socialism.

The Legitimist order had been a hollow imitation of the *ancien régime*, or of some medievalistic fantasy. The Orleanist regime was, by contrast, influenced by the British model of 'illegitimate monarchy'. In the aftermath of the Napoleonic Wars Britain's supposedly mixed constitution enjoyed more prestige than ever before. The Gallic edition was in some ways more tidy and logical than the original yet, beneath all differences of epoch and situation, it bore to it a definite family resemblance. The administrative apparatus of the state and army was larger but office-holding was not hereditary and the state collected its own taxes. The finances of the state were no longer confused with the monarch's household; the public funds and budget acted as a capitalist regulator. The monarch, in Thiers' phrase, was meant to 'reign not govern', though, as with George III, Louis Philippe did not quite see it this way. France was increasingly a land of financiers, of industrial promoters, of incipiently capitalist landlords and peasants. Defying any simple equation of politics and economics the Legitimist notables were often in the vanguard of agricultural improvement; the same could be said of some of their Antillean cousins, who began to adopt the new integrated methods of sugar extraction used in the beet sugar factories. The social weight of the smallholding peasantry was, of course, far greater in early nineteenth-century France than it had been in eighteenth-century Britain. This constituted an obstacle to the development of large-scale capitalist farming. And in France a semi-autonomous military caste was able to make large claims on national resources. But the state corresponded to the elementary expectations and needs of the notables: large landed proprietors, financiers and bankers, merchants and manufacturers operating on a national or international scale. They had passed through a baptism of fire with Jacobinism, Bonapartism and Legitimism. They wanted a sovereign power strong enough to overawe the democratic rabble and to guarantee the national debt; but too weak to invade their property rights and to embark on ruinous adventures. The government should be responsible to the tax-paying proprietors though not to the vast mass of citizens whose expenditures swelled the taxes on consumption; indeed the contribution of taxes in the sphere of circulation began to overtake taxes on property – and taxes on income were unthinkable. Charles X had been persuaded to flee in part by the collapse of confidence in public bonds and a threatened tax strike.

Louis Philippe perfectly fitted the bill for a French 'illegitimate monarch'. As the member of a cadet branch of the Bourbons he could not hope to impose a wilful royal power. As a monarch he could focus traditional loyalties in a harmless way. As the son of Philippe Egalité, supporter of the constitution in 1791 and veteran of Jemappes, he did not threaten the post-revolutionary social order. But, just as important, he lacked the dangerous legitimacy of popular assemblies and plebiscites.[24] These various attributes had made Louis Philippe as acceptable to the European powers as he was to a decisive nucleus of the French possessing classes. However, they did not equip the Orleanist regime for a confrontation with the great Antillean planters or for any policy that would jeopardise France's colonial possessions. Britain's 'illegitimate monarchy' had been underpinned by colonial expansion, and the North African projects of the Orleanist regime were now thought to supply a a safe outlet for martial energies and surplus population.

Abolitionism itself helped to provide the charter for colonisation in Africa. In the years 1842–8 an *Institut de l'Afrique* advocated 'a great work, the colonisation of Africa, and the regeneration of the African people by means of the abolition of slavery and the slave trade'. This body enjoyed the backing of British abolitionists like Thomas Fowell Buxton, of Isaac L'Ouverture (son of Toussaint) and of the Governor of Algeria, General Bugeaud, who warned that 'there can be no solid achievement in Africa without European colonisation'.[25] The colonialist ethos might permit attacks on the slave trade in Africa but it was not conducive to emancipation in the Antilles.

Just as the politics of the *juste milieu* echoed something of the outlook of the late Hanoverian oligarchy, so the frustrated abolitionism of Guizot or de Broglie had something in common with the meliorist gestures of a Pitt or Canning. It made the governments of the Orleanist regime vulnerable to the development of a more radical and consequent abolitionism, with republican inclinations. The *Société pour l'Abolition de l'Esclavage* had attracted a somewhat more secular and radical membership than the *Société pour la Morale Chrétienne* though one drawn exclusively from the ranks of the wealthy; the mulatto Bissette did not become a member, either because he could not afford the subscription or because he was made to feel out of place.[26]

The outstanding younger abolitionist was Victor Schoelcher, son of a large porcelain manufacturer; he had encountered the daily reality of slavery when his father sent him on a tour of the Caribbean in 1829–30 in search of colonial outlets. Schoelcher was in Mexico City when the decree abolishing slavery there was announced. He sent accounts of slave markets and slave punishments to a Paris magazine and advocated a gradual ending of slavery. On his return he was attracted by the projects of the republican and socialist opposition but soon devoted himself mainly to agitation on the slavery question, eventually becoming convinced that half-way houses to emancipation could not work because of the bad faith of the planter class. In a series of articles he pointed to the weakness of the parliamentary schemes of amelioration and to their frustration by recalcitrant officials and planters. In 1840 he published a booklet entitled *L'Abolition de l'Esclavage*, with the subtitle *Examen Critique des Préjugés contre la Couleur des Africains et des Sang-mêlés*, and in 1842, following another trip to the Antilles, a substantial work on the French colonies subtitled *Abolition Immédiate de l'Esclavage*.[27]

In the years 1839–40 the *Société pour l'Abolition de l'Esclavage* received a new influx of members including Victor Hugo, Louis Blanc, Lamartine and Cavaignac. Those like de Broglie who were now thoroughly implicated in the government's colonial policy were not well placed to prevent a more radical approach from making itself felt in the abolitionist ranks. In 1840 Lamartine was elected President of the society. Despite Lamartine's radical, indeed republican, sympathies his position on colonial slavery had up to this point been fairly cautious. In 1836 he had warned the Chamber:

> We must not forget that each inflammable word pronounced here touches not simply the conscience of our colleagues or the anxiety of the *colons*, but also reaches the ears of three hundred thousand slaves; that which we discuss calmly and without danger from this tribune, concerns the property, the fortune and the life of our compatriots in the colonies.[28]

By the 1840s the liberal poet and statesman saw that the whole issue of colonial slavery could not be indefinitely fudged and that it exposed the regime to very damaging attacks. Indeed the demoralising fiasco of Orleanist policy with respect to colonial slavery could be seen as symptomatic of the regime's failure to propose solutions to the 'social question' at home. Schoelcher and Lamartine were prepared to urge immediate abolition, but they still thought it politic to propose compensation to the slave-owners. Likewise they envisaged regimes of transition from slavery which would encourage the former slaves not simply to abandon large-scale or cash crop cultivation.

The Abolition Society broadened the scope of its activities in the mid-1840s. With financial help from British anti-slavery bodies the society began publication of a journal, the *Abolitioniste Français*. A petition against slavery drawn up by Schoelcher and Bissette attracted the signature of 7,000 workers in the Paris region in 1844. The King was himself aware that the paralysis of his government looked bad; in 1846 he issued an *ordinance* freeing all slaves belonging to the royal domain. In April 1847 Fabien, a mulatto colleague of Bissette, presented to the

Chamber a petition calling for immediate emancipation signed by 11,000 citizens. Liberal Catholics and Protestants combined in supporting this petitition which contained the signatures of several hundred priests and pastors. The liberal Catholics around the newspaper *L'Univers* called for the abolition of slavery and declared their willingness to back a new petition in 1848 that would be aimed at a broader public than those who had signed in 1847. The Archbishop of Paris announced that he saw nothing wrong with this activity on the part of the Catholic laity.[28]

The issue of slavery in the colonies, though difficult, was easy compared with the harsh choices and polarisations which confronted France itself. Desperate class conflicts, such as the uprising of silk-weavers in Lyons in 1834, were erupting in the wake of capitalist industrialisation, while large numbers of workers and their families were threatened by actual starvation when there were bad harvests and an economic downturn as in 1846–8. The political classes were increasingly dissatisfied with the workings of the electoral system. Oppositionists like Lamartine urged a wider franchise, even 'universal suffrage' to produce a government which would cater to all Frenchmen and not simply a narrow elite. Since legal political activity was subject to stiff police regulations a banquet campaign was organised in 1847 to urge an extension of the franchise, an 'end to corruption', the restoration of 'political integrity', and programmes for the 'abolition of poverty through work.' About 22,000 citizens subscribed to the banquets while about three times that number came to listen to the toasts and speeches. The anti-slavery campaign was only a descant to this chorus of agitation, but both had a momentum dangerous for the prevailing order.[29]

The King refused to countenance any electoral reform and called on Molé to form a government. Following the attempted cancellation of a banquet in Paris there were clashes with troops that resulted in fifty dead. The National Guard in the capital refused any longer to defend the government and a threatening crowd approached the Tuileries. On February 24th the seventy-five-year-old Louis Philippe abdicated in favour of his infant grandson. In its critical hour the Orleanist regime failed to find a strong man and even if it had it might still have been engulfed by the tide of popular republicanism. In Britain in 1832 the far better rooted Hanoverian regime had been more skilfully defended by William IV, who had known when to give way and when to stand his ground; and in Lord Grey he had found a more capable accomplice in his hour of need than had been forthcoming from the discredited ranks of Orleanist politicians.

In an attempt to rein in the surging popular movement a provisional government was formed at the Hotel de Ville on February 24th. Its members were drawn from the Paris municipality and the parliamentary opposition. Amongst them were Louis Blanc, Lamartine at the Foreign Ministry, Ledru–Rollin at Home Affairs and Arago at the Navy Ministry – all former sponsors or members of the Abolition Society. One of the few members of the provisional government of whom this could not be said was Albert, leader of one of the proletarian secret societies whose members had played a critical part by erecting barricades throughout the capital. Arago was immediately pressed by planters' representatives in Paris to give a commitment that the colonists' property would be respected. He was inclined to reassure them but invited Victor Schoelcher to join him as chief of the Colonial Bureau of the Ministry. Schoelcher arrived at the Ministry on the night of March 3rd and persuaded Arago that an immediate decree should be issued by the provisional government. He produced a draft which read: 'In the name of the French people, the provisional government of the Republic, considering that no French territory can any longer hold slaves, Decrees that: a Commission is set up within the provisional Ministry of the Navy and Colonies to prepare within the shortest time possible an act of immediate emancipation in all the colonies of the Republic. The Ministry of the Navy is charged with execution of the present decree.'[30]

On March 3rd Schoelcher had just returned from Senegal. Prior to his arrival at the office of the Navy Ministry Arago had sent a reassuring message to the Governors of the Antilles confirming them in their posts. However, when Schoelcher insisted that immediate action was needed Arago and other members of the provisional government supported him. At least one member of the provisional government, Marrast, future *maire* of Paris, was sympathetic to the planters. Several members of the commission argued that it was wrong to proceed immediately to emancipation without waiting for the Constituent Assembly to convoke; and *a fortiori* it was wrong to pre-empt the Assembly from deciding whether the freedmen should be given citizenship. Schoelcher, who knew that the hour to strike had come, cut through all objections and diversions. He was able to impose his will on the commission and on the government because both bodies contained a majority which respected him – and obstructionist minorities who feared to become the target of his considerable talents as a polemicist.

Schoelcher was appointed Under-Secretary for the Colonies as well as President of the Commission on Slavery. The Commission comprised an official of the colonial bureau, a lawyer, a clockmaker, a mulatto artillery officer and Henri Wallon, author of a treatise on Christianity and slavery in the Ancient World. Schoelcher was given authority to arbitrate disagreements. By April 15th the commission had elaborated a detailed decree emancipating the slaves together with the text of twelve other decrees concerning civic rights, education, agricultural credit and every other branch of colonial administration. The slaves were to be entirely free two months from the date of the proclamation of the abolition decree. According to the fifth clause of the decree the National Assembly was to decide 'the size of the indemnity which should be given to the *colons*'.[31] Amongst the other edicts one provided the colonies with 26 million francs to finance the institutions of a society based on free labour, such as schools, nurseries, clinics, and labour courts. Adult males freed from slavery were immediately to qualify for the vote. The 'social decrees' extended to the colonies the system of *ateliers nationaux* (national workshops) which were to be such a controversial feature of the programme of the Provisional government. The former slaves were promised the 'right to work' while those who were ill or infirm enjoyed the *droit au secours* (social security). In the localities there were to be *jurys cantonaux* to arbitrate conflicts; these bodies had three representatives of the employers and three of the workers, with the local justice of the peace as chairman. A *Fête du Travail* was to be held each year to celebrate emancipation day.[32] The crucial decree on emancipation was approved by the Provisional government on April 27th and published in the *Moniteur* on May 2nd, the day before the opening of the Assembly.

In the years prior to 1848 there were no large-scale or violent outbreaks of slave resistance, a lull which might be compared with the absence of slave revolts in the French Caribbean in the 1780s or in the British Caribbean in the years before 1816. But the parallel does not itself explain the relative quiescence of the pre-1848 French Antilles. Sizeable military forces present in Martinique and Guadeloupe must have helped to deter slave resistance, as had also been the case in St Domingue in 1776–84 and in Jamaica in 1791–1815. In addition to a nominal garrison of 3,000 regular troops apiece the Governors of the two French colonies could also each call upon a militia force of 5,000 or so, drawn from the coloured as well as white population; the Orleanist concessions to free people of colour had broadened the base of the slave regime in the Antilles. *Marronage* was certainly still a problem; the regular troops stationed on the islands included mountain regiments specially trained to track down fugitives in the interior.

Schoelcher believed that the material position of the slaves had improved somewhat as a result of the new regulations and because the ending of the slave trade gave the planters a stronger interest in the survival and reproduction of their slave crews. However, he stressed that the slave was still in all essential respects subject to the arbitrary domination of the planters and *commandeurs*; since it was this as much as material conditions which inspired slave resistance, amelioration measures could even stimulate unrest, as they had done in British Guyana. It seems likely that slave awareness of the debates over abolition grew steadily in the decade or so prior to 1848. The Chamber of Deputies had held several major set-piece debates on slavery and had commissioned its most senior members to report on the subject. While there were some who came out openly in defence of slavery the most authoritative statements were by ministers who insisted that the only real dispute was over which methods would lead most securely and safely to emancipation. Some slaves may have hoped to benefit from the manumission and apprenticeship provisions of the 1845 law. The creole proportion of the slave population, which might be expected to follow such debates most attentively, was growing; in 1848 Africans constituted only 14 per cent of the slave populaton compared with 46 per cent in 1790. In the 1840s the authorities became concerned at the development of a subversive variety of Freemasonry; two important lodges on Martinique were ordered to be disbanded in 1846. There were also reports that labour discipline on the plantations was harder to maintain. The slaves of the French Antilles in the 1840s were biding their time. The relative ease with which it was possible for them to escape to nearby British islands may also help to explain the absence of plantation risings. Planters complained of slave escapes of this sort and Schoelcher publicised a number of both successful and failed attempts.

The news of the overthrow of the July Monarchy and of the decree of March 4th had an electric impact in the French Antilles. The colonial officials on the islands did their best to lower the expectations of the slaves. The chief of the interior department on Martinique issued a statement on March 31st warning: 'Nothing is changed up to the present. You remain slaves until promulgation of the law.' The Governor further dampened hopes on April 3rd. He conceded that the slaves would in due course receive their freedom because 'their masters wished it', and he added:

> During the time of your fathers a republic existed in France. It proclaimed liberty without indemnity for the owners, without organising labour. It thought that the slaves would understand that they would have to work and avoid creating disorder. But they deserted their work and became increasingly unhappy. They forced the government to put you back into slavery.[33]

The news that a Republic had been proclaimed was received favourably by many of the free people of colour. Towards the end of April the slaves on many plantations in Martinique began to move, thousands of them streaming into St Pierre and the other towns. The Governor of Martinique warned Paris on April 28th that the definitive emancipation law was expected with every steam packet and that the least incident could turn into a revolution. Slaves simply abandoned the plantations and groups of slaves were seen everywhere discussing the situation. The slave order was simply decomposing as blacks took their fate into their own hands. The colonial authorities hesitated to order repressive action and doubted that the coloured troops would obey orders. But on May 22nd there were several clashes, including one at St Pierre in which thirty-five slaves lost their lives. The Governor feared an explosion. On May 23rd, still with no news yet received of the abolition decree of April 27th, the Governor urged the municipality to declare slavery at an end without further ado; in a unanimous vote it did so. The Governor also urged all *anciens citoyens* to rally to the *agents de la force publique*.[34]

News of the demonstrations and clashes in Martinique helped to stir similar unrest in Guadeloupe. The planters' journal the *Commercial* of April 5th had already urged the authorities to seize the initiative:

> If one consults history one sees, on every page, that failure to take the initiative leads to large and irreparable disasters. . . . Let us fear divisions, parliamentary struggles, noxious experiments in communism, all of which would have their repercussions in the colonies and will habituate the slave to public discussions, to parties and to disorders.[35]

This candid, and in its own way lucid, assessment of the situation from the planters' point of view was reinforced by their awareness that the political disturbances had led to a slackening of productive effort and discipline as the slaves tested the new situation. On May 27th the municipal council in Guadeloupe declared unconditional abolition of slavery. Only in French Guyana and Réunion did emancipation await the arrival of the decree of April 27th or respect the two-month delay for which it called.

With some justification Schoelcher argued that only the swift action of the provisional government had averted an explosion. The slave demonstrations of April and May and the subsequent municipal decrees of abolition came in the wake of the news that the new Republic had, as one of its first acts, declared that slavery would be ended. In default of such news there might well have been the further bloody clashes feared by the planters and colonial officials. With abolition declared in principle the troops and militia could no longer be relied on to repress the slaves and the planters retreated; their main preoccupations now became compensation and labour legislation. The speed with which

Schoelcher's commission had moved to elaborate a new colonial regime helped to consolidate the emancipation process. Members of the commission were sent to the Antilles to supervise implementation of the decrees: Perrinon, the mulatto artillery officer, was sent to Martinique, Gatine, a lawyer, to Guadeloupe. In most cases the former slaves returned to their plantations, animated by attachment to their homes and garden plots. The sugar harvest was not complete though in some instances the *libérés* were persuaded to work for a few weeks more. The republican constitution provided for the French colonies to elect representatives for the National Assembly on the basis of 'universal suffrage' (actually manhood suffrage). In the elections of August 1848 Schoelcher was elected by both Guadeloupe and Martinique; this was just as well since he had failed to be elected on the Paris list. Bissette was also elected for Martinique, while Perrinon was returned for Guadeloupe.

Schoelcher identified himself with the Mountain in the Assembly and described himself as a socialist; he was not a doctrinaire and had no relish for street-fighting but favoured ample civic rights and philanthropic solutions to popular misery. His emancipation programme had received the support of the provisional government in part because the question of colonial slavery, so long debated in Parliament and the press, offered them the opportunity for decisive and dramatic action at a time when popular expectations were mounting. The measures that might alleviate proletarian distress in the metropolis were more difficult to identify and agree upon. While insurrectionary and communist agitation spread in Paris and some other centres, the elections to the Constituent Assembly revealed that moderate liberals and conservative monarchists still held sway in many parts of the countryside. In June 1848 an order dismantling Louis Blanc's National Workshops provoked proletarian rebellion in the capital; this was suppressed by Cavaignac, the Republican General, with considerable bloodshed and the deportation of 15,000 of the insurrectionists. Cavaignac was soon appointed President of the Republic to appease a frightened and vengeful Assembly majority.

Schoelcher took no part in the June Days; his Minister urged the Paris crowd to respect republican legality only to be told: 'Ah, Monsieur Arago, you've never been hungry!'[36] Schoelcher was distressed by these events and urged the release of those who had been imprisoned and respect for the decree abolishing the death penalty — another cause for which he had laboured. Schoelcher left the Navy Ministry following the completion of the work of his commission in July. However, he continued to be consulted on policy by Tracy, the new Navy Minister; he urged the institution of a regular steam service to the Antilles and credit facilities to stimulate the colonial economy.

The aftermath of the June Days cut short the term of office of the republican Commissioners sent to the colonies; military Governors were appointed to the Antilles in September. However, the Commissioners had made good use of their four months establishing the foundations of a republican political culture, circulating literature and sponsoring the formation of clubs, notably Guadeloupe's *La Concorde*. One of the leaders of this club, Louisy Mathieu, a typographer who had been born in slavery, was elected as a *suppléant* to the National Assembly and took Schoelcher's seat when he opted to represent Martinique. The advent of the military Governors did not end the process of politicisation but it did lead to suspension of the social guarantees envisaged in the April decrees and the issuing in November 1848 of a new regulation that able-bodied adults without gainful employment would be liable to fines ranging from 5 to 25 francs. The new constitution of the Republic promulgated in December promised 'special laws' for the colonies, a menacing phrase used to deprive citizens in the colonies of rights they might enjoy in France itself.

With the election of Louis–Napoleon Bonaparte as President in December 1848 Schoelcher lost any remaining official influence and attempts were made to deprive him of his seat in the Assembly. Bissette aligned himself with Louis Napoleon and reached a new understanding with the planters. In what was almost certainly a rigged election Schoelcher and a fellow *montagnard* – Pory Papy, a mulatto lawyer and Freemason – were defeated in Martinique in the elections of 1849; the vote of Pory Papy plummeted from 19,000 to 500 in less than a year. However, in Guadeloupe Schoelcher and Perrinon were re-elected, while Bissette and his followers were defeated, thanks to support from the *nouveaux citoyens*; though women were not enfranchised the victors in Guadeloupe benefited from the campaigning endorsement of the *Société des Femmes Schoelcheristes de Fort de France*. The activities of the club *La Concorde* were now also supplemented by the publication of a *schoelcheriste* newspaper, entitled *Le Progrès*. In January 1850 the *schoelcheristes* elected Louisy Mathieu to the municipality in Point à Pitre.[37]

The relationship of forces in Guadeloupe helped to neutralise the influence of the military government; on the eve of abolition slaves in Guadeloupe comprised nearly 70 per cent of the population compared with 58 per cent in Martinique. The coloured militia in Guadeloupe was stronger, while in Martinique popular support for the *schoelcheristes* was more easily driven underground. Pory Papy had earned the special emnity of the proprietors on Martinique by agitating for the break-up of the large estates and a distribution of land to landless citizens, whether new or old. Similar demands had been made by Eugène Lacaille, attacked as 'the patriarch of incendiarism' because he had led six of his sons, it was alleged, on an expedition to burn the properties of some large planters. The role of Bissette weakened the radical abolitionists in Martinique; he had been able to capitalise on the prestige of his struggles in the 1820s and 1830s. Bissette no doubt had some grounds for distrusting the metropolitan abolitionists, though his decision to throw in his lot with the Bonapartists proved short-sighted in every respect since they dropped him soon afterwards.

In July 1849 the National Assembly voted to grant compensation to the former slave-owners to the extent of approximately half the value of their slaves; 6 millions francs in cash and 120 million francs in 5 per cent bonds. Schoelcher believed that the compensation should be paid to confirm emancipation and to stimulate colonial credit. The plantation colonies had long been short of coins and circulating medium which impeded the development of a wages system. But the root problem was the new relations between labourers and planters. The *nouveaux libres* displayed no zeal for the 1849 sugar harvest and the Antillean planters besieged the new President demanding stiff new labour laws against squatting, idleness and vagrancy. Louis Napoleon lent a ready ear to these complaints, partly because they chimed in so well with his general inclination to roll back the proletarian gains under the Republic and partly because the crisis of the colonial economy was clear for all to see. Guadeloupe's sugar exports had dropped from 38,000 tons in 1847 to 20,000 tons in 1848 and reached only 13,000 tons in 1849.[38] This sharp drop was a testimony to the reality of emancipation as the former slaves exercised their new-found freedom by refusing to work in the fields, concentrating instead on their own private plots. The years 1848–50 saw a drop in sugar prices and a rise in imports of foreign sugar.

The republican order in the colonies made a contribution to a crisis of the plantation economy, since neither the newly elected municipal authorities nor the local gendarmerie were willing to provoke a conflict with the *nouveaux libres*. The laws relating to vagrancy or squatting were often ignored. Schoelcher believed that republican institutions would enable a free labour system to emerge from bargaining between planters and labourers. In principle he did not favour the break-up of the plantations and no arrangements had been made to distribute land to the freedmen. The ability of the the *nouveaux libres* to secure an independent livelihood after emancipation owed as much to the slave property rights conceded by the previous amelioration schemes as to republican institutions.

Schoelcher himself had long believed that the plantations should be resuscitated by credit. His socialism was that of the idealistic *haute bourgeoisie*; he saw in petty production and smallholding a fetter on the size of the market, the productive forces and the scope for human self-realisation. In 1843 he wrote: 'Association has such powerful virtues that even slave labour performed thus in common presents an aspect less sad than the solitary and dismal labour of our peasants.'[39] In this area Schoelcher's ideas were congruent with the plans of some of the most ambitious entrepreneurs in the colonies, who were constructing a new system based on what they called 'an industrial revolution' in sugar-making, which required cultivation and processing to be separated so that the latter could achieve economies of scale. In this conception new sugar factories, *usines centrales*, would be built linking steam-powered mills with the highly integrated processing methods used by the beet sugar factories; the *usines centrales* would service several different plantations which would then concentrate wholly on cane cultivation and would receive back so much sugar for every ton of cane they supplied.[40]

The first experiments in this direction had been set up in 1844 by the *Compagnie des Antilles*, with backing from the Lafitte bank. By 1848 there were twelve *usines centrales* in operation in Guadeloupe and four in Martinique, each processing cane for between three and six plantations. Despite heavy initial investments the *usines centrales* had achieved a reasonable rate of return of 7–11 per cent net per year.[41] Because of the shortage of free labour the first *usines centrales* had used slaves as the basic labour force; the contracts with planters sometimes required them to make slaves available for work in the *usines*. Emancipation and the decline of sugar output temporarily checked the new system but the Republic removed the blockages to further productive reorganisation. It swept away the planters' protection against forfeiture as well as slavery. In principle this made it easier to organise factors of production profitably and to persuade smaller planters to enter agreements with the sugar companies rather than go it alone. The use of compensation payments to the slave-owners to fund development banks meant that further *usines centrales* could be set up. However, it was not until the advent of the Empire and the recovery of business confidence that further *usines* were constructed.

The Bonapartist regime endeared itself to the planters and sugar companies by taking immediate and vigorous measures to ensure a larger and more disciplined labour force. In Febuary 1852 an imperial edict suppressed all colonial representation and self-government; Guadeloupe's *Le Progrès* had already been banned. Draconian labour legislation was introduced. Every adult was obliged to carry a *livret* with details of employment and residence; those failing to comply could be subjected to penal labour. Subsequent regulations stipulated that those occupying plantation lands should render labour services to the planters, for which they might receive nominal payment. Contracts between employers and labourers were to be enforced by the local *maire*. All heads of household were required to pay a tax, as a further inducement to enter the labour market. Victor Schoelcher, who had been driven into exile, was to denounce the new colonial regime.[42] Ironically it had created the conditions in which his own enthusiasm for industrial credit and associated labour ceased to be a generous utopia, linked to education and civic rights, and became a grim reality, policed by the colonial state and furnishing rich pickings for metropolitan speculators. The accent of the new labour regime was on economic rather than physical coercion. The slave had been forced to work by the whip; the ex-slave was forced into an unequal contract by the need to prove gainful occupation or to pay a capitation tax. Further legislation to this end was enacted in 1854 and 1856; such reiterations, however, suggest that the legislation was not wholly effective. Many ex-slaves made good their occupation of plots in the hills or clubbed together to operate a fishing-boat; they could make some money by selling foodstuffs to the plantations. The continuing recalcitrance of the Antillean labourers and peasants explains the interest of both the planters and the authorities in securing alternative sources of labour.

An edict of March 1852 permitted the employers of the Antilles to buy African *engagés*, that is, contract labourers from Senegal. The *engagés* had supposedly entered a contract to work for a period of years; abolitionists urged that this was thinly veiled slavery and slave-trading. The British government complained that the traffic in *engagés* was in violation of the Anglo–French agreements against the slave trade; around the year 1860 it was brought to an end. In all about 16,000 African *engagés* had been brought to the Antilles.[43] Of greater significance was to be the steady introduction of East Indian contract labourers, also under a system of *engagements réguliers*. While many of the African *engagés* probably had been the victims of slave-raiding expeditions, the East Indians were more likely to be refugees from famine and poverty. Between 1852 and 1887 some 77,000 Indians, 1,300 Chinese and 500 Vietnamese were introduced to the French Antilles under contracts ranging from three to seven years. While most of the African *engagés* of the 1850s were sent to Martinique, Guadeloupe was later to take a higher proportion of the Indian indentures.[44]

Louis Napoleon also helped the colonial sugar interests in the years 1852–9 by lowering the duty payable on their product by about a fifth. The colonial regime of the Second Empire and the more buoyant conjuncture of the 1850s led to a recovery in plantation output. By 1857 the value of exports from Martinique and Réunion had reached a level 50 per cent higher than that of 1847. Recovery in Guadeloupe was slower, perhaps because of resistance from the labourers and peasants; in 1857 the value of exports from Guadeloupe had only reached the level of a decade earlier.[45] The rehabilitation of colonial output and the construction of new *usines centrales* was promoted by banks which enjoyed official encouragement and contracts, such as the Banque de Guadeloupe and the Credit Foncier Colonial.

Yet to suggest that slavery had come to an end in the French colonies in order to allow a more effective productive organisation of the sugar industry would be quite misconcieved. For, on the one hand, the sugar industry of the French Antilles could have been modernised without abolishing slavery and, on the other, the abolition of slavery created as many problems as it solved. Cutting cane and staffing the sugar-mills was still back-breaking toil even with the introduction of steam engines and vacuum pans. Indeed to some extent the new equipment simply extended and intensified the labour needed to produce sugar. A small number of highly qualified and salaried engineers were required in the *usines* but, as the figures for indentured labour show, the planters and sugar companies still preferred a tied labour force, earning only nominal wages and denied the possibility to move from one employer to another. It is true that the sugar earnings of Martinique and Guadeloupe had been stagnant for a decade or so before 1848; however, this was not true of Réunion where expansion continued. The ending of slave imports and the successive laws alleviating the slave condition, and the disposition of some slaves and free people of colour to invoke such laws, had set new limits to the super-exploitation which had been characteristic of the slave plantation. Planters who were heavily in debt were legally protected against *expropriation forcée* and were themselves legally prohibited from selling slaves to more profitable and efficient slave enterprises elsewhere in the Americas. In this sense the half-measures of moderate abolitionism created problems which then called for more radical solutions.

The protection of colonial sugar was costly for the metropolitan consumers and had become more so in the 1840s as foreign sugars were available at cheaper prices. Despite a tariff of 75–80 per cent, increasing quantities of foreign sugar were imported: in 1850 such imports totalled 30,000 tons. But metropolitan abolitionists did not agitate for the ending of colonial protection. No doubt some support for emancipation was forthcoming from sugar beet interests and sugar workers who reckoned that it would weaken colonial competition, as it did in the short-run. But the abolitionists of the 1840s combined advocacy of emancipation and support for favourable treatment of colonial commerce. With the slaves freed Schoelcher and other leading emancipationists were happy to be champions of the colonial interest. The free trade pamphlets of Say and Sismondi belonged to an earlier phase of abolitionism and had no bearing on the adoption of emancipation in 1848. The sugar beet interests themselves did not favour abandonment of protection; they came to fear foreign competition more than colonial competition.

The imperial government temporarily lowered the tariff on colonial sugar in the 1850s, judging it wise to promote colonial recovery. The Emperor, no less than Louis Philippe, also had to cater to the interests of the naval, military and colonial lobbies. But while Napoleon III sought to provide colonial sugar manufacturers and planters with the conditions they needed to stage a comeback, he did not allow the Antillean proprietors to dictate policy. The planters objected loudly that the compensation they had received – between 400 and 500 francs per slave – was only a third or a half of their value; at between £16 and £20 per slave it was quite close to what the British slave-owners had received, but without any period of 'apprenticeship'. However, no more money was forthcoming for the planters. Colonial sugar interests also asked for the exclusion of the foreign product from the French market, but Napoleon III did not comply. During the 1860s France imported large quantities of cheap raw sugar from Cuba; this stimulated the refining industry, brought down sugar prices and raised a reasonable revenue.[46] During the 'Liberal Empire' of the 1860s Napoleon III was less concerned to placate colonial special interests and more concerned to ingratiate himself with the populace of the metropolis who had, after all, played a major part in ejecting his royal predecessors. None the less it is surprising that Napoleon III did not do more for the beet producers, who would have benefited from more protectionism and less kindly treatment of the colonial planters.

While economic motives did not dictate abolition in the French case, at least emancipation did not entail intolerable costs. Colonial trade had dwindled to only 5 per cent of the total; even the revenue raised from sugar duties could as easily be raised from importing foreign sugars. The Republic sanctioned and the Empire honoured the promise to compensate the proprietors of the Antilles. The sum involved was not immense, and was financed almost entirely by a bond issue; its cost could easily be offset against the annual takings of the sugar tariff. British compensation, in total, cost nearly six times as much because there had been far more slaves in the British colonies.

French abolitionism succeeded in 1848 because, first, slavery had long been discredited, even in official doctrine, secondly, an incoming republican regime could not flout the new radical current of abolitionism in the metropolis, nor expect to control the situation in the colonies, without immediately moving against slavery. The association of so many of the prominent new politicians with the Abolition Society linked republicanism with emancipationism and gave Schoelcher a strong bargaining position in the vital early days of the provisional government. Positive justifications of slavery had long fallen out of fashion. Victor Hugo's story of a wronged black, *Bouk Jugal*, showed that the romantic imagination could still respond to the plight of the slave. Lamartine himself had written a verse drama on Toussaint Louverture's tragic fate, prior to becoming premier. The members of the provisional government were certainly aware of the weight of history they carried on their shoulders and of the pressure of a new type of class struggle. The Second Republic could not fall behind the emancipatory achievements of the First and must reassure the proletarian masses that its ideals were not to be degraded by the sordid interests of slaveholders. When Louisy Mathieu, the black deputy from Guadeloupe, entered the National Assembly he was greeted with applause and cheers – a reception only equalled by Louis Napoleon. The Assembly was here acclaiming its own generosity and virtue, qualities which it had all the more need of reaffirming in the aftermath of the June Days.

The French republican abolitionism of 1848 struck an answering chord in the Antilles not simply in the manifestations of May but also in the intense political mobilisation of 1848–51 and the tough struggle over the next two decades to keep alive the principles of *schoelcherisme*. The black Republicans of the Antilles had no difficulty in identifying with radical opposition to the Bonapartist regime; it is not surprising to find men such as Pory Papy amongst the *communards* of Paris. Schoelcher himself was happy neither with the Commune nor its bloody suppression. He was elected first as deputy from Martinique in 1871 amidst much acclaim and, as such, campaigned for a repeal of the colonial labour decrees, against the treatment of the indentured labourers, and against racist practices in the colonies. In Martinique and Guadeloupe the *schoelcheristes* encouraged the development of a public education system and of co-operative enterprises amongst the smallholders and fishermen. While Schoelcher's humanitarianism and good intentions could never be in doubt, his paternalistic social republicanism became the integument linking the coloured population to French colonialism. The former stalwarts of moderate abolitionism became pillars of the Third Republic; Henri Wallon, Schoelcher's colleague of 1848, drafted the constitution.

1848 and the Americas

The events of 1848 in Paris famously concentrated the attention of Europe; the events of the French Caribbean, notably the uprising of May 22nd in Martinique, had an impact throughout the Caribbean. The Governor of Cuba prevented the local press from reporting what had happened in Martinique and any papers relating to these events brought in by visitors were impounded. The Governors of the small Dutch islands of the Lesser Antilles – St Martin, St Eustatius and Saba – were unable to prevent the several hundred slaves they contained learning of the events in the nearby French Windward Islands since a small French enclave on St Martin was administered as a dependency of Guadeloupe. The sound of drums and conch shells greeted liberation and encouraged a defiant mood in the Dutch slaves. They simply refused to continue behaving as slaves and the Dutch colonists lacked the means to coerce them back into bondage. This was not a legal emancipation and the slave-owners did not receive compensation until many years latter.[47] From the Dutch islands the news of developments in Guadeloupe and Martinique reached the nearby Danish Virgin Islands.

In the Danish island of Ste Croix the first days of July witnessed an upheaval amongst the colony's 25,000 slaves which directly echoed the uprising in Martinique. Denmark had pioneered abolition of the slave trade in 1804 but in the 1830s and 1840s the royal Danish government had agonised over colonial slavery much after the fashion of the governments of the July Monarchy –with the difference that they had eventually endorsed a 'free womb' law, with a twelve-year 'apprenticeship' clause, in July 1847. The Governor of the Danish West Indies, Peter von Scholten, had made a name for himself as a supporter of equal treatment for the free people of colour. Many of the population of the Danish West Indies, whether free or slave, were members of the Moravian Church. So far from opposing slavery the Moravian Church had itself owned slaves. In 1842 the Moravian mission, which received considerable financial support from British Protestants, had been attacked for its tolerance of slaveholding by the British and Foreign Anti-Slavery Society. Fearing to become the targets of an international campaign the Moravians eventually agreed, in 1846, to manumit all slaves owned by the Church. The institution of slavery was already in a weakened condition when news of the events in the French island delivered the *coup de grace*.

The first sign of movement amongst the slaves of Ste Croix was given on the evening of Sunday July 2nd, when bands of rebels took over plantation buildings, rang bells and blew conch shells. At seven o'clock next morning a large party of rebels entered Fredrickstadt, the capital of Ste Croix, appealing to all blacks to leave their places of work and demand emancipation. The houses of several leading citizens were attacked, including those of the police chief, of the judge and of a merchant who had asked for repression of the rebels. The main body of rebels surrounded the fort and demanded freedom. In other parts of the island there were further noisy demonstrations but little or no bloodshed. The small garrison was powerless in the face of an enthusiastic but restrained crowd of rebels. Among those who emerged as leaders of the movement were Martin King and 'General' Buddhoe. With the island already in the hands of the rebels the Governor, on his own authority, decreed emancipation on July 3rd; while this decree suppressed slavery it added that 'estate negroes retain for three months from this date the use of the houses and provision grounds which they have hitherto possessed'.[48] Buddhoe accepted this decree and urged other rebels to do the same. However, some retreated to the interior. On July 8th 580 Spanish troops landed on the island, sent by the Governor of Puerto Rico in answer to an appeal from van Scholten; with these reinforcements the remnants of the rebellion were suppressed. Van Scholten left for Denmark on July 14th. Denmark experienced its own upheavals in 1848 and was menaced by the agitation over Schleswig–Holstein. Van Scholten succeeded in persuading the King to ratify his decree of emancipation on September 22nd.

The post-emancipation settlement in the Danish West Indies attempted to thrust the former slaves back into a position of dependence *vis-à-vis* their former masters and the colonial state, using devices similar to those found elsewhere in the post-emancipation Caribbean. A decree of 1849 obliged all those who wished to continue to live on the plantations and to work their provision grounds to enter labour contracts with the planters. Those identified as leaders of the July rebellion were either imprisoned or, as in the case of Buddhoe, deported. After many representations from the planters the Danish government eventually agreed in 1853 to pay compensation of $50 for each slave; a total of $2 million was paid out.[49]

With the events of 1848 slavery had been overthrown throughout the lesser Antilles and in all those Caribbean islands where it had flourished in the seventeenth and eighteenth century. Looking at the Americas as a whole, colonial slavery had been eclipsed. It survived only on the two Spanish islands and in Surinam.

Surinam had experienced a boost to plantation development during the Napoleonic Wars but following this it had reverted to being a colonial backwater. The ban on slave imports seems to have been fairly effective, with the slave population declining from about 50,000 in 1820 to about 33,000 in the 1850s. Over the same period the number of plantations dropped from 590 to 162. The royal Dutch government pursued a policy towards colonial slavery strongly reminiscent of that of the governments of Louis Philippe, with ministerial pronouncements favourable to abolition and ineffective, weakly funded schemes of slave education. British abolitionists brought pressure to bear on the Dutch Protestant Churches to manumit the slaves they owned; this pressure had some effect in part because the missionary activities of the Moravian and other Churches received considerable financial support from British Nonconformists. However Dutch governments shrank from emancipation because of the costs that would be involved in compensating slave-owners. The Dutch variant of oligarchic monarchy escaped unscathed from the revolutions of 1848, though William II conceded some moderate constitutional reforms and called on a Liberal–Catholic coalition to form the government. Emancipation was not enacted in Surinam until 1863, a time when the slavery issue had been brought to the fore by the Civil War in North America. By the 1860s the Dutch government was showing a considerable surplus on the colonial account, following the development of the so-called 'cultivation system' in Java, a system of colonial forced labour. The slaves in Surinam were renowned for their propensity to conspire against and desert their owners. There were thought to be as many as 8,000 maroons in the backlands in the 1850s; fugitive slaves also escaped to British Guyana after 1838. The maroon communities possibly acted as a safety valve drawing off the most rebellious slaves from the plantations and reducing the chances of mass outbreaks. The piecemeal manumission of the large slaveholdings of the Churches may also have made it seem that slavery was being wound down in Surinam.[50]

Spain also escaped the revolutionary commotions of 1848 and this no doubt helps to explain why slavery survived unscathed in the Spanish islands. But political life in the Spanish American Republics was stimulated by events in Europe and since the French Republic had a special prestige the ending of slavery in the French colonies was to have some echo in South America. The residual slavery in Colombia was brought to an end in 1851; within two or three years Argentina, Venezuela, Peru, Ecuador and Bolivia had all followed suit.

Slavery was, of course, in any case facing a sharp decline at this point, since the original emancipation laws had been decreed thirty or thirty-five years previously. *Manumisos* could claim their freedom between the ages of twenty-five and thirty, while the population that remained enslaved would contain a higher and higher proportion of those reaching the end of their working life. The value of the remaining slaves and *manumisos* either as a work-force or as collateral was now bound to diminish. The residual slavery created by 'free womb' laws was also in some respects more provocative and vulnerable than a full slave system. In Venezuela in the 1840s slaves had readily volunteered to take part in armed clashes between rival oligarchic factions. Since free birth only began in 1821, there would be slaves aged twenty-five or thirty-five condemned to lifelong slavery. The freeing of the first *manumisos* accentuated this tension and created a layer of free blacks whose parents and elder siblings were still enslaved.

The Spanish American emancipations of the early 1850s helped to confirm wider transformations in society and the state. They came at a time when the conservative *caudillos* of the post-independence period were being driven from the scene and a new attempt was being made to construct authoritative Liberal governments. In Venezuela Páez allowed himself to be replaced in 1847 by the Liberal general José Tadeo Monagas. When it became clear in 1848 that Monagas intended to be more than a puppet civil war broke out; amongst those who helped to defeat Páez was Renato Beluche the patriot privateer who had escorted Bolivar from Haiti to Venezuela. In 1849 the Governor of the Apure, a province where there were no slaves, wrote a letter to his fellow governors recommending the immediate ending of all remaining slavery. It was widely acknowledged that fugitive slaves aggravated the problem of rural banditry and were often willing to participate in rebellion. Conservative opposition to the Monagas regime escalated rapidly to armed action when José Tadeo handed over the Presidency to his brother José Gregorio in 1853. Emancipation was proclaimed in March 1854 partly in order to prevent the Conservatives enlisting slaves in the rebel forces. The act of liberation was, of course, also proclaimed as a fulfilment of the glorious heritage of Simon Bolivar. The owners of Venezuela's 12,000 or so slaves were promised compensation.[51]

The Colombian decree freeing all remaining slaves in 1851 and the Argentinian edict of 1853 originated in circumstances similar to those which favoured emancipation in Venezuela. In Argentina the measure followed shortly after the ejection of Rosas. In Colombia (known officially as the Republic of New Granada from the 1830s to the 1860s) there were still as many as 20,000 slaves in 1850. In 1849 the Conservative Tomás Mosquera was replaced by the Liberal José Hilario López, who was soon resisted by partisans of the conservative cause. The emancipation decree of 1850–1 came at a time when the López regime faced open rebellion and slave rebels had seized land in the mining districts. Once again slaveholders were offered compensation based on slave prices already deflated by the advance of manumission.[53]

The instability of the Spanish American Republics is such that the coincidence of emancipation and civil war might not be thought significant. But in each case an attempt was being made to renovate the formula of the state and to renew the Liberal republican tradition which, it was claimed, the conservative *caudillos* had travestied. In Argentina, Colombia and Ecuador the freeing of the slaves was accomplished as part of the promulgation of new constitutions. In Peru emancipation was an accompaniment to economic rather than political transformations. It coincided with the ending of the Indian tribute system and an attempt to restructure the economy according to free market principles in order to promote the more rapid exploitation of guano deposits. Those holding concessions entitling them to work the guano deposits found that neither residual slavery nor Indian labour were adequate to their needs. From the late 1840s tens of thousands of Chinese contract labourers, 'coolies', were introduced to supply the deficiency. The only South American state not to bring slavery to an end by the early 1850s was Paraguay, a Republic which retained its generally isolationist stance.

By 1860 there were only three territories in the Americas where slavery still led a vigorous existence: the south of the United States, the Spanish Caribbean islands, especially Cuba, and the Empire of Brazil. It is perhaps appropriate to end the above account of the ending of slavery in the French islands, the Danish islands and the South American Republics with the reflections on emancipation of a Colombian slaveholder, Joaquín Mosquera. This man, brother to Tomás Mosquera and himself President of Colombia in succession to Bolivar in 1830, had fought tenaciously to postpone or whittle away the emancipationist implications of the Cúcuta Law of 1821. But once emancipation arrived he met it with a strange blend of bitterness, arrogance and relief, giving an insight into the mentality of the patriot planters who have figured in earlier chapters of this book. In a letter to a friend he wrote:

I am replying tardily to your kind letter of March 3rd because I have been travelling in the district of Carloto visiting my mining properties; it is no rhetorical flourish to say that the simultaneous liberation of the slaves there has had an effect like that of an earthquake on a city. However, I have not lacked resignation, patience and a generous spirit with those who have been my slaves. It is only right that I should treat them with benevolence since they love me and respect me. I called them all together and congratulated them on their liberty, explaining their rights and duties as free men, just as if I was some abolitionist in the United States; and I told them that they had to forget all the customs and ideas of slavery and imagine that I was a stranger whom they were meeting for the first time, so that we would treat one another as man to man among free men. My meetings lasted a week at my mine *Ensoluado* and another at the *Aguablanca*. . . . I have rented out these properties at a miserable price; I have given the slaves the houses in which they live and their gardens, dividing them up by families and alloting some to old people and the sick; I have sold them equipment and tools at half the price they could buy them from the merchants around here and have let to them the cattle grounds for two *reales* annually per head. . . . They are now the lords of my properties, leaving to me a species of ownership that will bring only a fifth of the revenues I formerly obtained, if they pay me at all which I very much doubt. . . . I have lost much: but it has lifted an immense weight which bore down on me, against my character. The manumission of my slaves has freed me too.[53]

Notes

1. François–Auguste Chateaubriand, *Génie du Christianisme, ou Beauté de la Religion Chrétienne*, Paris 1802, 5 vols, IV, p. 189. This work was much reprinted. It contrasts the work of the Revolution with the Catholic tradition which made 'the masters more compassionate and the slaves more virtuous – it served the cause of mankind without any injury to the country, or subversion of public order and private property. With fine words of philanthropy all was lost – even compassion was paralysed . . .' Chateaubriand, *The Genius of Christianity*, Paris 1854, p. 187.

2. Estimated from David Eltis, 'The Direction and Fluctuation of the Transatlantic Slave Trade 1821–1843', in Gemery and Hogendorn, *The Uncommon Market*, pp. 273–302, pp. 287–8; and Serge Daget, 'British Repression of the Illegal French Slave Trade', also in *The Uncommon Market*, pp. 419–42.

3. Ministère de la Marine, *Budget de 1829: Rapport au Roi*, Paris April 1828, p. 185. The Ministry's budget at 57 million francs covered the cost of salaries, supplies and a major construction programme as well as the administration of the colonies. Taxes raised within the colonies themselves raised 7.4 million francs. For colonial customs revenue of 36–40 million francs see Alexandre Foignet, *Quelques Réflexions sur les Colonies*, Paris 1831, p. 30, and Poiré de Saint–Aurèle, *Du Droit de Colonies Françaises*, Paris 1832, p. 23. This latter author also pointed out that the colonial market took 50–55 million francs of French goods each year. He further insisted that France's commercial interest and geographical situation dictate policies favourable to the colonies: 'No colonies, no navy. Without a navy the merchant marine would have only a vulnerable and precarious existence' (p. 25). Of course Saint Aurèle was an apologist, but his appeal to commercial interest strikes a very different note from Choiseul's famous vindication of colonies as a prop of royal power.

4. Blet, *Histoire de la Colonisation Française*, II, pp. 47–56.

5. Shelby McCloy, *The Negro in the French West Indies*, Westport (Conn.), pp. 135–6.

6. Christian Schnakenbourg, *Histoire de l'Industrie Sucrière en Guadeloupe aux XIXe et XXe Siècles: Tome I, La Crise du Système Esclavagiste, (1835–1847)*, Paris 1980, p. 54.

7. Dale Tomic, *Prelude to Emancipation: Sugar and Slavery in Martinique, 1830–48*, PhD thesis, Madison 1978, p. 118; Schnakenbourg, *La Crise du Système Esclavagiste*, pp. 50, 137–43.

8. Benoit Joachim, 'L'Indemnité Coloniale de Saint Domingue et la Question des Rapatriés', *Revue Historique*, no. 500, October–December 1971, pp. 359–76; also Benoit Joachim, 'Commerce et Décolonisation: l'Experience Franco-Haitienne aux XIXe Siècle', *Annales*, 1972, pp. 1,497–1,525.

9. Quoted in André Jardin and André–Jean Tudesq, *Restoration and Reaction: 1815–1848*, Cambridge 1983, p. 95.

10. Daget, 'A Model of the French Abolitionist Movement', in Bolt and Drescher, *Anti–Slavery, Religion and Reform*, pp. 71–2.

11. Daget, 'A Model of the French Abolitionist Movement', in Bolt and Drescher, *Anti-Slavery, Religion and Reform*, p. 72. Criticism of the slave trade was not confined to the *Société de la Morale Chrétienne* though the latter's representations had the most political significance. The Abbé Grégoire continued to attack the slave traffic until his death in 1829, collaborating with the Abbé Guidicelly, a 'patriot priest' from Corsica, and J.E. Morenas, a Freemason from Provence. Morenas wrote a detailed indictment of the French slave traffic (*Précis Historique de la Traite des Noirs et de l'Esclavage Colonial*, Paris 1828). However, these men lacked the standing and prospects of the respectable dignitaries who supported the *Société*. Guidicelly eventually went to Haiti as a bishop, while Morenas worked for the British abolitionists in West Africa.

12. Daget, 'British Repression of the Illegal French Slave Trade', in Gemery and Hogendorn, *The Uncommon Market*, p. 429.

13. McCloy, *The Negro in the French West Indies*, pp. 137–8. The military establishment in the Antilles is given in the official *Notices Statistiques sur les Colonies Françaises*, Paris 1837, pp. 81, 192–3. Following the 1833 incidents the Martinique militia, both white and coloured, was suspended and the regular garrison raised to 4,103 troops (p. 81).

14. *Questions Relatives à l'Abolition de l'Esclavage*, Paris 1843, p. 7. The deliberations and evasions of the Orleanist abolitionists and politicians are well analysed in Seymour Drescher, *Dilemmas of Democracy: de Tocqueville and Modernization*, Pittsburg 1968, pp. 88–123, 151–97.

15. Auguste Cochin's typically indulgent account of the de Broglie reforms describes them as a judicious ten-year programme of emancipation which would 'encourage the slave family by marriage, property by the peculium, the peculium by the free day, morals by religion, intelligence by education'. *L'Abolition de l'Esclavage*, II, p. 53.

16. Antoine Gisler, *L'Esclavage aux Antilles Françaises, XVII–XIXe Siècles*, Fribourg 1965, p. 142; the impact of the reforms on slave conditions are discussed pp. 47–51, 133–8. See also Victor Schoelcher, *Esclavage et Colonisation*, ed. Emile Tersen and with an introduction by Aimé Césaire, Paris 1948, p. 120. This book is a useful collection of articles and other writings by the leading French abolitionist of the 1840s. Schoelcher's warnings were to be amply borne out by the exiguous signs of slave advancement and the trickle of manumissions that resulted from application of the *Loi Mackau*, see *Compte Rendu au Roi sur le Régime des Esclaves*, Imprimerie Royale, Paris 1847.

17. *Notices Statistiques sur les Colonies Françaises*, 4th part, Paris 1840, pp. 156–7; *Notices Statistiques sur les Colonies Françaises*, Part I, Paris 1837, p. 93. In Guadeloupe the free people of colour owned just under 10,000 slaves in 1835. (Brian Weinstein, 'The French West Indies', in M.L. Kilson and R.I. Rotberg, *The African Diaspora*, Cambridge, Mass. 1976, pp. 237–79, p. 244.)

18. Dale Tomic, *Prelude to Emancipation: Sugar and Slavery in Martinique, 1830–48*, PhD thesis, Madison 1978, p. 68.

19. The contribution of duties on colonial trade to the total of customs revenue is calculated from House of Commons, *Accounts and Papers*, 1849, vol. LIII, p. 168. The value and revenue of slave production is taken from Tomic, *Prelude to Emancipation*, p. 65.

20. Tomic and Schnakenbourg, authors of studies on Martinique and Guadeloupe respectively, have placed great emphasis on the thesis that the survival of slavery frustrated the economic development of the French Antilles because of planter indebtedness, the tying up capital resources in slaves as property, and the immobilisation of factors of production under the prevailing slave regime. See for Martinique, Tomic, *Prelude to Emancipation*, especially pp. 49–88 and 137–75; for Guadeloupe, Schnakenbourg, *La Crise du Système Esclavagiste*, especially pp. 120–36. Certainly the 1840s witnessed stagnation in the economy of the French Antilles, though if the French plantations are compared with those in Cuba the influence of abolitionism itself would have to be noted as one factor involved. The crisis of French colonial slavery was not essentially economic in character. This point, to which we return below, is forcefully

made by Edouard de Lépine, 'Sur l'Abolition de l'Esclavage', in *Questions sur l'Histoire Antillaise*, Fort–de–France 1978, pp. 25–166, especially pp. 96–102.

21. André–Jean Tudesq, *Les Grands Notables en France, 1840–9*, 2 vols, Paris 1964, II, p. 842. See also L.C. Jennings. 'La Presse Havraise et l'Esclavage', *Revue Historique*, CCLXXII, 1984.

22. Tudesq, *Les Grands Notables en France*, I, p. 837.

23. Jardin and Tudesq, *Restoration and Reaction*, p. 135.

24. Tudesq writes: 'The world of the notables represents not only the ruling class of a society in transition between two socio-economic structures but also the social form where there is a weakening of the centre' (*Les Grands Notables en France*, II, p. 1,231). His description of the *Juste Milieu* with its obsessive respect for property and concern for an 'equilibrium between order and liberty' is reminiscent of that Whig orthodoxy summarised by David Cecil as follows: 'All believed in ordered liberty, low taxation and the enclosure of land; all disbelieved in despotism and democracy' (*The Young Melbourne*, p. 8). Another observation by Cecil also had its counterpart under the July Monarchy: 'The Whigs despised the royal family; and there was certainly none of the hush and punctilio of court existence about them' (p. 6). The resemblances between the Orleanist regime and the Hanoverian order were, of course, deliberate; but, as the case of Spanish America had shown, constitutions could not always be successfully transplanted from one social formation to another. The viability of the Orleanist experiment in 'illegitimate monarchy', albeit short-lived, had been made possible by the deeper transformations in French society wrought by the Great Revolution.

25. Daget, 'A Model of the French Abolitionist Movement', in Bolt and Drescher, *Anti-Slavery, Religion and Reform*, p. 76.

26. Membership of the Abolition Society required two sponsors and cost 25 francs, for a worker equivalent to two weeks' wages. Bissette was apparently barred from giving evidence to the Parliamentary Commission on Emancipation because of his colour; see Drescher, *Dilemmas of Democracy*, p. 162–3.

27. For Schoelcher's critique of amelioration attempts see Schoelcher, *Histoire de l'Esclavage pendant les Deux Dernières Années* (a collection of articles and pamphlets, Paris 1847); extracts in *Esclavage et Colonisation*, pp. 108–39.

28. Quoted in Janine Alexandre–Debray, *Schoelcher*, Paris 1983, p. 68.

29. Seymour Drescher, 'Two Variants of Anti-Slavery', in Bolt and Drescher, *Anti-Slavery, Religion and Reform*, p. 52; Gaston–Martin, *Histoire de l'Esclavage dans les Colonies Françaises*, p. 291.

30. Schoelcher, *Esclavage et Colonisation*, p. 140. For an appreciation of Schoelcher's role see Edouard de Lépine, *Questions sur l'Histoire Antillaise*, pp. 36–45, 99–110.

31. Oruno Lara, *La Guadeloupe dans l'Histoire*, pp. 223–4.

32. Schoelcher, *Des Colonies Françaises*, pp. 101–12, 375–7. (*Esclavage et Colonisation*, pp. 63–9.)

33. Alexandre–Debray, *Schoelcher*, p. 129.

34. Tersen quotes the Governor's decree, Schoelcher, *Esclavage et Colonisation*, p. 134n. Once again there is an admirable discussion of how the slave mobilisations in Martinique accelerated and shaped emancipation in Edouard de Lépine, *Questions sur l'Histoire Antillaise*, pp. 125–47; see also the full account in Léo Elizabeth, *L'Abolition de l'Esclavage à la Martinique*, Memoires de la Société d'Histoire de la Martinique, Fort–de–France, Martinique 1983, especially pp. 33–80. Elizabeth draws attention to the considerable role of Freemasonry in preparing the ground for republicanism and emancipationism in Martinique.

35. Quoted in Schoelcher, 'La Verité aux Ouvriers et Cultivateurs de la Martinique' (1849), in *Esclavage et Colonisation*, p. 160. In this pamphlet Schoelcher replies to those who accused him of having brought chaos to the colonies by pointing out that the planters themselves were aware that slavery had become untenable; clearly fear of slave insurrection motivated the alarmed editorials he cites.

36. Maurice Agulhon, *The Republican Experiment: 1848–52*, Cambridge 1985, p. 57.

37. Oruno Lara, *La Guadeloupe dans l'Histoire*, pp. 231–3. This work, despite its

informality, gives a vivid idea of the enduring effects of the struggles in the Antilles in these years. It is interesting to note that Schoelcher did not visit the Antilles at this time but made himself the tribune of radical black and mulatto emancipationists in the colonies. Schoelcher insisted that his supporters never went beyond legal and peaceful forms of resistance to the planters, and the Bissettistes collaborating with them. While there is little doubt that the military Governors of the Antilles allowed the planters to intimidate the *nouveaux citoyens* with impunity, it is also the case that the latter resisted vigorously the provocations committed against them, for a time successfully in Guadeloupe and Marie Galante. Planters who took a hard line with labourers or tenants risked a fire in their cane fields and estate buildings; for the wave of suspected arson in 1849–50 see McCloy, *The Negro in the French West Indies*, pp. 155–6. For the eruption of demands for the break-up of the large estates in Martinique see Elizabeth, *L'Abolition de l'Esclavage à la Martinique*, pp. 90–7.

38. Weinstein, 'The French West Indies', in Kilson and Rotberg, *The African Diaspora*, pp. 248–9, 274–5.

39. Schoelcher, *Des Colonies Françaises*, quoted in Tomic, *Prelude to Emancipation*, p. 196.

40. Schnakenbourg, *La Crise du Système Esclavagiste*, pp. 212–20; Tomic, *Prelude to Emancipation*, pp. 125 et seq.

41. Schnakenbourg, *La Crise du Système Esclavagiste*, p. 238. These findings concerning the profitability of the Compagnie des Antilles show that despite slavery and the *Loi Mackau* the colonial system could yield reasonable profits right down to the end of the July Monarchy.

42. Victor Schoelcher, 'La Verité aux Ouvriers et Cultivateurs' and 'Polemique Coloniale' (1871–81), in *Esclavage et Colonisation*, pp. 168–74, 185–88.

43. Cochin, *L'Abolition de l'Esclavage*, II, pp. 472–3.

44. Eugène Revert, *La France d'Amérique*, Paris 1949, p. 61.

45. Cochin, *L'Abolition de l'Esclavage*, II, pp. 474–6.

46. Cochin, *L'Abolition de l'Esclavage*, II, pp. 472–7.

47. Goslinga, *A Short History of the Netherlands, Antilles and Surinam*, pp. 150–1.

48. Isaac Dookhan, *A History of the Virgin Islands of the United States*, Virgin Islands 1974, pp. 173–4.

49. Dookhan, *A History of the Virgin Islands*, pp. 175, 190–8.

50. Goslinga, *A Short History of the Netherlands, Antilles and Surinam*, pp. 153–61; Fieldhouse, *The Colonial Empires*, pp. 331–4.

51. Lombardi, *The Decline and Abolition of Negro Slavery in Venezuela*, pp. 135 et seq.

52. Carlos Restrepo Canal, *La Libertad de los Esclavos en Colombia*, Bogotá 1938, 2 vols, II, pp. 169–73. For the slaves' land seizures see Michael Taussig, *The Devil and Commodity Fetishism in South America*, Chapel Hill 1980, pp. 47–9. Tulio Halperín Donghi makes the point that these final emancipations coincided with a new configuration of political economy in the Spanish American Republics, 'Economy and Society in post-Independence Spanish America', in Leslie Bethell, ed., *The Cambridge History of Latin America*, vol III, Cambridge 1985, pp. 299–345, p. 341. According to Andrews full emancipation did not extend to Buenos Aires until 1860 when that province ratified the Constitution; Andrews, *The Afro-Argentines*, pp. 56–7.

53. Eduardo Posada, *La Esclavitud en Colombia*, Bogotá 1933, pp. 83–8.

XIII

Conclusion:

Results and Prospects

No more of rapine and its wasted plains
Its stolen victims and unhallowed gains,
Its Christian merchants, and the brigands bold
Who wage their wars and do their work for gold.
No more of sorrows sick'ning to the heart,
Commercial murders and the crowded mart;
The living cargoes and the constant trace
Of pain and anguish in each shrunken face! . . .

'No one perhaps, replied the Count, can more
The sad, but strong necessity deplore,
Of buying men to cultivate our plains
And holding these, our fellow men in chains.
The very name of slavery, to me
Is vile and odious to the last degree . . .
Think not, I pray, I advocate this cause,
Or speak of such a system with applause;
Sir in the abstract it must be condemned,
It is the practice only I defend
For ad quo morals, nothing can be worse
But ad quo sugar, 'tis the sole resource.'

The Sugar Estate (1840), R.R. Madden

Conclusion

In 1770 Britain, France, Spain and Portugal had possessed flourishing slave colonies in the Americas. In the succession of political and social struggles covered in this book colonial empire and slavery were both challenged. Down to the mid-nineteenth century these upheavals destroyed colonial rule on most of the mainland, and destroyed slavery in most of the Caribbean. The revolutionary events of this epoch thus brought about a simultaneous and fundamental restructuring of slavery and of empire. The broad picture is clear enough. In the United States and Brazil the colonial relationship was successfully rejected but slavery survived – indeed flourished. In Haiti and mainland Spanish America both slavery and colonial rule were defeated. In the British and French West Indies slavery was suppressed but colonial rule survived. The only flourishing slave colony left in the Americas by 1850 was Spanish Cuba: a new colonial pact had been negotiated, born of the slaveholders' fear of the slaves and the willingness of an impoverished metropolis to allow the development of a rich slave colony. Slave emancipation confirmed and probably reinforced colonial rule in the British and French West Indies. In the United States and Brazil independence confirmed and strengthened the vigour and dynamism of the slave system. The destruction of colonial slavery thus had contradictory aspects, whose implications must now be considered.

In this book no attempt has been made to give any detailed account of the major metropolitan revolutions and wars, or of the course of the industrial revolution; this backdrop of an 'age of revolution' has only been summarily introduced to the extent that it impinged on the fortunes of colonial slavery. In this period the advance of capitalism and the progress of bourgeois revolution had an uneven and contradictory character. The autonomy and power of wealth-holders was promoted by the dismantling of absolutism, the retreat of mercantilism, the elaboration of legal codes enshrining respect for contract and private property, the greater speed of communication, and the construction of political regimes more broadly representative of the possessing classes. But at the same time the underlying populations sought to check or control the power of the new or rejuvenated ruling classes. Increasing dependence on commodity production and consumption, greater ease of movement, the extension of passive or active citizenship created new hopes and fears, and created new forms of association and a new terrain of contestation. The advance of slavery and abolition must be seen in this context – it partook of similar cross-currents and contradictions.

There was a definite correlation between the rise of abolitionism as a significant mass movement and the onset of a phase of increasing 'dynamic density' in bourgeois society: Britain in 1788–92 and 1830–38; France, weakly in 1789–91, more strongly in the 1840s (and, to anticipate, the Northern US states of 1830–65). It is as if abolitionism had special resonance within social formations making the transition *from* the transition – where the exploiting classes had to contend with less particularistic forms of social contestation as riots or rick-burning merged into, and gave way to, more co-ordinated and politicised forms of class struggle. The failure of Spain, or the Netherlands or Denmark to develop abolitionist movements also correlates with the slower development of an industrial capitalist order in those countries. These broad correlations seem to invite the conclusion that there was a direct relation of cause and effect between capitalist advance and the rise of anti-slavery. The conclusion proposed here is different: such a simplified view would misconstrue the causal link and fail to account for the 'para-industrial' slavery of the epoch or for vital anti-slavery impulses that were not bourgeois in character and were even anti-capitalist. To the extent that capitalist advance did promote anti-slavery it was indirectly, because of the class struggles to which it gave rise and because of the capacities of the new type of state created in the wake of industrial revolution.

The main conclusion of the accounts presented in this book is that slavery was not overthrown for economic reasons but where it became politically untenable. Intense political and military struggles within and between the leading Atlantic powers created conditions in which slavery could be successfully challenged in many of the places where it had been of most importance in 1770. The slave systems overthrown in the period 1776–1848 were not stricken down by rival economic interests, or condemned because they no longer contributed to capital accumulation, or driven out of existence by market pressure. The solid ranks of the bourgeoisie inclined, when they favoured anti-slavery at all, to a moderate species of abolitionism. The slave systems perished in stormy class struggles in both colonies and metropolis. The economic beneficiaries of the overthrow of colonial slavery were not industrialists but other American slave-owning planters, still able and willing to supply the industrialising regions. St Domingue was at the height of its prosperity in 1789. The British West Indies had achieved a pinnacle of commercial profitability around 1807 and the West Indian slave plantations were still quite profitable in the 1820s. The Dutch farmers in New York in the 1790s, the Venezuelan planters in the 1810s, the French Antillean planters of the 1840s lost their slaves because of wider social and political conflicts, revolutions and class struggles. In each of these cases slavery was politically vulnerable not economically unprofitable; and in a politically viable slave system the slave-owner's natural response to poor profits was not emancipation but the sale of surplus slaves to more dynamic sectors of the slave economy. Slave emancipation was put on the agenda by englobing political crises and social contestation. The key dates for the rise of the challenge to slavery and the slave trade marked moments of exceptional tension in the polity and social formation: 1780 in Pennsylvania, 1793–4 in France and St Domingue, 1804 in Haiti, 1807 in Britain, 1821 in Gran Colombia, 1833 in Britain, 1848 in the French Lesser Antilles. As regimes, governments and states were made and unmade so anti-slavery forces, including the slaves themselves, gained the opportunity to isolate and defeat the slaveholders. The slave based enterprises and households had a considerable, but never fully adequate, capacity to reproduce the subjection of slaves. Political events which opened a rift between the slaveholders and the government gave opportunities to slave resistance; any state challenged by slaveholders, as Britain in the 1770s, or France in the 1790s, or Spain after 1811 in South America, would be tempted to retaliate by withdrawing support for slavery. Likewise those seeking to establish or shape a new political system found in abolitionism a potent symbol of legitimacy, a social programme calculated to evoke the spontaneous consent of wide layers of the non-slaveholding population.

But a qualification should be noted. If prevailing economic interests did not dictate bans on the slave trade or slave emancipation it remains true that neither did they lose much by the anti-slavery moves at the time they were made. The suppression of particular national slave trades benefited some planters and involved no expropriation. The slave system in the French Caribbean had been buoyant in 1789 but it was in full disintegration by the time of the decree of Pluviôse 1794. North American emancipation only made headway where slavery was already weak and generally freed only those not yet born. Likewise anti-slavery gained ground in Spanish South America, where slaves were few, but not in Cuba or Brazil, where slavery thrived. While slave plantations may still have been profitable in the British West Indies in the 1820s and in the French Antilles in the 1840s, the economic significance of slaveholding to the metropolitan ruling classes was small and trade with the colonial Caribbean in eclipse. In both cases incipient slave resistance was a factor reconciling the planters to a compensated emancipation. The resources available to these metropolitan governments allowed them to finance compensation schemes without great strain, essentially because slaveholding represented only a tiny fraction of total imperial wealth. In the British case generous compensation helped to buy off opposition from the West Indian proprietors; in the French compensation was promised out of general respect for private property and paid following the rallying of the party of order around Louis Napoleon.

Slave emancipation triumphed in this period where three factors favourable to such an outcome coalesced: (i) a political crisis marginalising slaveholders and giving birth to a new type of state; (ii) the actuality or prospect of slave resistance or rebellion; (iii) social mobilisations encouraging the partisans of reform or revolution to rally popular sentiment with anti-slavery acts.

Political crisis, by itself, did not necessarily destroy slave subordination or disorganise and discredit slave-owners, as the example of North America after 1776 amply shows. Where there was a native, resident and strongly entrenched planter class it could exploit political crisis to sponsor political forms which fortified rather than menaced slave-holding. Political crisis did nevertheless strongly correlate with the rise of anti-slavery; this was true even of those parts of North America where slaveholders could be isolated. A challenge to the established order could set the scene for slave outbreaks or desperate class struggles; it could also lead to a dramatic widening of a secular public space in which the workings of slavery became more visible and controversial.

During this period there were, broadly speaking, three types of political regime corresponding to different phases in the development of capitalism and producing different contexts and possibilities for anti-slavery. First, there were the late feudal absolutist regimes in which slavery was an accepted but regulated social relationship; mercantile capital could sponsor slave-based development in special enclaves; the slave status was defined, in principle, by royal statute not by the play of economic forces; if the defence of royal power required it slaves might be armed and freed; free people of colour would have their own duties and privileges as a regulated caste or estate. The second type of regime, produced in the wake of the first wave of bourgeois revolution, that of the early capitalist state – whether republic, Commonwealth or 'illegitimate monarchy' – gave much greater scope to privatised wealth and power, and typically sponsored a further and more intensive phase of colonial slavery and mercantile/manufacturing accumulation; while some moderate abolitionist aspirations might be ventilated these regimes furnished inhospitable terrain for the triumph of anti-slavery. The third type of regime, often thrown up as a consequence of the crisis of the regimes of absolutism or bourgeois oligarchy, was that in which bourgeois forces found themselves forced to make concessions to small property owners, artisans and skilled labourers, clerical workers and the humbler layers of professional people; the state was called upon to regulate capitalist forces and to undertake more ample functions to ensure social reproduction; anti-slavery had a greater chance of progress under this type of regime. Before briefly considering the different scope of anti-slavery in these settings it should be made clear that this proposed threefold typology does not exactly correspond to a chronological sequence since some 'intermediary' phases of bourgeois revolution – Philadelphia in 1778–80, Paris in 1793–9 – anticipated later dilemmas and developments without being able to contain or stabilise them; premonitions of the 'third' type they were unable to prevent regression to the second.

Because late feudal and absolutist regimes uniformly claimed divine sanction they possessed ready-made ideological resources for concealing and normalising the social relations of slavery. Fortified by such a traditional framework the royal authorities in Madrid responded to the pressures of the age with the new slave code of 1789 and a military policy of selective and opportune slave manumission in Santo Domingo or Venezuela. Slavery as such only became the object of controversy in Spain during the short-lived constitutional period (1811–14). The eccentric absolutist regimes in Portugal and Denmark took particular and limited measures against the slave trade but under duress and with the aim of avoiding abolitionist mobilisation. So long as they lasted the colonial structures of absolutism did encourage opponents to adopt a rhetoric of enlightened universalism. Absolutist autocracy and mercantilism provoked patriot radicalism, but its ability to resist the Patriots was sapped by the Atlantic boom even before it was shattered by the shocks of war and revolution. The slave regime in French St Domingue had been the first to break because of the depth of the crisis of the metropolitan order and because colonial structures had not enabled a sufficiently cohesive and hegemonic planter class to develop.

The political structures of 'illegitimate monarchy' did not prevent slaveholding becoming controversial but they did legitimate and enfranchise economic interest as a defence of slavery; and they represented a form of the state with a limited ability to intervene in civil society. A moderate species of abolitionism was to become typical of such regimes but not until 'illegitimate monarchy' itself was in question – as in Britain in 1831–3 or France in 1848 – did anti-slavery triumph. The advent of republicanism did not automatically ensure anti-slavery success, especially where a cohesive planter class retained hegemony over a sizeable non-slaveholding free population. But republican institutions did put slave-owners to a demanding test, requiring them to develop new justificatory ideologies and new political instruments for ensuring their hegemony. The North American emancipation laws of the 1780s, for all their limitations, did prepare the ground for the more radical challenges to slavery that were to appear within the French and British Empires; and they bequeathed an unresolved contradiction to republican institutions in the United States itself. Just as the advance of capitalism brought class struggle in its train, making slavery more difficult to defend, so the advance of bourgeois revolution created a secular political space which also created openings for anti-slavery.

The cycle of bourgeois revolutions created states that were not only more responsive to the dynamic of independent property and commerce but could also, for that very reason, mobilise greater socio-economic and military resources than the absolutist polities that they replaced. Asking more from their citizens they also sought to give, or at least promise, more. Civic freedom was an indispensable component of the package offered by Patriots, Republicans and Liberals; and at least sufficient civic equality to outlaw naked tyranny or plutocracy. The popular patriotic songs of the period probably bring us even closer to the new type of inter-subjectivity characteristic of the period than do political tracts: and in 'Rule Britannia' (1740), the 'Marseillaise' (1791), the 'Star-Spangled Banner' (1814), or Peru's national anthem (1821), we find the proud boast that citizenship banishes slavery. As the dates make clear patriot ideology was far from having consistent anti-slavery implications. But the tension it introduced between practice and ideology was different from that characteristic of the feudal-clerical order. It raised the question not of whether slaves were being fairly treated but of whether slavery should be tolerated.

From the slaveholders' standpoint 'illegitimate monarchy' or the limited bourgeois Republic could be attractive, promising release from absolutist regulation or colonial tutelage. But for this to apply slaveholding had to be protected by an exclusionary principle based on property or race, or some combination of the two, and the competence of the state had to be strictly circumscribed. Britain's original model of 'illegitimate monarchy' extended recognition and guarantees to propertied interests, including the interests of slaveholders; while it provided the setting for the rise of abolitionism, it so moderated, deflected and delayed the impact of anti-slavery that an eventful half-century elapsed between the founding of the abolition committee and the emancipation of the slaves in the British colonies.

In the United States slaveholding was protected by respect for private property, by a system of racial privilege and by strict limits on the legal scope for state intervention. In Brazil the ethnic balance was such that a US-style bi-polar racial ideology would not have strengthened the defences of slavery. Brazil's slaveholders, numbers of whom were themselves of partly coloured extraction, could draw on the Luso-

Conclusion

Brazilian tradition of a hierarchical racial spectrum in which dress, manners and money 'lightened' the skin. The Brazilian slave social formation was embedded within and protected by a strongly oligarchic political system and socio-economic order. The larger *fazendeiros* enjoyed almost untrammelled local power in the countryside through a combination of patronage and thuggery; the property franchise and National Guard directly empowered the wealthier urban citizens; the Emperor could make and unmake governments but not interfere with life on the estates.

Respect for property was certainly a powerful factor in neutralising or diminishing anti-slavery pressure. The blockages and delays encountered by British and French abolition stemmed more from the solidarity of the propertied classes than from racial solidarity. In the early bourgeois Republics and monarchies the ideological challenge of anti-slavery could be met by a moderate species of abolitionism which shunned expropriation, confining its objectives to ending the slave trade, encouraging voluntary manumission and regulating the plantations. British abolitionism did not aim at more than this prior to the 1820s. The French *Société des Amis des Noirs*, as we have seen, did not demand emancipation but took its stand on equal rights for free people of colour.

The new secular ideology of patriotism nourished a civic ideal that cohabited uneasily with slavery but refrained from attacking important sources of national wealth. In the Americas the patriotic abolitionism of the early nation-builders aimed to stop the import of Africans and gradually reduce reliance on slavery in the plantation zone. The slave trade bans adopted by North Americans between 1775 and 1807 had no direct anti-slavery consequences, though they encouraged opposition elsewhere to the slave traffic. Where slavery remained strong patriot abolitionists respected the property rights of slaveholders, even while lamenting their fate in the manner of Jefferson, Arango and Feijó. But while many Patriots did reconcile themselves to slaveholding, there was still a tension provoked by the outsize powers of slaveholders within a framework that supposedly offered equal rights to all free citizens. It would be wrong to dwell on 'cognitive dissonance' within patriot ideology and miss the fact that conflicting patriot ideals became most embarrassing when non-slaveholding free citizens were best placed to dispute slaveholder hegemony. It was the pressure of the political conjuncture and the aspirations of smallholders, artisans, port-workers or the maritime fraternity that could make planter Patriots anxious to disavow slavery. The spread of Methodism in the US South in the 1780s or the intense anti-planter patriotism of the white *colons* of the French

Windward Islands in the 1790s showed a latent animosity to slaveholders which was hidden in stable periods but of which planters were themselves aware.

In normal periods the parliamentary abolitionism of the 'illegitimate monarchies' was a typically weak and contradictory formation. Anti-slavery breakthroughs were made rather under the pressure of revolutionary or proto-revolutionary events, and the actuality or threat of slave resistance. The narrative of emancipation presented in this book has tried to bring out the cumulative character of the challenge to colonial slavery, even though each individual chapter pursues a national or imperial story. Each abolitionist advance derived some impetus from that which preceded it, in a sequence which zigzagged across the Atlantic every five or ten years between 1780 and 1848. Imperial or national boundaries remain significant not because anti-slavery impulses or motives had a purely local character but because slave emancipation could only be stabilised within national state structures, even if this meant creating a new state as it did in St Domingue/Haiti. Of course in the period 1776–1825 warfare challenged territorial divisions far more sweepingly than the wars of the previous epoch. Wars broke up empires and became instruments of revolutionary transformation. They mobilised secular ideologies in a new way, subjecting rival regimes to the most severe test, and requiring new rallying cries and material sacrifice. The French emancipation of 1794 and the English slave trade abolition of 1807 were greatly facilitated by the emergency atmosphere of military conflict.

Patriotism called into political existence wider layers of the populations of the Atlantic states. Its development has been traced from Hanoverian Britain, to North America, back to revolutionary Europe and on to South America. At the extreme, where the patriot cause itself faced a life and death struggle, some radical Patriots were prepared to envisage arming blacks and extending promises of emancipation. The previously noted safety catches of property and race would still inhibit, however. The most radical patriot abolitionists were the Spanish Americans yet even they chose slow and partial means to emancipation. Patriot abolitionism was not a stable formation, tending to disintegrate or dissipate in the aftermath of revolutionary crisis. In its most radical and exalted moments secular universalism, national messianism and emancipationism were difficult to disentangle. The Patriots who contributed most to anti-slavery often nourished cosmopolitan aspirations (Paine, the Jacobins and Hébertistes, Bolivar), while crucial contributions were made by individual Quakers, Freemasons, and former slaves like Equiano who owed allegiance to no state. Radical patriotism might offer anti-slavery tactical or conjunctural support, but the critical breakthrough fell to 'Black Jacobins' whose commitment was to social freedom rather than national identity.

The negotiation of the alliance between slave insurgency and French republicanism in the 1790s changed the history of New World slavery by transforming both parties to the alliance. It led to the construction of a black power and government which defeated the two leading imperial powers of the day: Britain and Napoleonic France. The revolutionary emancipationism of the French Caribbean did not confine itself to vague promises and postnate manumission but laid low what had been the most successful slave system in the Americas. It set a standard against which the evasions and betrayals of moderate abolitionism could be measured. The figure of Toussaint Louverture impressed itself on the imagination of the epoch, while the armies he created demonstrated the unconquerable spirit of those who had thrown off slavery. The slaves' willingness to fight for freedom persuaded Sonthonax, Laveaux and Vincent to defy the vagaries of metropolitan intrigue and defend the grandeur of the emancipation policy; likewise the stubborn resistance to Leclerc persuaded Dessalines and Christophe to break with him. The impact of the Haitian Revolution on the Caribbean and the rest of the Americas inspired groups of slaves and free people of colour and helped to radicalise a section of Spanish American Patriots. As Genovese stressed in *From Rebellion to Revolution* slave resistance itself acquired a new meaning and potential in the context of the revolutionary struggles of the 1790s. There was an incipient 'politicisation' of slave resistance as it achieved forms which aimed at, and could guarantee, general emancipation. In the conditions of the Atlantic world of the early nineteenth century this had to take the form of legislation backed by an effective territorial state.

The progress of abolition crucially depended on black witness, on slave resistance, and on the 'Black Jabobin' breakthrough of the 1790s. Whether small or large, and the proportions varied in different times and places, the black contribution to anti-slavery was absolutely critical to establishing a wider response. Without the early 'freedom suits' and black petitions, without the writings of Equiano and Cugoano, without Toussaint Louverture and Moyse, Christophe and Dessalines, Pierrot and Goman, Julien Fédon, Padilla and Romero, Jordan and Sharpe, Mary Prince, Bissette and Pory Papy, Pétion and Buddhoe and so many other black rebels and abolitionists, the challenge to colonial slavery could not possibly have triumphed. As the colonial slave formations 'matured' they also multiplied the likelihood of black contestation. The escalating slave resistance in Barbados in 1816, Guyana in 1823 and Jamaica in 1831–2 achieved both a larger scale and a more intimate engagement with the slave regime than any previous revolts in the British Caribbean. They were also more clearly aimed at contesting the whole slave system. The armed demonstrations of slaves in Martinique in 1848 also marked an advance for the black masses of the French Windwards, since on this occasion they did not entrust emancipation to agents from the metropolis.

Black resistance and revolt revealed both the unity and the diversity of the slave community and the latent antagonism of free blacks to slavery. Skilled or 'elite' slaves often played a leading role in plantation revolts and urban conspiracies. In the Caribbean colonies of Britain and France, as was noted in the Introduction, plantation management was particularly reliant on the 'head people' within the slave crew because of the shortage of free labourers available to work as drivers or artisans. In these colonies slave participation in local markets was also more extensive. In a political crisis, with the legitimacy of slavery itself in question, the elite slaves were well placed both to relay information and to foment collective resistance. Plantation security in the United States, Cuba and Brazil was less vulnerable because there were more free workers available for hire as overseers or their assistants and because there was a much larger number of small estates worked by only a few slaves. But while the disposition of the 'head people' was often a critical factor slave resistance did not get beyond the level of conspiracy without the involvement of the mass of field slaves. The field slaves on Caribbean sugar plantations had a notable capacity for resistance, partly because of the large average size of these estates and partly because their standard agricultural implement – the cane cutting *machete* – could also be used as a weapon. The 'maturing' of the slave colonies meant that kinship ties increasingly linked the slaves to the free blacks, creoles to Africans, field slaves to house slaves, those on one estate to those on another. The ferocious pressure of the slave systems itself tended to weld the enslaved and coloured population into a common, if differentiated, antagonism to the ruling order. It gave rise to the demand that slaves should work for themselves and their families rather than for their exploiters. Slave resistance was in this sense as much a form of class struggle as were the revolts of Captain Swing's followers or of the proletariat of Lyons. And while the point of production might provide the initial site of conflict the character and control of public authority were vital issues of contestation in both colonies and metropolis.

The defeats inflicted on British and French colonial slavery in the Caribbean reflected the special vulnerability of a slaveholding order dependent on a distant metropolitan state. In the colonies themselves property and race defined very small privileged minorities. The mobilisation of racial identity as a support of slaveholding was short-sighted where there were large black majorities and where there were growing minorities of free blacks. And so far as the metropolis was concerned it was scarcely possible to argue, as Jefferson did in Virginia, that emancipation would be a disaster for white citizens, since the slaves were thousands of miles away. It is not clear how much popular racism was to be found in Britain or France at the time of the struggles over emancipation – possibly rather little – but even if this estimate is faulty the slave-owners could not get much mileage out of it; likewise in certain parts of North and South America where there were very few slaves racial animosities could even favour laws banning the introduction of any more black slaves. By the time of emancipation the British and French planters were an embarrassment to the ruling authorities and lacked effective political instruments to defend themselves; colonial assemblies were discredited, and planter lobbies isolated or dispersed. Many British and French proprietors were absentees; their situation made them more prone to compromise than residents. Unable to enforce slave subjection through their own social weight these proprietors needed metropolitan support; but as colonial slavery became more discredited and troublesome this support eventually ebbed away, despite continuing and lively bourgeois distaste for expropriation. The dialectic of slave resistance, abolitionism and class struggle was a complex one and only worked itself out over several decades.

A friend who was good enough to read a draft of this book was disconcerted by the space allotted in it to British abolitionism when compared with that accorded to the overthrow of colonialism and slavery in Spanish America. 'I can't help feeling . . . that it is wrong to devote so much more space to British abolitionism than to these gigantic upheavals across two continents – the activities of a parcel of mewling vicars and parliamentary hypocrites studied so microscopically, while the broadest of brushes is reserved for the heroic twenty-year wars of the Liberators!' In explanation and justification I would plead that British emancipation, however unappealing some of its protagonists, involved the destruction of a major slave system and the speedy liberation of some 700,000 slaves. The anti-slavery actions of the Spanish American liberation movements were aimed at weak slave systems and, so far as many slaves were concerned, took a very gradual or risky form; during the twenty-year liberation struggle it is unlikely that more than about 70,000 slaves were freed, out of a total of roughly three times that number. Yet undeniably the achievements of the Liberators should not be measured only in these quantitative terms, partly because their example itself shamed Britain's parliamentary hypocrites and partly because they closed a vast extent of American territory to slavery. If Venezuela or Colombia or Peru or Central America had remained Spanish like Cuba, or had failed to enact emancipation like Brazil, then formidable new slave systems could have been built there. Because Britain was the leading Atlantic power of the age, struggles relating to the British slave trade and British slavery must be considered in depth, though I hope that the resulting account shows wider forces at work than the 'parcel' referred to.

The chapters on British and French emancipation aim to underline the many-sided process whereby anti-slavery forces converged and slaveholders were isolated. There are two ready-made but deceptive approaches to emancipation which I have sought to challenge. One of these concentrates all attention on respectable metropolitan abolitionism; the other nourishes a romantic regard for the pristine virtues of rebellion. The very revulsion prompted by the idea of slavery can lead to an oversimplified view of how easy it was to end it. If the historical record is examined, it becomes clear that abolitionism was often timid and ineffective, that the defenders of slavery had great resources of procrastination and diversion, and that the critical advances brought into play elemental social forces untouched by 'literary' anti-slavery. But from this it does not follow that a spontaneous anti-slavery carried all before it. The record also shows the odds were stacked against slave resistance, that unifying the oppressed was extraordinarily difficult and that the different forms of anti-slavery often did not mesh together. Constructing an anti-slavery alliance and post-slavery order were most demanding and arduous undertakings.

Among the ready-made ideas which fail to advance understanding are all those which locate the anti-slavery dynamic in an essentially dyadic relationship of master and slave. Hegel's well-known theses on the master-slave dialectic fails, as Jean–Paul Sartre pointed out in *The Critique of Dialectical Reason*, to take account of the dialectic between one master and another.[1] The 'dialectic of the subject' also fails to address the problem of how *inter-subjectivity* could develop between slaves in differing situations and of different extraction; and likewise it fails to consider the role played by such 'third' groups as free people of colour or non-slaveholding whites. The political crisis of the slaveholding order was always aggravated when slaveholders lost their ability to hegemonise the non-slaveholding population of the slave zone; the presence of alienated and mobilised free people of colour in St Domingue in 1791, or in Jamaica in the 1830s, was a major ingredient in precipitating the crisis of the slave order, despite the numbers of them who were themselves slaveholders.

The systems of colonial slavery required a complex of means and instruments in order to ensure the reproduction of slavery and colonialism – racial privileges, militia forces, slave-catchers, local assemblies, laws concerning property, commercial regulations and so forth. Their disintegration was bound to be a many-sided affair. This book has traced the circumstances in which the power of slaveholders was contested and an anti-slavery bond could spring up between slave rebels and anti-slavery radicals, metropolitan abolitionism and wider democratic upheavals. This political process was jerky and uneven if also cumulative. The half-way houses constructed along the road were often neither elegant nor durable, anti-slavery planks being held together with the unreliable mortar of patriotism or demagogy or political opportunism. But such way-stations could scarcely have been avoided unless emancipation had been the working out of a single master contradiction.

This book has attempted to identify relevant links between the class struggles of the metropolis and those of the plantation zone, and place both within a wider context of capitalist development and bourgeois revolution. While such an account will at best be an approximation, it aims to avoid the problem of an 'idealist' historiography in which the unfolding of events is already pre-programmed – whether by the contents of abolitionist ideology or by the tragedy of romantic rebellion. At the risk of appearing disrespectful to works of admirable scholarship, I will cite as examples of studies in which the foregoing problems have not been satisfactorily resolved *Slavery and Human Progress* by David Brion Davis and *Testing the Chains* by Michael Craton. Greatly illuminating though these books are, they risk trapping us in a closed history where the imperative of progress cannot be escaped (Davis), or slave rebels are doomed to cyclical repetition (Craton).

It is in the context of the messy and uneven growth of an anti-slavery alliance that I can address an apparent contradiction between the conclusions drawn here and the narratives presented in preceding chapters. I have suggested that anti-slavery grew in the secular space opened up by the arc of bourgeois revolution. Yet manifestly anti-slavery often received strong sponsorship from religious enthusiasts: Quakers, Methodists, radical *abbés*, black deacons, revolutionary deists and voodoo *houngans*. The conclusion I wish to suggest is not that anti-slavery was itself purely secular in inspiration, but that its achievements required a secular setting. Enforcement of the various emancipation laws was entrusted to magistrates and commissioners, civil servants and policemen and, within limits, to the vigilance of the former slaves themselves. They did not rely upon any appeal to divine providence or to the conscience of the slaveholder. The generally ineffective and half-baked attempts made to regulate slavery by moderate abolitionists did sometimes give responsibilities to priests and missionaries – as in the British West Indies in the 1820s or the French Antilles in the 1830s – but religious bodies had little or no formal role in the post-emancipation order. In the British case missionaries and black deacons did play an outstanding role in the 1820s and 1830s. Despite their many conservative features Methodism and Baptism in the British Empire helped to de-stabilise colonial slavery and to develop an implicit alliance between layers of the slave population and of the metropolitan populace. The activities of Sharpe or Knibb bear comparison with those of William Loveless and the Tolpuddle martyrs and in both cases it would seem that the experience of Nonconformist self-organisation both tempered and directed the impulse to resist, strengthening its secular and instrumental content at the expense of purely expressive, symbolic or ritual elements (though not, of course, entirely displacing the latter). The achievements of the black preachers and white missionaries in the West Indies had a secular context and character. They were enforced by civil magistrates and police, albeit with some ancillary mobilisation by missionaries and black deacons. Religion helped to give identity and self-respect to some populations of former slaves; but so did land-ownership, the freedom to move about, memories of resistance to slavery, music and song, local languages. Religion was probably a more significant element in this mixture in the British West Indies; a weaker element in the French and former Spanish territories. The colonial state itself often enjoyed some legitimacy as a consequence of emancipation; the resulting ideological complex in the colonial Caribbean was more open to social radicalism than to anti-colonial nationalism.

While endorsement of anti-slavery was convenient for ruling groups who could afford to dispense with slaveholding it would be wrong to ignore the real gains made by emancipatory interests. It might seem that abolition of abject personal dependence merely sugared the bitter pill of more encompassing state powers over the citizen of the new states and regimes. But whether in the metropolis or the plantation zone anti-slavery was also a doctrine that bound citizens to one another irrespective of the state, and even against the state. The resort to anti-slavery by political authorities in a tight corner noted in many of the foregoing chapters powerfully suggests that they sought thereby to enhance their standing, anticipating an adhesion of popularity from many sectors of the free population as well as from slaves.

The period 1776–1848 witnessed intense class struggles as exploiters and exploited, 'masters and servants', office holders and tax-payers, landed notables and farmers or peasants, monopolistic merchants and independent small producers, each sought to defend or advance their essential interests. The rise of industrial manufacture and the decline of the old mercantilism held out both opportunities and dangers to all social groups. Abolitionism, with its roots in a centuries-old popular anti-slavery reflex, also appeared to offer guarantees for the future – basically a guarantee that the enlarged circuit of capital accumulation would not simply reinforce and extend personal bondage. Anti-slavery as a doctrine had a special appeal to those who were caught in the middle or were seeking to construct a cross-class bloc. And as we have seen hostility to the slave trade often tapped more general resentment at the power or wealth of merchants. Emancipationism was certainly compatible with ideal projections of wage labour and thus congruent with capitalist industrialisation. But the ideal of 'free labour' or 'independent labour' which abolitionism claimed to protect had popular appeal because it could also be taken to refer to the small producer, the artisan or the professional, each of whom were free to work on their own account rather than for a capitalist. Women, normally excluded from political life, played a significant part in anti-slavery; while abolitionism idealised the family it directly inspired the first campaigns for civic equality for women.[2]

Anti-slavery sometimes drew strength from those nostalgic for a traditional order which prevented the excesses of a 'commercial age'. But the anti-slavery movements did not, in fact, aim to restore medieval regulation of economic life. The laws at which they aimed assumed some form of representative government responsive to popular interests and demands. Many of the pioneers of anti-slavery were attracted to democratic and anti-capitalist ideas. Wilberforce, the most famous abolitionist of them all, is in this respect not typical; and of course, the main target of his campaigns was the slave trade rather than slavery. The anti-slavery of Wallace, Sharp, Pechmeja, Paine, Grégoire, Hidalgo, Artigas or Schoelcher had to be prepared to challenge private property, and was often prepared to do so. These men were not in any modern sense socialists or communists or social democrats. But they were critics of private property in an age when it was a sacred and central institution throughout the Atlantic world. Moreover all the anti-slavery movements thrived at moments when radical social movements were posing a profound challenge to those possessed of wealth and privileges: ranging from North America in the early 1780s, to Paris in 1794, to the Mexican Bajío in 1811–4, to South America in the throes of revolution, to Britain in 1830–4, and France in 1848.

There were, as we have seen, moderate species of abolitionism and moderate uses of anti-slavery. There was certainly a specifically capitalist anti-slavery which insisted on generous compensation for slave-owners and which accompanied the suppression of slavery with attempts to develop labour disciplines which did not depend on a troublesome or expensive apparatus of direct coercion. Many advocates of anti-slavery were also ardent prison reformers or devotees of new poor law or vagrancy systems. Abolitionism as an ideology was capable of directly articulating a fairly comprehensive projection of bourgeois ideals and capitalist disciplines. Nevertheless it appealed to an idealistic minority rather than to the mass of capitalists or to such leaders of the business community as Sir Robert Peel (who headed a list of over a hundred manufacturers and merchants petitioning against abolition of the slave trade as late as 1806) while banking houses like Baring, Lafitte, Rothschild and Ardouin jostled for the privilege of investing in the slave colonies.

The sincere and dedicated bourgeois abolitionists of the nineteenth century usually had a generous and even utopian side to them. Their schemes of reform can not all be reduced to recipes for more effective social discipline since many campaigned to extend civic rights and to establish checks on economic and political power. These reformers and revisers of capitalism and bourgeois revolution may be compared to those who have tried, or are trying, to check or reverse the inegalitarian, authoritarian and ecologically destructive consequences of the accumulation process in our own times; an ideal projection of contemporary possibilities was undertaken in the cause of rescuing the progressive potential of newly released social powers, not of refining oppression.

Abolitionists like Sturge or Schoelcher remained eminently bourgeois without ever being in the mainstream or even specifically pro-capitalist. The term 'bourgeois' meant roughly middle class townsman, a social category which was by no means coextensive with that of capitalist, since there were agrarian capitalist landlords as well as middling town-dwellers without capital. It is as well to retain a sense of the discrepancy as well as the overlap between the bourgeois and the capitalist; this may also help us to understand why bourgeois revolutions did not simply advance capitalist interests, despite their ground-clearing function so far as the old order was concerned. The abolitionist alliance did sometimes fuse bourgeois and capitalists in one bloc but there were important periods when bourgeois radicals directed their main efforts at challenging the prevailing pattern of capitalist economy, with its slave trade, slave plantations, slave-related commerce, child labour, unregulated factory system and so forth; bourgeois radicals were also willing to challenge the prevailing bourgeois political regimes, with their many oligarchic and exclusionary principles. Sturge's support for the Chartists in the 1840s or Schoelcher's sympathy with 'socialism' testify to the existence of a current of bourgeois progressivism that was characteristic but also eccentric.

What of the thesis that abolitionism was itself the product of the new scope and freedom given to market forces by capitalist social relations? Had growing participation in market transactions educated the moral perceptions of the masses, enlarging their horizons and broadening their 'moral economy'? The accounts given in foregoing chapters show that this view fails to identify the anti-slavery impulse. Market forces often worked with an impersonality and ruthlessness that actually permitted and promoted a circuit of capitalist accumulation nourished by slave exploitation. The abolitionists found that it was not easy to win over those most directly involved in the slave-related trades; consumer boycotts had neglible effect while businessmen faced with a profitable investment saw no reason to leave it to a rival. While a few individuals did withdraw for ethical reasons from involvement in slavery there was not a shortage of those willing to take their place. Markets set up a structure which appeared to erase individual responsibility for the pattern of resultant action. Very often bankers and trustees would have been negligent of their clients' interests if they had not seized profitable openings available to them in the slave-related sector.

But there is more to be said on this topic since the popular reaction to the increasing 'marketisation' of social relations did help to evoke support for anti-slavery. Slaves like Mary Prince, quoted in chapter 11, saw the prospect of participation in a free labour market as a substantial advance over slavery; and, even under slavery, many slaves found petty commodity production and trading to be one way of acquiring some small measure of autonomy from their owner. Another way of putting these points would be to say that Mary Prince saw a market in labour power as preferable to a market in human beings and that slaves used local markets in subsistence goods to acquire some leverage against those who controlled the market in export crops. While preferring free wage labour former slaves carried into the post-emancipation period substantive expectations, some of them nourished by the market, which their prospecive employers could not satisfy. Likewise in the metropolis popular anti-slavery often tapped anxieties bred by the new sense of dependence which generalised commodity production entailed. Colonial slavery was both an extreme and a distant mode of exploitation; Atlantic commerce brought it closer, in terms of social space, allowing metropolitan abolitionism to awaken popular anxieties about extreme dependence on employers or on the fickle market mechanism. The attack on slaveholding and slave trading set minimum ground rules for fair dealing. While some anti-slavery writers certainly saw emancipation as a self-sufficient and adequate programme for taming and reforming the prevailing pattern of society this was not the case for the majority of anti-slavery activists and enthusiasts, who saw their work as part of a wider effort to extend freedom in ways congruent with respect for universal human interests. In the eyes of radical abolitionists this often meant refusing to accept the notion of a homogenous market system and instead challenging and suppressing, restraining or restructuring, particular markets by legislation or by the redistribution of wealth, and by promoting new forms of social co-operation.

In Britain and France anti-slavery themes had a resonance within all social classes. The rulers could find anti-slavery gestures a convenient way to stave off pressure for reform. The wider bourgeoisie and middle class could seek to impose itself on the oligarchy behind abolitionist rallying cries; and they might even hope to subdue the restiveness of the labouring classes through abolitionist lectures and sermons. And last but not least small producers, domestics, artisans and all types of wage or salary earner could see in anti-slavery measures a check on the powers of the wealthy. These various interpretations were even offered at the time by leading abolitionists; Wilberforce was not at all averse to pointing out the salutary political and socio-economic side-effects of official anti-slavery. But such declarations do not decide the matter. The historical record suggests that anti-slavery gestures did little or nothing to undermine popular opposition to oligarchy, or working class opposition to capital. The high tide of British anti-slavery in 1831–8 was almost immediately followed by the rise of Chartism, the most radical popular challenge to the ruling oligarchy in modern British history. Not only did leading abolitionists support Chartism but leading Chartists articulated their ideas by drawing on the anti-slavery tradition, as in Bronterre O'Brien's influential tract *The Rise and Progress of Human Slavery*. The term 'wage slavery' helped to introduce a social dimension into the perhaps 'over-political' radicalism of the time. In France in 1848 the abolitionist breakthrough was made when socialist and proletarian currents were at the height of their strength.

The fact that few of even the most radical abolitionists advanced a systematic critique of capitalism is not good grounds for supposing them to be capitalist ideologues. It was not, of course, until the very end of the period considered in this book that Karl Marx began to analyse the workings of capitalism, distinguishing between particular abuses and the essential functioning of capitalist accumulation. Capitalist relations, market relations and slavery did not constitute for Marx a necessary or homogenous totality, since tensions existed between them and each could exist in some form without the other. But at a given moment they could well constitute a complex structure of domination and exploitation with a historical logic of its own. Moreover Marx himself saw resistance to particular abuses generated by capitalism as a necessary preparation for a more fundamental onslaught. He followed many of the early socialists in attacking slavery in the Americas, seeing the overthrow of the 'open slavery' of the New World as a necessary prelude to an attack on the 'veiled slavery' of the Old. Moreover in so doing he did not mind associating with liberal reformists such as John Stuart Mill. The social formations of the Atlantic zone in the mid-nineteenth century were in flux and even an observer like Marx, attentive to the determinations of deep structures, could believe that the best way to assemble forces to contest the juggernaut of capital accumulation was to campaign for particular measures, such as slave emancipation, universal suffrage, the eight hour day and so forth. Marx would not, perhaps, have been surprised if he had learnt that such popular gains did not spell the end of capitalism or even that they had helped to create more expansive bourgeois societies. They still had value in themselves and as stepping stones for class struggle at a higher level; without them human collective powers could scarcely hope to take on the global system of capital accumulation.

Once all due credit has been paid to abolitionism in its various manifestations it must still be asked to what extent the abolitionists were in fact the authors of emancipation; and the results of emancipation must also be scrutinised to see to what extent they were shaped by metropolitan abolitionism, whether bourgeois or petty bourgeois, patrician or plebeian.

The events considered in this book do not show a one to one correspondence between emancipation and 'abolitionism', especially that official and respectable abolitionism which has been so copiously documented and thoroughly analysed. The Philadelphia emancipation was promoted by democratic radicals at a time when many anti-slavery enthusiasts were in political retreat. The decree of Pluviôse had been enacted at a time when the *Amis des Noirs* was a defunct organisation. Emancipation in Spanish America proceeded, for the most part, without the instigation of distinct abolitionist organisations. In the British case abolitionist mobilisations did indeed play an important role, but they did not win on their own; the prospect of escalating slave resistance and the pressure of domestic class struggle were needed to ensure victory. In France in 1848 there was no comparable abolitionist movement: emancipation was the work of the Revolution, of a bold abolitionist minister and of the pressure of slave insurgence. The distinction between radical and moderate abolitionists also had significance in the aftermath of emancipation, with radicals, such as Sturge or Schoelcher, inclined to support the new struggles of the former slaves while moderates, such as Buxton or de Tocqueville, turned to other matters. But while the representations of radicals could be helpful the former slaves had found ways of directly pursuing their own interests.

The facile pessimistic reflex which tells us that the former slaves were really no better off than they had been under slavery cannot be sustained. To begin with there is a large and impressive contrast between vital statistics before and after the ending of the slave systems. Around 1770 none of the Caribbean black populations had positive natural growth rates; a century later they all did, slaveholding Spanish Cuba alone excepted. In Haiti, Jamaica and a number of the smaller Caribbean islands former slaves and descendants of slaves now owned small plots of land on which they cultivated subsistence crops and perhaps some coffee. They built homes for themselves. They developed family life and cultural forms in ways that would have been quite impossible under slavery. Slavery still left marks on both the freed people and their rulers. Life was difficult for the former slaves – structures of class and racial inequality or oppression were not hard to identify. But the former slaves and their descendants now lived longer, and more freely, than in slavery days. While the majority of former slaves had no land or insufficient land they could move from one employer to another, or from one island to another. Back-handed acknowledgement of the new autonomy of the former slaves is provided by the fact that planters and other employers looked for other sources of unfree labour. The considerable influx of indentured labourers into the British and French West Indies and into Peru showed that economic demand for tied labour had by no means disappeared. The new resort to indentured labourers also demonstrated that emancipation itself had not been the end-product of capital's demand for a new type of labour but rather of capital's inability to sustain the given form of slavery.[3]

The results of emancipation vindicate the thesis that anti-slavery was linked to an over-arching process of 'bourgeois democratic' revolution while contradicting the narrower view that emancipation was simply an emanation of the bourgeois world-view or bourgeois progress. Petty producers, artisans and professionals had goals which cut across the pure bourgeois programme in the Caribbean just as they did in France.[4] Slave resistance itself often had, as we have seen, 'proto-peasant' characteristics. For good or ill many former slaves became peasants, rather few became wage labourers of any sort, let alone industrial wage labourers. The labour force released by emancipation in this epoch was not thereby made available to industrial capitalism or even, in most cases, to fully capitalist plantation agriculture, though enclaves of the latter were certainly to be found in Barbados, Martinique and some other smaller French and British islands. In 1780 nearly all American grown coffee had been slave-cultivated; by 1840 the bulk was grown by free or peasant labour. In the last days of slavery women had loomed large in the cane-cutting gangs; following emancipation they were more likely to be seen tending garden plots or carrying produce to market than working in the planters' fields. In some of the smaller islands the planters could find enough landless labourers to maintain sugar output at something like former levels but the big advances were made in territories where unfree labour could be mobilised. The improved position of former slaves often directly contradicted capitalist progress, by reducing their availability for plantation labour. But this incipient 'de-subordination' of the former slaves was generally seen with gathering disfavour by the public authorities, who looked for opportunities to make the former slaves more compliant: the ferocious repression carried out by Governor Eyre in Jamaica in the 1860s is a case in point. The new social freedoms enjoyed by the mass of former slaves were almost universally accompanied by effective exclusion from political power; in this sense the secular space opened up by the consolidation of bourgeois states set its own limits on emancipation.

The fate of the Republic of Haiti in the years 1825–50 has a special significance for the events considered in this book for reasons that have been alluded to above. Writing about his experiences as a slave and escaped slave in North America in the 1830s and 40s the outstanding anti-slavery advocate Frederick Douglass observed that his passionate interest in learning about Haiti led him to devour every scrap of news he could find concerning the first American state to outlaw slavery and the only American state to have a black government.[5]

President Boyer ruled Haiti until 1843. The Republic which he led was poor but dignified. While the President took all real decisions an Assembly of notables was allowed to debate them. So long as coffee prices held up, a layer of Haitian peasants and landowners could rise a little above subsistence. While a small educated elite wrote poetry or history the black masses elaborated a rich syncretistic folklore and threw up local irregulars as a check on predominantly mulatto rulers. Boyer's success in occupying the East and his willingness to allow an 'official opposition' eventually set the scene for his downfall in the 1840s when, as coffee revenues fell, he was challenged by secession in the East and revolt in the West. Boyer had sought to extend to the Spanish-speaking half of the island the mixture of smallholding and military administration which prevailed in the West. All remaining slaves had been emancipated in 1822–3 and those of military age formed into special regiments. An attempt had been made to divide up communal land and church land and to create a numerous small-holding peasantry. But this agrarian reform ran into strong opposition because it was accompanied by military favouritism and clumsy taxation; moreover it alienated those who preferred to let their cattle roam widely and to cut precious woods wherever they found them rather than become owners of little plots of land. Smuggling thrived. The inhabitants of the East believed that it was unjust that they should pay taxes to enable the Republic to reimburse the French former proprietors of estates in the West. Boyer's invasion in 1822 had enjoyed some internal support but this was entirely dissipated by the early 1840s. Boyer's troubles in the East were compounded by opposition in the West. On the one hand a young, predominantly mulatto urban elite chafed at Boyer's supposedly autocratic inclinations; on the other the black peasantry resented the influence of wealthy mulattos and the state's attempts to tax and control them. And there was a suspicion that Boyer or those close to him were willing to make further concessions to the French by allowing them to establish a naval base. The traditions and structures of the heroic revolutionary period led to some interesting echoes. The opposition to Boyer was led by a 'Society for the Rights of Man and the Citizen'. Following the departure of Boyer the Presidency was occupied in quick succession by four black veterans of the struggles against the French; Louis Pierrot, who had rallied to Sonthonax in 1793 at Le Cap, became President of Haiti in 1845, nominated by mulatto politicians who sought thus to reassure the black masses that their interests were safe. In 1848–9 a black military chief, Faustin Soulouque, destroyed the power of the mulatto political cliques and established an imperial regime supposedly modelled on that of Dessalines; reports of this had some impact in Martinique.[6]

However successive Haitian governments found it impossible to rehabilitate the finances of the state and failed to promote a prosperous peasantry. Large estates were broken up but the minifundist peasantry had no incentive to move out of subsistence cultivation. Any significant move into commodity production simply attracted taxation or official pillage. Soil erosion became a serious problem. The only large Atlantic state prepared to do business with Haiti was France – and French governments pressed for repayment of the compensation loan of 1825 and of its various successors. Down to the 1870s service payments accounted for at least a quarter of the national budget while military expenditures usually for at least a half. The major Atlantic powers were quite content to see the government of Haiti enfeebled and quarantined as a way of reducing its power to inspire troubles elsewhere.[7]

Conclusion

Post-revolutionary Haiti was no abolitionist utopia but neither was it the reincarnation of the old order. The compulsive image of the 'world turned upside down', the Carnivalesque reversal of roles, the Saturnalia does not really apply to this black state. While such images had a subversive appeal their permutation of social roles ended up by confirming the immutability of structure. Yet in Haiti the structures too had changed out of all recognition and quite new problems arisen. The problems of Haiti's public treasury had parallels in South America while the afflictions of the subsistence peasantry had more in common with the problems of peasants in Sardinia or Sicily than with those of the slaves incarcerated on the Cuban plantations. While the liberated blacks of the Caribbean no longer had the overseer's whip to contend with it is true that they still felt the pressure of competition from unfree labour; thus the decline in coffee prices reflected the steeply rising output of Brazil's slave plantations.

If the main concern of this book has been to trace the course of the challenge to slavery it has also sought to identify the blockage encountered in the two strongest newly independent states and in the remodelled slave colony of Cuba. Bourgeois revolution had developed in these lands in ways which enabled slaveholders to retain the leadership of the slaveholding social formation and to suppress any stirrings of emancipationism.

American slaveholders had proved themselves capable of becoming outstanding revolutionaries and bold statesmen. They had greater self-confidence, not surprisingly, where they were resident in the Americas and on their estates. The slaveholding New World planters had a divided soul. They were products of the commercial revolution, of the Enlightenment, of the new rise of American agriculture and of the liberal pattern of society and politics; they wished to build new nations yet their most splendid achievements were built on the brutal exploitation and oppression of enslaved blacks. Their possession of slaves gave them confidence, and sometimes allowed them to pursue a revolutionary vocation, yet it also set limits on the type of political participation they would offer non-slaveholders and it involved them in an Atlantic system of exchanges dominated by the industrialising regions.

The planters of the United States, Cuba and Brazil eagerly rushed to fill the gaps left by the decline of exports from St Domingue; they also paid the Haitian Revolution the homage of insulating themselves against its example by all means possible. While Haiti was subjected to diplomatic and commercial isolation the United States and Brazil were rapidly admitted to the concert of nations. The reaction of the slave powers was scarcely surprising; the complicity with them of supposedly abolitionist governments is more remarkable and instructive. Britain prided itself on its international campaign against the Atlantic slave trade but could not bring itself to boycott slave-produced cotton, sugar or coffee. US cotton was admitted free of duty from the beginning; between 1846 and 1851 all duties on sugar were lifted in deference to the agitation for free trade. Some prominent champions of free trade had earlier supported anti-slavery but the majority of organised abolitionists were outraged at the encouragement thus given to slave agriculture. Britain's official abolitionism did not prevent British merchants conducting a thriving and increasingly unfettered commerce with the slave plantations. France after 1848 also moved, though more cautiously, in the direction of free trade. Around mid-century the prospects for marketing the slave produce of the Americas had never been better. Capitalism as an economic system – and as a social formation in which the economic had a quite new salience and independence – thoroughly permeated and integrated the expanding slave systems of the Americas in the 1850s. British capital found advantageous outlets in each of the expanding slave states of the Americas, helping to build railways, equip plantations and finance trade. Capitalism thus 'outflanked' the newly liberated blacks of the Caribbean, battening on the sturdier slave systems of the mainland.[8]

The slaveholders of the United States, Brazil and Cuba had been able to anticipate or repress slave resistance and to retain or reassert their leadership over sizeable numbers of free persons who did not own slaves. The slave-based economy was extensive and rural in character but the slaveholders had formed strategic alliances with urban-based elites in the challenging epoch of bourgeois revolution. The vigour of the slave systems was such that they gave a good livelihood to a layer of businessmen, lawyers and politicians in such centres as New York, Washington, Havana, Madrid, Barcelona and Rio de Janeiro. The alliances made by these bourgeois factions showed a promiscuous ability to compromise with non-capitalist forces, in a symmetrically opposite direction to the impulse of bourgeois reform noted above.

The American slave systems were strong enough and flexible enough to take advantage of the new market opportunities presented by the collapse of colonial mercantilism and the vigorous demand for plantation produce. The conquest of independence by the mainland territories led to economic growth in the states linked to the plantation boom but to stagnation or recession in much of Spanish South America, where slavery was weak. In the slave zone imperial mercantilism was an impediment to further advance, which received its impetus from the spontaneous and expansive dynamic of the slave social formations and Atlantic economy. In much of Spanish South America, notably Mexico and Peru, the infrastructure of empire had still conserved a productive rationale at the close of the colonial epoch. That 'liberation of civil society' which ushered in a new epoch of advance for the planters in the United States and Brazil weakened and fractured the extensive and state-imposed co-ordination of the mining, hacienda and village economy in mainland South America. In Cuba the metropolis stimulated development by withdrawing state regulation from the internal economy and standing back to extract revenue from the customs system.

Thus, from the standpoint of Atlantic economy, independence seemed to work best with slavery and slavery seemed to work best without metropolitan interference. As symbols of the new America splendid new government buildings were constructed at Washington, with its White House and Capitol, Rio de Janeiro, with its enlarged royal Palaces, and Havana, with its enlarged Intendancy and Governor's Palace and impressive new prison, reputed to be the largest and most modern in the hemisphere. These edifices were constructed by slave labour yet were monuments to enlightened classicism. The governments which inhabited them were soon able to claim jurisdiction over inland areas which had largely escaped colonial administration. The President of the United States, the Emperor of Brazil or the Captain General of Cuba could not regulate life on the plantations and in this sense the powers of the state were limited. But these states could effectively defend their own territory and did not succumb to the fissiparous tendencies of Gran Colombia or the 'United Provinces'.

The destiny of this new slavery on the American mainland, and on the largest of the Caribbean islands, forms the central subject matter of the sequel to this volume. But in the foregoing chapters it has already been seen that the survival of slavery in these territories depended not only on a favourable relationship of social forces – with slaves constituting a minority, albeit a very large one, of the population – but also on the economic vitality of the slave plantations. Slave plantations thrived most in territories with the highest index of participation in the Atlantic economy. This vitality stemmed from rising demand for plantation produce and a system of Atlantic exchanges that progressively approximated to free trade. The British, French, Spanish and Portuguese Empires had to be destroyed, or as in the Cuban case reorganised along quite new lines, to make this possible. The creation of the United States, of the Brazilian Empire, and of a new colonial pact between Cuba and Spain, partook of the sweep of bourgeois revolution in the Atlantic world, and contributed massively to its economic advance; it demonstrated that capital still made use of the crutch of more ancient forms of exploitation.

Seen from a certain perspective the defeats inflicted on empire had hardly weakened slavery at all but had simply promoted its growth in three territories where the slave-owners had immensely greater prospects and opportunities than in the old colonies. Small island slavery would in any case have been marginalised by railways, steamships, breech-loading rifles and cartridges. In 1770 there had been roughly 2,340,000 slaves in the Americas. Despite the overthrow of slavery in St Domingue the number of slaves in the Americas had risen to 3 million in 1800 and, despite further emancipations, to 6 million in 1860. The land area cultivated by slaves grew by a similar or larger proportion, as the interior of the South-western United States, Cuba and Brazil was opened up to extensive plantation agriculture. The small islands did not have the space to accommodate such a huge rise in plantation agriculture or the new large-scale methods of cultivating cotton, sugar and coffee. New World slavery was now not colonial but colonising.

It should be noted that where slavery survived there was continuity in the local forms of government, however dramatic the changes in the relationship to a wider polity and economy. In Cuba this is evident enough. And in Virginia no less than in Brazil the movement for independence was led by the already existing local institution of government; in the one case the House of Burgesses, in the other the Braganza dynasty. This contrasts with the already noted correlation between emancipation and the advent of new regimes: the French Republic of the 1790s, Haiti, the Spanish American Republics, Britain's Reform Parliament, the French Republic of 1848. And in so far as any appeal was made to abolitionist sentiment in North America, Cuba or Brazil it was at moments of rupture and renewal, such as Philadelphia in 1775, Cadiz in 1811 or Rio de Janeiro in 1824.

The collapse of the previously dominant forms of colonial slavery combined with the continuing expansion of Atlantic capitalism suggests that colonialism, monarchism, racism and slavery itself were only contingent superstructures upon capitalist relations of production. In theory, perhaps, capitalism could survive without all of them. But in practice it found these more or less anomalous social forms necessary and convenient. At root this was because capitalist social relations, and their presuppositions, were not sufficiently deeply implanted and because potential sources of surplus would be battened upon so long as this was possible. Thus capital needed large numbers of propertyless labourers excluded from means of subsistence but could not find them. The industrialising regions also found that slave plantations brought new land for cane or cotton or coffee more rapidly into production than did smallholders.

In 1770 Britain was the only major Atlantic state in which capitalism had gained the upper hand, although even Britain artificially constricted the path of accumulation in its American colonies. The overthow of absolutism in France, Spain and Portugal, and the defeat of colonial mercantilism in most parts of the Americas, led to the emergence of a new state system in the Atlantic world, more attuned to the expansion of commerce and capitalist industry. These states no longer directly intervened in the process of production; they sought to tax but not incorporate overseas commerce and the sphere of circulation. But these were only preliminary steps. The appearance of new regimes of 'illegitimate monarchy' represented a sort of capitalist progress, but one still limited by the localism of agrarian magnates, some of them slaveholders.

The United States had made the most progress towards dismantling state parasitism just as Britain had taken the most thoroughgoing measures against colonial slavery. But conversely the North American Republic had triumphantly stabilised slavery while Britain's oligarchy had skilfully retrenched itself within the new 'reformed' Palace of Westminster. Both states faced the danger that this uneven and paradoxical advance would skewer them on its contradictions. The Constitution of the North American Republic had recognised slavery but not resolved the question of the rights of the constituent states; at the Hartford Convention of 1814 New Englanders had raised the spectre of secession. Down to 1860 the slaveholder Republic and the abolitionist Empire contended for domination of the hemisphere, a circumstance which was to lead to some bizarre alliances.

Britain claimed to police the oceans as scourge of the slave-traders yet the main slave powers of the Atlantic were client states within Britain's informal Empire; the 'illegitimate monarchies' of Spain, Brazil and Portugal had been established with vital British support – the latter embracing diplomacy, naval shows of strength, loans, volunteers, and secret agents. British commercial predominance in the Atlantic zone drew British interests back into collusion with the slave trade as well as slavery, as British manufactures, now more freely available than ever to Luso–Brazilian and Hispano–Cuban slave-traders, were briskly exchanged for captives on the coast of Africa.

The ending of the Atlantic traffic had been one of the first and most moderate goals of respectable anti-slavery. In 1815 the Atlantic slave trade had been solemnly denounced by all the powers and by 1820 the preparatory interval allowed in the Anglo–Spanish Treaty had come to an end. In the decade of the 1820s a total of just over 600,000 Africans entered the Americas as slaves, a volume somewhat below that of the 1780s but above that of the eighteenth century decadal average of just over 500,000. During most of the 1820s the Brazilian slave trade was only semi-illegal in the sense that though vague declarations had been made specific international agreements had not been entered into. From 1830 the Anglo–Brazilian Treaty suppressing the slave traffic supposedly came into force and for a year or two the volume of slave imports did decline. In 1835 Britain and Spain entered into a new and supposedly more rigorous agreement but this had little impact on Cuban import figures. Altogether 560,000 slaves were introduced to the Americas in the 1830s. In the 1840s slave imports fell somewhat, partly due to more vigorous patrolling, but still totalled 445,000 in the decade. The million slaves who had entered the Americas between 1830 and 1850 had done so in violation of both national legislation and international treaty. In the years 1851–2 the imperial authorities, responding both to domestic sentiment and a menacing squadron of British warships, began to take more effective action within Brazil itself to stop the Atlantic slave-traders. But for how long this would continue to be the case was uncertain. The Captain General of Cuba brought slave imports to a temporary halt in 1853 but the traffic soon returned to its old level once he was replaced.[9]

So long as slavery flourished in the Americas it was going to be difficult to stop the Atlantic slave trade. A flourishing slave system meant high slave prices. Control of the trade was made exceptionally difficult by the length of coast-lines involved and the expanse of ocean; natural obstacles were greatly compounded by the slave-traders' ability to buy the fastest steam clippers and to pay large bribes. All these factors meant that any slave trade suppression policy required co-ordination between the maritime powers and the governments of the importing and exporting regions. The US ban of 1808 was quite effective in stopping the importation of slaves to North America; a clandestine trade did, however, continue and introduced a thousand slaves or more a year. With the price of slaves in the US South rising to over $1,000 each by mid-century there was certainly an incentive to smuggle slaves in. The British ban of 1808 was fairly effective but became far more so from the mid-1830s with the abolition of slavery. The French ban was quite ineffective before 1831 but thereafter clandestine imports would have been very small because of the ease of invigilating access to the small French islands. Down to 1850 both Cuba and Brazil imported large numbers of slaves, regardless of international agreements; there was certainly some involvement in this trade by North American, British and French traders. Control of the slave traffic was rendered particularly difficult by the failure of Britain, the United States and France to agree on a joint approach to policing the oceans. For a few years in the 1830s there was a joint Anglo–French agreement but this was not renewed in 1838. Attempts to reach agreement were bedevilled by national belligerence and imperial rivalries. As the largest maritime power Britain stood to gain most by apparently reciprocal and equal agreements conceding rights of search and detention. British bullying further aggravated the problem, as in Palmerston's outrageous treatment of a Portuguese government in the 1830s that had a genuine desire to suppress slave trading, that of Sa de Bandeira. In fact the British government came close to declaring war on both the United States and France in the early and mid 1840s on issues largely unconnected with slavery; and in 1853–4 the British and US governments again came close to war. A British disposition to claim to 'rule the waves' and lack of zeal in Washington for prosecuting slave traders helped to inflame Anglo–US relations, as did the concern of both powers to spread their influence in the Americas, especially in the sensitive Caribbean and Central American zone. Even at times when there were relatively good relations between London and Paris, or London and Washington, slave trade suppression benefited little unless there was a co-operative reaction from the governments of the territories involved in the traffic. Many slaves were exported from parts of the African coast under nominal Portuguese sovereignty. There were forces in Portugal hostile to the slave traffic but the Portugese state was not strong enough to withstand the interests bound up in the slave trade. Not only were slaves the most valuable export of Angola, Guinea and Mozambique but the combined value of slave exports from Portuguese Africa was considerably in excess of the Portuguese national budget. Colonial officials from the Governors downwards would receive rich pickings if they co-operated with the slave-traders. Moreover the whole social formation of the Portuguese colonies was geared to this highly lucrative business, making it extraordinarily difficult for metropolitan officials to find local allies.[10]

Between 1770 and 1850 well over five million slaves were taken from Africa for a New World destination; more, that is, in these eighty years than in the preceding two hundred and eighty years. During this period the Napoleonic wars had a greater immediate, if temporary, impact on the volume of the traffic than the slave trade bans and diplomacy. The future prospects of the trade very much depended on political developments in the United States, Brazil, Spain, France and Britain. Anti-slavery was to remain or to become a force in all these states but the outlook in the 1850s was ominous indeed. The spread of European colonial rule had given a new impetus to doctrines of white supremacy.

In the purple prose of Carlyle and Gobineau a romantic racism furnished a literary counterpart to widespread pseudo-scientific notions of racial hierarchy. The rulers of Britain and France might still draw the line at slave-traders but were quite prepared to accept the respectability of American slaveholders, and to compete for diplomatic and commercial advantage in the slave zone.

Colonial slavery had foundered in the Americas in this epoch because the colonial form was not strong enough to contain concerted challenges from either slaveholders or slaves. But as in some social Darwinian struggle for the 'survival of the fittest' the stronger slave regimes had pulled through, obliging us to admit a 'functional' level of explanation into our account of how it was that some were swept away while others flourished.

Despite anti-slavery gains in this period the actual area of land cultivated by slaves had been constantly expanding. Millions upon millions of acres in the cotton lands of the American South-west, the plains of Matanzas in Cuba and Paulista West in Brazil were opened to plantation development for the first time. Moreover this spread of slavery was coupled with aggravated international and imperial rivalries which created bad prospects for abolition in the 1850s. The major slave powers themselves were in the full flood of expansion and seemed poised to conquer new territory for slavery. After the war between the United States and Mexico in 1845–8, following which Mexico lost a third of her national territory, it did not need the bluster of successive US Presidents speaking of their country's imperial destiny to make clear the seriousness of the threat from that quarter. North American fillibusters invaded Nicaragua in 1856–7; 'President' Walker thereupon legalised slaveholding once again. With the help of a buoyant Cuban treasury, Spain reoccupied Santo Domingo in 1859, converting it once more into a slave colony. A Franco–Spanish expedition landed in Mexico, supposedly to recover unpaid debts, and a quarrel simmered between Spain and Chile that was soon to lead to war. The Brazilian Empire entered the 1860s with its own plans for asserting Brazilian interests in the River Plate region; this too contained the seeds of a future war.

The sequel to this volume will consider the character and dynamic of the new slave systems and of the new anti-slavery challenges they met. The memory and the lessons of the struggles against colonial slavery from 1776 to 1848 itself played a role in precipitating and informing the crisis of the states which defended slavery. The new challenges had formidable obstacles to overcome, precisely because these states had already been tested by the storms of a revolutionary epoch, but they principally derived from internal antagonisms accumulated by the advance of slavery itself. In that sense the full significance of the events recounted in this book remains to be assessed and the conclusions offered here must remain partial and provisional.

Such is the pressure of hindsight that the 1850s may seem an awkward and arbitrary time to close this narrative, even with the prospect of a sequel. I would contest this not simply because the new American slavery did differ from colonial slavery but also because whatever closing date is chosen there will be contradictions and ambiguities. It is salutary today to consider the world as it must have appeared to those living in the 1850s, aware of the ideals and example of the revolutionary epoch but aware, too, of the surging tide of Atlantic, slave-based commerce. Privileging incandescent dates like 1776, 1789 and 1848 simply encourages complacency unless the years of disappointment, reversal or restoration are also given their due. Is 1945 really a more reassuring date than 1940? While it added new peril, had it really laid to rest the menace of 1940? William Blake's advice should apply to historical work too; 'Damn braces, bless relaxes.'

Notes

1. Sartre observes: 'Hegel can be criticised for describing *the* Master and *the* Slave, that is to say, ultimately, for describing the relations of *a* master and *his* slave through universals, without reference to their relations to other slaves or other masters. In reality the plurality of masters and the serial character of every society cause the Master as such, even in idealist terms, to find *a different truth* within the ensemble of his class.' J–P. Sartre, *The Critique of Dialectical Reason*, vol. I, London 1976, pp. 158 n. In the second volume of the *Critique* Sartre pursues this line of thought in an examination of racism and violence; *Critique de la Raison Dialectique*, II, Paris 1985, pp. 470–1. For an illuminating discussion of slave dispositions see Harry Fineberg, 'Resources in Class Conflict and Collective Action with Reference to Slavery and Slave Revolts', Manchester University, Government Department 1987.

2. On the role of women see Louis Billington and Rosamund Billington. ' "A Burning Zeal for Righteousness": Women in the British Anti-slavery Movement', in Jane Rendall, ed., *Equal or Different: Women's Politics in Britain 1800–1914*, Oxford 1987. On radical or 'populist' elements in the anti-slavery of this period see Di Tella, *La Rebelión de los Esclavos de Haiti*, pp. 95–6.

3. For an insightful discussion and survey see Robert Miles, *Capitalism and Unfree Labour: Anomaly or Necessity*, London 1987.

4. Hobsbawm, *The Age of Revolution*, pp. 177–9, for a discussion which goes from obstacles to capitalist advance in France to obstacles in the United States. George Comninel has recently used evidence such as this to cast doubt upon the whole concept of 'bourgeois revolution' (George Comninel, *Re-thinking the French Revolution*, London 1987). Hobsbawm certainly attributes some of the obstacles to capitalist advance in France to the eruption of popular class struggle in the shape of Jacobinism. But he does not conclude from the prevalence of peasant ownership in France that no bourgeois revolution had taken place. And while Comninel allows Marx to lead him into greatly

exaggerating the role of state autonomy under Napoleon III, Hobsbawm elsewhere points out that the Second Empire actually anticipated many features of liberal economics and politics. E.J. Hobsbawm, *The Age of Capital*, London 1975, chapter 6.

5. Frederick Douglass, *Narrative of the Life of Frederick Douglass, a Slave; Written by Himself*, Boston 1845.

6. Frank Moya Pons, 'The Land Question in Haiti and Santo Domingo: The Socio-Political Context of the Transition from Slavery to Free Labor, 1801–1843', in *Between Slavery and Free Labor: The Spanish-speaking Caribbean in the Nineteenth Century*, edited by Manuel Moreno Fraginals, Frank Moya Pons and Stanley Engerman, eds, Baltimore 1985, pp. 181–214.

7. Sir Spenser St John, *Hayti or the Black Republic*, London 1884, pp. 380–9.

8. My use of this term owes something to Michael Mann, *The Sources of Social Power*, though Mann himself would probably not agree that the constitution of the economic level in a social formation dominated by capitalism gives such outflanking power to exploiters.

9. Murray, *Odious Commerce*, pp. 92–113, 208–70.

10. These patterns, referred to in chapter 9 above, are much illuminated by Bethell, *The Abolition of the Brazilian Slave Trade*, and Alexandre, *Origens do Colonialismo Português Moderno*.

Index

Index

Index